INSTITUTES
OF THE CHRISTIAN RELIGION

John Calvin

1536 edition, translated and annotated
by Ford Lewis Battles

COLLINS

Collins Liturgical Publications
8 Grafton Street, London W1X 3LA

Distributed in Ireland by
Educational Company of Ireland
21 Talbot Street, Dublin 1

Distributed in Southern Africa by
Lux Verbi
Box 1822, Cape Town 8000

Collins Liturgical Australia
PO Box 316, Blackburn, Victoria 3130

Collins Liturgical New Zealand
PO Box 1, Auckland

Revised edition published 1986 by Wm. B. Eerdmans Publishing Co. in the USA
and Wm Collins Sons & Co in Great Britain
in collaboration with the H. Henry Meeter Center for Calvin Studies at
Calvin College, Grand Rapids, MI.
This translation is the first volume in *Bibliotheca Calviniana*, a library of books
by and about John Calvin.

Acknowledgements
From *Melanchthon and Bucer*, Volume XIX,
The Library of Christian Classics, edited by Wilhelm Pauck.
Copyright 1969, The Westminster Press

ISBN 0 00 599995 2

Made and printed in the USA by
Eerdmans Printing Company

CONTENTS

PREFACE TO THE REVISED EDITION

1536 was not a particularly memorable year. No events of world-historical importance seem to have occurred. Not even the outrageous Franco-Turkish alliance was to have more than a temporary impact. The tumults and intrigues and territorial shifts in religious affiliation express continuity rather than discontinuity with that which was initiated in prior years and which was to be consummated in future years. Even the work of Luther was not fully established in 1536. There was still much uncertainty about what would be its lasting impact institutionally and spiritually on Christendom.

Yet in 1536, in the city of Basel, a subtle but lastingly significant transition was at least symbolically indicated. In that year, in that city, an aging scholar died, and a younger scholar published the first edition of his "little book," as he affectionately called it. They were, respectively, Erasmus and Calvin. Erasmus, the preeminent Christian humanist of his generation, was a scathing critic of ecclesiastical abuses and religious phoniness, and the most accomplished student of the Greek New Testament of his times. Calvin, building on the work of both Erasmus and Luther, wrote with brilliance and passion of the many ways the church and its theology had been "deformed." He did not write of "reform." Rather he presented a case for restoring the church and theology to its pristine purity. The "little book" he had published in Basel was the first edition of *The Institutes of the Christian Religion*. A book of 514 pages, printed in small octavo format (hence "little"), it was published in March, some four months prior to the death of Erasmus. In recognition of the four hundred and fiftieth anniversary of its appearance this present revised edition of Ford Lewis Battles' English translation is being published in 1986.

This edition has been revised in several ways. Two of the most obvious differences from the first edition are that it is now set in type rather than photocopied from typewritten pages, and that the title has been changed from *Institution* to the more familiar *Institutes*. After having completed the translation of the much larger *Institutes* of 1559, which is still available in the Library of Christian Classics series, Ford Lewis Battles became convinced that the more appropriate translation of the Latin "institutio" was "institution" rather than "institutes." He may well have been right about that, but the more familiar and common title is used in this revised edition for the convenience of readers and to express the continuous use of "institutio" in the title of the successive editions from 1536 to 1559.

The text of the Introduction and translation remains the same except for correction of mainly typographical errors. Revisions have been made through an expansion of footnotes to the introductory essay where the author alluded to but did not specify sources, and by revisions to the endnotes for the elimination of repetitive citations and references. There was no general bibliography in the first edition, nor is there one in this edition. A list of frequently used abbreviations and short author-title references has been placed in the front of the endnotes. The page and folio citations of generally unavailable sixteenth century editions have been eliminated from the endnotes and corresponding index, and page citations from modern editions and translations substituted for them.

A fourth appendix has been added. It is the text of the previously untranslated Latin preface by Calvin to the French Bible of Pierre Robert Olivétan of 1535. The translation is mine, but I utilized a rough draft of a translation found among the papers of Ford Lewis Battles in the archives of the Meeter Center.

The indices have also been revised so that all page references are to the pagination of this edition. The fifth index has been both abbreviated and made more complete. The sixth index, a kind of brief bibliography, has been eliminated, and the seventh index has been added to the end of the text where it originally appeared in the 1536 edition. All the revisions have been made to enhance the clarity and correctness of the book.

Three kinds of readers are anticipated. The first are those who simply wish to read this earliest expression of Calvin's thought. They may want to get a better understanding of the roots of Reformed theology, or they may want to get to know the young (twenty-seven years old) Calvin. For such readers the introductory essay by Ford Lewis Battles and the text itself are all that need be read. A second kind of reader, however, will in addition be well served by reading the endnotes with their extensive citations from the writings of Calvin's predecessors and contemporaries, both those loyal to and breaking from the Roman church. They will thus have a fuller picture of the significance of the text in its historical context than could be acquired in any other way. And a third kind of reader will be the scholar for whom the many other citations in the endnotes may lead to further research.

The copy of the 1536 edition used by Ford Lewis Battles in the preparation of this translation was that of the Bibliotheque National (Paris) [Res D° 6386]. The *Index Aureliensis* notes seven other copies in European libraries. Recently an Afrikaans translation was published [Potchefstroom, 1980] which utilized the copy in Strasbourg. In North America the following five libraries have copies: Harvard [FC5/C1394c], Huntington [340000], New York Public [KB/1536/W. Eames Coll.], Princeton Seminary [Rare/D-1/C1393], and Princeton University

[11.3.2.W.H.S.]. There may be others, but they are presently unknown to the writer.

In the margins of the 1536 edition, as in all later editions, Scriptural and other references were noted. These are incorporated in the body of the text in brackets. In the 1536 and 1539 editions the citations of Scripture were given in the form of an abbreviated title of the book and followed simply by the chapter. In the 1559 edition the verses were also indicated and many more were noted than in the 1536. Readers are cautioned that the indications of Scripture given in brackets are from and in the form of the corresponding parts of the 1559 edition. Further, the translator has added the references which are preceded by a "cf." Thus there are more Scriptural references in brackets in the text than Calvin explicitly acknowledged in the 1536 edition. The marginal references to the present text indicate the corresponding parts of the 1559 edition by book, chapter, and section number.

As in the first edition the pagination of the three Latin editions is indicated in the text as follows: [ ] for the 1536; ( ) for the *Opera Calvini* [OC] text of 1853; and / / for the *Opera Selecta* [OS] text of 1926.

M. HOWARD RIENSTRA, Director
H. H. Meeter Center for Calvin Studies
January 1986

PREFACE TO THE FIRST EDITION

When the Library of Christian Classics was in the planning stage, the proposal was made that not the last Latin (1559) edition but the first Latin (1536) edition of Calvin's *Institutio Christianae Religionis* be translated into English. It was pointed out that the 1536 text, heretofore never completely rendered into the English language, represents Calvin's thought concisely and without tedious polemic. This suggestion, while possessing some merit, was laid aside in favor of retranslating the much longer text of 1559, for it was rightly stated that Calvin deemed this final version the authoritative form of his thought for posterity. As he says in his "To the Reader," prefacing the 1559 edition: ". . . I was never satisfied until the work had been arranged in the order now set forth" [LCC 20.3].

The 1536 *Institutio* is introduced by the famed *Epistola Nuncupatoria*, John Calvin's impassioned plea, on behalf of the persecuted Evangelicals of France, to King Francis I, dated 23 August 1535. The book was issued by Platter and Lasius at Basel in March of the following year. A second edition of the 1536 text was published by W. Baum, E. Cunitz and E. Reuss as Volume 29 of the Corpus Reformatorum (*Calvini Opera*, vol. 1), cols. 1-252 (Braunschweig, 1853). A third edition was published by P. Barth and W. Niesel in *Joannis Calvini Opera Selecta*, vol. 1, pp. 19-283 (Munich, 1926).

While the 1559 edition has been translated many times and into many languages, that of 1536 has been rendered twice into Spanish and once into German. The portions unchanged or slightly altered which were carried into the Latin of 1539 were of course put into French in the 1541 Geneva edition. Dryander (Francisco Enziñas) of Burgos made the first Spanish translation [Ghent, 1540]. The second was by Jacinto Teran, *Juan Calvino Institución de la Religión Cristiana* (Buenos Aires, 1936), reprinted in two volumes in 1958. The German translation, by Bernhard Spiess (Wiesbaden, 1887) bears the title: *Joh. Calvins Christliche Glaubenslehre nach der aeltesten Ausgabe vom Jahre 1536 zum ersten mal ins Deutsche übersetzt*. The German rendering of the original title (p. VII) is: *Joh. Calvins aus Noyon Unterweisung in der christlichen Religion*, etc. Spiess provides a Scriptural Index (pp. 423-429), an Index of references to other authors (pp. 430-431), and a German translation of Calvin's original topical index with parallel references to the original edition, the CR text, and the German translation of the treatise (XII-XVI).

The first three chapters of the 1536 edition were translated into English by Walter G. Hards in his unpublished doctoral dissertation: *A Critical Translation and Evaluation of the Nucleus of the 1536 Edition of Calvin's Institutes*, Princeton Theological Seminary, 1955. Chapter II, On Faith, in Hards' translation, was separately printed and circulated at Pittsburgh Theological Seminary subsequent to that date.

The English translation here presented had its inception in my work on the edition of 1559, done in collaboration with John Thomas McNeill (Philadelphia, 1960: Library of Christian Classics, vols. 20-21). In 1967-68, I offered a course on the Young Calvin at Pittsburgh Theological Seminary. *Calvin's Commentary on Seneca's De Clementia*, his letters prior to 1536, the *Concio Academica* of Nicolas Cop (?) of 1533, the Preface to P. Robert's French New Testament (1534/5), and the *Psychopannychia* (1535/42) were provided in English for the students. The *pièce de resistance* of the seminar was a complete English translation of the 1536 *Institutio* printed in parallel columns with a reproduction of the Bibliothèque Nationale (Paris) exemplar of the original text [Res D° 6386]. The present edition contains a revision of that draft translation, minus the textual apparatus, but with a full complement of endnotes.

A few remarks should be made on the character and sources of the endnotes. Dr. John Thomas McNeill and I annotated the edition of 1559 in our translation of 1960 [LCC vols. 20-21]. Although in a few instances explicit reference is made to the LCC edition notes here, it would be superfluous to repeat these notes in the present writing, particularly since they reflect the more than two decades of history between the first and last Latin editions. I have been content, therefore, to confine the selection of materials to what throws light upon Calvin's sources, upon the political and religious situation on the eve of publication, and upon Calvin's views at this beginning point of his theological career. It has neither been possible nor desirable to annotate the *Institutes* of 1536 solely from Calvin's known or putative original sources. Grateful thanks are therefore expressed to all previous researchers and especially to the following: Peter Barth and Wilhelm Niesel, whose Opera Selecta editions of *Institutio* 1536 (vol. 1) and 1559 (vols. 3-5) have been a basic resource. The French editions of 1541 (ed. Pannier, 1936-39) and 1560 (ed. Benoît, 1957-63) have been helpful at certain points. A. Ganoczy's *Le Jeune Calvin* (Wiesbaden: 1966), especially chapter 2.1 (pp. 139-195) has provided a useful summary of previous scholarship and has added much fresh documentation. The work of others, such as A. Lang, P. Wernle, R. Seeberg, J. Bohatec, A.L. Herminjard, G.H. Williams, has also been drawn upon.

Since the present edition is intended for the use of readers whose working language is English, reference is generally made to standard English translations or, where such are lacking, pertinent passages have been translated by the editor.

The intent is to put in the hands of the general reader, in a non-technical language, what he needs to understand this earliest form of Calvin's famed theological work.

The apparatus provides the following: marginal references to the corresponding book, chapter and section of the 1559 *Institutio*; descriptive headings within each chapter and internal paragraph numbering; page limits of the original 1536 imprint [ ], of the CR text ( ), and of the text as printed in Barth and Niesel, *Opera Selecta Calvini*, vol. 1, pp. 1-283 / /; endnotes to the sources of the text; a comparative table of the 1536 and 1559 editions; an index of Biblical references; an index to other writers.

The text has been typed for publication by my secretary, Mrs. Betty Henry; the endnotes for the Epistle Dedicatory by Mrs. Ruth Davidson; Miss Kathy A. Herrin has made corrections and typed the appendices. My wife Marion and daughter Emily have assisted with the original typing and the checking of the translation and notes, and have typed the endnotes for Chapters 1-6. Emily has also provided the Biblical references in the early chapters. Glenn Masters of Geneva College and the Reformed Presbyterian Seminary has compared all the Biblical references with Calvin's original marginal notes. Dr. John R. Walchenbach has proofread the text and has, by his constant support and assistance, made this a better book than it would otherwise have been. Dr. John Thomas McNeill has given valuable criticism on the Introduction and Endnotes. Father Thomas Thompson has checked references and obtained reproductions of pages of early imprints at the Center for Reformation Research in St. Louis, Missouri. To all of these persons, as well as to Dr. Richard Ray of the John Knox Press and to Professor John Leith of Union Theological Seminary, Richmond, Virginia, go my grateful thanks.

The completion of this book was made possible by a generous sabbatical and other assistance given by the Pittsburgh Theological Seminary; to President William Kadel and Dean David Shannon I would like to acknowledge a special debt.

Among the many libraries, through the years, that supplied me with research materials, I should like especially to mention the following:

> Barbour Library, Pittsburgh Theological Seminary: Professor Dikran Y. Hadidian, Librarian, and Mrs. Eunice Paul, Order Librarian.
>
> Case Memorial Library, The Hartford Seminary Foundation: The Reverend Duncan Brockway, Librarian.
>
> The Center for Reformation Research, St. Louis, Missouri: Dr. Robert Kolb, Acting Executive Director.
>
> The Centre for Reformation and Renaissance Studies, University of Toronto: Professor Harry Secor, Director; also Mr. Kenneth R. Bartlett, Assistant at the Centre for Medieval Studies, Toronto, Canada.

Other libraries at which I have worked or which have sent materials to me include: The Library of Union Theological Seminary, New York City; The Library of Yale Divinity School, New Haven, Connecticut; The Bodleian Library,

Oxford University, Oxford, England; Bibliothèque Nationale, Paris, France; British Museum, London, England; The Library of the Seminary of the Free Church, Lausanne, Switzerland; The National Library of Wales, Aberystwyth, Wales; Dartmouth College Library, Hanover, New Hampshire; The Library of St. Vincent's College, Latrobe, Pennsylvania.

FORD LEWIS BATTLES
Advent 1974

INTRODUCTION

Ford Lewis Battles

I. THE ROAD TOWARD THE INSTITUTES OF 1536 (1532-35)

A. The Prelude to the First Edition of the Institutes

1. The Dilemma of the French Evangelicals. Behind the writing of the *Institutes of the Christian Religion* as well as overshadowing the development of the Gospel faith in France in the 1520's and 1530's stands the enigmatic figure of Francis I, Most Christian King of the French, Most Mighty and Most Illustrious Monarch—to quote the high-sounding titles with which the apologies of Calvin and other religionists introduce their appeal.

John Calvin's first direct contact with the anger of Francis I came after All Saints' Day (1 November) 1533, marked in the city of Paris by the address of Nicolas Cop upon assuming the rectorship of the University of Paris, actually a sermon expounding the lectionary Gospel text of the day, Matthew 5:1-12. Whether Calvin wrote that discourse or at least had a hand in its composition is still a matter of scholarly debate; that he was presumed by the authorities to have had a part in it may be assumed by his sudden flight from the city. In my opinion, enough parallels can be adduced to Calvin's later works to substantiate what Theodore Beza has written about his authorship of it.[1]

Near the close of Cop's Address, we read the following call to the Gospel cause:

> "Blessed will you be," he says, "when men hurl insults at you and reproach you, and say all evil against you falsely, for my sake." [Matt. 5:11]. Why, then, do we conceal the truth rather than speak it out boldly? Is it right to please men rather than God; to fear those who can destroy the body, but not the soul? O the ingratitude of mankind which will not

---

1. ". . . Calvin furnished him [Nicholas Cop] with one in which religion was treated more purely and clearly than it was previously wont to be." Beza's "Life of Calvin," in *John Calvin's Tracts and Treatises*; H. Beveridge, translator (Grand Rapids: 1983 [Edinburgh: 1844]), Vol. I, p. lxiii.

bear the slightest affliction in the name of him who died for the sins of all, him whose blood has freed us from eternal death and the shackles of Satan! The world and the wicked are wont to label as heretics, imposters, seducers and evilspeakers those who strive purely and sincerely to penetrate the minds of believers with the Gospel; (in such evildoing) "they think they are offering service to God." [John 16:2] But happy and blessed are they who endure all this with composure, giving thanks to God in the midst of affliction and bravely bearing calamities. "Rejoice," he says, "for great is your reward in heaven."[2]

The response to these fighting words was not long in coming. Cop and Calvin fled from the city. The Sorbonne did its work well. On the tenth of December, Francis sent instructions to the Parlement of Paris on how to ferret out and dispose of the heretical sect responsible for this seditious message. Francis makes specific reference to the Cop incident:

> Dear faithful friends! . . . We are very troubled and displeased at what has taken place in our beloved city of Paris, chief and capital of our kingdom, and where at the principal university of Christendom that accursed heretical Lutheran sect swarms. Its further spread we wish with our might and power to prevent. And to that end we wish and understand that such grievous punishment should be meted out that it would be a correction to the accursed heretics and an example to all others.[3]

The letter just quoted, and the letter of the same date from Francis I to Jean du Bellay, Archbishop of Paris, provide for two counsellors of the Parlement of Paris to be assigned to the Archbishop to investigate the clergy and prepare a trial of those who are espousing heretical opinions. The letter also calls for an investigation "of the Doctor who has preached certain propositions . . . and his Rector . . ."; apparently, the king did not realize that "doctor" and "rector" were the same person, Nicolas Cop, who had by this time taken refuge in Basel.

It would be impossible within the compass of this brief introduction to review the complex history of church-state relations and political events leading to the writing of Calvin's appeal to Francis I. We can only sketch in a few broad strokes the character of that background and of its chief political actor.

Throughout his reign, Francis I was a beleaguered monarch, fighting in his vacillating and inconstant way for the integrity of his realm. The growth in the heart of his kingdom of a movement of protest against the ecclesiastical establishment, one of the few bulwarks of his regime, could only be looked at by him and by his chief religious advisers as seditious. Frustrated in being passed over for election as Emperor, frustrated three times in Italian campaigns (one of which led to a savage sack of the city of Rome), imprisoned for a time in Madrid by his archrival the Emperor Charles, repeatedly threatened by in-

---

2. For the full text see Appendix III.
3. A.-L. Herminjard, *Correspondance des Réformateurs.* . . . (Genève et Paris: 1870), Vol. III, No. 440, pp. 114-115.

vasion, shorn of some of his territories, Francis I was indeed desperate for support. That is why he went to such lengths as concluding a treaty of peace with the Protestant princes of Germany in January 1534, while at the same time actively persecuting the "Lutherans" in his own kingdom. That is why he entered into an ill-conceived concordat with Leo X in 1515 and conferred with Clement VII in October-November 1533 at Marseilles. That is why he even proposed at one time settling the conflict with the Empire by a duel between him and Charles; and went so far as to enter into an abortive alliance with the Sultan against his Christian foes. The whole reign of Francis I is one of vacillation and uncertainty. How, then, could his religious policy not reflect the character of this monarch?

It was this unstable monarch, "whose opinion was often that of the last man with whom he had talked," with whom the French Evangelicals had to deal. The intense diplomatic activity of the French king reached its height in 1534; between May and August there were consultations with the German and Swiss theologians on Church reunion after a secret treaty had been signed the preceding January between Francis and the German Protestant princes. Of all the foreign Protestants with whom Francis' envoy, Guillaume du Bellay, negotiated, the Swiss Protestants were least taken in by the false peace moves of the French king. The Reformation had already spread through the Swiss cities, beginning in Zürich, then passing to Berne, Basel and other cities in German Switzerland, and ultimately to the French-speaking territories in the west, although not yet to Geneva. Many French Protestants had sought refuge in Switzerland from the threat of death at home. The city of Neuchâtel, which had declared for the Reform in 1530, was the haven to which two Frenchmen from Lyons had fled: Antoine Marcourt and Pierre de Vingle, minister and printer respectively. With the help of Pierre Viret and at the behest of Guillaume Husson de Blois, a pungent critique was prepared from a tract of Viret's colleague, Antoine Marcourt. This critique in the form of placards done at de Vingle's press was smuggled into France to be affixed in public places so that the "poor ignorant" ones could be told the truth about the abomination of the Mass.

These posters mysteriously appeared in Paris and other places on the night of 17 October 1534. One was even tacked, it is claimed, to the door of the King's bedchamber in Blois! They provoked a bloody persecution and had fateful effects on all subsequent European religious history. Thanks to the chance discovery of strips of the original placards, used in the binding of other books, it is now possible to read for the first time in over four hundred years the authentic original text of this important pronouncement. Let us pause to quote from it and to discuss its significance.

Four simple trenchant points are made:
(1) that the once-for-all character of Christ's high-priestly self-sacrifice as described in the Letter to the Hebrews is set aside by the oft-repeated sacrifice of Christ in the Roman Mass;

(2) the Mass is an act of idolatry, localizing in countless earthly places for adoration a glorified human body which is really in heaven;

(3) the so-called priestly miracle of transubstantiation is an utter denial of Scriptural teaching about the Supper and about examination of self before communicating, for which auricular confession to a priest is substituted;

(4) the benefits of the Mass are clean contrary to those taught in Scripture as coming from the Supper.[4]

Let us sketch in a few words now the development of transubstantiation. Transubstantiation is in actuality a philosophical effort to explain a real presence of Christ in the Supper, physically perceived. Transubstantiation first took a canonical status at the Fourth Lateran Council of 1215. It was placed among those canons to counter the anti-clerical, anti-sacramental teachings of the Albigensians that were imperilling the medieval church, especially in France. The theological outworking of this canon took more than two generations, reaching its formulation at the hands of Thomas Aquinas in his two *Summae,* and also its liturgical fruition in the establishment of the feast of Corpus Christi for which he also wrote the service and its hymns.

Rapidly the Mass and its attendant priestly miracle became the kingpin of the whole medieval ecclesiastical system in the west. With the related withholding of the cup from the laity by the doctrine of concomitance, it had to stand unchallenged if the delicately poised system of Church and State was to survive. Hence, any questioning of its scriptural validity, any hesitation about its attendant features—the remainder of the seven-fold sacramental system, indulgences, treasury of merits, invocation of saints and all the rest was fought fiercely by Church and State equally.

Wyclif's determined campaign against transubstantiation at the end of the fourteenth century, despite the weakened and divided condition of the papacy at that time, was firmly suppressed. Even Hus' milder efforts to reform the Supper met with conciliar condemnation and a martyr's death at Constance in 1415.

When Luther's theses of 1517 entered these sacred precincts questioningly, and when in 1520 he unmistakably dealt a body blow to the medieval ecclesiastical system in his *Babylonian Captivity of the Church,* the long-suppressed criticism of this central dogma of a repressive and unscriptural church could flow freely. Luther was, however, mild in his critique alongside his Swiss counterpart, Huldreich Zwingli, whose views are in part reflected in the statement of the placards.

The point we would make here is that the most necessary and most dangerous critical act the Reform party could perform was to question the Mass. In the slashing strokes of this popular document, the authors first aroused the reactionary theologians of the Sorbonne (e.g. Robert Ceneau) who had unsuc-

---

4. The full text is given in Appendix I.

cessfully been trying to suppress "Lutheranism" ever since it appeared in France; secondly, highly placed "Catholic" humanists like Guillaume Budé and Jacopo Sadoleto who raised the flag of warning with the King; thirdly, the King himself who saw grave danger to his political designs, the threat to religious and civil order, and to his plans (however hollow) for religious peace; and finally, the common folk whether of superstitious traditional belief or moderately interested in the reform of the Church.

2. *Calvin's Seneca Commentary (1532): A First Apology to Francis I?* It is into this troubled chapter of France's history that Calvin was reborn an evangelical Christian. To these first steps of his we now turn. In April 1532, he published his first book, the *Commentary on Seneca's De Clementia*. Here we shall view it as a first step on his religious journey. Much has been written about the relationship of this humanist commentary to Calvin the Christian. Some have confidently tied it to his faith; others have noted that it is virtually devoid of religious reference, if not religious interest.

A problem in dealing with the question is the long-held notion that Calvin's theological views never really changed and that what he wrote in the final edition of 1559 of the *Institutes of the Christian Religion* applies more or less indiscriminately to his whole Christian life. This is simply not true: great consistency there is throughout his literary expression of the faith, but also much movement, reconsideration and recasting of his thought. Even a brief comparative glance at the five chief editions of the *Institutes* will show this.

Hence, most scholars have either directly or instinctively compared the mature Christian with the pre-conversion author of the Seneca. If, however, we concentrate our vision on the 1536 *Institutes* and view the Seneca in the light of it, a different picture begins to emerge. The *Institutes* opens with the famous letter to Francis I, an eloquent appeal to that monarch on behalf of Calvin's Reformed compatriots in France in the troubled year of 1535. Taken as a whole, this letter and the theological essay that follows, especially the final chapter, are a literary whole and hold up to Francis a model of the Christian monarch.

This search for "mirrors for magistrates," "instructions for a Christian prince," and the like constituted one of the most prolific literary genres of the sixteenth century. Few indeed were the Renaissance humanists who did not try to show their scholarly excellence and their political sagacity to the monarchs they wished to shape to more humane dimensions. Francis I had his Guillaume Budé; Philip II had his Erasmus. The threat on the one hand of political chaos due to internal revolutionary tendencies and external wars, and of oppressive tyranny by frightened rulers on the other, led sensitive and moderate men to scour antiquity for models of political behavior.

No worse tyrant appeared in Roman imperial history than Nero, yet no monarch ever had better political and moral instruction at the outset of his imperial career. Is it not possible that Calvin took up Nero's old Stoic teacher's advice not only to carve out a place for himself among the humanists, but also to bring, somehow, to the attention of Francis I, the right way to rule: between perilous laxity on the one hand and overbearing severity on the other? As a nominal Christian at least already of great ethical sensitivity, Calvin perhaps felt his modest learned little commentary might come to the attention of the King who had just assured Renaissance humanism a central place in French culture by the establishment of the Royal Lectureships, of which Calvin was then at least briefly availing himself. Perhaps Calvin knew Budé's as yet unpublished *L'Institution du Prince* in which that architect of the Royal Lectureships had already provided a classic treatise of guidance for his King.

That Calvin had his eye on Francis I when he chose the *De Clementia* of Seneca to test his newly acquired linguistic and historical skills, is a view that had been advanced before: J. Bohatec, among others, suggests that ". . . his Seneca *Commentary* signifies an open struggle of the young humanist against the absolutist claims of his native country."[5] Nowhere does Calvin explicitly say this, but looked at in the light of the 1536 *Institutes* and the use the latter book makes of material from the former, the theory becomes more plausible. It suggests a forensic dimension to Calvin's conversion explicitly prepared for in the *Seneca Commentary*. Let us for the moment suppose that the *Seneca Commentary* was Calvin's first apology to Francis I.

3. Theological First Steps of Calvin. We have already noted the comparative absence of explicitly religious teaching from the *Seneca Commentary*. It therefore would seem quite difficult to bring this early work into a discussion of Calvin's conversion. We hestitate to launch out on this topic, which has tantalized the minds of many greater scholars with as yet no clear answer in sight. Calvin's personal reticence on this point, the slenderness of the direct sources in his own writings, and the mysterious gaps in our information as to his whereabouts at this crucial time in his career make any precise dating of the conversion impossible. John T. McNeill's summary of past guesses, that it probably took place between 5 April 1534 (when he visited LeFèvre d'Étaples at Marguerite's court at the castle of Nérac) and 4 May 1534 when he returned to his native city of Noyon in Picardy to resign his benefice, seems as plausible as any, although Ganoczy more recently pleads for an even later date. Fortunately for our purpose, dating is not important; the content and structure of his conversion are. On this latter we are, I think, on firmer ground.

Before we examine formally the sources for our knowledge of his conversion, let us look at whatever religious content can be found in the *Seneca Commentary*. Basically, three religious questions seem to concern this young man on the eve of his conversion: (1) the contrast between paganism and Christianity or, more broadly stated, between superstition and true religion; (2) the origin and nature of the human soul; (3) the question of governance, divine and human, or in other words, the place of human authority within the divine prov-

5. J. Bohatec, *Calvins Lehre von Staat und Kirche* (Breslau: 1937), p. 43.

idential frame. Let us take a moment to look at these three points in a little more detail.

A constantly reiterated Calvinian criticism of Roman Catholicism concerns the "humanly devised" character of its liturgical practices. Always strongly questioned, such things are frequently the subject of Calvin's most biting satire: one thinks of the *Treatise on Relics* as the chief example of this. One sees this predilection already in Calvin's remarks in the *Seneca Commentary* on public recognition of the ruler among the Romans:

> Clemency kept Augustus secure during his lifetime; after his death, it has kept his reputation alive. Decrees of the senate made in praise of living princes can seem to be either forced out by fear, or precipitated by rashness. Servile rites which are performed by the people, acclamations also . . . serve the presence of a ruler. The praises given to a dead man are spontaneous and thus to be preferred. So the Roman people believed Augustus a god, not because they were bidden to do so, but because they knew by experience that he was a good prince. It was a solemn custom of the Romans to place their Caesars amongst the gods through apotheosis. . . . Herodian sets forth the rites and ceremonies for the consecration of emperors. As often as I reread that passage, I cannot keep from laughing, so silly was that religion of the Romans. [*Comm. Sen. de Clem.* p. 187][6]

Such rites are the product of superstition rather than of true religion. In another place Calvin sums up the difference between the two: "Superstition bears the same relationship to religion as pity does to clemency; just as cruelty stands in the same relationship to clemency as impiety does to religion" [*Comm. Sen. de Clem.* p. 363]. It is true that Calvin at this point quotes the obvious philosophical authorities on the meaning of these terms. But when we look at the clear Christian use to which this material is later put in the *Institutes* (1.12.1) we must admit that the fundamental issue of true versus false religion was already on Calvin's mind in early 1532.

A second fundamental theological question which was later to shape Calvin's faith is that of the soul, its nature and origin. Again, to turn to the *Seneca Commentary,* Calvin says:

> In passing he lightly touches upon the contradictory notions of the philosophers, who have not yet settled upon a sure and definite location for the soul. Herophilus has located it in the ventricle of the brain; for Plato and Democritus it seems more likely to rest in the entire head, Erasistratus considers it to be around the membrane of the brain, Strato in the space between the eyebrows; Parmenides and Epicurus in the whole breast; Diogenes in the arterial ventricle of the heart; the Stoics assign it to the whole heart or spirit; others the whole cervix of the heart; others

---

6. *Calvin's Commentary on Seneca's De Clementia,* edited and translated by Ford Lewis Battles and André Malan Hugo (Leiden: 1969). All page references are to this edition.

the diaphragm; Empedocles the concretion of the blood. [*Comm. Sen. de Clem.* p. 93]

Here he is quoting Plutarch in Budé's Latin translation and citing Cicero's *Tusculan Disputations*. This with other passages in the *Seneca Commentary* mark the topic as one of importance for Calvin, later crucial for his whole theology.

A third theological concern is the divine governance of the world and its relation to human political rule, barely hinted at in this early document:

> This statement, moreover, derives from the opinion of the Stoics, who attribute the superintendence of human affairs to the gods, assert providence, and leave nothing to mere chance. The Epicureans, although they do not deny the existence of the gods, do the closest thing to it: they imagine the gods to be pleasure-loving, idle, not caring for mortals, lest anything detract from their pleasures: they deride Stoic providence as a prophesying old woman. They think everything happens by mere chance. But he who professes himself vicar of the gods, surely confesses that the gods look after human needs. [*Comm. Sen. de Clem.* pp. 29-30]

There follows a significant string of classical proof-texts for the vicegerent character of earthly monarchs. After quoting Plutarch, "Princes are God's ministers, for the welfare and care of men; as God bestows upon them, they distribute part; keep part," he adds (following Romans, ch. 13) "Our religion, too, has such a confession: 'Power comes from God alone, and those that exist have been ordained by God.' " [*Comm. Sen. de Clem.* p. 31]

These three small points, expressed as they are in what seems to be a humanistic if not outright pagan tone, may not say much by themselves about the later champion of the faith. But less than two years after these lines were published, they began to take a new and unmistakably Christian turn in Calvin's first theological writings.

In Calvin's first explicitly "Evangelical" writing, his French preface to his cousin's translation of the New Testament probably penned in late 1534 or early 1535, we find emerging what may have already been in his mind when he compared, by implication, the silly rites of the pagan Romans with Christian worship. Here he succinctly rehearses the whole salvation history in a few pages "for those who love Christ and his Gospel."

> It is true enough that the Gentiles, astonished and convinced by so many goods and benefits which they saw with their own eyes, have been forced to recognize the hidden Benefactor from whom came so much goodness. But instead of giving the true God the glory which they owed him, they forged a god to their own liking, one dreamt up by their foolish fantasy in its vanity and deceit; and not one god only, but as many as their temerity and conceit enabled them to forge and cast; so that there was not a people or place which did not make new gods as seemed good to them. Thus it is that idolatry, that perfidious panderer, was able to exercise

dominion to turn men away from God, and to amuse them with a whole crowd of phantoms they themselves had given shape, name and being itself.[7]

From this fairly conventional Scriptural treatment of idolatry it is a short step to the identification of the current Roman Catholic cultus with idolatry.

Calvin's learned parrotting of various classical views on the location of the soul just quoted from the *Seneca Commentary* rather quickly gives way in the *Psychopannychia* written perhaps two years later (1534/5) to the following:

> Here let human wisdom give place; for though it thinks much about the soul it perceives no certainty with regard to it. Here, too, let Philosophers give place, since on almost all subjects their regular practice is to put neither end nor measure to their dissensions, while on this subject in particular they quarrel, so that you will scarcely find two of them agreed on any single point! Plato in some passages, talks nobly of the faculties of the soul and Aristotle, in discoursing of it, has surpassed all in acuteness. But what the soul is, and whence it is, it is vain to ask them, or indeed the whole body of Sages, though they certainly thought more purely and wisely on the subject than some amongst ourselves, who boast that they are disciples of Christ.[8]

In the previously cited *Preface to Pierre Robert's New Testament,* Calvin begins his discussion with Genesis 1:27, the making of man in the image of God. More precisely, the *Psychopannychia* identifies this image with the spirit or soul of man: "Whatever philosophers or these dreamers [the Anabaptists] may pretend, we hold that nothing can bear the image of God but spirit, since God is a spirit."[9] Later this identification of the divine image *par excellence* with man's rational faculty will be more fully developed. We see here, beginning in the *Seneca Commentary,* the early stages of that development in Calvin.

Our third theological concern noted in the *Seneca Commentary,* that of divine and human sovereignty, is marked in the very structure of the first edition of the *Institutes of the Christian Religion,* penned in 1535. Read the letter to Francis I; then skip over to the final chapter, or even the very last section. You will then observe that the *Institutes* is set in a political frame. At the heart of Calvin's thought was the relation between the King and the King of Kings, between the providential rule of our Heavenly Father and the sometimes capricious and cruel rule of him who should be the father of his country. Having

---

7. *Calvin's Commentaries,* edited and translated by Joseph Haroutunian and Louise Pettibone Smith, The Library of Christian Classics, Vol. XXIII (Philadelphia: n.d.), pp. 60-61. The original text may be found in the *Corpus Reformatorum* edition of Calvin's works: *Opera Calvini* [OC], Vol. IX, p. 797. The preface to the entire French Bible of Pierre Robert Olivetan, in Latin, may be found in OC, IX, 787-8.

8. *Psychopannychia,* in *John Calvin's Tracts and Treatises,* Vol. III, p. 420. The original text may be found in OC, V, 178.

9. *Psychopannychia,* op. cit., Vol. III, p. 424. The original text may be found in OC, V, 181.

looked at what may have been Calvin's first theological steps—or at least his paramount religious interests immediately before and after his conversion—let us turn to the conversion itself.

B. Some Speculations on the Shape and Content of Calvin's Conversion

1. The Conversion Viewed from the Sources. In the present essay we propose to lay aside the vexed question of the dating of Calvin's *conversio subita* as he calls it; this will free us to speculate on the theologically more interesting features of that obscurely documented event in his life. Perhaps we should rehearse first the sources themselves. Here we are on oft-trodden ground.[10] Where does Calvin in his own words speak of his conversion? Very briefly but directly in the preface to his *Commentary on the Psalms* a late writing (1555) but one of prime importance. Obliquely, Calvin in 1539 refers to his conversion in his account of the Evangelical layman before the judgment seat of God. This is in his eloquent response to Cardinal Sadolet's appeal to the city of Geneva (now that Calvin is exiled therefrom) to return to the bosom of the true Church. Cardinal Sadolet in his appeal to the people of Geneva had penned a dramatic scene before the judgment seat of God where a loyal Catholic made his last confession, and contrastingly a protestant (Calvin, thinly disguised) also made his final fruitless appeal. Calvin skillfully turns this around: in place of the schismatic pictured by Sadolet, he presents essentially a sketch of himself as churchman struggling against error after his conversion. These are the two usually cited sources for the conversion. To them I should like to add what I call "the kernel of Calvin's faith" contained in the first few pages of Chapter I of the 1536 *Institutes*; to it might be appended also, possibly, the *Preface to Pierre Robert's New Testament* as a whole. This is not a very impressive list, but it is what we have.

In many of the great conversions recorded in Christian history there is a particular verse of Scripture which is reputed to have "triggered" the experience. Without making a long list of such potent texts we shall be satisfied with recalling that Romans 1:17 so functioned for Luther; "The just shall live by faith." Now we have no such clear record for Calvin. It is probably foolish to speculate whether a particular verse so moved Calvin. For him as for Luther, Paul's Letter to the Romans was the prime book of Scripture in his grasp and formation of the Christian faith. Yet one is tempted to single out one verse or at least a larger context as determinative of his faith. Unquestionably, the first chapter of Romans can be so marked; I think one can be even more precise in noting Romans 1:18-25. If one verse is to be selected I would suggest Romans 1:21: "For

---

10. The voluminous literature on Calvin's conversion has been thoroughly surveyed and the question reconsidered by Alexandre Ganoczy, *Le Jeune Calvin* (Wiesbaden: 1966), pp. 6-15 and 271-303.

although they knew God they did not honor him as God or give thanks to him, but they became futile in their thinking and their senseless minds were darkened." Why? The central feature of Calvin's piety is the two knowledges, of God, of man. Initially mentioned in the edition of 1536, they became by 1559 almost an organizing principle of his thought. In summing up the knowledge of God, Calvin lists the *"virtutes Dei,"* excellences or powers of God—too dynamic to be called attributes. The list of these given at the head of Chapter I of the 1536 *Institutes* is almost identical with those given in the *Romans Commentary* (1540) at 1:21. The same passage in Romans is alluded to in Calvin's *Reply to Cardinal Sadolet* (1539), when he sets forth his true confession of faith before God's judgment seat, to replace the false one Sadolet had in his letter put into Calvin's mouth. Calvin, speaking of the false faith against which he had reacted, wrote in the form of a prayer; "They [the people], indeed, called thee the only God, but it was while transferring to others the glory which thou hast claimed for thy Majesty. They figured and had for themselves as many gods as they had saints, whom they chose to worship."[11] To sum up, the emphasis on honoring God and being thankful to him are central themes in Calvin's piety.

To look at this probable Scriptural base of Calvin's conversion more broadly we see that as with Luther so with Calvin, it is *the constellation of Psalms and Romans* that holds the secret of their faith. Luther's first commentary was on Psalms; his second on Romans, years before the 1517 experience, but leading to it. Calvin's first commentary was on Romans; in fact the *Institutes* itself may be thought of as an extended commentary on Romans. While his *Psalms Commentary* came much later, it is his most explicitly personal commentary (with sometimes veiled references to his own spiritual states under those attributed to David), and as we have seen contains in its preface the one explicit testimony to Calvin's conversion.[12] Also, statistically, whatever mere quantities mean in religious scholarship!—Romans and Psalms are far and away the chiefly used Scriptural books in the *Institutes*. In the final Latin (1559) edition Romans is cited or quoted at least 598 times; Psalms, 580. The third most-used book is Matthew with 542 references. Thus, when Calvin characterizes Psalms as "An Anatomy of All the Parts of the Soul," we see what a high place he gives it; and add to this the fact that he makes the Psalter the hymnbook of the Reformed Church.

Louis Goumaz, whose pioneer work, *La Doctrine du Salut d'après les Commentaires de Jean Calvin sur le Nouveau Testament* (Lausanne: 1917) set the pattern of correlating the theology of the *Institutes* with the exegesis of his commentaries, sums up the crucial place of the Scriptures in Calvin's conversion:

11. "Calvin's Reply to Sadoleto," in *Tracts and Treatises,* Vol. I, p. 57.
12. See J. Walchenbach, *The Influence of David and the Psalms on the Life and Thought of John Calvin* [unpublished Th.M. thesis, Pittsburgh Theological Seminary, 1969].

Scripture was the instrument for Calvin's conversion . . . he found in it the food which fed his religious nature and the document consonant with his humanistic and legal spirit.[13]

Let us now construct, out of the pieces given in the above-mentioned documents, a coherent picture of Calvin's conversion. There are five "moments" to the conversion experience: (1) the preparation, (2) the travail of conscience, (3) the call of the Gospel, (4) the conversion, (5) first steps in the Christian life. Here in a strophic translation are Calvin's own words, with the bracketed lines taken from the Psalms commentary.

I The Preparation

O Lord, as I had from childhood been so brought up,
I have always professed the Christian faith.
From the beginning I had no other sort of faith
Than what everywhere prevailed at that time.
Thy word which like a lamp ought
To have shined upon thy whole people,
Had been taken away or at least had been suppressed among us.
And lest anyone might desire a greater light
This notion had been planted
In the souls of all, that the search
For that heavenly and secret philosophy
Were better delegated to a few
From whom oracles were to be sought:
No higher intelligence befitted lowly minds
Than for them to yield themselves
In obedience to his Church.
Now the rudiments to which I had been introduced
Were of such sort as would not instruct me
To the lawful worship of thy presence.
Nor would they open the way for me
To a sure hope of salvation.
I indeed had learned to worship thee as my God:
But since the true way to worship thee
Utterly eluded me,
I was stumbling at the very threshold
As I had been taught, I believed
Myself redeemed by the death of thy Son,
From the claim of eternal death;
But I was imagining that redemption
As powerless to reach me.
The coming day of resurrection I awaited
But its memory as a luckless thing
I loathed.

13. Goumaz, p. 429.

And this sense had not come to me
Privately at home,
But from the very teaching which at that time
Conceived by the ministers of the Christian people
Was passed on to the people.
These persons were then preaching thy mercy
Toward me, but only toward those
Who had shown themselves worthy of it.
Worth they were lodging in works-righteousness
So that at last only he would be received
By thee into grace
Who reconciled himself toward thee with works.
Yet in the meanwhile they were now deceiving us
That we are miserable sinners,
Who would often slip because of the weakness
Of the flesh,
And that accordingly thy mercy ought to be
The gate of salvation for all:
But the way to obtain it, they showed,
Was to make satisfaction to thee
For our offenses.
Then they enjoined satisfaction upon us;
First, having confessed all our sins to a priest
We should humbly seek pardon and absolution;
Then by good works blot out
From thy remembrance our bad deeds;
Lastly, to make up for what we lacked,
We should add sacrifices and public expiations.
They now showed thou wert a stern judge,
A strict avenger of iniquity,
And thus, how dreadful
Thy presence must be.
Therefore they urged us to flee to the saints
That by their intercession
We might render thee open to our plea
And more favorable to us.
[From my early childhood
My father had destined me
For theology:
But after a time,
Having considered that the knowledge of the law
Commonly enriches those who follow it,
This hope suddenly made him change his mind.
That was the reason
I was withdrawn
From the study of philosophy
And put into the study of law,
To which, although, in obedience to my father,

I tried to apply myself faithfully,
God nevertheless by his secret providence
Finally made me turn
In another direction.]

II The Travail of Conscience

Though I performed all these rites
And they afforded me intervals of repose,
Still I was far away indeed
From real peace of conscience.
As often as I descended into myself
Or raised my mind to thee,
I was struck with utter horror
That no expiations,
No satisfactions could cure.
The more closely I looked at myself,
The keener the darts that pricked my conscience,
Leaving me no other solace
Than to delude myself in oblivion.
Yet nothing better offered itself,
So I kept to the road on which
I had already set out.

III The Call of the Gospel

At this point a far different sort of teaching arose,
Not one to lead us away
From the profession of Christianity
But to lead us back
To its very source,
And, purging it of the dregs,
To restore it to its purity.
Still, I was offended by novelty
And lent a reluctant ear,
Even at first, I confess,
Stoutly and vigorously resisted.
Such is the persistence of stubbornness
With which men cling to a course once undertaken,
That only with the greatest reluctance
Was I led to confess
My whole past life had been steeped
In ignorance and error.
One thing especially averted my mind
From these things:
Reverence for the Church.
[For I was so obstinately devoted
To the superstitions of the Papacy
That it was difficult to pull me

Out of that very deep morass.]
But when I let my ears be opened
And myself be taught,
I understood that fear of departing
From the Church's majesty
Was groundless.
For they reminded me what a big difference
There was between leaving the Church
And trying to correct the faults
Corrupting it.
Eloquently they spoke of the Church
Showing the highest zeal
To cultivate its unity.
Lest they seemed to quibble
Over the name "Church,"
They showed it nothing new
That anti-Christs preside over it
In place of pastors.
They set forth plenty of examples
Which showed their sole concern
To be the upbuilding of the Church.
In this they were making common cause
With many servants of Christ
We had counted among the number
Of the saints.
They inveighed rather freely
Against the Roman pontiff
Revered as Christ's vicar,
Peter's successor,
And prince of the Church:
This they excused on the grounds
That such titles are empty bugbears
Which should not so seal
The eyes of the godly
As to frighten them from looking into
And investigating the matter.
When the world was oppressed by dull ignorance
As by a deep slumber,
Then it was that the pope
Rose up to such a peak.
Surely it was not by God's Word
He was established,
Not by the lawful calling of the Church
Was he ordained prince of the Church,
But self-elected by his own will.
If we would have Christ's kingdom
Safe amongst us,
Such tyranny preying upon God's people

Is not to be borne.
And these preachers had the strongest arguments
To confirm all their charges.
First, they clearly disposed of everything
Then commonly adduced
To establish the papal primacy.
After they had withdrawn all its supports,
By God's word they also tumbled it
From its lofty eminence.
They made it abundantly clear,
As far as they could,
Both to the learned and the unlearned,
That the true order of the Church had perished;
The keys holding the Church's discipline
Had been dreadfully perverted;
Christian liberty had collapsed—
In short, Christ's kingdom lay prostrate
After this primacy had been set up.
To prick my conscience
Lest I should nonchalantly wink
At these matters as having nothing to do with me—
This is why they talked to me.
Far, far art thou from supporting
Any voluntary error
That not even one may err with impunity
Who is seduced from the path
By mere ignorance.
This they proved by the Son's testimony:
"If a blind man leads a blind man,
Both fall into the ditch." [Matt. 15:14]

IV The Conversion

[My mind which, despite my youth,
Had been too hardened in such matters,]
Now was readied for serious attention.
[By a sudden conversion
God turned and brought it
To docility.]
I realized as light broke upon me
In what a dunghill of errors
I had been wallowing,
How infected I had been
With filth and spots.
Thunderstruck at the misery
In which I had slipped,
And even more at the misery
Which threatened me
With awareness of eternal death,

I made it my first concern
To condemn, not without groaning and tears,
My previous life
And to betake myself into thy life.
And now, O Lord,
What remains for a wretch like me
But to offer thee my prayer of pardon
In place of trying to defend myself,
Lest thou hold to strick account
My dreadful desertion of thy Word,
Desertion from which
Thou once for all didst
By thy marvellous kindness
Vindicate me?

V First Steps in the Christian Life

[Having therefore received
Some taste and knowledge
Of true piety,
I was suddenly fired
With such a great desire to advance
That, even though I had not forsaken
The other studies entirely,
I nonetheless worked at them
More slackly.
But I was utterly amazed
That before a year had passed
All those who yearned
For pure doctrine
Were coming again and again to me
To learn it.
Even though I had scarcely commenced
To study it myself.
For my part, being of a nature
Somewhat unpolished and retiring,
I always longed for repose and quiet.
Hence I began to seek
Some hiding place
And way to withdraw from people.
But, far from attaining my heart's desire,
All retreats and places of escape
Became for me like public schools.
In short, although I always cherished
The goal of living in private, incognito,
God so led me and caused me to turn
By various changes
That he never left me at peace in any place
Until, in spite of my natural disposition

He brought me into the limelight.
Leaving my native France,
I departed into Germany
With the express purpose
Of being able to live,
At peace in some unknown corner,
As I had always longed.]

These are Calvin's own words drawn mainly from the Reply to Sadoleto of 1539, and the Commentary on Psalms of 1555. In them is reviewed the whole conversion, its preparation and its immediate aftermath. His was a conversion which cannot be confined to a merely personal, inward change. The inner change that took place was truly brought about within the larger context of stirring events in the history of the Church; in turn the new-born Calvin left his own impress on that history. We may therefore be pardoned if we call his conversion *forensic* for it involves a total reorientation to history and to the institutions— political, social and ecclesiastical—of Calvin's own time. This is one reason why his theology defies ultimate systematization: it is a salvation-history faith. It must be told as the story of Israel, narrowly begun in the Old Testament, but in Christ embracing all nations.

That is why we cannot leave our discussion of his conversion without examining what may be called the "first" and "second" drafts of his theological restatement of the conversion experience.

2. The Conversion Theologically Restated: the History of Salvation. Encouraged by Bucer and Farel, Calvin's cousin Pierre Robert completed on 12 February 1535 his French translation of the New Testament, published at Neuchâtel by the printer Pierre de Vingle on 4 June 1535. Calvin was asked to provide two prefaces for the book, one in Latin,[14] and one in French. It is the latter that we would like to call his "first draft" of the theological restatement of his conversion experience. Since Calvin was in Basel by January 1535, at the latest the Preface must be dated early in that year when his full energies were being given to writing or completing his first edition of the *Institutes of the Christian Religion* (finished 23 August 1535; published by March 1536).

The Preface to the New Testament expressed in a succinct fashion the familiar Pauline-Augustinian summary of human history: man's creation in the image of God . . . continuing mercy of God through conscience (Gentiles) and law (Israel) . . . further apostasy . . . coming of the Savior . . . call of the Gospel. The preface ends with an appeal to kings and magistrates and to bishops and pastors to support the right preaching of the Gospel and the health of the church. From our point of view, the center of this brief essay, as a theological restatement of Calvin's conversion, is the section we have labeled "The Call of the Gospel." There is no question that the fundamental shift in Calvin's outlook, the insight that led him, inwardly, to abandon the search for wisdom among the

14. For a translation of the Latin see Appendix IV.

philosophers, was the crucial place of the fall of man. The fall, not understood by the philosophers in their glorification of human wisdom and their speculation upon the soul [cf. *Inst.* 1.15.8], is the point at which weak human wisdom is to be differentiated from the divine wisdom of Christ, what Calvin has elsewhere called the *philosophia Christi*. It is the pursuit of this higher wisdom that imparts joy to Christians joyously serving their Lord even in the midst of persecution. In Jesus Christ all Old Testament types of great men converge. "All that we think or desire, all that we express, is to be found in Jesus Christ, whom to know the whole of Scripture calls us."

From this reading of the Gospel Calvin moves out from personal experience to reflect upon the whole history of salvation. It is all in this brief preface, Calvin's first theological reflection upon his conversion. Here is the reason why Calvin abandoned the literary career of a humanist, or to put it in his own words:

> Having therefore received
> Some taste and knowledge
> Of true piety,
> I was suddenly fired
> With such a great desire to advance
> That, even though I had not forsaken
> The other studies entirely,
> I nonetheless worked at them
> More slackly [see Strophic translation above].

The "second draft" as well call it, of this theological restatement of the conversion experience followed the first by a few weeks or months during the first half of the year 1535. We have already alluded to it as "the Kernel of Calvin's faith." It occupies the initial nine pages of Chapter I of the 1536 *Institutes*. It covers the same ground as the *Preface to the New Testament* but more explicitly theologically than the earlier document, which is more narrowly Scriptural in its emphasis. It commences with the "two knowledges," of God and of man, passes to the law—unwritten and written—and concludes with "another way," i.e., Christ.

In the summary of Calvin's conversion there is an important phrase for all later Calvinism:

> As often as I descended into myself
> Or raised my mind to thee. . . .

These two movements of the human mind lead to the antithetical knowledge of God and knowledge of ourselves, the gulf between the all-holy God and the fallen sinner which only the incarnate Son of God can bridge. Calvin felt this deeply in his conversion and sought to express it in concentrated form in these first few pages of his critical chapter on the law. Successive editions of the *Institutes* were to see these thoughts dispersed through the growing bulk of the work, ultimately offering for it a kind of organizing principle. But, here, and here alone, they stand in a coherent brief theological summary of Calvin's religious experience.

What is the knowledge of God? God is infinite wisdom, righteousness, goodness, mercy, truth, power and life; all things have been created for his glory; he is a just judge; he is merciful and gentle.

What is the knowledge of ourselves? Adam, our common parent, was created in God's image with all the virtues; by his fall into sin this image was effaced and canceled; he was stripped of the virtues, which were replaced by the corresponding vices; all of us born of Adam are ignorant and bereft of God, powerless to do his will, deserving of eternal death.

Into this impasse in his creation, the merciful Father brings the law: the unwritten law upon the conscience; and then the written law. To keep us from ignorance of our true condition, God stamped upon our hearts a witness of what we owe him: conscience, the law within. Still blinded by self-love, we have been provided by God with a written law to teach us how to keep perfect righteousness; since, however, we do not perform the law's requirements, we still deserve the curse of eternal death.

To this second impasse of man, God in his infinite mercy offers another way. In our despair we must seek help from another quarter, in deepest humility: in Christ God gives us all the gifts we cannot earn for ourselves; but we must grasp Christ with a true and living faith in order to avail ourselves of his benefits; through him is the only way to reach eternal blessedness in the Father.

Stamped upon this summary is not only Calvin's fresh study of the Scriptures but the memory of his crisis of faith so recently experienced. Here are the deep currents of faith which issued in a life of dedication to Christ and his church. Here are the sources of Calvin's *Institutes of the Christian Religion,* of his exegesis, his preaching, and of all his other multifarious activities in behalf of the Reform.

II. THE FIRST EDITION OF THE INSTITUTES OF THE CHRISTIAN RELIGION (1536)

A. Catechism or Apology?[15]

1. The Original Catechetical Intent. One of the results of Calvin's conversion was the demand placed upon him, almost as soon as he began his new

15. Luchesius Smits, *Saint Augustin dans l'Oeuvre de Jean Calvin.* 2 vol. (Assen: 1957). In Vol. I, p. 28 Smits notes the lack of "homogeneity" in the 1536 edition due to the combined catechetical and apologetic purposes of the work. He suggests that this double purpose has an example in Seneca's *De Clementia.* Smits quotes Calvin's Seneca Commentary [p. 337] to this effect: "It seems, moreover, that Seneca's plan in this book was different from his plan in the first. While in the first Seneca accommodated himself to the popular understanding, the second he sprinkled with Stoic paradoxes and scholastic subtleties." Frankly, I think this "parallel" falls short of the mark.

Scriptural studies, as a teacher of those hungry for the true faith. His new popularity has already been set forth in the words of the Preface to the *Commentary on the Psalms*. Despite his own comparative inexperience, seekers flocked to him for true doctrine. He concludes with the characteristic phrase: "God never left me at peace in any place. . . ."

There are scattered references to Calvin's early preaching in France but these are fragmentary and impossible to date in a coherent way. They do suggest, however, that what Calvin says of his unsought popularity as a preacher and teacher is true. Unquestionably, his mind was drawn to the need for a good catechism which might answer the demands of his acquaintances. It was in the brief leisure of Basel, where the unknown French exile who knew no German lived in 1535 and early 1536, that he found time to write down the first fruits of his theological studies. The long title tells the story: "Institutes of the Christian Religion, Embracing almost the Whole Sum of Piety, and Whatever is Necessary to Know of the Doctrine of Salvation: A Work most Worthy to be Read by All Persons Zealous for Piety. . . ." How much of his projected catechism he brought already written or in notes from France one cannot say. Some older authorities thought that the Dedicatory Letter to the French King and possibly chapters 5-6 were written at Basel, the first four chapters coming from his earlier intervals of leisure, especially in the library of his friend Louis du Tillet at Claix in Angoulême. Ganoczy, the most recent writer on this period of Calvin's life, credits the whole book (although not necessarily the entire preparatory study for it) to the first seven months of Calvin's Basel sojourn, pointing out the incredible speed with which the reformer worked. We will not try to settle this question here.

In the French Reformed tradition, Calvin did not have many predecessors as catechism-writers. Besides translations of Luther, there had appeared in the French language, Guillaume Farel's *Sommaire et briefve declaration dauscuns lieux fort necessaires a ung chascun chrestien pour mettre sa confiance en dieu et ayder son prochain*, first published at Basel in 1525 at the urging of the Basel Reformer Oecolampadius.[16] An English translation of the long title would read: "Summary and brief declaration of some passages very necessary for each and every Christian to put his confidence in God and help his neighbor." The *Sommaire* went through numerous editions. A second French summary of the Reformed faith was written in 1529 by Francis Lambert of Avignon, entitled *Somme Chrestienne*. It was to this rather meager store that Calvin proposed to add his own "short" work.

Farel's *Sommaire*, Piaget tells us, was "the first work in French to expound the principal points of Reformed Christian doctrine, in a simple and popular fashion for the use of those 'who knew no Latin.' " It was written "in order that

---

16. N. Weiss identifies a 1523 imprint, *La Summe de l'Escripture Saincte*, as likely of Farel's authorship. See *Bulletin de l'Histoire du Protestantisme Français* 68 (1919) 63-79.

all those of the French language could have a more correct understanding and knowledge of Jesus, who by so few is purely known and served." Based on Holy Scripture, "which contains God's plan and will," it is addressed to all those who "love truth."[17] While there may be some echoes of Farel's tone and general position, Calvin's work seems to owe nothing to it in style, structure, or even content, although two such works, covering as they do the same field from the same general theological vantage point, would necessarily overlap.

Calvin very clearly describes his literary intention on the first page of the Letter to Francis I:

> When I first set my hand to this work, nothing was farther from my mind, most glorious King, than to write something that might be offered to your Majesty. My purpose was solely to transmit certain rudiments by which those who are touched with any zeal for religion might be shaped to true godliness. And I undertook this labor especially for our French countrymen, very many of whom I saw to be hungering and thirsting for Christ; very few who had been imbued with even a slight knowledge of him. The book itself witnesses that this was my intention, adapted as it is to a simple and, you may say, elementary form of teaching.

This, then, was Calvin's catechetical intent. If we take his words at face value, he must have planned a French version to follow soon after, for a Latin work, however simply conceived, would be a closed book for most of his "French countrymen . . . thirsting for Christ." That he put it first in Latin may in part be due to the fact that he wanted it as an apology to reach foreign nations that they "might at least be touched with some compassion and concern" for the persecuted French Protestants. Latin was the lingua franca of the time, the logical medium to bring his case before the world. A lively debate among scholars of a generation ago discussed whether in fact such a French work was ever published. The first extant French edition of the *Institutes* is dated 1541, a translation of the second Latin edition of 1539. However, Calvin adapted from the 1536 Latin the Geneva *Catechism* of 1537. Obviously, he found the 1536 *Institutes* too long and complicated for a mere catechism; in fact, even the 1537 Catechism proved too learned for this popular use and was replaced, as Calvin gained pastoral experience at Geneva and Strasbourg, by the familiar Genevan question-and-answer type of catechism.[18]

2. *The Institutes becomes an Apology.* But Calvin's plan for a simple catechism was not to be. History dictated otherwise, and at the heart of the bloody events which changed the book was Francis I, Most Christian King of the French.

The stirring of religious reform in the early Sixteenth Century brought a

17. A. Piaget, ed., *Guillaume Farel, Sommaire et Briefue Declaration* (Paris: 1935) pp. 7-8.

18. For the relationship between the 1536 *Institutes*, the 1537 (French) and 1538 (Latin) *Catechism*, and the 1539 *Institutes*, see *John Calvin: Catechism 1538*, tr. ann. F.L. Battles (Pittsburgh: 1972).

wide variety of movements, from a most conservative effort to cleanse the existing church to radical attacks on the entire social fabric. George H. Williams has well shown the almost hopeless complexity of the varied personages who put forward their plans for the amelioration of humanity during the first half of the century.[19] In church history it had long been characteristic of the supporters of the establishment not to differentiate too precisely between moderate and radical critics. To offer but one example of many, the medieval church lumped the simple Bible faith of the early Waldensians with the Manichaean dualism of the Cathari of the Thirteenth Century. And in actuality it has always been difficult to differentiate movements of religious reform: there are shades and combinations of all kinds. The defenders of the establishment, too, have reasons of their own for perpetuating such confusion. The most reasonable demand for reform of corrupt or outmoded institutional forms and practices can be blunted and discredited if it can be attached to more exaggerated and dangerous demands for change. Perhaps this failure to discriminate is only partly conscious and deliberate: the beleaguered supporters of the *status quo* may in fact see the threatening forces as a single entity.

In both Luther and Zwingli we see a certain effort to prove their essential orthodoxy to Rome, especially in their forcible repudiation of radical movements which seemed to threaten their own recently constructed establishment. Luther against the Peasants' Revolt, Zwingli against the nascent Anabaptist movement in Zürich, in fact Luther over against Zwingli's more radical handling of the Lord's Supper—all may serve to illustrate our point.

When Lutheran ideas reached France in the 1520's, moderate reform was already represented by Jacques Lefèvre d'Étaples, Bishop Guillaume Briçonnet,[20] and the so-called Cercle de Meaux. But travelers brought more radical views from the Low Countries, from Germany and Switzerland. There was already a ferment at work in France; medieval sectarian ideas had been kept alive underneath the surface. Thus, there was ample evidence of revolutionary tendencies which might prove subversive to church and state. The spreading of French translations of the Bible through printing encouraged even uneducated persons to reflect on the meaning of Scripture. The Sorbonne saw all these tendencies as one threat to the ecclesiastical establishment and labeled them all as heretical. The impressive machinery for the suppression of heresy inherited from the Thirteen-Fourteenth Century fight to extirpate the Cathari was brought into action to cope with "Lutheranism," the name under which all dissident movements were now lumped.

Francis I, who in his humanist sympathies had earlier resisted Sorbonne

19. George H. Williams, *The Radical Reformation*. (Philadelphia: 1962).

20. On Bishop Briçonnet's tragic recantation of the Evangelical cause, see Herminjard, I, Nos. 77, 78. He officially decreed against Luther and his doctrines on 15 October 1523. On the work of Lefèvre d'Étaples see now: P.E. Hughes, *Lefèvre: Pioneer of Ecclesiastical Renewal in France* (Grand Rapids: 1984).

attempts to suppress Erasmus and other advocates of Christian humanism, went along with the Sorbonne's demands to purge France of heresy. This internal campaign of persecution, particularly as it threatened Germans resident in France, became an embarrassment to Francis' negotiations with the German Protestant princes and their theological advisers. The diplomatic accomplishments of 1534 were dashed by the affair of the Placards in October of that year, as we have seen. So, in the continued negotiations with the Lutherans of early 1535, in the midst of persecutions at home, it became expedient to picture the whole matter as an affair of national security and to isolate the French Evangelical party from the respectable Protestants outside France. Three groups of supporters of this reading of French Reform emerged: Catholic theologians like Cochlaeus and Ceneau wrote that Calvin was to call "lying pamphlets, tarring all French evangelicals with the same dire Anabaptist brush; otherwise respectable humanists like Budé and Sadolet snobbishly treated the whole movement as that of an ignorant rabble; finally, Francis' memorandum to the German Protestant princes on 1 February 1535 (drafted by his diplomatic envoy Guillaume du Bellay) presented this view of the whole movement toward Reform in France. To summarize the memorandum: the sovereign attempted to justify to his Protestant allies the persecutions undertaken in France following the affair of the Placards, an act of anarchy and revolt against the internal order of the kingdom. The government not only had the right but the duty to take vigorous steps. The French Evangelicals, the memorandum asserted, unlike the German Protestants, were seditious persons in no respect different from the Anabaptists. Were not such persons quite justly put to death even in Protestant Germany?

So went the reasoning of the royal memorandum. It did not serve its purpose of allaying the fears and misgivings of the Germans, but it did convince the more conservative spokesmen of the French Evangelical party of the need to dissociate themselves, theologically and politically, from more radical forces of reform, and to make their distinction very clear not only in the minds of their fellow Protestants outside France but to their own monarch and his advisers. The immediacy of this was borne out by the tragic events of Münster now approaching their apocalyptic climax: the polygamous Kingdom of Münster was to fall on 25 June 1535.

Calvin's response to this question: how can the true Evangelicals be proved of a different stamp from their more radical brethren? took two forms. He first set out to deal with what he considered the most damning theological aspect of the question in his *Psychopannychia*, written in 1534/5, published finally in 1542. He then mounted a more comprehensive literary campaign in the 1536 *Institutes*. Let us look at each of these documents in turn.

The *Psychopannychia* poses considerable critical problems. Against what groups or group was it originally intended? How much of the 1542 published version represents, actually, what Calvin originally wrote in 1534/5? Fortunately for us, these questions are not central to our present task, so they can be laid aside. We are concerned with only the message of the book.

Why did Calvin choose for his first theological essay obscure questions of what happened to soul and body at the time of physical death? If the book is directed against the Anabaptists, the doctrine of soul-sleep or soul-death was not one widely held in that movement.[21] By whatever groups it was held, unquestionably the doctrine was accepted more in France than in other lands that had been touched by Reform. Calvin must have felt the need to refute it in the interests both of protecting his fellow religionists from it and in assuring the Catholics that this heretical notion was not held by the authentic Evangelicals of France.

Among the Catholic doctrines rejected by the Protestants was that of purgatory and of prayers for the dead, and of the intercession of the saints. The Catholics who supported these doctrines thought their opponents must of necessity be rejecting the continued existence of the soul after the death of the body, a doctrine dictated to Pope John XXII by the University of Paris in the Fourteenth Century, and reiterated recently at the Fifth Lateran Council, against dangerous Aristotelian tendencies of Averroist origin stemming from the University of Padua. Did the Evangelicals in fact, by rejecting prayers for the dead, assume the death of the soul?

This question was posed to Calvin by Cardinal Sadolet in 1539:

> Nor would I say anything either of the prayers of the saints of God for us, or of ours for the dead, though I would fain know what these same men would be at when they despise and deride them. Can they possibly imagine that the soul perishes along with the body? This they certainly seem to insinuate, and they do it still more openly when they strive to procure for themselves a liberty of conduct set loose from all ecclesiastical laws, and of a license for their lusts. For, if the soul is mortal, Let us eat and drink, says the Apostle, for tomorrow we die; but if it is immortal, as it certainly is, how, I ask, has the death of the body made so great and so sudden a disruption, that the souls of the dead have no congruity, in any respect, no communion with those of the living, and have forgotten all their relationship to us and common human society? And this, especially, while charity, which is the principal gift of the Holy Spirit to a Christian soul, which is ever kind and fruitful, and which, in him who has it, never exists to no purpose, must always remain safe and operative in both lives.[22]

Just as the rejection of prayers for the dead, invocation of the saints, etc., was the key to overcoming the whole oppressive Catholic system of indulgences against which Luther had already taken his stand, so the continued assertion of the life of the soul, independent of the body, was requisite to dissociate the Evangelicals from fantastic and subversive tendencies which could, theologi-

21. On this question now see: Willem Balke, *Calvin and the Anabaptist Radicals* (Grand Rapids: 1981), pp. 25-33.

22. Op. cit. in Note 11 above, p. 15.

cally, be tied to a doctrine of soul-death and soul-sleep. We shall later take up the sacramental and political consequences of this.

And so, in his first theological essay, Calvin had set out, through painstaking word studies of "soul," "spirit," and other scriptural terms to assert the immortality of the soul against those who claimed either that it died or went to sleep until tbe general resurrection. The theological presupposition upon which Calvin's view rests is that the soul, pre-eminently, is to be identified with the image of God. If this be so, to assert that that image is destroyed for a time or even for a period sleeps, is unthinkable. As God never dies, never sleeps, so the image of him in man must be ever watchful until the blessed reunion of soul with body at the general resurrection. To this essentially Christian doctrine, however, Calvin was to add the Protestant insistence that communication between the souls in living bodies on earth and the disembodied souls of the dead awaiting the day of resurrection was impossible. To postulate such would be to detract from Christ's sole mediatorship.

The *Psychopannychia* itself went through several literary stages with the first of which we are primarily concerned at this point. Writing on 3 September 1535 to his friend Christopher Libertet, he speaks of his first draft in these terms:

> As for that essay . . . it contained my first thoughts, rather thrown together in the shape of memoranda or commonplaces than digested after any definite and certain method, although there was some appearance of order.[23]

The first draft bears a preface dedicated to a certain friend (unidentified) who stands ". . . firm in prudence and moderation . . ." ". . . amid those tumults of vain opinions with which giddy spirits disturb the peace of the church." In the preface Calvin anticipates the charge that his writing will disturb the unity and charity of the church, to which he responds: "We acknowledge no unity except in Christ, no charity of which he is not the bond; and therefore, the chief point in preserving charity is to maintain faith sacred and entire."[24] This in 1534 at Orléans, perhaps in the late summer. Calvin sent a copy of the first draft to the Reformer Wolfgang Capito at Strasbourg for his advice on publishing it. Capito's response which Herminjard dates toward the end of 1534 dissuaded Calvin from this and sent him "back to the drawing board" so to speak. Here are Capito's words:

> . . . As to publishing it, if you pay attention to us, you will by all means make plans for it at a more appropriate time. Now sects are raising an uproar everywhere, and the Germans in the great religious calamity have found that fighting errors makes them better known; that the surest way to take care of the afflicted churches is to depict Christ most carefully.

23. OC X, 51-2.
24. Op. cit. in note 8 above, p. 416.

. . . I would prefer that you begin your literary endeavors in a more praiseworthy matter. . . . To sum up: the tortured state of the French churches demands that you rather withdraw from all contentions.[25]

Capito suggests that constructive scriptural exegesis would be more appropriate, pointing to his own work on Hosea. But this advice came during the negotiations of the German princes and reformers with the French authorities looking toward a religious peace and a reforming council. October 1534 was to see the affair of the Placards at Paris, the bloody persecutions of the French Evangelicals in the months that followed, then the cataclysm of Münster and the official justification of internal religious oppression by the French crown, that the offenders were all, indiscriminately, subversives. Calvin took Capito's advice concerning the *Psychopannychia* (which he however revised in 1535 during his Basel sojourn after completing the *Institutes*). But remain silent he could not to the charge that he and his compatriots were trying to destroy political order in France. And so in his preface to the French King, having alluded to his original catechetical intent—which we have already quoted—he immediately and passionately launched on why he decided to give his work a second purpose:

> But I perceived that the fury of certain wicked persons has prevailed so far in your realm that there is no place in it for sound doctrine. Consequently, it seemed to me that I should be doing something worthwhile if I both gave instruction to those I had undertaken to instruct and made confession before you with the same work. From this you may learn the nature of the doctrine against which those madmen burn with rage, who today disturb your realm with fire and sword. And indeed I shall not fear to confess that I have here embraced almost the sum of that very doctrine which they shout must be punished by prison, exile, proscription, and fire and be exterminated on land and sea. Indeed, I know with what horrible reports they have filled your ears and minds, to render our cause as hateful as possible to you. But, as fits your clemency you ought to weigh the fact that if it is enough merely to make accusations, then no innocence will remain either in words or deeds. [*Inst.* p. 1]

Essentially the same story is told by Calvin in his Preface to the *Commentary on the Psalms*, but perhaps even more pointedly:

> But it happened that while I was dwelling at Basel,
> Hidden there as it were, and known only to few people,
> Many faithful, holy men were burned in France,
> And reports of this having spread to foreign countries,
> A great part of the Germans
> Reacted with grave disapproval
> So as to conceive a hatred
> Toward the authors of that tyranny.
> In order to quiet things down,

25. Herminjard, III, No. 490

It was arranged to circulate
Certain shameful pamphlets
Full of lies, to the effect
That only Anabaptists and seditious person
Were being treated so cruelly,
Who by their dreams and false opinions
Were overturning not only religion
But the whole political order.
It appeared to me that these tools of the court[26]
Were by their disguises trying
Not only to keep this shameful shedding
Of innocent blood
Buried under false charges and calumnies
Brought against the holy martyrs after their death,
But also that thereafter they might have a means
Of proceeding to the ultimate extremity
Of murdering the poor faithful
Without anyone having compassion for them.
Unless, then, I strongly opposed them
To the best of my ability,
I could not justify my silence
Without being found lax and disloyal.
This was the reason that roused me
To publish my *Institutes of the Christian Religion*:
First, to answer certain wicked charges
Sowed by the other,
And to clear the memory of my brethren
Whose death was precious
In the presence of the Lord; [Ps. 116:15]
Secondly, as the same cruelties
Could very soon thereafter
Be exercised against many poor people,
That foreign nations might at least
Be touched with some compassion
And concern for them.
For at that time I did not publish
The book as it now is,
Full and laborious,
But it was only a little booklet
Containing in summary form
The principal matters.
I had no other purpose
Than to acquaint others
With the sort of faith
Held by those
Whom I saw

26. ab aulicis artificibus . . . See Bohatec, op. cit., p. 128.

These wicked and faithless flatterers
Villainously defaming.[27]

We see, then, that two things led Calvin to write his first edition of the famous *Institutes*: the catechetical needs of his religious brethren; and the need to plead their case before the King, that persecution might cease. And the latter purpose called forth a double theological response from Calvin, the rejection of institutionalized Roman Catholicism and at the same time of its extreme opposite, the revolutionary, disruptive spiritualism of what at that time he lumped under the name "Catabaptists." Hence, Calvin's future theological course was determined: to hold a middle direction between the right and left. This was not a prudent compromise, but a judgment securely grounded on Calvin's own independent study of Scripture. The later development of his theological system is an extending and perfecting of this initial polarity.

B. The Dedicatory Letter to the French King

1. An Apology among Christian Apologies. A study of the classic apologies of the Christian religion, particularly those early writings of the Church Fathers prompted by pagan Roman persecutions of the infant Christian Church, will demonstrate the creative impulse apologetic gave to Christian theology. The church found itself caught between Jew and Gentile, and more intimately between tendencies within its ranks which sought on the one hand to perpetuate its Jewish heritage and on the other to repudiate that heritage. Already in the experience of Paul himself these forces are at work; by the Second Century the future of the faith lay in holding to the unity of the testaments against the Jews who would deny the New and the Gnostics who would reshape the New shorn of its historic roots in the Old. The Apologists also had to convince the authorities that the Christian movement did not wish to destroy the Roman state and that its refusal to go along with official paganism and the emperor cult was not an act of political sedition but a religious preference which in no way weakened the Christian's support of the state. Even in Paul, and especially in the Pastoral Epistles of the New Testament this assurance of peaceful, nonrevolutionary coexistence is sounded.

In trying to bridge the gulf which these conflicts seemed to open, the Apologists, Justin Martyr notably, began the long process of the domestication of Greek philosophy in the Christian tradition, following Philo Judaeus, in the First Century of our era.

It may seem an unwarranted digression to speak of these early writers here but for the fact that a significant parallel in literary tone and even in argument may be pointed out between their writing and Calvin's. To mention but one striking item: the early Apologists were faced with the pagans' question: what

27. *The Piety of John Calvin*, Ford Lewis Battles, trans. & ed. (Grand Rapids: 1978), pp. 31-32.

xlv

authority does this new cult born a little over a hundred years ago have in comparison with other faiths such as the Egyptian that goes back thousands of years? To this the Apologists, insisting on Christian continuity with the Jewish Scriptures, said: "Our faith is as old as creation itself." To the charge that they were plotting to overthrow established religion and in fact the whole political establishment, they pointed to the purity of their life, the exemplary character of their worship and their loyalty to the emperor. To the charge that their faith was a thing of patches hastily sewn together from bits filched from ancient philosophy, they asserted that on the contrary their faith was the original from which these later pagan aberrations derived.

No wonder that Calvin eagerly scanned the whole history of the church and especially its earliest centuries! Like his fellow apologists of the early church, Calvin was by his apologetic effort really constructing a new synthesis of the faith. To the charge of novelty leveled by the Sorbonnists, Calvin asserted his faith was the authentic apostolic message, theirs the late medieval aberration. To the charge that the French Evangelicals were plotting to topple the monarchy, Calvin pledged the political loyalty of the Evangelical party. No man ever put to better use the force of history in the service of the faith.

The letter to Francis I is, therefore, to be set beside the apologies of Justin Martyr and his mid-second Century contemporaries, also beside the apologies of Tertullian, Origen and Eusebius.

2. The Content of the Dedicatory Letter. Let us look at the structure of the Letter. Calvin does not break it up into sections as he did the chapters of the latest editions of the *Institutes*. The printers set it in solid type. But one may discern eight parts, already noted in our translation of the 1559 edition, and here reproduced.

(1) We have already quoted from and discussed the first section, which we may entitle: "Circumstances in which the book was first written." Here, after outlining his double purpose, Calvin asks Francis I, a truly Christian King (as his title claims) for a full and fair inquiry into the Evangelicals' case.

(2) Next Calvin pleads for the persecuted Evangelicals, casting in stark relief their Scriptural faith and heroic martyrdom over against the Romanists' neglect of that Scriptural faith and insistence upon the Mass, purgatory, pilgrimages and like trifles.

(3) Thereupon Calvin takes up four basic charges of the Catholics against the Reformed faith: that it is new, unknown, uncertain and unsupported by miracles. The antithetical approach once again had come to Calvin's aid: God's word is hardly new! Unknown the Reformed faith may be, but the reason is that true doctrine has long lain buried and forgotten through man's impiety. How can you call our faith "uncertain" seeing our assurance over against their doubt? As for supporting miracles, you should sift the difference between true and false miracles.

(4) In the next section, Calvin disposed of the oft-repeated argument that the Evangelicals have thrown out the Church Fathers because they fail to support

their teaching. Calvin has read his fathers and the standard historians of the church. From them he produces an impressive series of sharp antitheses. We summarize them here:

(a) God doesn't need gold or silver / Look at their lavish rites
(b) Christians may either eat meat or abstain from it / Lenten fasts
(c) Monks must work / idle, licentious monks of our day
(d) no images of Christ or saints / churches crawling with images
(e) after burial of the dead let them rest / perpetual solicitude for the dead
(f) bread and wine remain in the eucharist / transubstantiation
(g) all present must partake of the Lord's Supper / public and private masses put grace and merit of Christ up for sale
(h) rash verdicts without basis in Scripture disallowed / jungle of constitutions, canons, etc., unbased on God's Word
(i) marriage affirmed for clergy / celibacy enjoined
(j) God's Word to be kept clear of sophistries / look at their speculative theological brawls!

(5) After this heavy cannonade of the Roman Catholic position, Calvin turns to the next circle of defense of the papal stronghold, the appeal to custom. Most Roman Catholic polemicists had stood firm in the assertion that these Protestant Johnny-come-latelies were sacrilegiously mangling the established and hallowed customs of Mother Church. Here, Calvin's humanist training shows its clearest strength. Most custom, he asserts, is the result of the private vices of the majority which become public error and wrongly take on the force of law. Over against such public error stands the eternal justice of God's Kingdom which we are called upon fearlessly to follow. In ringing terms Calvin asserts that, though the whole world may fall into the same wickedness, strength of numbers does not sanction or excuse it.

(6) Where then is the true church to be found? The Romanists have asserted that the form of the church is always observable; that this form of the church rests in the Roman church and its hierarchy. To this Calvin makes rejoinder with the Pauline marks of pure preaching and lawful sacraments, the same marks Luther had earlier asserted in the ecclesiological debate with Rome. Historically, both in the Old Testament and in subsequent Christian history, this true church often went underground and was without visible form. Yet though it seemed to disappear, a thin line of true witnesses to it was marvelously preserved by God even through the darkest times. When Elijah asked where the true worshipers were, God told him seven thousand there were who had not bowed the knee to Baal. The remnant still lived when mankind as a whole lay in spiritual slumber.

(7) Now, one of the most telling criticisms of the Romanists against the Reformed preachers, an argument to which harassed monarchs were especially sensitive, was that the renewed preaching of the Gospel was destroying peace and bringing in its train tumult and revolution. Calvin's reply to this rather strong

argument is to postulate a two-fold Satanic strategy. For centuries Satan kept the church asleep in worldly luxury. When, however, it started to wake up, in this new Apostolic age so to speak, he countered with a new strategy. He raised up contentions of all sorts, prompted religious strife, especially centering his ingenious new strategy on those Calvin calls the "Catabaptists." In this time of strife, we are in the same boat as the Apostles, but like them we have assurance of our faith.

(8) In the last section Calvin realistically sizes up the likelihood that his appeal will actually reach the King, and if it does, sway him in the least. Whether their earthly King listens or not to their plea, really recognizes them as loyal Frenchmen, the Evangelicals will ultimately put their faith in the King of kings, whose rule is perfect justice and who will hear their plea. So ends the letter to Francis I.

If we now turn from this impassioned appeal, to the very end of the *Institutes*, whether the third portion of the sixth chapter of the 1536 edition, or Book 4, chapter 20 in the edition of 1559, we will see a final plea of obedience to the earthly monarch, but at the very last the ringing assertion that obedience to man must not become disobedience to God. "We must obey God rather than men." This is the "political frame" of the *Institutes*.

At the heart of this letter, then, is the acute sense of contrast, not only between the evangelical faith and the doctrine and practice of the Roman Church, but also a contrast, not elaborated here, but to be worked out more fully later on, between the Evangelicals and the loose congeries of extremists (from Calvin's point of view) which he here conveniently if inaccurately labels "Catabaptists," the very term Zwingli had made current in his famous *Elenchus*, and which Bucer used in his commentaries to denominate that group. We may conclude that the *Institutes* took shape between these two opposing religious tendencies. We shall now turn to the six chapters that comprise the 1536 *Institutes*.

C. Analysis of the "Catechetical" Chapters (1-5).

The catechetical literature of the later middle ages, both in Latin and in the vernacular, took the form of simple expositions of the Law, Apostles' Creed, Lord's Prayer, etc. Luther found this form ready at hand when he compiled his *Small Catechism* of 1522 and the *Large Catechism* of 1529. It was natural, then, that Calvin would construct his first edition of the *Institutes* from the successive expositions of the Ten Commandments (ch. 1), the Apostles' Creed (ch. 2), the Lord's Prayer (ch. 3), the Sacraments (ch. 4). To this he appends first a refutation of the papal mass (end of ch. 4) and a long chapter rejecting on Scriptural and historical grounds the so-called five "false sacraments" (ch. 5). The concluding chapter contains three related essays, on Christian Freedom, Ecclesiastical Power, and Political Power, which we propose to treat separately as really a part of the apologetic aspect of the book, more perhaps than the catechetical.

In dealing with these basic documents of the faith, Calvin quite often seems to follow, but always in his own independent way, Martin Luther. This is especially true in his treatment of the Decalogue. (Later editions of the *Institutes* will show a greater independence of treatment of the separate commandments.) Yet we must candidly remark that the well-known difference between Luther and Calvin on the Law is already apparent. Our analysis of these chapters will not be exhaustive but will concentrate on the polarities they present.

1. *Chapter 1: On the Law.* After the theological restatement of Calvin's faith which serves as a preface and which we have already discussed, Calvin launches into an exposition of the Decalogue. Most of the commandments are paraphrased in the briefest terms, but four of them call for fuller discussion: the Third evokes an essay on images and idolatry with application to the Roman Catholic cultus; the Fourth offers an opportunity to reject the Anabaptist teaching on oaths; the Fifth on Sabbath observance, since it stands between the moral and ceremonial law, calls for something other than a literal exegesis; the Tenth or "Deuteronomic" Commandment is more extensively discussed because of its practical consequences: if the family is extended to include the larger political groupings (one is reminded here of Aristotle's *Politics*) one may subsume under it the honoring of the king, prince, magistrates, etc. Here is a scriptural restatement of the classical notes on the *Pater Patriae* as set forth in the *Seneca Commentary.*[28]

The concluding discussion of the chapter moves on to the uses of the law and to justification: this logically brings in the contrast between faith-righteousness and works-righteousness, and such subsidiary Roman Catholic notions as works of supererogation. The influence of Luther (and of Paul) is obvious here. In later editions fuller support will be drawn from Augustine as this material is broken up, expanded and distributed to new chapters.

2. *Chapter 2: On Faith.* This chapter, containing an exposition of the Apostles' Creed, was the chief casualty of the later editions, being fragmented to provide substance for a radically altered structure. The centrality, existentially speaking, of faith to Calvin's whole religious view, demanded more than a mere reliance on an ancient and post-Scriptural epitome of evangelical teaching, such as the Apostles' Creed.

Basically, in 1536, the chapter consists of a theological essay on the nature of faith and the Trinity, an exposition of the Creed, and a concluding section on the relation of faith, hope and love. Strong antitheses, some against the Roman Catholics and others against the Anabaptists and anti-trinitarians mark the chapter.

Let us look at the chapter in more detail. True vs. false notions of faith mark the opening pages, largely against the Roman Catholics. The section on the Trinity seems to be directed against unnamed contemporary antitrinitarians, who are credited with "mocking us for confessing one God in three persons," the indiscriminate use of "Spirit" by some, the criticisms of others leveled against the use of technical non-Biblical theological terms are refuted by Calvin

28. See *Calvin's Commentary on Seneca's De Clementia* (cited in Note 6 above), pp. 105, 121, 171, 237, 107.

with the help of ancient church history parallels. Some authorities think that the proposed meeting of Calvin with Servetus in Paris in 1534 (?) which never occurred may be hinted at here; at any event, these kernels of refutation were later reused and expanded in the Servetus quarrel as reflected in the latest edition of the *Institutes* (1559). Our endnotes mark points of contact with Servetus' two earliest treatises.

In discussing the Creed, Calvin utilizes the first article to assert God's omnipotence and providence against any vestigial Pelagianism of the Sorbonne.

The second article carries a strong critique by Calvin of an unidentified position which had asserted Christ was God's Son only according to his humanity (by the virgin birth) and charged Calvin and his party with a "two-Christ" doctrine.

Calvin in dealing with the descent into hell reiterates the nonliteral interpretation of the *Psychopannychia*, thus setting a further antithesis with the Anabaptists; but this position of Calvin is also taken implicitly over against the Roman Catholics. The session at God's right hand is simply stated in a way that presages the remarks on Christ's risen body in Chapter 4 (On the Sacraments): "Therefore, although lifted up to heaven, he has removed the presence of his body from our sight, yet he does not refuse to be present with his believers in help and might, to show the manifest power of his presence." Here we see his distinction not only from the Roman Catholics but from Luther and from Zwingli as well. This affords the clue to Calvin's Christological difference from the Lutherans.

The fourth article is chiefly a brief positive statement of Calvin's view of the church, based on a thorough-going theology of grace, marked by election and predestination, but the most corporate and least developed statement of his doctrine in all of Calvin's voluminous writings on this hotly contested doctrine.[29] It is very much here a churchly doctrine, cast as it is in the midst of the discussion of the ecclesiastical article of the Apostles' Creed. Not all of Calvin's ecclesiology is confined to this chapter, however; aspects are dealt with in Chapters 3-6 as well.

The concluding essay of Chapter 2, on faith, hope and love, argues the primacy of faith, rejects the Roman Catholic notion of *fides informis* and also the Roman Catholic teaching that we are justified by love rather than faith.

It is interesting to note that the antitheses sketched here against the "left wing" of the Reformation are utilized in much expanded form later on against Servetus, other Antitrinitarians, and also against certain Anabaptists (as Menno Simons on Christology).

3. Chapter 3: On Prayer. This chapter owes a great deal to Martin Bucer's *Commentary on the Gospels* (1530), as Alexandre Ganoczy has shown, and as

---

29. Smits' previously cited (Note 15 above) careful study of Calvin's use of Augustine reveals that Calvin does not quote *On the Predestination of the Saints* until the edition of 1539.

1

is documented in our endnotes. Here let us be content with summing up the antitheses it contains. The most obvious antithesis is between Christ as sole Mediator and the many human mediators in the invocation of the saints. Implied throughout the chapter is the general antithesis between the false aspects of Roman Catholic worship and the purity of Evangelical worship, a subject to be more polemically treated in the following chapters. This included the localization of the holy, the superstitious use of set times (cf. Calvin's earlier exegesis of the Fifth Commandment, and his later adiaphoric treatment of rites in the second essay of Chapter 6), the use of Latin rather than the vernacular, and passivity vs. action of the congregation (implied in his remarks on singing). These points were later to be greatly expanded by Calvin.

4. *Chapter 4: On the Sacraments.* This chapter is divided into four sections, the first three corresponding roughly to the order of the sacramental chapters of the 1559 *Institutes* (4.14-18): the initial essay deals with the sacraments in general: it is followed by essays on baptism and the Lord's Supper, and the short concluding piece discusses the administration of the two dominical sacraments. In the marriage of physical with spiritual which is a sacrament, Calvin uses the exegetical principle of accommodation.

Parenthetically, we would like to note that many years later, in 1556, when Calvin was writing his Second Defense against Westphal, his chief Lutheran opponent on the Lord's Supper, he referred to his early reading on this topic:

> Beginning gradually to leave the darkness of the Papacy and having taken a little taste of healthy doctrine, when I read in Luther that Oecolampadius and Zwingli left nothing in the sacraments but bare figures and representations without truth, I confess that I turned from their books, with the result that I abstained from reading them for a long time. But before I began to write they had conferred together [1529] at Marburg.[30]

That Calvin had read Zwingli, or through some other source knew his position when he wrote this chapter, will be apparent from the position our reformer took. In defining a sacrament, Calvin rejects on the one hand "those who weaken the force of the sacraments and completely overthrow their use," and on the other hand "those who attach to the sacraments some sort of secret power with which one nowhere reads that God had endowed them." This latter tendency embraces two groups: those who teach that the sacraments of the new Law justify and confer grace, "provided we do not set up a barrier of mortal sin" (obviously referring to the Roman Catholics); and those who believe a hidden power is "joined and fastened to the sacraments to distribute in them the graces of the Holy Spirit, but only if the Holy Spirit accompanies them." Calvin does not identify this last group. So we may see that Calvin's *general* sacramental position lies between Zwinglianism and Roman Catholicism, emphasizing as it

30. "Second Defense . . . to the Calumnies of Joachim Westphal," *Tracts and Treatises,* II, 252-3.

does the sacraments as "seals" upon the document of faith, as God's accommodation to our weak capacity to understand.

Calvin's chief opponent in his discussion of baptism would seem to be the Anabaptists whose demand for believer baptism and Donatistical insistence on rebaptism he rejects; but Calvin also refutes the Roman Catholic view, resting upon a defective grasp of original sin, that baptism releases us from original sin and restores us to the righteousness and purity of Adam before the fall. Briefly alluded to is the Zwinglian minimal view of baptism as "but a token and mark by which we confess our religion before men." That Calvin senses his mediating position may be seen in his refutation of the Anabaptist demand for rebaptism by identifying them with the ancient Donatists: "Such today are our Catabaptists who deny that we have been duly baptized because we were baptized by impious and idolatrous men under the papal government."

Calvin's essay on the Lord's Supper sets forth in a briefer fashion the essential points made at greater length in his mature theological expression. There are several striking features of this earliest eucharistic discussion of his: first, it shows remarkably wide reading and independent reflection upon the infinitely varied views previously expressed on the Lord's Supper. While deeper study of Augustine and Chrysostom was to be evidenced in the 1539 edition, Calvin had in the edition of 1536 canvassed historically the development of the Lord's Supper, had examined the pertinent Scriptural passages deeply, and had reviewed the various positions on the Supper expressed in his own time. Two testimonies to this preparation for his task come from later writings. We have the text of two speeches he gave at the Colloquy of Lausanne in early October 1536, a discussion organized by the Bernese authorities between the Roman Catholics and the Reformed spokesmen on the Lord's Supper.[31] In this, Calvin quoted extensively from the Church Fathers. In 1556 in writing his *Second Defense* against the Lutheran Westphal he made the statement previously quoted about his early reading on the sacraments. Taken literally as some scholars do, this statement in the Westphal essay would push Calvin's theological awakening back to his days at Bourges and associate this interest with the influence of his teacher Melchior Wolmar. But it probably refers rather to Calvin's post-conversion religious studies in 1534-35.

A second feature of Calvin's earliest eucharistic statement is that it enters the debate not as a new voice just beginning its labors, but as if Calvin had long been debating the points at issue, either as spokesman for a party he does not identify or possibly as the self-appointed continuator of true Christian orthodoxy as he, fresh from his initial studies, understands it.

A third feature is that Calvin's grasp of the various tendencies, combinations and alignments of parties is so deep that he in brief anticipates later full-blown developments of theological controversy; in fact, much of his material

31. OC IX, 877-886

here possessing a general application is later adapted and augmented to apply to specific controversies in which he is subsequently engaged.

Without entering into all the subtleties and details of Calvin's eucharistic teaching, one may ask the question, where does his position lie with regard to the major alignments of parties? He sees two opposing faulty views on the Lord's Supper, expressed perhaps more succinctly in his exposition of the *Consensus Tigurinus* (1551): if the dignity of the sacraments is too highly extolled, superstition easily creeps in; on the other hand a cold and less elevated discussion of their virtue and fruit leads to profane contempt of them. The main cause of controversy over the Supper, he asserts in the *Institutes* of 1536, is that men have asked the wrong question: "How do we eat Christ's body?" They should have asked: "How does Christ's body become ours?" He rejects the idolatry of the Mass. He rejects a discipline that allows only the perfect (Anabaptists) or the perfectly shriven (Roman Catholics), to communicate. He rejects the rationalistic reductionism of Zwingli but sides with him on the limits of the glorified body against the real presence (differently advanced by the Roman Catholics on the one hand and by the Lutherans on the other); he accepts an "as if" physical presence, a sort of ubiquity of God's power which marvelously bridges the otherwise unbridgeable spiritual gulf between heaven and earth. These are subtle distinctions taken in conscious differentiation from the manifold positions taken by other theologians both of the past and of his own time, but dictated primarily by a living faith proclaimed to men in the Scriptures but fortified, "sealed," by the sacraments for the sake of man's weakness and incapacity. Faith does not make the sacraments mere signs, nor do the sacraments by themselves do the work of faith: they work together—faith and sacraments. At bottom, these differences in eucharistic theology mark corresponding differences in theology and Christology.

The strong *pastoral* intent of Calvin is seen in his rejection of any theological position or liturgical practice that denies the benefits of the sacraments to the faithful.[32] He therefore concludes his chapter with a discussion on the administration of the sacraments. Briefly but succinctly he sets forth the evidence from the New Testament for sacramental practice, then discusses details which can be varied according to time and place without harm to sacrament or receiver. The touchstone of *true* vs. *false* sacramental theology and practice is Scriptural authority: all else is of human invention.

5. *Chapter 5: On the Five False Sacraments.* This chapter was perhaps to be in later editions the least altered in basic content and structure of all the chapters of the 1536 *Institutes*. From the copious side-notes of the original text at this point it is clear that Calvin has both the Scriptures and Gratian's *Decretum* and Peter Lombard's *Sentences* beside him as he writes this chapter. It is of course directed against the false sacramental teachings and practices of the Ro-

---

32. One of the worst features of the Roman Mass, in Calvin's view, is that it makes the laity into "second-class citizens" of the kingdom.

man Church, and draws at least some of its initial inspiration from Luther's *Babylonian Captivity of the Church* (1520). Each "sacrament" is examined in terms of the claims made for it, its actual history and the true teaching that should replace it. While Calvin lives up to his promise of brevity in discussing Confirmation, Extreme Unction and Marriage, he deals with Penance and Orders at length. Under Penance he treats such related topics as repentance, confession, absolution (the power of the keys), indulgences, the treasury of merits, satisfaction for sins, and purgatory. In later editions these will be detached to separate chapters, leaving only the original nucleus. Over against this false ecclesiastical structure Calvin lays the Scriptural view of repentance and forgiveness. In like manner, he deals at length with the "Sacrament" of Orders and its various divisions, setting over against it the Scriptural doctrine of ministry, a topic to be much more fully dealt with in the edition of 1543, after Calvin's pastoral experience at Strasbourg.

We have in this chapter, in a sense, the nucleus of Calvin's detailed refutation of the foundations of the medieval church order, if we add to it some details from the middle essay of Chapter 6, On Ecclesiastical Power. These two portions, taken together and skillfully patched, were to become the first half of Book IV in the final edition of 1559. In reaction to the ecclesiastical abuses of his time he reaches back through history for a better way. Much of what he says here is an expansion of the lean antitheses already set forth in the Letter to Francis I.

D. Chapter Six: Conclusion of the Letter to Francis I?

1. General Considerations. A comparison of the Dedicatory Letter to Francis I and the final chapter of the 1536 *Institutes* suggests that this, and not the end of the letter itself, is the real conclusion of the apology to the king. Chapter 1-5 are primarily the catechism Calvin initially had set out to write, although Chapter 5, as we have seen, is a careful examination of the unscriptural sacramental structure and related features of the Roman Catholic Church as well as a catechetical chapter. The three-fold structure of Chapter 6, however, particularly relates to the appeal to Francis I. The first essay, on Christian Freedom, claims on a Scriptural basis freedom for Christians in the spiritual (ecclesiastical) as opposed to the political (temporal) sphere. The second essay, On Ecclesiastical Power, both rejects humanly devised ecclesiastical laws and customs as violations of this freedom, and also tries to demonstrate to the monarch the fact that the Roman Catholic ecclesiastical establishment has usurped some portion of the secular power. There ought to be two kings: Christ over His church, and the earthly monarch over his domain. This latter topic is the subject of the third essay, On Civil Government, designed both to assure Francis of the Evangelicals' political loyalty, and to apprise him of their utter rejection of the false political views of the Anabaptists, and warn him that the ultimate spiritual stakes are in the hands of God the King of kings. While many details summarily covered in the Dedicatory Letter are dealt with in other chapters in passing, the chief arguments of the letter are formally rehearsed in Chapter 6 and rounded out.

In Chapter 6 Calvin specifically alludes to arguments of the Sorbonne theologians in support of the current Roman Catholic ecclesiastical structures and practices. By skillful Scriptural and historical arguments set antithetically against their views, Calvin seeks both to refute them, justify his own religious party in the king's eyes, and also (by implication) to detach Francis from his malign ecclesiastical advisers.

2. Specific Content. It will be useful, perhaps, to look in more detail at the three essays that comprise the final chapter.

A. Christian Freedom. In a sense the problem of freedom is the central theme of Chapter 6. Later editions, in fragmenting this chapter and distributing its elements to widely separated contexts, have sacrificed the pointed message. But, as the immediate apologetic task of the first edition receded into the past, new and more multifarious questions arose that called for the expansion of, and regrouping of the thought of this chapter.

Calvin throughout Chapter 6 is steering a middle course between the piling up of laws and the rejection of all laws; he is pleading for a spiritual freedom even in the midst of civil tyranny, unburdened by the yoke of illicit church regulations and at the same time unplagued by wild unbridled license.

Christian freedom means three things: (1) freedom from the law, (2) freedom of conscience willingly obeying without compulsion of the law, (3) freedom in "things indifferent." Such freedom must never be exercised to the harm of the poor or the weak. We should avoid offensive opulence in living, and sometimes should show our freedom by abstaining from exercising it, especially when by so doing we may endanger weak consciences. But the final determination is not offense against neighbor but offense against God. In pressing the freedom of the Christian conscience from human traditions and laws, Calvin postulates the distinction between spiritual and political government, more or less paralleling his distinction between soul and body.

This first essay on Christian freedom which with little alteration is ultimately moved to a new context (between justification and prayer) in the 1559 edition, serves in the 1536 edition as the introduction to the discussion of the two kingdoms, a concept already familiar in Luther. The constitutions of the Roman Church enslave consciences, and thus deprive the Christian man of his God-given spiritual freedom.

B. Ecclesiastical Power. Calvin lays down his views of church order between the radical rejection of all church laws (currently evidenced in the revolutionary kingdom of Münster) and the senseless heaping up of all sorts of doctrinal, disciplinary, and ritual requirements which (however recently originated) are claimed by the Romanists to have an apostolic or even dominical origin. The radical or Anabaptist notions are but mentioned in passing here; the main butt of Calvin's argument in his second essay is the Roman Church. Against claims that the faith rests solely upon the church's decision, that the clergy and councils of the church are inerrant, Calvin brings both scriptural and historical counter-evidence. In an interesting digression he displays the patrimony of the church—its usurpation of temporal power and perquisites—as due to the misguided but pious generosity of princes. Was this an oblique appeal to Francis I?

The church needs laws to govern itself, to achieve concord in the diversity of human customs; but such are not necessary for salvation: consciences are not to be bound by them. Here Calvin's view of Christian freedom, already enunciated in the prior essay is reiterated. And so Calvin distinguishes between impious ecclesiastical constitutions and legitimate church ordinances made either for public decency or based on the common usage of men—hours of worship and the like. The details are not important; that definite procedures are set is important. We see here how his adiaphoric principle, elucidated in the previous essay on Christian freedom, is put to use.

C. Civil Government. In the final essay, on civil government, the Anabaptists figure much more prominently. As we read these final pages of the book we clearly see Calvin lecturing the French King both on what loyal Evangelical Frenchmen believe, and how he as monarch of the French ought to conduct himself in his office. Calvin first discusses the necessity of civil government.

Earlier, we mentioned in passing that the defective teaching of the Anabaptists on soul and body, already criticized in the *Psychopannychia*, has political implications as well.

> Certain men, when they hear that the Gospel promises a freedom that acknowledges no king and no magistrate among men, but looks to Christ alone, think that they cannot benefit by their freedom so long as they see any power set over them. They therefore think that nothing will be safe unless the world is shaped to a new form where there are neither courts, nor laws, nor magistrates, nor anything similar which in their opinion restricts their freedom. But whoever knows how to distinguish between body and soul, between this present fleeting life and that future eternal life, will without difficulty know that Christ's spiritual kingdom and the civil jurisdiction are things completely distinct.[33]

The distinction between body and soul, infant baptism, and the distinction between the spiritual and political realms, are all of one piece. Also, the contrast between perfectionism held by at least some Anabaptist groups and by Calvin attributed to them all, and the Calvinian notion of gradual spiritual growth during the present life, is to be associated with this general antithesis.

Calvin's picture of the function of the establishment and protection of true religion by the civil authority is consciously constructed against Anabaptist repudiation of all government but also against Romanist usurpation of temporal functions to the ecclesiastical sphere. Yet we must admit that in his delicate balancing of church and state, Calvin laid himself and the city of Geneva open to frequent conflict between council and consistory.

33. See text below: p. 207.

Let no man be disturbed that I now commit to civil government the duty of rightly establishing religion, which I seem above to have put outside of human decision. For, when I approve of a civil administration that aims to prevent the true religion which is contained in God's law from being openly and with public sacrilege violated and defiled with impunity, I do not here, any more than before, allow men to make laws according to their own decision concerning religion and the worship of God.[34]

Calvin's second topic, a discussion of civil government, is divided into three parts: magistrates, laws, and people.

What, then, does Calvin have to say on the office of *magistrate*? In what sense may the word "god" be applied to man? In their perfectionism the Anabaptists fancied themselves "gods," or so Calvin inferred; in their ecclesiastical usurpations, the Romanists took unto themselves, their saints, and their images and eucharistic hosts the name of "god." To Calvin, like Luther, following especially Psalm 82 and Romans chapter 13, the only human beings who could scripturally bear the name of "gods" were the magistrates. And so explicitly against the Anabaptist rejection of kings and civil authorities, and implicitly against Romanist incursions into the civil sphere, Calvin ringingly asserts the "godship" of the ruler. We are shocked by this sort of teaching until we read the high demands Calvin laid upon his civil magistrate. For him "civil authority is the most sacred calling before God, and the most honorable of all callings in the life of mortal men." As if reminding Francis I of his superlative title "Most Christian," Calvin pictures the high office:

This consideration ought continually to occupy the magistrates themselves, since it can greatly spur them to exercise their office and bring them remarkable comfort to mitigate the difficulties of their task, which are indeed many and burdensome. For what great zeal for uprightness, for prudence, gentleness, self-control and for innocence ought to be required of themselves by those who know that they have been ordained ministers of divine justice? How will they have the brazenness to admit injustice to their judgment seat, which they are told is the throne of the living God? How will they have the boldness to pronounce an unjust sentence by that mouth which they know has been appointed an instrument of divine truth? With what conscience will they sign wicked decrees by that hand which they know has been appointed an instrument of divine truth? With what conscience will they sign wicked decrees by that hand which they know has been appointed to prescribe the acts of God? To sum up, if they remember that they are vicars of God, they should watch with all care, earnestness, and diligence, to represent in themselves to men some image of divine providence, protection, goodness, benevolence, and justice. And they should perpetually set before themselves the thought that 'all are cursed who do in deceit the work of God' [Jer. 48:10].[35]

34. Ibid., pp. 208-9.
35. Ibid., p. 210.

Revolutionaries who rail against this holy ministry as abhorrent to Christian religion and piety are reviling God himself. It is quite apparent that the conflict between Calvin and the Anabaptists is one concerning the use of Scripture. The Anabaptists rest their case primarily in Jesus' sayings viewed apart from their Jewish roots; for Calvin the teachings of Jesus must be seen in the light of the Old Testament as well as the New; and the Pastoral Epistles, at the other end of the Scriptures, also buttress his case. You confuse the office of Apostle and King, Calvin warns the Anabaptists. Applying to Scripture the ancient classical distinction between the private and public man (on which Calvin had laid so much emphasis in his *Seneca Commentary*), he uses this in the remaining pages of the chapter as the foundation principle in discerning the interworking of magistrate, laws, and people.

The sole endeavor of the magistrate should be to provide for the common safety and peace of all. In fulfilling his function the magistrate has the power of judicial murder, for in sentencing to death he is but carrying out God's judgments. This would be an unpopular stand to take in modern penology! Here again, an exegetical principle is at stake. The pacifist Anabaptists took a simple Biblical prohibition against killing both as a Christian repudiation of the judicial process and especially of capital punishment and the right to wage war. Other radicals were not pacifists, but still repudiated worldly government. It is not improbable that Calvin had in mind the chaos of Münster when he wrote:

> Now if their [the magistrates'] true righteousness is to pursue the guilty and the impious with drawn sword, should they sheath their sword and keep their hands clean of blood, while abandoned men wickedly range about with slaughter and massacre, they will become guilty of the greatest impiety, far indeed from winning praise for their goodness and righteousness thereby![36]

Throughout this essay on the civil government, there are strong echoes of the *Seneca Commentary*. Earlier, we tentatively spoke of the former as the "first draft" of Calvin's apology to Francis I; unquestionably Calvin is here reworking from this new evangelical Christian vantage point the whole classical teaching on the monarch. This connection between the two writings is especially close as he turns to clemency, clue to the best king, and *epiekeia*, the well-spring of law-giving and its application.

True leadership in the state lies between excessive cruelty and exaggerated gentleness. Thus, the use of war must be only as a last resort. Kings must restrain their wrath; they must also restrain their greed and their passion for magnificence; for ultimately the public chest, raised through the right to tax his subjects, is "almost the very blood of the people."

Calvin now turns to the *laws*, the second aspect of civil government, reworking again materials already familiar to readers of the *Seneca Commentary*. As he often does, Calvin begins with the repudiation of an exaggerated position.

36. Ibid., p. 213.

Jacob Strauss, Andreas Carlstadt, and others had proposed literally substituting the entire Mosaic code of the Old Testament for the civil laws of the European nations. In response to this Calvin sets forth his famous distinction (shared with Melanchthon) of law into three layers: moral, ceremonial, and judicial or civil. Moral law, which has already been discussed in Chapter I (but without benefit of this tripartite distinction) is nothing else than a testimony of natural law and of that conscience which God has engraved in the minds of men. In his discussion of the Fourth Commandment in Chapter 1 and of rites and ceremonies in Chapter 5 and Chapter 6, part 2, Calvin has already dealt with the ceremonial law. He now concentrates on judicial law. *Epiekeia* (equity) and adiaphora are two principles that inform his discussion of the topic. Equity is the goal and limit of all laws, determining their right framing and their right application in later generations. Among the nations of the world there is and has always been an incredible variety of laws and punishments to be meted out; these varying details are adiaphoric. Fundamental to all laws, however, is their identical end: to punish those crimes which God's eternal law has condemned, but according to the specific needs of particular times and places.

The final topic is the *people*, for whom magistrates and laws exist, and who are to respond in obedience to him. Again, Calvin sets the stage for his discussion by sketching exaggerated views: in I Corinthians Paul had referred to the passionate litigiousness of certain Corinthian Christians. These constitute one extreme—the persons who use the law courts to excess. At the other end are the Anabaptists who hold the courts of law to be superfluous among Christians. Calvin's exposition of the Christian people's course is a mean between these two extremes. Use the law courts? Yes, with Christian love toward one's legal opponent. To repudiate the courts is for Christians to repudiate God's holy ordinance. Do not lust for revenge, but with equity and moderation of mind use the God-given office of magistrate and court to seek justice.

Calvin reserves to the very end of the *Institutes* the vexed question of what sort of obedience the subjects owe their sovereign. Here he is speaking both to Francis I and to his own countrymen. To the magistrate (under whatever political system one lives) is owed obedience because he is the vicegerent of God. Amassing evidence especially from the Old Testament history (e.g., Daniel, Jeremiah) Calvin argues for obedience not only to the just ruler, but even to the unjust, for the latter is a judgment of God upon the people. Private men have no right to take the law into their own hands.

However, God does provide some relief from oppression, in his own good time. He raises up, history teaches us, two kinds of avengers against unjust rulers: his public servants, lesser magistrates whose task it is to defend the people (ephors in Sparta, tribunes in Rome, and the three estates in France are given as examples); secondly, others who in their rage unwittingly do God's will.

Lastly, Calvin reminds Francis I and his persecuted Evangelical Frenchmen that there is but one King of kings. When obedience to the ruler leads away from obedience to God then: "We must obey God rather than men." The last lines of the Book then re-echo and amplify the closing words of the Dedicatory Letter.

TO THE MOST MIGHTY AND
MOST ILLUSTRIOUS MONARCH FRANCIS,
MOST CHRISTIAN KING OF THE FRENCH,
HIS ESTEEMED PRINCE AND LORD,
JOHN CALVIN SENDS PEACE
AND GREETING IN THE LORD*

1. CIRCUMSTANCES IN WHICH THE BOOK WAS WRITTEN

When I first set my hand to this work, nothing was farther from my mind, most glorious King, than to write something that might be offered* to Your Majesty. My purpose was solely to transmit certain rudiments by which those who are touched with any zeal for religion might be shaped to true godliness. And I undertook this labor especially for our French countrymen, very many of whom I saw to be hungering and thirsting for Christ; very few who had been imbued with even a slight knowledge of him. The book itself witnesses that this was my intention, adapted as it is to a simple and, you may say, elementary form of teaching.

But I perceived [4] that the fury* of certain wicked persons has prevailed so far in your realm that there is no place in it for sound doctrine. Consequently, it seemed to me that I should be doing something worthwhile if I both gave instruction to those I had undertaken to instruct and made confession before you with the same work. From this you may learn the nature of the doctrine against which those madmen burn with rage who today disturb your realm with sword and fire.* And indeed I shall not fear to confess that I have here embraced almost the sum of that very doctrine which they shout must be punished by prison, exile, proscription, and fire, and be exterminated on land and sea.* Indeed, I know with what horrible reports* they have filled your ears and mind, to render our cause as hateful as possible to you.* But as fits your clemency, you ought to weigh the fact that if it is enough merely to make accusation, then no innocence will remain either in words or in deeds.

Suppose anyone, to arouse hatred, pretends that this doctrine, an account of which I am now trying to render to you, (10) has long since been condemned both by the verdict of all estates, and trans[5]fixed by many judgments of the courts. This will surely be saying nothing other than that it has in part been violently rejected by the partisanship and power of its opponents, and in part insidiously and fraudulently oppressed by their falsehoods, /22/ subtleties, and slanders. It is sheer violence that bloody sentences are meted out against this doctrine without a hearing; it is fraud that it is undeservedly charged with treason

1

and villainy. So that no one may think we are wrongly complaining of these things, you can be our witness, most noble King, with how many lying slanders it is daily traduced in your presence. It is as if this doctrine looked to no other end than to subvert all orders and civil governments, to disrupt the peace, to abolish all laws, to scatter all lordships and possessions—in short, to turn everything upside down! And yet you hear only a very small part of the accusation, for dreadful reports are being spread abroad among the people. If these were true, the world would rightly judge this doctrine and its authors worthy of a thousand fires and crosses. Who now can wonder that public hatred is aroused against it, [6] when these most wicked accusations are believed? This is why all classes with one accord conspire to condemn us and our doctrine. Those who sit in judgment, seized with this feeling, pronounce as sentences the prejudices which they have brought from home.̈ And they think they have duly discharged their office if they order to be brought to punishment no one not convicted either by his own confession or by sure testimony. But of what crime? Of this condemned doctrine, they say. But with what right has it been condemned? Now, (11) the very stronghold of their defense was not to disavow this very doctrine but to uphold it as true. Here even the right to whisper is cut off.

2. PLEA FOR THE PERSECUTED EVANGELICALS

For this reason, most invincible King, I not unjustly ask you to undertake a full inquiry into this case, which until now has been handled with no order of law and with violent heat rather than judicial gravity. And do not think that I am here preparing my own personal defense, thereby to return safely to my native land. Even though I regard my country with as much natural affection as becomes me, [7] as things now stand I do not much regret being excluded. Rather, I embrace the common cause of all believers, that of Christ himself—a cause completely torn and trampled in your realm today, lying, as it were, utterly forlorn, more through the tyranny of certain Pharisees than with your approval.

But here is not the place to tell how it has come about: certainly our cause lies afflicted. For ungodly men have so far prevailed that Christ's truth, even if, driven away and scattered, it did not die, still lies hidden, buried and inglorious. The poor little church has either been wasted with cruel slaughter or banished into exile, or so overwhelmed by threats and fears that it dare not even open its mouth. And yet, with their usual rage and madness, the ungodly continue to batter a wall already toppling and to complete the ruin toward which they have been striving. Meanwhile, no one comes forward to defend the church against such furies. But any who wish to appear as greatly favoring truth feel that they should pardon /23/ the error and imprudence of ignorant [8] men. For so speak they, calling error and imprudence the most certain truth of God; calling untutored men those on whom the Lord bestowed the mysteries of the heavenly wisdom! So ashamed are they all of the gospel!

It will then be for you, most Serene King, not to close your ears or mind to such just defense, especially when a very great question is at stake: how God's glory may be kept safe on earth, how God's truth may retain its place of honor, how Christ's Kingdom may be kept in good repair·among us? Worthy indeed is this matter of your hearing, worthy of your cognizance, worthy of your royal throne! Indeed, this consideration makes a true king: to recognize himself a minister of God in governing his kingdom [Rom. 13:3f.]. Now, that king who in ruling over his realm does not serve God's glory exercises not kingly rule but brigandage. (12) Furthermore, he is deceived who looks for enduring prosperity in his kingdom when it is not ruled by God's scepter, that is, his Holy Word; for the heavenly oracle that proclaims that "where prophecy fails the people are scattered" [Prov. 29:18] cannot lie. [9] And contempt for our lowliness ought not to dissuade you from this endeavor. Indeed, we are quite aware of what mean and lowly little men we are. Before God we are miserable sinners: in men's eyes most despised—if you will, the offscouring and refuse [cf. I Cor. 4:13] of the world, or anything viler that can be named. Thus, before God nothing remains for us to boast of, save his mercy alone [cf. II Cor. 10:17-18], whereby we have been saved through no merit of our own [cf. Titus 3:5]: and before men nothing but our weakness [cf. II Cor. 11:30; 12:5, 9], which even to admit is to them the greatest dishonor. But our doctrine must tower unvanquished above all the glory and above all the might of the world, for it is not of us, but of the living God and his Christ whom the Father has appointed King to "rule from sea to sea, and from the rivers even to the ends of the earth" [Ps. 72:8; 71:7, Vg]. And he is so to rule as to smite the whole earth with its iron and brazen strength, with its gold and silver brilliance, shattering it with the rod of his mouth [10] as earthen vessels, just as the prophets have prophesied concerning the magnificence of his reign [Dan. 2:32-35; Is. 11:4; Ps. 2:9, conflated]. Indeed, our adversaries·cry out that we falsely make the Word of God our pretext, and wickedly corrupt it.· By reading our confession you can judge according to your prudence not only how malicious a calumny but also what utter effrontery this is.

Yet we must say something here to prepare the way for you to read our confession. When Paul wished all prophecy to be made to accord with the analogy of faith·[Rom. 12:6], /24/ he set forth a very clear rule·to test all interpretation of Scripture. Now, if our interpretation be measured by this rule of faith, victory is in our hands. For what is more consonant with faith than to recognize that we are naked of all virtue, in order to be clothed by God? That we are empty of all good, to be filled by him? That we are slaves of sin, to be freed by him? Blind, to be illumined by him? (13) Lame, to be made straight by him? Weak, to be sustained by him? [11] To take away from us all occasion for glorying, that he alone may stand forth gloriously and we glory in him [cf. I Cor. 1:31; II Cor. 10:17]? When we say these and like things our adversaries interrupt and complain that in this way we shall subvert some blind light of nature,· imaginary preparations,· free will,· and merits.· For they cannot bear that the whole praise and glory of all goodness, virtue, righteousness, and wisdom

3

should rest with God. But we do not read of anyone being blamed for drinking too deeply of the fountain of living water [John 4:14]. On the contrary, those have been harshly rebuked who "have dug for themselves cisterns, broken cisterns that can hold no water" [Jer. 2:13]. Besides, what befits faith more than for God to promise to be a propitious Father where Christ is recognized as brother and propitiator? Than confidently to look for all happy and prosperous things from Him whose unspeakable love toward us went so far that "he . . . did not spare his own Son but gave him up for us all" [Rom. 8:32]? Than to repose in certain expectations of salvation and eternal life, when we meditate upon Christ, given by the Father, [12] in whom such treasures are hidden? Here they seize upon us, and cry out that such certainty of trust is not free from arrogance and presumption. But as we ought to presume nothing of ourselves, so ought we to presume all things of God; nor are we stripped of vainglory for any other reason than to glory in the Lord [cf. II Cor. 10:17; I Cor. 1:31; Jer. 9:23-24].

What further? Examine briefly, most mighty King, all the parts of our case, and think us the most wicked of wicked men, unless you clearly find that "we toil and suffer reproach because we have our hope set on the living God" [I Tim. 4:10]; because we believe that "this is eternal life: to know the only true God, and Jesus Christ whom he has sent" [John 17:3 p.]. For the sake of this hope some of us are shackled with irons, some beaten with rods, some led about as laughingstocks, some proscribed, some most savagely tortured, some forced to flee. All of us are oppressed by poverty, cursed with dire execrations, wounded by slanders, and treated in most shameful ways.

Now look at our adversaries (I speak of the order of priests, [13] at whose nod and will the others treat us hostilely), and consider with me for a moment what zeal moves them. They readily allow themselves and others to ignore, neglect, and despise the true religion, (14) which has been handed down in the Scriptures, and which ought to have a recognized place among all men. /25/ They think it of no concern what belief anyone holds or does not hold regarding God and Christ, if only he submits his mind with implicit faith to the judgment of the church. The sight of God's glory defiled with manifest blasphemies does not much trouble them. Why do they fight with such ferocity and bitterness for the Mass, purgatory, pilgrimages, and trifles of that sort, denying that there can be true godliness without a most explicit faith, so to speak, in such things, even though they prove nothing of them from God's Word? Why? unless for them "their God is the belly" [Phil. 3:19]; their kitchen their religion! If these are taken away, they believe that they will not be Christians, not even men! For, even though some glut themselves sumptuously while others gnaw upon meager crusts, still all live out of the same pot, a pot that without this fuel [14] would not only grow cold but freeze through and through. Consequently, the one most concerned about his belly is the sharpest contender for his faith. In fine, all men strive to one goal: to keep either their rule intact or their belly full. No one gives the slightest indication of sincere zeal.

4

3. CHARGES OF ANTAGONISTS REFUTED

Despite this, they do not cease to assail our doctrine and to reproach and defame it with names that can render it hated or suspect.* They call it "new" and "of recent birth." They reproach it as "doubtful and uncertain." They ask what miracles have confirmed it. They inquire whether it is right for it to prevail against the agreement of so many holy fathers* and against most ancient custom. They urge us to acknowledge that it is schismatic because it wages war against the church, or that the church was lifeless during the many centuries in which no such thing was heard.* Finally, they say that there is no need of many arguments, for one can judge by its fruits what it is, seeing that it has engendered such a heap of sects, [15] so many seditious tumults, such great licentiousness. Indeed, it is very easy for them to revile a forsaken cause before the credulous and ignorant multitude. But if we too might speak in our turn, this bitterness which they spew at us from swollen cheeks would subside.

First, by calling it "new" they do great wrong to God, (15) whose Sacred Word does not deserve to be accused of novelty.* Indeed, I do not at all doubt that it is new to them, since to them both Christ himself and his gospel are new. But they who know that this preaching of Paul is ancient, that "Jesus Christ died for our sins and rose again for our justification" [Rom. 4:25 p.], will find nothing new among us.

That it has lain long unknown and buried is the fault of man's impiety. Now, when it is restored to us by God's goodness, /26/ its claim to antiquity ought to be admitted at least by right of recovery.*

The same ignorance leads them to regard it as doubtful and uncertain. This is precisely what the Lord complains of through his prophet, that "the ox knew [16] its owner, and the ass its masters' crib; but his own people did not know him" [Is. 1:3 p.]. But however they may jest about its uncertainty, if they had to seal their doctrine in their own blood, and at the expense of their own life, one could see how much it would mean to them. Quite the opposite is our assurance, which fears neither the terrors of death nor God's judgment-seat.

In demanding miracles of us, they act dishonestly. For we are not forging some new gospel, but are retaining that very gospel whose truth all the miracles that Jesus Christ and his disciples ever wrought serve to confirm. But, compared with us, they have a strange power: even to this day they can confirm their faith by continual miracles! Instead they allege miracles which can disturb a mind otherwise at rest—they are so foolish and ridiculous, so vain and false! And yet, even if these were marvellous prodigies, they ought not to be of any moment against God's truth, for God's name ought to be always and everywhere hallowed, [17] whether by miracles or by the natural order of things.

And we may also fitly remember that Satan has his miracles, which, though they are deceitful tricks rather than authentic acts, are of such sort as to mislead the simple-minded and untutored [cf. II Thess. 2:9-10]. Magicians and enchanters have always been noted for miracles. Idolatry has been nourished by won-

5

derful miracles, yet these do not sanction for us the superstition either of magicians or of idolaters.

The Donatists of old overwhelmed the simplicity of the multitude with this battering-ram: that they were mighty in miracles. We, therefore, now answer our adversaries (16) as Augustine then answered the Donatists: the Lord made us wary of these miracle workers when he predicted that false prophets with lying signs and prodigies would come to draw even the elect (if possible) into error*[Matt. 24:24]. And Paul warned that the reign of Antichrist would be "with all power, and signs and lying wonders" [II Thess. 2:9]. But these miracles, they say, are done neither by idols, nor by magicians, nor by false prophets, but by the saints. [18] As if we did not understand that to "disguise himself as an angel of light" [II Cor. 11:14] is the craft of Satan! The Egyptians of old worshiped Jeremiah, who was buried in their land, rendering to him sacrifices and divine honors.* Did they not misuse the holy prophet of God for idolatrous purposes? And yet, they acquire the cure of snake-bite from such veneration of his tomb. What shall we say except /27/ that it has always been, and ever will be, a very just punishment of God to "send to those" who have not received the love of truth "a strong delusion to make them believe a lie" [II Thess. 2:11]?

Well, we are not entirely lacking in miracles, and these very certain and not subject to mockery. On the contrary, those "miracles" which our adversaries point to in their own support are sheer delusions of Satan, for they draw the people away from the true worship of their God to vanity [cf. Deut. 13:2ff.].

4. MISLEADING CLAIMS THAT CHURCH FATHERS OPPOSE REFORMATION TEACHING

Moreover, they unjustly set the ancient fathers against us* (I mean the ancient writers of a better age of the church) as if in them they had supporters of their own impiety. If the contest were to be determined by patristic authority, the tide of victory would turn to our side. [19] Now, these fathers have written many wise and excellent things. Still, what commonly happens to men has befallen them too, in some instances. For these so-called pious children of theirs, with all their sharpness of wit and judgment and spirit, worship only the faults and errors of the fathers. The good things that these fathers have written they either do not notice, or misrepresent or pervert. You might say that their only care is to gather dung amid gold.* Then, with a frightful to-do, they overwhelm us as despisers and adversaries of the fathers! But we do not despise the fathers; in fact, if it were to our present purpose, I could with no trouble at all prove that the greater part of what we are saying today meets their approval. Yet we are so versed in their writings as to remember always that all things are ours [I Cor. 3:21-22], to serve us, not to lord it over us [Luke 22:24-25], and that we all belong to the one (17) Christ [I Cor. 3:23], whom we must obey in all things without exception [cf. Col. 3:20]. He who does not observe this distinction will have nothing certain in religion, inasmuch as these holy men were ignorant of

6

many things, often disagreed among themselves, [20] and sometimes even contradicted themselves. It is not without cause, they say, that Solomon bids us not to transgress the limits set by our fathers*[Prov. 22:28]. But the same rule does not apply to boundaries of fields, and to obedience of faith, which must be so disposed that "it forgets its people and its father's house [Ps. 45:10 p.]. But if they love to allegorize so much, why do they not accept the apostles (rather than anyone else) as the "fathers" who have set the landmarks that it is unlawful to remove [Prov. 22:28]? Thus has Jerome interpreted this verse, and they have written his words into their canons.* But if our opponents want to preserve the limits set by the fathers according to their understanding of them, why do they themselves transgress them so willfully as often as it suits them?

It was one of the fathers who said that our God neither drinks nor eats, and therefore has not need of plates or cups.* Another, /28/ that sacred rites do not require gold, and those things not bought with gold do not please with gold.* They therefore transgress this limit when in their ceremonies they take so much delight in gold, silver, ivory, marble, precious stones, and silks; [21] and think that God is not rightly worshiped unless everything swims with excess.*

It was a father who said that he freely ate meat on the day others abstained from it, because he was a Christian.* They transgress the limits, therefore, when they execrate any person who has tasted of meat in Lent.*

There were fathers, one of whom said that a monk who does not labor with his hands must be considered equal to a thug; the second father, that it is not lawful for monks to live off the goods of others, even though they may be assiduous in contemplation, in prayer, and in study.* They have also transgressed this limit when they have put the lazy bellies of monks in these stews and brothels to be sated with the substance of others.

It was a father who termed it a dreadful abomination to see an image in the churches of Christians.* They are far from remaining within these limits when they leave not (18) a corner free of images. Another father counseled that, after having exercised in burial the office of humanity to the dead, we should let them rest.* They break these limits when [22] they stir up perpetual solicitude for the dead. It was one of the fathers who said the true body was not in the sacrament of the Supper, but only the mystery of the body: for thus he speaks to the word.* Therefore they overstep the bounds when they make it real and substantial.*

There were two fathers, one of whom decreed that those content with partaking in one kind, but abstaining from the other, were to be excluded entirely from participation in the Sacred Supper of Christ; the other /29/ strongly contends that one must not deny the blood of their Lord to Christian folk, who, in confessing him, are bidden to shed their own blood. They have removed these landmarks when they have commanded by an inviolable law the very thing that the former father punished by excommunication and the latter reproved with a valid reason.*

It was a father who affirmed it rashness, when judging of some obscure matter, to take one side or another without clear and evident witness of Scripture.

7

They forgot this limit when they established so many constitutions, canons, and doctrinal decisions, without any word of God. It was a father who reproached Montanus [23] for, among other heresies, being the first to impose laws of fasting.* They also passed far beyond those limits when they ordained fasts by very strict law.*

It was a father who denied that marriage should be forbidden to the ministers of the church, and declared cohabitation with one's wife to be chastity.* And other fathers agreed with his opinion.* By severely enjoining celibacy for their priests, they have gone beyond this limit.* It was a father who deemed that one must listen to Christ alone, for Scripture says, "Hear him" [Matt. 17:5]; and that we need not be concerned about what others before us either said or did, but only about what Christ, who is the first of all, commanded.* When they set over themselves and others any masters but Christ, they neither abode by this boundary nor permitted others to keep it.* (19)

All the fathers with one heart have abhorred and with one voice have detested the fact that God's Holy Word has been contaminated by the subtleties of sophists and involved in the squabbles of dialecticians.* When they do nothing in their whole life [24] but enshroud and obscure the simplicity of Scripture with endless contentions and worse than sophistic brawls, do they keep themselves within these borders? Why, if the fathers were now brought back to life, and heard such brawling art as these persons call speculative theology, there is nothing they would less suppose than that these folk were disputing about God! But my discourse would overflow if I chose to review how wantonly they reject the yoke of the fathers, whose obedient children they wish to seem. /30/ Indeed, months and even years would not suffice me! Nevertheless, they are of such craven and depraved impudence as to dare reproach us for passing beyond the ancient boundaries.

5. THE APPEAL TO "CUSTOM" AGAINST TRUTH

Even in their appeal to "custom" they accomplish nothing. To constrain us to yield to custom would be to treat us most unjustly. Indeed, if men's judgments were right, custom should have been sought of good men. But it often happens far otherwise: what is seen being done by the many has obtained the force of custom; while the affairs of men have scarcely ever been so well regulated [25] that the better things pleased the majority. Therefore, the private vices of the many have often caused public error,* or rather a general agreement on vices, which these good men now want to make a law. Those with eyes can perceive it is not one sea of evils* that has flooded the earth, but many dangerous plagues have invaded it, and everything is rushing headlong. Hence, one must either completely despair of human affairs or grapple with these great evils—or rather, forcibly quell them. And this remedy is rejected for no other reason save that we have long been accustomed to such evils. But, granting public error a place in the society of men, still in the Kingdom of God his eternal truth must alone be listened to and observed, a truth that cannot be dictated to by length of time, by long-standing custom, or by the conspiracy of men* In such manner Isaiah of old instructed God's elect not (20) to "call conspiracy all that this people call conspiracy," that is, not to conspire in the conspiracy of the people and in consent with it, "not" to "fear what they fear, nor be in dread" thereof, [26] but rather to "hallow the Lord of Hosts and let him be their fear and their dread" [Is. 8:12-13].

Now, then, let our adversaries throw at us as many examples as they wish, both of past and present ages. If we hallow the Lord of Hosts, we shall not be greatly afraid. Even though many ages may have agreed in like impiety, the Lord is strong to wreak vengeance, even to the third and fourth generation [Num. 14:18; cf. Ex. 20:4]. Even though the whole world may conspire in the same wickedness, he has taught us by experience what is the end of those who sin with the multitude. This he did when he destroyed all mankind by the Flood, but kept Noah with his little family; and Noah by his faith, the faith of one man, condemned the whole world [Gen. 7:1; Heb. 11:7]. To sum up, evil custon is nothing but a kind of public pestilence in which men do not perish the less though they fall with the multitude.

6. ERRORS ABOUT THE NATURE OF THE CHURCH

/31/ By their double-horned argument they do not press us so hard that we are forced to admit either that the church has been lifeless for some time or that we are now in conflict with it. Surely the church of Christ has lived and will live so long as Christ [27] reigns at the right hand of his Father* It is sustained by his hand; armed with his protection; and is strengthened through his power. For he will surely accomplish what he once promised: that he will be present with his own even to the end of the world*[Matt. 28:20]. Against this church we now have no quarrel. For, of one accord with all believing folk, we worship and adore one God, and Christ the Lord [I Cor. 8:6], as he has always been adored by all godly men. But they stray very far from the truth when they do not recognize the church unless they see it with their very eyes, and try to keep it within limits to which it cannot at all be confined*

Our controversy turns on these hinges: first, they contend that the form of the church is always apparent and observable. Secondly, they set this form in the see of the Roman Church and its hierarchy* We, on the contrary, affirm that the church can exist without any visible appearance, and that its appearance is not contained within that outward magnificence which they foolishly admire* Rather, it has quite (21) another mark, [28] namely, the pure preaching of God's Word and the lawful administration of the sacraments* They rage if the church cannot always be pointed to with the finger. But among the Jewish people how often was it so deformed that no semblance of it remained?*What form do we think it displayed when Elijah complained that he alone was left*[I Kings 19:10, or 14]? How long after Christ's coming was it hidden without form? How often has it since that time been so oppressed by wars, seditions, and heresies that it did not shine forth at all? If they had lived at that time, would they have believed that any church existed? But Elijah heard that there still remained seven thousand men who had not bowed the knee before Baal. And we must not doubt that Christ has reigned on earth ever since he ascended into heaven. But if believers had then required some visible form, would they not have straightway lost courage? Since the Lord alone "knows who are his" [II Tim. 2:19], let us therefore leave to him the fact that he sometimes removes from men's sight the external notion of his church. That is, I confess, a dreadful [29] visitation of God upon the earth. But if men's impiety deserves it, why do we strive to oppose divine justice? In such a way the Lord of old punished men's ingratitude. For, because they had refused to obey his truth and had extinguished his light, he allowed their blinded senses to be both deluded by foolish lies and plunged into profound darkness, so that no form of the true church remained. Meanwhile, he preserved his own children though scattered and hidden in /32/ the midst of these errors and darkness. And this is no marvel: for he knew how to preserve them in the confusion of Babylon, and in the flame of the fiery furnace [Dan. ch. 3].

Now I shall point out how dangerous is their desire to have the forms of the church judged by some sort of vain pomp. This I shall sketch rather than explain at length lest I endlessly prolong my discourse. The Roman Pope, they say, who occupies the Apostolic See, and the other bishops represent the church, and must be taken for the church; therefore they cannot err. Why so? Because, they reply, they are pastors of the church and have been consecrated by the Lord. Were not Aaron and the other leaders [30] of the people of Israel also pastors? Aaron and his sons, though designated priests, still erred when they fashioned the calf [Ex. 32:4]. Why, according to this reasoning, would not those four hundred prophets who deceived Ahab [I Kings 22:12] have represented the church? (22) And the church was on the side of Micaiah, a single contemptible man, yet one who spoke the truth. Did not the prophets who rose up against Jeremiah, boasting that "the law could not perish from the priest, nor counsel from the wise, nor the word from the prophet" [Jer. 18:18 p.], bear the name and form of the church? Against the whole tribe of the prophets, Jeremiah alone is sent from the Lord to announce that "the law was going to perish from the priest, counsel from the wise, the word from the prophet" [Jer. 18:18; cf. ch. 4:9]. Was not such pomp manifested in that council where the priests, scribes, and Pharisees assembled to deliberate concerning the execution of Christ [John 11:47 ff]? Now, let them go and cling to this outward mask making Christ and [31] all the prophets of the living God schismatics; Satan's ministers, conversely, the organs of the Holy Spirit!

But if they speak from the heart, let them answer me in good faith: in what region or among what people do they think the church resided after Eugenius, by decree of the Council of Basel, was deposed from the pontificate and replaced by Amadeus? If they were to burst, they could not deny that the council was lawful as to its outward arrangements, and was summoned not only by one pope but by two.* Eugenius was there condemned for schism, rebellion, and obstinacy, with the whole company of cardinals and bishops who had plotted the dissolution of the council with him. Nevertheless, subsequently supported by the favor of princes, he recovered his papal office unscathed.* That election of Amadeus, duly solemnized by the authority of a general and holy council, went up in smoke, except that the aforesaid Amadeus was appeased by a cardinal's hat, as a barking dog by a morsel. From these rebellious and obstinate heretics [32] have come forth all future popes. cardinals, bishops, abbots, and priests. Here /33/ they must be stopped and held fast. For on which side will they bestow the name of church? Will they deny that the council was general, which lacked nothing of outward majesty, was solmenly convoked by two bulls, consecrated by the presiding legate of the Roman see, well ordered in every respect, and (23) preserving the same dignity to the end? Will they admit that Eugenius and all his company, by whom they were consecrated, were schismatic? Let them, therefore, either define the form of the church in other terms, or we will adjudge them—however numerous they are—who knowingly and willingly have been ordained by heretics, to be schismatic. But if it had never been discovered before, they who under that fine title "church" have for so long superciliously hawked themselves to the world, even though they have been deadly plagues upon the church, can furnish us with abundant proof that the church is not bound up with outward pomp. I speak not concerning their morals [33] and tragic misdeeds, with which their whole life swarms, since they speak of themselves as the Pharisees, who are to be heard but not imitated*[Matt. 23:3]. If you will devote a little of your leisure to the reading of our words, you will unmistakably recognize that this, this very doctrine itself whereby they claim to be the church, is a deadly butchery of souls, a firebrand, a ruin, and a destruction of the church.

7. TUMULTS ALLEGED TO RESULT FROM REFORMATION TEACHING

Lastly, they do not act with sufficient candor when they invidiously recount how many disturbances, tumults, and contentions the preaching of our doctrine has drawn along with it, and what fruits it now produces among many. The blame for these evils is unjustly laid upon it, when this ought to have been imputed to Satan's malice. Here is, as it were, a certain characteristic of the divine Word, that it never comes forth while Satan is at rest and sleeping. This is the surest and most trustworthy mark to distinguish it from lying doctrines, which readily present themselves, are received with attentive ears by all, and are listened to by an applauding world. Thus for some centuries during which everything was submerged in deep darkness, [34] men were the sport and jest of this lord of the world, and, not unlike some Sardanapalus, Satan lay idle and luxuriated in deep repose. For what else had he to do but jest and sport, in tranquil and peaceable possession of his kingdom? Yet when the light shining from on

11

high in a measure shatterd his darkness, when that "stronger man" had troubled and assailed his kingdom [cf. Luke 11:22], he began to shake off his accustomed drowsiness and to take up arms. And first, indeed, he stirred up men to action that thereby he might violently oppress the dawning truth." And when this profited him nothing, he turned to stratagems: he aroused disagreements and dogmatic contentions through his Catabaptists° and (24) other monstrous rascals in order to obscure and at last extinguish the truth. And now he persists in besieging it with both engines. /34/ With the violent hands of men he tries to uproot that true seed, and seeks (as much as lies in his power) to choke it with his weeds, to prevent it from growing and bearing fruit. But all that is in vain, if we heed the Lord our monitor, [35] who long since laid open Satan's wiles before us, that he might not catch us unawares; and armed us with defenses firm enough against all his devices. Furthermore, how great is the malice that would ascribe to the very Word of God itself the odium either of seditions, which wicked and rebellious men stir up against it, or of sects, which imposters excite, both of them in opposition to its teaching! Yet this is no new example. Elijah was asked if it was not he who was troubling Israel [I Kings 18:17]. To the Jews, Christ was seditious [Luke 23:5; John 19:7 ff.]. The charge of stirring up the people was laid against the apostles [Acts 24:5 ff.]. What else are they doing who blame us today for all the disturbances, tumults, and contentions that boil up against us? Elijah taught us what we ought to reply to such charges: it is not we who either spread errors abroad or incite tumults; but it is they who contend against God's power [I Kings 18:18].

But as that one answer is enough to check their rashness, so must it, in turn, meet the foolishness of others who often happen to be moved by such scandals and, thus perturbed, to waver. [36] In order not to give way under this perturbation and be driven from their ground, let them, however, know that the apostles in their day experienced the same things that are now happening to us. There were unlearned and unstable men who, to their own destruction, distorted things that had been divinely written by Paul, as Peter says [II Pet. 3:16]. They were despisers of God who, when they heard that sin abounded that grace might more abound, immediately concluded: "We shall remain in sin, that grace may abound" [cf. Rom. 6:1]. When they heard that believers were not under the law, straightway they chirped: "We shall sin because we are not under the law, but under grace" [cf. Rom. 6:15]. There were people who accused Paul of being a persuader to evil [Rom. 3:8]. Many false apostles were intruding themselves to destroy the churches he had built [I Cor. 1:10 ff.: II Cor. 11:3 ff.; Gal. 1:6 ff.]. "Some preached the gospel out of envy and strife" [Phil. 1:15 p.], "not sincerely," even maliciously, "thinking (25) thereby to lay further weight upon his bonds" [Phil. 1:17 p.]. Elsewhere the gospel made little headway. "They all sought their own interests, not those of Jesus Christ" [Phil. 2:21]. Others returned to themselves, as "dogs . . . to their vomit, [37] and swine . . . to their wallowing in the mire" [II Pet. 2:22 p.]. Many degraded the freedom of the Spirit to the license of the flesh [II Pet. 2:18-19]. Many brethren crept in by whom the godly were exposed to dangers [II Cor. 11:3 ff.]. Among these very brethren various contentions broke out [Acts, chs. 6; 11; 15]. What were the apostles to do here? Ought they not to have dissembled for a time, or utterly laid aside that gospel and deserted it /35/ because they saw that it was the seedbed of so many quarrels, the source of so many dangers, the occasion of so many scandals? Yet in tribulations of this sort they were helped by the thought that Christ is "a rock of offense, a stone of stumbling" [Rom. 9:33; cf. I Pet. 2:8; Is. 8:14], "set for the fall and rising of many . . . and for a sign that is spoken against" [Luke 2:34]. Armed with this assurance, they boldly advanced through all the dangers of tumults and offenses. It is fitting that we too be sustained by the same consideration, inasmuch as Paul testifies to this everlasting quality of the gospel, that "it may be a fragrance of death unto death" [II Cor. 2:15] for those who perish; for those who have been saved, "to be a fragrance of life unto life" [II Cor. 2:16].

8. LET THE KING BEWARE OF ACTING ON FALSE CHARGES: THE INNOCENT AWAIT DIVINE VINDICATION

But I return to you, O Generous King. [38] May you be not at all moved by those vain accusations with which our adversaries are trying to inspire terror in you: that by this new gospel (for so they call it) men strive and seek only after the opportunity for seditions and impunity for all crimes. "For God is not author of division, but of peace" [I Cor. 14:33 p.]; and the Son of God is not "the minister of sin" [Gal. 2:17], for he has come to "destroy the devil's works" [I John 3:8].

And we are unjustly charged, too, with intentions of a sort such as we have never even given the least suspicion. We are, I suppose, contriving the overthrow of kingdoms—we, from whom not one seditious word was ever heard; we, whose life when we lived under you was always acknowledged to be quiet and simple; we, who do not cease to pray for the full prosperity of yourself and your kingdom, although we are now fugitives from home! We are, I suppose, wildly chasing after wanton vices! Even though in our moral actions many things are blameworthy, nothing deserves such great reproach as this. And we have not, by God's grace, (26) profited so little by the gospel [39] that our life may not be for these disparagers an example of chastity, generosity, mercy, continence, patience, modesty, and all other virtues. It is perfectly clear that we fear and worship God in very truth since we seek, not only in our life, but in our death, that his name be hallowed [cf. Phil. 1:20]. And hatred itself has been compelled to bear witness to the innocence and civic uprightness of some of us upon whom the punishment of death was inflicted for that one thing which ought to have occasioned extraordinary praise. But if any persons raise a tumult under pretext of the gospel—hitherto no such persons have been found in our realm— if any deck out the license of their own vices as the liberty of God's grace—I have known very many of this sort—there are laws and legal penalties by which they may be severely restrained according to their deserts. Only let not the gospel of God be blasphemed in the meantime because of the wickedness of infamous men.

The wicked poison of our calumniators has, O most Noble King, in its many details, been sufficiently disclosed [40] that you may not incline an ear credulous beyond measure to their slanders. /36/ I fear even that too many details have been included, since this preface has already grown almost to the size of a full-scale apology. In it I have not tried to formulate a defense, but merely to dispose your mind to give a hearing to the actual presentation of our case. Your mind is now indeed turned away and estranged from us, even inflamed. I may add, against us; but we trust that we can regain your favor, if in a quiet, composed mood you will once read this our confession, which we intend in lieu of a defense before Your Majesty. Suppose, however, the whisperings of the malevolent so fill your ears that the accused have no chance to speak for themselves, but those savage furies, while you connive at them, ever rage against us with imprisonings, scourgings, rackings, maimings, and burnings* [cf. Heb. 11:36-37]. Then we will be reduced to the last extremity even as sheep destined for the slaughter [Is. 53:7-8; Acts 8:33]. Yet this will so happen that "in our patience we may possess our souls" [Luke 21:19 p.]; and may await the strong hand of the Lord, which will surely appear in due season, coming forth armed to deliver the poor from [41] their affliction and also to punish their despisers.

May the LORD, THE KING OF KINGS, establish your throne in righteousness [cf. Prov. 25:5], and your dominion in equity, most Mighty and most Illustrious King.

AT BASEL,
10th day before the Kalends of September. [1535]

CHAPTER I

THE LAW:*
CONTAINING AN EXPLANATION
OF THE DECALOGUE

A. KNOWLEDGE OF GOD*

1. Nearly the whole of sacred doctrine* consists in these two parts: knowl-   1.1.1
edge of God and of ourselves.* Surely, we ought for the present to learn the   1.2.1
following things about God. To hold with sure faith, first that he is infinite
wisdom, righteousness, goodness, mercy, truth, power and life [Baruch 3:12-14;
James 1:17]. And all of these things, [43] wherever seen, come from him. [Prov.
16:4]. Secondly, that all things in heaven and on earth have been created for his
glory [Ps. 148:1-14; Dan. 3:59-63]. To serve him for his nature's sake alone, to
keep his rule, accept his majesty, and in obedience recognize him as Lord and
King [Rom. 1:20]—all this is due him by right. Thirdly, that he is himself a
just judge, and therefore, is going to take harsh vengeance upon those who have
turned aside from his precepts, who have not followed his will through all things,
who think, say and do things other than those that pertain to his glory [Ps.
7:9-11; Rom. 2:1-16]. Fourthly, that he is merciful and gentle, ready to receive
the miserable and poor that flee to his mercy and put their trust in him; prepared
to spare and pardon, if any ask a favor of him; willing to succor and give aid,
if any, ask for his help; willing to save any who put all their trust in him and
cleave to him [Ps. 103:3-4, 8-11; Is. 55:6; Ps. 25:6-11; 85:5-7, 10].

B. KNOWLEDGE OF MAN

2. In order for us to come to a sure knowledge of ourselves, /38/ we must   1.15.3
first grasp the fact that Adam, parent of us all, was created in the image and
likeness of God [Gen. 1:26-27]. That is, he was endowed with wisdom, righ-   1.15.4
teousness, holiness, and was so clinging by these gifts of grace to God (28) that
he could have lived forever in Him, if he had stood fast in the uprightness God
had given him. But when Adam slipped into sin, [44] this image and likeness

15

of God was cancelled and effaced, that is, he lost all the benefits of divine grace,
by which he could have been led back into the way of life [Gen. 3]. Moreover,
he was far removed from God and became a complete stranger. From this it
follows that man was stripped and deprived of all wisdom, righteousness, power,
life, which—as has already been said—could be held only in God. As a consequence, nothing was left to him save ignorance, iniquity, impotence, death,
and judgment [Rom. 5:12-21]. These are indeed the "fruits of sin." [Gal. 5:19-21].
This calamity fell not only upon Adam himself, but also flowed down into us,
who are his seed and offspring. Consequently, all of us born of Adam are
ignorant and bereft of God, perverse, corrupt, and lacking every good. Here is
a heart especially inclined to all sorts of evil, stuffed with depraved desires,
addicted to them, and obstinate toward God [Jer. 17:9]. But if we outwardly
display anything good, still the mind stays in its inner state of filth and crooked
perversity. The prime matter or rather the matter of concern for all rests in the
judgment of God, who judges not according to appearance, nor highly esteems
outward splendor, but gazes upon the secrets of the heart [I Sam. 16:7; Jer. 17:10].
Therefore, however much of a dazzling appearance of holiness man may have on
his own, it is nothing but hypocrisy [45] and even an abomination in God's sight,
since the thoughts of the mind, ever depraved and corrupted, lurk beneath.

3. Even though we have been so born that nothing is left for us to do
which could be acceptable to God, nor has it been put in our power to please
him—yet we do not cease to owe the very thing we cannot supply. Inasmuch
as we are God's creatures, we ought to serve his honor and glory, and obey his
commandments. And we are not allowed to excuse ourselves by claiming that
we lack ability and, like impoverished debtors, (29) cannot pay our debt. For
the guilt that binds us is our own, arising from our own sin, leaving us without
the will or the capacity to do good [John 8:34-38; Rom. 7:15-25]. Now, since
God justly avenges crimes, we must recognize that we are subject to the curse
and deserve the judgment of eternal death. Indeed there is no one of us with
either the will or the ability to do his duty.

C. THE LAW

4. For this reason Scripture calls us all "children of God's wrath" and
/39/declares we are hurtling to death and destruction [Eph. 2:1-3; Rom. 3:9-20].
To man is left no reason why he should seek in himself his righteousness, power,
life, and salvation; for all these are in God only; cut off and separated from Him
by sin [Hos. 13:4-9], man will find in himself only unhappiness, weakness,
wickedness, [46] death, in short, hell itself. To keep men from being ignorant
of these things, the Lord engraved and, so to speak, stamped the law upon the
hearts of all [Rom. 2:1-16]. But this is nothing but conscience; for us the witness
within of what we owe God; it sets before us good and evil, thus accusing and
condemning us, conscious as we are within ourselves that we have not discharged
our duty, as was fitting. Yet man is swollen with arrogance and ambition and

16

blinded by self-love. Consequently, he is unable to see himself and, as it were, to descend into himself, and confess his misery. Seeing our condition, the Lord has provided us with a written law to teach us what perfect righteousness is and how it is to be kept: that is, firmly fixed in God, we turn our gaze to him alone, and to him aim our every thought, yearning, act, or word. This teaching of righteousness clearly shows how far we have strayed from the right path. To this end also look all promises and curses, set forth for us in the law itself. For the Lord promises that, if anyone should perfectly and exactly fulfill by his effort whatever is commanded, he will receive the reward of eternal life [Lev. 18:5]. By this he undoubtedly points out to us that the perfection of life taught in the law [47] is truly righteousness, is so considered with him, and would be worthy of such a reward if any could be found among men. But he pronounces a curse and announces the judgment of eternal death upon all who do not fully and without exception keep the whole righteousness of the law [Deut. 27:26; Gal. 3:10].

    Surely by this punishment he constrains all men that ever were, are, or will be. Among them not one can be pointed out who is not a transgressor of the law. The law teaches us God's will, which we are constrained to fulfill and to which we are in debt; it shows us how we are able to carry out exactly nothing of what God has commanded us [Rom. 3:19; 7:7-25]. Consequently, it is clearly a mirror for us wherein we may discern and contemplate our sin and curse, just as we commonly gaze upon the scars (30) and blemishes of our face in a mirror. Properly speaking, this very written law is but a witness of natural law, a witness which quite often arouses our memory, and instills in us the things we had not sufficiently learned, when natural law was teaching within. Now we are ready to understand /40/ what we are to learn from the law. God is the Creator, our Lord and Father. For this reason we owe him glory, honor, and love. Since, however, not one of us performs these duties, we all deserve the curse, judgment, in short, eternal death. Therefore we are to seek another way to salvation [48] than the righteousness of our own works. This way is forgiveness of sins. Then, since it is not in our power or ability to discharge what we owe the law, we must despair of ourselves and must seek and await help from another quarter. After we descend to this humility and submission, the Lord will shine upon us, and show himself lenient, kindly, gentle, indulgent. For of him it is written: "he resists the proud, gives grace to the humble" [James 4:6; I Pet. 5:5]. And first, if we pray him to avert his wrath, and ask his pardon, he will without doubt grant it to us. Everything our sins deserved he forgives, and receives into grace.

2.8.5

2.8.4

2.7.7

2.8.2
2.8.3

D. GOD'S LOVE IN CHRIST

    5. Then, if we implore his helping hand, surely we will be persuaded that, equipped with his protection, we will be able to do all things. He bestows upon us according to his own good will a new heart in order that we may will, and a new power, whereby we may be enabled to carry out his commandments [Ezek. 36:26]. And all these blessings he showers upon us for the sake of Jesus

Christ our Lord, who—even though he was one God with the Father [John 1:1-14]—put on our flesh, to enter a covenant with us and to join us (far separated from God by our sins) closely to him [Is. 53:4-11]. He also by the merit of his death paid our debts to God's justice, and appeased his wrath [Eph. 2:3-5]. He redeemed us from the curse and judgment [49] that bound us, and in his body the punishment of sin, so as to absolve us from it [Col. 1:21-22]. Descending to earth, he brought with him all the rich heavenly blessings and with a lavish hand showered them upon us [John 1:14-16; 7:38; Rom. 8:14-17]. These are the Holy Spirit's gifts. Through him we are reborn, wrested from the power and chains of the devil, freely adopted as children of God, sanctified for every good work. Through him also—so long as we are held in this mortal body— there are dying in us the depraved desires, the promptings of the flesh, and everything the twisted and corrupt perversity of our nature brings forth. Through him we are renewed from day to day [II Cor. 4:16], that we may walk in newness of life [Rom. 6:4] and live for righteousness.

6. God offers to us and gives us in Christ our Lord all these benefits, which include free forgiveness of sins, peace and reconciliation with God, the gifts and graces of the Holy Spirit. They are ours if we embrace and receive them with sure faith, utterly trusting (31) and, as it were leaning upon divine goodness, not doubting /41/ that God's Word, which promises us all these things, is power and truth [Rom. 3:21-26; 5:1-11]. In short, if we partake of Christ, in Him we shall possess all the heavenly treasures and gifts of the Holy Spirit, which lead us into life and salvation. Except with a true and living faith, we will never grasp this. [50] With it, we will recognize all our good to be in him, ourselves to be nothing apart from him; we will hold as certain that in him we become God's children and heirs of the heavenly kingdom [John 1:12; Rom.

3.14.4   8:14-17]. On the other hand, those who have no part in Christ, whatever their nature, whatever they may do or undertake, depart into ruin and confusion and into the judgment of eternal death; they are cast away from God and are shut off from all hope of salvation [John 3:18-20; I John 5:12]. This knowledge of ourselves and of our poverty and ruin teaches us to humble ourselves and cast ourselves before God and seek his mercy [Jer. 31:18-20]. Not from ourselves is the faith that furnishes us a taste of divine goodness and mercy, wherein God in his Christ has to do with us. Rather, it is God who is to be asked to lead us, unfeignedly repentant, to the knowledge of ourselves; to lead us, by sure faith, to the knowledge of his gentleness and of his sweetness, which he shows forth in his Christ in order that Christ as our leader, who is the only way to reach the Father, may bring us into eternal blessedness [Phil. 1:6; John 14:6; Rom. 5:1-11].

E. EXPOSITION OF THE DECALOGUE

2.8.11   7. The ten commandments of the law were divided into two tables (Ex. 32:15; 34:1; Deut. 10:1]. The first table includes the first four commandments, which instruct us in what we owe God: to recognize and profess him as the only

God, to love, honor and fear him above and before all else, to repose in him [51] alone all our hopes and needs, and always to ask his help. The second table comprises the six remaining commandments, which explain love and the duties of love to be practiced, for God's sake, toward our neighbor. As the gospel writers state, our Lord sums up the law under two heads: we are to love God with all our heart, all our soul, and all our strength, and our neighbor as ourselves [Matt. 22:37, 39; Luke 10:27]. Even though the whole law has been included under these two heads our Lord, to deprive us of all pretext of excuse, has willed to proclaim more deeply and explicitly by ten commandments, both everything that pertains to honor, fear, and love of him, and all that has to do with love which, for his own sake, he enjoins upon us toward our neighbors. But before he begins his commandments, he gives the following preface [Ex. 20:2; Deut. 5:6]: /42/

2.8.12

> I am the Lord your God, who led you out of the land of Egypt, and out of the house of bondage.

2.8.13

8. By these words he informs us that he is the Lord who has the right to give commandments, and to be obeyed. Besides, (32) he calls to mind how gloriously he manifested his strength and power, when he aided the Israelites in getting free from the bondage of Pharoah and the Egyptians; how he daily shows the same power, when he takes away his chosen ones [52] (the true Israelites) from bondage to sin (figured under the name 'Egypt'); when he releases them from the chains of the devil, spiritual Pharoah, Lord of the Egyptians (those who walk in their own lusts). He then adds the first commandment in this form:

2.8.14

2.8.15

First Commandment:
You shall not have other Gods before me. [Ex. 20:3]

2.8.13

9. This commandment forbids us to turn to another our trust, which ought to be placed wholly in him; or to transfer to another the credit (due him alone) for any good or virtue whatsoever [Is. 30:1-5; 31:1; Jer. 2:13, 32]. Rather, he is to be feared and loved by us, beyond all else, that we recognize him alone as our God, and fix all our hope and trust in him [I Tim. 1:17; Deut. 6:4-14; 10:12-13]. Meantime, we should ponder that every good thing comes to us from him, and permit nothing but that wherein he is honored and adored [I Cor. 10:23-31]. This we must do not only to declare, by tongue and bodily gesture, and by every outward indication, that we have no other God; but also with our mind, our whole heart, and all our zeal, to show ourselves as such. For not only are our words and outward works open to him, but the inmost recesses of our heart and deepest thoughts of our mind are better and more clearly revealed to him than to ourselves [I Chron. 28:9]. [53]

Second Commandment:
You shall not make a graven image for yourself nor any likeness of things which are in heaven above, or on earth beneath, or in the waters under the earth; and you shall not adore or worship them. [Ex. 20:4-5]

2.8.17f

10. This means: all worship and adoration is owed to the one God. He is incomprehensible, incorporeal, /43/ invisible, and so contains all things that he can be enclosed in no place. Let us then fervently pray against our imagining he can be expressed in any figure,* or represented in any idol whatsoever, as if it were God's likeness. Rather, we are to adore God, who is Spirit, in spirit and in truth [Deut. 6:13-16; 10:12-13; I Kings 8:22-27; I Tim. 1:17; John 1:9-14; 4:24]. The First Commandment therefore teaches that there is one God, apart from whom no other gods are to be thought of or held to. This commandment teaches God himself is such and is to be honored by such worship that we dare not attach anything (33) physical*to him, or subject him to our senses, as if he could be comprehended by our dull heads, or be represented in any form.

1.11.9 Those who are trying, with a miserable excuse, to defend an accursed idolatry that many ages ago had swamped and sunk true religion,* should attend to this. Images, they assert, are not to be taken for gods.* [54] Not so utterly unthinking were the Jews as to forget it was God by whose hand they had been led out of Egypt, before they fashioned the calf. Not so senseless are we to deem the gentiles as not to have understood God to be something else than wood or stones. They used to change images at will, but always keeping in mind the same gods. And though they consecrated many images to one god, they did not fashion as many gods for themselves as there were images. Besides, they daily consecrated new ones, but without thinking they were making new gods. What then? All idolaters, whether Jew or gentile, were convinced God was just as their empty minds had conceived him. To this emptiness, depravity was added:

1.11.9 as they had inwardly fancied, so they expressed. The mind therefore conceived the idol, the hand brought it to birth; nevertheless, the Jews thought they were worshiping the eternal God, the one true Lord of heaven and earth, under such images; while the gentiles were worshiping their own, although false, gods whom they still fancied to dwell in heaven. Furthermore, they did not believe God

1.11.8 present to them, unless he showed himself physically present. In obeisance to this blind longing, they raised up signs, wherein they believed God was set

1.11.9 before their physical eyes. Since they thought God saw himself in these, they also worshiped him in them. Finally, all men, [55] having fixed their minds and eyes upon them, began to grow more brutish and to be overwhelmed with

1.11.10 admiration for them, as if something of divinity inhered there. Those who assert that this was not done heretofore, and within our memory is still not being done, lie shamelessly. For why do they prostate themselves before these things? Why do they, when about to pray, turn to them as if to God's ears? Why do they take up the sword to defend these images as if they were altars and hearth fires, even to the point of butchery and carnage, so that they would more easily be deprived of the one God than of their idols? /44/ Nevertheless, I do not yet enumerate the crass errors of the multitude, which are well-nigh infinite, and which occupy the hearts of almost all men; I am only indicating what they profess when they especially wish to exculpate themselves of idolatry. We do not call them "our gods," they say. Neither did Jews nor pagans so speak of them, but only as signs and likenesses of God, and yet the prophets and all the Scriptures did not hesitate to accuse them of fornications with wood and stone [Jer. 2:27; Ezek. 6:4ff.; cf. Is. 40:19-20; Hab. 2:18-19; Deut. 32:37] only for doing the very things that are daily done by those who wish to be counted Christians, (34) namely, that they physically venerated God in wood and stone.

11. The ultimate evasion is that they call them "the books of the unedu-   1.11.7
cated." Suppose we grant them this (although it is completely vain, since it is more than certain, that the only purpose for prostration is to worship)—I still cannot see what benefit such images can provide for the unlearned [56] (especially for those for whom they wish to portray God) except to make them into anthropomorphites. The things they dedicate to saints—what are they but examples of the most abandoned lust and obscenity? If anyone wished to model himself after them, he would be fit for the lash. Indeed, brothels show harlots clad more virtuously and modestly than the churches show those objects which they wish to be seen as images of virgins. Therefore let them compose their images at least to a moderate decency, that they may with a little more modesty falsely claim that these are books of some holiness!

But then we shall also answer that this is not the method of teaching the people of God whom the Lord wills to be instructed with a far different doctrine than this trash. He has set forth the preaching of his Word as a common doctrine for all. What purpose did it serve for so many crosses—of wood, stone, even of silver and gold—to be erected, if this fact had been duly and faithfully taught: that Christ was offered on account of our sins that he might bear our curse and cleanse our trespasses? From this one word they could have learned more than from a thousand crosses of either wood or stone. For perhaps the covetous fix their minds and eyes more tenaciously upon gold and silver than upon any word of God.

And whom, pray, do they call the "unlearned"? Those, indeed, whom the   1.11.13
Lord recognizes as "God-instructed [John 6:45]." Here is the incomparable   2.8.18
boon of images, beyond price! [57] But he more pointedly states how gravely he detests all faithlessness and idolatry, adding to these two commandments:

> He is the Lord, our God, mighty and jealous, who visits the iniquity of the fathers upon the children, unto the third and fourth generation of those who hate his name, but shows mercy to thousands, to those who love him and keep his commandments. [Ex. 20:5-6 p.] /45/

This is as if he were saying that it was he alone to whom we ought to hold fast, nor can he bear any partner. Also he will vindicate his majesty and glory against any who may transfer it to graven images or other things. And not once, but against the fathers, the children, and the grandchildren. That is, at any time whatever. At the same time he manifests his everlasting mercy and kindness to those who love him and keep his law.

Third Commandment:

2.8.22   You shall not take the name of your God in vain [Ex. 20:7]

12. The meaning of this is: God is indeed so to be feared and loved by us, that we should not for any reason misuse his most holy name. (35) Rather, we should magnify him above all else for his holiness, give the glory to him in everything, whether favorable or adverse; we should wholeheartedly [58] ask of him all things which come to us from his hand, and give him thanks. To sum up, let us carefully keep away from all contumely and blasphemy, so as not to name him by any other name, or speak other of him than befits his lofty majesty. Let us not put that holy name of his to any other uses than those he has willed it to be put to, for that would be to profane and pollute it, as those do who make it serve the superstitions of necromancy, frightful curses, unlawful exorcisms, and other wicked incantations [Lev. 20:6f.; Deut. 18:10-12]. As far as pledges and oaths are concerned, we are not to call upon his holy name in any false way. For the eternal truth can be no more gravely dishonored than if it be cited
2.8.15   as witness to falsehood. In short, we are not to use even a true oath rashly, unless God's glory or the need of the brethren demands it as necessary. Save for
2.8.26   this cause, any kind of oathswearing is forbidden. As Christ's words teach us, when he interprets this head of the law, it means that all our speech is, yea, yea; nay, nay; and what goes beyond this, testifies that it comes from the evil one [Matt. 5:37]. At this point this must also be observed: everyone is forbidden to
2.8.27   use any oath out of his own private rashness. But that oath which we take when administered and required by the magistrate is not at all opposed to this commandment, [59] since in another passage God gave the magistrate the power to administer oaths, when the witness of truth was required for judgment [Ex. 22:11; Heb. 6:13-18]. Nay, all public oaths are exempted from this prohibition. Such are those that Paul used, to assert the dignity of the gospel [Rom. 1:9; 9:1f.]. /46/ For the apostles in their duties are not private men but public ministers of God. Such also are those oaths that can be used by princes in solemnizing treaties, or by a people swearing in the name of their prince, and any
2.8.25   others not done out of private greed, but for the public good. The first point therefore for us to remember is that oath-taking was permitted not for the sake of lust or desire, but because of necessity. But inasmuch as we are not permitted to call upon God's name except as was said, namely, to confirm our word, as often as there is such use, his very name, not another, is to be called on. For it pertains to his honor and glory that he is and is to be held the sole witness of
2.8.23   truth, who is the sole and eternal truth [Deut. 6:13; 10:20; Is. 45:23; 48:15ff.]. Finally, the more effectively to commend the excellent majesty of his name, the Lord has added the following words to this commandment:

2.8.25   He will not reckon as innocent him who has taken his name in vain.

By these words, he proclaims a particular curse against those who transgress this commandment. [60]

22

(36) Fourth Commandment:

Remember to keep holy the Sabbath Day. Six days you shall labor, and do   2.8.28
all your work; but on the seventh day is the Sabbath of the Lord your God.
You shall not do any work of yours, you and your son, and your daughter,
your man servant and your maid servant, your beast of burden and the
stranger who is within your gates. For in six days the Lord made heaven
and earth, the sea, and all that is in them; and on the seventh day he rested;
therefore he has blessed it, and hallowed it. [Ex. 20:8-11]

13. Observance of the Sabbath is related both to piety and to the worship
of God, since it has been included under the first table, and is called the "hallowing of the day." Therefore the Lord has never enforced anything more strictly   2.8.29
than this [Ex. 31:13-17]. And when, in the prophets, he intends to signify that
all religion has been subverted, he states that his Sabbaths have been polluted
and profaned, violated, not kept, not hallowed—as if by omitting this homage,
nothing further remained in which to honor him [Ezek. 20:12-13; 22:8; 23:38;
Jer. 17:21, 22, 27; Is. 56:2; Num. 15:32-35]. But there is absolutely no doubt that   2.8.28
this precept was a foreshadowing, and enjoined /47/ upon the Jews during the
era of ceremonies, in order to represent to them under outward observance the
spiritual worship of God. [61] Therefore at the coming of Christ, who is the   2.8.31
light of shadows and the truth of the figures, it was abolished, like the remaining
shadows of the Mosaic Law, as Paul clearly testifies [Gal. 4:8-11; Col. 2:16-17].
But, though the ceremonies and the outward rite have been abolished, with
which the faith of the Jews was exercised under the law's pedagogy, we still
retain the truth of the precept, that the Lord willed the Jews and us to have
forever and in common. This then is that truth: inasmuch as we ought to fear
and love God, we are to seek our rest in him. This will then come to pass, if
we clearly abjure our wicked desires, which do nothing but foment, disturb and
agitate the conscience: and, if we desist from all unclean works of our flesh, that
is, which bring wickedness to birth in our nature out of our concupiscence—
from all works (in a word) which are not of God's spirit, whatever appearance
of human wisdom they may put forth [Heb. 3:7-19; 4:9; Is. 35:5-8; 58:13-14].
All works of this sort are servile. From them the law of the Sabbath bids us
cease, that God may dwell in us, may effect what is good, and rule us by the
leading of his Holy Spirit,* whose kingdom imparts peace and tranquility to the
conscience.* This moreover is the true Sabbath, (37) whose type and, as it were,
shadow, that Jewish Sabbath was. Consequently, it had been assigned to the   2.8.30
seventh day, a number signifying perfection [62] in Scripture.* By it we are
taught, that God enjoined on us an eternal Sabbath, for which no limit is set;
secondly, its full and proper hallowing will never come to pass until the seventh
day [Heb. 4:1-11]. That seventh day, indeed, is ultimate and eternal. Although
all of us who are believers have in part entered into it, we have not yet fully
reached it. For we have now through faith begun our rest in God, in which we
are also daily making progress so that at least it may be completed when that
saying of Isaiah will be fulfilled, in which Sabbath upon Sabbath is promised

to God's church [Is. 66:23]. That is, when God will be all in all [I Cor. 15:28]. This also God showed us in the creation of the world, which he completed in six days; only on the seventh day did he rest from all work [Gen. 2:1-3], so that by his example we also, ceasing from our labors, may seek our rest in him, and aspire eagerly to this sabbath of the seventh day.*

2.8.33   14. This applies to the Lord's Day which we now observe: /48/ it was not established for us to hallow it before all others, that is, to count it more holy.
2.8.32 For this is the prerogative of God alone, who has honored all days equally [Rom. 14:5]. But it was established for the church to gather for prayers and praises of
2.8.33 God, for hearing the Word, for the use of the sacraments* [Gal. 4:8-11; Col. 3:16]. The better to devote all our effort, singlemindedly to [63] these tasks, we are to stop all mechanical and manual labor, and all pursuits which have to do with the conduct of this life. Of the same sort are other solmen days, wherein the mysteries of our salvation are called to mind. But if we drink that Word wholeheartedly (as is fitting) and through it mortify the works of the old man, not only on festal days but every day continuously do we hallow the Sabbath; and, because we are here so commanded, we begin to celebrate Sabbath after Sabbath. To sum up: it is not by religion that we distinguish one day from another, but for the sake of the common polity. For we have certain prescribed days not simply to celebrate, as if by our stopping labor God is honored and pleased, but because it is needful for the church to meet together on a certain
2.8.32 day. Moreover it is important for there to be a set and appointed day that all things may be done according to order and without disturbance [I Cor. 14:40].
2.8.34 Thus will vanish the nonsense of the sophists, who have infected the world with the Jewish notion that the ceremonial part of this commandment has been abrogated (in their phraseology they call it the 'appointing' of the seventh day); but that the moral part remains, namely, the observance of one day in the week.* Yet this is nothing but changing the day to spite the Jews, while at the same time retaining the observance of the day. [64] And we really see how much they profit by such teaching. For those who cling to their constitutions surpass the Jews three times over in crass and carnal sabbatarian superstition. (38) Hence the reproaches that we read in Isaiah apply to these today just as much as they did to those whom the prophet rebuked in his own time [Is. 1:13-15; Is. 58:13].

    15. The Jews had another task to see to in sabbatarianism, not one having to do with religion but with the preservation of equity among men. This means, actually, to remit the labor of servants and animals, lest inhuman taskmasters by persistent urging press them beyond due measure.* Moses was really pointing out the usefulness of something already taught rather than teaching something on his own [Ex. 23:11f; Deut. 5:14f.]. We are to have regard for equity today also, not out of any servile necessity, but according as love dictates. Here then are the first four commandments which set forth how we are to conduct ourselves toward God; these conclude the first table.

    16. But beyond the common /49/ form accepted almost everywhere, I include four commandments under the first table. Not without reason, nor even

for a light one, has this been done. For certain authorities divide them differently, erasing the Second Commandment from the number, as related by us, one to which the Lord undoubtedly gave a distinct place as a commandment. [65] Yet they absurdly tear in two the Tenth Commandment, on not coveting the possessions of one's neighbor, which is one single commandment. Besides, one can understand this manner of division was unknown in a purer age from the fact that Origen incontrovertibly set forth this division of ours. Admittedly the other was found in Augustine's time, but was not approved by all. Surely it pleased Augustine for a very insufficient reason, namely, that in the number "three" (if the first table consists of three commandments) the mystery of the Trinity shines forth more clearly. In other respects our division suited him better. I do not doubt it was by the devil's fraud that this commandment, whereby idolatry is so expressly forbidden, gradually slipped away from men's minds. This point had to be touched on in passing, lest anyone wonder or laugh at my division as if it were something new and recently devised. There remains the Second Table.

2.8.12

Fifth Commandment:
Honor father and mother. [Ex. 20:12]

2.8.35

17. Since God is to be loved and feared by us, we are neither to neglect our parents, nor offend them in any way. But we are to show great deference to them, reverence and honor them, obey them under the Lord's will; we are to endeavor to oblige and please those to whom our effort can be of use in these matters [Eph. 6:1-3; Matt. 15:4-6]. (39) A blessing is added: "Those who obey their parents with the honor due them will live long upon the earth." [66] It is as it were by way of a singular recommendation, which declares how pleasing to God is the observance of this commandment and which arouses our sluggishness, and urges at the same time that ungrateful children, who have neglected to reciprocate and show gratitude to their parents, may expect the surest curse.

2.8.37

/50/ Sixth Commandment:
You shall not kill. [Ex. 20:13]

2.8.39

18. Since God is to be feared and loved by us, we are not to harm anyone by any kind of offense, we are not to treat any man unjustly, not attack anyone, not do violence to anyone. Rather: if there is in us any fear and love toward God, we are to treat kindly all men friend or foe; we are to strive to please both, offer a helping hand to both if either is in any danger, struggle to be generous to both friend and foe, as much as we are able [Matt. 5:27-30].

Seventh Commandment:
You shall not fornicate. [Ex. 20:14]

2.8.41

19. The drift is this: that, since God is to be feared and loved by us, we are throughout life to regulate, speak, and carry out all our doings chastely and continently. And since virginity is a special gift of God, each one of us is to see

what has been given him [Matt. 5:43-48; Eph. 5:3-4; I Cor. 6:13-20; Matt. 19:11-12; I Cor. 7:1-40]. [67] For those who do not take up this word have a remedy for the impurity of their flesh, offered to them by the Lord. Unless they use it, they contend against God and resist his ordinance. And they are not to say (as many today do) that with God's help they can do all things. For God's help comes only to those who walk in his ways [Ps. 91:1-14], that is, in his calling, from which these fellows try to depart against God's will. In this stubbornness of theirs they are not to expect God's help, but should rather remember his statement: "You shall not tempt the Lord your God" [Deut. 6:16; Matt. 4:7]. To tempt God means to try to reject even his present gifts, counter to the nature with which he has endowed us. These fellows not only do this. They actually dare call "defilement" even the very matrimony God deigned to establish, declared honorable in all, the matrimony Christ our Lord hallowed by his presence, deigning to grace it with his first miracle [Gen. 2:18-24; Heb. 13:4; John 2:1-11]. This they do solely to extol with marvelous praises some sort of celibacy. As if celibacy were not one thing, virginity another! (40) They call it an "angelic life," in this doing particular injustice to the angels of God, by comparing fornicators, adulterers, and something much more evil and filthy, to them. Obviously, there is no need whatsoever for proofs here, where the very things themselves bear their own clear refutation. For we see how the Lord from time to time avenges [68] with frightful punishments, this sort of arrogance and contempt of his gifts. /51/ Nor are spouses to think all things allowed to them, but each man is to treat his wife soberly and modestly, and each wife her husband. So conducting themselves, they are not to brook anything at all unworthy of the honesty and restraint of marriage; in fine, they are to think of themselves as wedded in the Lord.

Eighth Commandment:
You shall not steal. [Ex. 20:15]

20. The commandment means: Since God is to be feared and loved by us, we are not to filch by fraud or seize by main force what belongs to another. We are not to catch anyone unawares in bargaining or contracts, either by selling too dear or by buying too cheaply from those who are ignorant of the prices of things; nor are we to lay hands on another's property by any sort of guile whatsoever. But, if there is in us any fear or love of God, we are rather to press with every effort to aid either friend or foe, as much as we can with advice and help, to hold onto his possessions, and we are rather to give up our own than take away anything from another. And not this alone, but if they are pressed by any material difficulty, we are to share their needs and relieve their penury with our substance [Is. 58:7-9; Rom. 12:20; II Cor. 8:14; Eph. 4:28, etc.]. [69]

Ninth Commandment:
You shall not speak false witness. [Ex. 20:16]

21. This means: Since God is to be feared and loved by us, we are not to press a false charge against anyone; we are not to impugn anyone's reputation:

not to yield our tongue or ears to evilspeaking or caustic wit, not to suspect or harbor a sinister thought about anyone. But, if there is in us any fear or love toward God, as far as we are able we are to think sincerely and speak honorably of all, that as fairminded interpreters toward all we may (as much as is permitted) take their words and deeds in the best part [Matt. 7:1-5; Rom. 13:8-10; 14:10]. This commandment is also extended to the point that we are not to delight in any lies, not to affect a fawning politeness, nor to accommodate ourselves to polite and idle talkativeness [Ps. 5:6; Matt. 12:36-37; Eph. 4:25-28; 5:6-11]. (41) /52/

Tenth Commandment:

2.8.49

You shall not covet your neighbor's house, you shall not desire his wife, his servant, his maidservant, his ox, his ass, nor anything that is his. [Ex. 20:17]

22. By this the Lord, who should be feared and loved by us, forbids all desire of another's wife, family, possessions, or any good whatsoever. In this way he forbids much more: we are not to conceive any stratagem, any fraud [70] or craft (even if it can be cloaked with an honest name) by which either a wife may depart from fellowship with her husband, or servants may escape, or other possessions may be wrested from his hand. We are not by flattery to separate wife from husband or servant from master. We are not to separate the husband himself from his wife in order that she, cast off by him, may become ours. We are not to separate the master from his servants in order that they, expelled, may cross over to us. In fine, we are not to play any tricks of this sort, to which greedy men are accustomed, to get our hands on another's property. That such an act is forbidden should be beyond doubt, where the will itself and the desire and the very thought of possession are forbidden. But if any fear or love of God is in us, let us rather so act that we may not only desire the wife and all the possessions of any man to remain safe and sound, but also foster love between husband and wife. Let us urge slaves to do their duty. In short, let us for all reasons preserve unto each his own, insofar as we are able.

23. The rule that forbids us to covet another's possessions ought also to be applied in this way in order that each person may, according to his calling, perform his own tasks, and render to another what pertains to his office [Eph. 4]. And he who does not bring forth from the gift of his own calling that which he gives to others, both covets and keeps another's belongings. For this reason a people should hold in honor its kings, princes, magistrates, and others in authority, [71] patiently bearing their government, obeying their laws and commands, refusing nothing which can be carried out under God's will [Rom. 13:1ff.; I Pet. 2:13ff.; Titus 3:1]. In turn, let the rulers take care of their own common people, render justice, keep the public peace and tranquillity, protect the good, punish the evil [Eph. 4:1, 7, 16, 28]. So let them manage all things as if they are about to render account of their services to God, the supreme King

2.8.46

and Judge [cf. Deut. 17:19; II Chron. 19:6-7; also Heb. 13:17]. Let bishops and ministers of churches faithfully attend to the ministry of the Word, not adulterating the teaching of salvation [cf. II Cor. 2:17], but delivering it pure and undefiled to God's people. And let them instruct the people not only through teaching, but also by the example of their life. In short, let them exercise authority as good shepherds over their sheep [I Tim. 3:1-5; II Tim. 2:15; 4:2, 5; Titus 1:6ff.; I Pet. 5:2f]. Let the people /53/ in their turn receive them as messengers and apostles of God, render to them that honor of which the Lord has deemed them worthy, and give them those things necessary for their livelihood [cf. Matt. 10:10ff.; Rom. 10:15 and 15:15ff; I Cor. 9:6-14; Gal. 6:6; I Thess. 5:12; I Tim. 5:17f.]. (42) Let parents undertake to nourish, teach, and govern the children committed to them by God, not provoking their minds with inhumanity and cruelty and turning them against their parents [Eph. 6:4; Col. 3:21]; but cherishing and embracing their children with such gentleness and kindness as becomes their character as parents. As we have already said, children owe obedience to their parents. Let youth reverence old age, as the Lord has willed that age to be worthy of honor. Also, let the aged guide the insufficiency of youth with their own wisdom and [72] experience wherein they excel the younger, not railing harshly and loudly against them but tempering their severity with mildness and gentleness. Let servants show themselves diligent and obedient to their masters, not serving for the eye, but from the heart, just as they render obedience to God. Also, let masters not conduct themselves peevishly and intractably toward their servants, oppressing them with undue rigor, or treating them abusively. Rather, let them recognize them as their brothers, co-servants of the same Lord, who is in heaven, whom they ought to love mutually and treat humanely [cf. Eph. 6:5-9; Col. 3:22-25; Titus 2:9-10; I Pet. 2:18-20; Col. 4:1; Philemon 16].

In this manner, let each man consider what, in his rank and station, he owes his neighbors, and pay what he owes.

F. SUMMARY

24. We have the whole law, unfolded in ten commandments, by which we are sufficiently instructed in those things that God either requires of us or forbids us do, both toward himself and toward others. It is easy to fathom the direction of all these things, namely, to teach love. The sum of the first table, by which we are especially instructed in godliness, consists in these things: to fear, love, and honor God; to confess him; call upon him; to ask and await all things from him; to find our protection in him; to repose in him [Matt. 7:12]. The sum of the second table is to cultivate love toward others for God's sake [73] by so doing toward all as we would have done to us, but not to love ourselves.

2.8.54　　In the entire law we do not read one syllable that lays down a rule for man on the things he may or may not do for his own advantage. And obviously, since men were born in such a state that they are completely inclined to self-love, there was no need of a law gratuitously to enkindle further that already immoderate love: Hence it is very clear /54/ that we keep the commandments not by loving ourselves but by loving God and neighbor; that he lives the best and holiest life who lives and strives for himself as little as he can; and that no one lives in a worse or more evil manner than he who lives and strives for himself alone, and thinks about and seeks only his own advantage:

25. But not to be passed over cursorily is the fact that not only outward works but also thoughts themselves and the inward affections of the heart are commanded or forbidden by God's law, lest anyone judge the law satisfied where merely the hand refrains from the deed. 2.8.6

There are some who (43) compose their eyes, feet, hands, and all parts of the body to some observance of the law. Meanwhile they keep the heart utterly aloof from all obedience, and think themselves well acquitted if they thoroughly hide from men what they do within before God. They hear: "You shall not kill; you shall not fornicate; you shall not steal." [Ex. 20:13-15] They do not unsheath a sword for slaughter; [74] they do not join their bodies to prostitutes; they do not lay hands on another's goods. So far so good. But wholeheartedly they breathe out slaughter, burn with lust, look with jaundiced eye upon the goods of all others and devour them with covetousness. They are now lacking in the chief point of the law. Against them Paul stoutly protests, affirming that "the law is spiritual" [Rom. 7:14]. By this he means that it demands a wholly obeying mind, soul and will. 2.8.6

When we say that this is the meaning of the law, we are not thrusting forward a new interpretation of our own, but we are following Christ, the law's best interpreter. The Pharisees had infected the people with the perverse opinion that he who has committed nothing by way of outward acts against the law fulfills the law. Christ reproves this most dangerous error, and he declares an unchaste glance at a woman to be adultery [Matt. 5:28]. He declares that all who hate a brother are murderers [I John 3:15]. For he makes "liable to judgment," those who even conceive anger in their hearts; he makes "liable to the council" those who by muttering and grumbling have given any indication of being offensive; he makes "liable to hell-fire" those who with railings and cursings burst forth into open anger [Matt. 5:21-22p.; cf. Matt. 5:43 ff.]. Those who did not comprehend these teachings fancied Christ another Moses, the giver of the law of the gospel, to supply what was lacking in the Mosaic law—a very false notion: For he there added nothing to the old law, but [75] only declared and recleansed the law, obscured by the Pharisees' lies and fouled with their leaven. 2.8.7

G. JUSTIFICATION

26. By the same ignorance or ill-will these commandments, not to take vengeance, to love one's enemies—which were once delivered to all Jews and then to all Christians in common—our opponents have turned into 'counsels' 2.8.56

which we are free either to obey or not to obey. Moreover, /55/ they saddled the requirement to obey these on monks, so that the latter might be even more righteous than simple Christians in this one respect, namely, that they voluntarily bound themselves to keep these 'counsels.' And the reason they assign for not receiving them as laws, is that they seem too burdensome and heavy, especially for Christians who are under the law of grace. Do they dare thus abolish God's eternal law that we are to love our neighbor? Did not Christ declare in a clear parable [Luke 10:29-37] that our neighbor is he for whom our works are of use, even someone very far away? Do not commandments occur here and there which require us to love our enemies: as when we are ordered to feed those who hunger [Prov. 25:21; Rom. 12:20], to lead their stray oxen and asses back to the path, or to assist them when overburdened [Ex. 23:4-5]. Is not the Lord's word ever-lasting: "Vengeance is mine, I will repay" [Heb. 10:30; cf. Deut. 32:35]. (44) And what, I ask you, do these statements mean? "Love your enemies; do good to those who hate you; [76] pray for those who persecute you, that you may be children of your Father who is in heaven" [Matt. 5:44-45]. Who, then, will be children of the heavenly Father? Monks? Well indeed will it go with us, if monks alone dare call God 'Father'! For this reason, those who so licentiously shake off the common yoke of the children of God truly betray themselves as sons of Satan. But how stupidly they argue! This would be a burden too heavy for Christians! As if we could think of anything more difficult than to love God with all our heart, all our soul, and all our strength! Compared with this law, every-thing could be considered easy—whether the requirement to love our enemy or to banish all desire for revenge from our hearts. All these are indeed hard and difficult for our feebleness, even to the least detail of the law [cf. Matt. 5:18; Luke 16:17]. It is the Lord in whom we act virtuously. "Let him give what he commands, and command what he will." To be Christians under the law of grace does not mean to wander unbridled outside the law, but to be engrafted in Christ, by whose grace we are free of the curse of the law, and by whose Spirit we have the law engraved upon our hearts [Jer. 31:33]. This grace Paul called "law," not in the strict sense, but alluding to the law of God, with which he was contrasting it [Rom. 8:2]. Under the term "law" these men are philosophizing over nothing.

27. Now you have previously heard that a heavy and dreadful sentence is pronounced by the Lord against all those who [77] have transgressed this law in any part, and have not completely fulfilled it, to fulfill which is not in our power. We are all therefore adjudged transgressors of the law. And the curses decreed for sinners in it are owed not to some of us but to everyone of us and hang over our necks. /56/

Therefore if we look merely to the law, we can only be despondent, con-fused, and despairing in mind, since from it all of us are condemned and ac-cursed [Gal. 3:10]. That is, as Paul says, all those under the law are accursed. And the law cannot do anything else than to accuse and blame all to a man, to convict, and, as it were, apprehend them; in fine, to condemn them in God's judgment: that God alone may justify, that all flesh may keep silence before him

30

[Rom. 3:19f.]. But we do not gabble about what many are accustomed today to   3.14.13
boast of. After they have been compelled to confess that it is an impossibility
for them to achieve perfect and ultimate righteousness through the merit of
works, since they never fulfill the law, they indeed confess it. But lest they seem
deprived of all glory, that is, to have yielded completely to God, they claim they
have kept the law in part and are, in respect to this part, righteous. What is
lacking they contend has been made up and redeemed by satisfactions and works
of supererogation. They consider this to be compensation for their lack. [78]
Forgetfulness of their own true nature, contempt of God's justice and ignorance
of their own sin have plunged them into this error. Surely those cut themselves
off from self-knowledge who judge themselves to be other (45) than Scripture
describes all the children of Adam to be. Their excellence Scripture sets off with
these titles: that they are of wicked and inflexible heart [Jer. 17:9]; that the whole
imagination of men's hearts is evil from their first years [Gen. 8:21]; "that all
their thoughts are vain" [Ps. 94:11]; that they are "the light of darkness" [cf. Job
10:22]; that all like sheep have gone astray, each having departed from his path
[Matt. 6:23]; that not a single one has been found who does good [Is. 53:6]:
that no one of them understands or seeks after God [Ps. 14:2]; that they do not
have the fear of God before their eyes [cf. Ex. 20:20]; in short, that they are   3.14.1
flesh [Gen. 6:3]. By this word are meant all those works which Paul lists:
"fornication, impurity, immodesty, licentiousness, service of idols, sorcery, party
spirit, envy, murder," and everything foul or abominable that can be imagined
[Gal. 5:19-21, cf. Vg]. So great indeed is the worth on which we are proud to   3.13.2
rely against God! For we must hold this as a universal principle: whoever glories
in himself, glories against God. Indeed, Paul calls upon the world to become
subject to God [cf. Rom. 3:19] while men are utterly deprived of any occasion
for glorifying. Does a man of such great ill-repute, condemned by God, [79]
dare assign any remnant to himself? Does he still think himself to be anything?
Has he not yet learned that he is laid low and cast down, and gives all to God?
Has he not yet learned in his humility to exalt God? For if /57/ anyone thinks
he has anything left to himself, I do not call it humility. And those who have   3.12.6
hitherto joined these two things together—namely, that we must feel humble
concerning ourselves before God and must know that we have some merits—
have taught a pernicious hypocrisy. For if we confess before God contrary to
what we feel, we lie to him. If we truly and earnestly recognize this, not only   3.15.3
will all confidence in merit vanish, but the very notion. In man, therefore, if he   3.14.1
be judged according to natural gifts, not one spark of good will be found in him
from the top of his head to the sole of his feet. Whatever there is in him that   3.12.1
deserves praise is the grace of God. But our evil intent is always to excuse even
our foulness, but to seize upon God's gifts for our own credit.

     28. Also God's righteousness is despised where it is not recognized as
such and so perfect, that nothing is accepted by him except what is whole and
perfect, and uncorrupted by any filth. But if this is so, all our works, if judged   3.12.4
by their own worth, are nothing but corruption and filth. Thus our righteousness

3.14.9 is iniquity, our uprightness pollution, our glory dishonor.* For the best thing that can be brought forth from us [80] is still always spotted and corrupted with some impurity of our flesh, and has, so to speak, some dregs mixed with it.

3.14.10 Next, even if it were possible for us to have some wholly pure and righteous works, yet, as the prophet says, one sin is enough to wipe out and extinguish every memory of that previous righteousness [Ezek. 18:24]. (46) James agrees with him: "Whoever," he says, "fails in one point, has become guilty of all" [James 2:10]. Now since this mortal life is never pure or devoid of sin, whatever righteousness we might attain [Prov. 24:16; I John 1:8], when it is corrupted, oppressed and destroyed by the sins that follow, could not come into God's sight or be reckoned to us as righteousness.

In short, in God's law we must have regard not for the work but for the commandment. Therefore, if righteousness is sought from the law, not one work or another, but unceasing obedience to the law will make one righteous. More-
3.14.13 over sin is an utterly execrable thing in God's sight and of such gravity that men's whole righteousness, gathered together in one heap, could not make compensation for a single sin. For we see that man was so cast away and abandoned by God for one transgression that he lost at the same time all capacity to receive and regain his salvation [Gen. 3:17]. Therefore, the capacity to make satisfaction was taken away.

29. Those who preen themselves on it surely will never satisfy God, to whom nothing is pleasing or acceptable that comes forth from his enemies. [81] But God's enemies are all those to whom he imputes sins. Therefore, our sins must be covered and forgiven before the Lord will recognize any work of ours [Ps. 31:1; cf. Rom. 4:1]. From this it follows that forgiveness of sins is free, /58/ and those who trust in their satisfactions obscure and blaspheme it. Let us therefore, after the apostle's example, "forgetting what lies behind and straining forward to what lies before us," run our race, pressing "on toward . . . the prize of the upward call" [Phil. 3:13-14 p.].

3.14.14 To boast about works of supererogation—how does this square with the injunction laid upon us that, when we have done whatever is commanded us, we call ourselves "unworthy servants," and say that "we have done no more than we ought to have done" [Luke 17:10 p.]? To speak before God is not to pretend or lie but to reckon honestly and truly to feel so. Therefore, the Lord bids us sincerely determine and consider within ourselves that we perform no unrequired duties for him but render him our due service. And so it is when we have done whatever has been commanded us, to wit, if all our thoughts and all our members were turned to the duties of the law or even if to one man belonged all the righteous works of all men. They who are far, far away from doing what has been commanded, still dare boast they have added a heap to the fair measure.

3.14.15
cf. 3.12.1 But some are ready at the drop of a hat [82] to dispute these matters under the shade in benches and chairs. But when that supreme Judge sits in his judgment seat every mouth will have to be stopped and all boasting will have to vanish. This it is we should have sought: what trust in our defense we could bring to

32

this judgment seat, not what we could gossip about in schools and corners. Besides, what sort of supererogations do such persons wish to hawk to God? Trifles that he never either commanded or approves, nor will he accept them when account of them is to be rendered before him! In this sense only (47) we agree that there are works of supererogation—namely, those of which it is said by the prophet: "Who has required this of your hands?" [Is. 1:12, cf. Vg.].

30. The fact, then, remains that through the law the whole human race is proved subject to God's curse and wrath, and in order to be freed from these, it is necessary to depart from the power of the law and, as it were, to be released from its bondage into freedom. This is no carnal freedom, which would draw us away from the observance of the law, incite us to license in all things, and let our concupiscence play the wanton, as if locks were broken or reins slackened. Rather, it is spiritual freedom to comfort and raise up the stricken, prostrate conscience, showing it to be free from the curse and condmenation with which the law was pressing it down, bound and fettered. [83] When through faith we lay hold on the mercy of God in Christ, we attain this liberation and, so to speak, manumission from subjection to the law, for it is by faith we are made sure and certain of forgiveness of sins, the law having pricked and stung our conscience to the awareness of them. [I Cor. 15:56] /59/ But God does not, as many stupidly believe, once for all bestow on us this forgiveness of sins in order that, having obtained pardon for our past life, we may afterward seek righteousness in the law;* this would be only to lead us into false hope, to laugh at us, and mock us. For since no perfection can come to us so long as we are clothed in this flesh, and the law moreover announces death and judgment to all who do not achieve perfect righteousness in works, it will always have grounds for accusing and condemning us unless, on the contrary, the Lord's mercy counters it, and by continual forgiveness of sins repeatedly acquits us. Therefore, what I was saying at the beginning always holds good: if we are judged by our own worth, whatever we plan or undertake, with all our efforts and attempts we still deserve death and confusion.

In this way, the promises also that are offered us in the law are all ineffectual and void. For this condition, that we should carry out the law—upon which the promises depend and by which alone they are to be performed—will never be fulfilled.

31. The apostle further presses this argument: [84] "If the promise of the inheritance comes from the law, faith is made powerless and the promise is void" [Rom. 4:14, cf. Vg.]. He infers two things: first, that faith has been made powerless and cancelled if the promise looks to the merits of our works or depends upon the observance of the law. For no one can ever confidently trust or rest secure in it because no one will ever come to be really convinced in his own mind that he has satisfied the law, as surely no one ever fully satisfies it through works. Not to seek evidences of this too far afield, every man willing to look upon himself with an honest eye can be his own witness. First, then, doubt would enter the minds of all men, and at length despair, while each one

3.17.1

3.14.10

3.17.2

3.13.3

reckoned for himself how great a weight of debt still overwhelmed him, and how far away he was from the condition imposed upon him. See faith already oppressed and extinguished! For to have faith is not to waver, to vary, (48) to be borne up and down, to hesitate, to remain in suspense, finally, to despair! Rather, to have faith is to strengthen the mind with constant assurance and perfect confidence, to have a place to rest and plant your foot [cf. I Cor. 2:5; II Cor. 13:4]. From this another point follows: also the promise itself has been abolished and vanishes. Indeed it will be fulfilled for none except those who possess a sure and unvarying persuasion that it has to be fulfilled for them, or (to put it in one word) for those who have faith. [85] When, therefore, faith fails, the promise will not remain in force. As a consequence, to hold out some hope of salvation, new promises would have to be offered which could be kept for us. There are moreover gospel promises, which our merciful Lord freely offers to us, not by reason of any worth or good deed of ours, /60/ but out of his fatherly goodness [Rom. 10:20], imposing on us no other condition than that we embrace wholeheartedly the very great gift of his good pleasure. This is what Paul adds: for this reason it is from faith that the inheritance of our salvation comes to us, to make the promise firm [Rom. 4:16]. Certain indeed is that faith which rests upon God's mercy alone, knowing as it does that mercy and truth are met together [Ps. 85:10], that is to say, whatsoever God mercifully promises, he also faithfully performs. And a firm promise follows that sure faith, one that can be fulfilled only for believers.

32. Therefore, we must now recognize that our salvation consists in God's mercy alone, but not in any worth of ours, or in anything coming from us. Accordingly, on this mercy we must establish and as it were deeply fix all our hope, paying no regard to our works nor seeking any help from them. Indeed, the nature of faith is to arouse the ears but close the eyes, to await the promise but turn thoughts away from all worth or merit of man. For never [86] will we have enough confidence in God unless we become deeply distrustful of ourselves. Never will we lift up our hearts enough in him unless they be previously cast down in us. Never will we have consolation enough in him unless we have already experienced desolation in ourselves. Never will we glory enough in him unless we dethrone all glory in ourselves. Consequently, when all our confidence is utterly cast down yet we still rely on his goodness, we grasp and obtain God's grace, and (as Augustine says) forgetting our merits, we embrace Christ's gifts. This is what it means to have true faith, as is fitting. But no one can attain this assurance except through Christ, by whose blessing alone we are freed from the law's curse. The curse was decreed and declared for us all, since, on account of the weakness inherited from our father Adam, we could not fulfill the law by our own works, as was required of those who desired to obtain therefrom righteousness for themselves. By Christ's righteousness then are we made righteous and become fulfillers of the law. This righteousness (49) we put on as our own, and surely God accepts it as ours, reckoning us holy, pure, and innocent. Thus is fulfilled Paul's statement: "Christ was made righteousness, sanctification, and redemption for us" [I Cor. 1:30]. For our merciful Lord first indeed kindly

34

received us into grace according to his own goodness and freely-given will, [87] forgiving and condoning our sins, which deserved wrath /61/ and eternal death [Rom. 5:11; 6:22]. Then through the gifts of his Holy Spirit he dwells and reigns in us and through him the lusts of our flesh are each day mortified more and more. We are indeed sanctified, that is, consecrated to the Lord in complete purity of life, our hearts formed to obedience to the law. To make it our undivided will to serve his will and by every means to advance his glory alone, we hate all the filth of our flesh reposing in us.

3.14.9

Then lastly, even while we walk in the Lord's ways by the leading of the Holy Spirit, to keep us from forgetting ourselves and becoming puffed up, something imperfect remains in us to give us occasion for humility, to stop every mouth before God and to teach us always to shift all trust from ourselves to him [Rom. 7:23]. As a consequence we always need forgiveness of sins. Accordingly those works also which are done by us while we rush along the Lord's way (as if they please God since they are done in faith!) cannot of themselves render us acceptable and pleasing to God.

But Christ's righteousness, which alone can bear the sight of God because it alone is perfect, must appear in court on our behalf, and stand surety for us in judgment [Heb. 11:6; Rom. 8:34]. [88] Received from God, this righteousness is brought to us and imputed to us, just as if it were ours. Thus in faith we continually and constantly obtain forgiveness of sins; none of the filth or uncleanness of our imperfection is imputed to us, but is covered over by that purity and perfection of Christ as if it were buried that it may not come into God's judgment until the hour arrives when, the old man in us being slain and plainly destroyed, the divine goodness receives us into blessed peace with the new Adam (who is Christ). There let us await the Day of the Lord when, having received incorruptible bodies, we will be carried into the glory of the heavenly kingdom [cf. I Cor. 15:45ff.].

3.14.12

H. USES OF THE LAW

33. From these things one can gather what the function and use of the law are. Now, it consists of three parts. (1) First, while showing God's righteousness, that is, what God requires of us, it admonishes each one of his unrighteousness and convicts him of his sin. All men, without exception, are puffed up with insane confidence in their own powers, unless the Lord proves their vanity. When all this stupid opinion of their own power has been laid aside, they must needs know they stand and are upheld by God's hand alone. Again, since by the righteousness of their works they are aroused against God's grace, it is fitting that this /62/ arrogance be cast down and confounded that, naked and empty-handed, they may flee to God's mercy, (50) repose in it, hide within it, [89] and seize upon it alone for righteousness and merit. For God's mercy is revealed in Christ to all who seek and wait upon it with true faith. (2) Then, since the law declares God will be the avenger, sets the punishment for trans-

2.7.6

2.7.8

35

gressors, and threatens death and judgment, it serves at least by fear of punish-
2.7.10 ment to restrain certain men who, unless compelled, are untouched by any
concern for what is just and right. But they are restrained, not because their
inner mind is stirred or affected, but because, being bridled, so to speak, they
keep their hands from outward activity, and hold inside the depravity that otherwise they would wantonly have indulged. Consequently, they are neither better
nor more righteous before God. Even though hindered by fright or shame, they
dare neither execute what they have conceived in their minds nor rage according
to their lust. Still, they do not have hearts disposed to fear and obey God.
Indeed, the more they restrain themselves, the more are they inflamed, burn and
boil within, and are ready to do anything or burst forth anywhere—but for the
fact that this dread of the law hinders them. Not only that—but so wickedly do
they also hate the law itself, and curse God the Lawgiver, that if they could they
would most certainly abolish him, for they cannot bear him either when he
commands them to do right, or when he takes vengeance on the despisers of his
majesty. But this constrained and forced righteousness [90] is necessary for the
public community of men, for whose tranquility the Lord so provided in guarding against complete and violent confusion. This would happen if all things were
2.7.12 permitted to all men. (3) Lastly, to the believers, too, in whose hearts the Spirit
of God already lives and reigns it provides no unimportant use, warning them
as it does, more and more earnestly what is right and pleasing in the Lord's
sight. For even though they have the law written and engraved upon their hearts
by the finger of God [Jer. 31:33; Heb. 10:16] that is, have been so moved and
quickened that they long to obey the Lord's will, they still profit by the law
because from it they learn more thoroughly each day what the Lord's will is like.
It is as if some servant, already prepared with complete earnestness of heart to
commend himself to his master, must search out and observe his master's ways
in order to conform and accommodate himself to them. Moreover, however
much they may be prompted by the Spirit and eager to obey God, they are still
weak in the flesh, and would rather serve sin than God. The law is to this flesh
like a whip to an idle and balky ass, to goad, stir, arouse it to work.
2.7.14 To sum up, the law is an exhortation to believers. This is not something
to bind their consciences with a curse, but to shake off their sluggishness, by
repeatedly urging them, and to pinch them awake to their imperfection.
[91] Therefore, many persons, wishing to express this /63/ liberation from the
curse of the law, have said that for believers the law has been abrogated. Not
that the law no longer enjoins believers to do what is right, but only that it is
not for them what it formerly was: it may no longer condemn and destroy their
consciences by confounding and frightening them with the message of death.
Just as, on the contrary, (51) good works detract from justification, not that no
good works are done, or works are denied to be good which are good, but lest
we put our confidence in them, lest we boast of them, lest we credit our salvation
to them. For this is our assurance: that Christ the Son of God is ours and has
been given to us so that in him we also may be sons of God, and heirs of his

heavenly Kingdom [Is. 9:6; I Thess. 4:14-18]. By God's kindliness, not our skill, have we been called into the hope of eternal life. We have been called, moreover, not to uncleanness and iniquity, but to be clean and spotless in God's sight, in love [Eph. 1:4].

I. JUSTIFICATION (CONTINUED)

34. If these matters had in bygone ages been treated and dealt with in proper order, so many tumults and dissensions would never have arisen. Paul says that in the upbuilding of Christian teaching we must keep the foundation that he laid [cf. I Cor. 3:10], "beside which no other can be laid, which is Jesus Christ" [I Cor. 3:11]. What sort of foundation is this? Is it that Jesus Christ was the beginning of our salvation? Is it that he opened the way when he merited for us occasion for meriting? Certainly not. But, [92] it is that "he has chosen us in him" from eternity "before the foundation of the world" through no merit of our own, "but according to the purpose of divine good pleasure" [Eph. 1:4-5, cf. Vg.]. It is that by his death we are redeemed from the condemnation of death and freed from ruin [cf. Col. 1:14, 20]. It is that we have been adopted unto him as sons and heirs by the Father [cf. Rom. 8:17; Gal. 4:5-7]. It is that we have been reconciled to the Father through his blood [Rom. 5:9-10; Rom. 9:11]. It is that, by the Father given unto his protection, we may never perish or fall [John 10:28; 17:12]. It is that thus engrafted into him [cf. Rom. 1:19] we are already, in a manner, partakers of eternal life, having entered the Kingdom of God through hope [John 1:12f; Eph. 3:6-11; 1:7; 1:4f.; II Tim. 1:9]. This is too little: we experience such participation in him that, although we are still foolish in ourselves, he is our wisdom before God; while we are sinners, he is our righteousness; while we are unclean, he is our purity; while we are weak, while we are unarmed and exposed to Satan, yet ours is that power which has been given him in heaven and on earth [Matt. 28:18] to crush Satan for us and shatter the gates of hell; while we still bear about with us the body of death, he is yet our life [Rom. 8:34; Eph. 4:24; 2:1-5; I Cor. 1:30; Col. 3:4]. In brief, because all his things are ours and we have all things in him, in us there is nothing. Upon this foundation we must be built if we would grow into a holy temple to the Lord [cf. Eph. 2:21].

Once the foundation is laid, wise master builders build upon it. /64/ For if there is need of teaching and exhortation, they inform [93] us that "the Son of God manifested himself in order to destroy the works of the devil"; that those who are of God may not sin [I John 3:8-9]; that the time past suffices for carrying out the gentiles' wishes [I Pet. 4:3]; that God's elect are vessels of mercy chosen for honor and ought to be purged of uncleanness [II Tim. 2:20-21].

35. But everything is said once for all when it is shown that (52) Christ wants disciples who deny themselves, take up their cross, and follow him [Matt. 16:24; Luke 9:23]. He who has denied himself has cut off the root of all evils so as to seek no longer the things that are his own. He who has taken up his

3.15.5

3.15.8

37

cross has readied himself for all patience and gentleness. But the example of Christ embraces both this and all other duties of piety and holiness. He presented himself to the Father as obedient even to death [Phil. 2:8]. He entered completely into the accomplishing of God's works [cf. John 4:34; also Luke 2:49; John 17:4]. He breathed heart and soul the glory of the Father [cf. John 8:50; John 7:16-18]. He laid down his life for his brothers [John 10:15; cf. John 15:13]. He did good to his enemies and prayed for them [cf. Luke 6:27, 35; Luke 23:34].

But if there is use for consolation, the following passages bring a wonderful consolation: "We are afflicted yet not made anxious, we fail but are not deserted, are humbled but not confounded, we are cast down but have not perished, ever bearing the mortification of Jesus Christ about in our bodies that Jesus' life may be manifested in us" [II Cor. 4:8-10 p.; Phil 2:5-8]. "If we died with him, we shall also live with him; if we suffer with him [94] we shall also reign with him" [II Tim. 2:11-12]; we are conformed to his sufferings [Phil. 3:10-11], because "the Father has predestined those whom he has chosen in himself to conform to the image of his Son that Christ himself may be the firstborn among many brethren" [Rom. 8:29 p.]. Therefore, "neither death nor life, nor things present, nor things to come, . . . will separate us from the love of God which is in Christ" [Rom. 8:38-39 p.]. Take note that we do not justify man by works before God, but all who are of God we speak of as being "reborn" [cf. I Pet. 1:3], and as becoming "a new creation" [II Cor. 5:17], so that they pass from the realm of sin into the realm of righteousness; we say that by this testimony they confirm their calling [II Pet. 1:10], and, like trees, are judged by their fruits [Matt. 7:20; 12:33; Luke 6:44].

3.16.1   36. This, in one word, is enough to refute the shamelessness of certain impious persons who slanderously charge us with abolishing good works when we condemn all pursuit of them by men; with preaching too easy forgiveness of sins when we make it free; and, by this enticement, with luring into sin men who are already too much inclined to it of their own accord; also with leading men away from zeal for good works, when we teach they are not justified by works or merit salvation. These false charges, I say, are sufficiently refuted by that simple statement. Still, I shall briefly reply to each. We do not deny good works, /65/ but those that are good we contend to be from God, and ought to be credited to him, because Paul calls all such works "the fruits of the Spirit of

3.15.3   God" [Gal. 5:22f.], so that he who glories, [95] should glory in the Lord. And we are not dividing the credit for good works between God and man, as they do, but we are preserving it whole, complete, and unimpaired for the Lord. To man we assign only this in good works: that he pollutes and contaminates by his impurity those very things which were good. For nothing proceeds from a man, however perfect he be, that is not defiled by some spot. Let the Lord, then, call to judgment the best in human works and he will not recognize in them his own righteousness (53) but man's confusion!

3.15.7   For this reason we condemn men's efforts, that is, whatever man has or does by himself we declare accursed. But by our teaching the hearts of believers

38

are cheered with a remarkable consolation; by it they are taught that these good works are given to them by God and are theirs because they have been given by God. At the same time, they are taught that the works are acceptable to God, and the believers are pleasing to him in these: not that they are thus deserved, but because the divine goodness has established this value for them. But indeed we require that no man attempt or go about any work without faith, that is, unless with firm assurance of mind he determines with himself that it will please God.

Good works indeed they always have in their mouths; meanwhile they so instruct consciences as never to dare have confidence that God shows himself kindly and favorable to their works. We are not [96] inviting men to sin when we affirm the free forgiveness of sins*, but we are saying that it is of such great value that it cannot be paid for by any good of ours. Therefore, it can never be obtained except as a free gift. Now for us indeed it is free, but not so for Christ, who dearly bought it at the cost of his most sacred blood, beyond which there was no ransom of sufficient worth to satisfy God's justice. When men are taught this, they are made aware that his most sacred blood is shed as often as they sin. Furthermore, we say that our foulness is such that it can never be cleansed except by the fountain of this purest blood. Those who hear these things—if they have any sense of God—how can they but dread wallowing in the mire, so as to befoul, as much as they can, the purity of this spring? "I have washed my feet," says the believing soul according to Solomon, "how shall I defile them anew?" [S. of S. 5:3]

3.16.4

37. Now it is plain which persons prefer to cheapen the forgiveness of sins. They make believe that God is appeased by their wretched satisfactions, that is, dung*[Phil. 3:8]. We affirm that the guilt of sin is too heavy to be atoned for by such light trifles, that it is too great an offense against God to be remitted by these worthless satisfactions, that this is the prerogative of Christ's blood alone. /66/

We do not seduce men's hearts from desiring to do good when we take from them their occasion for meriting. [97] For in saying men will take no care to regulate their lives aright unless hope of reward is held out to them, they are completely in error* For if it is only a matter of looking for reward when they serve God, and hiring or selling their labor to him, it is of little profit. God wills to be freely worshiped, freely loved. That worshiper, I say, he approves who, when all hope of receiving reward has been cut off, still does not cease to serve him.

3.16.2

Indeed, if men have to be aroused to good works no one could put sharper spurs to them than Paul admonishes, when he says: "We have been raised with Christ that we may live for righteousness" [Rom. 6:4; I Pet. 2:24]; when he enjoins us to offer our bodies as a living sacrifice, holy, pleasing to God [Rom. 12:1; Eph. 4:15f.]; when he enjoins us, after we are the one body of Christ, to bear witness by our mutual tasks [I Cor. 12:25] that we (54) are members of the same body [I Cor. 6:15, 17; 12:12]; when he tells us that our bodies are temples of the Holy Spirit [cf. II Cor. 6:16], that there is no agreement between Christ and Belial [II Cor. 6:15], between light and darkness [II Cor. 6:14]; when he shows that God's will is our sanctification [I Thess. 4:3], in order that we may abstain from unlawful desires; when he proves that we have been freed from the bondage of sin that we may be obedient to righteousness [Rom. 6:18]. Or can we be spurred to love by any livelier argument, than John's: that "we love one another, as God has loved us" [I John 4:11; cf. John 13:34]? That herein [98] God's children differ from the devil's children as children of light from children of darkness, because they abide in love [I John 3:10; 2:10-11]? Can we be more forcefully summoned to holiness than when we hear from the same that "all who have this hope . . . sanctify themselves" because their God is holy [I John 3:3]?

Or again, than when we hear Christ himself putting himself forward as our pattern in order that we may follow his footsteps [I Pet. 2:21; cf. John 15:1-10; 13:15]?

3.16.3 These few scriptural proofs, indeed, I have set forth as a mere taste. For if it were my purpose to go through every one, a large volume would have to be compiled. The apostles are full of exhortations, urgings, reproofs and consolations with which to instruct the man of God in every good work [cf. II Tim. 3:16-17], without mention of merit. And surely this one reason ought to have been enough: that God ought to be glorified in us [Matt. 5:16]. But if anyone is still not so forcibly affected toward the glory of God, the remembrance of God's benefits, nevertheless, suffices to arouse such persons to well-doing. These men, since by stressing merits they perchance force out some slavish and coerced observances of the law, say falsely that we have no basis for exhorting men to good works because we do not enter by the same road. As if such obedience were highly pleasing to God, who declares that he "loves a cheerful giver" and forbids anything to be given as if "grudgingly or of necessity" [II Cor. 9:7]! /67/

38. Although Scripture, not to omit any sort of exhortation, very often [99] recalls how "God will render to every man according to his works" [Rom.
3.18.2 2:6-7; Matt. 16:27; I Cor. 3:8, 14-15; II Cor. 5:10; etc.]. Consequently, let no man reason that our works are the cause of this retribution. Indeed the Kingdom of heaven is not servants' wages but sons' inheritance [Eph. 1:18], which only those who have been adopted as sons by the Lord will obtain; and for no other reason than this adoption.

3.18.4 Therefore, let us not consider that the Holy Spirit means to approve the worthiness of our works by this sort of promise, as if they merited such a reward. For Scripture leaves us no reason to be exalted in God's sight. Rather, its whole end is to restrain our pride, to humble us, cast us down, and utterly crush us. But our weakness, which would immediately collapse and fall if it did not sustain and comfort itself by this expectation, is relieved in this way. First, let everyone consider with himself how hard it would be for him to leave (55) and renounce not only all his possessions but himself as well. Still, it is with this first lesson that Christ initiates his pupils [Matt. 16:24-26], that is, all the godly. Then he so

instructs them throughout life under the discipline of the cross not to set their   cf. 3.8.1f.
hearts upon desire of, or reliance on, present benefits. In short, he usually so
deals with them that wherever they turn their eyes, as far [100] as this world
extends, they are confronted solely with despair. Consequently, Paul says, "We
are of all men most to be pitied if we are hoping only in this world" [I Cor.
15:19 p.]. Lest they fail amidst these great tribulations, the Lord is with them,
warning them to hold their heads higher, to direct their eyes farther so as to find
in him that blessedness which they do not see in the world. He calls this blessedness "prize," "reward," "recompense" [cf. Matt. 5:12; 6:1ff., etc.], not weighing
the merit of works, but signifying that it is a compensation for their miseries,
tribulations, slanders*, etc. For this reason, nothing prevents us, with scriptural
precedent [cf. II Cor. 6:13; Heb. 10:35; 11:26], from calling eternal life a "recompense,"* because in it the Lord receives his own people from toil into repose,
from affliction into consolation, from sorrow into joy, from disgrace into glory.
In brief, he changes into greater goods all the evil things that they have suffered.
Thus also it will be nothing amiss for us to regard holiness of life to be the way,
not indeed that leads, but by which those chosen by their God are led, into the
glory of the Heavenly Kingdom. For it is God's good pleasure to glorify those
whom he has sanctified [Rom. 8:30]. For this reason, observances of com-   3.17.7
mandments are sometimes called "righteousness" of the Lord: not those by
which the Lord justifies, that is, holds and regards as righteous; but by which
[101] he trains his own to be righteous, whom /68/ he previously justified by
his grace. But, if anyone attributes even the slightest portion to works, he per-
verts and corrupts the whole of Scripture, which assigns complete credit to the
divine goodness. But he who uses the term "merit" blasphemes against God's
grace, which cannot stand with him. Surely this is full of arrogance and raging
vanity against God. God promises reward and pay, I agree. But our task is to
thank God for his very great kindness, through which we recognize that what
is not all owed is given to us: not to become elated in heart, and to seize more
than was given. If a person has received a usufruct to a piece of property—does
he not deserve by such ingratitude to lose the usufruct he possessed? In like
manner, will the Lord bear us with impunity when we are ungrateful toward his
abundant grace? [102] (56)

CHAPTER II

FAITH:
CONTAINING AN EXPLANATION
OF THE CREED (CALLED APOSTOLIC)

A. FAITH AND FAITH IN THE ONE GOD

3.2.1   1. From the discussion just concluded we can understand what the Lord prescribes for us to do through the law. If we should fall down in any part of it, it decrees wrath and the dread judgment of eternal death. On the other hand, it shows not only how difficult but how utterly beyond our power and outside all our capacity it is to carry out the law as required. Therefore, if we but look upon ourselves and ponder what worth we possess, there is no remnant of good hope, but death and the surest confusion remain ours, cast down as we are by God. It also was explained that there is one way to avoid this calamity, and restore us to a better condition, namely the Lord's mercy, which we most surely will experience, if we receive it in perfect faith, and repose securely in it.

2.16.18   It now remains for us to learn what the nature of this faith ought to be—something we may readily learn from the Creed (which is called "Apostolic"), a brief compend [103] and, as it were, epitome, of the faith agreed upon by the catholic church.

3.2.9   2. But before proceeding farther, we must be advised that there are two forms of the faith. One is this: if someone believes that God is, /69/ he thinks that the history related concerning Christ is true. Such is the judgment we hold on those things which either are narrated as once having taken place, or we

3.2.10   ourselves have seen to be present. But this is of no importance: thus it is unworthy to be called "faith"; if anyone boasts of it, let him realize he has it in common with demons [James 2:19], for whom it accomplishes nothing except that they become more frightened, tremble, and are laid low.

The other is the faith whereby we not only believe that God and Christ are, but also believe in God and Christ, truly acknowledging Him as our God and Christ as our Savior. Now this is not only to adjudge true all that has been written or is said of God and Christ: but to put all hope and trust in one God

42

and Christ, and to be so strengthened by this thought, that we have no doubt about God's good will toward us. Consequently, we have been persuaded that whatever we need, either for the use of the soul or of the body, He will give us; we await with assurance whatever the Scriptures promise concerning him; we do not doubt [104] Jesus is our Christ, that is, Savior. But as we obtain through him forgiveness of sins and sanctification, so also salvation has been given, in order that we may at last be led into God's kingdom, which will be revealed on the last day. And this is indeed the head and almost the sum of all those things which the Lord by his sacred Word offers and (57) promises us. This is the goal set for us in his Scriptures; this the target he sets. 3.2.16

3. The Word of God, therefore, is the object and target of faith at which one ought to aim; and the base to prop and support it, without which it could not even stand. And thus this true faith—which can at last be called "Christian"—is nothing else than a firm conviction* of mind whereby we determine with ourselves that God's truth is so certain*, that it is incapable of not accomplishing what it has pledged to do by his holy Word [Rom. 10:11]. This Paul teaches in his definition, calling it "the substance of things hoped for, and the proof of things not seen" [Heb. 11:1]. By "substance" or "hypostasis" (as the Greek has it) [Heb. 13:1]; he understands a support on which we lean and recline. It is as if he said: faith itself is a sure and certain possession of those things God has promised us. 3.2.6

3.2.41

On the other hand, he would signify that the things pertaining to the last day (when the books will be opened) [Dan. 7:10] are loftier than those our sense can perceive, [105] or our eyes can see, or our hand can touch; meanwhile that we can only possess those things if we exceed the total capacity of our own nature, and press our keenness of vision beyond all things which are in the world, in short, surpass ourselves. He has added that this is the security of possessing /70/ the things that lie in hope and are therefore not seen. For (as he elsewhere writes) hope which is seen is not hope, nor does one hope for what he sees [Rom. 8:24]. While he calls it an indication and proof (in Greek *elenchus*, demonstration) of things not appearing, he is speaking as if to say that the evidence of things not appearing is the vision of things which are not seen, the perception of things obscure, the presence of things absent, the proof of things hidden. For God's mysteries pertaining to our salvation are of the sort that cannot in themselves and by their own nature (as is said) be discerned; but we gaze upon them only in his Word. So persuaded ought we to be of its truth that we must count its every utterance an accomplished fact.

4. This sort of faith is far different from the first one. Whoever has this kind of faith cannot but be accepted by God; on the contrary, without it, it cannot happen that anyone will ever please him [Heb. 11:6]. Through it whatever we desire and ask of God we obtain, insofar as he foresees it will be conducive to our larger good. [106] But this cannot have its seat in a devious, perverted and false heart*, nor can it be begun or sustained except by God's grace alone.

This is what God requires of us by the First Commandment of his law. Having first said that he is the one Lord our God, he adds that we are not to have other gods before him. This obviously means that in no one else but him are our hope and trust to rest, for they are owed to him alone. He also hints that, if our hope and trust look to another, we have another god.

We are now undertaking a discussion of this doctrine as summarized in the Creed. (58) The Creed is divided into four parts, of which the first three parts were devoted to the three Persons of the Sacred Trinity—Father, Son, and Holy Spirit—our one eternal and almighty God, in whom we believe. The fourth part explains what returns to us from this faith in God, and what we are to hope for.

1.13.21   5. But when certain impious fellows, to tear our faith up by the roots, raise an outcry over basic principles, and mock us for confessing one God in three persons, this passage required their blasphemies to be curbed. But, because my intention here is to lead teachable persons by the hand, not to fight hand to hand with contentious, rebellious men, I will not now combat them with troops in battle array. [107] I shall only point out briefly what is to be followed, what avoided in this matter, so those who lend ready and open ears to the truth may have a firm place to stand. Scripture teaches us one God, not many. Israel says, "The Lord thy God is one God" [Deut. 6:4]. In stating that the Father is God, the Son is God, and the Holy Spirit is God, the same Scripture is making no obscure assertion.

1.13.16   /71/ 6. We will bring forward only one proof but one that can stand for a thousand: Paul so connects these three—God, faith, and baptism [Eph. 4:5], that one may reason from one to another. Because there is one faith from it he proves there is one God; because there is one baptism, thence also he shows there to be one faith. For, since faith ought not to look around here and there, or dash about through various things, but to look upon the one God, to be united with him, to cleave to him—from this it is easily established that if there are many faiths, there also must be many gods. On the other hand, because baptism is the sacrament of faith, it confirms us in its unity by virtue of the fact that it is one. Yet no one can confess faith, except in the one God. Therefore, as we are baptized into one faith, so our faith believes in one God. And baptism is one and faith is one, for the reason that both belong to the one God.

From this also it follows that we are permitted to be baptized in one God, because we are baptized into faith [108] in him, in whose name we are baptized. Now, since Scripture meant us to be baptized in the name of the Father, and the

1.13.16   Son, and the Holy Spirit [Matt. 28:19], it at the same time intended all to believe with one faith in the Father, Son, and Holy Spirit. What else is this than a clear attestation that Father, Son, and Holy Spirit are one God? For if we are baptized in their name, we are baptized into faith in them. Consequently, they are one God if they are worshiped with one faith. Other clear testimonials also exist which assert partly one divinity of three persons, partly a distinction of persons.

The name called "ineffable" by the Jews is in Jeremiah [Jer. 23:6; 33:16] applied 1.13.9
to the Son.

7. He must therefore be the one eternal God who elsewhere denies he will give his glory to another [Is. 48:11]. (59) Yet when it is said that "he was in the beginning with God," [John 1:1], and the "Father made the world through him" 1.13.17 [John 1:2], moreover when it attests that "he had his own brightness with the Father before the world was made" [Heb. 1:3, 10]—the distinction between them is shown. Even more explicitly it is stated from the fact that the Father did not come and take on our flesh, but the Son came from the Father, to descend to us and become man [John 17:5; John 16:28; John 15:3, 5, 7, 10, 15, 17, 25-28]. In another prophet both were expressed at the same time, where the Father calls him "companion for kinsman" [Zech. 13:7]. But he is not kinsman or companion to God save insofar as he is God. Again, if he is companion, he must be distinct, [109] inasmuch as there is no fellowship but between two. In Acts, Peter declares the Holy Spirit to be God [Acts 5:3-9]. More than ten passages in the Gospel of John state the Spirit to be different from Christ [John 14:16, 25; 15:26]. But Paul most clearly of all explained this whole mystery 1.13.18 [Rom. 8:9-11], when he without distinction referred to the Spirit of Christ and the Spirit of him who raised Jesus from the dead. /72/ For if there is one Spirit 1.13.19 of the Father and of the Son, Father and Son must be one. Again, it is fitting that the Spirit himself be one with the Father and the Son, since no one is different from his own spirit.

Certain men cavil that they hear God is Spirit [John 4:24]; consequently they understand nothing else by "Spirit" than God the Father. But as they hear God is Spirit, so also they hear the Holy Spirit is the Spirit of God. Therefore there is no disagreement in the fact that the whole essence of God is spiritual, 1.13.20 and that in that essence there are Father, Son, and Spirit.

And individuals were not lacking who said that God is called sometimes Father, sometimes Son, sometimes Holy Spirit for no other reason than that He is both strong, good, glorious, and merciful. But these men also are easily refuted, because it is apparent that it is these epithets that show what God is like; it is those names that declare who he truly is. Persons who are not contentious or stubborn see the Father, Son, and Holy Spirit to be one God. For the Father [110] is God; the Son is God; and the Spirit is God: and there can be 1.13.2 only one God.

On the other hand, three are named, three described, three distinguished. One therefore, and three: one God, one essence. Why three? Not three gods, not three essences. To signify both, the ancient orthodox fathers said that there was one *ousia*, three *hypostaseis*, that is, one substance, three subsistences in one substance. The Latins, while they agreed in meaning in every respect with the Greeks, only gave two names to it, expressing something different in each name. For they said there was one essence (a term corresponding to the Greek word) but three persons, whereby they meant to point out a certain relationship.

8. The heretics bark that *ousia, hypostaseis*, essence, persons, are names 1.13.3

invented by human decision, nowhere read or seen in the Scriptures*. But since they cannot shake our conviction that three are spoken of, (60) who are one God, what sort of squeamishness is it to disapprove of words that explain nothing else than what is attested and sealed by Scripture!

It would be more than enough, they say, to confine within the limits of Scripture not only our thoughts but also our words, rather than scatter foreign terms about, which would become seedbeds of dissension and strife. For thus are we wearied with quarreling over words, thus by bickering do we lose the truth, thus do we destroy love*. [111]

If they call a foreign word one that cannot be shown to stand written syllable by syllable in Scripture*, they are indeed imposing upon us an unjust law which condemns all discourses not patched together out of the fabric of Scripture. But if that is "foreign" which has been curiously devised and is superstitiously defended, which conduces more to contention than edification, which is made use of either unseasonably or fruitlessly, /73/ which by its harshness offends pious ears, which detracts from the simplicity of God's Word—I wholeheartedly embrace their moderation. For I do not feel that concerning God we should speak with less conscientiousness than we should think, since whatever by ourselves we think concerning him is foolish, and whatever we speak, absurd. Yet some measure ought to be preserved: we ought surely to seek from Scripture a rule for thinking and speaking. To this yardstick all thoughts of the mind and all words of the mouth must be conformed.

But what prevents us from explaining in clearer words those matters in Scripture which perplex and hinder our understanding, yet which faithfully serve the truth of Scripture itself, and are made use of sparingly and modestly and not at the wrong occasion?* Daily examples occur. Men often debate on faith-righteousness, but few comprehend how we are made righteous by faith. Let us add that this is Christ's [112] righteousness, not ours; it is lodged in him, not in us; but it becomes ours by imputation, since it is said to have been received by us. Thus the fact that we are not truly righteous, but imputatively so; or we are not righteous, but are reckoned righteous by imputation, inasmuch as we possess Christ's righteousness through faith, will be a matter plain and uncomplicated.

2.4.1-5 It is said that God works in the reprobate, whose works have been condemned—a difficult and involved question. Is God the author of sin? Is evil to be imputed to God? Ought unrighteousness to be considered his work? Let us bring to mind that in the same act we are to discern the work of a perverse man and of a just God. We are to see that depraved man has the root of evil fixed in himself, by himself thinks evil, by himself wills it, by himself attempts it, by himself carries it out. For this reason we must impute to him whatever evil and guilt there is in his works. For he is striving against God in intention, in will, and in deed. But God as he wills, now bends, now forces and controls man's evil will and his evil effort; now gives a happy issue and adds strength. But God does all things justly.

46

Thus Pharaoh, Nebuchadnezzar and Sennacherib waged war against the living God, they laughed at his power; they persecuted—as much as they could—a people undeserving of such treatment; (61) by main force, without any right, they seized possession of another's property. Yet God had aroused them all to carry out all these acts [Ex. 9:16; Jer. 5:15]. [113] He had turned them, willing evil and thinking evil—or rather, turned their evil will and their evil intention against Israel, and was making it prevail, sometimes to avenge the ungodliness of His people, sometimes to enhance their deliverance. Thus Job's affliction was the work of God and of the devil, and yet one must distinguish the devil's injustice from God's justice: what the devil was trying to destroy God was training [Job 1:12; 2:6]. Thus Assyria was the rod of the Lord's anger [Is. 10:5], Sennacherib the axe of his hand [Is. 10:15]; /74/ all were summoned by Him, aroused, impelled by Him, in short, were His ministers. But why? While they were obeying their own unbridled lust, they were serving, unknowing, God's righteousness [Jer. 27:4-8]. See! There is God; there they are—authors of the same work! But in the same work shines God's righteousness; their iniquity. 1.18.1

By this distinction this tangled knot is untied; if anyone interrupts and growls that these distinctions for him go unproved, because the Sophists stuff their quarrels with such paltry quibbles, who will not hate such insolence? If anyone finds fault with the novelty of the words, does he not deserve to be judged as bearing the light of truth unworthily, since he is finding fault only with what renders the truth plain and clear? 1.13.3

However, the novelty of words of this sort (if such it must be called) becomes especially useful when the truth is to be asserted against false accusers, who evade it by their shifts. Of this today [114] we have abundant experience in our great efforts to rout the enemies of truth. With such crooked and sinuous twisting these slippery snakes glide away unless they are boldly pursued, caught, and crushed. Thus men of old, stirred up by various struggles over depraved dogmas, were compelled to set forth with consummate clarity what they felt, lest they might leave any devious shift to the impious, who cloaked their errors in layers of verbiage. 1.13.4

9. Because he could not oppose manifest Scriptures, Arius confessed that Christ was God and the Son of God, and, as if he had done what was right, pretended some agreement with the other men. Yet in the meantime he did not cease to prate that Christ was created and had a beginning, as other creatures. The ancients, to drag the man's tortuous craftiness out of its hiding places, went farther, and declared Christ the eternal Son of the Father, consubstantial with the Father. Here the impiety of the Arians boiled over, when they began most wickedly to hate and curse the word *homoousios*. But if at first they had sincerely and wholeheartedly confessed Christ to be God, they would not have denied him to be consubstantial with the Father. Who would dare inveigh against those upright men as wranglers and contentious persons because they became aroused to such heated discussion through one little word, and disturbed the peace of

the church? Yet that mere word [115] marked the distinction between Christians of pure faith and sacrilegious Arians.

(62) Afterwards Sabellius arose, who argued that the names of Father, Son, and Holy Spirit were empty, not put forward because of any distinction, but that they were diverse attributes of God, of which sort there are very many. If it came to a debate, he was accustomed to confess that he recognized the Father as God, the Son as God, and the Spirit as God; but afterward he wriggled out, by claiming he had said nothing else than if he had spoken of God as strong, and just, and wise. And so he reechoed another old song, that the Father is the Son, and the Holy Spirit /75/ the Father, without rank, without distinction. To shatter the man's wickedness, those men who had piety at heart, loudly countered that three properties must truly be recognized in the one God. And that they might fortifiy themselves against this tortuous cunning with the simple truth, they truly affirmed that a trinity of persons subsists in the one God, or, what was the same thing, subsists in the unity of God.

1.13.5   If, therefore, these terms were not rashly invented, they are rashly repudiated. Would that they had been buried, provided only among all men this faith were agreed on: that Father, Son, and Holy Spirit are one God, yet that the Son is not the Father, nor the Holy Spirit the Son; but that they have been differentiated by a peculiar quality. But where one has to resist the Arians on the one hand, the Sabellians on the other, [116] while indignant that the opportunity to evade the issue is cut off from both of them, they arouse some suspicion that they are disciples either of Arius or of Sabellius.

Arius says that Christ is God, but mutters that He was made and had a beginning. He says that Christ is one with the Father, but secretly whispers in the ears of his own partisans that He is united to the Father as other believers are, although by a singular privilege. Say "consubstantial" and you will tear off the mask of this turncoat, and yet you add nothing to Scripture. Sabellius says that Father, Son, and Spirit signify no distinctions in God. Say they are three, and he will scream that you are naming three Gods. Say that in the one essence of God there is a trinity of persons; you will say in one word what Scripture states, and cut short empty talkativeness.

And if they do not put up with these names, let them at least concede to us, what they cannot deny, even if they should burst, that when we hear "one" we are to understand unity of substance; that when we hear "three" we are to distinguish in this one essence, nevertheless, three properties. Indeed Scripture so distinguishes these as to attribute to the Father the beginning of acting and the fountain and source of all things; to assign to the Son the wisdom and plan of acting; to refer to the Spirit the power and effective working of action. Hence also the Son is said to be the Word of the Father, not as men speak and think, but eternal and unchangeable, coming forth in an ineffable way from the Father" [117] just as the Holy Spirit is called "Power," "Finger," "Might." Now let us hear the simple confession of truth. (63)

are cheered with a remarkable consolation; by it they are taught that these good works are given to them by God and are theirs because they have been given by God. At the same time, they are taught that the works are acceptable to God, and the believers are pleasing to him in these: not that they are thus deserved, but because the divine goodness has established this value for them. But indeed we require that no man attempt or go about any work without faith, that is, unless with firm assurance of mind he determines with himself that it will please God.

Good works indeed they always have in their mouths; meanwhile they so instruct consciences as never to dare have confidence that God shows himself kindly and favorable to their works. We are not [96] inviting men to sin when we affirm the free forgiveness of sins*, but we are saying that it is of such great value that it cannot be paid for by any good of ours. Therefore, it can never be obtained except as a free gift. Now for us indeed it is free, but not so for Christ, who dearly bought it at the cost of his most sacred blood, beyond which there was no ransom of sufficient worth to satisfy God's justice. When men are taught this, they are made aware that his most sacred blood is shed as often as they sin. Furthermore, we say that our foulness is such that it can never be cleansed except by the fountain of this purest blood. Those who hear these things—if they have any sense of God—how can they but dread wallowing in the mire, so as to befoul, as much as they can, the purity of this spring? "I have washed my feet," says the believing soul according to Solomon, "how shall I defile them anew?" [S. of S. 5:3]

3.16.4

37. Now it is plain which persons prefer to cheapen the forgiveness of sins. They make believe that God is appeased by their wretched satisfactions, that is, dung*[Phil. 3:8]. We affirm that the guilt of sin is too heavy to be atoned for by such light trifles, that it is too great an offense against God to be remitted by these worthless satisfactions, that this is the prerogative of Christ's blood alone. /66/

We do not seduce men's hearts from desiring to do good when we take from them their occasion for meriting. [97] For in saying men will take no care to regulate their lives aright unless hope of reward is held out to them, they are completely in error.* For if it is only a matter of looking for reward when they serve God, and hiring or selling their labor to him, it is of little profit. God wills to be freely worshiped, freely loved. That worshiper, I say, he approves who, when all hope of receiving reward has been cut off, still does not cease to serve him.

3.16.2

Indeed, if men have to be aroused to good works no one could put sharper spurs to them than Paul admonishes, when he says: "We have been raised with Christ that we may live for righteousness" [Rom. 6:4; I Pet. 2:24]; when he enjoins us to offer our bodies as a living sacrifice, holy, pleasing to God [Rom. 12:1; Eph. 4:15f.]; when he enjoins us, after we are the one body of Christ, to bear witness by our mutual tasks [I Cor. 12:25] that we (54) are members of the same body [I Cor. 6:15, 17; 12:12]; when he tells us that our bodies are temples of the Holy Spirit [cf. II Cor. 6:16], that there is no agreement between Christ and Belial [II Cor. 6:15], between light and darkness [II Cor. 6:14]; when he shows that God's will is our sanctification [I Thess. 4:3], in order that we may abstain from unlawful desires; when he proves that we have been freed from the bondage of sin that we may be obedient to righteousness [Rom. 6:18]. Or can we be spurred to love by any livelier argument, than John's: that "we love one another, as God has loved us" [I John 4:11; cf. John 13:34]? That herein [98] God's children differ from the devil's children as children of light from children of darkness, because they abide in love [I John 3:10; 2:10-11]? Can we be more forcefully summoned to holiness than when we hear from the same that "all who have this hope . . . sanctify themselves" because their God is holy [I John 3:3]?

Or again, than when we hear Christ himself putting himself forward as our pattern in order that we may follow his footsteps [I Pet. 2:21; cf. John 15:1-10; 13:15]?

3.16.3   These few scriptural proofs, indeed, I have set forth as a mere taste. For if it were my purpose to go through every one, a large volume would have to be compiled. The apostles are full of exhortations, urgings, reproofs and consolations with which to instruct the man of God in every good work [cf. II Tim. 3:16-17], without mention of merit. And surely this one reason ought to have been enough: that God ought to be glorified in us [Matt. 5:16]. But if anyone is still not so forcibly affected toward the glory of God, the remembrance of God's benefits, nevertheless, suffices to arouse such persons to well-doing. These men, since by stressing merits they perchance force out some slavish and coerced observances of the law, say falsely that we have no basis for exhorting men to good works because we do not enter by the same road. As if such obedience were highly pleasing to God, who declares that he "loves a cheerful giver" and forbids anything to be given as if "grudgingly or of necessity" [II Cor. 9:7]! /67/

38. Although Scripture, not to omit any sort of exhortation, very often [99] recalls how "God will render to every man according to his works" [Rom.
3.18.2   2:6-7; Matt. 16:27; I Cor. 3:8, 14-15; II Cor. 5:10; etc.]. Consequently, let no man reason that our works are the cause of this retribution. Indeed the Kingdom of heaven is not servants' wages but sons' inheritance [Eph. 1:18], which only those who have been adopted as sons by the Lord will obtain; and for no other reason than this adoption.

3.18.4   Therefore, let us not consider that the Holy Spirit means to approve the worthiness of our works by this sort of promise, as if they merited such a reward. For Scripture leaves us no reason to be exalted in God's sight. Rather, its whole end is to restrain our pride, to humble us, cast us down, and utterly crush us. But our weakness, which would immediately collapse and fall if it did not sustain and comfort itself by this expectation, is relieved in this way. First, let everyone consider with himself how hard it would be for him to leave (55) and renounce not only all his possessions but himself as well. Still, it is with this first lesson that Christ initiates his pupils [Matt. 16:24-26], that is, all the godly. Then he so

B. EXPOSITION OF THE CREED

First Part*
I believe in God the Father Almighty, Creator of heaven and earth.　　3.2.1

10. By this we confess that we have all our trust fixed in God the Father, 　1.16.1
whom we acknowledge to be Creator of ourselves and of absolutely all things
that have been created, /76/ which have been established by the Word, his
eternal Wisdom (who is the Son) and by his Power (who is the Holy Spirit) [Ps.
33:6; 104:24; Acts 17:24; Heb. 1:2-10]. And, as he once established, so now
he sustains, nourishes, activates, preserves, by his goodness and power, apart
from which all things would immediately collapse and fall into nothingness.

But when we call him almighty and creator of all things, we must ponder
such omnipotence of his whereby he works all things in all, and such providence 　1.16.3
whereby he regulates all things [I Cor. 12:6; Lam. 3:37-38]—not of the sort
those Sophists* fancy: empty, insensate, idle*. By faith are we to be persuaded
that whatever happens to us, happy or sad, prosperous or adverse, whether it
pertains to the body or to the soul, comes to us from him [118] (sin only
excepted, which is to be imputed to our own wickedness); also by his protection
we are kept safe, defended, and preserved from any unfriendly force causing us
harm [Hos. 13:14]. In short, nothing comes forth from him to us (since we
receive all things from his hand) which is not conducive to our welfare, howsoever things may commonly seem at one time prosperous, at another adverse
[Rom. 8:28].

Indeed all these things are done to us by him, not through any worth of
ours, nor by any merit to which he owes this grace, not because we can force
his beneficence to make any reciprocal payment. Rather it is through his fatherly
kindness and mercy that he has to do with us, the sole cause of which is his
goodness. For this reason, we must take care to give thanks for this very great 　1.17.2
goodness of his, to ponder it with our hearts, proclaim it with our tongue, and
to render such praises as we are able. We should so reverence such a Father
with grateful piety and burning love, as to devote ourselves wholly to his service*,
and honor him in all things. We should also so receive all adverse things with
calm and peaceful hearts, as if from his hand, thinking that his providence so
also looks after us and our salvation while it is afflicting and oppressing us [Job
2:10]. Therefore, whatever may finally happen, we are never to doubt or lose
faith that we have in him a propitious and benevolent Father, and no less are to
await salvation from him. For it is [119] something utterly certain and true that
the faith we are each of us taught to hold by this first part of the Creed is the
right faith* /77/ (64)

Second Part*
And in Jesus Christ, his only Son, our Lord; who was conceived of the 　2.16.1
Holy Spirit, born of the Virgin Mary, suffered under Pontius Pilate, was 　2.16.5
crucified, dead, and buried; he descended into hell; on the third day he 　2.16.7

2.16.13
2.16.17

rose again from the dead; he ascended into heaven, sits at the right hand of the Father; thence he shall come to judge the living and the dead.

2.14.6

11. By this we confess that we believe in Jesus Christ who we are convinced is the only Son of God the Father. He is the Son, not as believers are—by adoption and grace only—but by nature, begotten of the Father from eternity. When we call him "only" Son we are distinguishing him from all others. Inasmuch as he is God, he is one God with the Father, of the same nature and substance or essence, not otherwise than, distinct as to the person which he has as his very own, distinct from the Father [Ps. 100:3a]. It is fitting that anything there is of human wisdom be here submitted and as it were held captive. And neither prattling inquisitively nor hesitating [120] will advance the worship of such mysteries at all, which far surpass all the capacity of human understanding. And lest we conceive with the mind, or experience or speak anything in this respect other than we are taught by the Scriptures, let us be stricken with terror by the examples of the heretics, who were driven into extreme danger while they wanted to luxuriate in their own understanding. Since therefore God the Son is one and the same God with the Father, we hold him to be true God, Creator of heaven and earth. And just as we have established all our trust in the Father, so also must we establish it in the Son, since God is one.

1.13.24

Moreover, the Father is particularly called Creator of heaven and earth [Heb. 1:2, 10] because (as we previously said) of the distinction of properties, whereby the beginning of acting is referred to the Father that he may be said indeed to act by himself, but through the Word and his Wisdom, yet in his Power. That nevertheless there was a common action of the three persons in creating the world is made plain by that statement of the Father: "Let us make man in our image and likeness" [Gen. 1:26]. In these words he is not taking counsel with the angels, not speaking with himself, but addressing his Wisdom and Power.*

12. We confess moreover that we believe Christ, sent by the Father out of divine kindness and mercy, descended to us for our sake to release us from the devil's tyranny, to which we had been bound; from the bonds of sin, by which we were held tied; from the bondage of death, both of body and of soul, into which [121] we had been thrust; from eternal punishment, to which we had been given over (since our ability was not equal to releasing and extricating us from it). /78/ We confess that he, sent by the Father out of divine kindness and mercy, descended to us (65) to take on our flesh, which he joined to his divinity. Thus it was for our benefit that he who was to become our Mediator was true

2.12.1

God and man.* For since all things were scattered when our sin interposed a cloud between us and our God, who could reach Him [Is. 59:2]? Man? And yet all men together with their parent Adam bristled with dread at the Lord's sight. An angel [Gen. 3:10-12]? And yet even they had need of a Head, in whom they might cleave to their God [Col. 1:16-20; Eph. 1:21-23]. What then? The matter was hopeless if the very majesty of God would not descend to us, since it was

50

not in us to ascend to Him. And so God's Son became for us Immanuel, that is, God with us [Is. 7:14].

Again, since our lowliness in all respects differs from God's majesty, who would even have dared trust enough that God was near him, dwelt with him, was present with him? Not yet, therefore, was there sufficiently close nearness, not yet sufficiently firm affinity, except, as he had joined his divinity to us, he might so also join our humanity to his divinity. Thus Paul, since he set Him forth as Mediator to us, expressly called him "Man": [122] "A Mediator between God and men, the man Jesus Christ" [I Tim. 2:5]. He could have said "God"; or he could at least have omitted this word, just as he did the word "God," but he knew our weakness. Therefore, lest anyone should be troubled about where to seek the Mediator, or how we might come to him, he immediately added: "He is man." It is as if he said "He is near you, indeed, touches you, he is your flesh." Obviously he means to designate by this what he has more explicitly explained elsewhere: "We have not a high priest who is unable to sympathize with our weakness, but one who in every respect has been tempted as we are, yet without sin" [Heb. 4:15].

No common thing it was that the Mediator was to accomplish: to make children of God out of children of men; out of heirs of Gehenna to make heirs of the heavenly kingdom. Who could have done this had not the Son of God become the Son of man, and had not so taken what was ours as to impart what was his to us, and to make what was his by nature ours by grace? This therefore is our hope, that we are sons of God, for God's natural son fashioned for himself a body from our body, flesh from our flesh, bones from our bones, that he might be one with us [Gen. 2:23-24; Eph. 5:29-31]. What was ours, he willed to belong to himself, so that what was his might belong to us, and thus to be both Son of God and Son of man in common with us. This is our hope, that the inheritance [123] of the heavenly kingdom may be ours, because God's only Son, whose perfect inheritance it was, has adopted us as his brothers. "For if brothers, then also fellow heirs with him" [Rom. 8:17 p.]. /79/   2.12.2

Moreover it was for our benefit that he who was to become our Redeemer was true God and true man. It was his task to swallow up death. Who but Life could do this? It was his task to conquer sin. Who but very Righteousness could do this? Indeed, who is life or righteousness but (66) God alone? Therefore our most merciful Lord, when he willed that we be redeemed, made himself our Redeemer [cf. Rom. 5:8].   2.12.3

The other article of our redemption was this: that man, who by his disobedience had become lost, should by obedience remove his confusion, satisfy God's justice, and pay the penalties of sin. Accordingly, our Lord came forth, true man. He took the person of Adam, received his name in order to show himself obedient to the Father on man's behalf, to set our flesh as satisfaction for God's justice, to pay in our flesh the penalty of sin.

Those who despoil Christ of either his divinity or his humanity either blaspheme God's majesty or obscure his goodness. But they just as much weaken and overthrow our faith, which cannot stand except on this foundation.

The Word was therefore made flesh [John 1:14]; he who was God likewise became man [124] so that the very same one might be both man and God, not by confusion of substance, but by unity of person.

2.14.1   13. This can be understood by the example of man, whom we see constituted of two parts*. Yet neither part is so mingled with the other as not to retain its own distinctive nature. For the soul is not the body, and the body is not the soul. Therefore, some things are said exclusively of the soul that can in no wise apply to the body; and of the body, again, that in no way fit the soul; of the whole man, that cannot refer—except inappropriately—to either soul or body separately. Finally, the characteristics of the soul are sometimes transferred to the body, and those of the body to the soul. Yet he who consists of these parts is one man, not more than one. Such expressions signify both that there is one nature in man composed of two elements joined together, and that there are two diverse underlying natures that make up this person.* Thus, also, the Scriptures speak of Christ; they sometimes attribute to him what must be referred exclusively to his humanity, sometimes, what refers particularly to his divinity; sometimes what embraces both natures but fits neither one alone. Finally, through "communication of properties"* they assign to his divinity the things that belonged to his humanity, and to his humanity those that pertained to his divinity. [125]

2.14.2   These would mean nothing to me, were there not clear examples in Scripture. What Christ said of himself, "Before Abraham came to be, I am" [John 8:58], was far different from his humanity. For he did not become man until many centuries after Abraham. This therefore was peculiar /80/ to his divinity. That he is called "the servant of the Father" [Is. 42:1, and other passages]; that he "increased in age and wisdom . . . with God and men" [Luke 2:52], that he did not "seek his own glory" [John 8:50]—all these referred solely to his humanity. Indeed inasmuch as he is God, he is equal to the Father, and cannot in any wise be increased, and he accomplishes all things for his own sake [Phil. 2:9-11]. And peculiar neither to his divinity nor to his humanity, but to both (67) at once, was the fact that he received from the Father the power to forgive sins, to raise the dead, that he was appointed judge of the living and the dead [Luke 5:20-24; John 5:21; 6:40-54; Acts 10:42].

2.14.3   For the Son of God was endowed with such privileges when he was manifested in the flesh. These, he, along with the Father [I Pet. 1:20], held before the creation of the world [Eph. 1:4], and they could not have been given to a man who was nothing but a man.

There are very many passages of this form in John's Gospel, which agree well neither with the divinity nor the humanity, but best fit the person of Christ in which God and man have been manifested. In this sense also we must understand what we read in Paul: "Christ will deliver the Kingdom to his God and Father" [I Cor. 15:24 p.]. [126] For the Kingdom of the Son of God, which had no beginning, will have no end. But, just as after his humiliation he was crowned with glory and honor, and set over all; just as, after he emptied himself and gave himself to the Father, obedient unto death, he was exalted, and received the name before which every knee is bowed [Phil. 2:8-10]—so then he will subject to the Father both the name itself and whatever he has received from the Father, that God may be all in all [I Cor. 15:28].

But the communicating of characteristics or properties consists in what Paul says: "God purchased the church with his blood" [Acts 20:28 p.], and "the Lord of glory was crucified" [I Cor. 2:8 p.]. For God, properly speaking, does not have blood, does not suffer. But since Christ, who was true God and also true man, was crucified and shed his blood for us, the things that he carried out in his human nature are transferred to his divinity. Again, when Christ said: "No one has ascended into heaven but the Son of man who was in heaven" [John 3:13 p.], surely he was not in heaven in the body he had taken upon himself. But because the selfsame one was both God and man, for the sake of the unity of both natures, he gave to the one what belonged to the other. These I pursue more fully on account of those persons who cannot by any reason be convinced that in Christ's one person they observe the properties of both natures. So do they confess Christ to be God, and man, and the Son of God. [127] 2.14.2

Yet if you press more closely, you will observe that they say "God" and the "Son of God" for no other reason than that he was conceived in the virgin's womb of the Holy Spirit. The Manichees of old fancied the same thing: that man has his soul by derivation from God* for they read that "God breathed upon him the breath of life" [Gen. 2:7]. 2.14.8

They clamorously argue /81/ in defense of their error that God is said not to have spared his own Son [Rom. 8:32], that the angel enjoined that he who was to be born of the virgin be called "the Son of the Most High"* [Luke 1:32]. Obviously we are not making two Christs*, but are simply confessing that he, who was God's eternal Son, took our flesh. Thus he is one and the same Christ, God and man, but with natures united, not commingled* To keep them at this point from glorying in their futile objection (with which they contend against us)—that Christ was God's Son only according to his humanity, because it was he, not another, who as man was born of a virgin, and suffered, is called God's Son (68)—let them learn how Scripture speaks, from one passage of a prophet, in which the Lord speaks as follows: "You Bethlehem Ephrata, are tiny among the thousands of Judah; from you shall be born to me a ruler to rule my people Israel, whose going forth is from the beginning, from eternal days"[Micah 5:2 and Matt. 2:6, conflated (Vg)]. Do they not hear of this very Christ, who is born in Bethlehem, that his "going forth was from eternal days"? Yet if we gaze upon the "eternity of days" [128] not yet was Christ. True indeed is this: but the Son of God was, who afterward was made Christ. So speaks the author of the Letter to the Hebrews: "In recent days the Lord spoke to us in his beloved Son, whom he appointed heir of all things, through whom also he made the worlds." [Heb. 1:2]. Assuredly he had to be Son before he became man, if through him 2.14.7

the worlds were made, without our being required also to infer from this that the Word of God is the Son of God. For when John says that "all things were made through the Word" [John 1:3], the Apostle says, "through the Son" [Heb. 1:2]. Paul also so clearly distinguishes the two titles, "Son of God" and "Son of man," that to oppose his distinction forthwith would be a mark not only of obstinacy but of blindness.

2.14.6   First, when he says that he was "set apart for the gospel of God which God had promised beforehand through the prophets concerning his Son, who was made* from the seed of David according to the flesh and declared Son of God in power" [Rom. 1:1-4, cf. Vg). Why would Paul distinctly name him Son of David according to the flesh, unless he meant to intimate the Son of God, not according to the flesh? Elsewhere: "From them," he says, "is Christ, according to the flesh, who is God blessed for ever" [Rom. 9:5]. What clearer statement do they want, than that Christ is called "the seed of Abraham according to the flesh," but beyond flesh is "God blessed for ever"? Again, I wish it to be attested

2.14.4 that we do not deny the one [129] Christ is true God and man, nor through this to tear his divinity from his humanity, but to distinguish them. These statements beautifully agree in the hands of a sober expositor who treats such great mysteries as devoutly as they deserve.* But there is nothing that these mad and frantic spirits will not stir up! They seize upon the attributes of his humanity* to take away /82/ his divinity;* upon those of his divinity to take away his humanity; and upon those spoken of both natures so conjointly that they are applicable to neither, to take away both. But what else is this than to contend that Christ is not man because he is God; that he is not God because he is man; that he is

2.16.1 neither man nor God because he is man and God at the same time? Therefore Christ, besides being God, was made man when he took on true flesh.

    14. As he has been called by the Father's voice and by a heavenly oracle [Luke 1:30-35; 2:21], so do we believe Jesus to be truly he, and that this name, no other, "was given to men in which we must be saved" [Acts 4:12]. We also

2.15.2 believe that Christ himself was sprinkled with all the graces of the Holy Spirit.
2.15.5 These are called "oil" [Ps. 45:7; 89:20] because without these we waste away, dry (69) and barren. And as the Spirit has rested upon him, and has poured itself out wholly upon him, in order that we may all receive from his fulness (that is, whoever of us are partners and partakers of him through faith) [Is. 11:1-5; 61:1-3; John 1:16], so do we believe in short that by this anointing he was appointed king* by the Father [130] to subject all power in heaven and on earth [Ps. 2:1-6], that in him we might be kings, having sway over the devil,

2.15.6 sin, death, and hell [I Pet. 2:9; Acts 10:36]. Then we believe that he was appointed priest, by his self-sacrifice to placate the Father and reconcile him to us, that in him we might be priests, with him as our Intercessor and Mediator, offering our prayers, our thanks, ourselves, and our all to the Father [Rev. 1:6; Ps. 110:1-4; Heb. 5:1-10; 13:15-16]. Therefore also, as he has been set over us by the Father, we acknowledge him to be the only Lord. We believe him to have been conceived a man for us by the wonderful and unspeakable power of the

Holy Spirit, in the womb of the sacred virgin [Luke 1:26-38; 2:17]. Born a mortal man from her, in order to accomplish our salvation (for whose sake he had come), he delivered up his body to a most miserable death, and poured out his blood as the price of redemption [cf. Matt. 26:28; Eph. 1:7].

He suffered, moreover, under Pontius Pilate, condemned indeed by the judge's sentence, as a criminal and wrongdoer, in order that we might, by his condemnation, be absolved before the judgment seat of the highest Judge. He was crucified, that in the cross, which had been cursed by God's law, he might bear our curse which our sins deserved [Deut 21:22-23; Gal. 3:10]. He died, that by his death he might conquer death which was threatening us, and might swallow it which was to have swallowed us [Hos. 13:14; I Cor. 15:54]. He was buried, that through his grace we might be buried to sin, freed from the sway of the devil and of death [Heb. 2:14-15; Rom. 6:4]. [131]

15. That he descended to hell*means that he had been afflicted by God, and felt the dread and severity of divine judgment [Ps. 21:9], in order to intercede with God's wrath and make satisfaction to his justice in our name [Is. 53:4, 11], thus paying our debts and lifting /83/ our penalties, not for his own iniquity (which never existed) but for ours.

Yet it is not to be understood that the Father was ever angry toward him. For how could he be angry toward his beloved Son, "in whom he was well pleased" [Matt. 3:17]? Or how could he appease the Father by his intercession, if the Father regarded him as an enemy? But it is in this sense that he is said to have borne the weight of divine severity, since he was "stricken and afflicted" [cf. Is. 53:5] by God's hand, and experienced all the signs of a wrathful and avenging God, so as to be compelled to cry out in deep anguish: "Father, Father, why hast thou forsaken me?" [Ps. 22:1; Matt. 27:46]. It is obviously said that "he descended into hell," but did not enter a certain place (for which the term "limbo"*was invented), where the fathers who had lived under the Old Testament were as it were imprisoned, there awaiting their release from bondage and captivity, and forcibly broke through the gates of that place, to set them free from it.* For this story, although it is repeated by great authors,* (70) and even today is earnestly defended as true by many persons, still is nothing but a story.* Nor ought the passage in Peter to be taken in that sense, which they [132] who wish to preserve the story are always thrusting at us: "Christ, coming by the Spirit, preached to those spirits who were in prison" [I Pet. 3:19]. By this Peter only meant that the power of redemption imparted through Christ was shown forth and plainly manifested to the spirits of those who had died before that time.* For the believers who had always awaited their salvation from him, at that time plainly and face to face perceived his visitation. On the other hand, the reprobate, comprehending too late that Christ was their sole salvation, from which they had been excluded, then more plainly recognized that no hope remained to them.

But the fact that Peter, without distinction, says that godly and ungodly were together in the prison is not to be understood as if the godly were shut up, bound in such straits, but that they were gazing on Christ at a distance, obscurely

2.16.5

2.16.6

2.16.7

2.16.10

2.16.11

2.16.9

and enshrouded in clouds—not yet shown forth. By a certain figure of speech he calls this anxious waiting "a prison." But Scripture attests that they were then in Abraham's bosom*[Luke 16:22-23; Rev. 6:9-11], as they now also are, that is, in repose and quiet, which is for them the beginning of blessedness. For they understand that they live in God, and cleave inseparably to him. In this sense, they receive extraordinary comfort, awaiting the day of blessed resurrection. Although, moreover, this portion of the descent into hell [133] has been left out by some, it is not at all superfluous, containing as it does the greatest mysteries of the greatest things.

2.16.13

16. Moreover, we believe that "on the third day he rose from the dead," that is, from the same death that other men die by the law of nature; and that he rose again to life, a true man, /84/ yet now not mortal, but incorruptible, glorified by receiving body and soul. And we believe the power of his resurrection is such that, being justified, we are through it aroused from the death of sin into newness of life and righteousness [Rom. 6:4]; and likewise we are assured that all men who have passed through the same death are to be raised up at the same time. For his resurrection is the surest faith and the substance of man's resurrection [I Cor. 15:13; Acts 1:22].

2.16.14

17. We believe that "he ascended into heaven." By this ascent the entrance to the Kingdom of Heaven, which had been closed to all in Adam [John 14:1-3], he opened to us. Indeed he entered heaven in our flesh, as if in our name, that already in him we may possess heaven through hope, and thereafter may sit, so to speak, among the heavenly ones [Heb. 2:10, 13; Eph. 1:3; 2:6].

2.16.15

We believe likewise that just as he was manifested in the flesh "he sits there at the Father's right hand." By this is meant that he has been appointed and declared King, Judge, and Lord over all. All creation, without exception, has been subjected to his lordship, in order that, by his power, he may lavish spiritual gifts upon us [I Cor. 15:27; Heb. 2:8; Eph. 4:8]. Therefore he sanctifies us, [134] cleanses the filth of our sins, governs and leads us, until (71) we reach to himself, through death, which will bring an end indeed to our imperfection, but a beginning to our blessedness, which we shall receive in him, so that his Kingdom and glory may be our mainstay, power, and glorying against hell.

2.16.16

And it is indeed for our great benefit that he is now in the Father's presence: in order to provide us access to Him, and to pave the way, to present us to Him, to implore grace for us from Him, to intercede with Him on our behalf as everlasting pleader and mediator, to make intercession on our behalf with Him for our sins, and unceasingly to reconcile Him with us [Heb. 7:24f; 9:11ff; Rom. 8:26-27; I John 2:1]. Therefore, although, lifted up into heaven, he has removed the presence of his body from our sight, yet he does not refuse to be present with his believers in help and might, and to show the manifest power of his presence. This also he has promised: "Behold, I am with you even until the end of the age" [Matt. 28:20].

2.16.17

18. Finally, we believe that "he will descend" in the same visible form from heaven, as he was seen to ascend [Acts 1:11; Matt. 24:27, 44], namely on

the last day, when he will appear at once to all, with the ineffable majesty of his reign to judge the living and the dead. That is, both those still alive at that day, and those who had previously been taken away by death [I Thess. 4:14-17; Matt. 16:27-28]. And he will recompense all according to their works, as each proves himself faithful or unfaithful in his works. [135]

19. Since therefore we see the whole sum of our salvation and also all its parts comprehended in Christ, we must take care not [85] to think that the least particle of our salvation is lodged elsewhere. For in him alone have all the heavenly treasures been hid. Accordingly, let those who with their whole expectation depend upon him alone, drink their fill of whatever good can be sought. Indeed, if all these things (mentioned above) without doubt come from him to us, all of us who with sure faith wait upon them from his Word cannot be completely bereft of some part of good. $\quad$ 2.16.19

Third Part
I believe in the Holy Spirit

20. Here we confess that we believe in the Holy Spirit, but that He is with the Father and the Son, the third person of the most holy Trinity, consubstantial and co-eternal with the Father and the Son, almighty, and Creator of all things. For there are three distinct persons, but one esssence, as has been said. As these are deep and hidden mysteries, they ought rather to be adored than investigated, inasmuch as neither our intelligence nor our tongue—by nature or capacity— ought, or is able, to encompass these mysteries. Therefore, as we have all our trust reposing in God the Father and his only Son, so ought we to have the same trust in the Holy Spirit. [136] Indeed he is our God, one with the Father and the Son. $\quad$ cf. 3.1

We are persuaded that there is for us no other guide and leader to the Father than (72) the Holy Spirit, just as there is no other way than Christ; and that there is no grace from God, save through the Holy Spirit. Grace is itself the power and action of the Spirit: through grace God the Father, in the Son, accomplishes whatever good there is; through grace He justifies, sanctifies, and cleanses us, calls and draws us to himself, that we may attain salvation [Rom. 8:11-17; Eph. 2:18; I Cor. 12:1-13]. $\quad$ 1.13.14

Therefore, the Holy Spirit, while dwelling in us in this manner, illumines us with his light, in order that we may learn and plainly recognize what an enormous wealth of divine goodness we possess in Christ [I Cor. 2:10-16; II Cor. 13]. He kindles our hearts with the fire of love, both toward God and toward neighbor, and day by day He boils away and burns up the vices of our inordinate desire [Rom. 8:13], so that if there are in us any good works they are the fruits and powers of his grace. But our gifts, apart from him, are darkness of mind and perversity of heart [Gal. 5:19-21].

And all these gifts depend not upon any duties or merits of ours, but are given freely to us from the divine bounty, and gratuitously. Therefore we believe in the Holy Spirit, acknowledging him, with the Father and the Son, to be our one God, holding as sure [137] and firm /86/ that the work and power are his, because we have heard the sacred word of the gospel, because we have received him in faith, because we now stand firm in that faith. His work, I say, is freely-given, that nothing may be credited to our merits. Since these things happen to all believers equally, this ought to be the faith of all.

Fourth Part

4.1.2   I believe the Holy Catholic Church, the communion of saints, the for-giveness of sins, the resurrection of the flesh, eternal life.

3.22.1ff   21. First, we believe the holy catholic church—that is the whole number of the elect,* whether angels or men [Eph. 1:9-10; Col. 1:16]; of men, whether dead or still living; of the living, in whatever lands they live, or wherever among the nations they have been scattered—to be one church and society, and one people of God. Of it, Christ, our Lord, is Leader and Ruler, and as it were Head of the one body, according as, through divine goodness, they have been chosen in him before the foundation of the world [Eph. 1:4], in order that all might be gathered into God's Kingdom.*

4.1.2   Now this society is catholic, that is, universal, because there could not be two or three churches. But all God's elect are so united and conjoined in Christ [cf. Eph. 1:22-23] that, [138] as they are dependent on one Head, they also grow together into one body, being joined and knit together [cf. Eph. 4:16] as are the limbs of one body [Rom. 12:5; I Cor. 10:17; 12:12, 27]. These are made truly one who (73) live together in one faith, hope, and love, and in the same Spirit* of God, called to the inheritance of eternal life.

4.1.17   It is also holy, because as many as have been chosen by God's eternal providence to be adopted as members of the church—all these are made holy by the Lord [John 17:17-19; Eph. 5:25-32].

3.24.1, 6   22. And Paul indeed describes this order of God's mercy: "Those whom he has chosen from men he calls; those whom he has called, he justifies; those whom he has justified, he glorifies."* [Rom. 8:30]. He calls when he draws his own to himself, showing himself to be acknowledged by them as their God and Father. He justifies when he clothes them with the righteousness of Christ, with which as their perfection he also adorns them, and covers up their own imper-fection. And those who from day to day are cleansed of the corruption of their flesh, he refreshes with the blessings of his Holy Spirit,* and they are reborn into newness of life, until they clearly appear holy and stainless in his sight. He will glorify when the majesty of his Kingdom will have been manifested in all and through all things. /87/

Consequently, the Lord, when he calls his own, justifies and glorifies his own, is declaring nothing but his eternal election,* by which he had destined them to this end before they were born. Therefore no one will ever enter into the glory [139] of the Heavenly Kingdom, who has not been called in this manner, and justified, seeing that without any exception the Lord in this manner sets forth and manifests his election in all men whom He has chosen.

Scripture often, in accommodating itself to our capacity,* calls "the election of God" only what has already been manifested by this calling and justification. The reason is this: that often among His people God numbers some in whom He has worked His own powers although they were not elect. On the other hand, those who have truly been chosen, he may not reckon among the people of God, because they have not yet been declared to be such [Rom. 9:11, 25-26; 10: 20; 11:7, 24, 28; Hos. 2:23]. For here Paul is not referring to that one and unchangeable providence of God, but is describing to us the children of God in such a way that they can be recognized by us, namely those who are moved by the Spirit of God*[Rom. 8:1, 14].

23. Moreover, since the church is the people of God's elect [John 10:28], it cannot happen that those who are truly its members will ultimately perish [John 10:28], or come to a bad end. For their salvation rests on such a sure and solid bed, that, even if the whole fabric of the world were to fall, it itself could not tumble and fall. First, it stands with God's election, nor can it change or fail, unless along with that eternal wisdom. Therefore they can totter and waver, even fall, but not contend against one another for the Lord supports [140] their hand; that is what Paul says, "for the gifts and calling of God are without repentance" [Rom. 11:29]. Then those whom the Lord has chosen, have been turned over to the care and keeping of Christ his Son so that "he may lose none of them but may revive all on the last day." [John 6:39f.]. Under such a good watchman [cf. II Cor. 4:9] they can wander and fall, but surely they cannot be lost.* Besides, it must have been so decreed that there was no time from the creation of the world when (74) the Lord did not have his church upon the earth, also that there will be no time, even to the end of the age, when he will not have it, even as he himself promises [Joel 3:20; Ps. 89:27, 35-37; Ps. 132:12-18]. For even if at once from the beginning the human race was, by Adam's sin, corrupted and vitiated, yet from this as it were polluted mass, he sanctifies some vessels unto honor [Rom. 9:21], so there is no age that does not experience his mercy [II Tim. 2:20f.]. Finally, if we are so to believe the church that, relying upon the faithfulness of divine goodness, we hold for certain that we are a part of it, and with the rest of God's elect, with whom we have been called and already in part justified, let us have faith that we shall be perfectly justified and glorified.

We indeed cannot comprehend God's incomprehensible wisdom, nor /88/ is it in our power to investigate it so as to find out who have by his eternal plan been chosen, who condemned [Rom. 11:1-36]. But this is not needed by our faith, which is rendered abundantly [141] secure by this promise: God will recognize as his sons those who have received his only-begotten Son [John 1:12]. Who can there be with such shameless desire as, not content to be God's son, to seek something beyond?

24. When, therefore, we have found in Christ alone the good will of God

3.22.7, 10
3.24.6

4.1.3

4.1.17

3.22.7
3.24.4ff

the Father toward us, life, salvation, in short, the very kingdom of heaven itself, he alone ought to be more than enough for us. For this we must ponder: that utterly nothing will be lacking to us which can conduce to our salvation and good, if he is ours; that he and all things of his become ours, if we lean in sure faith upon him, if we rest in him, if we repose in him salvation, life, in sum, all our possessions, if we rest assured that he is never going to forsake us. For with ready hands he gives himself to us only that we may receive him in faith.

3.21.2   But those who, not content with Christ, strive to penetrate more deeply, arouse God's wrath against themselves and, because they break into the depths of his majesty, from his glory cannot but be oppressed [Prov. 25:2-6]. For since Christ our Lord is he in whom the Father, from eternity has chosen those he has willed to be his own and to be brought into the flock of his church, we have a clear enough testimony that we are among God's elect and of the church, if we partake in Christ. Then, since the very same [142] Christ is the constant and unchangeable truth of the Father, we are by no means to doubt that his word truly proclaims to us the Father's will as it was from the beginning and ever will be [John 1:1; 14:7-11].

When therefore by faith we possess Christ and all that is his, it must certainly be established that as he himself is the beloved Son of the Father and heir of the Kingdom of Heaven, so we also through him have been adopted as children of God, and are his brothers and companions in such a way as to be partakers of the same inheritance; on this account we are also assured that we are among those whom the Lord has chosen from eternity, whom he will ever protect and never allow to perish [Rom. 8:31-39].

25. Otherwise if each one of us did not believe himself to be a member of it, we would vainly and fruitlessly believe (75) there to be a church catholic.

4.1.8   But it is not for us to determine for certain whether others are of the church, nor to distinguish the elect from the reprobate. For this is God's prerogative alone, to know who are his own, as Paul attests [II Tim. 2:19]. And to keep men's rashness from getting out of hand, we are warned by daily events how far the Lord's judgments surpass our perception. For those who seemed utterly lost and had obviously been given up as hopeless, are recalled to the pathway by his goodness, /89/ and those who seemed to stand before the rest, often tumble down. Only God's eyes see who will persevere to the very end [Matt. 24:13], because he alone is the Head of salvation [Heb. 2:10]. [143]

4.12.10   Not indeed because Christ has declared that those things which the ministers of his Word loose or bind on earth will be loosed or bound in heaven [Matt. 16:19], does it follow from this that we can discern who are of the church, and who are strangers to it. For by this promise he did not mean to give some external criterion to point out to us openly and lay before our eyes the bound and loosed, but only to promise this: that they who shall hear and receive in faith the gospel promise by which Christ is offered upon earth as redemption and liberation, that is, proclaimed in this life by man to himself—that they, I say, are truly loosed and freed in heaven, that is, in God's presence and by His judgment; but those who will reject and hold it in contempt, to them there is from this promise the testimony that, in heaven and in God's presence, they remain in their chains and so in their condemnation.

26. The elect cannot be recognized by us with assurance of faith, yet Scripture describes certain sure marks to us, as has previously been said, by which we may distinguish the elect and the children of God from the reprobate and the alien, insofar as He wills us so to recognize them. Consequently, all who profess with us the same God and Christ by confession of faith, example of life and participation in the sacraments, ought by some sort of judgment of love to be deemed elect and members of the church. They should be so considered, even if some imperfection [144] resides in their morals (as no one here shows himself to be perfect), provided they do not too much acquiesce and flatter themselves in their vices. And it must be hoped concerning them that they are going to advance by God's leading ever into better ways, until, shed of all imperfection, they attain the eternal blessedness of the elect. For by these marks and traits Scripture delineates for us the elect of God, the children of God, the people of God, the church of God, as they can be understood by us. But those who either do not agree with us on the same faith, or, even though they have confession on their lips, still deny by their actions the God whom they confess with their mouth (as those whom we see wicked and lost throughout life, drunk with the lust of sinning, and quite unconcerned over their own wickedness)—all of this sort show themselves by their traits that they are not members at present of the church. 4.1.8

For this use have excommunications been instituted, in order that those may be withdrawn and expelled from the gathering of the believers who, (76) falsely pretending faith in Christ, by worthlessness of life and unbridled license of sinning, are nothing else than a scandal to the church, and therefore unworthy to boast in Christ's name [I Cor. 5:1-5; Matt. 18:15-19; I Tim. 1:20]. First, lest they be named among Christians with reproach to God, as if his holy church would be /90/ a conspiracy of evildoers and publicly wicked men; second, lest by frequent intercourse [145] they corrupt others by the example of a perverse life; finally, that they may commence to repent, confounded by shame, and from that repentance they may at last learn to "wise up." 4.12.5

27. Such persons we can adjudge, for the time being, to be estranged from the church, insofar as one is permitted to discern, and according to the rule of that knowledge which we have mentioned. But we are not so to despair of them as though they were cast outside God's hand. And utterly wicked is it to wipe anyone of these from the number of the elect, or to despair of him as though he were already lost, unless perchance it is very certain that such persons have already been condemned by God's Word. Included among these is anyone who, with set purpose and with resolute evil intent, should attack the truth, oppress the gospel, snuff out God's name, and resist the Holy Spirit. For the Lord's mouth already pronounced these condemned, when he said that the sin against the Holy Spirit is not forgiven, either in this age or in the future [Matt.

12:32]. This can only rarely be sensed by us (if it is ever possible), so it would be a more discreet plan to await the day of revelation, and not rashly go beyond God's judgment [Heb. 6:6; 10:26; John 5:28-29; I Cor. 4:3-5].

4.12.9   Let us not claim for ourselves more license in judgment, unless we wish to limit God's power and confine his mercy by law. For God, whenever it pleases him, changes the worst men into the best, engrafts the alien, and adopts the stranger into the church. And He does this to frustrate men's opinion and restrain their rashness—which [146] venture to assume for themselves a greater right of judgment than is fitting.

Rather, we are to take care to treat one another with mutual candor, to the best of our ability. Let each of us accept the acts done to one another in the best part; let us not twist them deviously and sinisterly as suspicious persons are accustomed to do [Matt. 7:1-5; Rom. 12:9-10; 14:13, 19; I Thess. 5:15; Heb. 12:14]. But if any are so perverse, as not to let others think well of them, nevertheless let us commit them to God's hand, commend them to his goodness, hoping for better things from them than we now see. For thus it will come to pass that as we bear with one another in mutual equity and patience and nourish peace and love, not stupidly bursting into God's more secret judgments, we will not entangle ourselves in the darkness of error. To put the matter in a word: let us not sentence the person himself (who is in the hand and judgment of God) to death; but let us only weigh the works of each according to God's law, the rule of good and evil.

4.12.5   28. In this sense are to be taken excommunications, not those by which persons who have (before men) separated from the church's flock, are cast outside the hope of salvation; but only those by which they are chastised until they return to the path from the filth of their previous life. (77) As Paul writes, he turned over a man to Satan, /91/ to physical death, in order that his spirit might be made safe in the day of the Lord [I Cor. 5:5; II Thess. 3:14-15]. That is, (as I interpret it) he consigned him to temporal condemnation, [147] that he might be made safe in eternity [II Thess. 3:14-15].

4.12.10   Consequently, though ecclesiastical discipline does not permit us to live familiarly or have intimate contact with excommunicated persons, we ought nevertheless to strive by whatever means we can, whether by exhortation and teaching or by mercy and gentleness, or by our own prayers to God, that they may turn to a more virtuous life and may return to the society and unity of the church. And not only those are to be so treated, but also Turks and Saracens, and other enemies of religion. Far be it from us to approve those methods by which many until now have tried to force them to our faith, when they forbid them the use of fire and water and the common elements, when they deny to them all offices of humanity, when they pursue them with sword and arms.

4.1.9   29. Although, while we are as yet uncertain of God's judgment, we are not allowed to distinguish individually those who belong to the church or not, yet where we see the Word of God purely preached and heard, where we see the sacraments administered according to Christ's institution, there, it is not to be doubted, the church of God exists*[cf. Eph. 2:20]. For his promise cannot fail: "Wherever two or three are gathered in my name, there I am in the midst of them" [Matt. 18:20].

No surer or even other knowledge concerning the church of God can be held on earth [148] nor can one otherwise discern who are of it, who not. Rather, nothing is known of these except by faith. This is what we mean when we say, "we believe the church." For by faith are believed things that cannot be seen with the naked eye. By this it is made plain that it is not a physical thing which ought to be subjected to our sense perception, or enclosed within a definite space, or fixed in some spot.

30. "We" likewise "believe the communion of saints." That is, in the catholic church all the elect (who with true faith worship God together) have reciprocal communication and participation in all goods. By this one does not deny that individuals have various gifts (as Paul teaches that the gifts of the Spirit have been divided and been variously distributed) [I Cor. 12:4-11], but not without each one holding duly and in order his own place which he possesses from the constitution of the civil order (as is necessary, under the elements of this world, for there to be separate possessions among men). But the community of believers looks to the end that they may share among themselves, with kindness and due charity, all such goods both of the spirit and of the body insofar as is fair and according as use demands. And obviously whatever gift of God is reserved for each one, all are truly made /92/ sharers of it, even though by God's dispensation it has been especially given to one, not to others [Rom. 12:4-8; I Cor. 12:12, 26]. Just as the members of one body [149] (78) share among themselves by some sort of community, each nonetheless has his particular gift and distinct ministry; for, as has been said, they are gathered and fastened together into one body. This is the catholic church, the mystical body of Christ [Eph. 1:22-23]. Thus under the next head we have attested that "we believe the church." By this we truly declare of what sort we believe it to be. Yet I know this part is passed over by some, is taken in a different sense by others, but I have interpreted it with the best faith of which I am capable. *4.1.3*

31. "We believe forgiveness of sins." That is, by divine liberality, with Christ's merit interposed, forgiveness of sins and grace come to us who have been adopted and engrafted into the body of the church; but no forgiveness of sins is given either from another quarter, or for any reason, or to others*[Acts 10:43; I John 2:1-12; Is. 33:24]. For outside this church and this communion of saints there is no salvation. *4.1.20f*

Now the church itself stands and consists in this forgiveness of sins, and is supported by this as by a foundation [Hos. 2:18-23]. Since forgiveness of sins is the way that leads to God, and the means by which he is reconciled to us, for this reason forgiveness of sins alone opens for us the entrance into the church (which is the city of God; and the tabernacle which the Most High has sanctified as his dwelling place); and keeps and protects us therein [Ps. 46:4-5; 87:1-3; I Tim. 3:15]. Believers receive this forgiveness, when [150] oppressed, afflicted, *3.3.20* and confounded by the awareness of their own sins, they are stricken by the sense of divine judgment, become displeased with themselves, and as it were groan and toil under a heavy burden. And by this hatred of sin and by their own confusion, they mortify their flesh and whatever derives from it.

And, as they persistently pursue this repentance (for so they must) as long as they dwell in the prison of their body, thus repeatedly and persistently they obtain that repentance. Not because their repentance is thus deserved, but it seemed good to the Lord, to show himself in this order to men that after they have divested themselves of all arrogance through recognition of their own poverty, have wholly cast themselves down, and have plainly become worthless to themselves, then at long last they may begin to taste the sweetness of the mercy which the Lord holds out to them in Christ. When this is perceived, they will recover their breath and take comfort, securely assuring themselves in Christ both of forgiveness of sins and of blessed salvation. On the other hand, those who do not strive by these steps to God will never attain this forgiveness of sins, which is the hinge of salvation [Luke 16:15, 26]. Although they may abound in a shining magnificence of works, even to the point of miracles, to God all their saying, doing, thinking is an abomination. /93/The greater the appearance of holiness, the more are men deceived by it, for their eyes are often dulled by that empty dazzlement of works. [151]

3.25.1

32. We believe the resurrection of the flesh. That is, it will come to pass that all human bodies will at one and the same time be raised from corruption into incorruption, from mortality into immortality [I Cor. 15:20-56; I Thess.

3.25.2,8
4:13-17; Acts. 23:6-9]. (79) And even those who previously died will receive their flesh—whether they had been eaten by worms, or decayed in the earth, or had been reduced to ashes, or scattered in some other way [John 5:28-32]. But those who still survive at that time, will also put off the corruption of their flesh. All will, by a sudden change, cross over into an immortal nature: the godly indeed into glory of life, the reprobate into condemnation of death* [Matt. 25:31-46].

33. Lastly, we believe eternal life. That is, it will come to pass that at that time the Lord will receive His own folk, glorified in body and soul, into blessedness, a blessedness which will endlessly endure, beyond all chance of change or corruption. This will be a true and complete perfecting into life, light, righteousness, when we shall cleave inseparably to the Lord, who like an inex-

3.25.10
haustible fountain, contains the fulness of these in himself [I Cor. 15:28-53]. That blessedness will be the Kingdom of God, crammed with all brightness, joy, power, happiness—things far removed now from human sense, and which (as Paul says) neither ear has heard, nor eye seen, nor the mind of man perceived [I Cor. 2:9]. On the other hand, the ungodly and the reprobate, who have not sought and reverenced God with pure faith, inasmuch as they [152] will have no

3.25.12
part in God and his Kingdom, will be cast with the devils into eternal death. Thus, outside all joy, power, and the other goods of the Heavenly Kingdom, condemned to eternal darkness and eternal punishment [Matt. 8:12; 22:13], they

will be eaten by a deathless worm [Is. 66:24; Mark 9:44], and burn in an unquenchable fire [Matt. 3:12; Mark 9:43-48; Is. 66:24].

34. And we are indeed so to believe both the communion of saints and forgiveness of sins, and the resurrection of the flesh, and eternal life that, trusting in the Lord's goodness, we may establish for certain that all these things will come to us along with all the saints.

And in order to signify how sure and unwavering is the truth of all these things, and in order that all may confirm themselves by this faith, each establishing for himself that the Lord is his God, Christ his Savior, and awaiting the resurrection of his flesh and life eternal, the whole confession is concluded with the word "Amen," the mark of proved certainty.

C. FAITH, HOPE, LOVE

35. Now indeed wherever this living faith is, which we previously showed to be trust in the one God and Christ, it certainly is a matter of no little significance /94/ that faith has at the same time as companions hope and love [I Cor. 13:13]. If these are utterly lacking, however learnedly and elaborately we may discuss faith, we are proved to have none. Not because faith is engendered in us from hope or love, but because it can in no wise come to pass without hope and love forever following faith. [153]   3.2.41

Let us first attest to the nature of hope: if faith (as we have heard) is a sure persuasion of the truth of God, a persuasion that cannot lie to us, deceive us, vex us, then those who have grasped this assurance, at the same time expect that it will straightway come to pass that God will fulfill his promises, since according to their opinion, they cannot but be true. To sum up, hope is nothing else than the expectation of those things which faith has believed truly promised by God.   3.2.42

Thus faith believes God to be truthful; hope waits for him to show his truth at the right occasion. Faith believes God to be our Father; hope waits for him always to act as such toward us. Faith believes eternal life has been given us; hope waits for it sometime to be revealed. Faith is the foundation on which hope leans. Hope nourishes faith and sustains it. For as no one can expect from God anything unless he has previously believed God's promises, so on the other hand ought our weak faith in patiently hoping and waiting to be sustained and heartened, lest it wearily fall.

Concerning love there is even clearer evidence. For since faith embraces Christ as offered to us by the Father [cf. John 6:29]—that is, he is not only forgiveness, righteousness, peace and reconciliation with the Father, but also sanctification and the fountain of living water—doubtless in him one finds love, which is the gift and fruit [154] of the Holy Spirit [Gal. 5:22], and the work of his sanctification [cf. Eph. 5:26]. See how hope and love are both equally born and come forth from faith, and are joined and attached to it by an indissoluble bond. Yet we are not to hold concerning love what we have just taught about   3.2.8

hope, namely, that through it faith is nourished, preserved and steadied. Indeed this belongs to hope because, while hope awaits the Lord in silence and patience, it restrains faith lest it hasten too much: and strengthens it lest it waver and doubt concerning the faithfulness of God's promises [Is. 28:16]. Far different is the character of love, which has nothing like these qualities.

3.2.9   There are some who are accustomed to throw at us Paul's words:* "If anyone has all faith so as to remove mountains, but has not love, he is nothing" [I Cor. 13:2]. From this they would prove that there is a kind of faith apart from love (which they call 'unformed faith')*. They do not consider what the apostle means by "faith" in this passage. For after he had discussed in the preceding chapter the various gifts of the Spirit—among which he had included powers, kinds of tongues, and prophecy [I Cor. 12:4-10]—and had exhorted the Corinthians to "seek after the better of these gifts," thereby to render greater benefit to the church of God, he added /95/ that he will show "a still more excellent way" [I Cor. 12:30]. All these gifts, however excellent they may be in themselves, are still to be considered as nothing unless they serve love. For they were given for the upbuilding of the Church [155] and unless they contribute to this they lose their grace. To prove this, Paul elaborates by repeating those same gifts which he had enumerated before, but under other names. Moreover, he uses the term "powers" and "faith" for the same thing, that is, for the gift of working miracles. Since this power or faith of miracles is a special gift of God, which anyone can abuse, just as the gift of tongues, prophecy, or the other graces, it is clear that this is far, far removed from true Christian faith. One can see it in the instance of Judas, who had it, yet was anything but a believer [Luke 10:17-20, 42].

3.18.8   From this same passage, and another which follows in the same chapter, they argue that he asserts love (81) to be greater than hope and faith, that we are justified by love rather than by faith, namely, by power, (and as they say) a stronger power.* This subtlety can be disposed of without any trouble. For we hold that what is said in the first passage has nothing to do with true faith. The second we also explain in terms of true faith. Paul says love is greater than faith, not as being more meritorious, but because it is more fruitful, because it extends farther, because it serves more, because it flourishes forever, while the use of faith continues only for time [cf. I Cor. 13:2ff.]. What man of sound judgment— indeed what man of wholly sound brain—would reason from this that love is more effective in justifying? The power of justifying does not lie in the worth of works. [156] Our justification rests upon God's mercy alone, and faith, when it lays hold of justification, is said to justify. But if at this point some wrangler should interrupt and ask why in such a short space I variously understand the term "faith," I have no light reason for this interpretation. For inasmuch as these gifts which Paul had enumerated are in a way subsumed under faith and hope, because they have to do with the knowledge of God, he includes them all by way of recapitulation under the terms "faith" and "hope." It is as if he said: "Prophecy and tongues, the gift of interpretation, and knowledge alike have the purpose of leading us to know God. But in this life we know God only through faith and hope. When, therefore, I name faith and hope, I at the same time include all these." "So faith, hope, love abide, these three" [I Cor. 13:13a.] that is, however great the variety of gifts, all are referred thereto—"the chief among them is love" [I Cor. 13:13b.], etc.

Now we must ponder that faith, hope and love are gifts of the Holy Spirit, nor can any of these either begin or stand firm except by God's mercy [I Cor. 4:7]. Therefore, let us learn to ask all these of God, not to seek them in ourselves; and, if we discern in ourselves anything either of hope, or of love, or of faith, let us credit the whole as received from God, with thanksgiving, asking with heart and mouth, /96/ but especially with heart, and [157] with restraint, that he may will to protect them in us, and daily to better them. For we need to have them increase constantly, while we are in this life. This (while it goes well with us) is nothing but progress on the road, until we clearly reach God, in whom the whole of our perfection rests.

CHAPTER III

PRAYER: WITH AN EXPOSITION OF THE LORD'S PRAYER

A. PRAYER IN GENERAL

3.20.1   1. From those matters so far discussed, we clearly see how destitute and devoid of all good things man is, and how he lacks all aids to salvation. (82) Therefore, if he seeks resources to succor him in his need, he must go outside himself and get them elsewhere. It was afterwards explained to you that the Lord willingly and freely reveals himself to us in his Christ. For in Christ he offers all happiness in place of our misery, all wealth in place of our neediness: in him the Lord opens to us the heavenly treasures [158] that our whole faith may contemplate that beloved Son of His, our whole expectation depend upon him, and our whole hope cleave to and rest in him. This, indeed, is that secret and hidden philosophy* which cannot be wrested from syllogisms. But they whose eyes God has opened surely learn it by heart, that in his light they may see light [Ps. 36:9]. But after we have been instructed by faith to recognize that whatever we need and whatever we lack is in God, and in our Lord Jesus Christ, in whom the Father willed all the fullness of his bounty to abide [cf. Col. 1:19; John 1:16] so that we may all draw from it as from an overflowing spring, it remains for us to seek in him, and in prayers to ask of him, what we have learned to be in him.* Otherwise, to know God as the Master and bestower of all good things, who invites us to request them of him, and still not go to him and not ask of him—this would be of as little profit as for a man to neglect a treasure, buried and hidden in the earth, after it had been pointed out to him. We must therefore more fully discuss this last point, since it was previously only mentioned in passing and, as it were, cursorily touched upon. /97/

3.20.8   2. Now, let this be the first rule of right prayer, that we abandon all thought of our own glory, that we cast off all notion of our own worth, that we put away all our self-assurance, in our abjection and our humility giving glory [159] to the Lord, so as to be admonished by the prophetic teaching: "We do not pour forth our prayers unto thee on the ground of our righteousness but on the ground of thy great mercies. O Lord, hear us: O Lord, be kindly unto us. Hear us, and

68

do what we ask . . . for thine own sake . . . because thy name is called upon over thy people, and over thine holy place" [Dan. 9:18-19, cf. Vg.]. Another prophet writes: "The soul that is sorrowful and desolate for the greatness of her evil, bowed down and feeble, . . . the hungry soul, and the eyes that fail give glory . . . to thee, O Lord. It is not for the righteousnesses of the fathers that we pour out our prayers before thee, and beg mercy in thy sight, O Lord our God" [Baruch 2:18-19 p., cf. Vg.]; but because thou art merciful, "be merciful unto us, for we have sinned before thee" [Baruch 3:2].

Let this be the second rule: truly to sense our own insufficiency, and earnestly ponder that we need the things we seek from God for ourselves and for our benefit, and that we seek them so as to attain them from him. For if we had another intent or mind, our prayer would be feigned and impure. If anyone were to ask of God forgiveness of sins, without surely and earnestly recognizing himself as sinner, he would be doing nothing but mocking God by his pretending. (83) Then, let us seek with great and ardent desire and eagerness those things which we seek only for God's glory. When, for example, we pray that "his name be hallowed" [Matt. 6:9; Luke 11:2], we should, so to speak, eagerly hunger and thirst after that sanctification. [160] If then we recognize ourselves pressed and belabored by the weight of sins, if we see ourselves empty of all things that could make us pleasing before God, let not this feeling terrify us, but rather let us betake ourselves to him, seeing that it is necessary for us to ponder and feel such things when we approach him [Luke 17:7-10]. For prayer was not ordained that we should be haughtily puffed up before God, or greatly esteem anything of ours, but by it we should confess our calamities and weep for them before him, as children intimately unburden their troubles to their parents. Rather, this sense of sin ought to be for us like a spur or goad the more to arouse us to pray.

3. To this awareness of our need our best Father adds two things to impel us to seek prayer intently: a command to bid us pray; a promise to assure us we will receive whatever we ask. We have the commandment very frequently repeated: "Seek," "come to me," "ask me," "turn back to me," "call upon me in your day of need." And this is expressed often elsewhere as it is also in the third chapter of the law, /98/ which forbids us to take the Lord's name in vain [Luke 11:9-13; John 16:23-29; Matt. 7:7; 11:28; Zech. 1:3; Ps. 50:15; Ex. 20:7]. For in being forbidden to take his name in vain, we are at the same time bidden to hold him in glory by deferring to him all credit for virtue, for good, for help, and protection [161] while we ask and await these very things from him. Therefore, unless we flee to him when any necessity presses us, unless we seek him and beg his help, we surely call down his anger upon ourselves just as much as if we were to make foreign gods for ourselves, or construct idols. Indeed in our contempt of all his commandments we just as much despise his will. On the other hand, those who call upon him, seek, render praise, enjoy great consolation, because they know that they are thus rendering something acceptable to him and serving his will. The promise is "Seek and you will receive" [Matt. 7:7; cf. Jer. 29:13f.], "It will be done to you" [Mark 11:24], "I will answer you"

3.20.6

3.20.12

3.20.13

69

[Is. 65:24], "I will rescue you" [Ps. 50:15; 91:2ff.], "I will refresh you" [Matt. 11:28], "I will comfort you," "I will feed you in abundance" [Ezek. 34:14f.], "You will not be confounded" [Is. 45:17].

3.20.14   4. All these, as they have been promised us by God, will without doubt be fulfilled, if we await them with sure faith. For prayer possesses no merit or worth to obtain what is requested, but the whole hope of prayer rests in such promises, and depends on them. Therefore, we are to determine in our hearts that we will be answered, just as much as Peter or Paul or any other saint was answered (even though they were equipped with a greater holiness of life than we), provided nevertheless we call upon God with the same and equally staunch faith. (84) When we have been equipped and armed with the same command to pray, and with the same promise the prayer will be answered, [162] God adjudges the value of the prayer not by the person's worth, but by faith alone, in which

3.20.11   men both obey his commandment and trust in his promise. On the other hand, those who are not sure of God's promise and call his truth into question, and so doubting and hesitating whether they are to be answered, invoke God himself, get nothing (as James says). He compares them to "waves which are driven with the wind and tossed." [James 1:6]. Then, since the Lord affirms that it will happen to each man according to his faith, it follows that nothing can happen

3.20.17   to us apart from faith [Matt. 8:13; 9:29; Mark 11:24]. Since no man is worthy to present himself to God and come into his sight, the Heavenly Father himself, to free us from this confusion, (which ought to have thrown the hearts of us all into despair,) has given us his Son, Jesus Christ our Lord, to be our advocate [I John 2:1] and mediator with him [I Tim. 2:5; cf. Heb. 8:6 and 9:15]. By his guidance we may confidently come to him, and with such an intercessor, /99/ trust that nothing we ask in his name will be denied us, as nothing can be denied to him by the Father. The throne of God, also, is not only a throne of majesty, but of grace, before which in his name we dare with all confidence appear, receive mercy, and find grace in timely help [Heb. 4:16].

     5. And as a rule for calling upon God [163] has been established, and a promise given that those who call upon him shall be heard, so too we are particularly bidden to call upon him in Christ's name; and we have his promise that we shall obtain what we have asked in his name [John 14:13; 16:24]. Hence it is incontrovertibly clear that those who call upon God in another name than that of Christ obstinately flout his commands and count his will as nought—in fact, have no promise of obtaining anything. Indeed, as Paul says, "all God's promises find their yea and amen in Christ" [II Cor. 1:20]. That is, they are

3.20.19   confirmed and fulfilled. Now, since he is the only way, and the one access, by which it is granted us to come to God [cf. John 14:6], to those who turn aside from this way and forsake this access, no way and no access to God remain; they have nothing left in his throne but wrath, judgment, and terror. Moreover, since the Father has designated him [cf. John 6:27] as our Head [Matt. 2:6] and Leader [I Cor. 11:3; Eph. 1:22; 4:15; 5:23; Col. 1:18], those who in any way lean away or turn aside from him are trying their level best to rub out and disfigure the mark imprinted by God.

6. Regarding the saints* who, having died, live in Christ, let us not dream   3.20.21
that they have any other way to petition God than through Christ, who alone is the way [Jn. 14:6], or that they are accepted by God in any other name. Accordingly, after Scripture recalls us from all these to Christ alone, [164] after our Heavenly Father wills that all things be gathered together in him [Col. 1:20; Eph. 1:10], it is an error for us to be so intent on gaining access through the saints, which they cannot even supply for themselves. (85) Also, since the saints   3.20.22
relate all their desires to the will of God alone, contemplate it, and abide in it, he who attributes to them any other prayer than that by which they pray for the coming of God's Kingdom is thinking of them stupidly and carnally and even contemptuously. But as much by the confounding of the reprobate as by the salvation of the godly will his kingdom be fulfilled. Therefore we are not to expect to be helped by any prayers of the saints (whatever they are able to do) unless we have a part in Christ, and are part of his Kingdom. On the other hand also, if we partake in Christ, we ought to be utterly convinced that whatever stands through our efforts is from God, and that the whole church of which those saints are members prays for us, while it is praying that the Lord's kingdom come. But now, even though they are praying for us in this way, we are still not   3.20.24
to call upon them. And that this is to be done [I Tim. 2:1-7; James 5:15-18] does not incontrovertibly follow from the fact that men who dwell on earth /100/ can reciprocally commend one another in prayers. This function serves to foster love in them, while they, as it were, share and mutually bear their necessities with one another. This practice does not apply to the dead whom the Lord [165] has withdrawn from our company. Even though their love toward us is ever growing, as they have been bound with us by the one faith in Christ, still no interchange of speech or hearing remains between us [I Cor. 13:10f.]. To declare otherwise—what is it but to wish (through a drunken dream of our brain) to penetrate and break into God's hidden judgments apart from his Word, and to trample upon Scripture? Scripture very often declares the prudence of our flesh to be the enemy of God's wisdom [Rom. 8:6-7, Vg.]; it wholly condemns the vanity of our mind; laying low our whole reason it bids us look to God's will alone [Deut. 12:32]. Scripture offers Christ alone to us, sends us to him, and   3.20.21
establishes us in him. "He," says Ambrose, "is our mouth, through which we speak to the Father; he is our eye through which we see the Father; he is our right hand, through which we offer ourselves to the Father. Unless he intercedes, there is no intercourse with God either for us or for all saints."*

7. Now, those who adopt and choose for themselves particular patrons from the saints, hoping to be helped by some special commendation of theirs, are no less insolent toward them. For they drag them back from that one will, a will which (as we have said) they hold to be set and unmoved in God, that his Kingdom come, while they forge for the saints some physical affection to make them more favorable to one worshiper or another of theirs. [166] But they make

71

the saints their mediators as if Christ failed them or were too severe for them. They dishonor him and strip him of the title of sole Mediator, which, as it has been given to him by the Father as a unique privilege, ought not to be transferred to another. Also, by this very thing they obscure the glory of his birth and make void the cross; in short, they strip and defraud of its rightful praise all that he has done or suffered for our salvation! (86) For all these things lead to the conclusion that he alone is, and is to be deemed, the Mediator. At the same time, they cast out the kindness of God, who manifested himself to them as Father. For he is not Father to them unless they recognize Christ to be their brother [cf. Heb. 2:11]. This they plainly deny unless they reflect that he has

3.20.26 brotherly affection toward themselves, than which nothing can be gentler. But some are obviously influenced by the fact that we often read of the prayers of the saints being heard. Why? Because they prayed, of course. "In thee they trusted," says the prophet, "and were saved . . . they cried . . . and were not /101/confounded." [Ps. 22:4-5; cf. 21:5-6, Vg. slightly modified.] Let us also, therefore, after their example pray that, like them, we may be heard. But our opponents unbecomingly and absurdly reason that only those who were once heard will be heard. How much better does James say it! "Elijah," he says, "was a man like ourselves, and he prayed fervently that it might not rain, and for three years and six months it did not rain on the earth. Then he prayed again and [167] the heavens gave rain, and the earth gave its fruit." [James 5:17-18 p.]. By this he does not infer some privilege of Elijah, but teaches the power of prayer in order to exhort us to pray in a like manner.

3.20.28 8. There are two parts to prayer (as we now understand this term): petition and thanksgiving. By petition we lay the desires of our heart before God, seeking from his goodness first what serves only his glory; secondly, what also is conducive to our use [I Tim. 2:1]. By thanksgiving we recognize his benefits to us, and confess them with praise, referring to his goodness all the good things, whatever they are. Both are encompassed in one verse of David, when in the person of God he writes as follows: "Call upon me in the day of need [cf. Ecclus. 6:10]; I will deliver you, and you shall glorify me" [Ps. 50:15]. We ought to use both constantly [cf. Luke 18:1; 21:36; Eph. 5:20], for our poverty is so great and such great anxieties urge and press us from all sides that there is reason enough for all, even the holiest, continually to groan and sigh to God, and to beseech him as suppliants. In short, we are well-nigh overwhelmed by so great and so plenteous an outpouring of God's benefactions, by so many and mighty miracles of his, discerned wherever one looks that we never lack reason and occasion for praise and thanksgiving. And let us explain these things somewhat more clearly, since (as has already been sufficiently proved) [168] all our hope and wealth so reside in God that neither we nor all our possessions can prosper unless by his blessing; we ought constantly to commit ourselves and all that we have to him [cf. James 4:14-15]. Then whatever we determine, speak, do, let us determine, speak, and do under his hand and will—in a word, under the hope of his help. For by God all are declared accursed who, placing confidence in themselves or someone else, conceive and carry out their plans; who undertake or try to begin anything apart from his will, and without calling upon him [cf. Is. 30:1; 31:1].

But since it has been said (87) that he is to be acknowledged as the author of all blessings, it follows that we ought so to receive all those things from his hand as to accompany them with continual thanksgiving; and that there is no proper manner for us to make use of his benefits, which ceaselessly flow and come to us from his generosity, except by continually uttering his praise and rendering him thanks. For Paul, /102/ when he testifies that these benefits "are sanctified by the word . . . and prayer" [I Tim. 4:5], at the same time hints that without the word and prayer they are not at all sanctified. ("Word" he evidently understands by metonymy, as "faith").

9. The reason why Paul elsewhere enjoins us to pray without ceasing [I Thess. 5:17-18; cf. I Tim. 2:1, 8] is, that he wishes all men to lift up their desires to God, at all times, in all places, and in all affairs; [169] to expect all things from him, and to give him praise for all things, since he offers us unfailing reasons to praise and pray.

This constancy in prayer is concerned with one's own private prayers, but has nothing to do with the public prayers of the church. These can neither be constant nor ought they even to take place in any other way than according to the polity agreed upon by common consent among all. For this reason, certain hours, indifferent to God but necessary for men's convenience, are agreed upon and appointed to provide for the accommodation of all, and for everything to be done "decently and in order" in the church, according to Paul's statement [I Cor. 14:40].   3.20.29

Hence public places have been appointed which we call "temples." These do not by any secret sanctity of their own make prayers more holy, or cause them to be heard by God. But they are intended to receive the congregation of believers more conveniently when they gather to pray, to hear the preaching of the Word, and at the same time to partake of the sacraments. Otherwise (as Paul says) [I Cor. 3:16; 6:19: II Cor. 6:16] we ourselves are the true temples of God. Let those of us who wish to pray in God's temple, pray in ourselves. But those who suppose that God's ear has been brought closer to them in a temple, or consider their prayer more consecrated by the holiness of the place, are acting in this way according to the stupidity of the Jews and Gentiles. In physically worshiping God, they go against what has been commanded, [170] that, without any consideration of place, we worship God in spirit and in truth [John 4:23].

10. But inasmuch as this goal of prayer has already been stated—namely, that hearts may be aroused and borne to God, whether to praise him or to beseech his help—we may understand from this that the essentials of prayer are set in the mind and heart, or rather that prayer itself is properly an emotion of the heart within, which is poured out and laid bare before God, the searcher of hearts [cf. Rom. 8:27].

Accordingly, Christ our Lord, when he willed to lay down the best rule for prayer, bade us enter into our bedroom and there, with door closed, pray to our Father in secret, that our Father, who is in secret, may hear us [Matt. 6:6]. For, when he has drawn us away from the example of hypocrites, who (88) grasp after the favor of men by vain and ostentatious prayers, he at the same time adds something better: that is, to enter into our bedroom and there, with door closed, pray. By these words, as I understand them, he taught us to descend into and enter our heart with our whole thought. /103/ He promises that God, whose temples our bodies ought to be, will be near to us in the affections of our hearts [cf. II Cor. 6:16]. For he did not mean to deny that it is fitting to pray in other places, but he shows that prayer is something secret, which is both principally lodged in the heart and [171] requires a tranquillity far from all our teeming cares. From this, moreover, it is fully evident that unless voice and song, if interposed in prayer, spring from deep feeling of heart, neither has any value or profit in the least with God. But they arouse his wrath against us if they come only from the tip of the lips and from the throat, seeing that this is to abuse his most holy name and to hold his majesty in derision as he declares through the prophet: "The people," he says, "draw near to me with their mouth, and honor me with their lips, but their hearts are far from me, and they have feared me by the command and teaching of men." [Is. 29:13; cf. Matt. 15:8-9]. "Therefore, behold, I will . . . do a great and marvelous miracle among this people; for the wisdom of their wise men shall perish, and the prudence of their elders shall vanish." [Is. 29:14 p., cf. Vg.].

3.20.31

11. Yet we do not here condemn speaking and singing provided they are associated with the heart's affection and serve it. For thus do they exercise the mind in thinking of God and keep it attentive which (as it is slippery) is easily relaxed and diverted in different directions. Moreover, since the glory of God ought, in a measure, to shine in the several parts of our bodies, it is especially fitting that the tongue has been assigned and destined for this task, both through singing and through speaking. For it was expressly created to tell and proclaim the praise of God. But the chief use of the tongue is in public prayers, which are offered in the assembly of believers, [172] by which it comes about that with one common voice, and as it were with the same mouth, we all glorify God together, worshiping him with one spirit and the same faith. And we do this openly, that all men mutually, each one from his brother, may receive confession of faith and be invited by his example.

3.20.33

12. From this also it plainly appears that public prayers must be couched not in Greek among the Latins, nor in Latin among the French or English (as has heretofore been the custom) but in the language of the people, which can be generally understood by the whole assembly. For this ought to be done for the edification of the whole church, which receives no benefit whatever from a sound not understood. Those who have no regard for love ought at least to have been moved by the authority of Paul, whose words are perfectly clear. "If you bless with the spirit," he says, "how can he who occupies the place of the unlearned say 'Amen' to your blessing, since (89) he is ignorant of what you are saying? /104/ For you give thanks, but the other is not edified" [I Cor. 14:16-17

p.]. Whether in public or in private prayer—as we must explicitly hold—the tongue without the heart is unacceptable to God. Furthermore, what the mind ponders should be of such great force and ardor as far to outstrip what the tongue in speaking can express. Lastly, the tongue is not even necessary for private prayer: [173] the inner feeling would be enough to arouse itself, so that sometimes the best prayers are silent ones. This can be seen for example in the prayers of Moses [Ex. 14] and Hannah [I Sam. 1:13].

13. Now we must learn not only a more certain way of praying but also the form itself: namely, that which the Heavenly Father has taught us through his beloved Son [Matt. 6:9ff.; Luke 11:2ff.], in which we may acknowledge his boundless goodness and clemency. For he warns us and urges us to seek him in our every need (as children are wont to take refuge in the protection of parents). Besides this, since he saw that we did not even sufficiently perceive how straitened our poverty was, what it was fair to request, and also what was profitable for us, he also provided for this ignorance of ours; and what had been lacking to our capacity he himself supplied and made sufficient from his own. For he composed a form for us in which he set forth as in a table all that he allows us to seek of him, all that is of benefit to us, all that we need ask. From this kindness of his we receive great fruit of consolation: that we know we are requesting nothing absurd, nothing strange or unseemly—in short, nothing unacceptable to him—since we are asking almost in his own words. 3.20.34

This form or rule of prayer consists of six petitions. The reason why I do not agree with those who distinguish seven headings* is that in [174] Luke [Luke 11:2-4] only six are read; obviously he would not have left the prayer in a defective form, so that what has been added in seventh place in Matthew exegetically ought to be referred to the sixth petition. But even though in all these God's glory is to be given chief place, and on the other hand, even though all have to do with us, and it is expedient for them to turn out as we ask, still the first three petitions have been particularly assigned to God's glory. And this alone we ought to look to in them, without consideration of our own advantage,* as they call it. The three others are concerned with the care of ourselves, and are especially assigned to those things which we should ask for our own advantage. So, when we ask that God's name be hallowed, we must then have no consideration for our own advantage [105] but must set before ourselves his glory, to gaze with eyes intent upon this one thing. And in petitions of this sort, we ought to be affected in precisely the same way. And, indeed, this yields a great advantage to us, because, when his name is hallowed as we ask, our own hallowing also comes about. But our eyes ought, as it were, to be blinded to this sort of advantage, so that they have no regard for it in any way, and so that, if all hope of our own private (90) good were cut off, still we should not cease both to desire and entreat with prayers this hallowing and the other things that pertain to God's glory. In the examples of Moses and Paul, we see them turning their minds and eyes away from themselves, [175] longing for their own destruction with fierce and burning zeal in order that, despite their own loss, God's glory and Kingdom might be advanced [Ex. 32:32; Rom. 9:3]. On the other 3.20.35

hand, when we ask to be given our daily bread, even though we desire what is to our advantage, here also we ought especially to seek God's glory so as not to ask it unless it redound to God's glory.*

B. EXPOSITION OF THE LORD'S PRAYER

"OUR FATHER who art in heaven."

3.20.36   14. First,* at the very threshold one meets what we previously mentioned: all prayer ought to be offered to God by us in Christ's name, as no prayer can be commended to him in another name. For in calling God "Father" we assuredly put forth Christ's name. If we had not been adopted to Christ as children of grace, with what assurance would anyone have addressed God as Father? Who would have broken forth into such rashness as to appropriate to himself the honor of a child of God? Christ, the true son, has been given to us as our brother by Him in order that what belongs to him by nature may become ours by benefit of adoption, provided we embrace with sure faith this great blessing. As John says, power has been given to those who believe in the name of the only begotten Son of God, to become children of God also [John 1:12]. Accordingly, He calls Himself our Father, and wills so to be called by us. [176] By this great sweetness of his name he frees us from unfaith, since there can be found no greater feeling of love elsewhere than in the Father. But his love toward us is as much greater and more excellent than all love of our parents, as He exceeds all men in goodness and mercy. It is as if, however many fathers there are on earth, stripped of all sense of fatherly piety, they were to forsake their children, yet He would never fail us [Ps. 27:10; Is. 63:16], since he cannot deny himself*[II Tim. 2:13]. For we have his promise: "If you when you are evil, know how to give good things to your children, how much more does your Father who is in heaven?" [Matt. 7:11] But a son cannot give himself over to the safekeeping of a stranger and an alien without at the same time complaining either of his father's cruelty or /106/ want of means. Thus, if we are his sons, we cannot seek help anywhere else than from him without reproaching him for poverty, or want of means, or

3.20.37   cruelty and excessive rigor. And let us not claim that the consciousness of our sins rightly makes us timid, for they have made our Father—although kind and gentle—displeased with us. Among men, a son can have no better advocate to plead his cause before his father, can have no better intermediary (91) to procure his lost favor, than if he himself, suppliant and humble, acknowledging his guilt, implores his father's mercy. Then will his father, unable to conceal his compassion, [177] not fail to be moved by such entreaties. How then will he who is the Father of mercies and God of all comfort [cf. II Cor. 1:3] respond? Will he not heed the tears and groans of his children entreating for themselves (since he particularly invites and exhorts us to this) rather than any pleas of other advocates, to whose help they have recourse, being doubtful of their Father's compassion and kindness? He depicts and represents for us in a parable [Luke 15:11-32] this abundance of fatherly compassion: a son had estranged himself from his father, had dissolutely wasted his substance [v. 13] had grievously offended against him [v. 18]; but the father embraces him with open arms, and does not wait for him to ask for pardon but anticipates him, recognizes him returning afar off, willingly runs to meet him [v. 20], comforts him, receives him into favor [v. 22-24]. For in setting forth this example of great compassion to be seen in man, he willed to teach us how much more abundantly we ought to expect it of him. For he is not only a father but by far the best and kindest of all fathers, provided we still cast ourselves upon his mercy, although we are ungrateful, rebellious, and froward children.

15. And to strengthen our assurance that he is this sort of father to us (if we are Christians), he willed that we call him not only "Father" but explicitly "our Father." It is as if we addressed him: "O Father, who dost abound with great devotion toward thy children, [178] and with great readiness to forgive, we thy children call upon thee and make our prayer, assured and clearly persuaded that thou bearest toward us only the affection of a father, although we are unworthy of such a father." However, we are not so instructed that each one of us should individually call him *his Father*, but rather that all of us in common should call him *our Father*. From this fact we are warned how great a feeling of brotherly love ought to be among us who are the common children of such a father. For if one father is common to us all [Matt. 23:9] and every good thing that can fall to our lot comes from him, it befits us to have nothing divided among ourselves that we are not prepared with great eagerness of heart to share with one another, as need demands. Now if we so desire, as is fitting, to extend our hand to one another [107] and to help one another, there is nothing in which we can benefit our brethren more than in commending them to the providential care of the best Father of all; for if he is kind and favorable, nothing else at all can be desired. Indeed, we owe even this very thing to our Father. Just as one who truly and deeply loves any father of a family at the same time embraces his whole household with love and good will, so it becomes us in like measure to show to his people, to his family and lastly, to his inheritance the same zeal and affection we have toward this Heavenly Father. [179] For he so honored these as to call them the fullness of his only-begotten Son [Eph. 1:23]. (92) The prayer of the Christian man ought then to be conformed to this rule in order that it may be in common and embrace all who are his brothers in Christ, not only those whom he at present sees and recognizes as such but all men who dwell on earth. For what the Lord has determined concerning them is beyond our knowing, except that we ought to wish and hope the best for them. Yet we ought to be drawn with a special affection to those, above others, of the household of faith, whom the apostle has particularly commended to us in everything [Gal. 6:10]. 3.20.38

To sum up, all prayers ought to be such as to look to that community which our Lord has established in his kingdom and his household. Nevertheless, this does not prevent us from praying especially for ourselves and for certain 3.20.39

others, provided, however, our minds do not withdraw their attention from this community or turn aside from it but refer all things to it. For although prayers are individually framed, since they are directed to this end they do not cease to be common. All this can easily be understoody by a comparison. There is a general command of God's to relieve the need of all the poor. Yet they obey it who to this end succor the indigence of those [180] whom they know or see to be suffering, even though they overlook many who are pressed by no lighter need because either they cannot know all or cannot provide for all. In this way those who, viewing and pondering this common society of the church, frame particular prayers of this sort, by which, in distinctive words, but words of public concern and common affection, they commend to God themselves or others whose need He has been pleased to make intimately known to them— such persons are not resisting God's will. However, not all aspects of prayer and almsgiving are alike. For liberality of giving can be practiced only toward those whose poverty is visible to us. But we are free to help by prayer even utterly foreign and unknown persons, however great the distance that separates them from us. This, too, is done through that general form of prayer wherein all children of God are included, among whom they also are. /108/

3.20.40   16. That he is in heaven [Matt. 6:9] is added. From this we are not to jump to the conclusion that he is bound, shut up, and surrounded, by the circumference of heaven, as by a barred enclosure. Indeed Solomon confesses that "the heaven of heavens cannot contain him" [I Kings 8:27]. And he himself says through the prophet that heaven is his seat, and the earth, his footstool [Is. 66:1; Acts 7:49; cf. ch. 17:24]. By this he obviously means that he is not confined to any particular region [181] but is diffused through all things. But our minds, so crass are they, could not have conceived his unspeakable glory otherwise. Consequently, it has been signified to us by "heaven," for we can behold nothing more sublime or majestic than this." Therefore it is as if he had been said to be mighty, lofty, incomprehensible. (93) But while we hear this, our thought must be raised higher when God is spoken of, lest we dream up anything earthly or physical about him, lest we measure him by our small measure, or conform his will to our emotions.

First Petition
"Hallowed be thy name." [Matt. 6:9b]

3.20.41   17. By God's name is indicated his power, which comprises all his excellences: as, his might, wisdom, righteousness, mercy, truth. For God is great and wonderful, because he is righteous, because he is wise, because he is merciful, because he is mighty, because he is truthful, etc. Therefore, we petition that this majesty be hallowed in excellences such as these, not in God himself, to whose presence nothing can be added, nothing taken away: but that it be held holy by all; namely, be truly recognized and magnified. And whatever God does, let all his works appear glorious, as they are. If he punishes let him be proclaimed

78

righteous; if he pardons, [182] merciful, if he carries out what he has promised, truthful. In short, let there be no thing at all wherein his graven glory does not shine, and thus let praises of him resound in all hearts and on all tongues. Finally, let all ungodliness—which besmirches and profanes his holy name (that is, which obscures and lessens this hallowing)—perish and be confounded. For even in such confounding God's majesty shines more and more. And so, in this petition, thanksgiving is also included. For while we are praying that God's name be hallowed everywhere, we give him praise for all good things, we relate all things, once received to him, and we recognize his benefits toward us. /109/

Second Petition
"Thy Kingdom come." [Matt. 6:10a]

18. The Kingdom of God is this: by his Holy Spirit, to act and to rule over his own people, in order to make the riches of his goodness and mercy conspicuous in all their works.* On the other hand, it is to ruin and cast down the reprobate, who do not acknowledge themselves to be for God and the Lord, who refuse to be subjected to His rule; and to destroy and lay low their sacrilegious arrogance, in order to make clear that there is no power which can withstand His power.* But these things daily come before our eyes, while His Holy Word [183] raised up like a sceptre, even under the cross and the world's contempt and disgrace, grows, reigns, prospers, is fruitful. This is to see that a kingdom of this sort also flourishes in this world, even if it is not of this world [I Cor. 1:21; John 17:14; 18:36; Rom. 14:17]: first, because, being spiritual, it consists of spiritual things; secondly, because it is incorruptible and eternal [Luke 1:33; Dan. 7:14]. (94)

19. Accordingly we pray that "God's kingdom come," that is, that the Lord may day by day add new believers to his people so that they may celebrate his glory in every way;* (also) that he may pour out ever more widely upon them his rich graces, through which he may live and reign day by day more and more in them, until he completely fulfills their perfect union with himself. At the same time we pray that he will cause his light and truth to shine with ever new increases, by which the darkness and falsehoods of Satan and his kingdom may vanish, be dispelled, be snuffed out, and perish. While we pray in this way, that "God's kingdom come," at the same time we desire that it may be at last perfected and fulfilled, that is, in the revelation of his judgment. On that day he alone will be exalted, and will be all in all, when his own folk are gathered and received into glory, but Satan's kingdom is utterly disrupted and laid low [I Cor. 15:28]. [184]

Third Petition
"Thy will be done, as in heaven, so on earth." [Matt. 6:10b]

20. By this petition* we ask him—both in heaven and on earth, namely, everywhere—to temper and compose all things according to his will, govern the

3.20.42

3.20.43

outcome of all things, use all his creatures according to his decision, subject all wills of all beings to himself. We ask that they equally obey his will: some by consent (his own folk), others unwillingly and reluctantly (the devil and the reprobate, who refuse and evade his rule and try to steal away from obedience to him). Indeed as we petition this, we are renouncing all our desires, /110/ resigning and turning over to the Lord any affections that are in us, and asking that God respond to our prayer not as we wish, but as he has foreseen and decreed. But we do not ask solely that God void and invalidate our affections that war against his will, but rather that God create in us new minds and new hearts, having extinguished our own [Ezek. 36:26]. We ask that no prompting of desire be felt in us, except one pure and in agreement with his will. To sum up, we ask not what we will of ourselves, but that his Spirit may will in us. While the Spirit teaches us within, let us learn to love those things which are pleasing to him; [185] but to hate or abhor all that displeases him.

21. Here are the first three sections of the prayer. In making these requests we are to keep God's glory alone before our eyes, while leaving ourselves out of consideration and not looking to any advantage for ourselves; even though we receive ample advantage from the prayer, we must not seek it there. But even though all these things must nonetheless come to pass in their time, without any thought or desire or petition of ours, still we ought to desire and request them. And it is of no slight value for us to do this. Thus, (95) we may testify and profess ourselves servants and children of God, serving his honor to the best of our ability. This we owe our Lord and Father. Therefore, men who do not, with this desire and zeal to further God's glory, pray that "God's name be hallowed," that "his Kingdom come," that "his will be done," should not be reckoned among God's children and servants; and inasmuch as all these things will come to pass even against such men's consent, the result will be their confusion and judgment.

Fourth Petition

3.20.44
22. This is the first of the three remaining petitions, by which we specifically ask of God the things that concern our own affairs, and help us in our need. [186]

"Give us this day our daily bread." [Matt. 6:11]

23. By this petition* we ask of God all things in general that our bodies have need to use under the elements of this world [Gal. 4:3], not only for food and clothing but also for everything God foresees to be beneficial to us, that we may eat our bread in peace. Briefly, by this we give ourselves over to his care, and entrust ourselves to his providence, that he may feed, nourish and preserve us. For our most gracious Father does not disdain to take even our bodies under his safekeeping and guardianship in order to exercise our faith in thsese small matters, while we expect everything from him, even to a crumb of bread and a drop /111/ of water. For since it has come about in some way or other through

our wickedness that we are affected and tormented with greater concern for body than for soul, many who venture to entrust the soul to God are still troubled about the flesh, still worry about what they shall eat, what they shall wear, and unless they have on hand abundance of wine, grain, and oil, tremble with apprehension. So much more does the shadow of this fleeting life mean to us than that everlasting immortality! Those who, relying upon God, have once for all cast out the anxiety about the care of the flesh, immediately expect from him greater things, even salvation and eternal life. [187] It is, then, no light exercise of faith for us to hope for those things from God which otherwise cause us such anxiety. And we benefit greatly when we put off this faithlessness, which sinks its teeth into the very bones of almost all men [Matt. 6:25-33].

24. Accordingly, we ask our bread of our Father. Now because we say "daily" and "this day," we are taught not to long with immoderate desire for those fleeting things, which we afterward flamboyantly squander in sensual pleasure, show, or other appearance of luxury. But we are to ask only as much as is sufficient for our needs and as it were from day to day. We are to do so with this certain assurance, that as our Heavenly Father nourishes us today, he will not fail us tomorrow. (96) Consequently, however abundantly goods may flow to us, even when our storehouses are stuffed and our cellars full, we ought always to ask for our daily bread, counting all possessions nothing except insofar as the Lord, having poured out his blessing, makes it prosper and bear fruit. And what is in our hand is not even ours except insofar as he bestows each little portion upon us hour by hour, and allows us to use it. Yet those who, not content with daily bread but panting after countless things with unbridled desire, or sated with their abundance, or carefree in their piled-up riches, nonetheless [188] supplicate God with this prayer are but mocking him. For the first ones ask him for what they do not wish to receive, indeed, what they utterly abominate— namely, mere daily bread—and as much as possible cover up before God their propensity to greed, while true prayer ought to pour out before him the whole mind itself and whatever lies hidden within. But others ask of him what they long for least of all, that is, what they think they have within themselves. In calling the bread "ours," God's generosity stands forth the more, for it makes ours what is by no reckoning owed to us [cf. Deut. 8:18]. The fact we ask it be given us signifies that it is a simple and free gift of God, however it may come to us, even when seemingly obtained from our own skill and diligence and supplied by our own hands. /112/

Fifth Petition
"Forgive us our debts, as we forgive our debtors." [Matt. 6:12]

25. By this petition* we ask that we be granted forgiveness of sins, necessary for all men, without exception. We call sins "debts" because we owe penalty or payment for them to God, and we could in no way satisfy it unless we were released by this forgiveness [Rom. 3:23-24]. This free pardon comes

3.20.45

from his mercy, [189] when he himself generously wipes out these debts, and releases us from them, exacting no payment from us for them but making satisfaction to himself by his own mercy in Christ, who once for all gave himself as a ransom to the Father [cf. Rom. 3:24]. Therefore, those who trust that God is satisfied with their own or others' merits, and that by such satisfaction forgiveness of sins is paid for and purchased, share not at all in this free gift. And while they call upon God according to this form, they do nothing but subscribe to their own accusation, and seal their condemnation by their own testimony. For they confess they are debtors unless they are released by the benefit of forgiveness, which they still do not accept but rather spurn, while they thrust their merits and satisfactions upon God. For thus they do not entreat his mercy but call down his justice.

26. Finally, we petition that forgiveness (97) come to us, "as we forgive our debtors" [Matt. 6:12]: namely, as we spare and pardon those who have in any way injured us, either treating us unjustly in deed or insulting us in word. Not that it is ours to forgive them the guilt of transgression or offense, for this belongs to God alone [cf. Is. 43:25]! This, rather, is our forgiveness: willingly to cast from the mind wrath, hatred, desire for revenge, and voluntarily to banish to oblivion the remembrance of injustice. For this reason, we ought not to seek forgiveness of sins [190] from God unless we ourselves also forgive the offenses against us of all those who do or have done us ill. If we retain feelings of hatred in our hearts, if we plot revenge and ponder any occasion to cause harm, and even if we do not try to get back into our enemies' good graces, by every sort of good office deserve well of them, and commend ourselves to them, by this prayer we entreat God not to forgive our sins. For we ask that he do to us as we do to others [Matt. 7:12]. This, indeed, is to petition him not to forgive us unless we ourselves forgive. What do people of this sort gain from their petition but a heavier judgment? Finally, we must note that this condition—that he "forgive us as we forgive our debtors" [Matt. 6:12]—is not added because by the forgiveness we grant to others we deserve his forgiveness. Rather, by this word /113/ the Lord intended only to comfort the weakness of our faith. For he has added this as a sign to assure us he has forgiven our sins just as surely as we are aware of having forgiven those of others, provided our hearts have been emptied and purged of all hatred, envy, and vengeance. Moreover, it is by this mark, as it were, that the Lord has excluded from the number of his children those persons who, being eager for revenge and slow to forgive [191] practice persistent enmity and foment against others the very indignation they pray to be averted in God. This the Lord does that such men dare not call upon him as Father.

Sixth Petition
"Lead us not into temptation, but free us from the evil one." [Matt. 6:13a]

3.20.46

27. The forms of temptation are many and varied. For wicked conceptions of the heart, provoking us to transgress the law, which either our own inordinate

desire suggests to us or the devil prompts, are temptations. These are not evil of their own nature yet become temptations through the devil's devices, when they are so thrust before our eyes that by their appearance we are drawn away or turn aside from God [James 1:2, 14; cf. Matt. 4:1, 3; I Thess. 3:5]. And these temptations are either from the right or from the left [cf. Prov. 4:27]. From the right are, for example, riches, power, honors, which often dull men's keenness of sight by the glitter and seeming goodness (98) they display, and allure with their blandishments, so that, captivated by such tricks and drunk with such sweetness men forget their God. From the left are, for example, poverty, disgrace, contempt, afflictions and the like. Thwarted by the hardship and difficulty of these, they become despondent in mind, cast away assurance and hope, and are at last completely estranged from God. We pray God, our Father, not to let us yield to these temptations which, either aroused in us by our inordinate desire or proposed to us [192] by the devil's guile, war against us. We pray, rather, that he sustain by his hand and encourage us so that, strengthened by his power, we may be able to stand firm against all the assaults of our malign enemy, whatever thoughts he may introduce into our minds. And we pray that whatever is presented to us tending either way we may turn to good—namely, that we may not be puffed up in prosperity or cast down in adversity. But we do not here ask that we feel no temptations at all, for we very much need, rather, to be aroused, pricked, and urged by them, lest with overmuch inactivity, we grow sluggish [James 1:2]. For it is not beside the point that David wished to be tempted [cf. Ps. 26:2], and it is not without cause /114/ that the Lord daily tests his elect [Gen. 22:1; Deut. 8:2; 13:3, Vg.], chastising them by disgrace, poverty, tribulation, and other sorts of affliction. But God tries in one way, Satan in another. Satan tempts that he may destroy, condemn, confound, cast down. But God tempts that he may prove and exercise his own children; that he may mortify, purify, and cauterize their flesh, which unless it were forced under this restraint would play the wanton and vaunt itself beyond measure. Besides, Satan attacks those who are unarmed and unprepared that he may crush them unaware. God, along with the temptation, provides a way of escape, that his own may be able patiently to bear all that he imposes upon them [I Cor. 10:13; II Pet. 2:9].

28. This then is our plea: that we may not be vanquished or overwhelmed by any temptations, [193] but may by the Lord's power stand fast against all hostile powers that attack us. This is not to yield to temptations. Our plea is that, received into his care and safekeeping and secure in his protection, we may stand unconquered over sin, death, the gates of hell [Matt. 16:28], and the devil's whole kingdom. This is to be freed from the evil one. Here we must carefully note that it is not in our power to engage that great warrior the devil in combat, or to bear his force and onslaught. Otherwise it would be pointless or a mockery to ask of God what we already have in ourselves. Obviously those who prepare for such a combat with self-assurance do not sufficiently understand with what a ferocious and well-equipped enemy they have to deal. Now we seek to be freed from his power, as from the jaws of a mad and raging lion [I Pet. 5:8];

if the Lord did not snatch us from the midst of death, we could not help being immediately torn to pieces by his fangs and claws, and swallowed down his throat. Yet we know that if the Lord be with us, and fight for us while we keep still, "in his might we shall do mightily" [Ps. 60:12; cf. 107:14]. Let others trust as they will in their free will and in those powers (99) which they have of themselves. For us let it be enough that we stand and are strong in God's power alone.

3.20.47   29. These three petitions, in which we especially commend to God ourselves and our possessions, clearly show what we have previously said: [194] that the prayers of Christians ought to be public, and to look to the public upbuilding of the church, and the advancement of the believers' fellowship. For each man does not pray that something be given to him privately, but all of us in common ask our bread, forgiveness of sins, not to be led into temptation, and to be freed from the evil one. Moreover, there is added the reason why we should be so bold to ask and so confident of receiving. /115/

"Thine is the kingdom, and the power and the glory, forever." [Matt. 6:13b]

30. This, this is firm and tranquil repose for our faith. For if our prayers were to be commended to God by our worth, who would dare even mutter at all in God's presence? Now, however miserable we may be, though unworthiest of all, however devoid of all commendation, we will yet never lack a reason to pray, never be shorn of assurance, since his Kingdom, power, and glory can never be snatched away from our Father.

At the end is added, "Amen" [Matt. 6:13, marg.]. By it is expressed the warmth of desire to obtain what we have asked of God. And our hope is strengthened that all things of this sort have already been brought to pass, and will surely be granted to us, since they have been promised by God, who cannot deceive.

C. THE PRACTICE OF PRAYER

3.20.48   31. We have everything we ought, [195] or are at all able, to seek of God, set forth in this form and, as it were, rule for prayer handed down by our best Master, Christ, whom the Father has appointed our teacher and whom alone he would have us heed and hearken to [Matt. 17:5]. For he both has always been the eternal Wisdom of God [Is. 11:2] and, made man, has been given to men, the angel of great counsel [Is. 9:6, conflated with ch. 28:29 and Jer. 32:19].

And this prayer is in all respects so perfect that any extraneous or alien thing added to it, which cannot be related to it, is impious and unworthy to be conceded by God. For in this summary he has set forth what is worthy of him, acceptable to him, necessary for us—in effect, what he would willingly grant.

For this reason, those who dare go beyond and ask anything from God apart from this; first, indeed wish to add to God's wisdom from their own store— something that cannot happen without insane blasphemy; secondly, do not confine themselves within God's will, but, holding it in contempt, stray farther away in their uncontrolled desire; lastly, will never obtain anything, since they pray without faith. But doubtless all such prayers are made apart from faith, for in these the word of God is absent, upon which faith, if it is to stand at all, must always rely. But these persons not only lack God's word but contend against it with all their strength. (100)

We would not have it understood [196] that we are so bound by this form of prayer that we are not allowed to change it in either word or syllable. For here and there in Scripture one reads many prayers, far different from it in words, yet composed by the same Spirit, the use of which is very profitable to us. In so teaching, we mean only this: that no man should ask for, expect, or demand, anything at all except what is included, by way of summary, in this prayer; and though the words may be utterly different, the sense ought not to vary. In this way it is certain all prayers contained in Scripture are referred to it. /116/ Truly, no other can ever be found that equals this in perfection, much less surpasses it. Here nothing is left out that ought to be thought of in praising God, nothing that ought to come into man's mind for his own advantage. And, indeed, it is so precisely framed that hope of attempting anything better is rightly taken away from all men. To sum up, let us remember that this is the teaching of Divine Wisdom, teaching what it willed and willing what was needful.

3.20.49

32. But, although it has already been stated above that, lifting up our hearts, we should ever aspire to God and pray without ceasing [I Thess. 5:17], still, since our weakness is such that it has to be supported by many aids, and our sluggishness such that it needs to be goaded, it is fitting each one of us should set apart certain hours for this exercise. [197] Those hours should not pass without prayer, and during them all the devotion of the heart should be completely engaged in it. These are: when we arise in the morning, before we begin daily work, when we sit down to a meal, when by God's blessing we have eaten, when we are getting ready to retire. But this must not be any superstitious observance of hours, whereby, as if paying our debt to God, we imagine ourselves paid up for the remaining hours. Rather, it must be a tutelage for our weakness, which should be thus exercised and repeatedly stimulated. We must take particular care that, whenever we either are pressed or see others pressed by any adversity, we hasten back to God, not with swift feet but with eager hearts. Then, that we should not let our prosperity or that of others go unnoticed, failing to testify, by praise and thanksgiving, that we recognize God's hand therein.

3.20.50

33. Lastly, in all prayer we ought carefully to observe that our intention is not to bind God to particular circumstances, or to prescribe at what time, in what place, or in what way he is to do anything. Accordingly, in this prayer we are taught not to make any law for him, or impose any condition upon him, but to leave to his decision to do what he is going to do, in what way, at what time, and in what place it seems good to him. Meanwhile, before we frame any prayer

for ourselves, [198] we pray that his will be done [Matt. 6:10]. By these words we subject our will to his in order that, restrained as by a bridle, it may not presume to control God but may make him the arbiter and director of all its entreaties.

3.20.51   If, with hearts (101) composed to this obedience, we allow ourselves to be ruled by the laws of divine providence, we shall readily learn to persevere in prayer and, with desires suspended, patiently to wait for the Lord. Then we shall be sure that, even though he does not appear, he is always present to us, and will in his own time declare how he has never turned deaf ears to the prayers that in men's eyes he seems to have neglected. /117/ This, then, will be an ever-present consolation: that, if God should not respond to our first requests, we may not faint or fall into despair. Such is the wont of those who, carried away with their own ardor, so call upon God that unless he attends upon their first act of prayer and brings them help at once, they immediately fancy him angry and hostile toward them and, abandoning all hope of being heard, cease to call upon him. Also, let us not tempt God and, wearing him with our depravity, provoke him against ourselves. This is usual with many who covenant with God only under certain conditions, and, as if he were the servant of their own appetites, bind him to laws of their own stipulation. If he does not obey them at once, [199] they become indignant, grumble, protest, murmur, and rage at him. To such, therefore, he often grants in wrath and fury what in mercy he denies to others to whom he is favorable. The children of Israel supply proof of this, for whom it would have been much better not to be heard by the Lord than to swallow his wrath with their meat [Num. 11:18, 33].

3.20.52   But if finally even after long waiting our senses cannot learn the benefit received from prayer, or perceive any fruit from it, still our faith will make us sure of what cannot be perceived by sense, that we have obtained what was expedient. And so he will cause us to possess abundance in poverty, and comfort in affliction. For though all things fail us, yet God will never forsake us, who cannot disappoint the expectation and patience of his people. He alone will be for us in place of all things, since all good things are contained in him and he will reveal them to us on the Day of Judgment, when his Kingdom will be plainly manifested. But believers need to be sustained by this patience, since they would not long stand unless they relied upon it. For the Lord proves his people by no light trials, and does not softly exercise them, but often drives them to extremity, and allows them, so driven, to lie a long time in the mire before he gives them any taste of his sweetness. And, as Hannah [200] says, "He kills and brings to life; he brings down to hell and brings back" [I Sam. 2:6 p.]. What could they do here but be discouraged and rush into despair if they were not—when afflicted, desolate, and already half dead—revived by the thought that God has regard for them and will bring an end to their present misfortunes? (102) /118/

CHAPTER IV

THE SACRAMENTS

A. THE SACRAMENTS IN GENERAL

1. On the nature of the sacraments, it is very important for us that some 4.14.1
definite doctrine be taught, to learn from it both the purpose for which they
were instituted and their present use. First, what is a sacrament? An outward
sign by which the Lord represents and attests to us his good will toward us to
sustain the weakness of our faith? Another definition: a testimony of God's grace,
declared to us by an outward sign. From this we also understand a sacrament 4.14.3
never lacks a preceding promise but is rather [201] joined to it by way of
appendix, to confirm and seal the promise itself, and to make it as it were more
evident to us. Thus God provides for the ignorance of our mind and for the
weakness of our flesh. Yet, it is not so much needed to confirm God's truth as
to establish us in it. For it is of itself firm and sure enough, and cannot receive
better confirmation from any other source than itself. But as our faith is slight
and feeble unless propped on all sides and sustained by every means, it trembles,
wavers, totters. Here our merciful Lord so tempers himself to our capacity* that
(since we are creatures who always creep on the ground, cleave to the flesh, and
do not think about or even conceive of anything spiritual) he leads us to himself
even by these earthly elements, and in the flesh itself causes us to contemplate
the things that are of his Spirit. It is not because the gifts have been endowed
with the natures of things set forth to us in the sacraments, but because sealed
by God to this signification. We must not listen to those who argue by such a 4.14.5
cavil as this. We either know, they say, or do not know that God's word preceding
the sacrament is His true will. If we know it, we learn nothing new from the
sacrament, which follows. If we do not know it, the sacrament (whose whole
force and energy rest in the word) also will not teach it? [202] To them here is
a brief answer: the seals attached to government documents and other public
acts are nothing taken by themselves, for they would be attached in vain if the
parchment had nothing written on it. Yet, added to the writing, they do not on
that account fail to confirm and seal what is written. And our adversaries* cannot
boast that this comparison has been recently devised by us, /119/ since Paul
himself used it, calling circumcision a "seal"* [Rom. 4:11].

87

4.14.6   Since the Lord calls his promises "covenants" [Gen. 6:18; 9:9; 17:2] and his sacraments "tokens" of the covenants, a simile can be taken from the covenants of men. (103) What can the slaughter of a sow accomplish unless words accompany the act, indeed, unless they precede it? For sows are often slain apart from any inner or loftier mystery. What can giving the right hand accomplish when hands are often joined in battle? Yet when words precede, the laws of covenants are by such signs obviously ratified, although they were first conceived, established, and decreed in words.

2. The sacraments, therefore, are exercises which make us more certain of the trustworthiness of God's Word. And because we are of flesh, they are shown us under things of flesh, to instruct us according to our dull capacity, and to lead us by the hand as tutors lead children. Augustine calls a sacrament "a visible word" for the reason that it represents God's promises [203] as painted in a picture and sets them before our sight, portrayed graphically and in the manner of images. Likewise, other comparisons can be adduced to designate the sacraments more plainly; thus we might call them "the pillars of our faith." For as a building stands and rests upon its own foundation but is more surely established by columns placed underneath, so faith rests upon the Word of God as upon a foundation; but when the sacraments are added, it rests more firmly upon them as upon columns. Or we might call them mirrors in which we may contemplate the riches of God's grace, which he lavishes upon us. For by them he manifests himself to us (as has already been said) as far as it is given to our dullness to perceive, and attests his good will toward us.

4.14.7   Not reasoning closely enough are those who argue that the sacraments are not testimonies of God's grace because they are also offered to the wicked, who, however, do not at all find God more favorable toward themselves but rather incur a heavier condemnation. For by the same argument, because the gospel is heard but rejected by many, and because Christ was seen and recognized by many but very few of them accepted him, neither gospel nor Christ himself would be a testimony of God's grace. It is therefore certain that the Lord offers us mercy and the grace of his good will both in his Sacred Word [204] and in his sacraments. But it is understood only by those who take Word and sacraments with sure faith, just as Christ was offered and held forth by the Father to all for their salvation, /120/ yet not all acknowledged and received him. In one place Augustine, meaning to convey this, said that the efficacy of the Word is brought to light in the sacrament, not because it is spoken, but because it is believed. We have determined, therefore, that sacraments have been set forth by God in order to serve our faith, namely, to nourish, exercise, and increase it.

3. The reasons which some are accustomed to raise against this opinion are too weak and trifling. Some say that our faith cannot be made better if it is already good, for it is not faith unless it leans unshaken, firm, and steadfast upon God's mercy. It would have been better for them to pray with the apostles that the Lord increase their faith [Luke 17:5] than stolidly to pretend such perfection of faith as no one (104) of the children of men ever attained or ever will attain

88

in this life. Let them answer what sort of faith they think he had who said, "I believe, O Lord; help thou my unbelief" [Mark 9:24]. For that faith, although as yet incomplete, was good and could have been made better once unbelief was taken away. But they will be refuted by no surer argument than their own conscience. For if they confess themselves sinners [205] (which, willy-nilly, they cannot deny), they must charge it to the imperfection of their own faith.

Yet, they say, Philip answers the eunuch that he was permitted to be baptized if he believed with all his heart [Acts 8:37]. What place does confirmation of baptism have here, where faith fills the whole heart? On the other hand, I ask them whether they do not feel a good portion of their heart devoid of faith, and whether they do not daily acknowledge new increases? An eminent man boasted that he grew old, learning. We are therefore thrice miserable Christians if we grow old without advancement, for our faith ought to progress through all stages of our life until it grows to full manhood [Eph. 4:13]. Accordingly, in this passage, to "believe with all our heart" is not to cleave to Christ perfectly, but only to embrace him from the heart and with a sincere mind; not to be sated with him, but to hunger, thirst, and aspire after him with fervent affection. It is customary in Scripture to speak of something as done "with the whole heart:" this means "sincerely and deeply." Of this sort are the following: "With my whole heart I have sought thee" [Ps. 119:10] likewise, "I shall confess unto thee with my whole heart"; and the like [Ps. 111:1; 138:1 p.]. 4.14.8

4. Others write: if faith be increased through sacraments, the Holy Spirit was given in vain, whose power and work is /121/ to begin, sustain, and consummate faith. I certainly admit to them that faith is the proper and entire work of the Holy Spirit, illumined by whom we recognize God [206] and the treasures of his kindness, and without whose light our mind is so blinded that it can see nothing; so dull that it can sense nothing of spiritual things. But for one blessing of God which they proclaim, we recognize three. For first, the Lord teaches and instructs us by his Word. Secondly, he confirms it by the sacraments. Finally, he illumines our minds by the light of his Holy Spirit and opens our hearts for the Word and sacraments to enter in, which would otherwise only strike our ears and appear before our eyes, but not at all affect us within.

Sacraments, moreover, are so much confirmations of our faith that the Lord sometimes, when he would remove confidence in the very things being promised in the sacraments, takes away the sacraments themselves. When He deprives Adam of the gift of immortality and withdraws it from him, He says, "Let him not take of the fruit of life, lest he live forever" [Gen. 3:22 p.]. What do we hear? Could that fruit restore to Adam his incorruption, from which he had already fallen? Not at all! But this is just as if the Lord had said, "Lest he enjoy vain confidence by clinging to the symbol of my promise, (105) let that which could bring him any hope of immortality be removed from him." For this reason, when the apostle urged the Ephesians to remember that they were "strangers to the covenants, foreigners to the commonwealth of Israel, without God and without Christ" [Eph. 2:12 p.], [207] he said that they had not been 4.14.12

participants in the circumcision [Eph. 2:11]. In this he signifies by metonymy that those who had not received the token of the promise were excluded from the promise itself.

To their other objection—that God's glory passes down to the creatures, and so much power is attributed to them, and his glory is thus to this extent diminished—our answer is ready: we place no power in creatures. I say only this: God uses means and instruments which he himself sees to be expedient, that all things may serve his glory, since he is Lord and Judge of all. He therefore feeds our bodies through bread and other foods, he illumines the world through the sun, and he warms it through heat; yet neither bread, nor sun, nor fire, is anything save in so far as he distributes his blessings to us by these instruments. In like manner, he nourishes faith spiritually through the sacraments, whose one function is to set God's promises before our eyes to be looked upon. And it is our duty to put no confidence in other creatures which have been destined for our use by God's good will, and through whose ministry he lavishes the gifts of his bounty upon us; nor to admire and proclaim them as the causes of our good. In the same way, neither ought our confidence to inhere in the sacraments, nor the glory of God /122/ be transferred to them. Rather, laying aside all things, both our faith and our confession ought to rise up to him, the author of the sacraments and of all things.

4.14.13   5. Some seek from the very term "sacrament," [208] a pretext for their error, but they do it very unwisely. Sacrament, they say, although it has many senses among reputable authors, has only one that accords with "signs." That is, it signifies the solemn oath the soldier took to the commander when he entered military service. For as recruits bind their fealty to their commander by this military oath and make profession of military service, so by our signs do we profess Christ our commander, and testify that we serve under his ensign. They add comparisons by which they make the matter clearer. As the Romans were distinguished by the toga from the pallium-clad Greeks, as at Rome the orders were differentiated from each other by their insignia (the senatorial from the knightly class by purple and by crescent-shaped shoes, and the knights in turn from the common people by a ring)—so we wear our symbols to distinguish us from profane men. Yet I steadfastly declare that the fathers who applied the name "sacraments" to signs had given no attention at all to the use of this word by Latin writers, but invented this new meaning for their own convenience, simply to designate sacred signs by it.

6. But if we wish to investigate more deeply, they can be seen to have transferred the term to the meaning (106) now in use by the same analogy as that which appears in the use of the word "faith." For although faith is [209] truthfulness in carrying out promises, yet they have called it certainty or sure persuasion which one has of truth itself. In this way, while the "sacrament" was the soldier's act of vowing himself to his commander, they made it the commander's act of receiving soldiers into the ranks. For by the sacraments the Lord promises that "he will be our God and we shall be his people" [II Cor. 6:16;

Ezek. 37:27]. But we pass over such subtleties, since I can indeed show with many and indeed plain arguments that in using the word "sacraments," the fathers had no other intention than to signify that they are signs of holy and spiritual things. We accept the comparisons which our adversaries bring forward, but we do not tolerate that what is secondary in the sacraments be regarded by them as the first and even the only point. Now, the first point is that the sacraments should serve our faith before God; after this, that they should attest our confession before men. As applied to this latter consideration, these comparisons have validity. /123/

7. On the contrary, we must be reminded that, as these men weaken the force of the sacraments and completely overthrow their use, so, on the opposite side, there are those who attach to the sacraments some sort of secret powers with which one nowhere reads that God has endowed them. By this error the simple and unskilled are dangerously deceived, while they are both taught to seek God's gifts where they cannot be found, and are gradually drawn away from God to go off after vanity. [210] Those who propagate such teaching are of two sorts. The first have taught that the sacraments of the new law (those now used in the Christian church) justify and confer grace, provided we do not set up a barrier of mortal sin. How deadly and pestilential this notion is cannot be expressed—and the more so because for many centuries it has obtained in a good part of the world, to the great loss of the church. Of a certainty it is diabolical. For in promising a righteousness apart from faith, it hurls souls headlong to confusion and judgment. Moreover, those immoderate praises of the sacraments which are read in ancient writers have deceived them. Such is Augustine's statement: "The sacraments of the old law only promised salvation; but ours give it." Failing to note that these and similar figures of speech were exaggerated, they also published their own exaggerated paradoxes, but in a sense wholly at variance from the writings of the ancients. For Augustine only meant there the same thing that he writes elsewhere: "The sacraments of the Mosaic law foretold Christ, but ours tell forth Christ." It is as if he had said: "Those represented him when he was still awaited; but ours show him as if present who has already been given." This can be easily adjudged, both by the very appearance of the passage, and from a certain homily, where he openly confesses that the sacraments of the Jews [211] (107) were different in their signs, but equal in the thing signified; different in visible appearance, but identical in spiritual power. Therefore, let it be regarded as a settled principle that the sacraments have the same office as the Word of God: /124/ to offer and set forth Christ to us, and in him the treasures of heavenly grace. But these avail and profit men nothing unless received by them in faith.

Others do not err so perniciously. Yet they do err. For they themselves believe that a hidden power is joined and fastened to the sacraments to distribute in them the graces of the Holy Spirit, just as wine is preferred in a cup. Actually, their sole office is to attest and confirm for us God's good will toward us. And they are of no further benefit unless the Holy Spirit accompanies them. For he

4.14.14

4.14.26

4.14.17

it is who opens our minds and hearts and makes us receptive to this testimony. There also varied and distinct graces of God brightly appear. For the sacraments are messengers which do not bring but announce and show those things given us by divine bounty. The Holy Spirit (whom the sacraments do not bring indiscriminately to all men but whom the Lord exclusively bestows on his own people) is he who brings the graces of God with him, gives a place for the sacraments among us, to make them bear fruit.

4.14.18   8. The term "sacrament," as [212] we have previously discussed its nature so far, embraces generally all those signs which God has ever signalled to men to render them more certain and confident of the truth of his promises. He sometimes willed to present these in natural things, at other times set them forth in miracles.

Here are some examples of the first kind. One is when he gave Adam and Eve the tree of life as a guarantee of immortality, that they might assure themselves of it as long as they should eat of its fruit [Gen. 2:9; 3:22]. Another, when he set the rainbow for Noah and his descendants, as a reminder that he would not thereafter destroy the earth with a flood [Gen. 9:13-16]. These, Adam and Noah regarded as sacraments. Not that the tree provided others with an immortality which it could not give to itself; nor that the rainbow (which is but a reflection of the sun's rays upon the clouds opposite) could be effective in holding back the waters; but because they had a mark engraved upon them by God's Word, so that they were proofs and seals of his covenants. And indeed the tree was previously a tree, the rainbow a rainbow. After they were inscribed by God's Word a new form was put upon them, so that they began to be what previously they were not. That no one may think these things said in vain, the rainbow even today is a witness to us of that covenant which the Lord made with Noah. As often as we look upon it, we read this promise of God in it, that the earth will never be destroyed by a flood. Therefore, if [213] any philosophizer, to mock the simplicity of our faith, (108) contends that such a variety of colors naturally arises /125/ from rays reflected upon a cloud opposite, let us indeed admit it, but laugh at his stupidity in failing to recognize God as the lord of nature, who according to his will uses all the elements to serve his glory. If he had imprinted such reminders upon the sun, stars, earth, stones, they would all be sacraments for us. Why are crude and coined silver not of the same value, though they are absolutely the same metal? The one is merely in the natural state; stamped with an official mark, it becomes a coin and receives a new valuation. And cannot God mark with his Word the things he has created, that what were previously bare elements may become sacraments?

Here are examples of the second kind: when, to promise Gideon the victory, he watered a fleece with dew while the earth was dry, and conversely bedewed the earth, leaving the fleece untouched [Judg. 6:37-38]; when he drew back the shadow of the sundial ten degrees to promise safety to Hezekiah [II Kings 20:9-11; Is. 38:7]. Since these things were done to support and confirm their feeble faith, they were also sacraments.

9. But our present intention is specifically to discuss those sacraments which the Lord willed to be ordinary in his church in order to nourish his own in one [214] faith and the confession of one faith. They were put, moreover, not only in signs, but in ceremonies. Or (if you prefer) the signs here given are ceremonies. Hence you could define sacraments of this sort as ceremonies by which the Lord wills to exercise and confirm the faith of his people. The sacraments themselves were also diverse, according to the varied dispensation of the times by which the Lord was pleased to reveal himself in one way or another to men. For circumcision was enjoined upon Abraham and his descendants [Gen. 17:10]. To it were afterward added purifications [Lev., chs. 11 to 15] and sacrifices [Lev. chs. 1 to 10] from the law of Moses. These were the sacraments of the Jews until the coming of Christ. When at his coming these were abrogated, two sacraments were instituted which the Christian church now uses, Baptism and the Lord's Supper*[Matt. 28:19; 26:26-28].

Yet those ancient sacraments looked to the same purpose to which ours now tend: to direct and almost lead men by the hand to Christ, or rather, as images, to represent him and set him forth to be known. We have already taught that they are seals by which God's promises are sealed, and, moreover, it is very clear that no promise has ever been offered to men except in Christ [II Cor. 1:20]. Consequently, to teach us about any promise of God, they must show forth Christ. There is only one [215] difference: the former foreshadowed Christ promised while he was as yet awaited; the latter attest him as already given and revealed. /126/ When these things are explained one by one, they will become much clearer. For the Jews, circumcision was the symbol to admonish them that whatever comes forth from man's seed, (109) that is, the nature of mankind, has been corrupted and needs pruning. Moreover, circumcision was a token and reminder to confirm them in the promise given to Abraham of the blessed seed in which all nations of the earth were to be blessed [Gen. 22:18], from which they were also to await their own blessing. Now that saving seed (as we are taught by Paul) was Christ [Gal. 3:16], in whom alone they trusted they were to recover what they had lost in Adam. Accordingly, circumcision was the same thing to them as in Paul's teaching it was to Abraham*, namely, a sign of the righteousness of faith [Rom. 4:11]; that is, a seal by which they were more certainly assured that their faith, with which they awaited that seed, is accounted to them as righteousness by God.

Baptisms and purifications disclosed to them their own uncleanness, foulness, and pollution, with which they had been defiled in their own nature; but these rites promised another cleansing to remove and wash away all their filth [Heb. 9:10,14]. And this cleansing was Christ. Washed by his blood [I John 1:7; Rev. 1:5], [216] we have been healed by his bruises [Is. 53:5; I Pet. 2:24]. Sacrifices made them aware of their unrighteousness and, at the same time, taught them that some satisfaction must be paid to God's justice. They were therefore taught that there should be some high priest, a mediator between God and men, to make satisfaction to God's justice by the shedding of blood and by the offering of a sacrifice to be received for the forgiveness of sins. This high priest was Christ [Heb. 4:14; 5:5; 9:11]; he poured out his own blood; he himself was the sacrificial victim; he offered himself obedient unto death, to the Father [Phil. 2:8]. By his obedience he canceled the disobedience of man [Rom. 5:19] which had aroused God's wrath.

4.14.22   10. As for our sacraments, the more closely Christ has been revealed to men, the more clearly do the sacraments present him to us from the time when he was truly revealed by the Father as he had been promised. For baptism attests to us that we have been cleansed and washed; the Eucharistic Supper, that we have been redeemed. In water, washing is represented; in blood, satisfaction. These two are found in Christ ". . . who," as John says, "came in water and blood" [I John 5:6]; that is, to wash and to redeem. The Spirit of God is also witness of this. Indeed, "there are three witnesses in one: the water, the blood, and the Spirit" [I John 5:8 p.]. In the water and the blood we have testimony of cleansing and redemption. But the Spirit, the primary witness, [217] makes us certain of such testimony. This lofty mystery has been admirably shown us in the cross of Christ, when water and blood flowed from his sacred side [John 19:34]. /127/ For this reason, Augustine* has called it the wellspring of our sacraments. Yet we shall have to discuss these things more amply. (110)

B. BAPTISM

4.15.1   11. Baptism was given to us by God: first, to serve our faith before him; secondly, to serve our confession before men. We shall treat in order the reason for both aspects of its institution. Baptism brings three things to our faith which must be dealt with individually.

    12. The first thing that the Lord sets out for us is that baptism should be a symbol and proof of our cleansing; or (that we may better explain it) be like a messenger sent to confirm to us that all our sins are so abolished, remitted, and effaced that they can never come to his sight, be recalled, or charged against us. For he wills that all who believe be baptized for the remission of sins [Matt. 28:19; Acts 2:38].

    13. Accordingly, they who dared write that baptism is nothing but a token and mark by which we confess our religion before [218] men, as soldiers bear the insignia of their commander as a mark of their profession*, have not weighed what was the chief point of baptism. It is that we are to receive baptism with

4.15.2   this promise: "He who believes and is baptized will be saved" [Mark 16:16]. In this sense we are to understand what Paul has written: that the church "has been sanctified" by Christ, the bridegroom, and "cleansed with the washing of water in the Word of life" [Eph. 5:26 p.]. And another passage: "He saved us . . . in virtue of his own mercy, through the washing of regeneration and of renewal in the Holy Spirit" [Titus 3:5]. And by Peter: "Baptism . . . saves us" [I Pet. 3:21 p.]. For Paul did not mean to signify that our cleansing and salvation are accomplished by water intervening, or that water is itself the instrument to cleanse, regenerate, and renew; nor that here is the cause of salvation, but only that in this sacrament are received the knowledge and certainty of such gifts. This the words themselves explain clearly enough. For Paul joins together the Word of life and the baptism of water, as if he said: "Through the gospel a message of our cleansing and sanctification is brought to us; /128/through such baptism the message is sealed." And Peter immediately adds that this baptism is not a removal of filth from the flesh but a good conscience before God [I Pet. 3:21], which is from faith.

14. But we are not to think [219] baptism conferred upon us only for past time, so that for newly committed sins into which we fall after baptism we must seek new remedies. In early times this error caused some to refuse the initiation by baptism unless in uttermost peril of life and at their last gasp, so that thus they might obtain pardon for their whole life. But we must realize that at whatever time we are baptized, we are once for all washed and purged for our whole life. Therefore, as often as we fall away, we ought to recall the memory of our baptism and fortify our heart with it, (111) that we may always be sure and confident of the forgiveness of sins. For, though baptism, administered only once, seemed to have passed, it was still not destroyed by subsequent sins. For Christ's purity has been offered us in it; his purity ever flourishes; it is defiled by no spots, but abolishes and cleanses away all our defilements. Now from this fact we ought not to take leave to sin in the future, as this has certainly not at all taught us to be so bold. Rather, this doctrine is only given to sinners who groan, wearied and forsaken under their own sins, in order that they may have something to lift them up and comfort them, so as not to plunge into confusion and despair. Paul speaks thus: "Christ was made our expiator for the forgiveness of past sins" [Rom. 3:25]. By this Paul does not deny [220] that we obtain in Christ continual and unceasing forgiveness of sins even unto death; but he indicates that he was given by the Father only to poor sinners who, wounded by the branding of conscience, sigh for the physician. To them the mercy of God is offered. Those who, counting on impunity, chase after the occasion and license to sin, provoke nothing but God's wrath and judgment.

4.15.3

15. Baptism also brings another consolation, for it shows us our mortification in Christ, and new life in him. Indeed (as the apostle says), "we have been baptized into his death," "buried with him into death, . . . that we may walk in newness of life" [Rom. 6:3-4 p.]. /129/ By these words he not only exhorts us to follow Christ as if he said that we are admonished through baptism by the example of Christ's death to die to our desires and by the example of his resurrection to be aroused to righteousness. But he also takes hold of something far higher, namely, that through baptism Christ makes us sharers in his death, that we may be engrafted in it [Rom. 6:5, cf. Vg.]. And, just as the twig draws substance and nourishment from the root to which it is grafted, so those who receive baptism with right faith truly feel the effective working of Christ's death in the mortification of their flesh, together with the working of his resurrection in the quickening of the Spirit [Rom. 6:8]. From this, Paul takes occasion for

4.15.5

exhortation: if we are Christians [221] we ought to be dead to sin and alive to righteousness [Rom. 6:11]. He uses this same argument in another place: we were circumcised and put off the old man after we were buried in Christ through

4.15.6 baptism [Col. 2:11-12]. And in this sense, in the passage which I have just quoted, he called it the washing of regeneration and of renewal [Titus 3:5]. So John first baptized, so later did the apostles, "with a baptism of repentance unto forgiveness of sins" [Matt. 3:6, 11; Luke 3:16; John 3:23; 4:1; Acts 2:38, 41]—

4.15.7 meaning by the word "repentance," such regeneration; and by "forgiveness of sins," cleansing. By this also we are utterly certain that John's ministry was exactly the same as that afterward committed to the apostles. For the different hands that administer baptism do not make it different; but the same doctrine shows it to be the same baptism. (112) John and the apostles agreed on one doctrine: both baptized to repentance, both to forgiveness of sins, both into the name of Christ, from whom repentance and forgiveness of sins came. John said that Christ was the Lamb of God, through whom the sins of the world would be taken away [John 1:29]. In this, he made also a sacrifice acceptable to the Father, and himself propitiator and savior. What could the apostles add to this

4.15.8 confession? What, then, is the meaning of John's statement that he baptizes with water but that Christ would come to baptize in the Holy Spirit and fire [Matt. 3:11; Luke 3:16]? [222] This can be explained in few words. John did not mean to distinguish one sort of baptism from another, but he compared his person with that of Christ—that he was a minister of water, but Christ the giver of the Holy Spirit; and that this power would be declared by a visible miracle on the day when he would send the Holy Spirit to the apostles under tongues of fire [Acts 2:3]. What could the apostles boast beyond this? And what those who baptize today? For they are only ministers of the outward sign, but Christ is the author of inward grace.

4.15.9 These things which we have said both of mortification and of washing were foreshadowed in the people of Israel, who were on this account said by the apostle to have been "baptized in the cloud and in the sea" [I Cor. 10:2]. /130/ Mortification was symbolized when the Lord, rescuing his people from the grasp and cruel bondage of Pharaoh, made a way for them through the Red Sea [Ex. 14:21] and drowned both Pharaoh himself and the Egyptian army, who were in hot pursuit and almost at their backs [Ex. 14:26-28]. For in the same way he also promises us in baptism and shows us by a sign given that by his power we have been led out and delivered from bondage in Egypt, that is, from the enslavement of sin; that our Pharaoh, that is, the devil, has been drowned, although he does not cease to harry us and weary us. As the Egyptian, however, was not cast into the depth of the sea, but left lying on the shore, [223] still terrified the Israelites by his frightful appearance, yet could not harm them [Ex. 14:30-31], so too this enemy of ours still threatens, brandishes his weapons, is felt, but cannot conquer. In the cloud [Num. 9:15; Ex. 13:21] there was a symbol of cleansing. For as the Lord covered them with a cloud and gave them coolness, that they might not weaken and pine away in the merciless heat of the sun, so do we recognize that in baptism we are covered and protected by Christ's blood, that God's severity, which is truly an unbearable flame, may not assail us.

16. Now, it is very clear how false is the teaching, propagated by some, that through baptism we are released and made exempt from original sin, and from the corruption that descended from Adam into all his posterity; and are restored into that same righteousness and purity of nature which Adam would have obtained if he had remained upright as he had first been created. For teachers of this type never understood what original sin, what original righteousness, or what the grace of baptism was. Original sin is the depravity and corruption of our nature, which first renders us liable to God's wrath, then (113) also gives rise in us to what Scripture calls "works of the flesh" [Gal. 5:19]. And that is what is properly called "sin" in the Scriptures. The works that come forth therefrom—such as adulteries, fornications, thefts, hatreds, contentions, murders, carousings—[224] ought according to this reckoning to be called "fruits of sin" [Gal. 5:19-21], although they are also often called "sins" in Scripture. 4.15.10

4.15.10

2.1.8

17. We must therefore carefully note these two points. First, as we are vitiated and corrupted in all parts of our nature, we are held rightly condemned on account of such corruption alone and convicted before God, to whom nothing is acceptable but righteousness, /131/ innocence, and purity. Even infants bear their condemnation with them out from their mother's womb [Ps. 51:5]; though they have not yet brought forth the fruits of their own iniquity, they have the seed enclosed within themselves. Indeed, their whole nature is a seed of sin; thus it cannot but be hateful and abominable to God. Through baptism, believers are assured that this condemnation has been removed and withdrawn from them, since (as was said) the Lord promises us by this sign that full and complete remission has been made, both of the guilt that should have been imputed to us, and of the punishment that we ought to have undergone because of the guilt. They also lay hold on righteousness, but such righteousness as the people of God can obtain in this life, that is, by imputation only, since the Lord of his own mercy considers them righteous and innocent. 4.15.10

Secondly, this perversity never ceases in us, but continually gives birth to new fruits [Rom. 7]—which we have previously described as "works of the flesh" [Gal. 5:19] [225]—just as a glowing furnace continually emits flame and sparks, or a spring ceaselessly gives forth water. Thus those who have defined original sin as "the lack of original righteousness" have still not expressed effectively enough its power and energy. For our nature is not only destitute and empty of good, but so fertile and fruitful of every evil that it cannot be idle. Those who have said that original sin is "concupiscence" have used a not too foreign word, if only they added—something they will by no means concede— that whatever is in man, from the understanding to the will, from the soul even to the flesh, has been defiled and crammed with this concupiscence. Or, to put it more briefly, the whole man is of himself nothing but concupiscence. For lust of this sort never actually dies and is extinguished in men until, freed by death 4.15.11

2.1.8

4.15.11

from the body of death, they are completely divested of themselves. Baptism indeed promises us the drowning of our Pharaoh [Ex. 14:28] and the mortification of our sin, but not so that it no longer exists or gives us trouble, but only that it may not overcome us. For so long as we live cooped up in this prison of our body, traces of sin will dwell in us; but if we faithfully hold fast to the promise given us by God in baptism, they shall not dominate or rule. [226] (114)

18. But let no one deceive himself, let no one cajole himself in his sinfulness, when he hears that sin always dwells in us. We do not /132/ say these things that sinners should slumber untroubled in their sins, but only that those who are disturbed, exercized, and pricked by their own flesh should not faint and be discouraged. Let them rather think that they are still on the road, and believe that they have made good progress when they feel that a bit is being taken away from their concupiscence each day, until they reach their destination, that is, the final death of their flesh, which shall be accomplished in the close of this mortal life. So, therefore, must we believe: we are baptized into the mortification of our flesh, which begins with our baptism and which we pursue day by day and which will, moreover, be accomplished when from this life we pass to the Lord.

4.15.6   19. Lastly, our faith receives from baptism the consolation of its sure testimony to us that we are not only engrafted into the death and life of Christ, but so united and joined to Christ himself that we become sharers in all his blessings. For he dedicated and sanctified baptism in his own body [Matt. 3:13] in order that he might have it in common with us as the firmest bond of the union and fellowship which he has deigned to enter into with us. Hence, Paul proves that we are children of God from the fact that we put on Christ in baptism [Gal. 3:26-27]. [227]

4.15.13   20. Moreover baptism thus serves as our confession before men. Indeed, it is the mark by which we publicly profess that we wish to be reckoned God's people; by which we testify that we agree in worshiping the same God, in one religion with all Christians; by which finally we openly affirm our faith. Thus not only do our hearts breathe the praise of God, but our tongues also and all members of our body sound his praise in every way they can. For thus, as is fitting, all our faculties are employed to serve God's glory, which ought to lack nothing, and by our example others are aroused to the same efforts. Paul had this in mind when he asked the Corinthians whether they had not been baptized in Christ's name [I Cor. 1:13]. He thus implied that, in being baptized in Christ's name, they had devoted themselves to him, sworn allegiance to his name, and pledged their fealty to him before men. As a result, they could no longer confess any other but Christ alone, unless they chose to renounce the confession they had made in baptism.

4.15.14   21. Now that we have explained our Lord's purpose in ordaining baptism, it will be easy for us to judge how we should use and receive it. For inasmuch as it is given for the consoling and confirming of our faith, it is to be received as from the hand of God. We ought to deem it certain and proved that it is God who speaks to us through the sign; [228] that it is he who purifies, washes away and wipes out the remembrance of sins; that it is he who makes us sharers in the death of his Son, who weakens the power of Satan and of our lust; /133/ indeed, who clothes us with his Son. These things, I say, (115) he does for our soul within as truly and surely as we see our body outwardly cleansed, submerged, and surrounded with water. For this analogy or similitude is the surest rule of the sacraments: that we should see and ponder spiritual things in physical. For the Lord was pleased to represent them by such figures—not because such graces are bound and enclosed in the sacrament or because the sacrament is an organ and instrument to confer them upon us, but only because the Lord by this token attests his will toward us, namely, that he is pleased to lavish all these things upon us.

Let us take as proof of this, Cornelius the centurion, who, having already received forgiveness of sins and the visible graces of the Holy Spirit, was baptized [Acts 10:48]. He did not seek an ampler forgiveness of sins from baptism, but a surer exercise of faith. Perhaps someone will object: why, then, did Ananias tell Paul to wash away his sins through baptism [Acts 22:16; cf. ch. 9:17-18] if sins are not washed away by baptism? I reply: we are said to receive, obtain, and acquire what we believe given to us by God, whether we then first recognize it, [229] or become more certain of it as previously recognized. Ananias meant only this: "To be assured, Paul, that your sins are forgiven, be baptized. For the Lord promises forgiveness of sins in baptism; receive it, and be secure." But from this sacrament, we obtain only as much as we receive in faith. If we lack faith, this will be evidence of our being accused before God, of not having believed the promise given there. But as far as it is a symbol of our confession, we ought by it to testify that our confidence is in God's mercy, and our purity in forgiveness of sins, which is through Jesus Christ; and that we enter God's church in order to live harmoniously with all believers in complete agreement of faith and love. This was what Paul meant when he said, "We have all been baptized in one Spirit that we may be one body" [I Cor. 12:13 p.]. 4.15.15

22. Now, suppose what we have determined is true—that a sacrament must not be taken from the hand of the one by whom it is ministered, but as if it were from the very hand of God, from whom it doubtless is sent. From this we may then infer that nothing is added to it or taken from it by the worth of him by whose hand it is administered. For example, among men, if a letter is sent—provided the handwriting and seal are sufficiently recognized—it makes no difference who or of what sort the carrier is. [230] In like manner, it ought to be enough for us to recognize the hand and seal of our Lord in his sacraments, whatever carrier may bring them. This argument neatly refutes the error of the Donatists, who measured the force and value /134/ of the sacrament by the worth of the minister. Such today are our Catabaptists, who deny that we have been duly baptized because we were baptized by impious and idolatrous men under the papal government. They therefore passionately urge rebaptism. 4.15.16

We shall be armed against their follies (116) with a strong enough argument if we think of ourselves as initiated by baptism not into the name of any man, but into the name of the Father and of the Son and of the Holy Spirit [Matt. 28:19]; and that baptism is accordingly not of man but of God, no matter who administers it. However ignorant or contemptuous those who baptized us were of God, they did not baptize us into the fellowship of either their ignorance or sacrilege, but into faith in Jesus Christ, because it was not their own name but God's that they invoked, and they baptized us into no other name. But if it was the baptism of God, it surely had the promise of forgiveness of sins, mortification of the flesh, spiritual quickening, and participation in Christ.

4.15.17 Now our opponents ask us what faith came to us during some years after our baptism. This they do to prove our baptism void, since it is not sanctified to us except when the word of promise [231] is accepted in faith. To this question we reply that we indeed, being blind and unbelieving, for a long time did not grasp the promise that had been given us in baptism; yet that promise, since it was of God, ever remained fixed and firm and trustworthy. Even if all men are liars and faithless, still God does not cease to be trustworthy [Rom. 3:3]. Even if all men are lost, still Christ remains salvation. We therefore confess that for that time baptism benefited us not at all, inasmuch as the promise offered us in it—without which baptism is nothing—lay neglected. Now when, by God's grace, we begin to repent, we accuse our blindness and hardness of heart—we who were for so long ungrateful toward his great goodness. But we believe that the promise itself did not vanish. Rather, we consider that God through baptism promises us forgiveness of sins, and he will doubtless fulfill his promise for all believers. This promise was offered to us in baptism; therefore, let us embrace it by faith. Indeed, on account of our unfaithfulness it lay long buried from us; now, therefore, let us receive it through faith.

4.15.18 But they fancy they are hurling a fiery dart at us when they assert that Paul rebaptized those who had once been baptized with John's baptism [Acts 19:2-7]. For suppose, by our confession, John's baptism and that which is now [232] ours are one and the same. Then, as those persons who had previously been wrongly instructed, after they were taught the right faith, were rebaptized into it, that baptism which was without true doctrine must be counted as nothing, and we ought to be baptized all over again into the true religion which we have now tasted for the first time.

I admit that that previous baptism was the true baptism of John /135/ and one and the same as the baptism of Christ, but I deny that they were rebaptized. What mean the words, "They were baptized in the name of Jesus" [Acts 19:5]? Some interpret it to mean they were only instructed with genuine doctrine by Paul; but I prefer to understand it more simply, that it is the baptism of the Holy Spirit, that is, the visible graces of the Spirit given through the laying on of hands. It is nothing new to signify these graces by the word "baptism." (117)

And what is afterward added does not conflict: "When he had laid his hands upon them, the Holy Spirit descended upon them" [Acts 19:6 p.]. For

Luke is not telling two different things, but he is following the form of narration familiar to the Hebrews, who first put forward a summary of the matter and then explain it more fully. Anyone can observe this from the context itself. For it is said: ". . . when they had heard these things, they were baptized in Jesus' name. And when Paul had laid his hands upon them then, the Holy Spirit descended upon them." [Acts 19:5-6] This latter expression describes the nature of the baptism.

23. But, from this [233] it has been said that there are two parts to the use of the sacrament: first, to instruct us in the Lord's promises; secondly, for us to confess our faith among men. It could then be doubted why the children of Christians are baptized while as yet infants who seem incapable of being taught anything by such numerous proofs, nor do they seem to have inwardly conceived a faith to which they can give outward testimony. We shall explain the reason for infant baptism in a few words.

Of those whom the Lord recalls in infancy from this mortal life, he makes some directly heirs of the heavenly kingdom. Now, eternal blessedness consists in the knowledge of God. Why then could he not here and now give some taste and first fruits of that good to those who are going one day to enjoy it fully? Why could he not be seen in a mirror and obscurely by those, by whom he will one day be seen face to face [I Cor. 13:12]? If we cannot comprehend it, let us ponder how wonderful are all his works, and how unfathomable his counsels to our minds.

Moreover, if we confess (something it is certainly necessary to confess) that even from this age vessels of mercy are chosen by the Lord [Rom. 5:1], we cannot deny faith to be the sole path to salvation [Hab. 2:4]. For if we live in Christ, and indeed through faith, when we depart from faith [234] we can do nothing but die in Adam [Rom. 1:17]. For the testimony is clear: "He who believes and is baptized will be saved; he who does not believe has already been condemned" [Mark 16:16]. Some persons, from the position of this passage, contend that this statement only is to be referred to those who were of sufficient age to be able to heed the gospel preaching, because in that passage the Apostles are sent out to preach the gospel; then it follows: /136/ "He who believes . . . will be saved." That means, they say, him to whom it will have been preached; but one preaches only to adults. But I assert to the contrary, that this is a general statement, again and again driven home and repeated in the Scriptures, so that it cannot be evaded by such a slight solution. No distinction of ages is established when it is said, "This is life eternal, to know the one true God, and him whom he has sent, Jesus Christ" [John 17:3]; when it is said: "God's wrath remains upon him who has not believed in the only-begotten Son of God" [John 3:36]; "Only those who have eaten the flesh of the Son of man will have life," [6:53], (118) and other passages of this sort. Therefore, the opinion stands firm, that no men are saved except by faith, whether they be children or adults. For this reason, baptism also rightly applies to infants, who possess faith in common with adults. Nor ought anyone to take this in the sense

101

that I am saying faith always begins from the mother's womb, when the Lord calls even adults themselves sometimes later, sometimes sooner. [235] But I am only saying that all God's elect enter into eternal life through faith, at whatever point in age they are released from this prisonhouse of corruption.

But if this reason were to fail us, we would still have abundant proof that in baptizing infants we are obeying the Lord's will: who willed that they be allowed to come to him [Matt. 19:14]. Those whom he forbids to be prevented, he at the same time commands to be helped. And since he said, "Of such is the Kingdom of Heaven," we are doing nothing but subscribing to his statement and sealing its truth, when we impart to them the sign of forgiveness of sins, without which the Kingdom of Heaven is closed and barred to all. But the precept laid down by the Lord concerning the circumcizing of the children of the Jews [Gen. 17:10-14] ought to stand for us as a commandment, since our baptism has taken the place of circumcision. For the very same thing the Lord promised the Jews in circumcision—namely, that he would be God for them and their offspring, and they and their offspring would be his people [cf. Lev. 26:12]—he today promises to Christians in baptism: not only to adults but also to infants, whom also for this reason Paul calls "saints," [I Cor. 7:14] just as the infants of the Jews of old could be called "saints," as compared with the unclean and profane gentiles. [236]

C. THE LORD'S SUPPER

4.17.1   24. The other sacrament instituted for the Christian church is the bread sanctified in Christ's body, and the wine sanctified in his blood. Moreover, we call it either the Lord's Supper* or the Eucharist*, because in it we are both spiritually fed by the Lord's goodness, and give thanks to him for his kindness. The promise added thereto very clearly asserts for what purpose /137/ it has been instituted, and the goal to which it looks, namely, to confirm to us that the Lord's body was once for all so handed over to us, as now to be ours, and also forever to be so; that his blood was once for all so poured out for us, as always to be ours. By this on the other hand is refuted the error of those who have dared deny that sacraments are exercises of faith,* given to protect, arouse and increase it. For his words are: "This cup is the New Testament in my blood" [Luke 22:30; I Cor. 11:25]. This is proof and witness of the promise. But wherever there is a promise, faith has the means to support itself, to comfort itself, to strengthen itself.

4.17.2   Great indeed is the fruit of sweetness and (119) comfort our souls can gather from this sacrament: because we recognize Christ to have been so engrafted in us as we, in turn, have been engrafted in him, so that whatever is his we are permitted to call ours, [237] whatever is ours to reckon as his. As a consequence, we may dare assure ourselves that eternal life is ours; that the Kingdom of Heaven can no more be cut off from us than from Christ himself; on the contrary, that we cannot be condemned for our sins any more than can he, because they are not now ours, but his. Not that any guilt is rightly to be imputed to him, but that he has set himself as debtor for them, and presents himself as the payer. This is the exchange˙which out of his measureless goodness he has made with us: that, receiving our poverty unto himself, he has transferred his wealth to us; that taking our weakness upon himself he has strengthened us by his power; that having received our mortality he has given us his immortality; that, descending to earth, he has prepared an ascent to heaven for us;˙ that, becoming Son of man with us, he has made us sons of God with him.˙

25. All these things are so perfectly promised in this sacrament, that we must certainly consider him truly shown to us, just as if Christ himself present were set before our gaze and touched by our hands. For this word cannot fool us or lie to us: "Take, eat, drink; this is my body which is given for you; this is blood, which is shed for forgiveness of sins" [Matt. 26:26-28; I Cor. 11:24; cf. Mark 14:22-24; Luke 22:19-20]. By bidding us take he points out that it is ours. [238] By bidding us eat he points out that it becomes one substance with us. When he says, "This is my body given for you," "This is my blood shed for you," he teaches that these are not so much his as ours, which he took up and laid down, not for his own advantage but for our sake and benefit.

4.17.3

And, indeed, we must carefully observe that the entire force of the Sacrament lies in these words: /138/ "which is given for you,"˙ "which is shed for you." The present distribution of the body and blood of the Lord would not greatly benefit us unless they had once for all been given for our redemption and salvation.˙ They are therefore represented under bread and wine so that we may learn not only that they are ours, but that they are as life and food for us.

And so as we previously stated, from the physical things set forth in the Sacraments we ought to be led by a sort of analogy to spiritual things. Thus, when we see bread set forth to us as a sign of Christ's body, we must at once grasp this comparison: as bread nourishes, sustains, and keeps the life of our body, so Christ's body is the food and protection of our spiritual life. When we see wine set forth as a symbol of blood, we must reflect on the benefits which wine imparts to the body, and so realize that the same are spiritually imparted to us by Christ's blood. These benefits are to strengthen, refresh, and gladden.˙ [239] For if we sufficiently consider what benefit we have received from the giving of that most holy body, (120) what benefit from the shedding of that blood, we shall clearly perceive that those qualities of bread and wine are, according to such an analogy, excellently adapted to express those things.

26. It is not, therefore, the chief function of the Sacrament simply to exhibit to us the body of Christ. Rather, it is, I say, to seal and confirm that promise by which he testifies that his flesh is food indeed and his blood is drink [John 6:56], feeding us unto eternal life [John 6:55], by which he declares himself to be the bread of life, whereof he who eats will live forever [John 6:48, 50]. And to do this, the Sacrament sends us to the cross of Christ, where that promise was indeed performed and in all respects fulfilled. In calling himself "the bread of life," he did not borrow that name from the Sacrament, as some

4.17.4

wrongly interpret. Rather, he had been given as such to us by the Father and showed himself as such when, being made a sharer in our human mortality, he made us partakers in his divine immortality; when, offering himself as a sacrifice, he bore our curse in himself to imbue us with his blessing; when, by his death, he swallowed up and annihilated death [cf. I Pet. 3:22, Vg., and I Cor. 15:54]; and when, in his resurrection, he raised up this corruptible flesh

4.17.5 of ours, which he had put on, to glory and incorruption [cf. I Cor. 15:53-54]. Therefore, the Sacrament does not make Christ to be the bread of life; [240] but since it reminds us that he was made bread which we continually eat, it gives us a relish and savor of that bread. In short, it assures us that all things that Christ did or suffered were done and suffered to quicken us; and again, that this quickening is eternal, we being ceaselessly nourished, sustained and preserved throughout life by it. For, as Christ would not have been the bread of life for us /139/ if he had not been born and had not died for us, and if he had not arisen for us, so he would not at all now have been these things if the effective working and fruit of his birth, death, and resurrection were not a thing eternal and immortal.

4.17.33 27. If this force of the sacrament had been examined and weighed as it deserved, there would have been quite enough to satisfy us, and these frightful contentions would not have arisen which of old, and even within our memory, have miserably troubled the church, when men in their curiosity endeavored to define how Christ's body is present in the bread. Some men, to prove themselves subtle, added to the simplicity of Scripture: that he is 'really' and 'substantially' present. Still others even went farther: they said he has the same dimensions in which he hung on the cross. Others devised a wondrous transubstantiation. Others said the bread itself was the body. Others, that it was under the bread. Others that only a sign and figure of the body were set forth. [241] This is indeed an important matter, over which great disputes, of words and minds, have arisen. So indeed is it commonly established; but those who feel thus, do not pay attention, in the first place, to the necessity of asking how Christ's (121) body, as it was given for us, became ours; how his blood, as it was shed for us, became ours. But that means to possess the whole Christ crucified, and to become a participant in all his benefits. Now, overlooking those highly important matters, in fact neglecting and well-nigh burying them, our opponents fight over this one thorny question: How is the body devoured by us?

28. Yet how in such a crowd and variety of opinions, will the one sure truth of God stand fast for us? First, let us ponder what sort of spiritual thing the sacrament is, whereby the Lord willed to feed not our bellies but our souls, and let us seek Christ in it, /140/ not for our body, nor as it can be understood by the senses of our flesh; but in such a way that the soul recognizes it as it were present and shown forth. In short, we have enough to obtain him spiritually. For thus we will obtain him as life, because to receive any fruits from the sacrament is to have received him. After anyone deeply grasps this thought and meditates upon it, he will readily understand how the body of Christ [242] is offered to

us in the sacrament, namely truly and effectively. And he will not be at all anxious over the nature of the body. Because these matters are less familiar (few persons having hit the nail on the head!) it will be necessary perhaps to explain them in more detail.

Therefore, we must hold the following by way of summary. Christ, as he took our true flesh when he was born of the virgin, suffered in our true flesh; when he made satisfaction for us, so also both in rising again received that same true flesh and bore it up to heaven. For we have this hope of our resurrection and of our ascension into heaven: that Christ rose again and ascended. But how weak and fragile that hope would be, if this very flesh of ours had not entered into the Kingdom of Heaven! But it is the unchangingly true nature of a body to be contained in a place, to possess its own dimensions and to have its own shape. 4.17.29

I know how certain obstinate fellows quibble to defend an error once rashly conceived, that the only dimensions Christ's flesh ever possessed, extended as far and wide as heaven and earth. That he was born as a child from the womb, that he grew, that he was stretched upon the cross, enclosed in the tomb—this came to pass by a certain dispensation, in order that he might discharge the office of birth, of death, and the other offices of men. That after [243] his resurrection he was seen in his customary bodily form [Acts 1:3; cf. I Cor. 15:5], that he was taken up into heaven [Acts 1:9; Luke 24:51; Mark 16:19], that finally also after his ascension he was seen by Stephen [Acts 7:55] and Paul [Acts 9:3]— this came to pass by the same dispensation, they assert, in order to make clear to men's sight that he was made king in heaven.* What is this but to raise Marcion from hell? For who will doubt that if Christ's body existed in this state, it was a phantasm?

They allege Christ himself has said: "No one has ascended into heaven but he who descended from heaven, (122) the Son of man, who is in heaven"* [John 3:13, cf. Vg.]. But are they so senseless as not to see that this was said through "communication of properties?"* Surely, when the Lord of glory is said by Paul to have been crucified [I Cor. 2:8], it is not because he suffered according to his divinity, but because /141/ Christ, who, cast down and despised, suffered in the flesh, was very God and Lord of glory. In this way he was also Son of man in heaven [John 3:13], for the very same Christ, who, according to the flesh, dwelt as Son of man on earth, was God in heaven. In this manner, he is said to have descended to that place according to his divinity, not because divinity left heaven to hide itself in the prison house of the body, but because even though it filled all things, still in Christ's very humanity it dwelt bodily [Col. 2:9], that is, by nature, and in a certain ineffable way.* 4.17.30

29. Some use a slightly more subtle evasion:*[244] this body which is set forth in the Sacrament is glorious and immortal; therefore, there is nothing absurd if under the Sacrament it is contained in several places, in no place, or in no form.* 4.17.17

But I ask: What sort of body did the Lord give to the disciples the day before he suffered? Do not the words testify that he gave them that very mortal body which immediately was to be given up? He had previously (these men say) presented his glory to be seen by three of his disciples on Mount Tabor [Matt. 17:2]. True, indeed, but by that splendor he afforded them at that hour only a foretaste of his immortality. But when he distributed his body at the Last Supper, the hour was already near at which, stricken and humbled by God [Is. 53:4], he should lie down uncomely like a leper [cf. Is. 53:2]—so far was he from intending to manifest then his glory. And what a large window is here opened to Marcion, if Christ's body seemed mortal and lowly in this one passage, in another was considered immortal and glorified?

4.17.29   But I overlook such a great absurdity. Only let them answer me on his glorious body:* Was it not nevertheless a body? It is, they say, but without place, in several places, without form, without measure. But that is, not in one word indeed, but by circumlocution to call it "spirit." Either we clearly deny the resurrection of the flesh, or confess that when it rose again, it would still be flesh, which differs from spirit in this respect, that it is enclosed in the space of a locality, that [245] it is seen, that it is touched. And it supports them not even a trifle to be objecting over and over again that Christ entered in the place where his disciples were through closed doors [John 20:19]. He surely did enter, by a wonderful manner of entry. For he did not break them by force, or wait until they were opened by a man's hand, but by his power caused every obstacle to fall. Moreover, having entered, he proved to his disciples the reality of his body. "See," he says, "and handle, for a spirit does not have flesh and bones" [Luke 24:39]. See! The glorious body of Christ is proved to be true body, for it can be handled and seen. Remove these, it will /142/ (123) then cease to be

4.17.24   a true body. Here to show us their ill-will, they accuse us of speaking evilly of the power of Almighty God. But either they are stupidly mistaken or they are basely lying. For here it is not a question of what God could do, but what he willed to do. Now, we affirm that what was pleasing to him was done. But it pleased him that Christ be made like his brethren in all things except sin [Heb. 4:15; cf. ch. 2:17]. What is the nature of our flesh? Is it not something that has its own fixed dimension, is contained in a place, is touched, is seen? And why (they say) cannot God make the same flesh occupy many and divers places, be contained in no place, or lack measure and form? Madman, why do you demand of God's power that he cause flesh to be and not to be flesh at the same time! It is as if you insisted that [246] he make light to be both light and darkness at the same time! But he wills light to be light; darkness, darkness; and flesh, flesh. Indeed, when he pleases he will turn darkness into light and light into darkness; but when you require that light and darkness not differ, what else are you doing than perverting the order of God's wisdom? Flesh must therefore be flesh; spirit, spirit—each thing in the state and condition wherein God created it. But such is the condition of flesh that it must subsist in one definite place, with its own size and form. With this condition Christ took flesh, giving to it incorruption and glory, and not taking away from it nature and truth.*

For there is a plain and clear testimony of Scripture, that he ascended into heaven, and so will return, in the way he was seen to ascend [Acts 1:9, 11]. And there is no reason why these stiffnecked opponents should make rejoinder that he ascended and will return visibly, but meanwhile dwells invisibly with us. Indeed, our Lord testified that he had flesh and bones, which could be handled   4.17.26
and seen [John 20:27]. Also, "departing" and "ascending" do not signify giving the appearance of one ascending and departing, but actually doing what the words state. But though he has taken his flesh away from us, and in the body   4.17.18
has ascended into heaven, yet he sits at the right hand of the Father—that is, he reigns in the Father's power and majesty and glory. [247] This Kingdom is neither bounded by any location in space nor circumscribed by any limits. Thus uncircumscribed, Christ can exert his power wherever he pleases, in heaven and on earth; he can show his presence in power and strength; he is always able to be among his own people to live in them, sustain them, strengthen, quicken, keep them, as if he were present in the body.

30. In this manner, the body and blood of Christ are shown to us in the Sacrament; but in the previous manner not at all.

By way of teaching, we say he is in truth and in effective working shown forth, but not in nature. By this we obviously mean that the very substance of his body or the true and natural body of Christ is not given there; but all those benefits which Christ has supplied us with in his body. /143/

Such is the presence of the body that the nature of the Sacrament requires: 4.17.32
one we say manifests itself here with a power and effectiveness so great that it not only brings an undoubted assurance (124) of eternal life to our hearts but also assures us of the immortality of our flesh. Indeed, it is now quickened by his immortal flesh, and in a sense partakes of his immortality. Those who are carried beyond this by their own exaggerations do nothing but obscure simple and plain truth with such involvements.

31. But if some intransigeant person raises a controversy with us over   4.17.22
Christ's words, [248] because he said this is his body, this is his blood, I should like him to ponder here for a little while with me, that we are now discussing a sacrament the whole of which must be referred to faith. But with this partaking of the body we have declared, we feed faith as sumptuously and copiously as those who draw Christ himself away from heaven. But if we so tenaciously stick to the words, the words also splendidly support me. Matthew and Mark state the Lord called the cup "his blood of the New Testament"; Luke and Paul say, "the testament in blood." Although you shout this is body and blood, I on the other hand will contend this is the testament in body and blood. Paul requires   4.17.32
interpretation of Scripture to conform to the analogy of faith [Rom. 12:3, 6]. No doubt in this case it remarkably supports me. See for yourself to what standard of faith you are conforming yourself. He who does not confess Jesus Christ came in the flesh is not of God [I John 4:3]. You, although you cover it up, deprive him of his true flesh.

32. This knowledge will easily draw us away also from physical adoration;   4.17.35

107

which certain persons with perverted rashness have set up in the Sacrament, because they reasoned as follows: if it is the body, then both soul and divinity are together with the body and cannot be separated from it: [249] consequently, we must adore Christ there: See the offspring of our excellence, once we have let ourselves wander in the dreams of our own brains! But if with becoming humility the masterminds of such reasonings had kept all these thoughts of their intellect under the Word of God, they would surely have heard what he said: "Take, eat, drink," [Matt. 26:26-27], and would have obeyed this command, by which he bids us receive the Sacrament, not adore it. Therefore, those who receive the Sacrament as the Lord has commanded, without adoration, are confident that they are not turning aside from God's command. No greater consolation can come to pass than this assurance /144/ when we undertake any task. They have the example of the apostles, who, as we read, did not adore it prostrate, but received and ate it as they reclined. They have the practice of the apostolic church which, as Luke tells, took communion not in adoration, but in breaking of bread [Acts 2:42]. They have the apostolic doctrine, with which Paul instructed the church of the Corinthians, professing that he had received from the Lord what he delivered [I Cor. 11:23]. But those who adore the Sacrament, relying only on conjectures and some sort of arguments born of themselves, cannot claim one syllable from God's Word. For though they greatly stress the words "body" and (125) "blood," still what sane and sober man can convince himself that Christ's body is Christ? [250] Indeed, they seem to themselves neatly to prove this with their syllogisms. But if their consciences happen to be troubled by some graver feeling, they will easily, along with their syllogisms, be overturned, be dissolved and melt away. So it will be when they see themselves bereft of God's sure Word, for upon it alone our souls stand fast when they are called to account; and without it they will faint the very first moment it dawns upon them that the Apostles' teaching and examples are against them, and that they themselves are the only authorities they have. To such impulses other sharp pricks will be added. What? Was it a matter of no importance to adore God in this form as if nothing were prescribed for us? Ought they to have undertaken so lightly what no word had anywhere stated, when the worship and glory of God were concerned?

4.17.36   Moreover, inasmuch as Scripture carefully recounted to us the ascension of Christ, by which he withdrew the presence of his body from our sight and company, to shake from us all carnal thinking of him and, whenever it recalls Christ, to warn our minds to be raised up, and seek him in heaven, seated at the right hand of the Father [Col. 3:1-2], we ought rather to have adored him spiritually in heavenly glory than to have devised some dangerous kind of adoration, replete with a carnal and crass conception of God and Christ. Therefore, those who have devised the adoration of the Sacrament [251] have dreamed it by themselves apart from Scripture in which no mention of this adoration can be shown—something that obviously would not have been overlooked if it had been acceptable to God. And they who no less forbid anything to be added to Scripture

108

than be taken away from it [Deut. 13:1] have in this despised God. While they have fashioned themselves a god after the decision of their own lust, they have forsaken the living God. Indeed they have worshiped the gifts instead of the Giver. In this there is a double transgression: for both the honor taken from God has been transferred to the creature [cf. Rom. 1:25], and he himself also has been dishonored in the defilement and profanation of his gift, when his holy Sacrament is made a hateful idol. But let us, on the other hand, /145/ to avoid falling into the same pit, fix our ears, eyes, hearts, minds, and tongues completely upon God's sacred teaching. For that is the school of that best schoolmaster, the Holy Spirit, in which we so advance that nothing need be acquired from elsewhere, but that we ought willingly to be ignorant of what is not taught in it.

33. We discussed before how it serves our faith before God. But the Lord in this sacrament recalls to our memory, as we have already explained, the abundance of his bounty, and arouses us to recognize it. At the same time he admonishes us not to be ungrateful for such lavish kindness, but rather to proclaim it with fitting praises, [252] and to celebrate it with thanksgiving. Therefore, when he gave the institution of the Sacrament itself to the apostles, he taught them to do it in remembrance of him [Luke 22:19]. This Paul interpreted (126) as "to declare the Lord's death" [I Cor. 11:26], that is, publicly and all with a single voice to confess openly before men that for us the whole assurance of life and salvation rests upon the Lord's death, that we may glorify him by our confession, and by our example exhort others to give glory to him. Here again the purpose of the Sacrament is made clear, that is, to exercise us in the remembrance of Christ's death. For the command to us to "declare the Lord's death till he come" [I Cor. 11:26] in judgment means nothing else than that we should by the confession of our mouth declare what our faith recognizes in the Sacrament: that the death of Christ is our life. Here is the second use of the Sacrament, which pertains to outward confession. *4.17.37*

34. Thirdly, the Lord also intended the Supper to be a kind of exhortation for us, which can more forcefully than any means quicken and inspire us to love, peace, and concord. For the Lord so communicates his body to us there that he is made completely one with us and we with him. Now, since he has only one body, of which he makes us all partakers, it is necessary that all of us also be made one body by such participation. [253] The bread shown as Sacrament represents this unity. As it is made of many grains so mixed and commingled that one cannot be distinguished from another, so it is fitting that in this way we should be joined and bound together by such great agreement of hearts that no sort of disagreement or division may intrude. I prefer to explain it in Paul's words: "The cup of blessing which we bless is a communicating of the blood of Christ; and the bread of blessing which we break is a participation in the body of Christ. . . . Therefore . . . we . . . are all one body, for we partake of one bread" [I Cor. 10:16–17, cf. Vg.]. We shall benefit very much from the Sacrament /146/ if this thought is impressed and engraved upon our *4.17.38*

minds: that none of the brethren can be harmed, traduced, mocked, despised, or in any way offended by us, without at the same time, our harming, traducing, mocking, and despising Christ; that we cannot disagree with our brethren without at the same time disagreeing with Christ; that we cannot love Christ without loving him in the brethren; that we ought to take the same care of our brethren's bodies as we take of our own; for they are members of our body; and that, as no part of our body is touched by any feeling of pain which is not spread among all the rest, so we ought not to allow a brother to be affected by any evil, without being touched with compassion for him. Accordingly, [254] Augustine with good reason frequently calls this sacrament "the bond of love."* For what sharper goad could there be to arouse mutual love among us than when Christ, giving himself to us, not only invites us by his own example to pledge and give ourselves to one another, but inasmuch as he makes himself common to all, also makes all of us one in himself.

4.17.40   35. We see that this sacred bread of the Lord's Supper (127) is spiritual food, sweet and delicate to those to whom Christ has shown it to be their life, whom it moves to thanksgiving, for whom it is an exhortation to mutual love among themselves. On the other hand, it is turned into a deadly poison for those whose faith it does not teach, and whom it does not arouse to thanksgiving and to love. "For," as Paul says, "any who eat unworthily are guilty of the Lord's body and blood, and eat and drink judgment upon themselves, not discerning the body of the Lord" [I Cor. 11:27 and 29, conflated]. We must note in this passage that "not to discern the body and blood of the Lord" and "to receive it unworthily" are taken to mean the same thing. Men of this sort who, without any spark of faith, without any zeal for love, rush like swine to take the Lord's Supper do not at all discern [255] the Lord's body. In so far as they do not believe that that body is their life, so far do they dishonor it, robbing it of all its dignity; and finally they profane and pollute it by so receiving it. And, since they are estranged from and out of accord with their brethren, and dare mix the sacred symbol of Christ's body with their discords, it is not on their account that Christ's body is not torn and dismembered. Therefore, they are deservedly held guilty of the Lord's body and blood, which they so fouly defile with sacrilegious impiety. Hence, by this unworthy eating they bring condemnation upon themselves. /147/ For while they have no faith fixed upon Christ, yet, in receiving the Sacrament, they profess that their salvation is nowhere but in him and abjure all other assurance. Therefore, they are their own accusers; they bear witness against themselves and seal their own condemnation. Then, although they are divided and separated by hatred and ill will from their brethren, that is, from the members of Christ, and thus have no part in Christ, they still testify that this alone is salvation—to partake of Christ and be united with him. We must however note in passing that they vainly put forth this passage repeatedly for the real presence of the body.* Paul, I admit, is speaking of Christ's actual body: but in what sense one must see—so that there is no need to make more excuses. [256]

    36. On this account, Paul enjoins that a man examine himself before

eating of this bread or drinking from this cup [I Cor. 11:28]. By this (as I indeed interpret it), he meant that each man descend into himself, and ponder with himself whether he recognizes with assurance of heart Christ as his Savior; whether he acknowledges it by confession of mouth; whether, after Christ's example, he is prepared to give himself for his brethren and to communicate himself to those with whom he sees Christ in common; whether, as he is considered a member by Christ, he in turn so holds all his brethren as members of his body; whether he desires to cherish, protect, and help them as his own members. Not that these duties both of faith and of love can now be made perfect in us, but that we should endeavor and aspire with all our heart toward this end in order that we may day by day increase our faith once begun, (128) and strengthen our weak love.

37. Certain ones, when they would prepare men to eat worthily, have tortured and harassed pitiable consciences in dire ways; yet they have not brought forward a particle of what would be to the purpose. They said that those who were in state of grace ate worthily. They interpreted "in state of grace" to mean to be pure and purged of all sin. Such a dogma would debar all the men who ever were or are on earth from the use of this Sacrament. For if it is a question [257] of our seeking our worthiness by ourselves, we are undone; only ruin and confusion remain to us. Although we try with all our strength, we shall make no headway, except that in the end we shall be most unworthy, after we have labored mightily in pursuit of worthiness.

4.17.41

To heal this sore, they have devised a way of acquiring worthiness: that, examining ourselves to the best of our ability, and requiring ourselves to account for all our deeds, we expiate our unworthiness by contrition, confession, and satisfaction. /148/ There will be later on a more appropriate place to state the nature of this expiation. As far as applies to the present task, I say that these remedies are too feeble and fleeting for consciences dismayed and dejected and stricken with the horror of their own sin. For if our Lord by his prohibition admits no one to participation in his Supper who is not righteous and innocent, grave caution is needed by anyone to assure himself of his own righteousness, which he hears that God requires. On what ground are we confirmed in the assurance that those who have done their best have performed their duty before God? But even if this were so, when will it come about that anyone dare assure himself that he has done his best? So, since no definite assurance of our worthiness is held out to us, the door will always remain locked by that dread prohibition which decrees that they [258] who eat and drink unworthily eat and drink judgment upon themselves [I Cor. 11:29].

Now, it is easy to judge the nature of that doctrine and from what author it sprang. For it so deprives and despoils poor sinners of the consolation of this Sacrament; yet in it, all the delights of the gospel were set before us. Surely the devil could find no speedier means of destroying men than by so maddening them that they could not taste and savor this food with which their most gracious Heavenly Father had willed to feed them.

4.17.42

38. In order, therefore, not to rush headlong to such confusion and ruin, let us remember that this sacred feast is medicine for the sick, solace for sinners, alms to the poor; but would bring no benefit to the healthy, righteous, and rich—if such could be found. For since in them Christ is given to us as food, we understand that without him we would pine away, starve, and fail. Then, since he is given us unto life, we understand that without him in us we are plainly dead. Therefore, this is the worthiness—the best and only kind we can bring to God—to offer our vileness and (so (129) to speak) our unworthiness to him so that by his mercy he may make us worthy of him; to despair in ourselves so that we may be comforted in him; to abase ourselves so that we may be lifted up by him; to accuse ourselves so that we may be justified by him; moreover, [259] to aspire to that unity which he commends to us in his Supper; and, as he makes all of us one in himself, we may desire one soul, one heart, one tongue for us all. If we have weighed and considered these things well, these thoughts will never trouble us. How could we, needy and bare of all good, befouled with sins, half-dead, eat the Lord's body worthily? Rather, we shall think that we, as being poor, come to a kindly giver; as sick, to a physician; as sinners to the Savior; that the worthiness, commanded by God consists chiefly in faith, /149/ which reposes all things in God, but nothing in ourselves; secondly, in love—and that very love, more imperfect, we offer to God, that he may increase it to something better than we supply.

39. Others, agreeing with us that worthiness itself consists in faith and love, still are far in error on the standard itself of worthiness, requiring, as they do, a perfection of faith which cannot at all be attained, and a love equal to that in which Christ has dealt with us. But, by so doing, they like those previously mentioned, drive all men from approaching this most holy Supper. For if their view obtained, no one would receive it except unworthily, since all to a man would be held guilty and [260] convicted of their own imperfection. And obviously it was excessive stupidity—not to mention foolishness—to require such perfection in receiving the Sacrament as would make the Sacrament void and superfluous. For it is a sacrament ordained not for the perfect, but for the weak and feeble, to awaken, arouse, stimulate, and exercise the lack of faith and love.

4.17.44

40. What we have so far said of the Sacrament abundantly shows that it was not ordained to be received only once a year—and that, too, perfunctorily, as now is the public custom. Rather, it was ordained to be frequently used among all Christians in order that they might frequently return in memory to Christ's Passion, by such remembrance to sustain and strengthen their faith, and urge themselves to sing thanksgiving and to proclaim his goodness; finally, by it to nourish mutual love, and among themselves give witness to this love, and discern its bond in the unity of Christ's body. For as often as we partake of the symbol of the Lord's body, as a token given and received, we reciprocally bind ourselves to all the duties of love in order that none of us may permit anything that can harm our brother, or overlook anything that can help him where necessity demands.

Luke related in The Acts that this was the practice of the apostolic church, when [261] he says that believers ". . . continued in the apostles' teaching and fellowship, in the breaking of bread and in prayers" [Acts 2:42, cf. Vg.]. Thus it became the unvarying rule that no (130) meeting of the church should take place without the Word, prayers, partaking of the Supper, and almsgiving. That this was the established order among the Corinthians also, we can sufficiently infer from Paul [cf. I Cor. 11:20].

Plainly this custom which enjoins us to take communion once a year is a veritable invention of the devil, whoever was instrumental in introducing it. They say that Zephyrinus was the author of this decree, although I am not persuaded that it was in the form in which we now have it. For perhaps by his ordinance he did not provide too badly /150/ for the church, as times were then. For there is not the least doubt that the Sacred Supper was in that era set before the believers every time they met together; and that a majority of them took communion; but since all scarcely ever happened to take communion at once, and since it was necessary for those who were mingled with profane and idolatrous men to attest their faith by some outward sign—the holy man, for the sake of order and polity, appointed that day on which all Christian people should, by partaking of the Lord's Supper, make a confession of faith. 4.17.46

Moreover, on that account they ceased to take communion as frequently, since not long before Anacletus had established that all Christians should take communion daily. [262] But posterity wickedly distorted Zephyrinus' otherwise good ordinance, when a definite law was made to have communion once a year. By this it has come about that almost all, when they have taken communion once, as though they have beautifully done their duty for the rest of the year, go about unconcerned. It should have been done far differently: the Lord's Table should have been spread at least once a week for the assembly of Christians, and the promises should have been declared to feed us in it spiritually. None indeed should have been forcibly compelled, but all should have been urged and aroused; also the inertia of indolent people should have been rebuked. All, like hungry men, would have flocked to such a bounteous repast. Not unjustly, then, did I complain at the outset that this custom was thrust in by the devil's artifice, which, in prescribing one day a year, renders men slothful all the rest of the year.

41. Out of the same shop came another regulation, which has either stolen or snatched half the Supper from the greater part of God's people. The symbol of the blood, denied to lay and profane persons (these are titles they apply to God's inheritance [I Pet. 5:3]), was given as a special property to a few shaven and anointed men. The edict of the eternal God is that all should drink [Matt. 26:27]; man dares supersede and abrogate it by a new and opposing law, decreeing that not /151/ all should drink. [263] And that such lawgivers may not irrationally contend against their God, they pretend perils that could occur if this sacred cup were commonly offered to all, as if those perils had not been foreseen and considered by God's eternal wisdom! Then, indeed, they subtly 4.17.47

reason that one is enough for two. "For if it is the body" (they say), "it is the whole Christ, who cannot be separated from his body. Therefore, the body contains the blood also."* (131) See how much our perception is in agreement with God, when with slackened reins it begins to go even a little wanton and wild! The Lord shows us bread and says that it is his body; he shows the cup and calls it his blood. Human reason brazenly contradicts this assertion: "bread is blood, wine is body." It is as if the Lord had to no purpose distinguished his body from his blood by both words and signs, and people had at any time heard it said that the body of Christ, or the blood, is called God and man. Obviously, if he had meant to signify his whole self, he could have said, "It is I"—as he was accustomed to speak in the Scriptures [Matt. 14:27; John 18:5; Luke 24:39]—

4.17.48 but not, "This is my body; this is my blood." I know, indeed, that the ministers of Satan (as it is their custom to mock the Scriptures) ridicule and quibble over this; that only the apostles, whom he had already chosen and enrolled in the order of "sacrificers," were admitted by Christ to participate in this Supper.*

But I should like them to answer me five questions, from which they cannot escape [264] without being easily refuted with their lies. First, what oracle has revealed this solution to them—so foreign to God's Word? Scripture lists twelve who reclined with Jesus [cf. Matt. 26:20], but it does not so obscure Christ's dignity as to call them "sacrificers." (We shall afterward deal with this term in its proper place.) Even though he then gave it to the Twelve, he still bade them do the same, namely, distribute it among themselves. Secondly, why from that better age, even to a thousand years after the apostles, did all, without exception, partake of both symbols? Did the ancient church not know whom Christ had admitted as guests to his Supper? It would be the most abandoned shamelessness to halt here and dodge the question! There are extant church histories, there are books of ancient writers, which give clear evidence of this

4.17.50 fact. /152/ Thirdly, why did Christ simply say of the bread that they should eat, but of the cup that they *all* should drink [Mark 14:22-23; Matt. 26:26-27]? It is as if he deliberately intended to oppose Satan's craftiness. Fourthly, if the Lord (as they would have it) deemed only "sacrificers" worthy of his Supper, what man would ever have dared call strangers who had been excluded by the Lord to partake of it? And even to partake of that gift whose power was not in their possession, without the command of him who alone could give it? Indeed, with what assurance do they today presume to distribute to the common folk the symbol of Christ's [265] body, if they have neither command nor example of the Lord? Fifthly, was Paul lying when he said to the Corinthians that he had received from the Lord what he had delivered to them [I Cor. 11:23]? For afterward he declares the thing delivered to be that all indiscriminately should partake of both symbols [I Cor. 11:26]. (132) If Paul had received from the Lord the practice that all be admitted without distinction, let those who drive away almost all God's people see from whom they have received their practice, since they cannot now pretend that its author is God, with whom there is no Yes and No [II Cor. 1:19]. And still we cloak such abominations with the name of church

114

and defend them on that pretext! It is as if these Antichrists, who so readily trample, scatter, and abolish the teaching and ordinances of Christ, were the church; or the apostolic church, in which religion flourished in full vigor, were not the church! By these and similar devices Satan has tried with thick darkness to obscure and to defile Christ's Sacred Supper—in order at least to prevent its purity from being preserved in the church.

4.18.1

42. But the height of frightful abomination* was when the devil raised up a sign by which it was not only to be obscured and perverted, but—being completely erased and annulled—to vanish and pass out of human memory. This happened when he blinded nearly the whole world with a most pestilential error—the belief that the Mass is a sacrifice and offering [266] to obtain forgiveness of sins*. I know how deeply this plague has taken root, how much it lurks under the appearance of good, how it displays the name of Christ, and how numerous persons believe that in the one word "Mass" they embrace /153/ the whole sum of faith. But when it is most clearly proved by the Word of God that this Mass, however decked in splendor, inflicts signal dishonor upon Christ, buries and oppresses his cross, consigns his death to oblivion, takes away the benefit which came to us from it, and weakens and destroys the Sacrament by which the memory of his death was bequeathed to us—will any of the roots be too deep for this most sturdy ax (I mean the Word of God) to hack out? Is there any covering so dazzling that this light cannot disclose the lurking evil underneath?

43. Let us therefore show what was set forth in the first place, that in it an unbearable blasphemy and dishonor is inflicted upon Christ* For he was consecrated priest and pontiff by his Father, not for a time, in the way in which we read of priests being appointed in the Old Testament. Their priesthood could not be immortal since their life was mortal. Consequently, successors were needed from time to time, to replace those who died. But Christ*, being immortal, needs no vicar to replace him. Therefore, the Father designated him "priest forever, according to the order of Melchizedek," that he should discharge an everlasting priesthood [Heb. 5:6, 10; 7:17, 21; 9:11; 10:21; Ps. 110:4; Gen. 14:18]. This [267] mystery had been long before prefigured in Melchizedek; when Scripture has once introduced him as priest of the living God, it nowhere afterward mentions him, implying that his life had been without end. From this similarity Christ was called priest according to his order.

4.18.2

But now those who sacrifice daily are required to appoint for their oblations priests whom they substitute for Christ as successors and vicars. By this substitution they not only deprive Christ of his honor, and snatch from him the prerogative of the eternal priesthood, but try to cast him down from the right hand (133) of his Father, where he cannot sit immortal without at the same time remaining eternal priest. And let them not allege that their priestlings are not substituted for Christ as if he were dead, but are only suffragans of his eternal priesthood, which does not therefore cease to stand. For they are too strongly constrained by the apostle's words to be able to escape thus. Namely, he says that many other priests were made because death prevented them from continuing in office [Heb. 7:23]. Therefore, Christ, who is not prevented by death, is unique and needs no partners.

4.18.3   44. Another power of the Mass was set forth: that it buries and suppresses the cross and Passion of Christ. This is indeed very certain: for if Christ offered himself as a sacrifice on the cross in order to sanctify us forever, and to seek eternal redemption for us [Heb. 9:12], no doubt the force and effectiveness of this sacrifice [268] continue without end. Otherwise, we would feel no more reverent about Christ /154/ than about the oxen and calves which used to be sacrificed under the law, the sacrifices of which are proved ineffective and weak by the fact that they were frequently repeated [cf. Heb. 10:1]. Therefore, we shall have to confess either that Christ's sacrifice, which he offered upon the cross, lacked the power to cleanse eternally, or that Christ carried out one sacrifice, once for all, unto all ages. This is what the apostle says: that this High Priest, Christ, "has appeared, once for all, at the consummation of the age to overthrow sin by the sacrifice of himself" [Heb. 9:26 p.]. Again: "By the will of God we have been sanctified through the offering of the body of Jesus Christ once for all" [Heb. 10:10]. Also: "Christ by a single offering has perfected for all time those who are sanctified" [Heb. 10:14 p.]. Christ also signified this by his last words, uttered with his last breath, when he said, "It is finished" [John 19:30, Vg.]. We commonly regard the last words of the dying as oracles. Christ, dying, testifies that by his own sacrifice everything that pertained to our salvation has been accomplished and fulfilled. We daily sew innumerable patches upon such a sacrifice, as if it were imperfect, when he has very clearly commended its perfection. When God's Sacred Word not only affirms but cries out and contends that this sacrifice was performed only once and all its force [269] remains forever, do not those who require another sacrifice accuse it of imperfection and weakness [cf. Heb. 7:28; 9:26; 10:18]? But to what purpose is the Mass, which has been laid down on this condition, that a hundred thousand sacrifices may be performed each day, except to bury and submerge Christ's Passion, by which he offered himself as sole sacrifice to the Father? Who, that is not blind, fails to see that it was Satan's boldness that grappled with such open and clear truth? Nor am I unaware of the tricks by which the father of lies is wont to disguise his fraud: that these are not varied or different sacrifices, but the same one often repeated. But such smoke clouds there is no trouble dispersing. For in the whole discussion the apostle contends (134) not only that there are no other sacrifices, but that this one was offered only once and is never to be repeated.

4.18.5   45. Now I come down to the third function of the Mass, where I must explain how it wipes out the true and unique death of Christ and drives it from the memory of men. For as among men the confirmation of a testament depends upon the death of the testator, so also our Lord has confirmed by his death the testament by which he has given us forgiveness of sins and everlasting righteousness [Heb. 9:15-17]. Those who dare alter, or add anything new to, this testament deny his death and hold it of no importance. What is the Mass but a

116

new [270] and wholly different testament? Why so? Do not individual masses promise new forgiveness of sins, and new acquiring of righteousness, /155/ so that there are now as many testaments as there are masses? Let Christ, therefore, come again and ratify by another death this new testament; or rather, by countless deaths, innumerable testaments of masses. Have I not therefore spoken the truth at the beginning, that the unique and true death of Christ is wiped out by masses? What of the fact that the Mass leads directly to the end that, if such can be, Christ is slain again?*For where there is a testament (says the apostle), there the death of the testator must take place [Heb. 9:16]. The Mass displays a new testament of Christ; therefore, it requires his death. Moreover, it is necessary that the victim offered be slain and sacrificed. If Christ is sacrificed in each and every Mass, he must be cruelly slain in a thousand places at every moment* This is not my argument, but the apostle's: if Christ had had to offer himself often, he ought to have suffered repeatedly from the beginning of the world [Heb. 9:25-26].

46. Now I must discuss the fourth function of the Mass, that it robs us of the benefit which was coming to us from Christ's death, while it causes us not to recognize or ponder it. For who can think himself redeemed by Christ's death, when he has seen new redemption in the Mass? Who [271] can trust that his sins are forgiven, when he has seen a new forgiveness? And it is no way out to say that we obtain forgiveness of sins in the Mass solely because it has already been purchased by Christ's death* This amounts to nothing else than to boast that we have been redeemed by Christ on condition that we redeem ourselves; for this is the kind of doctrine that is spread abroad by Satan's ministers, and today is defended with shouting, sword, and fire: that we, when we offer Christ to the Father in the Mass, by this act of oblation obtain forgiveness of sins and are made participants in Christ's Passion* What now remains of Christ's Passion, except that it is an example of redemption by which we learn that we are our own redeemers?

47. Now I come to the end: namely, that the Sacred Supper (in which the Lord had left graven and inscribed the remembrance of his Passion) has been taken away, destroyed, and abolished by the raising up of the Mass. Indeed, the Supper itself is a gift of God, which ought to have been received with thanksgiving. (135) The sacrifice of the Mass is represented as paying a price to God, which he should receive by way of satisfaction. There is as much difference between this sacrifice and the sacrament as there is between giving and receiving. And such is the most miserable ungratefulness of man that where he ought to have recognized and given thanks for the abundance of God's bounty, he makes God in this his debtor! The Sacrament promised that by Christ's death we are not merely once restored to life, [272] but are continually revived, for all the parts of our salvation have then been fulfilled. The sacrifice of the Mass sings the far different tune that Christ ought to be sacrificed daily to /156/ be of any benefit to us.

48. The Supper was to have been distributed in the public assembly of

4.18.6

4.18.7

the church to teach us of the communion by which we all cleave together in Christ Jesus. The sacrifice of the Mass dissolves and tears apart this community. For after the error prevailed that there ought to be priests to perform sacrifice on the people's behalf as if the Supper had been turned over to them, it ceased to be communicated to the believers' church according to the Lord's commandment. An opening was made for private masses, which would seem to suggest an excommunication rather than that community established by the Lord. For the petty sacrificer, about to devour his victim by himself, separates himself from all believing folk. I call it a private mass (that no man may be mistaken) whether he resound with bellowing and shouting, or only squeak with mumbling and whispering, since both kinds remove participation in the Supper from the church.

4.18.9
49. But before I conclude my discourse, I ask our Mass-doctors—since they know obedience to God is stronger than sacrificial victims and he requires men rather to hearken to his voice than offer sacrifices [I Sam. 15:22]—how they can believe that God is pleased by this way of sacrificing, for which [273] they have no command, and which they see cannot be proved by even one syllable of Scripture. Moreover, when they hear the apostle saying that no one takes upon himself the name and honor of the priesthood except him who has been called (as Aaron was)—indeed, that Christ himself did not rush into it, but obeyed his Father's call [Heb. 5:4-5]—either they must bring God forward as author and founder of their priesthood, or they must confess that the honor is not of God, into which, uncalled, they have broken with wicked rashness. But they cannot claim even an iota with which to support their priesthood. Whither, then, will their sacrifices vanish, which cannot be offered without a priest?

4.18.18
What remains but that the blind may see, the deaf hear, and even children understand this abomination of the Mass? Offered in a golden cup, it has so inebriated all kings and peoples of the earth, from highest to lowest, and has so stricken them with drowsiness and dizziness, that, more stupid than brute beasts, they have steered the whole vessel of their salvation into this one deadly whirlpool. Surely, Satan never prepared a stronger engine to besiege (136) and capture Christ's Kingdom. This is the Helen for whom the enemies of truth today do battle with so much rage, fury, and cruelty—a Helen indeed, with whom they so fornicate in spiritual fornication, the most abominable of all. [274]

Here I do not even touch with my little finger those gross abuses which they could offer as an excuse for the profanation of the purity of their sacred Mass; /157/ the base traffickings they practice; the unclean profits they make by their massings; the unrestrained greed with which they satisfy their covetousness. I only point out, and that in a few simple words, what sort of thing the holiest holiness itself of the Mass is, on account of which it has deserved for many centuries to be esteemed so respectable and venerable. For it would be a rather large task to set out these very great mysteries according to their dignity. And I am unwilling to mingle with them those obscene corruptions which show themselves before the eyes and faces of all men, in order that all may understand

118

that the Mass, taken in the highest purity it can claim, without its appurtenances, from root to top, swarms with every sort of impiety, blasphemy, idolatry, and sacrilege.

50. Now, that no wrangler may do battle against us over the words "sacrifice" and "priest," I shall also explain, but in brief, what I have meant throughout the discussion by "sacrifice" and "priest." Generally understood, the term "sacrifice" includes anything at all offered to God. We must therefore make a distinction, and for the purpose of teaching let us call one "a sacrifice of thanksgiving or praise." [275] the other "a sacrifice of propitiation or of expiation." 4.18.13

Now the sacrifice of expiation is that which is intended to appease God's wrath, to satisfy his justice, to wash sins, and to implore grace and salvation. A sacrifice of this sort was accomplished by Christ alone, because no other could have done it. And it was done but once, because the effectiveness and force of that one sacrifice accomplished by Christ are eternal, as he testified with his own voice when he said that it was accomplished and fulfilled [John 19:30]; that is, whatever was necessary to recover the Father's favor, to obtain forgiveness of sins, righteousness, and salvation—all this was performed and completed by that unique sacrifice of his. And so perfect was it that no place was left afterward for any other sacrificial victim.

Therefore, I conclude that it is a most wicked infamy and unbearable blasphemy, against Christ and against the sacrifice which he discharged for us through his death on the cross, for anyone to suppose that by repeating the oblation he obtains pardon for sins, appeases God, and acquires righteousness. But what else is done by performing masses except that by the merit of a new oblation we are made partakers in Christ's Passion? And that there might be no limit to their frenzy, they thought it a small thing to say that their sacrifice was made in common equally for the whole church, unless they added that it was their choice to apply it particularly to this man or that, as they pleased, [276] or rather to everyone who was willing to pay cash for such merchandise. Now, although they could not reach Judas' price, (137) still to resemble their author in some respect, they have kept a similarity in number. Judas had sold him /158/ for thirty pieces of silver [Matt. 26:15]; these persons sell him for thirty pieces of copper; Judas, once; these, as often as they find a buyer. 4.18.14

We also deny that they are priests in the sense that they by such oblation intercede before God for the people and, having appeased God, obtain atonement for sins. For Christ is the sole Pontiff and Priest of the New Testament [cf. Heb., ch. 9], to whom all priesthoods have been transferred, and in whom they have been closed and terminated. And even if Scripture had mentioned nothing of Christ's eternal priesthood, still because, when God discontinued the old priesthoods, he instituted none, the argument of the apostle remains invincible: "No one takes the honor upon himself, except him who has been called by God" [Heb. 5:4]. With what effrontery, then, do these sacrilegious persons, who boast that they are butchers of Christ, dare call themselves priests of the living God?

51. Under the second class of sacrifice, which we have called that of 4.18.16

119

"thanksgiving,"' are included all our prayers, praises, thanksgivings, and whatever we do for the worship of God, indeed ourselves and all that is ours ought to be consecrated and dedicated to him, so that everything that is in us may serve his glory and [277] manifest his magnificence.

This mode of sacrifice has nothing to do with appeasing God's wrath, nothing to do with obtaining forgiveness of sins, nothing to do with meriting righteousness; rather, it is concerned solely with magnifying and exalting God. Indeed, it cannot be performed, except by those who, after already having received forgiveness of sins, have been reconciled to God and justified. It is moreover so necessary for the church that it cannot be absent from her. Therefore it will be eternal, so long as the people of God stand. As it also was written in the prophet: "For from the rising of the sun, even to its setting, my name is great among the nations; and in every place incense is offered to my name, and a clean offering; for terrible is my name among the nations, says the Lord" [Mal. 1:11; cf. Vg.]. Far be it from us to remove it! Thus Paul bids us "offer our bodies a living sacrifice, holy, acceptable to God, a reasonable worship"

4.18.19   [Rom. 12:1; cf. I Pet. 2:5-6]. In this way David prayed that his prayer might ascend like incense into God's presence [Ps. 141:2]. Thus elsewhere the prayers of the saints are called "incense," and by the prophet "the calves of lips"

4.18.16   [Hos. 14:2; 14:3; Vg.]. Paul hit the nail on the head when he called it "worship"; for he had in mind the spiritual manner of worshiping God, which he tacitly

4.18.17   contrasted with the carnal sacrifices of the Mosaic law. The Lord's Supper cannot be without a sacrifice of this kind, [278] in which, while we proclaim his death [I Cor. 11:26] and give thanks, we do nothing but offer a sacrifice of praise. From this office of sacrificing, all Christians are called a royal priesthood [I Pet. 2:9], because through Christ we offer sacrifice of praise to God: "the fruit of lips /159/ confessing his name" [Heb. 13:15, Vg.]. And (138) we do not appear with our gifts before God without an intercessor. The Mediator interceding for us is Christ, by whom we offer ourselves and what is ours to the Father. He is our Pontiff, who has entered the heavenly sanctuary [Heb. 9:24] and opens a way for us to enter [cf. Heb. 10:20]. He is the altar [cf. Heb. 13:10] upon which we lay our gifts. In him we venture whatever we venture. He it is, I say, that has made us a kingdom and priests unto the Father [Rev. 1:6].

4.18.19   52. Our readers now possess, collected into summary form, almost everything that we thought should be known concerning these two sacraments, whose use has been handed down to the Christian church from the beginning of the New Testament even to the end of the world; that is, that baptism should be, as it were, an entry into the church, and an initiation into faith; but the Supper should be a sort of continual food on which Christ spiritually feeds the household of his believers. Therefore, as there is but one God, one faith, one Christ, and one church, his body; so baptism is but one [Eph. 4:4-6], and is not a thing oft-repeated. But the Supper [279] is repeatedly distributed, that those who have once been drawn into the church may realize that they continually feed upon Christ.

Apart from these two, no other sacrament has been instituted by God, so the church of believers ought to recognize no other; for erecting and establishing new sacraments is not a matter of human choice. We shall readily understand this if we remember what was explained plainly enough above: that sacraments have been appointed by God to instruct us concerning some promise of his own, and to attest to us his own good will toward us. Moreover, we shall realize this if we bear in mind that no man has been God's counselor [Is. 40:13; Rom. 11:34], that he should be able to promise anything certain concerning God's will, or assure us and make us confident of what attitude he bears toward us, what he intends to give and what to deny us. At once it is indicated that no man can set forth a sign to be a testimony of any intention or promise of His. It is He alone who has given the sign and can bear witness of himself among us. I will say it more briefly and perhaps more bluntly but more plainly: there can never be a sacrament without promise of salvation. All men assembled together can promise us nothing concerning our salvation. Therefore, they cannot of themselves produce or set up a sacrament.

Let the Christian church be content with these two sacraments, therefore. 4.18.20
And let the church not only refuse to admit and acknowledge [280] any third one for the present but also not desire or expect any, even to the end of the age.

Various sacraments besides these ordinary ones were given to the Jews, according to the changing condition of the times (as manna [Ex. 16:13; I Cor. 10:3], water flowing from the rock [Ex. 17:6; I Cor. 10:4], the brazen serpent [Num. 21:8; John 3:14], and the like). But by this variation the Jews were warned not to stop at such figures /160/ whose condition was impermanent, but to await from God something better, which would abide without any destruction or end. But conditions are far different with us, to whom Christ has been revealed. For in him "all treasures of knowledge and wisdom (139) are hid" [Col. 2:3, cf. Vg.] with such great abundance and richness that either to hope for or to seek any new addition to these treasures is truly to tempt God and provoke him against us. It is for us to hunger for, seek, look to, learn, and study Christ alone, until that great day dawns when the Lord will fully manifest the glory of his Kingdom [cf. I Cor. 15:24] and will show himself for us to see him as he is [I John 3:2]. And for this reason this age of ours is designated in the Scriptures as "the last hour" [I John 2:18], the "last days" [Heb. 1:2], the "last times" [I Pet. 1:20], that no one should delude himself with a vain expectation of some new doctrine or revelation. "For at many times and in many ways the Lord formerly spoke through the prophets; but in these last days [281] the Lord has spoken in his beloved Son" [Heb. 1:1-2 p.], who alone can reveal the Father [Luke 10:22].

But now, as the capacity to coin new sacraments in the church has been denied to men, so it is to be wished that as little as possible of human invention be mingled with those sacraments which come from God. For just as when water is poured in, wine is displaced and diluted, and with yeast sprinkled over it the whole lump of dough goes sour, thus the cleanness of God's mysteries is but polluted when man adds anything of his own. And yet we see how much the sacraments, as even today they are performed, have degenerated from their real purity. Everywhere there is too much of processions, ceremonies, and mimes; yet at the same time there is no consideration or mention of God's Word, without which even the sacraments themselves are not sacraments. Indeed, the very ceremonies established by God cannot lift their head in such a great crowd, but lie as if crushed down. In baptism how much does one see of that which alone ought to have shone and been looked upon, that is, baptism itself? The Supper has been completely buried, since it has been turned into the Mass, except that it is frequented once a year, although in a mangled, halved, and mutilated form.

D. ADMINISTRATION OF THE SACRAMENTS

4.15.19   53. How much more satisfactory it would be, whenever anyone is to be baptized, to present him to the assembly of believers and, with the whole church looking on as witness, [282] and praying over him, offer him to God; to recite the confession of faith with which the catechumen should be instructed; to recount the promises taken in baptism; to baptize the catechumen in the name of the Father and of the Son and of the Holy Spirit [Matt. 28:19]; lastly, to dismiss him with prayers and thanksgiving*. If this were done, nothing essential would be omitted; and that one ceremony, which came from God, its author, not buried in outlandish pollutions, /161/ would shine in its full brightness. But whether the person being baptized should be wholly immersed, nor should only be sprinkled with poured water—these details are of no importance, but ought to be optional to churches according to the diversity of countries. Yet the word "baptize" means to immerse, and it is clear that the rite of immersion was observed in the ancient church.

4.17.43   As far as the Sacred Supper is concerned, it could have been administered most becomingly if it were set before the church very often, and (140) at least once a week*. First, then, it should begin with public prayers. After this a sermon should be given. Then, when bread and wine have been placed on the Table, the minister should repeat the words of institution of the Supper. Next, he should recite the promises which were left to us in it; at the same time, he should excommunicate all who are debarred from it by the Lord's prohibition. Afterward, he should pray that the Lord, with the kindness wherewith he has bestowed this sacred food upon us [283] also teach and form us to receive it with faith and thankfulness of heart, and, inasmuch as we are not so of ourselves, by his mercy make us worthy of such a feast. But here either psalms should be sung, or something be read, and in becoming order the believers should partake of the most holy banquet, the ministers breaking the bread and giving the cup. When the Supper is finished, there should be an exhortation to sincere faith and confession of faith, to love and behavior worthy of Christians. At the last, thanks should be given, and praises sung to God. When these things are ended, the church should be dismissed in peace.

Whether or not the believers take it in their hands, or divide it among themselves, or severally eat what has been given to each; whether they hand the cup back to the deacon or give it to the next person; whether the bread is leavened or unleavened; the wine red or white—it makes no difference. These things are indifferent, and left at the church's discretion. However, it is certain that the practice of the ancient church was for all to take it in their hands. And Christ said, "Divide it among yourselves" [Luke 22:17, Vg.]. The histories narrate that common leavened bread was used before the time of the Roman Bishop Alexander, who was the first who delighted in unleavened bread. But I see no reason for this, unless to draw the eyes of the common people to wonderment by a new spectacle, rather than to instruct their minds in religion. [284] I adjure all who are in the least affected by a zeal for piety whether they do not clearly see both how much more brightly God's glory shines here, and how much richer sweetness of spiritual consolation comes to believers, than in these lifeless and theatrical trifles, which serve no other purpose than to deceive the sense of a people stupefied. They call this the holding of the people by religion when they lead them anywhere—dulled and befooled with superstition. If anyone should like to defend such inventions by appealing to antiquity, I also am not ignorant of how ancient the use of chrism and exsufflation is in baptism; how soon after /162/ the apostolic age the Lord's Supper was corrupted by rust. But this, indeed, is the stubborn boldness of men, which cannot restrain itself from always trifling and wantoning in God's mysteries. Let us, however, remember that God so esteems obedience to his Word that he would have you judge both his angels and the whole world in it [I Cor. 6:2-3; Gal. 1:8]. (141) [285]

CHAPTER V

IT IS DEMONSTRATED THAT THE FIVE REMAINING ONES, UNTIL NOW COMMONLY CONSIDERED SACRAMENTS, ARE NOT SACRAMENTS: THEN IT IS SHOWN OF WHAT SORT THEY ARE

INTRODUCTION

4.19.1   1. Our previous discussion of the sacraments could have been enough to persuade teachable and sober folk not to carry their curiosity any farther, or to accept any sacraments apart from God's Word, except those two which they knew to be ordained by the Lord. But the notion of seven sacraments, a commonplace of almost everybody's talk and pervading all schools and sermons, has taken root by its very antiquity and is still fixed in men's minds*. Consequently, it seemed to me that I should be doing something worthwhile if I were to examine individually and more closely the five remaining rites, which are commonly reckoned among the true and genuine sacraments of the Lord, and, tearing away all camouflage, were to expose, for simple folk to see, what they are like and how falsely they have hitherto been reckoned as sacraments.

4.19.2   First, it is to be kept in mind that [286] we previously confirmed with invincible argument, that the decision to establish a sacrament rests with God alone. Indeed, a sacrament ought, by God's sure promise, to encourage and comfort believers' consciences, which would never receive this certainty from man. A sacrament ought to be for us a testimony of God's good will toward us, of which no man or angel can be the witness, since no one was God's counselor [Is. 40:13; Rom. 11:34]. It is the Lord alone who /163/ testifies concerning himself to us through his own Word. A sacrament is a seal by which God's covenant, or promise, is sealed. But it could not be sealed with physical things and the elements of this world, unless it were shaped and designed for this by God's power. Therefore, man cannot establish a sacrament, because it is not in man's power to cause such great mysteries of God to be concealed under such humble things. The Word of God must precede, to make a sacrament a sacrament.

A. CONFIRMATION*

2. Confirmation (as they call it) is the first sign which, invented by the rashness of men, has been set out as a sacrament of God. Moreover, they have feigned that the power of confirmation is to confer [287] for the increase of grace, the Holy Spirit, who was conferred in baptism for innocence; to confirm for battle those who in baptism were regenerated to life. This confirmation moreover is performed with anointing and with this formula: (142) "I mark thee with the sign of the holy cross, and confirm thee with the chrism of salvation, in the name of the Father, and of the Son, and of the Holy Spirit." All beautifully and charmingly done! But where is the Word of God, which promises the presence of the Holy Spirit here? They cannot show us one jot. How will they assure us that their chrism is a vessel of the Holy Spirit? We see the oil—the gross and greasy liquid—nothing else. Augustine says, "Let the word be added to the element, and it will become sacrament." Let them, I say, bring forth this word, if they would have us see in the oil anything else than oil. But if they acknowledged themselves, as they ought, to be ministers of the sacraments, we would have no reason to contend longer. This is the first law of a minister, to do nothing without a command. Come now, let them produce some command for this ministry, and I will not say another word. If they are without a command, they cannot excuse their sacrilegious boldness. In this sense, the Lord asked the Pharisees whether John's baptism was from heaven or from men. If they had answered "from men," [288] he would have proved it trifling and vain; if "from heaven," they would be compelled to acknowledge John's doctrine. Therefore, in order not to slander John too much, they dared not confess it to be from men [Matt. 21:25-27]. If confirmation is therefore from men, it is proved vain and /164/trifling; if our opponents wish to convince us that it is from heaven, let them prove it.

3. Indeed, they defend themselves with the example of the apostles, who, they judge, did nothing rashly. Quite true; nor would we blame them if they showed themselves followers of the apostles. But what did the apostles do? Luke tells in The Acts that the apostles who were at Jerusalem, when they had heard that Samaria had received the word of God, sent Peter and John thither; these apostles prayed for the Samaritans that they might receive the Holy Spirit, who had not yet come upon any of them, for they had been baptized in Jesus' name only; when they had prayed, they laid their hands upon them, and through this laying on of hands the Samaritans received the Holy Spirit [Acts. 8:14-17, cf. Vg.]. And he frequently mentions this laying on of hands [Acts 6:6; 8:17; 13:3; 19:6]. I hear what the apostles did, that is, that they faithfully fulfilled their ministry. The Lord willed that those visible and wonderful graces of the Holy Spirit, which he then poured out upon his people, be administered and distributed by his apostles through the laying on of hands. I think that no deeper mystery underlies this laying on of hands, [289] but my interpretation is that

they made use of such a ceremony to signify by their gesture that they commended to God, and, as it were, offered him on whom they laid their hands.

If this ministry which the apostles then carried out still remained in the church, the laying on of hands would also have to be kept. But since that grace has ceased to be given, what purpose does the laying on of hands serve? Surely, the Holy Spirit is still present among God's people, for the church cannot stand unless he is its guide and director. For we have (143) an eternal and permanently established promise by which Christ calls to himself those who thirst, that they may drink living waters [John 7:37; cf. Is. 55:1; also John 4:10; 7:38]. But those miraculous powers and manifest workings, which were dispensed by the laying on of hands, have ceased; and they have rightly lasted only for a time. For it was fitting that the new preaching of the gospel and the new kingdom of Christ should be illumined and magnified by unheard-of and extraordinary miracles. When the Lord ceased from these, he did not utterly forsake his church, but declared that the magnificence of his Kingdom and the dignity of his word had been excellently enough disclosed. In what respect, then, will these actors say they are following the apostles? They should have brought it about with laying on of hands, in order that the evident power of the Holy Spirit might be immediately expressed. This they do not accomplish. Why, then, [290] do they boast that the laying on of hands is theirs, which we read was indeed in use

4.19.7
among the apostles, but for a wholly different end? This is as reasonable as to say that the breath which the Lord breathed upon his disciples [John 20:22] is a sacrament by which the Holy Spirit is given. But while the Lord did this once, /165/he did not mean that we should also do it. In the same way also, the apostles laid on hands for the time when it pleased the Lord that the visible graces of the Holy Spirit be distributed at their prayers, not in order that their descendants should in mimicry only and without profit counterfeit a cold and empty sign, as these apes do.

4. But if they prove that in the laying on of hands they follow the apostles (in which they have no similarity to the apostles except some sort of misguided imitation), yet whence that oil, which they call "the oil of salvation"? Who taught them to seek salvation in oil? Who taught them to attribute to it the power to confirm? Did Paul, who draws us far away from the elements of this world [Gal. 4:9], who condemns nothing more than clinging to such petty observances [Col. 2:20]? But I boldly declare this, not from myself, but from the Lord: Those who call oil "the oil of salvation" forswear the salvation which is in Christ; they deny Christ, and they have no part in God's Kingdom. For oil is for the belly and the belly for oil; the Lord will destroy both [cf. I Cor. 6:13]. For all these [291] weak elements which decay with use have nothing to do with God's Kingdom, which is spiritual and will never decay. What, then? Will someone ask, "Do you measure with the same stick the water with which we are baptized, and the bread and wine under which the Lord's Supper is set forth?" I reply: in the sacraments of the Lord two things are to be noted: the substance of the physical thing which is set forth to us, and the form which is impressed

126

upon it by God's Word, in which its whole force lies. In so far as they, therefore, retain their substance—bread, wine, water, that are offered to our sight in the sacraments—Paul's statement holds good always: "Food for the belly, and the belly for food; God will destroy both" [I Cor. 6:13, cf. Vg.]. For they pass away and vanish with the form of this world [I Cor. 7:31]. But in so far as they are sanctified by God's word to be sacraments, (144) they do not hold us within the flesh, but truly spiritually teach us.

5. But let us investigate still more closely how many monsters this grease feeds and nourishes. These anointers say that the Holy Spirit is given in baptism for innocence; in confirmation, for the increase of grace; that in baptism we are regenerated unto life; in confirmation we are equipped for battle. And they are so shameless as to deny that baptism can be duly completed without confirmation!* What wickedness! Have not we then been buried in baptism with Christ, made partakers in his death, [292] that we may also be sharers in his resurrection [Rom. 6:4-5]? Moreover, this participation in Christ's death and life Paul explains to be the mortifying of our flesh and the quickening of the Spirit, because "our old man has been crucified" [Rom. 6:6, Vg.] because "we walk in newness of life" [Rom. 6:5, Vg.]. What is it to be equipped for battle, but this? But Luke, /166/ in the passage we have cited, says that persons who had not received the Holy Spirit were baptized in the name of Jesus Christ [Acts 8:16]. In saying this, Luke does not simply deny that they who believe in Christ with their heart and confess him with their mouth are endowed with any gift of the Spirit [Rom. 10:10]. But he has in mind the receiving of the Spirit, by which manifest powers and visible graces were received. Thus the apostles are said to have received the Spirit on the Day of Pentecost [Acts 2:4], while Christ long before had said to them, "It is not you who speak, but the Spirit of your Father, who speaks in you" [Matt. 10:20, Vg.]. You who are of God observe here Satan's malicious and dangerous fraud. In order stealthily to draw the unwary from baptism, he lies in saying that what was truly given in baptism is given in his confirmation. Who now can doubt that this is a doctrine of Satan, which, cutting off from baptism the promises proper to baptism, conveys and transfers them elsewhere? We have now detected, I say, upon what foundation this wonderful anointing rests. The word of God is: "All who have been baptized in Christ have put on Christ with his [293] gifts" [Gal. 3:27]. The word of the anointers is: "No promise has been received in baptism to prepare us for combat." The former is the voice of truth; the latter must be that of falsehood. Therefore, I can more truly define this confirmation than they have hitherto defined it: it is an overt outrage against baptism which obscures and abolishes, its function; it is a false promise of the devil, to draw us away from God's truth. Or, if you prefer, it is oil, befouled with the devil's falsehood, to deceive and plunge the simpleminded into darkness.

6. Furthermore, they add that all believers ought to receive the Holy Spirit by the laying on of hands after baptism so that they may be found complete Christians; for there will never be a Christian unless anointed with chrism by

4.19.8

4.19.9

episcopal confirmation: These are their exact words. Yet I thought that everything pertaining to Christianity was set down (145) and comprised in the Scriptures. Now (as I see) the true form of religion is to be sought and learned elsewhere than from the Scriptures. Therefore, the wisdom of God, heavenly truth, Christ's whole teaching, only begin Christians; oil perfects them. By this sentence all the apostles and many of the martyrs are condemned, who most certainly never received the chrism—since there was not yet holy oil to pour out upon them and make them complete in all the details of Christianity, /167/ or rather [294] make Christians of those who were not yet Christians: But, though I remain silent, these persons abundantly refute themselves. For what portion of their own people do they anoint after baptism? Why, then, do they allow such half-Christians in their flock, whose imperfection they could easily remedy? Why do they with such craven negligence allow people to omit what could not be omitted without grave incrimination? Why do they not more strictly require a thing so necessary and requisite for the obtaining of salvation, unless, perhaps, one has been prevented by sudden death? That is, when they allow it to be despised so freely, they tacitly confess that it is not so important as they claim.

4.19.10   7. Finally, they determine that this sacred anointing ought to be held in greater veneration than baptism, because it is exclusively administered by the hands of the high priests, while baptism is commonly dispensed by all priests. What can you say here but that they are plainly mad who are so fond of their own inventions that by comparison they carelessly despise God's most holy institutions? O sacrilegious mouth, do you dare oppose to Christ's sacrament a grease befouled only with the stench of your own breath, and under the spell of mumbled words, and to compare it with water sanctified by God's Word? Yet to your audacity this was but a trifle—for you even preferred it. These are [295] the responses of the holy see, the oracles of the apostolic tripod. But some of these people begin to moderate a little this madness which even in their opinion was out of control. Anointing is to be held in greater reverence, they say, perhaps not because of the greater power and profit in confers, but because it is given by the more worthy, and on the more worthy part of the body, that is, on the forehead; or because it provides a greater increase of virtues, although baptism avails more for forgiveness of sins: But in the first reason, do they not betray themselves as Donatists, who reckon the force of the sacrament from the worthiness of the minister? However, I shall admit that confirmation may be called worthier by the worthiness of the bishop's hand. But if someone inquire of them the source of this very great privilege of the bishops, what reason will they bring forward but their own whim? The apostles (they will say) alone used that right, as they alone dispensed the Holy Spirit. Are the bishops alone apostles? Indeed, are they apostles at all? Still, suppose we concede this also. Why do they not contend by the same argument that bishops alone ought to touch the sacrament (146) of blood in the Lord's Supper, which they deny to laymen for the reason that it was given by the Lord to the apostles alone? If /168/ to the apostles alone, why do they not infer, therefore, to the bishops alone? But in that place they make the apostles simple priests; now a dizziness of the head carries them off in another direction, so that suddenly they make them bishops. Finally, Ananias was not an apostle, yet he was sent to Paul that Paul might receive [296] his sight, be baptized, and be filled with the Holy Spirit [Acts 9:17-19]. I shall also add this to the pile: If this office had belonged to the bishops by divine right, why did they dare transfer it to common presbyters, as we read in a letter of Gregory?*

8. How trifling, foolish, and stupid is their other reason for calling confirmation more worthy than God's baptism: that in it the forehead is smeared with oil, in baptism the top of the head*—as if baptism were performed with oil and not with water! I call all godly men to witness whether these rascals are not striving toward this one end, to corrupt the purity of the sacraments with their leaven. I have already said in another place that in the sacraments, amidst the throng of human inventions, what is of God scarcely glimmers through crannies. If anyone did not trust me then in this matter, let him now at least believe his own teachers. Behold, while they neglect the water and reckon it of no account, they esteem only oil in baptism! We therefore say, on the contrary, that in baptism the forehead is moistened with water. In comparison with this, we esteem your oil—whether in baptism or in confirmation—not worth one piece of dung. But if anyone will claim that it is sold for more, the answer is ready: your selling is an imposture, is worthlessness, is theft.

They betray their impiety in the third reason when they prate that a greater increase of virtues [297] is conferred in confirmation than in baptism.* By the laying on of hands the apostles administered the visible graces of the Spirit. In what respect does these men's grease show itself beneficial? But farewell to these directors, who cover one sacrilege with many sacrileges. It is a Gordian knot which it is better to cut than to toil so hard to untie.

9. But now, when they see themselves deprived of God's Word and of any demonstrable argument, they pretend, as usual, that this is a most ancient observance, confirmed*by the custom of many centuries. Even if this were true, they gain nothing. A sacrament is not of the earth, but of heaven; not of men, but of God alone. They must prove God the author of their confirmation if they wish to have it regarded as a sacrament.* But why do they claim antiquity, seeing that the ancient writers nowhere reckon more than two sacraments? If we had to seek from men a refuge for our faith, we have an impregnable citadel*in that the ancients never recognized as sacraments what these fellows falsely call sacraments. (147) /169/ The ancients speak of the laying on of hands, but do they call it a sacrament? Augustine openly affirms that it is nothing but prayer.* Now let them not snarl at me with their foul distinctions, [298] that Augustine meant this act not to be confirmatory, but curative or reconciliatory. The book is extant and circulates in men's hands; if I am twisting it into another meaning than Augustine himself wrote, I am content to let them not only rail at me as usual, but spit at me.

4.19.13   10. How I wish that we might have kept the custom which, I suspect, existed among the ancient Christians before this misborn wraith of a sacrament came to birth! Not that it would be a confirmation, which cannot be named without doing injustice to baptism; but a Christian catechizing, in which children or those near adolescence would give an account of their faith before the church. But the best method of catechizing would be to have a manual drafted for this exercise, containing and summarizing in a simple manner nearly all the articles of our religion, on which the whole believers' church ought to agree without controversy. A child of ten would present himself to the church to declare his confession of faith, would be examined in each article, and answer to each; if he were ignorant of anything or insufficiently understood it, he would be taught. Thus, while the church looks on as witness, he would profess the one true and sincere faith, in which the believing folk with one mind worship the one God. If this discipline were in effect today, it would certainly arouse some slothful parents, who carelessly neglect the instruction of their children as a matter of no concern to them; [299] for then they could not overlook it without public disgrace. There would be greater agreement in faith among Christian people, and not so many would go untaught and ignorant; some would not be so rashly carried away with new and strange doctrines; in short, all would have some methodical instruction, so to speak, in Christian doctrine.

B. PENANCE

4.19.14   11. In the next place they put penance, of which they discourse in such confused and disorderly fashion that consciences can gain nothing certain or solid from their doctrine. We will first explain in a few words what we have learned concerning repentance from the Scriptures, then what our adversaries teach and finally, with what trifling reason or no reason at all, they made it a sacrament. /170/

3.3.3   12. Certain men well versed in penance, even long before these times, meaning to speak simply and sincerely according to the rule of Scripture, said that it consists of two parts: mortification and vivification. Mortification they explain as sorrow of soul and dread conceived from the recognition of sin and the awareness of divine judgment. For when anyone has been brought into a true knowledge of sin, (148) he then begins truly to hate and abhor sin; then he is heartily displeased with himself, he confesses himself miserable and lost [300] and wishes to be another man. Furthermore, when he is touched by any sense of the judgment of God (for the one straightway follows the other) he then lies stricken and overthrown; humbled and cast down he trembles; he becomes discouraged and despairs. This is the first part of repentance, commonly called "contrition." "Vivification" they understand as the consolation that arises out of faith. That is, when a man is laid low by the consciousness of sin and stricken by the fear of God, and afterward looks to the goodness of God—to his mercy, grace, salvation, which is through Christ—raises himself up, he takes heart, he recovers courage, and as it were, returns from death to life.*

13. Others, because they saw the various meanings of this word in Scripture, posited two forms of repentance. To distinguish them by some mark, they called one "repentance of the law." Through it the sinner wounded by the branding of sin and stricken by dread of God's wrath, remains caught in that disturbed state and cannot extricate himself from it. The other they call "repentance of the gospel." Through it the sinner is indeed sorely afflicted, but rises above it and lays hold of Christ as medicine for his wound, comfort for his dread, the haven of his misery.* Examples of "repentance of the law" are: Cain [Gen. 4:13], Saul [I Sam. 15:30], and Judas [Matt. 27:4]. While Scripture recounts their repentance to us, it represents them as acknowledging the gravity of their sin, and afraid of God's wrath; but [301] since they conceived of God only as Avenger and Judge, that very thought overwhelmed them. Therefore their repentance was nothing but a sort of entryway of hell, which they had already entered in this life, and had begun to undergo punishment before the wrath of God's majesty.* We see "gospel repentance" in all those who, made sore by the sting of sin but aroused and refreshed by trust in God's mercy, have turned to the Lord. When Hezekiah received the message of death, he was paralyzed with fear. But he wept and prayed, and looking to God's goodness, he recovered confidence [II Kings 20:2; Is. 38:2]. The Ninevites were troubled by a dreadful threat of destruction; but putting on sackcloth and ashes, they prayed, hoping that the Lord might be turned toward them and be turned away from the fury of his wrath [Jonah 3:5, 9]. David confessed that he sinned greatly in taking a census of the people, but /171/ he added, "O Lord, . . . take away the iniquity of thy servant" [II Sam. 24:10]. When he was rebuked by Nathan, David acknowledged his sin of adultery, and he fell down before the Lord, but at the same time he awaited pardon [II Sam. 12:13, 16]. Such was the repentance of those who felt remorse of heart at Peter's preaching but, trusting in God's goodness, they added: "Brethren, what shall we do?" [Acts 2:37]. Such, also, was Peter's own repentance; he wept bitterly indeed [Matt. 26:75; Luke 22:62], but he did not cease to hope.*

14. Although all these things are true, yet the word "repentance" itself, so far as I can learn from Scripture, is to be understood otherwise. For [302] their inclusion of faith under repentance disagrees with what Paul says in Acts: (149) "Testifying both to Jews and Gentiles of repentance to God, and of faith . . . in Jesus Christ" [Acts 20:21]. There he reckons repentance and faith as two different things. What then? Can true repentance stand, apart from faith? Not at all. But even though they cannot be separated, they ought to be distinguished. For as faith is not without hope, yet faith and hope are different things, so repentance and faith, although they are held together by a permanent bond, are to be yoked rather than confused. On this account, in my judgment, repentance is mortification of our flesh and of the old man, which true and pure fear of God brings about in us. In that sense we must understand all those preachings

3.3.4

3.3.5

by which either the prophets of old or the apostles later used to exhort men of their time to repentance. For they were striving for this one thing: that, confused by their sins and pierced by the fear of God, they should fall down and humble themselves before the Lord, and return to the way and repent. Therefore these words are used interchangeably in the same sense: "Turn or return to the Lord," and "do penance"*[Matt. 3:2]. And John has said, "Bring forth fruits worthy of repentance" [Luke 3:8; cf Acts 26:20; Rom. 6:4]; lead a life befitting a repentance and conversion of this sort. [303]

3.3.19   15. Moreover the whole sum of the gospel is contained under these two headings, repentance and forgiveness of sins: John, a messenger sent before the face of Christ to prepare his ways [Matt. 11:10; cf. Mal. 3:1], proclaimed: "Repent, for the Kingdom of Heaven has come near" [Matt. 3:2; 4:17, Vg.]. By calling them to repentance, he was admonishing them to recognize they were sinners, and their all was condemned before God, that they might with all their hearts desire the mortification of their flesh, and a new rebirth in the Spirit. By proclaiming the Kingdom of God, he was calling them to faith, for by the Kingdom of God, which he taught was at hand, he meant the forgiveness of sins, salvation, life, and utterly everything we obtain in Christ. Hence we read in the other Evangelists: "John came preaching a baptism of repentance for the remission /172/ of sins" [Mark 1:4; Luke 3:3]. What else is this than that they, weighed down and wearied by the burden of sins, should turn to the Lord and conceive a hope of forgiveness and salvation? So, also, Christ entered upon his preaching: "The Kingdom of God has come near; repent, and believe in the gospel" [Mark 1:15 p.]. First he declares that the treasures of God's mercy have been opened in himself; then he requires repentance; finally, trust in God's promises. Therefore, when Christ meant to summarize the whole business of the gospel in brief, he said that he "should suffer, . . . and rise [304] from the dead, that repentance and forgiveness of sins should be preached in his name" [Luke 24:26, 46-47]. And after his resurrection the apostles preached this: "God raised Jesus . . . to give repentance to Israel and forgiveness of sins" [Acts 5:30-31]. Repentance is preached in the name of Christ when, through the teaching of the gospel, men hear (150) that all their thoughts, all their inclinations, all their efforts, are corrupt and vicious. Accordingly, they must be reborn if they would

3.3.9   enter the Kingdom of God; moreover, this is the manner of rebirth: if they have participation in Christ, in whose death our depraved desires die, in whose cross our old man is crucified, in whose tomb our body of sin is buried [Rom. 6:6].

3.3.19   Forgiveness of sins is preached when men are taught that for them Christ became redemption, righteousness, satisfaction, and life [I Cor. 1:30], that by his name they are freely accounted righteous and innocent in God's sight. In one word, then, I interpret repentance to be mortification.

3.3.20   This repentance first gives us access to the knowledge of Christ, who reveals himself to none but poor and afflicted sinners, who groan, toil, are heavy-laden, hunger, thirst, and pine away with sorrow and misery [Is. 61:1-3; Matt. 11:5, 28; Luke 4:18]. Accordingly, we must strive toward this repentance,

132

devote ourselves to it and pursue it throughout life. Plato said that the life [305] of a philosopher is a meditation upon death; but we may more truly say that the life of a Christian man is a continual effort and exercise in the mortification of the flesh; till it clearly dies. Therefore, I think he has profited greatly who has learned to be very much displeased with himself, not so as to stick fast in this mire and progress no farther, but rather to hasten to God and so yearn that, having been engrafted into the death of Christ, he may meditate on repentance. This thought, as it was the simplest of all, so has it seemed to me to agree best with the truth of Scripture.

16. Now, I come to discuss what the Scholastic Sophists have taught concerning repentance. This I will run through in as few words as possible because it is not my intention to pursue everything, lest this little book of mine which I mean to keep to the brevity of a handbook, /173/ burst all bounds. They have involved this matter, otherwise not very complicated, in so many volumes that there would be no easy way out if you were to immerse yourself even slightly in their slime. First, in giving their definition, they clearly disclose that they have never understood what repentance is. For they take certain clichés from the books of the ancient writers, which do not express the force of repentance at all. For example: to repent is to weep over former sins, and not to commit sins to be wept over; again, it is to bewail past evil deeds and not again to commit deeds to be bewailed; [306] again, it is a certain sorrowing vengeance that punishes in oneself what one is sorry to have committed; again, it is sorrow of heart and bitterness of soul for the evil deeds that one has committed, or to which one has consented. Let us grant that these things have been well said by the fathers (which it would not be difficult for a contentious man to deny). (151) Yet they were not spoken with the intent to define repentance, but only to urge their hearers not to fall again into the same transgressions from which they had been rescued.

They divide repentance, thus subtly defined, into contrition of heart, confession of mouth, and satisfaction of works. This division is no more logical than the definition—even though they wish to appear to have spent their whole life in framing syllogisms. Suppose someone reasons from their definition—a kind of argument prevalent among dialecticians—that anyone can weep for previously committed sins and not commit sins that ought to be wept over, can bewail past evil deeds and not commit evil deeds that ought to be bewailed, can punish what he is sorry to have committed, etc., even though he does not confess with his mouth. How, then, will they maintain their division? For if he does not confess though truly penitent, there can be repentance without confession. But if they reply that this division applies to penance only in so far as it is a sacrament, or is understood concerning the whole perfection of repentance, [307] which they do not include in their definitions, /174/ there is no reason to accuse me; let them blame themselves for not defining it more precisely and clearly. Now, for my part, when there is a dispute concerning anything, I am stupid enough to refer everything back to the definition itself, which is the hinge and

3.4.1

foundation of the whole debate. But let that be the teachers' license. Now let us survey in order the various parts themselves.

3.4.2   17. Now I would have my readers note that this is no contention over the shadow of an ass, but that the most serious matter of all is under discussion: namely, forgiveness of sins. For while they require three things for repentance—compunction of heart, confession of mouth, and satisfaction of works—at the same time they teach that these things are necessary to attain forgiveness of sins. But if there is anything in the whole of our religion that it is our business to know, the chief thing is clearly to understand and honestly to grasp by what reason, with what law, under what condition, with what ease or difficulty, forgiveness of sins may be obtained! Unless this knowledge remains clear and sure, the conscience can have no rest at all, no peace with God, no assurance or security; but it continuously trembles, wavers, tosses, is tormented and vexed, shakes, hates, and flees the sight of God. But if forgiveness of sins depends upon these conditions which they attach to it, nothing is more miserable or hopeless for us.

18. They make contrition the first step in obtaining pardon, and they require it [308] to be a due contrition, that is, just and full. But at the same time they do not determine when a man can be sure he has in just measure carried out his contrition. Here indeed miserable consciences are tormented in strange ways and troubled, when they see due contrition for sins imposed upon them. And they do not grasp the measure of the debt (152) so that they are able to discern within themselves that they have paid what they owed. If they were to say we must do what is in us, we are always brought back to the same point. For when will anyone dare assure himself he has applied all his powers to lament his sins? Therefore, when consciences have for a long time wrestled with themselves, and exercised themselves in long struggles, they still do not find a haven in which to rest. Consequently, to calm themselves, at least in part, they wrest sorrow from themselves and squeeze out tears that they may thereby accomplish

3.4.3   their contrition. But if they say I accuse them falsely, let them actually bring forward and exhibit anyone who, by a doctrine of contrition of this sort, either is not driven to desperation or has not met God's judgment with pretended rather than true sorrow. And we have said in some place that forgiveness of sins can never come to anyone without repentance, because only those /175/ afflicted and wounded by the awareness of sins can sincerely call upon God's mercy. But we added at the same time [309] that repentance is not the cause of forgiveness of sins. Moreover, we have done away with those torments of souls which they would have us perform as a duty. We have taught that the sinner does not dwell upon his own compunction or tears, but fixes both eyes upon the Lord's mercy alone. We have merely reminded him that Christ called those who "labor and are heavy-laden" [Matt. 11:28], when he was sent to publish good news to the poor, to heal the brokenhearted, to proclaim release to the captives, to free the prisoners, to comfort the mourners [Is. 61:1; Luke 4:18, conflated]. Hence are to be excluded both the Pharisees, who, sated with their own righteousness, do not recognize their poverty; and despisers, who, oblivious of God's wrath, do not seek a remedy for their own evil. For such do not labor, are not heavy-laden, are not brokenhearted, or prisoners or captives, and do not mourn. But it makes a great difference whether you teach forgiveness of sins as deserved by just and full contrition* which you can never perform; or whether you enjoin the sinner to hunger and thirst after God's mercy to show him—through the recognition of his misery, his vacillation, his weariness, and his captivity—where he may seek refreshment, rest, and liberation; in short, to teach him in his humility to give glory to God.

19. There has always been great strife between the canon lawyers and the Scholastic theologians* concerning confession. [310] The latter contend that confession is enjoined by divine precept; the former claim that it is commanded only by ecclesiastical constitutions* Now in that contest the marked shamelessness of the theologians is evident, who corrupted and forcibly twisted all the passages of Scripture they cited for their purpose. And when they saw that what they wanted could not even in this way be obtained, those who wished to appear more astute than others resorted to the evasion that confession is derived from divine law with respect to its substance, (153) but later took its form from positive law* Of course, the most incompetent among pettifogging lawyers thus relate the citation to the divine law because it is said: "Adam, where are you?" [Gen. 3:9]. The exception, too, because Adam answered as if taking exception: "The wife that thou gavest me," etc. [Gen. 3:12]. In both cases, however, the form is derived from the civil law. But let us see by what proofs they demonstrate this confession—formed or unformed—to be a command of God. The Lord, they say, sent the lepers to the priests* [Matt. 8:4; Mark 1:44; Luke 5:14; 17:14]. What? Did he send them to confession? Who ever heard it said /176/ that the Levitical priests were appointed to hear confessions [Deut. 17:8-9]? They therefore take refuge in allegories: it was laid down by the Mosaic law that priests should distinguish between stages of leprosy [Lev. 14:2-3]. Sin is spiritual leprosy: [311] it is the duty of priests to pronounce concerning this. Before I answer, I ask in passing why, if this passage makes them judges of spiritual leprosy, do they assume cognizance of natural and physical leprosy? As if this reasoning were not to mock Scripture: the law entrusts the recognition of leprosy to the Levitical priests, let us take this over for ourselves: sin is spiritual leprosy, let us also be judicial examiners of sin! Now I reply: "When the priesthood is transferred, there is necessarily a transference of the law as well" [Heb. 7:12]. All priestly offices have been transferred to Christ and are fulfilled and completed in him. The whole right and honor of the priesthood has therefore been transferred to him alone. If they are so fond of chasing after allegories, let them set before themselves Christ as their sole priest, and in his judgment seat concentrate unlimited jurisdiction over all things. We shall readily allow that. Moreover, their allegory, which reckons the merely civil law among the ceremonies, is unsuitable.

Why then does Christ send lepers to the priests? That the priests may not

3.4.4

charge him with breaking the law, which bade that one cured of leprosy be shown to the priest, and atoned for by offering sacrifice. He bids cleansed lepers do what the law enjoins. "Go." he says, "show yourselves to the priests" [Luke 17:14]; "and offer the gift that Moses prescribes in the law, for a proof to them" [Matt. 8:4 p.]. Truly, [312] this miracle was to be a proof for them. They had declared them lepers; now they declare them cured. Are they not, even against their will, compelled to become witnesses of Christ's miracles? Christ permits them to investigate his miracle. They cannot deny it. But because they still try to evade, this work serves for them as a proof. Thus, in another passage: "This gospel will be preached throughout the whole world, as a proof to all nations" [Matt. 24:14 p.]. Likewise, "You will be dragged before kings and governors . . . as a proof to them." [Matt. 10:18] That is, that they may be more strongly convicted by God's judgment.

3.4.5   They derive a second argument from the same source, that is from an allegory—as if allegories were of great value in confirming any dogma! But, let them be of value, unless I show that I can apply those very allegories more plausibly than they. Now they say: (154) the Lord bade the disciples unbind the risen Lazarus and let him go [John 11:44]. First, they falsely declare this, for nowhere does one read that the Lord said this to his disciples. It is much more probable that he said this to the Jews who were present, in order that his miracle might be demonstrated beyond any suspicion of fraud, and might display his greater power, in that he raised the dead by his voice alone, and not by his touch. So do I interpret the fact that the Lord, /177/ to relieve the Jews of all perverse suspicion, [313] willed that they roll away the stone, smell the stench, look upon the sure signs of death, see him rising up by the power of his Word alone, and be the first to touch him alive. But suppose we regard this statement as made to the disciples, what then will our opponents maintain? That the Lord gave the apostles the power of loosing? How much more aptly and skillfully this could be treated as an allegory if we should say that by this symbol the Lord willed to instruct his believers; to loose those raised up by him, that is, so that they should not recall to memory their sins which he himself had forgotten, nor damn as sinners those whom he himself had absolved, nor still upbraid them for those things that he himself had condoned, nor be harsh and captious to punish where he himself was merciful and ready to spare! Now let them go and peddle their allegories!

3.4.6   20. Now they come into closer combat when they fight, armed with plain (as they suppose) testimonies: those who came to the baptism of John confessed their sins [Matt. 3:6]; and James enjoins us to "confess our sins to one another" [James 5:16]. No wonder if those who wished to be baptized confessed their sins! For, as it was said before, "John . . . preached a baptism of repentance" [Mark 1:4]. He baptized with water unto repentance. Whom, therefore, would he have baptized but those who had confessed themselves sinners? Baptism is the symbol of forgiveness of sins. Who would have been admitted to this symbol but sinners and those who recognize themselves as such? [314] Therefore, they confess their sins in order to be baptized. It is with good reason that James enjoins us to "confess . . . to one another" [James 5:16]. But if they had paid attention to what follows immediately, they would have understood that this also gives them little support. "Confess," he says, "your sins to one another, and pray for one another" [James 5:16]. He joins together mutual confession and mutual prayer. If we must confess to priestlings alone, then we must pray for them alone. What? Suppose it followed from the words of James that only priestlings could confess? Indeed, while he wishes us to confess to one another, he addresses those alone who could hear one another's confession ἀλλήλοις, "mutually," "interchangeably," or, if they prefer, "reciprocally."

Away, then, with trifles of this sort! Let us take the apostle's view, which is simple and open: namely, that we should lay our infirmities on one another's breasts, to receive among ourselves mutual counsel, mutual compassion, and mutual consolation. Then, as we are aware of our brothers' infirmity, let us pray to the Lord for them. Why, (155) then, do they quote James against us though we so strongly urge the confession of God's mercy? But no one can confess the mercy of God unless he has previously confessed his own misery. Rather, we pronounce anathema upon everyone who has not confessed himself a sinner before God, before his angels, /178/ before the church, and in short, before [315] all men. For the Lord has "shut up all things under sin" [Gal. 3:22] "that every mouth may be stopped" [Rom. 3:19] and all flesh be humbled before God [cf. Rom. 3:20; I Cor. 1:29]. But let him alone be justified [cf. Rom. 3:4] and exalted.

21. But I marvel how shamelessly our opponents dare contend that the confession of which they speak is divinely ordained. Of course we admit its practice to have been very ancient, but we can easily prove that it was formerly free. Surely, even their records declare that no law or constitution concerning it had been set up before the time of Innocent III. And there are clear testimonies, both in histories and among other ancient writers, that teach this was a discipline of polity, instituted by bishops, not a law laid down by Christ or the apostles. I shall bring forward only one of these many testimonies, which will provide clear proof of this matter. Sozomen relates that this constitution of the bishops was diligently observed by the Western churches, especially at Rome. This means that it was not a universal practice of all the churches. Moreover, he says that one of the presbyters was especially designated for this office. This thoroughly refutes what these fellows falsely state concerning the keys given in common to the whole priestly order. Indeed, it was not a function common to all priests, but the exclusive function of one priest who had been chosen for it by the bishop. Then he adds that this also had been the custom at Constantinople [316] until a certain matron, pretending to confess, was found to have hidden under the guise of confession an affair which she was having with a certain deacon. On account of this crime, Nectarius, a man renowned for his holiness and learning, bishop of that church, abolished the rite of confession. Here, here, let these asses prick up their ears! If auricular confession were the law of God, why would

3.4.7

137

Nectarius have dared set it aside and uproot it? Will they accuse Nectarius—a holy man of God, approved by the consent of all the ancients—of heresy and schism? But with this same sentence they will condemn the church of Constantinople in which, Sozomen declares, the practice of confession was not only neglected for a time, but within his memory allowed to fall into disuse. Indeed, they will accuse of defection not only the Church of Constantinople but all the Eastern churches—if they speak the truth—that neglected an inviolable /179/ law enjoined upon all Christians.

3.4.9   22. But, to make the whole matter plainer and easier, we will first faithfully relate what kind of confession we are taught in the Word of God. (156) Then we will add an account of their inventions concerning confession—not indeed all, for who could empty such an immense sea—but at least those with which they embrace the sum of their confession. I need not recall here that it is common in many parts of Scripture to understand [317] "confession" to mean "praise," unless they had been so shameful as not to instruct themselves in such passages, as when they say, confession stands for joyousness of mind, according to the passage: "In the voice of exultation and confession" [Ps. 42:4; 41:5, Vg.]. Let the simple folk keep this meaning, and carefully distinguish it from that, lest they be deceived with such false colors.

      23. On confession of sins Scripture teaches as follows: since it is the Lord who forgives, forgets, and wipes out sins, let us confess our sins to him that we may obtain pardon. He is the physician; therefore, let us lay bare our wounds to him. It is he who is hurt and offended; from him let us seek peace. He is the discerner of hearts, the one cognizant of all thoughts [cf. Heb. 4:12]; let us pour out our hearts before him. He it is, finally, who calls sinners: let us come to God himself. "I acknowledged my sin to thee," says David, "and I did not hide my iniquity. I said, 'I will confess against me my iniquity to the Lord'; and thou forgavest the wickedness of my heart." [Ps. 32:5; 31:5, Vg.]. Of similar nature is another confession of David himself: "Have mercy upon me, O God, according to thy great loving-kindness" [Ps. 51:1; 50:3, Vg.]. Such, too, is Daniel's statement: "We have sinned and done wrong and acted wickedly and rebelled, O Lord, in turning aside from thy commandments." [Dan. 9:5] And there are other confessions that occur here and there in Scripture. "If we confess our sins," says John, "the Lord is faithful [318] . . . to forgive our sins." [I John 1:9, cf. Vg.] To whom should we confess? Surely to him, that is, if we fall down before him with troubled and humbled heart; if wholeheartedly accusing and condemning ourselves before him, we seek to be acquitted by his goodness and

3.4.10   mercy. He who will embrace this confession in his heart and before God will without doubt also have a tongue prepared for confession, whenever there is need to proclaim God's mercy among men. This he will do not only to whisper the secret of his heart to one man and at one time, and in the ear; but often, publicly, with all the world hearing, unfeignedly to recount both his own poverty and the Lord's magnificence. In this way, when David was rebuked by Nathan he was pricked by the sting of conscience, and confessed his sin before both

God and men. "I have sinned," he said, "against the Lord." [II Sam. 12:13] That is, I now make no excuse; I do not try to avoid /180/ being judged by all to be a sinner, nor to prevent what I tried to hide from the Lord being revealed also even to men.

Scripture, moreover, approves two forms of private confession: one made for our own sake, to which the statement of James refers that we should confess our sins to one another [James 5:16]. For he means that, sharing our weaknesses with one another, we help one another with counsel and consolation. (157) The other form we are to use for our neighbor's sake, to appease him and [319] to reconcile him to us if through fault of ours he has been in any way injured. Christ speaks of this in Matthew: "If you are offering your gift at the altar, and there remember that your brother has something against you, leave your gift there . . . and go; first be reconciled to your brother, and then come and offer your gift"* [Matt. 5:23-24]. For the love, which was dissolved by our offense, is thus repaired by our acknowledging the wrong we have committed, and asking pardon for it. Scripture does not know any other manner or form of confession at all.

24. What do [our adversaries] say? They decree that all persons of "both sexes," as soon as they attain the age of discretion, should confess all their sins to their own priest at least once a year, and that their sin is not forgiven unless they have a firmly conceived intent to confess it.* And if they do not carry out this intent when occasion is offered, no entrance to paradise is now open.* Now, they assert, the priest has the power of the keys with which to bind and loose the sinner because Christ's word is not void: "Whomever you bind,"*etc. [Matt. 18:18]. Yet they quarrel fiercely among themselves over this power. Some say that there is essentially only one key—namely, the power to bind and loose— that knowledge is indeed required for good use, but it is only like an accessory, not joined to the other in essence.* Others, because they saw that this was excessively unbridled license, [320] posited two keys: discretion and power.* Still others, since they saw the depravity of the priests restrained by such moderation, forged other keys: the authority to discern (to use in passing sentence), and the power to exercise in executing their sentence; and they added knowledge as counselor.* /181/ But they dare not interpret binding and loosing simply as remitting and blotting out sins, for they hear the Lord proclaiming through the prophet: "I am, I am he who blots out your transgressions, O Israel, I and no other but me"*[Is. 43:11, 25 p.]. But they say that it is the priest's task to declare who are to be bound or loosed, and to state whose sins are to be remitted or retained;* to declare this, moreover, either through confession when he absolves and retains sins or through sentence when he excommunicates or receives into the partaking of the sacraments.* Finally, suppose they understand that they have not yet removed this difficulty, but that the objection can always be raised against them, that unworthy persons are often bound and loosed by their priests, who will not therefore be bound or loosed in heaven. Their last refuge is then to reply that the conferring of the keys is to be understood with this one limitation: Christ

3.4.12

3.4.13

3.4.15

139

promised that the sentence of the priests would be approved before his judgment seat, provided it was justly pronounced according as (158) the deserts of the one bound or loosed required. Now, [321] they say that these keys have been given by Christ to all priests and are conferred upon them by the bishops at the time of promotion, but their free use remains only in the possession of those who perform ecclesiastical functions; that the keys indeed remain in the possession of the excommunicated and suspended clergy, but rusted and bound. And those who say these things may rightly be called modest and sober in comparison with those who have forged on a new anvil new keys, with which they teach the

3.5.2 treasury of the church is locked. The merits of Christ and the holy apostles, Peter, Paul, the martyrs, etc., our opponents call the "treasury of the church." They pretend that the prime custody of this storehouse has been entrusted to the Bishop of Rome, who controls the dispensing of these very great benefits, so that he can both distribute them by himself and delegate to others the prime management of their distribution. Consequently, plenary indulgences, as well as indulgences for certain years, stem from the pope; indulgences for a hundred days, from the cardinals; and of forty days, from the bishops!

3.4.16 25. I shall reply to each point in a few words. But I shall remain silent for the present as to what right or lack of right they have to bind the souls of believers with their laws, since this will be dealt with in its place. /182/ But it is utterly unbearable that they lay down a law on the recounting of all sins; that they deny that sin is forgiven except upon the condition that an intent to confess has been firmly conceived, [322] and that they prate that no entrance to paradise would remain if the office of confession were neglected. But this is unbearable.

Are all sins to be recounted? Now David, who in himself had, I believe, rightly pondered confession of sins, exclaimed: "Who will understand errors? Cleanse thou me from my secret errors, O Lord" [Ps. 19:12 p.]. And in another place: "My iniquities have gone over my head, and like a heavy burden they burden me beyond my strength" [Ps. 38:4; cf. Ps. 37:5, Vg.]. He understood only too well how deep is the pit of our sins, how many are the faces of crimes, how many heads this hydra bore, and what a long tail it dragged along. Therefore, he did not attempt to catalogue them. But from the depths of his evil deeds he cried out to the Lord: "I am overwhelmed, I am buried, I am choked, the gates of hell have encompassed me" [Ps. 18:6; cf. Ps. 17:6, Vg.], I am sunk down into the deep pit [Ps. 69:2-3, 15-16], may thy hand draw me out, weak and dying. Who would now think of reckoning up his sins when he sees that

3.4.17 David cannot begin to number his? The consciences of those who have been affected with some awareness of God are most cruelly torn by this butchery. First they called themselves to account, and divided sins into arms, branches, twigs, and leaves, according to their formulas. They then weighed the qualities, [323] quantities, and circumstances; and so the matter pressed forward a bit. But when they had progressed farther, and sky and sea were on every side, there was no port or anchorage. The more they had crossed over, the greater was the mass ever looming before their eyes, indeed, it rose up like high mountains;

(159) nor did any hope of escape appear, even after long detours. And so they were stuck between the victim and the knife. And at last no other outcome but despair was found. There these cruel butchers, to heal the wounds they had inflicted, applied certain remedies, asserting that each man should do what lay in his power. But again new anxieties crept in. Indeed, new tortures flayed helpless souls: "I have not spent enough time"; "I have not duly devoted myself to it"; "I have overlooked many things out of negligence, and the forgetfulness that has come about from my carelessness is inexcusable!"

Still, other medicines to alleviate this sort of pain were applied. Repent of your negligence; provided it is not utterly careless, it will be forgiven. But all these things cannot cover the wound, and are less an alleviation of the evil than poisons disguised with honey in order not to cause offense at the first taste because of their harshness, but to penetrate deep within before they are felt. Therefore, that dreadful voice always presses and resounds in the ears: "Confess all your sins." Nor could [324] this dread /183/ be calmed, except by sure consolation.

Moreover, the lulling of a good many people by the flatteries with which such deadly poison was tempered did not cause them to believe that these blandishments would satisfy God or even truly satisfy themselves. Rather, the effect was that of an anchor put down on the high seas, providing a brief respite from sailing; or of the wayside rest of a traveler drooping with exhaustion. I do not labor to prove this point. Every man can be his own witness of this. I shall sum up what sort of law this is. First, it is simply impossible; therefore it can only destroy, condemn, confound, and cast into ruin and despair. Then, depriving sinners of a true awareness of their sins, it makes them hypocrites, ignorant of God and of themselves. Indeed, while wholly occupied with the cataloguing of sins, they in the meantime forget that hidden slough of vices, their own secret transgressions and inner filth, the knowledge of which ought particularly to have brought home to them their own misery. 3.4.18

26. But a very sure rule for making confession was to recognize and confess that the abyss of our evil is beyond our comprehension. We see that the publican's confession was composed according to this rule: "Lord, be merciful to me a sinner" [Luke 18:13]. It is as if he said: "How great, how great a sinner I am; I am wholly a sinner, [325] nor can my mind grasp or my tongue utter the very magnitude of my sins! May the abyss of thy mercy swallow up this abyss of my sin."

What? you will ask. Is, then, not each single sin to be confessed? Is, then, no confession accepted by God unless it consists of these two words: "I am a sinner"? Nay, we must rather take care as much as we are able to pour out our whole heart in the Lord's presence; not only to confess ourselves sinners in one word, but to acknowledge ourselves as such, truly and sincerely; to recognize with all our thought how great and how varied is the stain of our sins; to acknowledge not only that we are unclean, but of what sort and how great (160) and how manifold the uncleanness is; to recognize not only that we are debtors, but with what great debts we are burdened and with how many obligations we are bound; not only wounded, but with how many and how deadly stripes we are wounded. Yet when, with this acknowledgment, the sinner has poured out himself entirely before the Lord, let him earnestly and sincerely consider that still more sins remain, and the recesses of their evils are deep beyond fathoming. Consequently, let him exclaim with David: "Who can understand errors? Cleanse thou me from my secret errors, O Lord" [Ps. 19:12]. Let us by no means concede to them their assertion that sins are forgiven only when there is a firmly conceived intent to confess, and that the gate to paradise is closed to one who [326] has neglected an opportunity offered him to confess. For there is now no other forgiveness of sins than there always has been. Whenever we read that men have obtained forgiveness /184/ of sins from Christ, we do not read that they confessed into the ear of some priestling.* Apparently, where there were neither priestling confessors, nor even confession itself, confession was impossible. For many centuries after, this confession was unheard of, yet all the while sins were being forgiven without this condition. But, that we may not too long dispute, as it were, over something doubtful, the word of God is clear and abides forever: "Whenever the sinner bewails his sins, I shall not recall all his iniquities" [Ezek. 18:21-22 p.]. He who ventures to add anything to this word binds not sins but the Lord's mercy.

3.4.19   27. No wonder, then, that we condemn this auricular confession and desire it to be banished from our midst—a thing so pestilent and in so many ways harmful to the church!* Even if of itself this were something indifferent, still, since it is useless and fruitless and besides has occasioned so many impieties, sacrileges, and errors, who would not consider that it should be abolished forthwith? They do, indeed, count on some uses that they peddle as very fruitful, but those are either false or utterly worthless. Yet by a special prerogative they [327] esteem only one of these: that the confessant's blush of shame is a heavy punishment by which the sinner both becomes more cautious afterward and, by punishing himself, turns aside God's vengeance.* As if we did not enough confound a man, with great shame, when we call him to that supreme heavenly judgment seat to be examined by God! What a remarkable gain it is if we cease to sin on account of the shame of one man, and are not ashamed to have God as witness of our evil conscience!

Nonetheless, that itself is also utterly false. For it is generally apparent that nothing gives greater confidence or license to sin than when, having made confession to a priest, men think themselves able to wipe their mouths and say. "I have not done it" [Prov. 30:20]. And not only are they emboldened throughout the year to sin; but, unbothered by confession for the rest of the year, they never sigh unto God, never return to their senses, (161) but heap up sins upon sins until they vomit all of them up at once, as they suppose. When, moreover, they have disgorged them, they seem to themselves unburdened of their load, and feel that they have transferred judgment from God and bestowed it upon the priest, and have made God forgetful when they have made the priest their con-

142

fidant. Indeed, who happily looks forward to the day of confession? Who hastens to confession with an eager mind and does not, rather, come to it against his will, reluctantly, as one is dragged by the neck to prison? Except, perhaps, [328] priestlings themselves, /185/ who delight in exchanging anecdotes of their misdeeds as if they were amusing stories. I will not defile many sheets of paper by relating those horrible abominations with which auricular confession swarms! I only say, if that holy man did not act unwisely who on account of one rumor of fornication removed confession from his church, or rather from the memory of his people; we are warned what must be done when, today, there are infinite whoredoms, adulteries, incests, and panderings.

28. Now we must examine the power of the keys in which the confessioners place the whole ship of their kingdom—"prow and poop," as the saying goes: Were the keys, then, given to no purpose? they ask, Was this, then, groundlessly said: "Whatever you loose on earth will be loosed in heaven also?" [Matt. 18:18] Do we, then, render void the word of Christ? I reply: It was for a weighty reason that the keys were given.

There are, then, two passages in which the Lord attests that what his own have bound and loosed on earth will be bound and loosed in heaven. Of slightly different meaning, these passages are tastelessly and ignorantly confused by these pigs (as they commonly do everything). One is in John, when, about to send the disciples out to preach, Christ breathes on them [John 20:22], and says, "Receive the Holy Spirit. If you forgive the sins of any, they will be forgiven; if you retain the sins of any, they will be retained" [John 20:23]. [329] The keys of the Kingdom of Heaven, which were previously promised to Peter [Matt. 16:19], are now shown to him together with the other apostles. And whatever had been promised to him is the same thing that he now equally receives with all the rest: It had been said to him: "I shall give you the keys of the Kingdom of Heaven." These words are spoken to them, that they may proclaim the Gospel, that is, to open the gates of the Kingdom of Heaven to those who have sought access to the Father through Christ; but to close and bar them to those who have strayed from this path. To them it had been said: "Whatever you have bound on earth, will be bound in heaven; whatever you have loosed, will be loosed." Now to all the apostles, among whom is Peter himself, it is said: "If you forgive the sins of any, they will be forgiven; if you retain the sins of any, they will be retained." To bind, then, is to retain sins; to loose, to forgive. And obviously by forgiveness of sins, consciences are truly loosed from the harshest fetters; while on the other hand, by retention, with the tightest bonds they are bound and tightened.

29. I shall bring to this an interpretation not subtle, not forced, not distorted; but simple, natural, fluent, and plain. (162) This command concerning forgiving and retaining sins and that promise made to Peter concerning binding and loosing have to be referred solely to the ministry of the Word, because when the Lord committed his ministry to his apostles, /186/ at the same time [330] he also equipped them for the office of binding and loosing. For what is the

3.4.20

4.11.1

4.11.1

sum total of the gospel except that we all, being slaves of sin and death, are released and freed through the redemption which is in Christ Jesus [cf. Rom. 3:24], but that they who do not acknowledge or receive Christ as their liberator and redeemer are condemned and sentenced to eternal chains [cf. Jude 6]? When the Lord entrusted this embassy to his apostles to be carried into all nations [cf. Matt. 28:19], in order to approve it as his own, as coming from himself and as commanded by him, he honored it with this noble testimony—and he did this to the particular consolation both of the apostles themselves and also of the hearers to whom this embassy was going to come. It was important for the apostles to have constant and perfect assurance in their preaching, which they were not only to carry out in infinite labors, cares, troubles, and dangers, but at last to seal with their own blood. I say that this assurance was not vain or empty, but full of power and strength. It was important for them to be convinced that in such anxiety, difficulty, and danger they were doing God's work; also, for them to recognize that God stood beside them while the whole world opposed and attacked them; for them, not having Christ, the Author of their doctrine before their eyes on earth, to know that he is in heaven to confirm its truth. [331] On the other hand, it was necessary to give an unmistakable witness to their hearers that the doctrine of the gospel was not the word of the apostles but of God himself;* not a voice born on earth but one descended from heaven. For these things—forgiveness of sins, the promise of eternal life, the good news of salvation—cannot be in man's power. Therefore, Christ has testified that in the preaching of the gospel the apostles have no part save that of ministry; that it was he himself who would speak and promise all things through their lips as his instruments. He has testified that the forgiveness of sins which they themselves preached was the true promise of God; the damnation which they pronounced, the sure judgment of God. This testimony, moreover, was given to all epochs, and remains firm, to make all men more certain and sure that the word of the gospel, whatever man may preach it, is the very sentence of God, published at the supreme judgment seat of God, written in the Book of Life, ratified, fixed and firm in heaven. We conclude that the power of the keys is simply the preaching of the gospel, and that with regard to men it is not so much power as ministry. For Christ has not given this power actually to men, but to his Word, of which he has made men ministers.*

4.11.2   30. The other passage,* which we have said is to be understood in another sense, has been written in Matthew. There Christ says: (163) "If any brother /187/[332] refuses to listen to the church, let him be to you as a Gentile and a publican. Truly, I say to you, whatever you bind on earth shall be bound in heaven; and whatever you loose [on earth] shall be loosed [in heaven]" [Matt. 18:17-18 p.]. But we do not make them out to be so different as not to possess considerable connection and likeness between them. Both are alike in this first respect; each is a general statement; in both is always the same power of binding and loosing (that is, through God's Word), the same command of binding and loosing, the same promise. But they differ in this respect: the first passage is

144

particularly concerned with the preaching which the ministers of the Word execute; the latter applies to the discipline of excommunication which is entrusted to the church. But the church binds him whom it excommunicates—not that it casts him into everlasting ruin and despair, but because it condemns his life and morals, and already warns him of his condemnation unless he should repent. It looses him whom it receives into communion, for it makes him a sharer of the unity which it has in Christ Jesus. Therefore, that no one may stubbornly despise the judgment of the church, or judge it immaterial that he has been condemned by the vote of the believers, the Lord testifies that such judgment by believers is nothing but the proclamation of his own sentence, and that whatever they have done on earth is ratified in heaven. For they have the Word of God with which to condemn the perverse; they have [333] the Word with which to receive the repentant into grace. They cannot err or disagree with God's judgment, for they judge solely according to God's law. which is no uncertain or earthly opinion but God's holy will and heavenly oracle. Moreover, he calls the church, not a paltry few tonsured, shaven, linen-wearers, but the assembly of the believing folk, gathered in his name [cf. Matt. 18:20]. Nor are those scoffers to be listened to, who argue as follows: How could any quarrel be referred to the church which is spread and scattered throughout the earth? Christ has sufficiently shown that he is speaking of all Christian congregations, as churches can be established in separate localities and provinces: "Wherever," he says, "two or three are gathered together in my name, there I am in the midst of them" [Matt. 18:20].

31. Upon these two passages—which I believe I have interpreted briefly,   4.11.2
familiarly, and truly—these madmen (as they are carried away by their own giddiness) indiscriminately try to establish now confession, now excommunication, now jurisdiction, now the right to frame laws, and now indulgences. But   3.4.20
what if with one sword I cut off the handle of every demand of this kind: their priestlings are not vicars or successors of the apostles? But this, also will be treated in another place. Now, out of greatly wishing to fortify themselves, they erect a siege engine, only to cast down thereby all their own contrivances. [334] For Christ did not give the power of binding and loosing to the apostles /188/ before he gave them the Holy Spirit. Therefore, I deny that the power of the keys belongs to any persons who have not received the Holy Spirit. I deny that anyone can use the keys (164) unless the Holy Spirit has first come to teach him and tell him what to do. They babble that they have the Holy Spirit, but in reality they deny it, unless perchance they fancy, as they surely do, that the Holy Spirit is something vain and of no account; but they will not be believed. And by this device, indeed, they are utterly overthrown; so that, of whatever door they boast that they have the key, they must always be asked whether they have the Holy Spirit, who is the judge and keeper of the keys. If they reply that they have him, they must, on the other hand, be asked whether the Holy Spirit can err. This they will not dare to say forthrightly, even though they hint at it obliquely in their teaching. We must therefore infer that no priestlings have the

power of the keys who without discrimination repeatedly loose what the Lord had willed to be bound, and bind what he had bidden to be loosed.

3.4.21   When they see themselves by very clear proofs convicted of loosing and binding the worthy and the unworthy indiscriminately, they usurp power without knowledge. And although they dare not deny that knowledge is required for the good use of power, they write that the power itself has been entrusted to evil ministrants. Yet this [335] is the power: "Whatever you bind or loose on earth will be bound and loosed in heaven." [Matt. 16:19 or 18:18 p.] Either Christ's promise must be a lie, or those who have been endowed with this power bind and loose rightly.

Nor can they evade the issue by saying that Christ's promise is limited according to the merits of him who is bound or loosed. We too admit that only those worthy of being loosed or bound can be loosed or bound; but the messengers of the gospel and the church have the Word to measure this worthiness. In this Word, the messengers of the gospel can through faith promise to all forgiveness of sins in Christ; they can proclaim damnation against all and upon all who do not embrace Christ. In this Word the church proclaims, "Neither whoremongers, . . . adulterers, . . . thieves, murderers, greedy, nor wicked will partake of the Kingdom of God" [I Cor. 6:9-10 p.]. The church binds such persons with the surest bonds. And with the same Word the church looses and comforts those who repent. But what power will this be—not to know what is to be bound or loosed, yet not to be able to bind or loose unless you know? Why, then, do they say that they absolve by the authority given them, when their absolution is uncertain? What is this imaginary power to us if it is useless? Now I hold that by this one passage it is either nothing or so uncertain that it ought to be considered as nothing. For since they admit that a good /189/ many priests [336] do not use the keys rightly, and that the power is ineffective without lawful use, who will convince me that he by whom I am loosed is a good dispenser of the keys? But if he is evil, what else does he have but this empty loosing of them! "I do not know what ought to be bound or loosed in you, since I lack a just use of the keys; but if you deserve it, I absolve you." I do not say, "A lay person," since they cannot bear to hear this, but a Turk or the devil could do as much. For that is to say: I do not have the Word of God, the sure rule of loosing, but authority (165) has been given to me to absolve you, provided your merits are such. We therefore see what they were aiming at when they defined the keys as the authority to discern and the power to carry out; knowledge being added as counselor, and like a counselor, for good use. That is to say, they wished to rule lustfully, licentiously, without God and his Word.

Accordingly, I shall tell in a few words how they fit their keys to so many locks and doors, sometimes to serve their own jurisdiction, sometimes confessions, sometimes constitutions, sometimes rites. In that commandment concerning forgiving and retaining sins which in John's Gospel Christ gives to his disciples, he is not appointing lawgivers, secretaries of confessions, officials, dataries, bullaries; but those whom he had made ministers of his Word [337] he

146

adorns with a singular testimony. In Matthew, when Christ turns over to his church the office of binding and loosing, he does not command that by the authority of some reverend mitered or two-horned person, the poor who are not intended for loosing be eliminated and destroyed, by the clash of cymbals and the snuffing of a candle, and be cursed by all threats. Rather he enjoins that the wickedness of evil men be corrected by the discipline of excommunication. And that is to be accomplished by the authority of his Word, and the ministry of the church.

32. But those madmen who fancy the keys of the church to be the distri-   3.5.1
bution of the merits of Christ and the martyrs, which the pope distributes by his bulls and indulgences, are fit to be treated by drugs for insanity rather than to be argued with. Nor is there need to toil greatly in refuting their indulgences, which under the onslaught of many battering-rams are of themselves now beginning to grow old and to show deterioration. And obviously the fact that indulgences have so long stood untouched, and in such unrestrained and furious license have retained such lasting impunity, can truly serve as a proof of how much men were immersed for centuries in a deep night of errors. Men saw themselves openly and undisguisedly held up to ridicule by the pope and his bull-bearers, their souls' salvation the object of lucrative trafficking, the price of salvation reckoned at a few coins, nothing offered free of charge. By this subterfuge they saw themselves cheated of their offerings, which were filthily spent on whores, pimps, and drunken revelries. [338] But they also saw that the greatest trumpeters of indulgences hold them in most contempt; /190/ that this monster daily runs more riotously and lecherously abroad, and that there is no end; that new lead is continually put forward and new money taken away. Yet with the highest veneration they received indulgences, worshiped them and bought them. And those who were more discerning than the rest, nevertheless considered them to be pious frauds by which they could be deceived with some benefit. Finally, when the world has ventured to become a trifle wise, indulgences grow cold and gradually even freeze up, until they altogether vanish.

33. But very many persons see the base tricks, deceits, thefts, and greed-   3.5.2
iness with which the indulgence traffickers have heretofore mocked and beguiled us, and yet they do not see the very fountain of the impiety itself. (166) As a consequence, it behooves us to indicate not only the nature of indulgences but also what in general they would be, wiped clean of all spots. Now these, to describe them rightly, are a profanation of the blood of Christ, a Satanic mockery, to lead the Christian people away from God's grace, away from the life that is in Christ, and turn them aside from the true way of salvation. For how could the blood of Christ be more foully profaned than when they deny that it is sufficient for the forgiveness of sins, for reconciliation, for satisfaction—unless the lack of it, as of something dried up and exhausted, be otherwise supplied and filled? [339] "To Christ, the Law and all the prophecies bear witness," says Peter, that "through him we are to receive forgiveness of sins." [Acts 10:43 p.] Indulgences bestow forgiveness of sins through Peter, Paul, and the martyrs. "The blood of

Christ cleanses us from sin," says John [I John 1:7 p.]. Indulgences make the blood of martyrs the cleansing of sin. "Christ," says Paul, "who knew no sin, was made sin for us" (that is; satisfaction of sin) "so that we might be made the righteousness of God in him" [II Cor. 5:21 p., cf. Vg.]. Indulgences lodge satisfaction of sins in the blood of martyrs. Paul proclaimed and testified to the Corinthians that Christ alone was crucified and died for them [cf. I Cor. 1:13]. Indulgences declare: "Paul and others died for us." Elsewhere Paul says, "Christ acquired the church with his own blood" [Acts 20:28 p.]. Indulgences establish another purchase price in the blood of martyrs. "By a single offering Christ has perfected for all time those who are sanctified" [Heb. 10:14], says the Apostle. Indulgences proclaim: "Sanctification, otherwise insufficient, is perfected by the martyrs." John says that "all the saints have washed their robes . . . in the blood of the Lamb" [Rev. 7:14]. Indulgences teach that they wash their robes in the blood of the saints.

3.5.3   Assuredly, while all their doctrine is patched together out of terrible sacrileges and blasphemies, this [340] is a more astounding blasphemy than the rest.

34. Let them recognize whether or not these are their judgments: that martyrs /191/ by their death have given more to God and deserved more than they needed for themselves, and that they had a great surplus of merits to overflow to others. In order, therefore, that this great good should not be superfluous, their blood is mingled with the blood of Christ; and out of the blood of both, the treasury of the church is fabricated for the forgiveness and satisfaction of sins. And Paul's statement, "In my body I complete what is lacking in Christ's sufferings for the sake of his body, that is, the church" [Col. 1:24], is to be understood in this sense.

What is this but to leave Christ only a name, to make him another common saintlet who can scarcely be distinguished in the throng? He, he alone, deserved to be preached; he alone set forth; he alone named; he alone looked to when there is a question of obtaining forgiveness of sins, expiation, satisfaction. But let us listen to their truncated syllogisms. Lest (167) the martyrs' blood be fruitlessly poured out, let it be conferred upon the common good of the church. Is this so? Was it unprofitable for them to glorify God through their death? to attest his truth by their blood? to bear witness by their contempt of the present life that they are seeking a better life? by their constancy, to strengthen the faith of the church while breaking the stubbornness of its enemies? But the fact is that they recognize no fruit if Christ alone [341] is the propitiator, if he alone has died for the sake of our sins, if he alone has been offered for our redemption.

3.5.4   How maliciously they twist the passage in Paul wherein he says that in his own body he supplies what was lacking in Christ's sufferings [Col. 1:24]! For he refers that lack or that supplement not to the work of redemption, expiation, and satisfaction but to those afflictions with which the members of Christ— namely, all believers—must be exercised so long as they live in this flesh. Therefore, Paul says that of the sufferings of Christ this remains: what once for

148

all he suffered in himself he daily suffers in his members. And Christ distinguishes us by this honor, that he accounts and calls our afflictions his own. Now, when Paul added "for the church," he did not mean for redemption, for reconciliation, or for satisfaction of the church, but for its upbuilding and advancement. As he says in another place: He endures everything for the sake of the elect, that they may obtain the salvation that is in Christ Jesus [II Tim. 2:10].

Away with the notion that Paul thought anything was lacking in Christ's sufferings with regard to the whole fullness of righteousness, salvation, and life; or that he meant to add anything! For Paul clearly and grandly preaches that the richness of grace was so bountifully poured out through Christ that it far surpassed the whole power of sin [cf. Rom. 5:15]. By this alone, [342] not by the merit of their life or death, have all the saints been saved, as Peter eloquently witnesses [cf. Acts 15:11]. So, then, one who would rest the worthiness of any saint anywhere save in God's mercy would be contemptuous of God and his Anointed. /192/ But why do I tarry here any longer, as if this were still something obscure, when to lay bare such monstrous errors is to vanquish them?

Now—to pass over such abominations—who taught the pope to enclose 3.5.5 in lead and parchment the grace of Jesus Christ, which the Lord willed to be distributed by the word of the gospel? Obviously, either the gospel of God or indulgences must be false. Christ is offered to us through the gospel, with all abundance of heavenly benefits, with all his merits, all his righteousness, wisdom, and grace, without exception. They affix some measured portion of indulgence, released from the pope's chest, with lead, parchment, and a certain place—and tear it away from the Word of God!

35. They assign the third place in penance to satisfaction.* With one word 3.4.25 (168) we can overthrow all their empty talk about this. They say that it is not enough for the penitent to abstain from past evils, and change his behavior for the better, unless he make satisfaction to the Lord for those things which he has committed.* But they say that there are many helps by which we may redeem sins: tears, fasting offerings, alms, and other works of charity. [343] With these we must propitiate the Lord. With these we must pay our debts to God's righteousness. With these we must compensate for our transgressions. With these we must merit his pardon.* And although the Lord has forgiven the guilt through the largeness of his mercy, yet by the discipline of his justice he retains punishment. It is this punishment which must be redeemed by satisfaction.

36. Over against such lies I put freely given remission of sins; nothing is more clearly set forth in Scripture [Is. 52:3; Rom. 3:24-25; 5:8; Col. 2:13-14; II Tim 1:9; Titus 3:5]! First, what is forgiveness but a gift of sheer liberality? For the creditor who gives a receipt for money paid is not the one who is said to forgive, but he who, without any payment, willingly cancels the debt out of his own kindness. Why, then, is the word "freely" added but to take away all thought of satisfaction? With what confidence,then, do they still set up their satisfactions, which are laid low by so mighty a thunderbolt? Moreover, since all Scripture bears witness to Christ—that through his name we are to receive

forgiveness of sins [Acts 10:43]—does it not exclude all other names? How then do they teach that forgiveness of sins is received through the name of satisfactions and not deny that it is /193/received through the name of satisfactions but rather through the name of Christ even if satisfactions intervene? When Scripture says "through the name of Christ," it means that we bring nothing, we claim nothing of our own, but rely solely upon the commendation of Christ. [344] As Paul declares: "God was in the Son reconciling the world to himself, not counting their trespasses against men on his account" [II Cor. 5:19 p.].

3.4.26   I fear lest (such is their perversity) they say that both forgiveness of sins and reconciliation take place once for all when in Baptism we are received through Christ into the grace of God; that after Baptism we must rise up again through satisfactions; that the blood of Christ is of no avail, except in so far as it is dispensed through the keys of the church. But John speaks far differently: "If anyone has sinned, we have an advocate with the Father, Jesus Christ . . . ; and he is the propitiation for our sins" [I John 2:1-2]. Again: "I am writing to you, little children, because your sins are forgiven in his name" [I John 2:12 p.]. Surely he is addressing believers, to whom, while he sets forth Christ as the propitiation of sins, he shows that there is no other satisfaction whereby offended, God can be propitiated or appeased. He does not say: "God was once for all reconciled to you through Christ; now seek for yourselves another means of reconciliation." But he makes him a perpetual advocate in order that by his intercession he may always restore us to the Father's favor; (169) an everlasting propitiation by which sins are expiated. For what John said is ever true: "Behold the Lamb of God, who takes away the sins of the world!" [John 1:29; cf. ch. 1:36]. He, I say, not another, takes them away; that is, since he alone is the Lamb of God, he alone also the offering for sins, he alone [345] the expiation, he alone

3.4.27   the satisfaction. Here we ought to consider two things: that Christ's honor be kept whole and undiminished; that consciences assured of pardon for sin may have peace with God.

Isaiah says that the Father laid upon the Son the iniquities of us all [Is. 53:6] to heal us by his stripes [Is. 53:6, 5]. Peter repeats this in other words: Christ in his body bore our sins upon the tree [I Pet. 2:24]. Paul writes: sin was condemned in his flesh when he was made sin for us [Gal. 3:13 and Rom. 8:3, conflated]; that is, the force and the curse of sin were slain in his flesh when he was given as a victim, upon whom the whole burden of our sins—with their curse and execration, with the judgment of God and the damnation of death—should be cast.

3.4.30   And whenever he mentions that redemption was accomplished through Christ, he customarily calls it ἀπολύτρωσιν [Rom. 3:24; see also I Cor. 1:30; Eph. 1:7; Col. 1:14]. This is why he sets forth elsewhere: "Christ gave himself as a ransom for us" [I Tim. 2:6].

3.4.27   Establish now forgiveness of sins in works—/194/ will these things spoken of remain intact in Christ's possession? What a vast difference there is between saying that our iniquities have been lodged with Christ in order that they be expiated in him and saying that they are expiated by our works; that Christ is the propitiation for our sins, and that God must be propitiated by works! [346] But if it is a question of quieting the conscience, what will this quieting be if a man hears that sins are redeemed by satisfactions? When can he at length be certain of the measure of satisfaction? Then he will always doubt whether he has a merciful God; he will always be troubled, and always tremble. For those who rely upon trifling satisfactions hold the judgment of God too much in contempt, and reckon of little account the great burden of sin, as we have stated elsewhere. And even though we should grant that they redeem some sins by appropriate satisfaction, still, what would they do when they are overwhelmed by so many sins for the satisfaction of which a hundred lives, even if they were wholly devoted to this purpose, could not suffice?

37. At this point they take refuge in the foolish distinction that certain sins are venial, others mortal; for mortal sins a heavy satisfaction is required; venial sins can be purged by easier remedies*—by the Lord's Prayer, by the sprinkling of holy water, by the absolution afforded by the Mass. Thus they dally and play with God. Though they are incessantly talking about venial and mortal sin, they still cannot distinguish one from the other, except that they make impiety and uncleanness of heart a venial sin. But we declare, (something which Scripture teaches by the rule of just and unjust) that the wages of sin (170) is death [Rom. 6:23]; and that "the soul that sins [347] is worthy of death" [Ezek. 18:20 p.]; but that the sins of believers are venial, not because they do not deserve death, but because by God's mercy "there is no condemnation for those who are in Christ Jesus" [Rom. 8:1], because they are not imputed, because they are wiped away by pardon* [cf. Ps. 32:1-2].

38. I know how unjustly they slander this doctrine of ours, for they call it the paradox of the Stoics, concerning the equality of sins, but they will be easily refuted by their own mouth. For I ask whether among those very sins which they confess as mortal they recognize one as less than another. It does not therefore immediately follow that sins that are mortal are at the same time equal. Since the Scripture precisely states that "the wages of sin is death" [Rom. 6:23], but obedience to the law is the way of life [cf. Lev. 18:5; Ezek. 18:9; 20:11, 13; Gal. 3:12; Rom. 10:5; Luke 10:28]—transgression of the law, death [cf. Rom. 6:23; Ezek. 18:4, 20]—they cannot evade this verdict. Amid such a great heap of sins, what will be the result of performing satisfaction? If /195/ it takes one day to make satisfaction for one sin, while they are contemplating it they sin seven times (I speak of the most righteous); if they gird themselves to seven satisfactions, they accumulate forty-nine sins [cf. Prov. 24:16]. Now that the assurance of being able to make satisfaction for their sins has been cut off, why do they tarry? How dare they still think of making satisfaction?

Indeed, they try to extricate themselves, but "the water," as the proverb goes, "clings to them."* They fashion a distinction between penalty and guilt. They confess that guilt is remitted by God's mercy, even if they teach that we merit it by tears and prayers; but that after guilt has been remitted [348] there remains the penalty which God's justice demands to be paid.* Therefore, they hold that satisfactions properly are concerned with the remission of the penalty.*

Yet all that we are taught in Scripture concerning forgiveness of sins directly opposes this distinction. This is the new covenant that God in Christ has made with us, that he will remember our sins no more [Jer. 31:31, 34]. What he meant by these words we learn from another prophet, where the Lord says: "If a righteous man turns away from his righteousness, . . . I will not remember his righteous deeds" [Ezek. 18:24 p.]; "if a wicked man turns away from his impiety, I will not remember all his iniquities" [Ezek. 18:21-22 p. cf. v. 27]. His statement that he will not remember their righteous acts means virtually this: he will not keep an account of them to reward them. The statement that he will not remember their sins therefore means that he will not demand the penalty for them. The same thing is said elsewhere: "not to reckon them to his account and to keep them hidden" [cf. Ps. 32:1-2]. By such expressions the Holy Spirit clearly would have explained his meaning to us, if we had listened to him attentively. Surely, if God punishes sins, he charges them to our account; if he takes vengeance, he remembers them; if he calls to judgment, he does not hide them.

But let us hear from another prophet by what laws the Lord forgives sins: "Though your sins," he says, "are as scarlet, they shall be as white as snow; though they are red like crimson, they shall be as wool" [Is. 1:18]. Here I must [349] adjure my readers not to heed my glosses, but only to yield some place to the Word of God. (171)

3.4.30   What, I ask you, would Christ have bestowed upon us, if the penalty for sins were still required? For when we say that he bore all our sins in his body upon the tree [I Pet. 2:24], we mean only that he bore the punishment and vengeance due our sins. Isaiah has stated this more meaningfully when he says: "The chastisement (or correction) of our peace was upon him" [Is. 53:5]. What is this "correction of our peace" but the penalty due sins that we would have had to pay before we could become reconciled to God—if he had not taken our place? Lo, you see plainly that Christ bore the penalty of sins /196/ to deliver his own people from them.

Would that we might sincerely understand what Christ has promised his believers! "He who believes in me has not come into judgment, but has passed over from death into life" [John 5:24]. The assurance of this promise, Paul firmly declares: "There is no condemnation for those who are in Christ Jesus" [Rom. 8:1].

39. I do not doubt that they will laugh at me for taking judgment and condemnation in a sense other than eternal punishment. But that has nothing to do with the satisfactions which they teach are paid by temporal punishments. But if they had not determined to resist the Holy Spirit, they would feel within themselves a greater power by Christ's and Paul's words, [350] namely, that believers are so freed from the curse of sin through Christ, that in God's sight they appear as if clean and pure.

But inasmuch as they arm themselves with testimonies from Scripture, let   3.4.31
us see what sort of arguments they put forward. David, they say, rebuked by the
prophet Nathan for adultery and murder, received pardon for his sin, and yet he
was afterward punished by the death of his son born of adultery* [II Sam.
12:13-14]. We are taught to recompense with satisfaction such punishments as
had to be inflicted even after remission of guilt.* For Daniel enjoined Nebuchadnezzar to make recompense for his sins with alms* [Dan. 4:27]. And Solomon writes: "Love covers a multitude of sins" [Prov. 10:12; I Pet. 4:8]. In Luke
the Lord says of the sinning woman: "her many sins are forgiven, for she loved
much"* [Luke 7:47 p.]. How perversely and wrongheadedly do they always judge
God's deeds!

40. Yet if they had observed—and it is something they ought not at all
to have overlooked—that there are two kinds of divine judgment, they would
have seen something far different in this rebuke of David than the punishment
and avenging of sin. One judgment we call, for the sake of teaching, that of
vengeance; the other, of chastisement. By the judgment of vengeance, the Lord
exercises his wrath against the reprobate, takes vengeance, confounds, scatters
them, brings them to nought. That, properly speaking, is to punish [351] and
avenge sin. And that can properly be called "penalty" or "punishment." In the
judgment of chastisement he does not punish, is not angry, does not take vengeance, but instructs his own, admonishes, chastises, pinches awake. That is not
penalty or vengeance, but correction and admonition. The one is the act of a
judge; (172) the other, of a father. When a judge punishes an evildoer, he
censures the transgression itself and applies the penalty to the crime itself. When
a father quite severely corrects his son, he does not do this to take vengeance
on him or to manhandle his transgressions, but rather to teach him and to render
him more cautious thereafter. Briefly, wherever there is penalty, there are the   3.4.32
curse and wrath of God, which he keeps away from the believers. Chastisement
is God's blessing, and a testimony of love. /197/ We read that all the saints
always prayed that wrath be averted, while they received chastisement with a
calm mind. "Correct me, O Lord, but in judgment, not in thine anger, lest
perchance thou bring me to nothing. Pour out thy wrath," etc. [Jer. 10:24].
Although I do not even oppose calling this sort of punishment of trespasses,
"chastisement," I caution as to how it is to be understood.

Therefore, when He deprived Saul of the kingdom, He was punishing   3.4.33
[I Sam. 15:23]. When He took away David's little son from him [II Sam. 12:18]
he was rebuking. Paul's statement is to be understood in this sense: "When we
are judged, we are rebuked by the Lord so that we may not be condemned along
with the world" [I Cor. 11:32]. That is, while we as children of God are afflicted
by the hand of the Heavenly Father, this is not a penalty [352] to confound us,
but a chastisement to instruct us.

In the bitterness of afflictions, the believer must be fortified by this thought.   3.4.34
"The time has come for judgment to begin with the household of the Lord"
[I Pet. 4:17], . . . in which his name has been called upon [cf. Jer. 25:29].

What would the children of God do if they believed the severity they feel is God's vengeance? For he who, struck by the hand of God, thinks God a punishing Judge, cannot conceive of God as other than wrathful and hostile to him; cannot but detest the very scourge of God as curse and damnation. In short, he who feels that God still intends to punish him can never persuade himself that he is loved by God. Whether the penalty is everlasting or temporal makes no difference. For wars, famines, plagues, diseases, are just as much curses of God as the very judgment of eternal death.

3.4.35

41. All see (unless I am deceived) the purpose of the Lord's punishment against David. It is that it might be a proof that murder and adultery gravely displease God. He had declared himself so greatly offended against this that David himself might have instruction not to dare commit such a crime thereafter; but not that it might be a penalty by which he should make a payment to God. So also should we judge concerning the other correction, whereby the Lord afflicted his people with a violent plague [II Sam. 24:15], on account of David's disobedience, which he had committed in taking a census of his people. [353] For he freely forgave David the guilt of his sin, but because it was appropriate both for the public example of all times and also for the humiliation of David that such a crime should not go unpunished, he very harshly chastised him with his scourge. But it is strange why they thus cast their eyes upon the one example of David, and are not moved by so many other examples in which they were free to contemplate the free forgiveness of sins. We read that the publican went down from the Temple justified; no punishment (173) ensues [Luke 18:14]. Peter obtained pardon for transgression [Luke 22:61]; we read of his tears says Ambrose, we do not read of satisfaction. And the paralytic heard: /198/ "Rise up, your sins are forgiven" [Matt. 9:2]; no punishment is imposed. All the absolutions mentioned in Scripture are described as free. The rule ought to have been sought from these frequent examples rather than from a single one that contained some special feature.

3.4.36

Daniel, by the exhortation with which he persuaded Nebuchadnezzar to make recompense for his sins by righteousness and his iniquities by pity for the poor [Dan. 4:27], did not mean to imply that righteousness and mercy were the propitiation of God and the recompense of punishments. Banish the thought that there should be any other ransom than the blood of Christ! But in the phrase "to make recompense," [354] he referred to men rather than to God. It was as if he said: "O King, you have exercised unjust and violent mastery, you have oppressed the humble, you have despoiled the poor, you have treated your people harshly and unjustly. Now replace with mercy and righteousness your unjust exactions, your violence and oppression." Similarly, Solomon says "love covers a multitude of sins" [Prov. 10:12], not before God, but among men themselves. The whole verse reads: "Hatred stirs up strife but love covers all offenses." [Prov. 10:12] In this Solomon, as his habit is, through antithesis, contrasts the evil things that arise out of hatreds with the fruits of love. His meaning is that those who hate one another bite, harry, reproach, one another and make a fault

154

of everything; that those who love one another conceal many things among themselves, wink at many things, condone many things in one another—not that one man approves of another's faults, but that he tolerates them, and heals them by admonishing instead of aggravating them by reproaches. Undoubtedly, Peter quotes this passage in the same sense, unless we would accuse him of debasing and craftily twisting Scripture [cf. I Pet. 4:8].

As far as the passage in Luke is concerned [Luke 7:36-50], no one who has read with sound judgment the parable set forth there by the Lord, will pick a quarrel with us over it. The Pharisee thought to himself that the Lord did not know the woman [355] whom he had so readily received. For he felt that Christ would not have received her if he had known what sort of sinner she was. And he inferred from this that Christ was not a prophet, since he could be deceived to this extent. The Lord, to show that she whose sins he had already forgiven was not a sinner, set forth a parable. "A certain moneylender had two debtors. One owed five hundred denarii, the other fifty. The debt of each was forgiven. Which one has the greater gratitude? The Pharisee answered, 'The one, I suppose, to whom he forgave more.' The Lord said: 'From this know that this woman's sins are forgiven, for she loved much' " [Luke 7:41-43, 47 p.]. By these words, you see, he does not make her love the cause, but the proof, of forgiveness of sins. For they are taken from the parable of that debtor who (174) was forgiven five /199/ hundred denarii; to him he did not say that they were forgiven because he loved much, but that he loved much because they were forgiven. And it is necessary to apply these words to the parable in this manner: You think this woman is a sinner, yet you ought to have recognized that she is not such, since her sins have been forgiven her. Her love, by which she gives thanks for his benefit, ought to have convinced you of the forgiveness of her sins. Now this is an argument *a posteriori*, by which something is proved from the evidences that follow. [356] The Lord clearly testifies in what way she obtained forgiveness of sins: "Your faith," he says, "has saved you" [Luke 7:50]. By faith, therefore, we gain forgiveness; by love we give thanks and testify to the Lord's kindness.

42. The opinions widely expressed in the books of the ancient writers concerning satisfaction move me little. I see, indeed, that some of them—I will simply say almost all whose books are extant—have fallen down in this respect. But I will not admit that they were so rude and untutored as to write those things in the sense in which they are understood by our new exponents of satisfaction. For they have largely called satisfaction not a payment to be rendered to God but a public testimony whereby those who had been sentenced with excommunication, when they wished to be received back into communion, assured the church of their repentance. For there were imposed upon those repentant ones certain fastings and other duties with which to prove that they truly and heartily loathed their former life, or rather, to wipe out the memory of their previous actions, and thus were said to have made satisfaction not to God but to the church. From that ancient rite, the confessions and satisfactions that today are

3.4.37

3.4.38

3.4.39

in use took their origin. Truly viperous offspring [cf. Matt. 3:7; 12:34], these, by which it come to pass that not even a shadow of that better form remains! I know that the old writers sometimes speak rather harshly; and, as I have just said, [357] I do not deny that they erred; but those of their writings sprinkled with very few spots here and there become utterly defiled when handled by these men's unwashed hands. And if we must contend by the authority of the fathers, what ancient writers, good God, do these men thrust upon us? A good part of these authors from whom Lombard, their leader, has sewn together his patch-works, were collected from the senseless ravings of certain monks, which pass under the names Ambrose, Jerome, Augustine, and Chrysostom; as in the present argument almost all his evidence is taken from Augustine's book *On Repentance*, which was bunglingly patched together by some rhapsodist from good and bad authors indiscriminately. Indeed, it bears the name of Augustine, but nobody of even mediocre learning would deign to acknowledge it as his. /200/

3.5.6   43. Now let them no longer trouble us with their "purgatory," because with this ax it has been broken, hewn down, and overturned from its very foundations. And I do not agree with certain persons who think that one ought to dissemble on this point, and make no mention of purgatory, from which as they say, fierce conflicts arise but little edification can be obtained. (175) Certainly, I myself would advise that such trifles be neglected if they did not have their serious consequences. But, since purgatory was constructed out of many blasphemies and is daily propped up with new ones, and since it incites to many grave offenses, it is certainly not to be winked at. One could for a time perhaps in a way [358] have concealed the fact that it had been devised apart from God's Word in curious and bold rashness; that men had believed in it by some sort of "revelations" forged by Satan's craft; and that some passages of Scripture had been ignorantly distorted to confirm it. Still, the Lord does not lightly allow man's effrontery so to break in upon the secret places of his judgments; and he sternly forbade that men, to the neglect of his Word, should inquire after truth from the dead [Deut. 18:11]. Neither does he allow his Word to be so irreligiously corrupted.

44. Let us, however grant that all those things could have been tolerated for a time as something of no great importance; but when expiation of sins is sought elsewhere than in the blood of Christ, when satisfaction is transferred elsewhere, silence is very dangerous. Therefore, we must cry out with the shouting not only of our voices but our throats and lungs that purgatory is a deadly fiction of Satan, which nullifies the cross of Christ, and overturns and destroys our faith. Moreover, what means this purgatory of theirs but the penalty which the souls of the dead undergo as satisfaction for sins? But if it is perfectly clear from our preceding discourse that the blood of Christ is the sole satisfaction for the sins of believers, the sole expiation, the sole purgation, what remains but to say that purgatory is simply a blasphemy against Christ? I pass over the sacrileges by which it is daily [359] defended, the minor offenses that it breeds

in religion, and innumerable other things that are accustomed to come forth from such a fountain of impiety.

To make an end at some time, let us now look at the sacrament itself of penance (the topic proposed for the last place). Moreover, they toil anxiously to find a sacrament there. No wonder, for they are seeking a knot in a bulrush.* Yet when they have done as best they can, they leave the matter involved, hanging, uncertain, confused by a variety of opinions and troubled. They therefore say: either outward penance is a sacrament, and if it is, ought to be regarded as a sign /201/ of inner repentance, that is, of contrition of heart,* which will be the matter of the sacrament; or both together are a sacrament, not two, but one complete. But they say: outward penance is solely sacrament; inner repentance is both sacramental matter and sacrament. Furthermore, forgiveness of sins is matter only and not sacrament.* Let those who bear in mind the definition of sacrament given by us above examine against this what the Romanists say is a sacrament, and they will find that it is not an outward ceremony instituted by the Lord to confirm our faith. (176) But if they reply that my definition is not a law they must obey, let them hear Augustine, whom they pretend to consider sacrosanct. He says, "Visible sacraments [360] were instituted for the sake of carnal men, that by the steps of sacraments they may be transported from things discernible by the eyes to those understood."* What similar thing do they themselves see or can they show to others in what they call "the sacrament of penance"? In another place,* he says: "A sacrament is indeed so called because in it one thing is seen, another understood. What is seen has bodily form; what is understood has spiritual fruit." These words in no wise fit the sacrament of penance (as they fancy it), where there is no bodily form to represent spiritual fruit.

And (to kill these beasts in their own arena)* if any sacrament were here, could it not be far more plausibly boasted that the priest's absolution is a sacrament than is penance, either inward or outward? For it was easy to say that it is a ceremony to confirm our faith in forgiveness of sins, and has "the promise of the keys," as they call the statement, "Whatever you bind or loose on earth will be loosed and bound in Heaven" [Matt. 18:18; cf. ch. 16:19]. But someone might have objected that many who are absolved by priests get nothing by such absolution, although according to their dogma the sacraments of the new law ought to carry out what they represent. Absurd. As they postulate a double eating in the Supper, [361] a sacramental (common to good and bad equally) and a spiritual (confined to the good alone)—why shouldn't they imagine that a two-way absolution is also received? I have not hitherto been able to understand what they mean with their dogma; we explained how far it differs from God's truth when we specifically dealt with that argument. Here I only mean to show that this scruple offers no hindrance to prevent them from calling the priest's absolution a sacrament. For they will answer through Augustine's mouth /202/ that there is sanctification without a visible sacrament and a visible sacrament without inner sanctification. Again: "that in the elect alone sacraments carry out

4.19.15

4.19.16

what they represent."* Again: "Some put on Christ as far as the receiving of the sacrament; others, as far as sanctification.* The former, good and bad do equally; the latter, the good alone."* Obviously, they were more than childishly deceived, and were blind in the sunshine, who, while they strove with much difficulty, still did not perceive a thing so plain and obvious to everyone.

4.19.17 But, to keep them from becoming puffed up, regardless of what they posit their sacrament upon, I deny that it is rightly reckoned a sacrament. First, because no promise of God—the only basis of a sacrament—exists. Secondly, because every (177) ceremony displayed here [362] is a mere invention of men, although we have already proved that the ceremonies of sacraments can be ordained only by God. What they fabricated about a sacrament of penance was therefore a falsehood and an imposture. They have adorned this feigned sacrament with an appropriate title, "the second plank after shipwreck," for if anyone has stained, by sinning, the garment of innocence received in baptism, he can restore it by penance.* But it is, they assert, Jerome's saying. No matter whose it may be, it cannot be excused of manifest impiety. As if baptism were wiped out by sin, and is not rather to be recalled to the memory of the sinner whenever he thinks of forgiveness of sins, so that from it he may gather himself together, take courage, and confirm his faith. Thus will he obtain the forgiveness of sins promised him in baptism! You will therefore speak most aptly if you call baptism the sacrament of penance, since it has been given as a consolation to those practicing repentance.*

C. EXTREME UNCTION (AS THEY CALL IT)*

4.19.18 45. The third false sacrament is extreme unction, which is performed only by the priest, [363] and that in *extremis* (as they say), with oil consecrated by the bishop, and with this formula: /203/ "Through this holy anointing and through his most kindly mercy, may God pardon thee for whatever sins thou hast committed through seeing, hearing, smelling, touching, or tasting."* They fancy its two powers are forgiveness of sins and easing of bodily sickness, if such be expedient; if not, health of the soul.* They say moreover that its institution was set by James, whose words are: "Is any among you sick? Let him call for the presbyters of the church, and let them pray over him, anointing him with oil in the name of the Lord [James 5:14, Vg.]; and if he has committed sins, he will be forgiven"* [James 5:15]. This anointing is of the same sort as we demonstrated above the laying on of hands to be, namely, merely play-acting, by which, without reason and without benefit, they wish to resemble the apostles. Mark relates that the apostles on their first mission, according to the command which they had received from the Lord, raised up the dead, cast out demons, cleansed lepers, healed the sick, and in curing the sick used oil. "They anointed," he says, "many sick persons with oil, and they were cured" [Mark 6:13, cf. Vg.]. James had reference to this when he enjoined that the presbyters should be called to anoint the sick man. That no deeper mystery underlies such cermonies will readily [364] be decided by those who have observed how much freedom both the Lord and his apostles exercised in these outward matters. The Lord, about to restore sight to the blind man, made a clay of dust and spittle [John 9:6]; (178) some he healed by touch [Matt. 9:29]; others by a word [Luke 18:42]. In the same way, the apostles cured some diseases by word alone [Acts 3:6; 14:9-10], some by touch [Acts 5:12, 16], some by anointing [Acts 19:12].

But it is likely that this anointing, like all the other methods, was not used without discrimination. I admit this: yet not that it was an instrument of healing, but only a symbol, by which the unschooled in their ignorance might be made aware of the source of such great power, that they might not give the credit for it to the apostles. It is a well-worn commonplace that by oil the Holy Spirit and his gifts are signified [Ps. 45:7].

But that gift of healing, like the rest of the miracles, which the Lord willed to be brought forth for a time, has vanished away in order to make the new preaching of the gospel marvelous forever.

46. Therefore, even if we grant to the full that anointing was a sacrament 4.19.19 of those powers which were at that time administered by the hands of the apostles, it now has nothing to do with us, to whom the administering of such powers has not been committed.

And for what greater reason do they make a sacrament out of this unction than out of all the other symbols mentioned to us in Scripture? Why do they not appoint some bathing pool of Siloam [John 9:7] into which [365] the sick at certain times may plunge themselves? That, they say, would be done in vain. Surely, no more in vain than anointing. Why not let them lie upon dead men, since Paul raised a dead child by lying upon him [Acts 20:10]? /204/ Why is not clay made of spittle and dust a sacrament? But the others (they reply) were individual examples, while this was commanded by James. That is, James spoke for that same time when the church still enjoyed such a blessing of God. Indeed, they affirm that the same force still inheres their anointing, but we experience otherwise. Let no one now marvel how with such great boldness they have mocked souls, whom they knew to be senseless and blind when deprived of the Word of God, which is life and light; for they are not ashamed to wish to deceive the living and feeling senses of the body. Therefore, they make themselves ridiculous when they boast that they are endowed with the gift of healing. The Lord is indeed present with his people in every age; and he heals their weaknesses as often as necessary, no less than of old; still he does not put forth thus these manifest powers, but does not dispense miracles through the apostles' hands.

Therefore, as by the symbol of oil the apostles have with good cause 4.19.20 designated that the gift of healing committed to them was not their own power but that of the Holy Spirit, so on the other hand those persons wrong the Holy Spirit who make a putrid and ineffectual oil [366] his power. That is as if someone were saying that all oil is the power of the Holy Spirit, because it is called by that name in Scripture [I John 2:20, 27]; that every dove is the Holy

Spirit, because he appeared in that form [Matt. 3:16; John 1:32]. But let them look into these things.

47. As for us, it suffices for the present to recognize as a certainty that their anointing is not a sacrament, for neither is it a ceremony instituted by God, nor (179) has it any promise. Indeed, when we require these two things in a sacrament—that it be a ceremony instituted by God, and that it have God's promise—at the same time we demand that that ceremony be delivered to us, and the promise apply to us. For no one argues that circumcision is now a sacrament of the Christian church, even though it both was an institution of God and had a promise attached. For it was neither enjoined upon us, nor was the promise which had been joined with it given to us. That the promise which they fiercely claim in extreme unction was not given for us we have clearly proved, and they themselves make clear by experience. The ceremony ought not to have been used except by those endowed with the gift of healing, not by these butchers who are more able to slay and hack than to heal.

4.19.21   However, even if they should win their point, (which they are very far from doing) that what James prescribes [367] concerning anointing applies to this age, even at that they would not make much headway in proving their anointing, with which they have hitherto daubed us.

48. James wishes all sick persons to be anointed [James 5:14]; these fellows smear with their grease not the sick but half-dead corpses when they are already drawing their last breath, or (as they say), in /205/ extremis.* If in their sacrament they have a powerful medicine with which to alleviate the agony of diseases, or at least to bring some comfort to the soul, it is cruel of them never to heal in time. James would have the sick man anointed by the elders of the church; these men allow only a priestling as anointer. It is highly absurd that they interpret "presbyters" in the passage of James as "priests,"* and imagine that the plural number is put there as embellishment—as though the churches of that time swarmed with sacrificers, so that they could proceed in a long parade, bearing holy oil on a litter. James, when he bids simply that sick persons be anointed, to my mind indicates no other anointing than with common oil, and no other is found in Mark's narrative [Mark 6:13]. These men do not deign to use any oil but that consecrated by a bishop,* that is, warmed with much breathing, muttered over with long incantations, and saluted with nine kneelings thus: thrice, "Hail, holy oil"; thrice, "Hail, holy chrism"; thrice, "Hail, holy balm."* [368] From whom have they drawn such exorcisms? James says when the sick man has been anointed with oil and been prayed over, if he be in sins, they will be forgiven [James 5:14-15], not meaning that sins are wiped out with grease, but that the prayers of believers, with which the afflicted brother has been commended to God, will not be in vain. These fellows impiously lie that sins are forgiven through their "sacred," that is, accursed, unction.* Lo, how beautifully they profit when they have been allowed freely to abuse James's testimony according to their own whim! (180)

D. ECCLESIASTICAL ORDERS*

49. The sacrament of order occupies the fourth place in their list, but it is so fruitful that it breeds of itself seven sacramentlings. But this is quite ridiculous, that, while they affirm that there are seven sacraments, when they set out to count them, they reckon thirteen. And they cannot allege that these constitute one sacrament because all tend to one priesthood and are as steps to it. For since it is clear that there are different ceremonies in each, and they say that there are different gifts, no one doubts that [369] they ought to be called seven sacraments, if these men's opinions are accepted. Anyway, why do we argue over it as something doubtful, when they themselves plainly and distinctly proclaim seven? /206/

And seven orders, or ecclesiastical grades are named. These are: doorkeepers, readers, exorcists, acolytes, subdeacons, deacons, priests. Indeed they are seven by reason of the sevenfold grace of the Holy Spirit, with which they who are promoted to these offices ought to be endowed.* But this grace is increased and more liberally heaped upon them as they are promoted.*

50. Now the number itself has been consecrated by perverted interpretation of Scripture, because they think that they have read in Isaiah of seven powers of the Holy Spirit, when Isaiah actually refers to no more than six [Is. 11:12]; and the prophet did not wish to confine them all to that passage. For He is elsewhere called "the Spirit of life" [Ezek. 1:20, Vg.], "of sanctification" [Rom. 1:4, Vg.], "of adoption of sons" [Rom. 8:15, Vg.]; while he is there called "the Spirit of wisdom, understanding, counsel, fortitude, knowledge, and fear of the Lord." [Is. 11:2].

However, others who are more discerning make not seven orders,* but nine,* after the likeness, as they say, of the church triumphant. And there is a conflict among them because some would have the clerical tonsure as the first order, and the episcopate the last; others, excluding tonsure, include the archiepiscopate in the orders.* Isidore divides them differently: he distinguishes between psalmists and readers. He puts the psalmists in charge of the singing; the readers of the reading of the Scriptures [370] for the instruction of the people. And this distinction is observed in the canons.*

Amidst such great variety, what do they wish us to follow or flee? Should we say that there are seven orders? So teaches the Master of the School;* but the most enlightened doctors determine otherwise. But again they disagree among themselves. Moreover, the most sacred canons call us in another direction. This obviously is how men agree when they argue over divine things apart from God's Word!

51. But now, when they contend over the origin (181) of their orders, do they also make themselves as ridiculous as these boys? They are called "clerics" from the lot, or because chosen by lot by the Lord, or because of the lot of the Lord, or because they have God as portion.* Yet it was a sacrilege for them to apply to themselves this title which belonged to the whole church.* For that

4.19.22

4.4.9

inheritance is of Christ, given by the Father [cf. I Pet. 5:3]. Nor is Peter calling a few shaven men (as they wickedly imagine) "the clergy," /207/ but the whole people of God. This is how it goes with them: The clergy are shaved on the top of the head, that the crown may signify royal dignity, since clerics ought to be kings, to rule themselves and others. For Peter speaks of them as follows: "You are a chosen race, a royal priesthood, a holy nation, a people of his possession" [I Pet. 2:9, Vg.]. Here again I prove them false. Peter is speaking of the whole church; these fellows twist it to a few men, as if to them alone it was said, "Be holy" [I Pet. 1:15-16; Lev. 20:7; cf. Lev. 19:2]; as if they alone were purchased by Christ's blood [I Pet. 1:18-19]; as if they alone were made a kingdom and [371] priesthood to God through Christ [I Pet. 2:5, 9]! Then they also give other reasons: the top of the head is made bare to show their mind free to the Lord so "with face unveiled" [II Cor. 3:18, Vg.] to contemplate God's glory, or to teach them that the faults of the mouth and the eyes must be cut off. Or the shaving of the head is the putting away of temporal things; but the hairs remaining around the crown are remnants of the good things which are retained for their sustenance. Everything in symbols, obviously because "the veil of the Temple has" not yet "been rent" [Matt. 27:51]. Persuaded, then, that they have discharged their duties with distinction because they have symbolized such things by their crown, they actually perform none of them. How long will they mock us with such deception and trickery? By shaving off a few hairs the clerics signify that they have cast away abundance of temporal goods, that they contemplate God's glory, that they have mortified the lust of the ears and eyes. And is there no class of men more greedy, stupid, and lustful? Why do they not manifest holiness rather than make an outward show of it with false and lying signs?

Now, when they say that the clerical crown has its origin and reason from the Nazarites, what else do they claim but that their mysteries have arisen from Jewish ceremonies, or rather, are mere Judaism?

But when they add that Priscilla, Aquila, and Paul himself, taking a vow, shaved themselves that they might be purified [372] [Acts 18:18], they show their gross ignorance. For it is nowhere recorded of Priscilla, and in Aquila's case it is also uncertain; for that tonsure can be referred as much to Paul as to Aquila. But not to leave to them what they claim—that they have an example from Paul—simpler readers should note that Paul never shaved his head for any sanctification, but only to serve his weaker brethren. (182) It is my custom to call such vows the vows of love, not of piety; that is, not undertaken for any worship of God, but to treat gently the ignorance of the weak, /208/ as he himself says that to the Jews he became a Jew, etc. [I Cor. 9:20]. But he was doing this to accommodate himself temporarily to the Jews. When these fellows pointlessly aim to imitate the purifications of the Nazarites, what else are they doing but raising up another Judaism [Num. 6:18; cf. ch. 6:5]?

With the same religious scruple was composed that decretal epistle which forbids clerics (according to the apostle) to let their hair grow, but requires them

4.19.25

4.19.26

162

to shave it like a ball. It is as if the apostle, teaching what is comely for all men [I Cor. 11:4], were concerned about the ball-like tonsure of the clergy!

52. From this let my readers judge what those other orders are like, which have such a beginning as these. But it surpasses all folly that in each order they make Christ their companion. First, they say, he fulfilled the office of doorkeeper [373] when he cast the buyers and sellers from the Temple with a whip made of cords [John 2:15; Matt. 21:12, conflated]. And he indicates that he is a doorkeeper when he says, "I am the door" [John 10:7, Vg.]. He assumed the function of reader when he read Isaiah in the synagogue [Luke 4:17]. He discharged the office of exorcist when he touched with saliva the tongue and ears of the deaf-and-dumb man and restored his hearing [Mark 7:32-33]. He testified that he was an acolyte by saying, "He who follows me does not walk in darkness" [John 8:12, Vg.]. He performed the office of subdeacon when, girded with a linen cloth, he washed the disciples' feet [John 13:4-5]. He played the role of deacon when he distributed body and blood in the Supper to the apostles [Matt. 26:26]. He fulfilled the function of priest when he offered himself as a sacrifice on the cross to his Father [Matt. 27:50; Eph. 5:2]. These things cannot be heard without such laughter that I marvel at their being written without laughter, if, after all, those who wrote them were men. But their subtlety is especially remarkable when they philosophize over the title "acolyte," calling him a taper-bearer, a magic word (suppose), certainly unheard of in all nations and languages, since ἀκόλουθος to the Greeks simply means "lackey."

53. However, if I should tarry over seriously refuting these opinions, I also would rightly be laughed at—they are so trifling and absurd. Nevertheless, in order that they may not deceive even mere women, their vanity must be exposed in passing. With great pomp and solemnity they create their readers, psalmists, doorkeepers, and acolytes, to perform these services [374] to which they appoint either boys or at least those whom they call "laymen." For who most often lights the candles, pours wine and water into the cruet, but a boy or some wretched layman who gains his livelihood thereby? Do not the same men sing? /209/ Do not the same men shut and open the church doors? For whoever saw either an acolyte or a doorkeeper performing his function in their churches? Rather, (183) he who as a boy did the office of acolyte, when he is taken into the order of acolytes, ceases to be what he has begun to be called; so that they seem to intend deliberately to throw off the office itself when they assume the title. See, why they hold it needful to be consecrated by sacraments and to receive the Holy Spirit—just to do nothing!

If they pretend that it is due to the perversity of the age that they forsake and neglect their duties, let them at the same time confess that today their sacred orders (which they wonderfully exalt) are of no use or benefit in the church, and that their whole church is full of anathema, inasmuch as it allows candles and cruets to be handled by boys and profane persons who are not worthy to touch them unless consecrated as acolytes, and since it relegates to boys, the chanting, which ought to have been heard only from consecrated lips.

4.19.23

4.19.24

But to what purpose do they consecrate exorcists? I hear [375] that the Jews had their exorcists, but I see that they were called after the exorcisms they exercised [Acts 19:13]. Whoever heard it said of these fake exorcists that they showed one instance of practicing their profession? It is pretended that they have the power of laying hands on the insane, catechumens, and demoniacs; but they cannot persuade the demons they are endowed with such power, because the demons not only do not yield to their commands but even command the exorcists! For you scarcely find a tenth of them not led by an evil spirit. Whatever, then, they babble about their petty orders—whether they count six or five—is a patchwork of ignorant and unsavory falsehood.

4.19.28
4.19.27
Moreover I include the subdiaconate among these, even if it was transferred to the major orders after that crowd of minor orders began to sprout. It is clear that these certainly ought to be considered at the level of sacraments, since by our opponents' confession, they were unknown to the primitive church and devised many years after. But since sacraments contain a promise of God, they can be instituted neither by angels nor by men, but by God alone, to whom alone it belongs to give the promise.

4.19.28
For the two remaining, they seem to have authorization from God's Word, and for this reason they especially call them "holy orders" for honor's sake. But we must see how dishonestly they abuse it as an excuse for themselves. [376]

54. We shall begin moreover with the order of the presbyterate or priesthood. For by these two names they signify the same thing, and they so /210/ call those whose duty it is, they say to perform the sacrifice of Christ's body and blood on the altar, to say prayers, and to bless God's gifts. Therefore, in ordination they receive the chalice and paten with the host as tokens of the power conferred to offer sacrifices of expiation [cf. Lev. 5:8] to God; and their hands are anointed (184), by which token they understand that they have been given the power to consecrate. So unauthorized by God's word to do such things are they, that they could not more wickedly pervert the order laid down by God. First, what we have asserted in the previous discussion ought to be an acknowledged fact: all who call themselves priests in order to perform expiatory sacrifice are wronging Christ. Christ was appointed and consecrated priest by the Father with an oath [Heb. 7:20f.] according to the order of Melchizedek [Heb. 5:6; 6:20; 7:17; cf. Ps. 110:4], without end, without successor [Heb. 7:3]. He once for all offered a sacrifice of eternal expiation and reconciliation [Heb. 7:27; 8:3]; now, having also entered the sanctuary of heaven [Heb. 9:24], he intercedes for us [Heb. 7:25]. In him we are all priests [Rev. 1:6; cf. I Pet. 2:9], but to offer praises and thanksgiving, in short, to offer ourselves and ours to God. It was his office alone to appease God and atone for sins by his offering. What remains [377] but that their priesthood is an impious sacrilege?

4.5.4
55. But since they are not ashamed to boast of themselves as the apostles' successors, it is worthwhile to investigate how credibly they perform their offices. Yet they ought to have agreed among themselves, if they craved credibility. Now the bishops, the mendicants, and the petty sacrificers fiercely fight over

the succession of the apostles. The bishops contend that twelve men were assigned to the apostolate by a singular privilege, and that they (as ones surpassing the others in honor) belong to the position and rank of the apostles. The common presbyters correspond to the seventy who were afterwards appointed by the Lord [cf. Luke 10:1]. But this is too absurd a reckoning, and obviously does not require a long refutation. Indeed they recognize this from their tables.

Before devilish division arose in the church, and one said, "I am of Ce-
phas," another "I am of Apollos," [I Cor. 1:12] there was no distinction between presbyters and bishops. Those to whom this distinction seemed to have been taken from the pagans reasoned much more correctly. The pagans had their flamens, curial priests, luperci, /211/ salii, pontiffs, and the like, distinguished according to rank. The mendicant monks peddle themselves as vicars of the apostles by a comparison (which actually shows them to be far different) because they dash about here and there, and feed off others. The Apostles did not aimlessly flit from place to place, as these vagabonds do, but set forth [378] whither they were called by the Lord to propagate the fruit of the gospel; and they did not feed idle bellies by others' toil, but according to the freedom allowed them by the Lord, they utilized the benefits of those they were instructing in the word. And there was no reason for the monks to cover themselves with another's plumage, as if testimony were lacking, since Paul has described their title clearly enough. "We have heard," he says, "that some among you are walking about in idleness, not working, (185) but mere busybodies" [II Thess. 3:11]. Elsewhere: "Among them are those who make their way into households and capture weak women, burdened with sins, always learning, and never arriving at a knowledge of the truth" [II Tim. 3:6-7]. Since I say, they can by a valid interdict claim these titles, let them leave to others the office of the apostles, from which they are as far distant as from heaven itself.

Therefore let us see concerning the order of the priesthood in general how fairly it squares with the office of the apostles. Our Lord, when as yet no form of the church had been established, commanded the apostles to preach the gospel to every creature, and to baptize believers unto forgiveness of sins [Matt. 28:19-20; Mark 16:15]. Moreover, he had previously commanded that they distribute the sacred symbols of his body and blood after his example [Luke 22:19]. No mention of sacrifice! Here is the holy, inviolable and perpetual law, imposed upon those who are the successors of the apostles, by which they receive the command to preach the gospel [379] and administer the sacraments. Therefore those who do not devote themselves to the preaching of the gospel and the administration of the sacraments, wickedly impersonate the apostles. On the other hand, those who sacrifice boast falsely of a common ministry with the apostles.

56. There is a difference between the apostles and those who ought to be set over the governing of the church today. First, there is the name. Even though by the meaning and derivation of the word, both can be called "apostles," because both have been sent by the Lord [Rom. 10:14f; Luke 6:13], still, the

4.4.2

4.3.6

4.3.5

former were twelve men specially chosen by the Lord /212/ to spread the new preaching of the Gospel on earth. And the Lord willed them especially to be called "apostles," for it was of great importance to have sure knowledge of the

4.3.4 mission of those who were to bring a new and unheard of thing. The latter are rather called "presbyters" and "bishops." Secondly, there is the office. Even though it is common to both to minister Word and sacraments, still to those

4.3.7 twelve men it had been commanded to spread the gospel in various regions, with no limits established [Act. 1:8]: to the latter individual churches are assigned.

Yet it is not here denied that it is lawful for him who is in charge of one church to aid other churches, either because some sort of disturbance has broken out which requires his presence, or, absent, he can teach the absent ones by his writings. But to keep peace in the church, this order is necessary: that to each be assigned his task so that all may not raise a tumult at once, [380] to keep all from being in confusion, at the same time dashing about aimlessly without an assignment, rashly gathering together in one place, and forsaking their churches

4.3.15 at pleasure. Paul laid down this distinction, writing as follows to Titus: "This is why I left you in Crete, that you might correct what was defective, and appoint presbyters in every city [Titus 1:5]. The same is shown by Luke in The Acts, when he introduces Paul speaking as follows (186) to the elders of the Church at Ephesus: "Take heed to yourselves and to all the flock for which the Holy Spirit has appointed you bishops, to rule the church of God, which he acquired by his blood" [Acts 20:28]. Thus Paul reminds Archippus bishop of the Colossians [Col. 4:17]; and elsewhere, the bishops of the Philippians [Phil. 1:1].

4.3.8 57. Having properly considered these matters, we are now ready to define the office of presbyter, who are to be included in the order of presbyters, or rather, what the order itself in general is. The office is to proclaim the gospel and administer the sacraments. (I now pass over how the elders ought to excel in uprightness of conduct, and how they should as individuals act toward one another. For it is not our present intention to cover all the gifts of a good pastor, but only to point out what those who call themselves pastors should profess.) A bishop is he who, called to the ministry of word and sacraments, carries out his office in good faith. I call bishops and presbyters indiscriminately [381] "ministers of the church." Order is the calling itself.

4.3.10/11 58. This is the place to explain the meaning of the call. It consists of two things, namely, that we should understand who are the ones to institute bishops

4.3.13 or presbyters, and by what rite or ceremony to initiate them. Evidence for lawful institution cannot be sought from the institution of the apostles, who awaited no human call, but by the command of the Lord alone girded themselves for their task. It is clear enough that the apostles themselves did not hold this order, except that Paul, whom we cited a moment ago in that passage, /213/ stated that he left Titus in Crete to appoint bishops in every city [Titus 1:5]. And elsewhere he advises Timothy not to lay hands upon anyone rashly [I Tim. 5:22].

4.3.7 And Luke in The Acts refers to presbyters appointed by Paul and Barnabas over the separate churches of Lystra, Iconium and Antioch [Acts 14:22-23]. The mitered pontiffs have strongly alleged these passages, as they are accustomed to note all the passages which seem grist for their mill. From this they have inferred that the power of ordaining and consecrating presbyters (as they say) belongs to them alone*. And to make their consecration venerable and pious to the uninstructed with a shining mask, they delineate it with many ceremonies. But they are mistaken when they think that to consecrate and ordain is anything else than to appoint [382] the bishop and pastor of a church, if they consecrate and ordain according to Paul's rule. But if they do otherwise, they are most wickedly twisting these passages of Paul to their own fancy. And obviously they are doing far otherwise. For they do not ordain to the episcopate, but to the pristhood. So we destine them, they say, for the ministry of the church. But do they think the ministry of the church to be anything else than the ministry of the Word? I know indeed how repeatedly they sing this song: that their paltry sacrificers are ministers of the church. But no sane man believes this. In fact the truth of the Scripture vanquishes them, recognizing as it does no other minister of the church than the herald of God's Word, (187) called to govern the church, whom it sometimes calls "bishop" [Acts 20:28], sometimes "presbyter" [Acts 14:23], and even occasionally "pastor" [I Pet. 5:4].

59. But now, if they object that the canons forbid anyone being admitted without a title*, this fact is not unknown to me. But the titles they put forth I do not consider lawful. Are not the better part of their titles, dignities, parsonages, canonries, prebendaries, chaplaincies, priories, and even monasteries? Are these not taken partly from cathedral churches, partly from collegiate churches, partly from deserted shrines, partly from cloisters? All these I take to be stews of Satan and boldly so affirm. For do not all those ordained to that office but sacrifice and immolate Christ? In short, they ordain no one [383] except to sacrifice, which is not to consecrate to God, but to demons. But the true and only ordination is to call to the governing of the church a man of proved life and teaching, and to appoint him to that ministry. In this sense are these passages of Paul to be taken: whatever ceremony /214/and rite of calling they contain is along with the call itself. But concerning the ceremony we will speak thereafter in its place.

60. Now let us deal with the matter in hand: by whom the ministers of the church are to be ordained, that is, called. What then? Did Paul give Timothy and Titus the rights of collations, such as are now exercised by crowned princes? Not at all. But when Paul had given to each the command to establish and gather the churches of the provinces in which they had been left, he urged the one not to let the churches be deserted; the other he warned not to accept anyone except a proved man. Did not Paul and Barnabas confer the possessions of churches, as some metropolitans do now? By no means. Moreover, I do not estimate that all those by their own decision imposed men who seemed good to them upon churches without their knowledge and consent, but having shared counsel with the churches, they called to that office those of the brethren whom they considered to be of purer doctrine and more upright life. And it was necessary if they wished the churches to remain inviolate, when a church was going to deliberate

on choosing a minister, before proceeding to the election, that they should call [384] from the neighborhood one or two bishops, eminent beyond the others in holiness of life and purity of doctrine, with whom to discuss what person ought rather to be chosen. Whether it is enough for the bishop to be created by the meeting of the whole church, or by the vote of a few to whom this responsibility is delegated, or by the magistrate's decision, no definite law can be determined. But counsel is to be taken according to the circumstances of the times and

4.4.15

customs of the people. Cyprian strongly argues that an election is not properly made except by the common vote of all the people. The histories attest that this observance prevailed at that time in many regions.

4.4.12

61. But because it scarcely ever happens that so many heads can unanimously settle any matter, and it is generally (188) true that "the uncertain crowd is divided into contrary interests," it seems better to me, that either the magistrate or the senate or the elders perform this office of choosing, always (as I have said) with some bishops as advisers whose good faith and probity they respect. But this can be better provided for, according to the exigencies of the time, by the princes or by free cities, having godliness at heart. Certainly, the horned prelates have utterly corrupted right ordination, by their rights of collations, presentations, representations, patronages, and other sorts of tyrannical lordships.

4.5.2

62. But, they say, the corruption of the times [385] /215/ required that, since among people and magistrates hatred and party spirit prevailed more in selecting bishops than did right and sound judgment, the decision of this matter should be delegated to a few chief bishops. Obviously, this was a remedy for an extreme evil in hopeless circumstances! But when the medicine has seemed more deadly than the disease itself, why is this new evil not also remedied?

63. But the canons have very explicitly warned bishops not to abuse their power to the ruin of the church. Although, if I were to speak the truth, the canons themselves are firebrands ignited for the total destruction of the earth rather than cautions to keep the moderation of good discipline. Yet I pass over this. But what do these canons thrust at me—mere mockeries that they are even to their authors, though all the while pleasing to them.

But do we doubt that the common people of old, when they were meeting to choose a bishop, understood they were bound by most holy laws, since they saw the rule laid down for them out of God's Word? Indeed, a single utterance of God justly ought to have been of more weight for the people than countless tens of thousands of little canons. Nonetheless, corrupted by a most ignoble passion, they had no regard for law or equity. Thus today, even if the best laws have been drawn up, they remain buried in documents. Meanwhile public morality has condoned the fact that almost exclusively barbers, cooks, muleteers, bastards and such dregs of men are created pastors of churches. [386] I am not exaggerating: bishoprics are the rewards for panderings and adulteries. For when they are given to hunters and falconers, we are to suppose that things have turned out admirably! Such great indignity is unseasonably defended by the canons. The people once had an excellent canon, I say, prescribed by the Word of God, that a bishop ought to be above reproach, a teacher, not contentious, not greedy, etc. [I Tim. 3:1-7; cf. Titus 1:7-9]. Why, then, has the responsibility of choosing ministers been transferred from the people to these officials? Because the Word of God was not being heeded among tumults and factions of the people. And why is it not today transferred back by the bishops, who not only violate all laws, but casting away shame, wantonly, selfishly, and ambitiously mingle and confuse human things with divine?

Is it tolerable even to hear the name (189) "pastors of the church" applied to those who have never seen any one of their flock, who have violently rushed into possession of a church as upon enemy booty, who have obtained it by lawsuits, who have bought it for a price, who have earned it by sordid currying of favor, who as children scarcely able to babble have received it as an inheritance from their uncles and relatives? 4.5.6

Would the licentiousness of the lay folk—corrupt and lawless as they were—ever have gone as far as this? Whoever can gaze with dry eyes upon this picture of the church /216/ seen in our age, are cruel and ungodly men who, when they could restore it, neglect it, and surpass all inhumanity. [387]. 4.5.7

64. Now let us examine what is secondary in the calling of presbyters, by what kind of ceremony they are to be initiated. Our Lord, when he sent forth the apostles to preach the gospel, breathed upon them [John 20:22]. By this symbol he represented the Holy Spirit's power which he gave them. These good men have retained this insufflation, and, as if they are putting forth the Holy Spirit from their own throat, they mutter over those they are making priestlings, "Receive the Holy Spirit" [John 20:22, Vg.]. They leave nothing which they do not preposterously counterfeit: I do not say like actors whose gestures have some reason and mean, but like apes, which imitate everything wantonly and without any discrimination. We are preserving (they say) the Lord's example. But the Lord did many things which he did not intend as examples for us. The Lord said to his disciples, "Receive the Holy Spirit" [John 20:22, Vg.]. He also said to Lazarus, "Lazarus, come forth" [John 11:43, Vg.]. He said to the paralytic, "Rise up and walk" [Matt. 9:5, Vg.; cf. John 5:8]. Why do they not say the same to all dead men and paralytics? He gave evidence of his divine power when in breathing upon the apostles he filled them with the grace of the Holy Spirit. If they try to do this, they rival God and all but challenge him to a contest, but are very far from being effective, and by their inept gesture do nothing but mock Christ. Indeed, they are so shameless as to dare affirm [388] that they confer the Holy Spirit. But how true that is, experience teaches, which cries out that all those who are consecrated as priests are turned from horses into asses, from fools into madmen. Nevertheless, it is not over this that I have a quarrel with them. I am only condemning the ceremony itself, which ought not to have been taken as an example, since Christ used it as symbol of a particular miracle—so far is the excuse of following him from being a just defense of their claim! 4.19.29

Finally, from whom have they received anointing? They answer that they 4.19.30

have received it from the sons of Aaron, from whom their order took its beginning. They constantly prefer, therefore, to defend themselves by perverse examples, rather than to confess that what they rashly use they have themselves devised; but meanwhile they do not notice, when they profess themselves successors of the sons of Aaron, that they do wrong to Christ's priesthood, (190) which alone was foreshadowed and prefigured by all the ancient priesthoods. In Him, therefore, all those were contained and fulfilled, in him they ceased, as we have already repeated several times /217/ and as The Letter to the Hebrews, without the aid of glosses testifies. But if they are so delighted with the Mosaic ceremonies, why do they not take oxen, calves, and lambs to sacrifice? Indeed, they have a good part of the ancient Tabernacle and of the whole Jewish worship; but their religion is lacking in that they do not sacrifice calves and oxen. Who can fail to see that this observance of anointing [389] is much more dangerous than circumcision; especially when they add superstition and a Pharisaical notion of the worthiness of the work? The Jews rested their assurance of righteousness in circumcision; these men, spiritual graces in anointing.

4.19.31   This indeed is (if it please God) the sacred oil, which imprints an indelible character. As if oil could not be wiped away with dust and salt, or (if it clings harder) with soap! But (they tell us), the character is a spiritual one. What has oil to do with the soul? Do they forget what they parrot from Augustine: "If the word be withdrawn from the water, it will be nothing but water; but it is the word that makes it a sacrament"? What word will they show to accompany their grease? That Moses was commanded to anoint the sons of Aaron [Ex. 30:30; cf. chs. 28:41; 29:7]? There also he was commanded concerning the coat, the ephod, the turban, the crown of holiness, with which Aaron was to be adorned [Lev. 8:7,9] and the caps, which his sons were to wear [Lev. 8:13]. He was commanded concerning the slaughtering of the calf, the burning of its fat [Lev. 8:14-16], concerning the slaying and burning of rams [Lev. 8:18-21], concerning the consecration of ear tips and garments with the blood of another ram [Lev. 8:22-24], and innumerable other observances. Since these are passed over, I wonder how it is that mere anointing with oil pleases them. But if they are glad to be sprinkled, why are they sprinkled with oil rather than with blood? Obviously, they are attempting something ingenious: to shape one religion out of Christianity and Judaism and paganism by sewing patches together. Their unction therefore stinks [390] because it lacks salt, that is, the word of God.

4.3.16   65. There remains the laying on of hands, which, it is clear, the apostles observed whenever they admitted any man to the ministry of the church. In this 4.19.31 way, Paul calls the laying on of hands of the presbytery, "ordination," by which Timothy had been taken into the episcopate [I Tim. 4:14]. Although I know "presbytery" in that passage is taken by some in the sense of the assembly of 4.3.16 elders, one may understand it more simply, in my view, of the ministry. I judge that this rite derived from the custom of the Hebrews, who, as it were, presented to God by the laying on of hands that which they wished to be blessed and sanctified. /218/ So Jacob, about to bless Ephraim and Manasseh, laid his hands on their heads [Gen. 48:14]. (191) With this meaning, I suppose, the Jews laid their hands upon their offerings according to the prescription of the law [Num. 8:12; 27:23; Lev. 1:4; 3:2; 8:13; 4:4, 15, 24, 29, 33, etc.]. The apostles, accordingly, signified by the laying on of hands that they were offering to God him on whom they were laying their hands. What then? Were they pursuing the shadows of the Law? Not at all. But they were employing this symbol with no superstition when they used it. For they laid hands upon those for whom they prayed the Holy Spirit to come from the Lord, and they administered Him by this sort of symbol, in order that they might teach that He comes not from them but descends from heaven. To sum up: it was the symbol by which they commended to the Lord him for whom they wished to implore the grace of the Holy Spirit. [391] It pleased the Lord, then, that grace be distributed by their ministry. But whatever it was, was it to be considered a sacrament completely? The apostles prayed on bended knee [Acts 7:60; 9:40; 20:36; 21:5; 26:14]: therefore, will men not kneel without its being a sacrament? The disciples are said to have prayed toward the east; looking toward the east should be a sacrament for us. Paul wishes men to lift up pure hands in every place [I Tim. 2:8], and it is recalled that holy men often prayed with hands raised up [Ps. 63:4; 88:9; 141:2; 143:6]; the stretching up of hands also should become a sacrament. In the end, all the gestures of the saints would turn into sacraments. **4.19.2**

All quarreling aside, I will pursue briefly what use we are not to make of this ceremony. If we use it to the end that we may confer the gifts of the Spirit, just as the apostles did, we are acting foolishly. For this mystery was neither committed to us by the Lord, nor was it established as a symbol by him. Yet the Pope and his minions incessantly roll this stone, as if they believed that they confer the Holy Spirit by such signs, just as we discussed more fully when we were dealing with that confirmation of theirs. But if the person being installed as bishop is placed in the midst of the church assembly, and is instructed in this office, is prayed over, with the hands of the elders laid upon him (by no rite, except in order to feel himself to be offered as a minister to God), and the church is moved to commend him with its common prayers to God—no sane man will disapprove of such laying on of hands. [392]

66. The origin, ordination, and office of the deacons* are described by Luke in The Acts [Acts 6:3]. For when the Greeks started a rumor that their widows were being neglected in the relief of the poor, the apostles, making the excuse that they were unable to fulfill both functions (preaching the Word and serving at table), asked the multitude /219/ to choose seven upright men to whom they might entrust this task [Acts 6:1ff.]. This was the office of deacons: to attend to the care of the poor and minister to them; from this they took their name. For they are so called, as ministers. Then Luke added an account of their institution. Those they had chosen, he says, they ordained in the presence of the apostles: praying, they laid their hands upon them [Acts 6:6]. Would that the church today had such deacons, and appointed them by such a ceremony; namely, the laying on of hands. On this we have said what (192) seemed to be sufficient. **4.3.9**

4.19.32 Paul also speaks of the deacons: he wishes them to be modest, not double-tongued, not wine-bibbers, not pursuing filthy gain, well established in the faith [I Tim. 3:8-9] husbands of one wife, governing their households and children well [I Tim. 3:12]. By what likeness to this is there in the deacons which these men devise? I am not speaking of men (lest they complain that I am unfairly judging their doctrine from the faults of men), but I contend that it is dishonorable to seek from the example of those whom the apostolic church ordained as deacons a testimony for these very ones whom our opponents present to us in their doctrine. [393] They say that it is the office of their deacons "to assist the priests; to minister in everything done in the sacraments, that is, in baptism, in chrism, in paten, and in chalice; to bring in the offerings and lay them upon the altar; to set the Lord's Table and cover it; to carry the cross and to pronounce the gospel and epistle to the people." Is there one word here of the true ministry of deacons?

Now, let us learn how they are installed: "when a deacon is ordained, the bishop alone lays his hand upon him. That is, he lays a napkin, i.e., a stole on the ordinand's left shoulder, that he may understand he has received the Lord's light yoke [Matt. 11:30], by which he may subject to the fear of God those things pertaining to his left side. The bishop gives him the text of the gospel, that he may understand himself as a proclaimer of it." What does all of this have to do with deacons? The papists do just as if someone said that he had ordained as apostles persons whom he had appointed only to burn incense, to dust images, to sweep churches, to catch mice, and to chase away dogs. Who would allow this class of men to be called apostles and be compared with the very apostles of Christ? Therefore, let them hereafter not falsely say that these are deacons, whom they have ordained only for their play-acting. They even call them Levites, and refer their reason and origin to the sons of Levi. I indeed allow this, provided they confirm (what is true) that they are reverting to the Levitical rites and the shadows of the Mosaic law, having denied Christ. [394]

4.19.33 67. Now let us establish once for all what is to be thought of the sacrament of order. There is no need to repeat at greater length /220/ the things explained above. This will suffice for modest and teachable persons (such as I have undertaken to instruct): there is no sacrament of God except where a ceremony is shown joined to a promise, or rather, except where a promise is seen in a ceremony. In this rite one finds not even one syllable of any definite promise; hence, it would be fruitless to seek a ceremony to confirm the promise. Again, one reads of no ceremony ordained by God. Therefore, there cannot be any sacrament.

E. MARRIAGE

4.19.34 68. The last one is marriage. All men admit that it was instituted by God [Gen. 2:21-24; Matt. 19:4ff.]; (193) but no man had ever seen it administered as a sacrament until the time of Gregory. And what sober man would ever have thought it such? Marriage is a good and holy ordinance of God; and farming, building, cobbling, and barbering are lawful ordinances of God, and yet are not sacraments. For it is required that a sacrament be not only a work of God but an outward ceremony appointed by God to confirm a promise. [395] Even children will discern that there is no such thing in matrimony.

69. But it is, they say, "the sign of a sacred thing, that is, of the spiritual joining of Christ with the church." If by the word "sign" they understand a symbol set before us by God to raise up the assurance of our faith, they are wandering far from the mark; if they simply understand "sign" as what is adduced by way of comparison, I will show how keenly they reason. Paul says, "As star differs from star in billiance, so will be the resurrection of the dead" [I Cor. 15:41-42]. There you have one sacrament. Christ says, "The Kingdom of Heaven is like a grain of mustard seed" [Matt. 13:31, Vg.] Here you have another. Again, "The Kingdom of Heaven is like leaven" [Matt. 13:33, Vg.]. Behold a third. Isaiah says, "Behold, the Lord will feed his flock like a shepherd" [Is. 40:10-11, cf. Vg.]. Behold a fourth. In another place, "The Lord shall go forth as a giant" [Is. 42:13 p., cf. Comm.]. Here you have a fifth. Finally, what end or measure will there be? There is nothing that by this reasoning will not be a sacrament. There will be as many sacraments as there are parables and similitudes in Scripture. In fact, theft will be a sacrament, inasmuch as it is written, "The Day of the Lord is like a thief" [I Thess. 5:2, Vg.]. Who can bear these Sophists when they prate so ignorantly? I admit that whenever we see a vine, it is a very good thing to recall what Christ said: "I am the vine, you are the branches" [John 15:5, Vg.]; "My Father is the vine-dresser" [John 15:1]. Whenever we meet a shepherd with his flock, /221/it is good that this also come to mind: [396] "I am the good shepherd" [John 10:14, Vg.]; "My sheep hear the voice" [John 10:27, Vg.]. But anyone who would classify such similitudes with the sacraments ought to be sent to a mental hospital.

70. But they press us with Paul's words, by which they say the term "sacrament" is applied to marriage: "He who loves his wife loves himself. For no man ever hated his own flesh, but nourishes and cherishes it, as Christ does the church, because we are members of his body, of his flesh, and of his bones. 'For this reason a man shall leave his father and mother and be joined to his wife, and the two shall become as one flesh.' This is a great sacrament. But I say, in Christ and the Church" [Eph. 5:28-31, Vg.]. Yet so to handle the Scriptures is to mix earth with heaven. Paul, to show to married men with what singular love they ought to embrace their wives, sets forth Christ to them as prototype. For as he poured out his godly compassion upon the church, which he had espoused to himself, thus he wishes every man to feel toward his own wife. Then the words follow: "He who loves his wife loves himself . . . as Christ loved the church" [Eph. 5:28]. Now to teach how Christ loved the church (194) as himself, nay, how he made himself one with his bride the church, Paul applies to Christ what Moses relates that Adam said of himself. For when Eve (who he knew was formed from his rib) [397] was brought into his sight, he

said, "She is bone of my bones, and flesh of my flesh" [Gen. 2:23, Vg.]. Paul testifies that all this was spiritually fulfilled in Christ and in us, when he says that we are members of his body, of his flesh, and of his bones, and thus one flesh with him. Finally, he adds this summation: "This is a great mystery." And that nobody may be deceived by an ambiguity, he explains that he is not speaking of carnal union of man and woman, but of the spiritual marriage of Christ and the church. Truly, indeed, this is a great mystery, that Christ allowed a rib to be removed from himself to form us; that is, when he was strong, he willed to be weak, in order that we might be strengthened by strength; so that we ourselves should now not only live, but he should live in us [Gal. 2:20].

4.19.36 The term "sacrament" has deceived them. But was it right that the whole church should suffer the punishment of their ignorance? Paul had said "mystery." The translator could have left this word, as one not unfamiliar to Latin ears, or rendered it as "secret." He preferred to use the word "sacrament" [Eph. 5:32, Vg.], but in the same sense that the word "mystery" had been used in Greek by Paul. Let them now go, and clamorously rail against skill in languages, through ignorance of which they have so long been most shamefully deceived in a matter easy and obvious to anyone. But why do they press so hard for this word "sacrament" in this one place, but overlook it at other times? [398] For in the first letter to /222/ Timothy [I Tim. 3:9], and in this same letter to the Ephesians itself [Eph. 1:9; 3:3, 9, Vg.], the translator of the Vulgate has used it consistently for "mystery."

71. Still, let this slip be pardoned them; liars at least ought to have good memories.

But, having graced marriage with the title of sacrament, to call it afterward uncleanness and pollution and carnal filth—what giddy levity is this? How absurd it is to bar priests from this sacrament! If they say they do not debar them from the sacrament, but from the lust of copulation, they will not give me the slip. For they teach that copulation itself is a part of the sacrament, and that it alone is the figure of the union which we have with Christ, in conformity to nature; for man and woman are are made one flesh only by carnal copulation. However, some of them have found two sacraments here: one of God and the soul, in the bridegroom and bride; the other, of Christ and the church, in the husband and wife. However, copulation is still a sacrament, from which it is unlawful to bar any Christian. Unless, perhaps, the sacraments of Christians are so out of accord that they cannot stand together. There is also another (195) absurdity in their grand offices. They affirm that in the sacrament the grace of the Holy Spirit is conferred; they teach copulation to be a sacrament; and they

4.19.37 deny that the Holy Spirit is ever present in copulation. Not to have mocked the church simply in one thing, what a long [399] train of errors, lies, frauds, and misdeeds have they attached to this one error? Thus, you may say that they sought nothing but a den of abominations when they made a sacrament out of marriage. For when they once obtained this, they took over the hearing of matrimonial cases; as it was a spiritual matter, it was not to be handled by secular judges. Then they passed laws by which they strengthened their tyranny, laws in part openly impious toward God, in part most unfair toward men.* Such are these: That marriages between minors contracted without parental consent should remain firm and valid.* That marriages between kinsfolk even to the seventh degree are not lawful, and if contracted, must be dissolved.* They forge the very degrees*, against the laws of all nations /223/ and also against the ordinance of Moses [Lev. 18:6 ff.]: that a man who has put away an adulterous wife is not permitted to take another.* that godparents may not be coupled in matrimony.* that marriages may not be celebrated from Septuagesima to the octave of Easter, and in the three weeks before the nativity of John, and from Advent to Epiphany.* and innumerable like regulations which would take too long to recount. At length, we must extricate ourselves from their mire, in which our discourse has already stuck longer than I should have liked. Still, I believe that I have accomplished something in that I have partly pulled the lion's skin from these asses.* [400].

CHAPTER VI

CHRISTIAN FREEDOM, ECCLESIASTICAL POWER, AND POLITICAL ADMINISTRATION

A. CHRISTIAN FREEDOM

3.19.1   1. We must now discuss Christian freedom. No summary of gospel teaching ought to omit an explanation of this topic. It is a matter of prime necessity, and without a knowledge of it consciences dare undertake almost nothing without faltering; often hesitate and draw back; constantly waver and are afraid. But we have put off a fuller discussion of it to this place (having lightly touched upon it above). For, as soon as Christian freedom is mentioned, (196) either passions boil or wild tumults rise, unless these wanton spirits (who otherwise most wickedly corrupt the best things) are opposed in time. Partly, on the pretext of this freedom, men shake off all obedience toward God and break into unbridled license; partly, they disdain it, thinking such freedom cancels all moderation, order, and choice of things. [401] What are we, boxed in by such perplexities, to do here? Shall we say goodbye to Christian freedom, thus cutting off occasion for such dangers? /224/ But, as we have said, unless this freedom be grasped, neither Christ nor gospel truth is rightly known. Rather, we must take care that so necessary a part of doctrine not be suppressed, yet at the same time that those absurd objections which commonly arise from it be met.

3.19.2   2. Christian freedom, in my opinion, consists of three parts. The first: that the consciences of believers, while having to seek assurance of their justification before God, should rise above and advance beyond the law, forgetting all law-righteousness. For since, as we have elsewhere shown, the law leaves no one righteous, either we are excluded from all hope of justification or we ought to be freed from it. And in such a way, indeed, that utterly no account is taken of works. For he who thinks that in order to obtain righteousness he ought to bring some trifle of works, is incapable of determining their measure and limit but makes himself debtor to the whole law. Removing, then, mention of law, and laying aside all consideration of works, we should, when justification is being discussed, embrace God's mercy alone, turn our attention from ourselves,

176

and look only to Christ. For there the question is not how we may become righteous, but how, [402] being unrighteous and unworthy, we may be reckoned righteous. If consciences wish to attain any certainty in this matter, they ought to give no place to the law. Nor can any man rightly infer from this that the law is superfluous for believers*, since it does not stop teaching and exhorting and urging them to good*, even though before God's judgment-seat it does not have a place in their consciences. For, as these two things are completely different, we must rightly and conscientiously distinguish them. The whole life of Christians ought to be a sort of practice of godliness, because we have been called to sanctification [I Thess. 4:7; cf. Eph. 1:4; I Thess. 4:3]. The function of the law consists in this: by warning men of their duty, to arouse them to pursue holiness and innocence. But where consciences are worried how to make God favorable, what to respond and with what assurance to stand, if called to his judgment—there we are not to reckon what the law requires, but Christ alone, who surpasses all law-perfection, must be set forth for righteousness.

Almost the entire argument of the letter to the Galatians hinges upon this point. For those who teach that Paul in this contends for freedom only from ceremonies are absurd interpreters*, as can be proved from his proof-passages. (197) Such passages are the following: That Christ "became a curse for us" to "redeem us from the curse of the law" [Gal. 3:13]. Likewise: [403] "Stand fast in the freedom with which Christ has set us free, and do not submit again to the yoke of salvery. Now I, Paul, say . . . that if you become circumcized, Christ will become of no advantage to you. . . . And every man who becomes circumcized is a debtor to the whole law. For you Christ has become of no advantage. Any of you who are justified by the law /225/ have fallen away from grace" [Gal. 5:1-4 p.]. These passages surely contain something loftier than freedom from ceremonies!   3.19.3

3. The second part, dependent upon the first, is that consciences observe the law, not as if constrained by the necessity of the law, but that freed from the law's yoke willingly obey God's will. For since they dwell in perpetual dread so long as they remain under the sway of the law, they will never be eager and ready to obey God, unless they have already been given this sort of freedom. By an example we shall more briefly and clearly arrive at the meaning of this. The precept of the law is that "we should love our God with all our heart, with all our soul, and with all our strength." [Deut. 6:5] To bring this about, our soul must previously be emptied of all other feeling and thought, our heart cleansed of all desires, and our strength gathered and concentrated upon this one point. They who have progressed farther than the others on the Lord's way are yet far distant from that goal. For even though they love God deeply and with sincere affection of heart, they have a great part of their heart and soul still occupied with fleshly desires, by which [404] they are drawn back and prevented from hastening at full speed to God. Indeed, they struggle manfully but the flesh partly weakens their strength, partly appropriates it to itself. What are they to do here, while they feel that there is nothing they are less able to do than to   3.19.4

fulfill the law? They will, they aspire, they try, but not at all with due perfection. If they look at the law, whatever work they may attempt or intend they see accursed. And there is no reason for any man to deceive himself by concluding that his work is not entirely evil because it is imperfect, and that God nonetheless finds acceptable what is good in it? For the law in requiring perfect love condemns all imperfection. Let him therefore ponder his own work, which he wished to be adjudged in part good, and by that very act he will find it, just because it is imperfect, to be a transgression of the law.

3.19.5   See how all our works are under the curse of the law if they are measured by the standard of the law! But how, then, would unhappy souls gird themselves eagerly for a work for which they might expect to be able to receive only a curse? But if, freed from this severe requirement of the law, or rather from the entire rigor of the law, they hear God calling them with fatherly gentleness, they will cheerfully and with great eagerness answer his call, and follow his leading. To sum up: Those bound by the yoke of the law are like servants assigned certain tasks for each day by their masters. These [405] servants think they have accomplished nothing, (198) and dare not appear before their masters unless they have fulfilled the exact measure of their tasks. But sons, who are more generously and candidly treated by their fathers, do not hesitate to offer them incomplete and half-done and even defective works, /226/ trusting that their obedience and readiness of mind will be accepted by their fathers, even though they have not quite accomplished what their fathers wished. Such children ought we to be, firmly trusting that our services will be approved by our most merciful Father, however small, rude, and imperfect these may be.

And we need this assurance in no slight degree, for without it we will attempt everything in vain. For God considers that he is revered by no work of ours unless we truly do it in reverence toward him. But how can this be done amidst all this dread, where one doubts whether God is offended or honored by our works?

3.19.6   And this is the reason why the author of The Letter to the Hebrews refers to faith and judges by faith alone all the good works of the holy fathers (as we read) [Heb. 11:2ff.; 11:17; etc.]. In the Letter to the Romans, there is a famous passage on this freedom, wherein Paul reasons that sin ought not to dominate us [Rom. 6:12 and 6:14, conflated], for we are not under the law but under grace [Rom. 6:14]. For after he had exhorted believers not to let "sin reign in" their "mortal bodies" [Rom. 6:12], nor to "yield" their "members to sin as weapons of iniquity," but to "give" themselves "to God as those who have come to life from the dead, [406] and "their members to God as weapons of righteousness" [Rom. 6:13]—yet they could object that they still bore with them their flesh, full of lusts, and that sin dwelt in them—Paul adds this consolation, derived from freedom from the law, as if to say: "'Even though they do not yet clearly feel that sin has been destroyed or that righteousness dwells in them, there is still no reason to be afraid and cast down in mind as if God were continually offended by the remnants of sin, seeing that they have been emancipated from the law by grace, so that their works are not to be measured according to its rule." Let those who infer that we ought to sin because we are not under the law understand that this freedom has nothing to do with them. For its purpose is to encourage us to good.

4. The third part of Christian freedom is that we are bound before God by no religious obligation to outward things of themselves "indifferent;"* but are permitted sometimes to use them, sometimes to leave them, indifferently.* And the knowledge of this freedom is very necessary for us. For if it is lacking, our consciences will have no repose and there will be no end to superstitions. Today we seem to many to be unreasonable because we stir up discussion over the unrestricted eating of meat, use of holidays and of vestments, and similar vain frivolities* (as it seems to them). But these matters are more important than is commonly believed. For when consciences have once ensnared themselves, they enter a long and inextricable maze, not easy to get out of. [407] If a man begins to doubt whether he may use linen for sheets, shirts, handkerchiefs, and napkins, he will afterward be uncertain also about hemp; (199) finally, doubt will even arise over tow. For he will turn over in his mind whether /227/ he can sup without napkins, or go without handkerchiefs. If any man thinks daintier food unlawful, in the end he will not be at peace before God, when he eats either black bread or common victuals, while it occurs to him that he could sustain his body on even coarser foods. If he boggles at sweet wine, he will not with clear conscience drink even flat wine, and finally he will not dare touch water if sweeter and cleaner than other water. To sum up, he will come to the point of considering it wrong to step upon a straw across his path, as the saying goes. Here begins a weighty controversy, for what is in debate is whether God, whose will ought to precede all our plans and actions, wishes us to use these things or those. As a consequence, some, in despair, are of necessity cast into confusion; others, despising God, and abandoning fear of him, must make their own way in destruction, where they have none ready-made. For all those entangled in such doubts, wherever they turn, see offense of conscience everywhere present. "I know," says Paul, "that nothing is common" (taking "common" in the sense of "profane"), but it is common for anyone who thinks it common [Rom. 14:14 p.]. With these words [408] Paul subjects all outward things to our freedom, provided our minds are assured that the basis for such freedom stands before God. But if any superstitious opinion poses a stumbling block for us, things of their own nature formerly pure are for us defiled. For this reason, he adds: "Happy is he who does not judge himself in what he approves. But he who judges, if he eats, is condemned, because he does not eat from faith. For whatever is not from faith is sin [Rom. 14:22-23 p.].

5. Amidst such perplexities, do not those who show themselves rather courageous by daring all things confidently, nonetheless to this extent turn away from God? But those who are quite deeply moved with some fear of God, when they are compelled to commit many things against their consciences, are overwhelmed and fall down with fright. All such persons receive none of God's gifts

3.19.7

3.19.8

with thanksgiving, yet as Paul testifies, it is by this alone that all things are sanctified for our use [I Tim. 4:4-5]. Now I mean that thanksgiving which proceeds from a mind that recognizes in his gifts God's kindness and goodness. For many of them, indeed, understand them as good things of God which they use, and praise God in his works; but, unpersuaded that these good things have been given to them, how can they thank God as the giver?

To sum up, we see the direction this freedom tends; namely, that we should use God's gifts for the use [409] for which he gave them to us, with no scruple of conscience, no trouble of mind. With such confidence our souls will be at peace with him, and will recognize his liberality toward us. But we must carefully note that Christian /228/ freedom is, in all its parts, a spiritual thing. Its whole force consists in quieting frightened consciences before God (200) whether they are disturbed and troubled over forgiveness of sins; or anxious whether unfinished works, corrupted by the faults of our flesh, are pleasing to God; or tormented about the use of things indifferent. Accordingly, it is perversely interpreted either by those who allege it as an excuse for their desires that they may abuse God's good gifts to their own lust or by those who think that freedom does not exist unless it is used before men, and consequently, in using it have no regard for weaker brethren.

6. Today men sin to a greater degree in the first way. There is almost no one whose resources permit him to be extravagant who does not delight in lavish and ostentatious banquets, bodily apparel, and domestic architecture; who does not wish to outstrip his neighbor in all sorts of elegance; who does not wonderfully flatter himself in his opulence. And all these things are defended under the pretext of Christian freedom. They say that these are things indifferent. I admit it, provided one uses them indifferently. But when these things are coveted too greedily, when they are proudly boasted of, when they are lavishly squandered [410] they are defiled by these vices.

Paul's statement very well distinguishes among things indifferent; "To the clean all things are clean, but to the corrupt and unbelieving nothing is clean, inasmuch as their minds and consciences are corrupted" [Titus 1:15, cf. Vg.]. For why are the rich cursed, who have their consolation, who are full, who laugh now [Luke 6:24-25], who sleep on ivory couches [Amos 6:4], "who join field to field" [Is. 5:8], whose feasts have harp, lyre, timbrel, and wine [Is. 5:12]? Surely ivory and gold and riches are good creations of God, permitted, indeed appointed, for men's use by God's providence. And we have never been forbidden to laugh, or to be filled, or to join new possessions to old and even ancestral ones, or to delight in musical harmony, or to drink wine. True indeed. But where there is plenty, to wallow in delights, to gorge oneself, to intoxicate mind and heart with present pleasures and be always panting after new ones—such are very far removed from a lawful use of God's gifts.

Away, then, with uncontrolled desire, away with immoderate prodigality, away with vanity and arrogance in order that men may with a clean conscience cleanly use God's gifts.

7. Where the heart is tempered to this soberness they will have a rule for lawful use of such blessings. But should this moderation be lacking, even base and common pleasures are too much. It is a true saying that under coarse and [411] rude attire there often dwells a heart of purple, while sometimes under silk and purple is hid a simple humility. Thus let every man live in his station, whether slenderly, or /229/ moderately or plentifully, so that all may remember God nourishes them to live, not to luxuriate. And let them regard this as the law of Christian freedom; to have learned with Paul, "in whatever state" they are, to be content; to know how to be humble and exalted; to have been taught, in any and all circumstances, "to be filled and to hunger, to abound and to suffer want." [Phil. 4:11-12] (201)

8. In this respect also many err; they use their freedom indiscriminately and unwisely, as though it were not sound and safe if it did not have men witness it. By this heedless use, they very often offend weak brothers. You can see some persons today who reckon their freedom does not exist unless they take possession of it by eating meat on Fridays. I do not blame them for eating meat, but this false notion must be driven from their minds. For they ought to have pondered that from their freedom they obtain nothing new in men's sight but before God, and that it consists as much in abstaining as in using. If they understand that it makes no difference in God's sight whether they eat meat or eggs, wear red or black clothes, this is enough and more. The conscience, to which the benefit of such freedom was due, has now been set free. Consequently, even if [412] men thereafter abstain from meat throughout life, and ever wear clothes of one color, they are not less free. Indeed, they are free, because they abstain with a free conscience. But in having no regard for their brothers' weakness they slip most disastrously, for we ought so to bear with it that we do not heedlessly allow what would do him the slightest harm. But it is sometimes also important for our freedom to be declared before men. This I admit. Yet we must with the greatest caution hold to this limitation, not to abandon the care of the weak, whom the Lord has so strongly commended to us.

9. Here, then, I shall say something about offenses—how they are to be distinguished, which ones avoided, which overlooked. From this we may afterward be able to determine what place there is for our freedom among men. Now I like that common distinction between an offense given and one received, inasmuch as it has the clear support of Scripture* and aptly expresses what is meant. If you do anything with unseemly levity, or wantonness, or rashness, out of its proper order or place, so as to cause the inexperienced and the weak to stumble, such will be called an offense given by you, since by your fault it came about that this sort of offense arose. And, to be sure, one speaks of an offense as given in some matter when its fault arises from the doer of the thing itself. An offense is spoken of as received when something, otherwise not wickedly or unseasonably [413] committed, is by others' ill will or malicious intent of mind turned into occasion for offense. Here was no "given" /230/ offense, but those malicious interpreters baselessly so understand it. Only the weak are made to

stumble by the first kind of offense, but the second gives offense to persons of bitter disposition and pharisaical severity. Accordingly, we shall call the one the offense of the weak, the other that of the Pharisees. Thus we shall so temper the use of our freedom as to allow for the ignorance of our weak brothers, but for the rigor of the Pharisees, not at all!

For Paul fully shows us in many passages what must be yielded to weakness. "Receive," he says, "those weak in faith" [Rom. 14:1 p.]. Also: "Let us no more pass judgment upon one another, (202) but rather not put a stumbling block or occasion to fall in the way of our brother" [Rom. 14:13 p.]; and many passages with the same meaning, which are more suitably sought in their place than referred to here. The sum is: "We who are strong ought to bear with the infirmities of the weak, and not to please ourselves; but let each of us please his neighbor for his good, to edify him" [Rom. 15:1-2 p.; for v. 2, cf. Vg.]. In another place: "But take care lest your freedom in any way cause offense to those who are weak" [I Cor. 8:9 p.]. Likewise: "Eat whatever is sold in the meat market without raising any question on the ground of conscience" [I Cor. 10:25]. "Now I say your conscience, not another's. . . . In short, so act that you may give no offense to Jews [414] or to Greeks or to the church of God" [I Cor. 10:29, 32 p.]. Also, in another passage; "You were called to freedom, brothers, only do not use your freedom as an opportunity for the flesh but through love serve one another" [Gal. 5:13]. So indeed it is. Our freedom has not been given against our feeble neighbors, for love makes us their servants in all things; rather it is given that, having peace with God in our hearts, we may also live peaceably among men. We learn from the Lord's words how much we ought to regard the offense of the Pharisees: He bids us let them alone because they see blind leaders of the blind. [Matt. 15:14] His disciples had warned him that the Pharisees had been offended by his talk. [Matt. 15:12] He answered that they were to be ignored and their offense disregarded. Still the matter will remain in doubt unless we grasp whom we are to consider weak, whom Pharisees. If this distinction is removed, I do not see what use for freedom really remains in relation to offense, for it will always be in the greatest danger.

10. But Paul seems to me most clearly to have defined, both by teaching and by example, how far our freedom must either be moderated or purchased at the cost of offense. When Paul took Timothy into his company, he circumcised him [Acts 16:3]. But he could not be brought to circumcise Titus [Gal. 2:3]. Here was a diversity of acts but no change of purpose or mind. That is, in circumcising Timothy, although he was "free from all," he made himself "a slave to all"; and "to the Jews" he "became [415] as a Jew" in order to win Jews; /231/ to those under the law he "became as one under the law . . . to win those under the law" [I Cor. 9:19-20 p.]; "to those without the law," "as one without the law," "to win those without the law"; "to the weak," "as weak," "to win the weak" [I Cor. 9:21 p.]; "all things to all men that" he "might save many" [I Cor. 9:22 p.], as he elsewhere writes. We have due control over our freedom if it makes no difference to us to restrict it when it is fruitful to do so.

3.19.12

What he had in view when he strongly refused to circumcise Titus he testifies when he thus writes: "But even Titus, who was with me, was not compelled to be circumcised, though he was a Greek, but because of false brethren surreptitiously brought in, who slipped in to spy out our freedom, which we have in Christ Jesus, that they might bring us into bondage—to them we did not yield submission, even for a moment, (203) that the truth of the gospel might be preserved among you" [Gal. 2:3-5 p.]. We have need also to assert our freedom if through the unjust demands of false apostles it endanger weak consciences. We must at all times seek after love and look to the upbuilding of our neighbor. "All things," he says elsewhere, "are lawful to me, but not all things are helpful. All things are lawful, but not all things build up. Let no one seek his own good but another's" [I Cor. 10:23-24 p.]. Nothing is plainer than this rule: that we must use our freedom if it results in the upbuilding of our neighbor, but if it does not help our neighbor, then we must forego it. [416] There are those who pretend a Pauline prudence in abstaining from freedom, while there is nothing to which they apply it less than to the duties of love. To take care of their own repose, they wish all mention of freedom to be buried; when it is no less important sometimes to use our neighbors' freedom for their good and edification than on occasion to restrain it for their own benefit. All that I have taught about avoiding offenses I mean to be referred to things intermediate and indifferent. For those things that have to be done must not be omitted for fear of some offense. Surely, it is fitting here also to take love into consideration, even up to the altar [cf. Matt. 5:23-24]. that is, that for our neighbor's sake we may not offend God.

11. I do not approve the intemperance of those who do nothing without raising a tumult and who prefer to tear into everything rather than open a matter gently. But I do not listen to those who, after making themselves leaders in a thousand sorts of wickedness, pretend that they must so act in order not to cause offense to their neighbors [cf. I Cor. 8:9]. As if they were not in the meantime building up their neighbors' consciences into evil, especially when they ever stick fast in the same mud without hope of getting out! And suave fellows are they who, whether their neighbor is to be instructed in doctrine or in example of life, say he must be fed with milk while they steep him in the worst and deadliest opinions. Paul recalls that he fed the Corinthians with milk. /232/[I Cor. 3:2] But if the Mass had then been among them, would he have performed sacrifice to [417] furnish them with milk food? No, for milk is not poison. They are therefore lying when they claim to be feeding those whom they are cruelly killing under seeming delights. Granted that this sort of dissimulation is to be approved for the moment—still how long will they give their children this same milk to drink? For if these never grow up sufficiently to be able to bear even some light food at least, it is certain that they were never brought up on milk.

12. Now, since believers' consciences, having received the privilege of their freedom, which we previously described, have, by Christ's gift, attained to this, that they should not be entangled with any snares of observances in those

matters in which the Lord has willed them to be free, we conclude that they are released from the power of all men. For Christ does not deserve to forfeit our gratitude for his great generosity—nor consciences, their profit. And we should not put a light value upon something that we see cost Christ so dear. For he valued it not with gold (204) or silver but with his own blood [I Pet. 1:18-19], so that Paul does not hesitate to say that Christ's death is nullified if we put our souls under men's subjection [cf. Gal. 2:21]. For in certain chapters of The Letter to the Galatians, Paul is solely trying to show how to us Christ is obscured, or rather extinguished, unless our consciences stand firm in their freedom. They have surely fallen away from it if they can, at men's good pleasure, be ensnared by the bonds of laws and constitutions [cf. Gal. 5:1, 4]. [418] But as this is something very much worth knowing, so it needs a longer and clearer explanation. For immediately a word is uttered concerning the abrogating of human constitutions, huge troubles are stirred up, partly by the seditious, partly by slanderers—as if all human obedience were at the same time removed and cast down.

3.19.15   13. Therefore, in order that none of us may stumble on that stone, let us consider that there is a twofold government in man:* one aspect is spiritual, whereby the conscience is instructed in piety and in reverencing God; the second is political, whereby man is educated for the duties of humanity and civil life that must be maintained among men. These are usually called the "spiritual" and the "temporal" jurisdiction (not improper terms) by which is meant that the former sort of government pertains to the life of the soul, while the latter has to do with the concerns of the present life—not only with food and clothing but with laying down laws whereby a man may live his life among other men honorably, and temperately. For the former resides in the mind within, while the latter regulates only outward behavior. The one we may call the spiritual kingdom, /233/ the other, the political kingdom. Now these two, as we have divided them, must be examined separately; and while one is being treated, we must call away and turn aside [419] the mind from thinking about the other. There are in man, so to speak, two worlds, over which different kings and different laws have authority.

B. ECCLESIASTICAL POWER

4.10.1   14. Since, therefore, whatever we have said concerning Christian freedom pertains to this spiritual kingdom, in this discussion we have no contention against the political order of laws or lawgivers.* Rather, our contention is against the power which those who wish to seem pastors of the church usurp for themselves: but they are actually the most savage butchers. The laws they frame they call "spiritual," pertaining to the soul, and declare them necessary for eternal life.* But thus the Kingdom of Christ is invaded; thus the freedom given by him to the consciences of believers is utterly oppressed and cast down. I am not now discussing the great impiety with which they fashion the observance of their laws, while they teach men to seek forgiveness of sins and righteousness from this observance, and while they establish the whole of religion and the sum of piety in it. I assert the one point that necessity ought not to be imposed upon consciences in those matters from which they have been freed by Christ; and unless freed, (as we have previously taught) they cannot rest with God. They should acknowledge one King, their deliverer Christ, and should be governed by one law of freedom, (205) namely, the holy Word of the gospel, if they would retain the grace which they have once for all obtained in Christ. They must be held in no bondage, [420] and bound by no bonds. These Solons* even fancy that their constitutions are laws of freedom, a gentle yoke, a light burden* [Matt. 11:30]. But who cannot see that this is pure falsehood? They do not feel their laws oppressive when, casting aside the fear of God, they heedlessly and actively neglect both their own and divine laws. But those men who are moved by some concern for their own salvation are far indeed from regarding themselves as free so long as they are entangled in these snares. We see how cautiously Paul dealt with this matter, not daring in even one thing to lay a restraint upon men [I Cor. 7:35]. And with good reason! He surely foresaw how great a wound would be inflicted upon consciences if in those matters which the Lord had left free, necessity were imposed. On the contrary,* one can scarcely count the constitutions which these men have very grievously decreed under pain of eternal death, and which they with the greatest severity require as necessary for salvation. And among these are very many extremely difficult to observe, but all, if in a crowd, are impossible, so great is the pile. How, then, can they who are so burdened with great difficulties escape being perplexed and tortured with extreme anguish and terror? Therefore, in brief, from these matters which I have already taught, it is to be established /234/ that our consciences are constrained before God by no such constitutions, made to bind souls inwardly in God's presence, [421] and to lay scruples on them, as if enjoining things necessary to salvation. Such, moreover, are all today called "ecclesiastical constitutions,"* thrust upon men as true and necessary worship of God. And, as these are innumerable, so limitless are the traps to catch and ensnare souls. 4.10.2

4.10.6

15. What then? Is there no ecclesiastical power? This reasoning grips with anxiety many of the simpler folk, for whom we above all are writing. We reply: obviously this is so: but this power has been given for upbuilding, as Paul attests, and not for destruction [II Cor. 10:8; 13:10]. Those who use it lawfully deem themselves no more than ministers of Christ, and stewards of God's mysteries [I Cor. 4:1, 9]. He will rightly define this power who will call it the ministry of God's Word.* Christ set it within these limits when he commanded the apostles to go and teach everything he had taught them to all nations. [Matt. 28:18ff.] Would that those who were once in charge of the church of God and are now in charge of it had remembered that the law of this commandment was laid down for themselves! Thus, for true pastors* their dignity would be kept intact preeminently and they would not boast of the false power which plagues God's people with a more than tyrannical wickedness. For here is to be committed to memory 4.8.1

4.8.2

what we have in passing pointed out elsewhere. Whatever authority and dignity Scripture accords to either prophets or priests, or apostles, or successors of apostles, [422] is wholly (206) given not to the men themselves, but to the ministry to which they have been appointed; or (to speak more briefly) to the Word, whose ministry is entrusted to them. For if we examine them all in order—prophets and priests as well as apostles and disciples—we shall not find that they have been endowed with any authority to command, to teach or to

4.8.3 answer, except in the name and Word of the Lord. The Lord willed Moses to be heard as the first of all the prophets. But what did he command or announce at all, except from the Lord? Nor could he do anything else. Of old "he set his prophets over nations and kingdoms, to pluck up and to root out, to destroy and to overthrow, to build and to plant" [Jer. 1:10]. But at the same time it is added: because he had put his words into their mouths [Jer. 1:9]. For none of the prophets opened his mouth without the Lord anticipating his words. Hence, these expressions are so often repeated among them: "the Word of the Lord," "the burden of the Lord," "The mouth of the Lord has spoken," "A vision from the Lord," "the Lord of Hosts speaks." And rightly! For Isaiah exclaimed that his lips were unclean [Is. 6:5]; Jeremiah admitted that he knew not how to speak, because he was a child [Jer. 1:6]. What could have come forth from the defiled mouth of Isaiah or the foolish mouth of Jeremiah /235/ but filth and folly, if they had spoken their own word? But they had holy and pure lips when they began to be instruments of the Holy Spirit. [423]

4.8.3 Ezekiel beautifully describes the general function of the prophets: "O Son of man, I have appointed you as a watchman for the house of Israel; you will therefore hear a word from my mouth and will declare it to them from me" [Ezek. 3:17 p.]. Is not he who is bidden to hear a word from the Lord's mouth forbidden to invent anything of his own? What is it to bring tidings from the Lord? So to speak that one could confidently boast that the word he has brought is not his own, but the Lord's. Jeremiah expresses the same thought in other words: "Let the prophet who has a dream tell the dream, and let him who has my word speak my true word. What is the chaff to the wheat? says the Lord"

4.8.2 [Jer. 23:28 p.]. Concerning priests also the Lord has commanded that "the word of the law should be sought from their mouth" [Deut. 17:10f.] but at the same time adds the reason, "for they are the messengers of the Lord of Hosts" [Mal.

4.8.4 2:7]. Now let us also look upon the apostles. They are indeed adorned with many notable titles. They are "the light of the world" and "the salt of the earth" [Matt. 5:13-14]; they are to be heard for Christ's sake [Luke 10:16]; whatever they "bind or loose on earth shall be bound or loosed in heaven" [Matt. 16:19; 18:18; cf. John 20:23]. But they show by their name how much is permitted to them in their office. Those ought to be "apostles," who do not prate whatever they please, but faithfully report the commands of Him by whom they have been sent. "Behold," Christ said to them, "as the living Father has sent me, so also I send you" [John 20:21]. But how he was sent by the Father, he attests in another saying. [424] "My teaching is not mine (207) but his who sent me, the

Father's" [John 7:16]. It would be wicked to reject this law, which Christ even imposed on Himself, then on the apostles, and on the successors of the apostles. Yet the manner [of imposition] is far different. He, the eternal and sole counselor of the Father [cf. Is. 40:13; Rom. 11:34], who was always in His bosom [cf. John 1:18], was so received by the Father, that he had hidden in himself at one and the same time all the treasures of knowledge and wisdom [Col. 2:3]. From this fountain all the prophets have drunk every heavenly oracle they have given forth. From the same fountain Adam, Noah, Abraham, Isaac, Jacob, and others, whoever God deigned from the beginning to give a knowledge of Himself, have also drunk all they have taught of heavenly teaching. For if what John the Baptist was saying was always true (as surely it was): "No one has ever seen God, but the only-begotten Son, who is in the bosom of the Father, has proclaimed Him to us" [John 1:18]; and another word of Christ Himself: "No one has ever seen 4.8.5 the Father except the Son and anyone to whom the Son has chosen to reveal him" [Matt. 11:27]—how could they either have comprehended God's mysteries with the mind, /238/ or have uttered them, except by the teaching of the Son to whom alone the secrets of the Father are revealed? Therefore, holy men knew God only by beholding him in his Son as in a mirror* [cf. II Cor. 3:18]. Nor have the prophets prophesied concerning God in any other way than by the Spirit of the same Son. But if someone prefers it to be stated thus: [425] God has never manifested himself to men in any other way than through the Son, that is, his sole wisdom, light, and truth. But this wisdom, even though it had manifested 4.8.7 itself formerly in various ways, was not as yet shining forth fully. But when it was at length revealed in the flesh, it declared loudly and clearly to us whatsoever can be comprehended and ought to be pondered concerning God by the human mind. Truly the apostle meant to proclaim no common thing when he wrote, "In many and various ways God spoke of old to the fathers through the prophets; but in these last days he has spoken to us in his beloved Son [Heb. 1:1-2]. For Paul means, nay, openly declares: God will not speak hereafter as he did before, intermittently through some and through others; nor will he add prophecies to prophecies, or revelations to revelations. Rather, God has so fulfilled all functions of teaching in his Son that we must regard this as the final and eternal testimony from him. In this way the whole New Testament time, from the point when Christ appeared to us with the preaching of his gospel even to the Day of Judgment, is designated (as we have elsewhere noted in passing)* by "the last hour" [I John 2:18], "the last times" [I Tim. 4:1; I Pet. 1:20], "the last days" [Acts 2:17; II Tim. 3:1; II Pet. 3:3]. This is done that, content with the perfection of Christ's teaching, we may learn not to fashion anything new for ourselves beyond this or to admit anything contrived by others. It was therefore with good reason that the Father [426] sent the Son, and by a singular privilege appointed him as our teacher, commanding him, and not any man, to be heard. In few words, indeed, he commended Christ's teaching office to us when (208) he said, "Hear him" [Matt. 17:5]. But these words contain more weight and force than would be commonly thought. For it is as if, having led us away from the doctrines of all men, he conducted us to his Son alone; bade us seek all teaching of salvation from him alone; depend upon him, cleave to him alone; in short (as the words themselves pronounce), hearken to him alone.

16. And what, indeed, ought we now either to expect or to hope from man, when the very Word of life has intimately sojourned with us in our flesh? Unless perchance there were hope that a man could overcome God's wisdom. But the mouths of all men should be stopped after he has once spoken, in whom the Heavenly Father willed all the treasures of knowledge and wisdom to be hid [Col. 2:3]. And he has, indeed, so spoken as befitted the wisdom of God (which is in every part seamless) [cf. John 19:23], and the Messiah (from whom /237/ the revelation of all things was awaited) [John 4:25]; that is, after himself he left nothing for others to say. It is right (I say) that—while all men keep silent, neglected and held in contempt—Christ alone be heard. For it is proper to him

4.8.8 to teach as one having power [Matt. 7:29]. And nothing could be said more clearly than what he says to his disciples: "But you are not to be called rabbi, for you have one teacher, . . . the Christ" [Matt. 23:8, 10]. Then [427] to fix this word more deeply upon their minds, he repeats it twice in the same passage [Matt. 23:9-10]. This one thing, therefore, has been left to the apostles, and also now remains to their successors: diligently to keep the law by which Christ set bounds to their embassy when he ordered them to go and teach all nations not what they had thoughtlessly fabricated among themselves, but all that he had

4.8.9 commanded them [Matt. 28:19-20]. The Apostle, Peter, perfectly instructed by the Master as to how much was permitted to him, reserves nothing else for himself or others: "Let him who speaks," he says, "speak only the words of God" [I Pet. 4:11]. What else is this but to reject all inventions of the human mind (from whatever brain they have issued) in order that God's pure Word may be taught and learned in the believers' church? What is it but to remove the ordinances of all men (whatever their rank) in order that the decrees of God alone may remain in force?

17. These are those spiritual "weapons . . . with power from God to demolish strongholds;" by them God's faithful soldiers "destroy stratagems and every height that rises up against the knowledge of God, and take every thought captive to obey Christ" [II Cor. 10:4-5, Comm.], "and have vengeance ready against all disobedience [v. 6]. Here, then, is the plainly and clearly defined power with which the pastors of the church, by whatever name they be called, ought to be endowed. That is, that they may boldly dare do all things by God's Word, whose ministers and stewards they have been appointed; may compel all worldly power, glory, loftiness [428] to yield to (209) and obey his majesty; may for him command all from the highest even to the last; may build up Christ's household and cast down Satan's kingdom; may feed the sheep and kill the wolves; may exhort and instruct the teachable; may accuse, rebuke, and subdue the rebellious and stubborn; may bind and loose; and finally may launch light-

4.8.10 nings and thunderbolts; but do all things in God's Word.* But suppose we compare this power of which we have spoken, with that power whereby these spiritual tyrants who pretend to be bishops and directors of souls have until now ingratiated themselves among God's people—the agreement between these will be no better than that of Christ with Belial [II Cor. 6:15]. First indeed, they would have our faith stand or fall on their decision. Accordingly, whatever they have determined on either side may be firmly established in our minds and either what they have approved /238/ may itself be approved by us beyond question, or what they have condemned may itself also be regarded as condemned. Hence that principle among them: the church has the power to frame articles of faith; the authority of the church equals that of Holy Scripture; a man is not a Christian unless he surely consents to all their dogmas, whether affirmative or negative— either with implicit or explicit faith.* And there are others of the same form. Then they wish our consciences to be subject to their authority, so that whatever laws they have framed, the necessity of obeying them remains with us. [429] Meanwhile, contemptuous of God's Word, they coin dogmas after their own whim, which they afterward require to be subscribed to as articles of faith. And they write laws, whose observance they make necessary. Yet they unlawfully claim for themselves leave to assert new dogmas and to coin articles of faith, a right even the apostles were deprived of, as we showed a little while ago.* But if they are not yet satisfied, Paul surely denied he was lording it over the faith of Corinthians whose apostle he had been ordained by the Lord [II Cor. 1:24]. If he had recognized such freedom to teach, he would never have handed down this teaching to their church that when two or three prophets speak, "let the others discriminate. But if a revelation is made to another sitting by, let the first be silent" [I Cor. 14:29-30 p.]. Thus no one was excepted from having his authority subject to the judgment of God's Word. But elsewhere much more clearly Paul frees our faith from all human traditions and fictions, when he says: "Faith comes from what is heard, but what is heard comes through God's Word" [Rom. 10:17 p.]. Well, then, if faith depends upon God's Word alone, if it looks to it and reposes in it alone, what place is now left for the word of men? Since the power to frame laws was both unknown to the apostles, and many times denied the ministers of the church by God's Word, I marvel that anyone, contrary to the example of the apostles and against the clear prohibition of God, dared seize this power for himself. [430] What James writes is not ambiguous: "He who judges his brother . . . judges the law, he who judges the law is not a keeper of the law but a judge. There is one lawgiver . . . who is able to save and destroy" [James 4:11-12 p.]. And he had said this previously through Isaiah, albeit a little less (210) clearly: "The Lord is our king, the Lord is our lawgiver, the Lord is our judge; he has saved us" [Is. 33:22]. We hear James declaring the power of life and death is his who has jurisdiction over the soul. Since, however, no man can take this to himself, we ought, therefore, to acknowledge God as sole ruler of souls, with whom alone is the power to save and to destroy, or (as those words of Isaiah declare) that he is at once ruler and judge and lawgiver and savior [Is. 33:22]. Peter, also, when admonishing the shepherds as to their office, /239/ exhorts them to feed their flock, without domineering over the "clergy"

4.8.9

4.10.6

4.10.7

189

[I Pet. 5:2-3]; by this term he means the inheritance of God, that is, the believing flock. Cut off, uprooted, indeed, is the power claimed for themselves by those who wish to operate outside God's Word. For it is not something given to the apostles to prop their doctrine and their rule, but only to magnify God's rule and doctrine.

4.10.17   18. I hear the answer they make for themselves—that their traditions are not from themselves but from God.* For it is not [431] to babble their own fictions, but to transmit as if by hand to the Christian people what they have received from the Holy Spirit: that they have been appointed by divine providence to rule. They add reasons also with which to confirm it. There exist shining promises, by which Christ promises the presence of his Spirit never to be lacking to the church [cf. John 14:16]. There exist bright praises, with which the church has been marked by the divine voice: that she is holy and stainless, without blemish, without stain, [Eph. 5:27] and other things which can be interpreted in the same sense from the Scriptures. Therefore, if to anyone the authority of the church is doubtful, he is impious and contentious not only to the church but also to the Spirit of Christ, by whose direction the church is without doubt ruled. For this reason Christ wished him who did not listen to the church to be considered as a gentile and a publican [Matt. 18:17]. Therefore there must be unwavering agreement among all on their opinion: the church cannot err in those things necessary for salvation. But now everything that is said of the church they say belongs to them. Either the whole church falls or stands firm, being sustained
4.8.10   and standing firm on their shoulders. Councils of the church also have the same certainty of truth that reposes in the church; [432] directly governed by the Holy
4.10.17   Spirit, they truly represent the church and cannot err.* These points gained, it follows immediately that their traditions are the revelations by the Holy Spirit and cannot be despised except in impious contempt of God. And that they may not seem to have attempted anything without great authorities, they want us to believe that a good part of their observances has come down from the apostles.* Of such sort are prayers for the dead and almost one whole discipline of their
4.8.14   ceremonies. They set forth as incontrovertible that very many things were revealed to the apostles after Christ's ascension, which were not included in the writings,* as for example (221) when The Lord said to them: "I have many things to say to you which you cannot bear now," but you will know later [John 16:12].
4.10.17   One example, they contend, sufficiently shows what the apostles did in other situations, namely, when, assembled together [Acts 15:6], they ordered all Gentiles, by decree of council, to abstain from things offered to idols, from what is strangled and from blood* [Acts 15:29]. /240/
4.2.2   19. But I shall without difficulty enable those willing properly to consider these individual points with me to discern how trifling and plainly ludicrous they all are. Indeed, I would urge them to give serious attention to this, if I were confident I could benefit them by so teaching. But since their one purpose is to defend their own cause in any way they may without regard for truth, [433] I do not think I have any business with them. I shall say only a few things by which

good men and those zealous for truth whom we initially undertook to instruct, can extricate themselves from their deceits.

20. I must therefore warn such persons not to be moved by the false pretext of the church, on which these more than dangerous and deadly enemies of the church baselessly pride themselves. They make no other pretension than what the Jews once apparently claimed when they were reproved for blindness, ungodliness, and idolatry by the Lord's prophets. For they too boasted gloriously of Temple, ceremonies, and priestly functions, and these measured the church very convincingly, as it seemed to them. So in place of the church now are displayed to us certain outward appearances which are often far removed from the church and without which the church can stand at her best. Accordingly, we are to refute them by the very argument with which Jeremiah contended against the stupid confidence of the Jews. That is, "Let them not boast in lying words, saying 'This is the Temple of the Lord, the Temple of the Lord, the Temple of the Lord' " [Jer. 7:4]. For the Lord recognizes nothing anywhere as his save where his Word is heard and scrupulously observed. For this is the abiding mark with which our Lord has sealed his own people: "Everyone who is of the truth," he says, "hears my voice" [John 18:37]. Likewise: "I am the Good Shepherd: [434] I know my sheep, and they know me" [John 10:14]. "My sheep hear my voice, and I know them, and they follow me" [John 10:27]. But a little before, he had said: "The sheep follow their shepherd, for they know his voice. A stranger they do not follow but flee from him, for they do not know the voice of strangers" [John 10:4-5]. Why do we willfully act like madmen in searching out the church when Christ has marked it with an unmistakable token, which, wherever it is seen, cannot fail to show the church there; while where it is absent, nothing remains that can give the true meaning of the church? Nay, Jerusalem is to be distinguished from Babylon, (212) Christ's church from Satan's cabal, by the very difference with which Christ has distinguished between them. He says: "He who is of God hears the words of God. The reason why you do not hear them is that you are not of God" [John 8:47]. To sum up, since the church is Christ's Kingdom, and he reigns by his Word alone, will it not be clear to any man /241/ that those are lying words [cf. Jer. 7:4] by which the Kingdom of Christ is imagined to exist apart from his scepter (that is, his most holy Word)? But if, tearing away all masks and disguises, we truly look upon that which ought to be our first concern and is of greatest importance to us, that is, the kind of church Christ would have for himself, in order for us to fashion and fit ourselves to its standard. [435] We shall then easily see that it is not a church which, passing the bounds of God's Word, wantons and disports itself in framing new laws and in dreaming up new things with the appearance of religion. For does not that law once spoken to the church hold good forever? "Everything that I command you you shall be careful to do; you shall not add anything to it or take anything from it" [Deut. 12:32]. And another passage: "Do not add to" the Word of the Lord, or take away from it, "lest he perchance rebuke you, and you be found a liar" [Prov. 30:6 p.]. They cannot deny that this was spoken to the

4.2.3

4.2.4

4.10.17

church. What else, then, do they declare but its recalcitrance, for they boast that, after such prohibitions, there was nonetheless occasion to add and mix something of their own with God's word? Far be it from us to assent to their falsehoods, by which they bring so much insult upon the church! But let us understand that whenever one considers this inordinate human rashness—which cannot contain itself within the commands of God's Word but must, wildly exulting, run after its own inventions—the name "church" is falsely pretended. There is nothing involved, nothing obscure, nothing ambiguous in these words which forbid the church universal to add to or take away anything from God's

4.10.17   Word, when the Lord's worship and religion are concerned. The Lord, who long ago declared that nothing so much offended him as being worshiped by humanly devised rites, has not become untrue to himself. Here is the source of those brilliant utterances among the prophets [436] which ought continually to resound in our ears: "I did not speak to your fathers, nor did I command them in the day that I brought them out of the land of Egypt, words concerning burnt offerings and sacrifices. But this command I gave them, saying, 'Hear my voice, and I will be your God, and you shall be my people; and you shall walk in all the way that I command you' " [Jer. 7:22-23]. Again: "I earnestly warned your fathers, . . . 'Hear my voice' " [Jer. 11:7 p.]. There are other passages of the same kind, but this is among the first, and preeminent above all the rest: "Does the Lord delight in burnt offerings and sacrifices and not rather that Lord's voice be obeyed? For obedience is better than sacrifices, and to hearken than to offer the fat of rams. Since to rebel is as the sin of divination, and not to obey as the iniquity of idolatry" [I Sam. 15:22-23 p.]. (213) Therefore, since one cannot in this area excuse all human inventions of the charge of impiety which are sus-

4.10.18   tained by the authority of the church, they are easily proved to be falsely imputed to the church. /242/ For this reason we freely inveigh against this tyranny of human traditions which is haughtily thrust upon us under the title of the church.* For we do not scorn the church (as our adversaries, to heap spite upon us unjustly and falsely declare);* but we give the church the praise of obedience, than which it knows no greater.* [437] Rather, grave injury is done to the church by those who make it obstinate against its Lord, when they pretend that it has gone beyond what is permitted by God's Word. I leave unsaid what infamous shamelessness—as well as malice—it is to harp continually about the power of the church, while at the same time to conceal what the Lord has commanded it and what obedience it owes the Lord's command. But, if, as is fitting, we are minded to agree with the church, it is more to the point to see and remember what the Lord has enjoined upon us and the whole church, that we may obey it with one consent. For there is no doubt that we shall agree very well with the

4.8.11   church if we show ourselves in all things obedient to the Lord. But the church has the amplest promises that she is never to be forsaken by Christ, her spouse, but guided by his Spirit into all truth*[cf. John 16:13]. First, the various promises they habitually allege were given just as much to individual believers as to the whole believing folk. For even though the Lord was speaking to the twelve

apostles when he said, "Behold, I am with you even unto the end of the age"*
[Matt. 28:20]: also, "I will pray the Father, and he will give you another com-
forter, to abide with you forever . . . the Spirit of truth," whom the world cannot
receive: [438] because it does not see him or know him. But you know him, for
he remains with you, and will be in you [John 14:16-17]. Nevertheless he was
not promising it to the Twelve, but to those individuals, and even to the other
disciples, either those whom he had already received, or those whom he was
going afterward to receive into his kingdom. But when they so interpret such
promises, full of wonderful consolation, as if they were given to no individual
Christian but to the whole church together, what do they do but take away from
all Christians the consolation which ought to have come from this source to them?
I do not deny here that the Lord, rich in mercy and goodness, variously distributes to all into whom he nevertheless separately pours out himself more abundantly and richly (as it is necessary to endow with greater gifts those who have
been appointed as teachers for the rest); rather I say that these very gifts of his,
as they are varied and manifold, he variously distributes [I Cor. ch. 12]. In
short, not that the very fellowship of the godly, supplied with such diversity of
gifts, has not been endowed with a far fuller and richer treasure of heavenly
wisdom than each one separately. But we must not allow them /243/ perversely
to twist the Lord's words (214) into a meaning different from what the words
actually say.

21. Therefore, I simply admit what is true: that the Lord is ever present
with his people and governs them by his Spirit. I confess that this Spirit is not
the Spirit of error, ignorance, falsehood, or darkness; [439] but of revelation,
truth, wisdom and light, from whom they may learn without deceit what has
been given them by God [I Cor. 2:12]; that is, "what is the hope of their calling,
and what the riches of the glory of the inheritance of God and what is the
exceeding greatness of his power toward all believers" [Eph. 1:18f]. Moreover, 4.8.12
that the Lord set in his church a division of graces, in order that there might
always be those to excel in especial gifts for its upbuilding. "For he gave apostles,
prophets, teachers, pastors: all of these were to serve the common upbuilding
of the church, by their divers ministries, but with one mind, until we should
come together into oneness of faith, and of the knowledge of God's Son, into
the perfect man, into the measure of the age of the fullness of Christ" [Eph.
4:11-13]. But since believers, even those who have been given more excellent 4.8.11
gifts than the rest, in this flesh receive only the first fruits and some taste of his
Spirit [Rom. 8:23], being aware of their own weakness, nothing better is left for
them but to keep themselves carefully within the limits of God's Word, last, if
they wander far according to their own predilection, they stray quite out of the
right way. And obviously there ought also to be no doubt that if they turn aside
even a little from God's Word, it may come about that they fall away in many
things, insomuch as they are void of that Spirit by whose teaching alone the
mysteries of God are perceived. For, as Paul writes, [440] Christ cleansed the 4.8.12
church "with the washing of water in the word of life, that she might present

herself to him as his glorious bride, without wrinkle or spot"* [Eph. 5:26-27, cf. Vg.], or anything of this sort, but that she should be holy and spotless. He rather teaches what Christ does each day in the church rather than what he has already accomplished. For if he daily sanctifies all his people, cleanses and polishes them, and wipes away their stains, it is obvious that they are still sprinkled with some defects and spots, and something is lacking to their sanctification. But to consider the church already holy and spotless when all her members are spotted and somewhat impure—how absurd and foolish this is! It is true, therefore, that Christ has cleansed the church with washing in the word of life; that is, has washed her with forgiveness of sins, the symbol of whose washing is baptism, and has done this to sanctify her to himself. But only the beginning of her sanctification is visible here: the end and perfect completion will appear when

4.8.13   Christ, the Holy of Holies [cf. Heb., chs. 9, 10], truly and perfectly fills the church with his holiness. Therefore the church of the believers, relying on such a great fulness of promises, /244/ has the wherewithal signally to sustain her faith, never doubting that she possesses in the Holy Spirit the best and surest guide on the right road. She does not rely on empty assurance. (215) For he is not the Lord to nourish his people in vain, and boil away faith once given. [441] Instructed with such great awareness and knowledge of her ignorance and lack of schooling, it befits her to be a chaste bride and sober pupil; then she will pay constant and careful attention to the words of her Teacher and Spouse. The church should not be wise of herself, should not devise anything of herself, but should set the limit of her own wisdom where Christ has made an end of speaking. In this way the church will at the same time distrust all the devisings of her own reason. But in those things where she rests upon God's Word, the church will not waver with any distrust or doubting, but will repose in great assurance and firm constancy.

4.8.15   22. No wonder, then, if Christ has by a singular word from God commended to us the authority of his church: in bidding us to regard as a Gentile and a publican anyone who will not hear her* [Matt. 18:17]! He also adds no common promise: where two or three are gathered in his name there he will be in the midst of them [v. 20]. But it is indeed a wonder that these rascals are so shameless that they dare go wild on this point. For what will their final conclusion be, except that one is not to despise the consensus of the church, which rests solely in the truth of God's Word? Men must listen to the church, they say* Who denies this? The reason is that the church makes no pronouncement except from the Lord's Word. If they require anything more, let them know that these words of Christ afford them no support. For when the promise has been given to those who gather together in Christ's name, and such an assembly is called "church," [442] we do not concede it to be a church unless it has been gathered together

4.9.2   in Christ's name. But is this "to be gathered in Christ's name" when God's commandment is cast aside that forbids anything to be added or taken away from his Word [Deut. 4:2; cf. Deut. 12:32; Prov. 30:6; Rev. 22:18-19], anything to be ordained according to their own decision?

23. We do not at all recognize their ultimate inference: that the church 4.8.13
cannot err in matters necessary to salvation. But here we take it in an entirely
different sense. We understand by the phrase, "cannot err," that the church,
having forsaken all her own wisdom, allows herself to be taught by the Holy
Spirit through the Lord's Word.

24. Their argument has this drift: inasmuch as the church is governed by
the Spirit of the Lord, it can proceed safely without the Word; no matter where
it may go, it can think or speak only what is true. Now, suppose we grant them 4.9.1
their every point on the church, even this would not much further their traditions.
For they do not think the truth abides in the church unless there is agreement 4.9.3
among the pastors; and that the church itself exists only if it becomes visible in
general councils. Yet this is far from /245/ having always been true, if the
prophets have left us true testimonies of their times. Isaiah speaks: "His watch-
men are all blind, and know nothing; they are all dumb dogs, they cannot bark.
Lying down, they sleep, and love sleep. . . . And the shepherds themselves know
and understand nothing: they all look to their own ways" [Is. 56:10-11].
Jeremiah moreover says: "From prophet even [443] (216) to priest, everyone
deals falsely" [Jer. 6:13]. Again: "The prophets are prophesying falsehood in
my name, since I did not send them, nor did I command them" [Jer. 14:14].
And Ezekiel says: "There is a conspiracy of her prophets in the midst thereof,
like a roaring lion who seizes prey. They have devoured souls; they have seized
what is precious and have mutiplied widows in the midst thereof. Her priests
have violated my law, and profaned my holy things. They have not distinguished
between the holy and the profane" [Ezek. 22:25-26]. "Her prophets have daubed
for them with untempered mortar, seeing vanity, and divining falsehood, saying:
'The Lord has spoken,' when he has not spoken" [Ezek. 22:28]. Likewise in
Zephaniah: "Her prophets are unstable, her men liars, her priests have polluted
holy things, and have transgressed the law" [Zeph. 3:4]. Moreover, how often 4.9.4
did Christ and his apostles foretell that pastors would pose the greatest dangers
to the church [Matt. 24:11, 24: Acts 20:29-30; II Thess. 2:3 ff; I Tim. 4:1;
II Tim. 3:1 ff.; 4:3 f; II Pet. 2:1 f]? And, not to fill many pages in reciting them,
we are warned by examples not only from their times but from almost every age
that the truth is not always nurtured in the bosom of the pastors, and the whole-
ness of the church does not depend upon their condition. It was indeed fitting
that they be executors and keepers of the peace and safety of the church, since
they were appointed for its preservation; but it is one thing to render what you
owe; another, to owe what you fail to render. Still, let no one understand these 4.9.5
words of ours [444] as if I meant to undermine the authority of pastors, in
general, rashly, and without distinction. I only wish discrimination to be made
among these pastors themselves, lest we also immediately regard as pastors those
who are so called. We are indeed entirely so to consider that their whole task
is limited to the ministry of God's Word, their whole wisdom to the knowledge
of his Word; their whole eloquence, to its proclamation. If they turn aside from
this task we are to consider them to be empty-headed and sluggish, stammerers,

195

faithless in all respects, deserters of their office—whether they be prophets, or bishops, or teachers, or even anything greater. I am not speaking of individuals but of the whole tribe of pastors together; if, abandoning God's Word, they are carried away by their own minds, they can become nothing but fools. Yet they betake themselves into dissolute license for no other reason than that they are

4.9.12 pastors who have shaken off and cast away obedience to God's Word. /246/ As if Joshua was a not a pastor, to whom it was said that he was not to turn aside to the right or to the left, but to keep and observe all the precepts of the law

4.9.5 [Josh. 1:7]. And meantime, they strive to persuade us that they cannot be bereft of the light of truth, that the Spirit of God dwells continually in them, that the church subsists in them, and dies with them. As if there were already no judgments of the Lord to prohibit in our day the very same events for which the

4.9.6 prophets in their day denounced men! [445] Such are these: "The priests shall become mute and the prophets astounded" [Jer. 4:9 p.]. (217) Also: "The law will perish from the priest and counsel from the elders" [Ezek. 7:26 p.]. It is as if there were false prophecies of Christ and the apostles. Of this sort are the following: "Many false prophets will come in my name" [Matt. 24:5, 24, confl.].

4.9.4 Likewise: "I know that after my departure fierce wolves will come in among you, not sparing the flock (Paul is here referring to the bishops of the Church of Ephesus); and from among your own selves will arise men speaking perverse things, to draw away disciples after them" [Acts 20:29-30]. Likewise: "There were false prophets among the people, just as among you there will be false teachers, who will introduce sects, treacheries," etc. [II Pet. 2:1]; and very

4.9.5 many others of this sort. Nor do these utterly stupid men realize that they are singing the same song that those once sang who were fighting against God's Word when they spoke with the same assurance upon which they now rely: "Come, and we shall hatch plots against Jeremiah, for the law shall not perish from the priest, nor counsel from the wise, nor the word from the prophet" [Jer. 18:18].

25. As a consequence, it will benefit them but little to mention councils of bishops a thousand times over; nor will they persuade us to believe what they contend—that councils are governed by the Holy Spirit—before they convince us that these have been gathered in Christ's name. Ungodly and evil bishops can just as much conspire against Christ as good and honest ones [446] can come together in his name. We have clear proof of this fact in a great many decrees

4.12.23 that have come forth from such councils. It would not be very difficult for me to show openly by clear proofs the wicked impiety of these were it not for the fact that I am striving for brevity (necessary in this little treatise). If one is permitted nevertheless to judge from one head of what sort the remaining ones could be: Paul declares that it is the hypocrisy of demons and falsehood to command celibacy and to forbid the eating of foods [I Tim. 4:1-3]. To refer these words to the Manicheans and Tatianists is no basis to clear and free our opponents of the charge that marriage and meat are completely condemned by them: by them marriage is forbidden only to certain persons; meat only on

196

certain days. For they are unable to excuse their decrees forbidding the contraction of matrimony and enjoining abstinence from foods—things /247/ God created to be received with thanksgiving. For the whole creation of God is good and holy to believers and to those who recognize the truth. But since these oracles of Satan have been promulgated by the ministry of councils, let each man consider for himself what further is to be expected from the instruments of Satan. Need I then recount how councils disagreed with councils, and that what had been decided [447] by one council was abrogated by another? In deciding moral questions, they say, this diversity commonly comes about by use; on these, there is nothing to forbid various laws from being given, according to the variety of the times. Indeed, in doctrine, customs appeared sometimes to be at loggerheads. Take for example the Council of Constantinople, which the Emperor Leo had summoned, and that of Nicea, which Irene (in envy of him) afterwards had convened. One of these decided to remove (218) and destroy images; the other to restore them. And rarely indeed has there been harmony between the eastern and western (to use their term) church. Let them go, now, and boast in their customary way that the Holy Spirit is attached and bound to their councils. And indeed, I am not arguing here either that all councils are to be condemned or the acts of all to be rescinded, and (as the saying goes) to be canceled at one stroke. For in certain councils, especially in those ancient ones, I see shining a true zeal for piety, and clear tokens of insight, doctrine, and prudence. I do not doubt that also in other ages the councils had their bishops of a better type. But the same thing happened in these later councils that Roman senators of old themselves complained of—senatorial decrees were badly framed. For so long as opinions are counted, not weighed, [448] the better part had often to be overcome by the greater. Still, in those ancient and purer councils one may count something lacking. For either otherwise learned and wise men who were then present, occupied with the business at hand did not foresee many other things; or some things of lesser importance escaped them, occupied as they were with graver and more serious matters; or they could have been deceived simply through lack of skill; or they were sometimes borne headlong with too much feeling. Of this last (which seems hardest of all), there is a notable example in the Council of Nicea whose eminence has been recognized by the consent of all with highest reverence. For when the chief article of our faith was there imperiled, the enemy Arius was ready for battle, and they had to fight with him hand to hand, so it was of greatest importance that there should be agreement among those who had come prepared to fight Arius' error. Despite this, heedless of such great dangers, /248/ even forgetful of gravity, modesty, and all civility, they let slip the battle that was in their hands, as if they had purposely come there to do Arius a favor. They began to revile one another with internal dissensions, and to turn against one another the pen which ought to have been wielded against Arius. Foul recriminations were heard; accusatory pamphlets flew back and forth; and the contentions would not have ended until [449] they had stabbed and wounded one another, if the Emperor Constantine had not

4.9.9

4.9.8

4.9.10

interfered. He, professing that an inquiry into their life was a matter beyond his competence, chastised such intemperance with praise rather than with blame.* In how many respects is it likely that other councils which followed this also failed? Perhaps someone will think me foolish because I labor to show such errors, since our opponents admit that councils can err in those matters which are not necessary to salvation.* But this is no superfluous labor! For although, being compelled, they confess it even by mouth, still, when they thrust upon us the decision of councils, on whatever matter, indiscriminately as an oracle of the Holy Spirit, (219) they require more than they had originally assumed. In doing this, what do they affirm but that councils cannot in any way err; or if they err, it is unlawful for us to discern the truth, or not to assent to their errors? Accordingly, no names of councils, pastors, bishops, church (which can either be falsely pretended or truly used) ought to prevent our being taught by such evidence to test all spirits of all men by the standard of the divine Word in order to determine whether or not they are from God.*

26. But to trace the origin of these traditions (with which the church has hitherto been oppressed) back to the apostles* is pure [450] deceit. For the whole doctrine of the apostles has this intent: not to burden consciences with new observances, or contaminate the worship of God with our own inventions. And if there is anything credible in the histories and ancient records, the apostles not only were ignorant of what the Romanists attribute to them but never even heard of it. And let them not prate that very many of the apostles' decrees not committed to writing had been received in use and customary practice. The reference is to those things which, while Christ was still alive, they could not understand but after his ascension learned by the revelation of the Holy Spirit [John 16:12-13]. What effrontery! I confess that the disciples were as yet untutored and well-nigh unteachable when they heard this from the Lord. But when they committed their doctrine to writing, were they even then beset with such dullness that they afterward needed to supply with a living voice what they had omitted from their writings through the fault of ignorance? Now, if they had already been led into all truth by the Spirit of truth [cf. John 16:13] when they put forth their writings, what hindered them from embracing in their writings a perfect knowledge of gospel doctrine and leaving it in signed and sealed? /249/Moreover, they make themselves ridiculous when they picture as huge mysteries, unknown for so long to the apostles, what were either partly Jewish or Gentile observances (some published long before among the Jews, others among the Gentiles); [451] partly foolish gesticulations and old-womanish little ceremonies which stupid priestlings (who ken neither swimming nor letters)* perform exceedingly well. In fact, children and jesters so aptly mimic these that they might seem to be the most suitable officiants of such holy rites!

27. With not much greater skill do they claim the apostles' example, to defend their tyranny. The apostles, they say, and the elders of the primitive church framed a decree outside the command of Christ, by which they enjoined all the Gentiles to abstain from meat offered to idols, from meat of strangled

198

animals, and from blood*[Acts 15:20, 29]. If this was allowed to them, why should it not be allowed to their successors to follow the same practice as often as the situation requires? Would that they always followed them both in other practices and in this! For I deny—and can easily prove by a strong reason—that the apostles instituted or decreed anything new there. Indeed when Peter in that council declares that God is being put to the test if a yoke is laid on the necks of the disciples [Acts 15:10], he subverts his own opinion if (220) he afterward consents to have any yoke laid upon them. But it is imposed, if the apostles on their own authority decree that the Gentiles are prohibited to touch meat offered to idols, blood, and meat of strangled animals [Acts 15:20, 29]. A scruple, indeed, still remains in that they nonetheless seem to forbid these. But this scruple will be easily removed if one [452] pays attention to the actual meaning of the decree* itself, of which the first and most important point is that the Gentiles are to be left their freedom, and are not to be troubled or exposed to the bother of legal observances [Acts 15:19, 24, 28]. So far it notably favors us. But an exception immediately follows [Acts 15:20, 29]. This is no new law laid down by the apostles, but the divine and eternal command to preserve love. It takes away not one tittle from that freedom but only warns the Gentiles how to accommodate themselves to their brethren so as not to offend them by abusing their own freedom. Let this then be the second point, that the Gentiles may enjoy a harmless freedom, without offending their brethren. Yet the apostles still prescribe a particular thing: they teach and designate, as far as was expedient for the time, what things might cause the brethren offense, in order to avoid them. But they bring nothing new of their own to God's eternal law, which forbids the offending of brethren. It is as if faithful pastors in charge of churches   4.10.22
not yet well established should command all their people that—until the weak with whom they live grow stronger—/250/ they should not openly eat meat on Friday, or publicly labor on holy days, or any such thing. For even though these things, superstition aside, are of themselves indifferent, still, [453] when offense to the brethren is added, they cannot be committed without sin.* But the times are such that believers cannot so appear in the sight of weak brethren without very gravely wounding the consciences of their brethren. Who but a slanderer will say that they thus make a new law, when it is clear that they are only forestalling scandals*which have been explicitly enough forbidden by the Lord? And it can no more be said of the apostles, who had no other intention than by removing the occasion for offenses to urge the divine law concerning the avoiding of offense. It is as if they had said: "The Lord's command is that you should not wound a weak brother; you cannot eat meat offered to idols, meat of strangled animals, and blood, without offending weak brethren. We therefore command you in the word of the Lord not to eat with offense." Paul is the best witness that the apostles had the same thing in mind. He surely writes this in accordance with the decision of the council: "Concerning foods offered to idols . . . we know that 'there is no image in the world.' . . . But some, conscious of idols, eat food as really offered to idols; and their weak conscience is defiled.

. . . Take care lest this freedom of yours . . . cause even a slight offense to the weak" [I Cor. 8:1, 4, 7, 9]. He who shall weigh these matters well will not afterward be deceived by the camouflage of those who make the apostles a pretext for their tyranny, [454] (221) as if the apostles by their decree had begun to encroach upon the freedom of the church.

4.11.8   28. Even though we have not mentioned everything that could be presented here, and also what we have said has been confined to a very few words, I trust we have won such a victory as to leave no reason for anyone to doubt that the spiritual power on which the pope with his whole royal entourage preens himself is an impious tyranny opposed to God's Word and unjust toward His people. Indeed, under the term "spiritual power" I include boldness in formulating new doctrines by which they turn the wretched people utterly away from the original purity of God's Word, and leave to formulate new laws*with which they have cruelly troubled unhappy consciences—in short, the whole ecclesiastical jurisdiction (as they call it) which they exercise through suffragans and officials. For if we allow Christ to rule among us, this whole kind of dominion is easily overturned and laid low.

29. Moreover, we are not presently concerned to discuss the other kind of dominion* which is confined to possessions and estates, because it is not exercised over consciences.* Yet in this respect it is worth noting that they are always like themselves, that is, far removed from what they wish to be called,

4.11.8   "pastors of the church." [455] /251/ I do not blame the individual faults of men; but the common crime of the whole order, the veritable plague of the order, since it is thought to be mutilated unless it be decked out with opulence and proud titles. Was it the bishops' duty to involve themselves in judicial proceedings and in the administration of cities and provinces, and to undertake activities far, far removed from their own? For in their own office they have so much work and business that if they devoted themselves wholly and continuously to it, and were not distracted by any interruptions, they would scarcely be adequate to the task. Was it fitting for them to rival the elegance of the princes in number of retainers, splendor of buildings, lavishness of clothing and table? Their life ought to have been a singular pattern of frugality, moderation, continence, and humility. How inconsistent with the function of those whom God's eternal and unchangeable decree forbids to seek after filthy lucre and to be greedy, and commands to be content with simple fare [I Tim. 3:3], is it for them not only to seize villages and fortified towns, but also to make off with entire provinces, and even to usurp civil authority? But they are so brazen as to dare even to cast about for an excuse and to boast that churchly dignity is not unfittingly sustained

4.11.9   by this magnificence, and that they meanwhile are not too much drawn away from the functions of their calling. As far as the first point [456] is concerned, if it is a fitting ornament of their rank that they have been raised to such a height as to inspire fear in lofty monarchs, they have reason to expostulate with Christ, who has in this way gravely injured their honor. For what more outrageous thing could be said, in their opinion, than these words: "The rulers and princes of the

Gentiles lord it over (222) them, . . . but you do not do so; rather, let the greatest among you become as the youngest, and the leaders as one who serves" [Matt. 20:25-26; Mark 10:42-44; Luke 22:25-26 p.]? For them obviously their 4.11.9 ministry is separated by the widest gap from all glory and loftiness of this world. Otherwise, I would that they could prove this by experience as easily as they can mouth it! It did not seem good to the apostles to give up the preaching of the Word of God to serve tables [Acts 6:2]. Since they do not wish to be taught by this, they are compelled to accept the fact that to be both a good bishop and a good prince is not the same man's task. For if the apostles (who, according to the largeness of the gifts with which they had been endowed by the Lord were able to cope with far more and heavier cares than any men born after them) still confessed that they could not shoulder the ministry of the Word and of tables together, without sinking under the burden—how could these little men, nothing compared to the apostles, outstrip their industry a hundred times? Even to attempt it was the most shameless [457] and brazen self-confidence! Yet we see it done—with what result is clear! /252/ For there could be no other outcome than that they should forsake their duties and move into the other camp. The generosity of the princes had some zeal for piety, when they devoted so much of their resources to the enrichment of the bishops. But they did not provide in 4.11.10 the best way for the welfare of the church by this absurd liberality of theirs, for they thus corrupted its true and ancient discipline. Indeed, to speak the truth, they completely abolished it! Those bishops who misused this great bounty of the princes to their own benefit, by showing this one example, have given proof enough and more that they are no bishops at all. In short, to speak once for all concerning both according to their power: when they daily struggle so manfully to keep these possessions, what they seek is nothing obscure. If they resign the 4.11.14 spiritual rule on the condition that it yield all to Christ, no danger will befall the glory of God, sound doctrine or the safety of the church. Even if they resign this secular power, there is no danger it will impair in any way the church's welfare. But they are carried away, blind and headlong, by one lust for dominion. For they think that nothing is safe unless (as the prophet says) they rule with harshness and with might [Ezek. 34:4]. Yet these few words on the patrimony of the church [458] were said in passing.

30. I return now to spiritual rule, the proper subject of this section. But 4.9.12 our opponents, where in defending their cause they see that all support of reason forsakes them, resort to this last and miserable evasion; even though these men themselves be stupid in mind and counsel, and utterly wicked in heart and will, still the Word of the Lord abides, which bids men obey their rulers [Heb. 13:17], even if they must bear evil and excessively harsh laws. Yet the Lord commands us to do whatever the scribes and Pharisees say, even when they lay upon us unbearable burdens, which they would not touch with their finger [Matt. 23:3-4]. Is this so? But if (223) we must accept the teaching of all pastors whatever without any doubting, what was the point of the Lord's frequent admonitions to us not to heed the talk of false prophets or false pastors? "Do not," the Lord

says, "listen to the words of the prophets who prophesy to you; for they teach you vanity, and they speak the vision of their heart not from the mouth of the Lord" [Jer. 23:16]. Likewise: "Beware of false prophets, who come to you in sheep's clothing but inwardly are ravenous wolves" [Matt. 7:15]. John also would vainly exhort us to "test the spirits to see whether they are of God" [I John 4:1]. Not even the angels are exempt from this judgment, much less Satan with his lies [Gal. 1:8]! But what is this saying: "If a blind man [459] lead a blind man, both will fall into the ditch" [Matt. 15:14]? Does this not sufficiently declare that it is very important what sort of pastors should be heard, and that not all are to be heard indiscriminately? /253/ There is consequently no reason why they should frighten us with their titles so as to drag us into sharing their blindness. For we see, on the contrary, that the Lord took particular care to alarm us, so that we should not allow ourselves to be led into others' error, masked under any name whatsoever. For if the word of the Lord is true, blind guides also, whether they are called high priests, or prelates, or pontiffs, can do nothing but hurtle their partners with them over the same precipice.

4.10.23   31. The other part of the laws remains; but though such laws be a hundred times unjust and injurious to us, still they contend that these should be obeyed without exception. For here there is no question of our consenting to errors, but only that as subjects we should bear the harsh commands of our leaders, which we have no right to reject. But here also the Lord best succors us with the truth of his word, and delivers us out of such bondage into the freedom that he has purchased for us by his sacred blood [I Cor. 7:23]. For here it is not only intended (as they maliciously pretend) that we endure some grave oppression in our body but that our consciences, deprived of their freedom (that is, of the benefit of the blood of Christ), should be tormented like slaves. [460] Let us, however, pass over this also, as if it were little to the point. But how important do we think it that the Lord is deprived of his Kingdom, which he so sternly claims for himself? But it is taken away whenever he is worshiped by laws of human devising, inasmuch as he wills to be accounted the sole lawgiver of his own worship. So that no one may think this something negligible, let us hear how highly the Lord regards it. "Because," he says, "this people . . . feared me by a commandment and doctrine of men, . . . behold, I will add, and cause them to wonder, with a great and amazing miracle; for wisdom shall perish from their wise men, and the understanding of the prudent shall be hidden" [Is. 29:13-14 p.]. Another passage: "In vain do they worship me teaching as doctrine

4.10.24   the precepts of men" [Matt. 15:9]. Many marvel why the Lord so sharply threatens to astound the people who worshiped him with the commands and doctrines of men [Is. 29:13-14] and declares that he is vainly worshiped by the precepts of men [Matt. 15:9]. But if they were to weigh (224) what it is to depend upon God's bidding alone in matters of religion (that is, on account of heavenly wisdom), they would at the same time see that the Lord has strong reasons to abominate such perverse rites, which are performed for him according to the willfulness of human nature. For even though those who obey laws having to do

202

with the worship of God have some semblance of humility in this obedience of theirs, they are nevertheless not at all humble in God's sight, since they prescribe for him these same laws which they observe. [461], Now, this is the reason why Paul so urgently warns us not to be deceived by the traditions of men [Col. 2:4 ff], or by what he calls ἐθελοθρησκεία that is, "will worship," devised by men apart from the Word of God [Col. 2:22, 23]. It is certainly true /254/ that our own and all men's wisdom must become foolish, that we may allow him alone to be wise. Those who expect his approval for their paltry observances contrived by men's will, do not at all hold to that path. So it has been done for some centuries past, and within our memory, and is done today also in those places in which the authority of the creature is more than that of the Creator [cf. Rom. 1:25]. There religion (if it still deserves to be called religion) is defiled with more, and more senseless, superstitions than ever any paganism was. For what could men's mind produce but all carnal and fatuous things which truly resemble their authors? Moreover, this utterly evil thing is added, that when religion once begins to be defined in such vain fictions, such perversity is always followed by another hateful curse, for which Christ rebuked the Pharisees. It is that they nullify God's commandment for the sake of the traditions of men [Matt. 15:3]. I do not wish to fight with words of my own against our present lawmakers; they will obviously have won, if they are able to excuse Christ's accusation as not applicable against them [462] But how could they excuse themselves, since among them it is far more wicked to have skipped auricular confession at the turn of the year than to have led an utterly wicked life the whole year through? to have infected their tongue with a slight taste of meat on Friday than to have fouled the whole body with fornication every day? to have moved the hand to honest work on a feast day than religiously to have exercised all the bodily members in the worst crimes? for a priest to be bound in one lawful marriage than to be entangled in a thousand adulteries? to have left unperformed an avowed pilgrimage than to have broken faith in all promises? not to have squandered something on monstrous, but no less superfluous and unprofitable, pomp of churches than to have failed the poor in their uttermost need? to have passed by an idol without honoring it than to have treated the whole race of mankind abusively? not to have murmured one senseless word at certain hours than never to have framed a true prayer in the heart? What is it to set at nought God's precept for the sake of their own traditions [Matt. 15:3] if it be not this? While commending the observance of God's commandments only coldly (225) and perfunctorily, they nonetheless zealously and busily urge an exact obedience to their own, as if these contained in themselves the whole force of piety? [463] While requiring that only light amends be made for the transgression of the divine law, they punish even the slightest infraction of a decree of theirs with no lighter penalty than prison, fire, or sword. While not so harsh and inexorable against those who despise God, they persecute to the hilt with an implacable hatred their own despisers: and they instruct all those whose simplicity they hold captive /255/ to see with greater equanimity God's whole law overthrown

4.10.10

than a tittle of the precepts of the church (as they call them) violated. First, it is a grave transgression for one man to despise, judge, and cast out another because of what are trivial and (in God's sight) indifferent matters. But now, as though this were but a slight evil, those trifling elements of this world (as Paul writing to the Galatians calls them [Gal. 4:9]) are more highly esteemed than the heavenly oracles of God. And he who is well-nigh absolved in adultery, is judged in food; he to whom a harlot is permitted is denied a wife. Here, then, is the fruit of this sham obedience which turns away from God as much as it

4.10.26 inclines to men. Why then did Christ will that those unbearable burdens be endured, which the scribes and Pharisees lay upon men [Matt. 23:2-3]? Nay, rather, why did the same Christ elsewhere will that men beware the leaven of the Pharisees [Matt. 16:6]? As explained by the Evangelist Matthew, "leaven" [464] means whatever of their own doctrine men mix with the purity of God's Word [Matt. 16:12]. What thing do we wish to be clearer than that we are commanded to flee and avoid their whole doctrine? By this it is made very clear to us that in the other passage, too, the Lord would not have the consciences of his people troubled by traditions peculiar to the Pharisees. And the words themselves, if they are not twisted, imply no such thing. For there the Lord meant to inveigh bitterly against the conduct of the Pharisees and was simply instructing his hearers at the outset, so that, although they saw nothing in the life of the Pharisees which they should follow, still they should not stop doing those things which the Pharisees taught by word of mouth, since they sat in Moses' seat, that is, as interpreters of the law [Matt. 23:2].

4.10.27 32. But many many unlettered persons, when they hear that believers' consciences are impiously bound by human traditions; and God is worshiped in vain, apply the same erasure to all the laws by which the order of the church is shaped. It is convenient here to deal also with their error. At this point it is exceedingly easy to be deceived, for it is not apparent at first sight how much difference there is between the former and the latter sort of regulations. But we shall briefly explain the whole matter so clearly that no one will be deceived by the similarity. First, let us grasp this consideration. We see that some form of organization is necessary in all human society to foster the common peace and [465] maintain concord. We further see that in human transactions there is some procedure which has to do with public decency, and even with humanity itself. This ought especially to be observed in churches, (226) which are best sustained when all things are under a well-ordered arrangement, and which without concord become no churches at all. Therefore, if we wish best to provide for the safety of the church, we must attend with all diligence to Paul's command that "all things be done decently and in order" [I Cor. 14:40]. Yet since such diversity exists in the customs of men, /256/ such variety in their minds, such conflicts in their judgments and dispositions, no organization is sufficiently strong unless constituted with definite laws; nor can any procedure be maintained without some set form. Therefore, we are so far from condemning the laws that conduce to this as to contend that churches, when deprived of them and their very sinews

204

disintegrated, are wholly deformed and scattered. Nor can Paul's requirement—that "all things be done decently and in order"—be met unless order itself and decorum be established through the addition of observances that form, as it were, a bond of union. But in these observances one thing must always be guarded against. They are not to be considered necessary for salvation and thus bind consciences by scruples; nor are they to be associated with the worship of God, so that piety is lodged in them. We pointed out a little while ago what single characteristic distinguishes between those impious constitutions [466] (which, as we have said, obscure true religion and subvert consciences) and legitimate church ordinances which always have a purpose different from these: either to pertain only to the decorum with which all things should be done in the assembly of believers in fitting order, or to keep that community of men within bounds by some sort of bonds of humanity. Yet when it is once understood that a law has been made for the sake of public decency, there is taken away the superstition into which those fall who measure the worship of God by human inventions. Again, when it is recognized that the law has to do simply with common usage of men, then that false opinion of obligation and necessity, which used to strike consciences with great terror when traditions were thought necessary to salvation, has been overthrown. For there nothing is required except that love be fostered among us by common effort.

4.10.28

33. There are examples of the first sort in Paul: that women should not teach in the church [I Cor. 14:34], that they should go out with heads covered [I Cor. 11:5ff.]. And examples can be seen in the everyday habits of living, such as: that we pray with knees bent and head bare; that naked human corpses be not cast into a ditch; that we administer the Lord's sacraments not profanely and negligently; and other practices that belong to the same class. What? Does religion consist in a woman's shawl, so that it is unlawful for her to go out with a bare head? [467] Is that decree of Paul's concerning silence so holy that it cannot be broken without great offense? Is there in bending the knee or in covering a corpse any holy rite that cannot be neglected without offense? Not at all. For if a woman needs such haste to help a neighbor that she cannot stop to cover her head, she does not offend if she runs to her with head uncovered. And there is a place where it is no less proper for her to speak than elsewhere to remain silent. (227) Also, nothing prohibits a man who cannot bend his knees because of disease from standing to pray. Finally, it is better to bury a dead man in due time than, where a shroud /257/ is lacking, to wait until the unburied corpse decays. Nevertheless, the established custom of the region, in short, humanity itself and the rule of modesty, dictate what is to be done or avoided in these matters. In them a man commits no crime if out of imprudence or forgetfulness he departs from them; but if out of contempt, this willfulness is to be disapproved. But if anyone loudly complains and wishes here to be wiser than he ought, let him see with what reason he can defend his overscrupulousness before the Lord. This saying of Paul's ought to satisfy us: "that it is not our custom to contend, or that of the churches of God" [I Cor. 11:16].

4.10.29

4.10.31

4.10.29   34. Of the other kind are the hours prescribed for public prayers, sermons, and baptisms. At sermons there are quiet and silence, appointed places, the singing together of hymns, [468] days set apart for the receiving of the Lord's

4.10.31 Supper, the discipline of excommunications, and any others. The days themselves, the hours, the structure of the places of worship, what psalms are to be sung on what day, are matters of no importance. But it is fitting to have definite days and stated hours, and a place suitable to receive all, if there is any concern for the preservation of peace. For confusion in such details would become the seed of great contentions if every man were allowed, as he pleased, to change matters affecting public order! For it will happen that the same thing will please all if matters as it were regarded as indifferent will be left to individual choice.

4.10.32 Therefore, we must strive with the greatest diligence to prevent error from creeping in, either to corrupt or to obscure this pure use. This end will be attained if all observances, whatever they shall be, display manifest usefulness, and if very few are allowed; but especially if a faithful pastor's teaching is added to bar the way to perverse opinions. But this knowledge will first assure that each one of us will keep his freedom in all these things; yet each one will voluntarily impose some necessity upon his freedom, in so far as this decorum* of which we spoke or considerations of love shall require. Secondly, that we occupy ourselves without superstition in the observance of these and not require it too fastidiously of others, [469] that we may not feel the worship of God to be the better for a multitude of ceremonies; and that one church may not despise another because of diversity of outward discipline. Finally, that, establishing here no perpetual law for ourselves, we should refer the entire use and purpose of observances to the upbuilding of the church. If the church requires it, we may not only without any offense allow something to be changed but permit any observances previously in use among us to be abandoned. This present age meanwhile offers proof of the fact that it may be a fitting thing to set aside, as may be opportune in the circumstances, certain rites that in other circumstances are not impious or indecorous. /258/ For (such was the blindness and ignorance of former times) (228) churches have heretofore stuck fast in ceremonies with corrupt opinion and stubborn intent. Consequently, they can scarcely be sufficiently cleansed of these frightful superstitions without removing many ceremonies probably established of old with good reason and not notably impious or vicious of themselves; obstinately to insist upon defending such would be a most harmful pursuit. For to judge any one of these by itself, we have already admitted, is nothing bad. But if they are considered in their circumstances, it will appear from the abuse of the ceremonies alone that an error resided in men's minds, so that it cannot be easily corrected, unless these shows be withdrawn from sight which repeatedly furnish new material for error. [470] Thus by the testimony of the Holy Spirit Hezekiah was praised because he destroyed the brazen serpent [II Kings 18:4] which had been set up at the Lord's command by Moses, and which to preserve as a reminder of divine benefits was not an evil thing, if it had not begun to serve the idolatry of the people. But, since the best

206

king would have no other means of correcting impiety, he had just as good reason to break it as Moses had had to set it up. For men's perverse judgments are to be taken care of just like sick or nauseated stomachs from which foods slightly difficult to digest are taken away, though these would be harmless to healthy ones.

C. CIVIL GOVERNMENT

35. Now, since we have established above that man is under a twofold government,* and since we have discussed already at sufficient length the kind that resides in the soul or inner man and pertains to eternal life, this is the place to say something also about the other kind, which pertains only to the establishment of civil justice and outward morality. First, before we enter into the matter itself, we must keep in mind that distinction which we previously laid down so that we do not (as commonly happens) unwisely mingle these two, which have a completely different nature. For certain men, when they hear that the gospel promises a freedom that acknowledges no king and no magistrate among men, but looks to Christ alone, [471] think that they cannot benefit by their freedom so long as they see any power set up over them. They therefore think that nothing will be safe unless the whole world is reshaped to a new form, where there are neither courts, nor laws, nor magistrates, nor anything similar which in their opinion restricts their freedom.* But whoever knows how to distinguish between body and soul,* between this present fleeting life and that future eternal life, will without difficulty know that Christ's spiritual Kingdom and the civil jurisdiction are things completely distinct. /259/ Since, then, it is a Jewish vanity to seek and enclose Christ's Kingdom within the elements of this world, let us rather ponder that what Scripture clearly teaches is a spiritual fruit, which we gather from Christ's grace; and let us remember to keep within its own limits all that freedom which is promised and offered to us in him. (229) For why is it that the same apostle who bids us stand and not submit to the "yoke of bondage" [Gal. 5:1] elsewhere forbids slaves to be anxious about their state [I Cor. 7:21], unless it be that spiritual freedom can perfectly well exist along with civil bondage? These statements of his must also be taken in the same sense: In the Kingdom of God "there is neither Jew nor Greek, neither male nor female, neither slave nor free" [Gal. 3:28, Vg.; order changed]. And again, "there is not Jew nor Greek, uncircumcised, circumcised, barbarian, Scythian, slave, freeman; but [472] Christ is all in all" [Col. 3:11 p.]. By these statements he means that it makes no difference what your condition among men may be or under what nation's laws you live, since the Kingdom of Christ does not at all consist in these things.

36. Yet this distinction does not lead us to consider the whole nature of government a thing polluted, having nothing to do with Christian men. That is what, indeed, some fanatics boast: after we have died through Christ to the elements of this world [Col. 2:20], are transported to God's Kingdom, and sit

among heavenly beings, it is a thing unworthy of us and set far beneath our excellence to be occupied with those worldly and vile cares which have to do with business foreign to a Christian man. To what purpose, they ask, are laws without trials and tribunals? But what has a Christian man* to do with trials themselves? Indeed, if it is not lawful to kill, why do we have laws and trials?* But as we have just now pointed out that this kind of government is distinct from that spiritual and inward Kingdom of Christ, so we must know that they are not at variance. For spiritual government, indeed, is already initiating in us upon earth certain beginnings of the Heavenly Kingdom, and in this mortal and fleeting life affords a certain forecast of an immortal and incorruptible blessedness. Yet civil government has as its appointed end, so long as we live among men, to adjust our life to the society of men, to [473] form our social behavior to civil righteousness, to reconcile us with one another, and to promote and foster general peace and tranquillity. All of this I admit to be superfluous, if God's Kingdom, such as it is now among us, wipes out the present life. But if it is the Lord's will that we go as pilgrims upon the earth while we aspire to the true fatherland, and if the pilgrimage requires such helps, those who take these from man deprive him of his very humanity. /260/

37. Our adversaries claim that there ought to be such great perfection in the church of God that its government should suffice for law. But they stupidly imagine such a perfection as can never be found in a community of men. For since the insolence of evil men is so great, their wickedness so stubborn, that it can scarcely be restrained by extremely severe laws, what may we expect them to do if they see that their depravity can go scot-free— when no power can force them to cease from doing evil? But there will be a more appropriate place to speak of the function of civil government. Now we only wish it to be understood that to think of doing away with it is outrageous barbarity. (230) Its function among men is no less than that of bread, water, sun and air; indeed, its place of honor is far more excellent. For it does not merely see to it (as all these serve to do) that men breathe, eat, drink, and are kept warm, [474] (even though it surely embraces all these activities when it provides for their living together). It does not, I repeat, look to this only, but also prevents idolatry, sacrilege against God's name, blasphemies against his truth, and other public offenses against religion from arising and spreading among the people; it prevents the public peace from being disturbed; it provides that each man may keep his property safe and intact; that men may carry on blameless intercourse among themselves. In short, it provides that a public manifestation of religion may exist among Christians, and that humanity be maintained among men. Let no man be disturbed that I now commit to civil government the duty of rightly establishing religion, which I seem above to have put outside of human decision. For, when I approve of a civil administration that aims to prevent the true religion which is contained in God's law from being openly and with public sacrilege violated and defiled with impunity, I do not here, any more than before, allow men to

4.20.3

208

make laws according to their own decision concerning religion and the worship of God.

38. But my readers, assisted by the very clarity of the arrangement, will better understand what is to be thought of the whole subject of civil government if we discuss its parts separately. These are three: the magistrate, who is the protector and guardian of the laws; the laws, according to which he governs; the people, who are governed by the laws and obey the magistrate. Let us, then first look [475] at the office of the magistrate, noting whether it is a lawful calling approved of God; the nature of the office; the extent of its power; then, with what laws a Christian government ought to be governed; and finally, how the laws benefit the people, and what obedience is owed to the magistrate.

39. The Lord has not only testified that the office of the magistrates is approved by and acceptable to him, but he also sets out its dignity with the most honorable titles and marvelously commends it to us. /261/ To mention a few: Since those who serve as magistrate are called "gods" [Ex. 22:8, Vg.; Ps. 82:1, 6], let no one think that their being so-called is of slight importance. For by it are signified that they have a mandate from God, having been invested with divine authority, and are wholly God's representatives, in a manner, acting as his vicegerents. This is no subtlety of mine, but Christ's explanation. "If Scripture," he says, "called them gods to whom the word of God came . . ." [John 10:35]. What is this, except that God has entrusted to them the business of serving him in their office, and (as Moses and Jehoshaphat said to the judges whom they appointed in every city of Judah) of exercising judgment not for man but for God [Deut. 1:16-17; II Chron. 19:6]? To the same purpose is what God's wisdom affirms through Solomon's mouth, that it is his doing "that kings reign, and counselors decree what is just, that princes (231) exercise dominion, and [476] all benevolent judges of the earth." [Prov. 8:14-16] This amounts to the same thing as to say: it has not come about by human perversity that the authority over all things on earth is in the hands of kings and other rulers, but by divine providence and holy ordinance. For God was pleased so to rule the affairs of men. Paul also plainly teaches this when he lists "ruling" among God's gifts [Rom. 12:8] which, variously distributed according to the diversity of grace, ought to be used by Christ's servants for the upbuilding of the church. But Paul speaks much more clearly when he undertakes a just discussion of this matter. For he states both that power is an ordinance of God [Rom. 13:2], and that there are no powers except those ordained by God [Rom. 13:1]. Further, that princes are ministers of God, for those doing good unto praise; for those doing evil, avengers unto wrath [Rom. 13:3-4]. To this may be added the examples of holy men, of whom some possessed kingdoms, as David, Josiah, and Hezekiah; others, lordships, as Joseph and Daniel; others, civil rule among a free people, as Moses, Joshua, and the judges. The Lord has declared his approval of their offices. Accordingly, no one ought to doubt that civil authority is a calling, not only holy and lawful before God, but also the most sacred and by far the most honorable of all callings in the whole life of mortal men.

4.20.4

4.20.6
40. This consideration ought continually to occupy the magistrates themselves, [477] since it can greatly spur them to exercise their office and bring
them remarkable comfort to mitigate the difficulties of their task (indeed many
and burdensome). For what great zeal for uprightness, for prudence, gentleness,
self-control, and for innocence ought to be required of themselves by those who
know they have been ordained ministers of divine justice? How will they have
the brazenness to admit injustice to their judgment seat which they are told is
the throne of the living God? /262/ How will they have the boldness to pronounce
an unjust sentence by the mouth they know has been appointed an instrument
of divine truth? With what conscience will they sign wicked decrees by the hand
they know has been appointed to prescribe the acts of God? To sum up, if they
remember they are vicars of God, they should watch with all care, earnestness,
and diligence, to represent in themselves to men some image of divine providence, protection, goodness, benevolence, and justice. And they should perpetually set before themselves the thought that "all are cursed who do in deceit the
work of God" [Jer. 48:10 p.]. Therefore, when Moses and Jehoshaphat wished
to urge their judges to do their duty, they had nothing more effective to persuade
them than what we have previously mentioned [Deut. 1:16]: "Consider what
you do, for you exercise judgment not for man but for God since he is beside
you in giving judgment. [478] Now then, let the fear of the Lord be upon you.
Take heed what you do, for there is no perversity with the Lord our God"
[II Chron. 19:6-7 p.]. And in another place it is said: "God stood in the assembly
of the gods, and holds judgment in the midst of the gods" [Ps. 82:1]. This is to
hearten them for their task (232) when they are taught that they are deputies of
God, to whom they will have to render account of the administration of their
charge. And this admonition deserves to have great weight with them. For if
they commit some fault, they are not only wrongdoers to men whom they
wickedly trouble, but are also insulting toward God himself, whose most holy
judgments they defile [cf. Is. 3:14-15]. On the other hand, they have the means
of comforting themselves greatly when they ponder in themselves that they are
occupied not with profane affairs or those alien to a servant of God, but with a
most holy office, since they are serving as God's deputies.

4.20.7
41. Those who, unmoved by so many testimonies of Scripture, dare rail
against this holy ministry as a thing abhorrent to Christian religion and piety—
what else do they do but revile God himself, whose ministry cannot be reproached without dishonor to himself? And these folk do not just reject the
magistrates, but cast off God that he may not reign over them. For if the Lord
truly said this of the people of Israel because they had refused Samuel's rule
[I Sam. 8:7], why will it less truly be said today of these who let themselves
rage against all governments ordained by God? [479] The Lord said to his
disciples that the kings of the Gentiles exercise lordship over Gentiles, but it is
not so among the disciples, where he who is first ought to become the least
[Luke 22:25-26]; by this saying, they tell us, all Christians are forbidden to
engage in kingdoms or governments. O skillful interpreters! There had arisen

a contention among the disciples over which one would excel the others. To silence this vain ambition, the Lord taught them that their ministry is not like kingdoms, in which one is pre-eminent above the rest. /263/ What dishonor, I ask you, does this comparison do to kingly dignity? Indeed, what does it prove at all, except that the kingly office is not the ministry of an apostle?

42. Moreover, among magistrates themselves, although there is a variety of forms, there is no difference in this respect, that we must regard all of them as ordained of God. For Paul also lumps them all together when he says that there is no power except from God [Rom. 13:1]. And that which is the least pleasant of all has been especially commended above the rest, that is, the power of one. This, because it brings with it the common bondage of all (except that one man to whose will it subjects all things), in ancient times could not be acceptable to heroic and nobler natures. But to forestall their unjust judgments, Scripture expressly affirms that it is the providence of God's wisdom that kings reign*[cf. Prov. 8:15], and particularly commands us to honor the king [Prov. 24:21; I Pet. 2:17]. Obviously, it is an idle pastime for men in private life, [480] who are disqualified from deliberating on the organization of any commonwealth, to dispute over what would be the best kind of government. Also this question admits of no simple solution but requires deliberation, since the nature of the discussion depends especially upon the circumstances. And if you compare the forms of government among themselves apart from the circumstances, (233) it is not easy to distinguish which one of them excels in usefulness, for they contend on such equal terms* The fall from kingdom to tyranny is easy; but it is not much more difficult to fall from the rule of the best men to the faction of a few; yet it is easiest of all to fall from popular rule to sedition* However, as you will surely find if you fix your eyes not on one city alone, but look around and glance at the world as a whole, or at least cast your sight upon regions farther off, divine providence has wisely arranged that various countries should be administered by various kinds of government. For as elements cohere only in unequal proportion, so countries are best held together according to their own particular inequality. However, all these things are needlessly spoken to those for whom the will of the Lord is enough. For if it has seemed good to him to set kings over kingdoms, senates or municipal officers* over free cities, it is our duty to show ourselves compliant and obedient to whomever he sets over the places where we live. [481]

43. Now in this place we ought to explain in passing the office of the magistrates, how it is described in the Word of God and the things in which it consists. Jeremiah admonishes kings to "do justice and righteousness," to "deliver him who has been oppressed by force from the hand of the malicious prosecutor," not to "grieve or wrong the alien, the widow, and the fatherless" or "shed innocent blood" [Jer. 22:3, cf. Vg.]. But Moses /264/ commands the leaders whom he had appointed as his representatives to "hear the cases between their brethren, and judge . . . between a man and his brother, and the alien" and "not recognize faces in judgment, and hear small and great alike, and be

4.20.8

4.20.9

211

afraid of no man, for the judgment is God's" [Deut. 1:16-17 p.]. But I pass over such statements as these: that kings should not multiply horses for themselves; nor set their mind upon avarice; nor be lifted up above their brethren; that they should be constant in meditating upon the law of the Lord all the days of their life [Deut. 17:16-19]; that judges should not lean to one side or take bribes [Deut. 16:19]—and like passages which we read here and there in Scripture. For in explaining here the office of magistrates, it is not so much my purpose to instruct the magistrates themselves as to teach others what magistrates are and to what end God has appointed them. We see, therefore, that they are ordained protectors and vindicators of public innocence, modesty, decency, and tranquillity, and that their sole endeavor should be to provide for the common safety and peace of all. [482] But since they cannot perform this unless they defend good men from the wrongs of the wicked, and give aid and protection to the oppressed, they have been armed with power with which severely to coerce the open malefactors and criminals (by whose wickedness the public peace is troubled and disturbed) [cf. Rom. 13:3]. For from experience we thoroughly agree with the statement of Solon that all commonwealths are maintained by reward and punishment; take these away and the whole discipline of cities collapses and is dissolved. For the care of equity and justice grows cold in the minds of many, (234) unless due honor has been prepared for virtue; and the lust of wicked men cannot be restrained except by severity and the infliction of penalties. And the prophet has included these two functions, when he bids kings and other rulers execute judgment and justice [Jer. 22:3; cf. ch. 21:12]. Justice, indeed, is to receive into safekeeping, to embrace, to protect, vindicate, and free, the innocent. But judgment is to withstand the boldness of the impious, to repress their violence, to punish their misdeeds.

4.20.10

44. But here a seemingly hard and difficult question arises: if the law of God forbids all Christians to kill [Ex. 20:13; Deut. 5:17; Matt. 5:21], and the prophet prophesies concerning God's holy mountain (the church) that in it men shall not afflict or hurt [Is. 11:9; 65:25]—how could it be permitted to magistrates to be pious men and shedders of blood at the same time? Yet if we understand that the magistrate in administering punishments does nothing by himself, [483] but carries out the very judgments of God, we shall not be hampered by this scruple. The law of the Lord forbids killing; but, that murders may not go unpunished, the Lord puts into the hand of his ministers a sword to be drawn against all murderers. It is not for the pious to afflict and hurt; yet to avenge, at the Lord's command, the afflictions of the pious is not to hurt or to afflict. Would that /265/ this were ever before our minds—that nothing is done here from men's rashness, but all things are done on the authority of God who commands it; and while his authority goes before us, we never wander from the straight path. Unless perhaps restraint is laid upon God's justice, that it may not punish misdeeds. But if it is not right to impose any law upon him, why should we level false accusation against his ministers? They do not bear the sword in vain, says Paul, for they are ministers of God to execute his wrath, avengers of

wrongdoers [Rom. 13:4]. Therefore, if princes and others rulers recognize that nothing is more acceptable to the Lord than their obedience, let them apply themselves to this ministry, if they are intent on having their piety, righteousness, and uprightness approved of God [cf. II Tim. 2:15]. Moses was obviously impelled by this desire when, realizing that he had been destined by the Lord's power to be liberator of his people, he laid his hand upon the Egyptian [Ex. 2:12; Acts 7:24]. This was the case again, when, by slaying three thousand men in one day, he took vengeance upon the people's sacrilege [Ex. 32:27-28]. David also, when at the end of his life he ordered his son Solomon to kill Joab and Shimei [I Kings 2:5-6, 8-9]. [484] How does Moses' gentle and peaceable disposition flame into such savageness that, sprinkled and dripping with the blood of his brethren, he dashes through the camp to new carnage? How can David, a man of such great gentleness throughout life, as he breathes his last, make that bloody testament, that his son should not allow the hoary heads of Joab and Shimei to go in peace to the grave [I Kings 2:5-6, 8-9]? But both men, by executing the vengeance ordained of God, hallowed by cruelty their hands, which by sparing they would have defiled. "It is an abomination among kings," says Solomon, "to do iniquity, for the throne is established in righteousness" [Prov. 16:12]. Again: (235) "A king who sits on the throne of judgment casts his eyes upon every evil" [Prov. 20:8 p.]. Again: "A wise king scatters the evildoers and turns them upon the wheel" [Prov. 20:26 p.]. Again: "Remove the dross from the silver, and a vessel will come forth from the metal caster; remove the impious from the king's sight, and his throne will be established in righteousness" [Prov. 25:4-5]. Now if their true righteousness is to pursue the guilty and the impious with drawn sword, should they sheathe their sword and keep their hands clean of blood, while abandoned men wickedly range about with slaughter and massacre, they will become guilty of the greatest impiety, far indeed from winning praise for their goodness and righteousness thereby! Begone, now, with that abrupt and savage harshness, and that tribunal which is rightly called "the reef of guilty men!"* [485] For I am not one either to favor undue cruelty or think that a fair judgment can be pronounced unless clemency, that best counselor of kings and surest keeper of the kingly throne (as Solomon declares) [Prov. 20:28] is always present—clemency, which by a certain writer of antiquity was truly called the chief gift of princes.* Yet it is necessary for the magistrate to pay attention to both, /266/ lest by excessive severity he either harm more than heal: or, by superstitious affectation of clemency, fall into the cruelest gentleness, if he should (with a soft and dissolute kindness) abandon many to their destruction. For during the reign of Nerva it was not without reason said: "It is indeed bad to live under a prince with whom nothing is permitted; but much worse under one by whom everything is allowed."*

45. But kings and peoples must sometimes take up arms to execute such public vengeance.* On this basis we may judge wars lawful which are so undertaken.* For if power has been given them to preserve the tranquillity of their dominion, to restrain the seditious stirrings of restless men, to help those forcibly

4.20.11

oppressed, to punish evil deeds—could they use it more opportunely than to check the fury of one who disturbs both the repose of private individuals and the common tranquillity of all, [486] who raises seditious tumults, and by whom violent oppressions and vile misdeeds are perpetrated? If they ought to be the guardians and defenders of the laws, they should also overthrow the efforts of all whose offenses corrupt the disciplines of the laws. Indeed, if they rightly punish those robbers whose harmful acts have affected only a few, will they allow a whole country to be afflicted and devastated by robberies with impunity? For it makes no difference whether it be a king or the lowest of the common folk who invades a foreign country in which he has no right, and harries it as an enemy. All such must equally, be considered as robbers and punished accordingly. But it is the duty of all magistrates* here to guard particularly against giving vent to their passions even in the slightest degree. Rather, if they have to punish, let them not be carried away with headlong anger, (236) or be seized with hatred, or burn with implacable severity. Let them also (Augustine says) have pity on the common nature in the one whose special fault they are punishing*. Or, if they must arm themselves against the enemy, that is, the armed robber, let them not lightly seek occasion when offered, unless they are driven to it by extreme necessity. For if we must perform much more than the heathen philosopher required when he wanted war to seem a seeking of peace,* surely everything else ought to be tried before recourse is had to arms. [487] Lastly, in both situations let them not allow themselves to be swayed by any private affection, but be led by concern for the people alone. Otherwise, they very wickedly abuse their power, which has been given them not for their own advantage, but for the benefit and service of others. Moreover, this same right to wage war furnishes the reason for garrisons, leagues, and other civil defenses.* /267/ Now, I call "garrisons," those troops which are stationed among the cities to defend the boundaries of a country; "leagues," those pacts which are made by neighboring princes to the end that if any trouble should happen in their lands, they may come to one another's aid, and join forces to put down the common enemies of mankind. I call "civil defenses," things used in the art of war.

4.20.12

4.20.13

46. Lastly, I also wish to add this, that tributes and taxes are the lawful revenue of princes, which they may chiefly use to meet the public expenses of their office; yet they may similarly use them for the magnificence of their household, which is joined, so to speak, with the dignity of the authority they exercise. As we see, David, Hezekiah, Josiah, Jehoshaphat, and other holy kings, also Joseph and Daniel (according to the dignity of their office) were, without offending piety, lavish at public expense, [488] and we read in Ezekiel that a very large portion of the land was assigned to the kings [Ezek. 48:21]. Nevertheless, he does so in such a way that princes themselves will in turn remember that their revenues are not so much their private chests as the treasuries of the entire people* (for Paul so testifies [Rom. 13:6]), which cannot be squandered or despoiled without manifest injustice. Or rather, that these are almost the very blood of the

people, which it would be the direst inhumanity not to spare. Moreover, let them consider that their imposts and levies, and other kinds of tributes, are nothing but supports of public necessity; but that to impose them upon the lowly common folk without cause is tyrannical extortion. These considerations do not encourage princes to waste and luxurious expenditures (as there is surely no need to add fuel to their cupidity, already too much kindled of itself). But as it is very necessary that, whatever they venture, they should venture with a pure conscience before God, they must be taught how much is lawful for them, that they may not in impious self-confidence come under God's displeasure. And this doctrine is not superfluous for private individuals in order that they should not let themselves rashly and shamelessly decry any expenses of princes, even if these exceed the common expenditures of the citizens. (237)

47. Next to the magistracy in the civil state come the laws, stoutest sinews* of the commonwealth, or, as Cicero* calls them, the souls, without which the magistracy cannot stand, even as they themselves cannot without the magistracy. Accordingly, nothing truer could be said [489] than that the law is a silent magistrate; the magistrate, a living law* But because I have undertaken to say with what laws a Christian state ought to be governed, this is no reason why anyone should expect a long discourse concerning the best kind of laws. This would be endless and would not pertain to the present purpose. I shall in but a few words, and as in passing, note /268/ what laws can piously be used before God, and be duly administered among men. I would have passed over this matter in utter silence if I were not aware that here many dangerously go astray. 4.20.14

48. For there are some who deny that a commonwealth is duly framed which, neglecting the political system of Moses, is ruled by the common laws of nations* Let other men consider how perilous and seditious this notion is; it will be enough for me to have proved it false and foolish. We must bear in mind that common division of the whole law of God, administered by Moses, into moral, ceremonial, and judicial laws* And we must consider each of these parts, that we may understand what there is in them that pertains to us, and what does not. In the meantime, let no one be concerned over the small point that ceremonial and judicial laws pertain also to morals. For the ancient writers* who taught this division, although they were not ignorant that these two latter parts had some bearing upon morals, still, because these could be changed or abrogated while morals remained untouched, [490] did not call them moral laws. They applied this name especially to the first part, without which the true holiness of morals cannot stand. The moral law (to begin first with it) is contained 4.20.15 under two heads, one of which simply commands us to worship God with pure faith and piety; the other, to embrace men with sincere affection. Accordingly, it is the true and eternal rule of righteousness, prescribed for men of all nations and times, who wish to conform their lives to God's will. For it is his eternal and unchangeable will that he himself indeed be worshiped by us all, and that we love one another. The ceremonial law was the tutelage of the Jews, with which it seemed good to the Lord to train this people, as it were, in their

childhood, until the fullness of time should come [Gal. 4:3-4; cf. ch. 3:23-24], in order that he might fully manifest his wisdom to the nations, and show the truth of those things which then were foreshadowed in figures. The judicial law, given to them for civil government, imparted definite formulas of equity and justice, by which they might live together blamelessly and peaceably. Those ceremonial practices indeed properly belonged to the doctrine of piety (inasmuch as they kept the church of the Jews in service and reverence to God) and yet could be distinguished from piety itself. In like manner, the form of their judicial laws (although it had no [491] (238) other intent than how best to preserve that very love which is enjoined by God's eternal law) had something distinct from that precept of love.

49. Therefore, as ceremonial laws could be abrogated while piety remained safe and intact, so too, when these judicial constitutions were taken away, the perpetual duties and precepts of love could still remain. /269/ But if this is true, surely every nation is left free to make such laws as it foresees to be profitable for itself. Yet these must be in conformity to that perpetual rule of love, so that they indeed vary in form but have the same purpose. For I do not think that those barbarous and savage laws (such as gave honor to thieves, permitted promiscuous intercourse and others both more filthy and more absurd) are to be regarded as laws at all. For they are abhorrent not only to all justice,

4.20.16 but also to all humanity and gentleness. What I have said will become plain if in all laws we examine (as we should) these two things: the constitution of the law, and the equity on which its constitution itself rests. Equity, because it is natural, cannot but be the same for all, and therefore, this same purpose ought to apply to all laws, whatever their object. Constitutions have attendant circumstances upon which [492] they in part depend. It therefore does not matter that they are different, provided all equally press toward the same goal of equity. It should be clear that the law of God which we call the moral law is nothing else than a testimony of natural law and of that conscience which God has engraved upon men's hearts. Consequently, the entire scheme of this equity of which we are now speaking has been recorded in it. Hence, this equity alone must be the goal and rule and limit of all laws. Whatever laws shall be framed to that rule, directed to that goal, bound by that limit, there is no reason why we should disapprove of them, howsoever they may differ from the Jewish law, or among themselves. God's law forbids stealing. The penalties meted out to thieves in the Jewish state are to be seen in Exodus [Ex. 22:1-4]. The very ancient laws of other nations punished theft with double restitution; the laws which followed these distinguished between theft, manifest and not manifest. Some proceeded to banishment, others to flogging, others finally to capital punishment. False testimony was punished by damages similar and equal to injury among the Jews [Deut. 19:18-21]; elsewhere, only by deep disgrace; in some nations, by hanging; in others, by the cross. All codes equally avenge murder with blood, but with different kinds of death. Against adulterers some nations levy severer, others, lighter punishments. [493] Yet we see how, with such diversity, all laws tend to the same end. For, together with one voice, they pronounce punishment against those crimes which God's eternal law has condemned, namely, murder, theft, adultery, and false witness. But they do not agree on the manner of punishment. Nor is this either necessary or expedient. There is a country (239) which, unless it deals cruelly with murderers by way of horrible examples, must immediately perish from slaughters and robberies. There is a century which /270/ demands that the harshness of penalties be increased. There is a nation inclined to a particular vice, unless it be most sharply repressed. How malicious and hateful toward public welfare would be a man offended by such diversity, a diversity perfectly adapted to maintain the observance of God's law? For utterly vain is the boast of some, that the law of God given through Moses is dishonored when it is abrogated and new laws preferred to it. For either others are not preferred to it when they are more approved, not by a simple comparison, but with regard to the condition of times, place, and nation; or that law is abrogated that had never been enacted for us. For the Lord through the hand of Moses did not give that law to be proclaimed among all nations; but when he had taken the Jewish nation into his safekeeping, defense, and protection, he also willed to be a lawgiver especially to it: and—as became a wise lawgiver—[494] he had special concern for it in making those laws.

50. It now remains for us to examine what was set in the last place: what usefulness the laws, judgments, and magistrates have for the common society of Christians; how much deference private individuals ought to yield to their magistrates, and what obedience should be owed. To very many the office of magistrate seems superfluous among Christians, because they cannot piously call upon them for help, inasmuch as it is forbidden to them to take revenge, to sue before a court, or to go to law. But Paul clearly testifies to the contrary that the magistrate is minister of God for our good [Rom. 13:4]. By this we understand that it is the will of the Lord, that, defended by his hand and supported against the wrongdoing and injustices of evil men, we may live a quiet and serene life [I Tim. 2:2]. 4.20.17

51. But if it is to no purpose that he has been given by the Lord for our defense unless we are allowed to enjoy such benefit, it is clear enough that the magistrate may without impiety be called upon and also appealed to. But here I have to deal with two kinds of men. There are very many who so boil with a rage for litigation that they are never at peace with themselves unless they are quarreling with others. And they carry on their lawsuits with bitter and deadly hatred, and in insane passion to revenge and hurt, and they pursue them with implacable obstinacy even to the ruin of their adversaries. Meanwhile, [495] to avoid being thought of as doing something wrong, they defend such perversity on the pretense of legal procedure. But if one is permitted to go to law with a brother, one is not therewith allowed to hate him, or be seized with a mad desire to harm him, or hound him relentlessly. Such men should therefore understand that lawsuits are permissible if rightly used. There is right use, both for the plaintiff in suing and for the accused in defending himself, if the defendant 4.20.18

presents himself on the appointed day /271/ and with such exception, as he can, defends himself without bitterness, but only with this intent, to defend what is his by right; and if on the other hand the plaintiff, (240) undeservedly oppressed either in his person or in his property, puts himself in the care of the magistrate, makes his complaint, and seeks what is fair and good. But he should be far from all passion to harm or take revenge, far from harshness and hatred, far from burning desire for contention. He should rather be prepared to yield his own and suffer anything than be carried away with enmity toward his adversary. On the other hand, where hearts are filled with malice, corrupted by envy, inflamed with wrath, breathing revenge, finally so inflamed with desire for contention, that love is somewhat impaired in them, the whole court action of even the most just cause cannot but be impious. For this must be a set principle for all Christians: that a lawsuit, however just, can never be rightly prosecuted by any man, unless he treat his adversary [496] with the same love and good will as if the business under controversy were already amicably settled and composed. Perhaps someone will interpose here that such moderation is so uniformly absent from any lawsuit that it would be like a miracle if any such were found. Indeed, I admit that, as the customs of these times go, an example of an upright litigant is rare; but the thing itself, when not corrupted by the addition of anything evil, does not cease to be good and pure. But when we hear that the help of the magistrate is a holy gift of God, we must more diligently guard against its

4.20.19 becoming polluted by our fault. As for those who strictly condemn all legal contentions, let them realize that they therewith repudiate God's holy ordinance, and one of the class of gifts that can be clean to the clean [Titus 1:15]; unless, perchance, they wish to accuse Paul of a shameful act, since he both repelled the slanders of his accusers, exposing at the same time their craft and malice [Acts 24:12 ff.], and in court claimed for himself the privilege of Roman citizenship [Acts 16:37; 22:1, 25], and, when there was need, appealed from the unjust judge to the judgment seat of Caesar [Acts 25:10-11]. This does not contradict the fact that all Christians are forbidden to desire revenge, which we banish far away from Christian courts [Lev. 19:18; Matt. 5:39; Deut. 32:35; Rom. 12:19]. For if it is a civil case, a man does not take the right path unless he commits his cause, with innocent simplicity, to the judge as public protector; [497] and he should think not at all of returning evil for evil [Rom. 12:17], which is the passion for revenge. If, however, the action is brought for some capital or rather serious offense, we require that the accuser be one who comes into court without a burning desire for revenge or resentment over private injury, but having in mind only to prevent the efforts of a destructive man from doing harm to society. For if then you remove a vengeful mind, /272/ that command which forbids revenge to Christians [cf. Rom. 12:19] is not broken. But, some will object, not only are they forbidden to desire revenge, but they are also bidden to wait upon the hand of the Lord, who promises that he will be present to avenge the oppressed and afflicted [Rom. 12:19]: while those who seek aid from the magistrate, either for themselves or for others, anticipate the Lord's vengeance: (241) Not at all! For we must consider that the magistrate's revenge is not man's but God's, which he metes out, as Paul says [Rom. 13:4], through the ministry of man for our good. We are not in any more disagreement with Christ's words in which he forbids us to resist evil, and commands us to turn the right cheek to him who has struck the left, and to give our cloak to him who has taken away our coat [Matt. 5:39-40]. He indeed wills that the hearts of his people so utterly recoil from any desire to retaliate that they should rather allow double injury to be done them than to increase their intention to pay it back. And we are not leading them away from this forbearance. [498] For truly, Christians ought to be a kind of men born to bear slanders and injuries, open to the malice, deceits, and mockeries of the most wicked men. And not that only, but they ought to bear patiently all these evils. That is, they should have such complete spiritual composure that, having received one affliction, they make ready for another, promising themselves throughout life nothing but the bearing of a perpetual cross. Meanwhile, let them also do good to those who do them harm, and bless those who curse them [Luke 6:28; cf. Matt. 5:44], and (this is their only victory) strive to conquer evil with good [Rom. 12:21]. So minded, they will not seek an eye for an eye, a tooth for a tooth (as the Pharisees taught their disciples to desire revenge) but, as they are instructed by Christ, they will so suffer their body to be maimed, and their possessions to be maliciously seized, that they will forgive and voluntarily pardon those wrongs as soon as they have been inflicted upon them [Matt. 5:38 ff.]. Yet this equity and moderateness of their minds will not prevent them from using the help of the magistrate in preserving their own possessions, while maintaining friendliness toward their enemies; or zealous for public welfare, from demanding the punishment of a guilty and pestilent man, who, they know, can be changed only by death. But the usual objection—that Paul has condemned lawsuits altogether—is also false [I Cor. 6:5-8]. [499] It can readily be understood from his words that there was an immoderate rage for litigation in the church of the Corinthians—even to the point that they exposed to the scoffing and evilspeaking of the impious the gospel of Christ and their whole religion. Paul first criticized them for disgracing the gospel among unbelievers by the intemperateness of their quarrels. Secondly, he rebuked them also for contending in this way among themselves, brethren with brethren. /273/ For they were so far from bearing another's wrongs that they greedily panted after one another's possessions, and without cause assailed and inflicted loss upon one another. Therefore, Paul inveighs against that mad lust to go to law, not simply against all controversies. But he expressly brands it an offense for them not to accept the loss of their goods, rather than to endeavor to keep them, even to the point of strife. Christians ought indeed so to conduct themselves that they always prefer to yield their own right rather than go into a court, from which they can scarcely get away without a heart stirred and kindled to hatred of their brother. (242) But when any man sees that without loss of love he can defend his own property, the loss of which would be a heavy expense to him, he does not offend against this statement of Paul, if he has recourse to law.

4.20.20

4.20.21

To sum up (as we said at the beginning), love will give every man the best counsel. Everything undertaken apart from love and all disputes that go beyond it, [500] we regard as incontrovertibly unjust and impious.

4.20.22   52. The first duty of subjects toward their magistrates is to think most honorably of their office*, which they indeed should recognize as a jurisdiction bestowed by God, and on that account to esteem and reverence them as ministers and representatives of God. For you may find some who very respectfully yield themselves to their magistrates and are not unwilling to obey them because they know that such is expedient for public welfare; nevertheless, they regard magistrates only as a kind of necessary evil* But Peter requires something more of us when he commands that the king be honored [I Pet. 2:17]; as does Solomon when he teaches that God and king are to be feared [Prov. 24:21]. For Peter, in the word "to honor" includes a sincere and candid opinion. Solomon, yoking the king with God, shows that the king is to be regarded with full veneration and dignity. There is also that famous saying in Paul: that we should obey "not only because of wrath, but because of conscience" [Rom. 13:5; cf. Vg.]. By this he means that subjects should be led not by dread alone of princes and rulers to remain in subjection under them (as they commonly yield to an armed enemy who sees that vengeance is promptly taken if they resist), but because [501] they are showing obedience to God himself when they give it to them; since the rulers' power is from God. From this also something else follows: that, with hearts inclined to reverence their rulers, the subjects should prove their obedience toward them, whether by obeying their proclamations, or by paying taxes, or by undertaking public offices and burdens which pertain to the common defense*, or by executing any other commands of theirs. "Let every soul," says Paul, "be subject to the higher powers. . . . For he who resists authority, resists what God has ordained" [Rom. 13:1-2, Vg.]. /274/ "Remind them," he writes to Titus, "to be subject to overseers and powers, to obey magistrates, to be ready for every good work" [Titus 3:1, cf. Vg.]. And Peter says, "Be subject to every human creature for the Lord's sake, whether it be to the king, as supreme, or unto governors who are sent through him to punish evildoers, but to praise doers of good" [I Pet. 2:13-14]. Now, in order that they may prove that they are not pretending subjection, but are sincerely and heartily subjects, Paul adds that they should commend to God the safety and prosperity of those under whom they live. "I urge," he says, "that supplications, prayers, intercessions, and thanksgivings be made for all men, for kings, and all that are in authority, (243) that we may lead a quiet and peaceable life, with all godliness and honesty" [I Tim. 2:1-2, cf. Vg.]. [502]

4.20.23   Let no man deceive himself here. For since the magistrate cannot be resisted without God being resisted at the same time, even though it seems that an unarmed magistrate can be despised with impunity still God is armed to avenge mightily this contempt toward himself.

53. Moreover, under this obedience I include the restraint which private citizens ought to bid themselves keep in public, that they may not deliberately

intrude in public affairs, or pointlessly invade the magistrate's office, or undertake anything at all politically. If anything in a public ordinance requires amendment, let them not raise a tumult, or put their hands to the task—all of them ought to keep their hands bound in this respect—let them commit the matter to the judgment of the magistrate, whose hand alone here is free. I mean, let them not venture on anything without a command. For when the ruler gives his command, private citizens receive public authority. For as the counselors are commonly called the ears and eyes of the prince, so may one reasonably speak of those whom he has appointed by his command to do things, as the hands of the prince.*

54. But since we have so far been describing a magistrate who truly is what he is called, that is, a father of his country,* and, as the poet expresses it, shepherd of his people,* guardian of peace, protector of righteousness, and avenger of innocence*—he who does not approve of such government must rightly be regarded as insane. [503] But it is the example of nearly all ages that some princes are careless about all those things to which they ought to have given heed, and, far from all care, lazily take their pleasure. Others, intent upon their own business, put up for sale laws, privileges, judgments, and letters of favor.* Others drain the common people of their money, and afterward lavish it on insane largesse. Still others exercise sheer robbery, plundering houses, raping virgins and matrons, and slaughtering the guiltless. Consequently, many cannot be persuaded that they ought to recognize these as princes /275/ and to obey their authority as far as possible. For in such great disgrace, and among such crimes, so alien to the office not only of a magistrate but also of a man, they discern no appearance of the image of God which ought to have shone in the magistrate; while they see no trace of that minister of God, who had been appointed to praise the good, and to punish the evil [cf. I Pet. 2:14, Vg.]. Thus, they also do not recognize as ruler him whose dignity and authority Scripture has commended to us. Indeed, this inborn feeling has always been in the minds of almost all men to hate and curse tyrants as much as to love and venerate lawful kings. But if we look to God's Word, it will lead us farther. [504] We are not only subject to the authority of princes who perform their office uprightly and faithfully as they ought, but also to the authority of all who, by whatever means, have got control of affairs, even though they perform not a whit of the princes' office.* (244) For despite the Lord's testimony that the magistrate's office is the highest gift of his beneficence to preserve the safety of men, and despite his appointment of bounds to the magistrates—he still declares at the same time that whoever they may be, they have their authority solely from him. Indeed, he says that those who rule for the public benefit are true patterns and evidences of this beneficence of his; that they who rule unjustly and incompetently have been raised by him to punish the wickedness of the people;* that all equally have been endowed with that holy majesty with which he has invested lawful power. I shall proceed no farther until I have added some sure testimonies of this thing. Yet, we need not labor to prove that a wicked king is the Lord's

4.20.24

4.20.25

wrath upon the earth [Job 34:30, Vg.; Hos. 13:11; Is. 3:4; 10:5], for I believe no man will contradict me; and thus nothing more would be said of a king than of a robber who seizes your possessions [Deut. 28:29], of an adulterer who pollutes your marriage bed [Deut. 28:30], or of a murderer who seeks to kill you. For Scripture reckons all such calamities among God's curses. But let us, rather, pause here to prove this [505] which does not so easily settle in men's minds. In a very wicked man utterly unworthy of all honor, provided he has the public power in his hands, that noble and divine power resides which the Lord has by his Word given to the ministers of his justice and judgment. And he should be held in the same esteem by his subjects, insofar as public obedience is concerned, in which they would hold the best of kings if he were given to them.

4.20.26 First, I should like my readers to note and carefully observe that providence of God, which the Scriptures with good reason so often recall to us, and its special operation in distributing kingdoms and appointing what kings he pleases. /276/ In Daniel, the Lord changes times and successions of times, removes kings and sets them up [Dan. 2:21, 37]. Likewise: "to the end that the living may know that the Most High rules the kingdom of men, he gives it to whom he will" [Dan. 4:17; cf. ch. 4:14, Vg.]. Although Scripture everywhere abounds with such passages, this prophecy particularly swarms with them. Now it is well enough known what kind of king Nebuchadnezzar was, who conquered Jerusalem—a strong invader and destroyer of other peoples. Nevertheless, the Lord declares in Ezekiel that He has given him the land of Egypt for the work he had done for him in devastating Egypt [Ezek. 29:19-20]. And Daniel said to him: "You, O king, are a king of kings, to whom the God [506] of heaven has given the kingdom, powerful, mighty, and glorious; to you, I say, he has given also all lands where the children of men dwell, beasts of the forest and birds of the air: these he has given into your hand and made you rule over them" [Dan. 2:37-38, cf. Vg.]. Again, Daniel says to Nebuchadnezzar's son, Belshazzar: "The Most High God gave Nebuchadnezzar, your father, kingship and magnificence, honor and glory, and because of the magnificence that he gave him, all peoples, tribes, and tongues were trembling and fearful before him" [Dan. 5:18-19, cf. Vg.]. (245) When we hear that a king has been ordained by God, let us at once call to mind those heavenly edicts with regard to honoring and fearing a king; then we shall not hesitate to hold a most wicked tyrant in the place where the Lord has deigned to set him. Samuel, when he warned the people of Israel what sort of things they would suffer from their kings, said: "This shall be the right of the king that will reign over you: he will take your sons and put them to his chariot to make them his horsemen and to plow his fields and reap his harvest, and make his weapons. He will take your daughters to be perfumers and cooks and bakers. Finally, he will take your fields, your vineyards, and your best olive trees and will give them to his servants. He will take the tenth of your grain and of your vineyards, and will give it to his eunuchs and servants. He will take your menservants, maidservants, and asses and set them [507] to his work. He will take the tenth of your flocks and you will be his servants"* [I Sam. 8:11-17, with omissions.] Surely, the kings would not do this by legal right, since the law instructed them to restrain themselves [Deut. 17:16ff.]. But it was called a right in relation to the people, for they had to obey it and were not allowed to resist. It is as if Samuel had said: The willfulness of kings will run to excess, but it will not be your part to restrain it; you will have this one thing left to you: to obey their commands and hearken to their word. But in Jeremiah* especially, there is a memorable passage, which (although rather long) it will not trouble me to quote because it very clearly defines this whole question. "I have made the earth and men, says the Lord, and the animals which are upon the face of the earth, with my great strength and outstretched /277/ arm; and I give it to him who is pleasing in my eyes. Now, therefore, I have given all these lands into the hand of Nebuchadnezzar . . . my servant. . . . All the nations and great kings shall serve him . . . , until the time of his own land comes. . . . And it shall be that any nation and kingdom that will not serve him and place their neck under the yoke of the king of Babylon, I shall visit that nation with sword, famine, and pestilence. . . . Therefore, serve the king of Babylon and live" [Jer. 27:5-8, 17; cf. Vg.]. We see how much obedience the Lord willed to be paid to that abominable and cruel tyrant for no other reason than that he possessed the kingship. But it [508] was by the Lord's decree that he had been set upon the throne of the kingdom and assumed into kingly majesty, which it would be unlawful to violate. If we have continually present to our minds and before our eyes the fact that even the most worthless kings are appointed by the same decree by which the authority of all kings is established, those seditious thoughts will never enter our minds that a king should be treated according to his merits,* and that it is unfair that we should show ourselves subjects to him who, on his part, does not show himself a king to us.* In the same prophet, there is also another command of the Lord by which he enjoins his people to seek the peace of Babylon, where they have been sent as captives, and to pray to the Lord on its behalf, for in its peace will be their peace [Jer. 29:7]. Behold, the Israelites, divested of all their possessions, driven from their homes, led away into exile, and cast into (246) pitiable bondage, are commanded to pray for the prosperity of their conqueror—not as we are commanded in other passages to pray for our persecutors [cf. Matt. 5:44], but in order that his kingdom may be preserved safe and peaceful, that under him they too may prosper. So David,* already designated king by God's ordination and anointed with his holy oil, when he was persecuted by Saul without deserving it, still regarded the head of his assailant as inviolable, because the Lord had sanctified it with the honor of the kingdom. "Far be it from me," he said, "that I should do this thing before the Lord, [509] to my lord, the Lord's anointed, to put forth my hand against him, since he is the Lord's anointed" [I Sam. 24:6, cf. Vg.]. Again: "My soul has spared you; and I have said, 'I shall not put forth my hand against my lord, for he is the Lord's anointed' " [I Sam. 24:11, cf. Vg.]. Again: "Who will put forth his hand against the anointed of the Lord and be innocent? . . . The Lord lives; unless the Lord strike him, or the day come for him to die,

4.20.27

4.20.28

223

or he fall in battle, far be it from me that I should put forth my hand against the Lord's anointed" [I Sam. 26:9-11, cf. Vg.].

4.20.29   55. We owe this attitude of reverence and therefore of piety toward all our rulers in the highest degree, whatever they may be like. I therefore the more often repeat this: that we should learn not to examine the men themselves, but take it as enough that they bear, by the Lord's will, a character upon which he has imprinted and engraved an inviolable majesty. /278/ But (you will say) rulers owe responsibilities in turn to their subjects.* This I have already admitted. But if you conclude from this that service ought to be rendered only to just governors, you are reasoning foolishly. For husbands are also bound to their wives, and parents to their children, by mutual responsibilities. Suppose parents and husbands depart from their duty. Suppose parents show themselves so hard and intractable to their children, whom they are forbidden to provoke to anger [Eph. 6:4], that by their rigor they tire them beyond measure. Suppose husbands most despitefully use their wives, whom [510] they are commanded to love [Eph. 5:25] and to spare as weaker vessels [I Pet. 3:7]. Shall either children be less obedient to their parents or wives to their husbands? They will still be subject even to those who are wicked and undutiful. Indeed, all ought to try not to "look at the bag hanging from their back,"* that is, not to inquire about the duties of others, but every man should keep in mind that one duty which is his own. This ought particularly to apply to those who have been put under the power of others. Therefore, if we are cruelly tormented by a savage prince, if we are greedily despoiled by one who is avaricious or wanton, if we are neglected by a slothful one, if finally we are vexed for piety's sake by one who is impious and sacrilegious,* let us first be mindful of our own misdeeds, which without doubt are chastised by such whips of the Lord [cf. Dan. 9:7; 9:11 ff.]. Let us then also call this thought to mind,* that it is not for us to remedy such evils; that only this remains, to implore the Lord's help, in whose hand are (247) the hearts of kings, and the changing of kingdoms* [Prov. 21:1 p.]. "He is God who will stand in the assembly of the gods, and will judge in the midst of the gods" [Ps. 82:1 p.]. Before His face all kings shall fall and be crushed, and all the judges of the earth, that have not kissed his anointed [Ps. 2:10-11], and all those who have written unjust laws to oppress the poor in judgment and to do violence [511] to the cause of the lowly, to prey upon widows and rob the fatherless [Is.

4.20.30   10:1-2, cf. Vg.]. Here are revealed his marvellous goodness, his power, and his providence. For sometimes he raises up open avengers from among his servants, and arms them with his command to punish the wicked government and deliver his people, oppressed in unjust ways, from miserable calamity. Sometimes he directs to this end the rage of men who intend one thing and undertake another. Thus he delivered the people of Israel from the tyranny of Pharaoh through Moses [Ex. 3:7-10]; from the violence of Chusan, king of Syria, through Othniel [Judg. 3:9]; and from other servitudes through other kings or judges. Thus he crushed and afflicted the insolence of the Egyptians by the Assyrians; thus the pride of Tyre, by the Egyptians; the violence of Babylon by the Medes and

Persians; the ungratefulness of the kings of Judah and Israel by the Babylonians. Yet /279/ all these actions were not executed in the same way. For the first kind of men, when they had been sent by God's lawful calling to carry out such acts, in taking up arms against kings, did not at all violate that majesty which is implanted in kings by divine ordination; but they subdued the lesser power with the greater, just as it is lawful for kings to punish their subordinates. But the latter kind of men, although they were directed by God's hand whither he pleased, and executed his work unwittingly, yet planned in their minds to do nothing but an evil act. [512] But however these deeds of men are judged in themselves, still the Lord accomplished his work through them alike when he broke the bloody scepters of arrogant kings and when he overturned intolerable governments. Let princes hear and be afraid. But we must, in the meantime, be very careful not to despise or violate that authority of magistrates, full of venerable majesty, which God has established by the weightiest decrees, even though it may reside with the most unworthy men, who defile it as much as they can with their own wickedness. For, if the correction of unbridled despotism is the Lord's to avenge, let us not at once think that it is entrusted to us, to whom no command has been given except to obey and suffer. (248) I am speaking all the while of private individuals. For if there are now any magistrates of the people, appointed to restrain the willfulness of kings (as in ancient times the ephors were set against the Spartan kings, or the tribunes of the people against the Roman consuls, or the demarchs against the senate of the Athenians; and perhaps, as things now are, such power as the three estates exercise in every realm when they hold their chief assemblies), I am so far from forbidding them to withstand, in accordance with their duty, the fierce licentiousness of kings, that, if they wink at kings who violently fall upon and assault the lowly common folk, [513] I declare that their dissimulation involves nefarious perfidy, for by it they dishonestly betray the freedom of the people, of which they know that they have been appointed protectors by God's ordinance.

56. But in that obedience which we have shown to be due the authority of rulers, we are always to make this exception, indeed, to observe it as primary, that such obedience is never to lead us away from obedience to him, to whose will the desires of all kings ought to be subject, to whose decrees their commands ought to yield, to whose majesty their scepters ought to be submitted. And how absurd would it be that in satisfying men you should incur the displeasure of him for whose sake you obey men themselves! The Lord, therefore, is the King of kings, who, when he has opened his sacred mouth, must alone be heard, before all and above all men, next to him we are subject to those men who are in authority over us, but only in him. If they command anything against him, let it go unesteemed. And here let us not be concerned about all that dignity /280/ which the magistrates possess; for no harm is done to it when it is humbled before that singular and truly supreme power of God. I know with what great and present peril this constancy is menaced, because kings bear defiance with the greatest displeasure, whose "wrath is a messenger of death," [Prov. 16:14]

4.20.31

4.20.32

say Solomon. But since this edict has been proclaimed by the heavenly herald, [514] Peter—"We must obey God rather than men" [Acts 5:29]—let us comfort ourselves with the thought that we are rendering that obedience which the Lord requires when we suffer anything rather than turn aside from piety. And that our courage may not grow faint, Paul pricks us with another goad: That we have been redeemed by Christ at so great a price as our redemption cost him, so that we should not enslave ourselves to the wicked desires of men—much less to their impiety [I Cor. 7:23; cf. 6:20].

THE END

IMPORTANT SUBJECTS
TREATED IN THIS BOOK

ABBREVIATIONS FREQUENTLY USED
IN ENDNOTES

ANF   *The Ante-Nicene Fathers.* 1885–.

BSHPF   *Bulletin de la Société de l'Histoire du Protestantisme Français.*

CC   Philip Schaff, *The Creeds of Christendom.* 1877–.

CSEL   *Corpus Scriptorum Ecclesiasticorum Latinorum.* 1866–.

CR   *Corpus Reformatorum.* 1834–. When followed by Cal, Calvin; by Melanch, Melanchthon; by Zw, Zwingli.

DCR   *Documents Illustrative of the Continental Reformation.* Edited by B. J. Kidd. 1911.

EvQ   *Evangelical Quarterly.*

LCC   *Library of Christian Classics.* 1953–.

LW   *Luther's Works.* 1958–.

LWZ   *The Latin Works and Correspondence of H. Zwingli.* 3 Vols. 1912–.

OC   *Opera Calvini.* 1869–. The 55 volumes of Calvin's works in the *Corpus Reformatorum* series.

OS   *Opera Selecta Calvini.* 1926–. The 5 volumes of the selected works of Calvin.

NPNF   *Nicene and Post-Nicene Fathers.* 1890–.

PG   J. P. Migne, *Patrologiae. Series Graeca.* 1857–.

PL   J. P. Migne. *Patrolgiae. Series Latina.* 1844–.

SC   *Supplementa Calviniana.* 1961–.

SWHZ   *Selected Works of H. Zwingli.* Edited by S. M. Jackson. 1901.

T&T   *John Calvin: Tracts and Treatises.* 3 Vols. 1844–.

WA   *D. Martin Luthers Werke.* Weimarer Ausgabe. 1883–.

ENDNOTES

EPISTLE DEDICATORY TO FRANCIS

Page 1.

Lord. Cf. Huldreich Zwingli's flattering appeals to Francis I in his *Commentary on True and False Religion* (1525) [Eng. tr., *Latin Works of Huldreich Zwingli* (LWZ) 3.43-54]; and his *Exposition of the Christian Faith* (1531) [Eng. tr., Library of Christian Classics (LCC) 24.245f].

offered. As has been stated in the Introduction, Calvin in his letter to Francis I describes his original purpose in writing the *Institutes* as catechetical, his second as apologetic. The latter purpose called forth a two-pronged theological response from the author. He must needs explicitly reject institutionalized Roman Catholicism and at the same time its extreme opposite, the revolutionary, disruptive spiritualism he then lumped under the name *Catabaptists*. Most of the prefatory letter concerns itself with the Roman Church, but at pp. 11ff he begins to deal with the Anabaptists. He is at great pains to dissociate the French Evangelical party from more revolutionary reformers, exemplified by the Münster incident of 1534-35, with which subversive colors Francis I's ecclesiastical mentors were trying to paint the Evangelicals. Calvin explicitly describes his two-fold struggle in his *Reply to Cardinal Sadolet* (1539) [OS 1.465; (Eng. tr., T&T 1:36)]: "We are being attacked by two sects which seem to differ greatly from one another. What likeness does that of the pope have with the Anabaptists? And yet, that you may see how Satan never transformed himself with such great cunning without in some part betraying himself, both sects have the same particular goal—to harass us."

Christ. Lambert of Avignon in a letter of 20 January 1525 wrote to the Elector of Saxony: "Almost all France is deeply stirred up; without a teacher, many people are seeking the truth." [Pannier, 1.7a, citing Herminjard, 1.113]. Guillaume Farel's *Sommaire et Briefve Declaration*, the first summary of the Evangelical faith in the French language, originally published in 1525 and reissued in 1534, bears the superscription: *To all those who love our Lord and desire to know the truth.* This eagerness for the truth is reflected autobiographically in Calvin's Preface to the *Commentary on the Psalms*. Less than a year after his sudden conversion, as he calls it, he confesses: ". . . all those who yearned for pure doctrine were coming again and again to me to learn it, even though I had scarcely commenced to study it myself." His efforts to seek solitude failed and "all retreats and places of escape became for" him "like public schools." Herminjard, 4.4n3, infers from this that Calvin had begun to write the *Institutes* before arriving in Switzerland.

231

NOTES TO PAGES 1 - 3

fury. The doctors of the Sorbonne and the counsellors of the Parlement of Paris. (Pannier, 1.7b).

fire. Francis I in his letter to the Estates of the Empire of 1 February 1535 (Herminjard, 3. no. 492) endeavored to answer charges that he indiscriminately imprisoned and put to death Germans living in France by asserting that he had had to act not against these, but against "certain seditious persons who were plotting to overthrow society. . . ." See Herminjard, 3.249-254, and especially nos. 10-11.

sea. Cf. Calvin, *Commentary on Seneca's De Clementia* (1532) [Eng. tr., Battles-Hugo, p. 321]: "Hence the Bull of Phalaris and Nero's mockeries against the Christians (Tacitus, *Annals*, 15.44.4): 'when they were covered with the hides of wild beasts and mangled to death by dogs.' "

reports. The Edict of Coucy (16 July 1535) of Francis I, which offered payment to informers, extended amnesty to all persons willing to abjure canonically within six months their heretical religious views and return to the Catholic faith. The "sacramentarians" are however to be punished according to their deserts, and all reading or teaching, public or private, of any doctrine contrary to the Catholic faith is subject to the death penalty. See Herminjard, 3.322n32. On 31 May 1536, the King issued a new and more liberal edict which "pardoned all heretics," even the sacramentarians and the lapsed, provided they undertook to abjure within six months (Herminjard, 4.6n6; 71n2).

you. See LCC 20.10n1. For original text of the Placards, see R. Hari, "Les Placards de 1534" in *Aspects de la Propaganda Religieuse* (1957), pp. 114-119. An English translation is supplied in Appendix I.

Page 2.

home. An echo, perhaps, of Cicero, *Pro Cluentio*, 2.6: "First, that, as is only just, you bring to this court no preconceived judgments (for indeed men will cease, not only to respect us as judges, but even to call us judges, unless in this place we base our judgments on the facts of the case instead of applying to the facts the ready-made judgments we have brought from home)."

Page 3.

repair. Plautus, *Trinummus*, 317.

adversaries. For a discussion of the Roman Catholic opponents of Reform, see LCC 20.12n4, 15n8, etc. J. Bohatec, *Budé und Calvin*, p. 127n2, comments on the documentation provided in Barth and Niesel, OS 3.9ff (utilized in the notes of LCC 20.9-31). One might say, summarizing Bohatec, that there are three concentric rings of opponents to the Evangelical position: (1) the outermost circle of traditional scholastics—Thomas Aquinas, Gabriel Biel, etc.; (2) the Roman Catholic controversialists who mounted the polemic against Luther and others—Eck, Clichtoveus, de Castro, Cochlaeus, etc., who drew their positions largely from the earlier scholastics; (3) the immediate opponents of Calvin—called by him the *aulici artifices* ("tools of the court"). See Introduction, p. xliv. These last, says Bohatec, have been left unidentified by Barth and Niesel. They include, *inter alia*, Robert Ceneau (Robertus Canalis), Bishop of Avranches, almoner of the Queen-mother and court preacher, author of *Appendix ad coenam dominicam* . . . (1534); Guillaume Budé, author of *De transitu Hellenismi ad Christianismum* (1534/35); and Cardinal Jacopo Sadoleto (Sadolet), author of *Commentaria in Epistolam Pauli ad Romanos* (1535).

Morelet du Museau, writing from Basel (16 September 1534) to Martin Bucer at

Strasbourg (Herminjard, 3. no. 478, pp. 207f) attempts to answer the latter's question as to the identity of Robert, Bishop of Avranches: "Now I must respond to the latter part of your letter, in which you write, that I inform you whether Robert, Bishop of Avranches, is known to me? I never had any intercourse or close acquaintance with him although I did however know the man; therefore I'll scrape together what I know of the man. He is a doctor of the Sorbonne, as you could recognize from the title of his book, which I have not seen, Ceneau by name, at least he is so called among us. I heard one or another sermons of his when I was at the chamber of the King, whose mother had called him to the palace to preach at certain festivals: there he transacted not the business of Christ, but his own. He was provided with several benefices, finally with a small bishopric located in Narbonne, which, to increase his income, he exchanged for another rather fat one over which he now presides, situated on the Normandy coast. Concerning his teaching I write you nothing; from his works you can judge of what sort he is; yet among the French he is of no or slight reputation, except among the scholastic doctors of the Sorbonne, who highly regard his teaching and erudition. If one considers only outward matters, no one could think ill of the man: for his life is not a scandal, as is true of many and of almost all bishops." Herminjard states (p. 207n9): "Ceneau's book is named in the title of the work published by Bucer in September 1534 in refutation of it: *Defense against the Catholic Axiom*, that is the accusation of the Rev. Father Robert, Bishop of Avranches, in which he importunately accuses all who are striving to follow Christ's teaching, of impious innovation in all the dogmas and rites of the Church, especially concerning the most holy Eucharist. . . . Strassburg, Matthew Apiarius, 1534." Obviously the *Catholic Axiom* and the *Appendix* are the same work. In it Ceneau calls upon the King to inflict the death penalty upon the Evangelical opponents of the Roman Mass. Many years later, in refuting the Augsburg Interim, Calvin concluded his Adultero-German Interim [*On the True Way to Reform the Church*] (1549) with a refutation of Robert Ceneau, who had from the Romanist side also opposed the Interim with his *Antidote to the Proposition of the Interim* [see Calvin, T&T 3.334-341]. That Ceneau laid some slight claim to humanist pursuits is suggested by a work published by him in 1535 *On the True Reckoning of Measures and Weights* [Herminjard, 3.366n22], the preface of which is followed by a panegyric to Francis I.

Guillaume Budé, the second of the three immediate opponents of the Evangelical cause espoused by Calvin, had earlier been a force in Calvin's humanist formation. On this, see Battles, "The Sources of Calvin's Seneca Commentary," in G. Duffield, ed., *Studies in John Calvin* (1965), pp. 38-66; also Calvin, *Comm. Sen. De Clem., passim*. While an enlightened humanist, the founder through the royal lectureships of the later Collège de France and thus an opponent of the obscurantist learning of the Sorbonne theologians headed by Noël Beda, Budé himself was religiously conservative, coming (as Bohatec asserts [p. 130]) under the influence of the Romanist controversialist Cochlaeus. This conservatism, which increased as Budé grew older, was primarily manifested in the *De Transitu* toward the dangers of paganizing humanism [see Calvin, *Comm. Sen. De Clem.* (Eng. tr., Battles-Hugo, pp. 53*-55*)], against which he espoused an Augustinian piety, even though the pages of the work are strewn with recondite references to his cherished classical authors. But secondarily, the *De Transitu*, in Bohatec's words [p. 128], ". . . subjected the most important portions of Evangelical doctrine to a sharp criticism." The dedication of the *De Transitu* celebrates Francis as the defender of orthodoxy, ". . . praising that monarch for having ordered a public procession (21 Jan. 1535) to expiate the crime committed by several fanatics against the sacrament of the altar

[*Opera Omnia* (1557/1966), 1.132f; Herminjard, 3.239n]. Budé closes the dedication with this distich:

To make more venerable the sure faith of the Word
In the world, Francis our prince lavished it with honor.

[*Opera*, 1.133]

Jacopo Sadoleto, the third immediate opponent of the Evangelical party, Cardinal and Bishop of Carpentras, was an eminent humanist, correspondent of Erasmus, Budé, Sturm, and others, chiefly known to Calvinists as the author of an appeal to the people of Geneva to return to Mother Church, now that they had exiled (1538) Calvin and Farel; to this letter, Calvin eloquently replied in 1539. Sadoleto, in his *Commentary on St. Paul's Epistle to the Romans* (1535), dedicated to Francis I, and sprinkled both with criticism of Protestantism and with praises of the King's support of Romanist orthodoxy, took a religious position which Calvin has in mind in his remarks on his opponents. In his preface to Book I, Sadoleto lauds the King: ". . . but chiefly through the virtue and vigilance of our Most Christian King Francis, not even a slight contagion of this great error could remain in these regions." The Dedicatory Epistle to the Commentary is even more explicit [quoted by Bohatec, p. 129]: "For although you have been graced with ancestors who deemed it their duty to do and endure all things for the protection and defense of the faith and religion, in coping with the overwhelming and extraordinary conditions of these times you surpass even their most illustrious courage. . . . Although in the past there were often grave disturbances and times rendered unsafe by conflicts among many persons, yet never did there exist in the Christian faith such dissension as exists today, nor did we meet with such a great mass of forces as you are warding off perils from the many nations which are under your rule, and are healing their misfortunes."

As Herminjard has shown [9.239n23], it took some time for the Protestants to realize that such Christian humanists as Budé and Sadoleto were not on their side: "Conrad Gessner, writing to Bullinger (27 Dec. 1534) still thought that G. Budé was 'wholly on our side, with certain other savants.' This illusion was dissipated when in March 1535 Budé published his *De Transitu*. . . . Budé's will, dated 23 June 1536 is equally instructive. After having declared that he has put all his hope of salvation in the mercy of Jesus Christ, he adds: 'having also great confidence in the intercession of the glorious and only mother and virgin, of St. Peter and St. Paul . . . and of the blessed Magdalene . . . to whom I have, in my life, made the commemoration recommended by the precept. . . .' " Melanchthon in his letter to Joachim Camerarius [CR Melanch 2.936f] of 2 Sept. 1535 sadly comments: "I hope you have seen Budé's *De Transitu Hellenismi ad Christianismum* and Sadolet's *Commentary on Romans*; both obviously tragically inveigh against us. . . . We are savagely wounded by Sadolet and Budé . . . both of whom have written to the King of France" [quoted by Bohatec, p. 128; Herminjard, 3.239].

corrupt it. Alfonsus de Castro, *Adversus omnes haereses* (1534), 1.4 [fol. 8Eff]. See also LCC 20.12n4.

faith. See LCC 20.12n5.

rule. Cf. Calvin, *Comm. Sen. De Clem.*, 51.18; also Erasmus, *Adagia*, 1.5.90.

nature. J. Cochlaeus, *De libero arbitrio* (1525), I [fol. E. 4^v.8-18]: "Nor does scripture, which you twist with your sacrilegious boldness to impieties, excuse you, but testifies that you are more impious and wicked and accuses you of profanely and shamelessly and impiously abusing sacred things, ungrateful toward God, the church, nature, and men—you who have cast out through heresy the light of grace which you received from God in baptism, you have trampled on the sacraments of the church, altered the natural light of reason into flesh and made the whole human race by your cursed tongue (as we have shown above) worse and more wretched than brute beasts, stones and stocks." This and the following passage from Cochlaeus are from a point-by-point refutation of Melanchthon's *Loci Communes* (1521). Cf. the latter work [Eng. tr., LCC 19.26]: "But if you think of the power of the human will as a capacity of nature, according to the human reason it cannot be denied that there is in it a certain freedom in outward works."

preparations. Cochlaeus, *De libero arbitrio,* II [fol. L. 6^v.10-19]: "Why are you not ashamed, Philip [Melanchthon], to cite two scripture passages, contrary to the sound of their language, as having the same meaning, without any annotation or admonition, and also to join them closely together? For if [you cite] 'The heart of a man disposes his way,' how can you immediately subjoin, 'A man's way is not his own doing'? Does it not also say in the same chapter of Proverbs [ch. 16]: 'It is man's task to prepare his soul'? What will you, who deny free will, answer to these verses?" Cf. I [fol. F.6^r.16-24]: "But you, Philip, like a forerunner of the devil, say to Christians: All things happen of necessity, you have no free will, all you did before justification is mortal sin, your repentance subsists on sorrow, attrition is of no value, auricular confession is nothing, satisfaction is nothing, good works are nothing, any merit of a righteous man is nothing, all the works of a righteous man, although proceeding from the Spirit of God, are unclean and venial sins."

free will. Cochlaeus, *De libero arbitrio,* I [fol. B.3^r.16-24]: "What man of sane mind is there who does not feel he has reason and will and free choice, by which he differs from the rest of the animals? Would he not rightly and deservedly be taken for a beast if he denied these were in him? How would it not be difficult for me to dispute with you, who are without reason (as you confess) and without free will?" I [fol. C.5^r.16-21]: "But if you take away reason and will and free choice from man (as you do), what, I beg of you, will remain in man, through which his heart can be made teachable, or through which he can discern between good and evil, or rightly judge? With these taken away, a man speaks just like a garrulous magpie or Balaam's ass." II [fol. I.1^v.26-2^r.2]: "Let them nonetheless beware of depriving man, made in the image of God, of free will (which you both brutally and impiously do)." Eck, *Enchiridion* (1532), c. 31 [Eng. tr., F. L. Battles, John Eck, *Enchiridion of Commonplaces* (Grand Rapids, 1974), p. 210]: "Here the heretics have revived the once extinct heresy of Mani who first indeed denied free will functions actively in good works, because such are wholly and totally done by God; thereupon Luther, having become insane, denied free will completely, because all things happen out of absolute necessity—something once said by the stupid Stoics, Empedocles, Critolaus, Diodorus and other mistaken ones." Commenting on Gen. 4:7 Eck says, "Here God makes free will master. Luther, to the ignominy of the Creator, makes it slave." On Deut. 30:14 Eck says, "Election pertains to free will; the wise man is in agreement."

merits. Cochlaeus, *De libero arbitrio,* I: "For you attack the merits of the saints who are in heaven, nay you close heaven to men on account of the kindling-wood of sin, and bid them stand outside, and wish to defend your utterly crude dogmas against all the blessed souls of the saints in heaven, nay even against all the angels, and against Christ himself." *Ibid.,* "We deny the good works of the justified are unclean and sins. We deny the merits of the saints are nothing good. We deny that our will does not work together with God's grace in good works." *Ibid.,* "That these works were meritorious, scripture testifies in more than one passage." Eck, *Enchiridion* (1532), c. 5 [Eng. tr., Battles,

p. 50]: (1) "It is abundantly shown from the scriptures of both Testaments that faith does not suffice without works, and works are something meritorious for eternal life, on the basis of divine preordination and God's accepting grace." (2) "The righteous man does not sin in all good works." Etc.

Page 4.

ways. Herminjard [3.253n12-13], "To repress the pretended 'sedition' of the Lutherans, Francis I had recourse to the following means: tortures, the solemn procession of 21 January [1535] sentences by default against those persons deferred who had not answered the summons the 28th of the same month, lastly the edict of 29th January, which threatened the concealers of the Lutherans with the same penalties as the Lutherans themselves, if they did not turn them over to justice, and which assigned to the denouncers a fourth of the confiscations. At the conclusion of the procession, the scaffold had devoured six victims."

faith. Thomas Aquinas, *S. Th.*, SS 2.5-8; Gabriel Biel, *Epitome*, 3 Dist 25 q. unica E ff. See also LCC 20.14n7.

Page 5.

suspect. The charges rehearsed here are reminiscent of those laid by the suffragan of the Bishop of Constance before the Greater Senate of Zurich that "certain persons were teaching obnoxious and seditious doctrines . . ." (Zwingli, *Epistle to Erasmus Fabricius*, April 1522 [Eng. tr., SWHZ, p. 12]).

birth. The charge of recent birth or novelty was widely laid against emerging Protestantism by the Romanist spokesmen, not only by polemicists like Eck, but by more moderate Christian humanists like Budé. Bohatec [p. 130] calls attention to several passages in the *De Transitu* where this note is sounded. Budé, *Opera*, 1.171.39-41: "This novelty had a gladsome and attractive appearance, before increasing stubbornness took on a more brazen shamelessness." 173.42-45: "For this reason, writing these and related things with a harsh comment, I testify that I am endeavoring to win over a people wrongheadedly imbued with this doctrine, as well as its shameless and absurd defenders, not perhaps the authors themselves and the undertakings of these new things." 154:30-33: "What, on the other hand, what, I say, if (as these counsels are both wonderful and hidden to mortals) God Almighty is, by this movement, this undertaking of new things, bringing forth the establishment of Christianity and the repair of the ancient discipline?" 174.34-38: "These matters are so averse to the common persuasion that even though the appearance of novelty may make their doubtful points seem gladsome, having a marvellous allure for erring minds or rather birds, still the army was composed of veterans and volunteers that flocked together under the banner of unwonted freedom." See also 182.41-44 and 177.37-43. Calvin turns the charge of novelty against his opponents at p. 200, below.

uncertain. De Castro, *Adv. Haer.*, c. 14 [fol. 29 D,E].

confirmed it. De Castro, *Adv. Haer.*, c. 14 [fol. 29 F].

fathers. De Castro, *Adv. Haer.*, c. 7 [fol. 15 E].

custom. Cf. J. Clichtoveus, *Antilutherus* (1524) [1.12.fol. 24f]. Clichtoveus rests his argument for ecclesiastical custom largely upon excerpts from Gratian, *Decretum*, 1.11 [Friedberg, 1.22-30]. "His tenth reason begins [fol. 24^r.28-30]: 'Of great authority and efficacy in binding [one to observe ecclesiastical constitutions] is the custom of the church and use, observed over a long period of time.'" Augustine, *Epist.*, 86 [Gratian, 1.11.7: Friedberg, 1.25], is quoted; then Clichtoveus comments [fol. 24^r.40-24^v.1]: "But who doubts that violations of God's laws incur a deadly punishment, and lay themselves under eternal condemnation? Therefore transgressors of praiseworthy customs long observed by the church fall under the same condemnation, according to the passage from Augustine just quoted."

church. Cf. Eck, *Enchiridion* (1532), c. 1 [Eng. tr., Battles, p. 10]: "Just as the church is one, so is there unity in the church. I beg of you, moreover, brethren, by the name of our Lord Jesus Christ that all of you say this, and that there not be schisms among you; be perfect in the same mind and the same knowledge. The Lutherans cause new schisms, and fight both among themselves and with others, so that now Carlstadt has broken off, and Egranus, and Luther, and Zwingli, and the Catabaptists. For God is not a God of dissension but of peace, just as I teach in all the churches of the saints."

heard. Eck, *Enchiridion* (1532), c. 1 [Eng. tr., Battles, p. 8]: "Christ is no bigamist: the church of the apostles and ours are one church. Before Luther was born, there was the church which believed the Mass a sacrifice, seven sacraments, etc. She was the bride of Christ. Therefore now let us remain with that same church, and not be joined to the church of the wicked. Christ, because he loves the church his bride, did not leave her; neither for five hundred nor a thousand years; how then would the head desert his body for so long a time?" De Castro, *Adv. Haer.*, c. 14 [fol. 29F].

licentiousness. Clichtoveus, *Antilutherus* (1524), c. 1 [fol. 4.ʳ29-31, 35-38]: "Therefore Luther gives the name of 'Christian freedom' to a laxer license of living without the observance of ecclesiastical constitutions. . . . He calls 'gospel freedom' an unbridled condition of life, with the observance of only those things which the holy gospel clearly contains, and with a repudiation of all the things instituted by the ancient fathers."

novelty. Bohatec, *Budé und Calvin,* p. 130, cites Cochlaeus, *Adversus novam reformationem* (1528/1534) [fol. 3, D. 2-3].

recovery. This is an interesting analogic use of a Roman legal concept, *postliminium.* The right of postliminium [*Dig.*, 8.50; 39.15] has to do with the recovery of something which has been alienated or lost, or with the restoration to his house of one who had been carried off into captivity, or with the return of one thought to be dead. Zwingli had used the analogy in 1522 in his *Supplicatio* ("The Petition of Eleven Priests to be Allowed to Marry") addressed to the Bishop of Constance. The gospel, long hidden "through the ignorance, not to say evil intentions, of certain persons," when God "had determined to recall and renew these teachings in our day as it were by right of postliminium, certain persons attack or defend them" [Eng. tr., SWHZ, p. 26]. Similarly, Calvin appeals to the right of postliminium for the renewal of the ancient teaching so long hidden. Budé, according to Bohatec, *Budé und Calvin,* p. 130, utilizes the term "postliminium." He cites *De Transitu* [Opera, 1.188.4-6; 201.12].

Page 6.

error. Augustine, *John's Gospel,* 13.17 [Eng. tr., NPNF¹ 7.93].

honors. Calvin's marginal note erroneously refers to Jerome in the Preface [of the Commentary on Jeremiah]. The reference is actually to Isidore of Seville, *De ortu et obitu patrum*, 38.74 [PL 83.143].

us. Clichtoveus, *Propugnaculum ecclesiae adv. Lutheranos* (Cologne, 1526), 3.2 [pp. 412f]; de Castro, *Adv. Haer.*, 1.7 fol. 15Cff; Cochlaeus, *De libero arbitrio,* I [fol. B.1. 14-26]: "No wonder then when you reject and despise the old churchmen as well as the recent ones, and all translators of the divine Scriptures, that you everywhere arrogantly despise and most impudently attack the schoolmen and theologians, men who not only by right and public custom, but also of their own will attribute merited honor to the Church Fathers. But you most libellously say, immediately after the Church began, Christian doctrine was overthrown by the Platonic philosophy. In these later times of the church we have embraced Aristotle in place of Christ and Christian discipline has finally degenerated into scholastic nonsense; concerning which you are not sure whether it is more impious rather than stupid." Also see LCC 20.18n12 for summary of Calvin's knowledge of the Fathers.

gold. Cassiodorus, *Institutes*, 1. [PL 70.1112].

Page 7.

fathers. Cf. Calvin, *Comm. Sen. De Clem.* [Eng. tr., Battles-Hugo, p. 361], quoting Cicero, *Paradoxes of the Stoics*, 3.20: "To transgress is to cross over the lines. . . ." Prov. 22:28 is used by Ratramnus of Corbie, *Contra Graecorum Opposita*, 3.1 [PL 121.271], in refutation of the Greeks.

canons. Gratian, *Decretum*, 2.24.3.33 [Friedberg 1.999]. "The princes of Judah have transferred the boundaries, which their fathers placed, when they change truth to falsehood, and preach something other than the Apostles accepted" [Jerome, *Comm. on Hosea*, 2, Hos. 5:10].

cups. Cassiodorus, *Tripartite History*, 11.16 [CSEL 71.651]. See LCC 20.19n15. Cf. Calvin, *Comm. Harm. 4 Bks. Moses.* Ex 25:23 (CTS 2.160n): Acacius, Bishop of Amida.

gold. Ambrose, *On the Duties of the Clergy*, 2.28 [Eng. tr., NPNF² 10.64].

excess. Clichtoveus (Paris, 1526), 1 [fol. 56]. On excessive splendor in churches cf. Calvin, *Inst. Chr. Rel.*, 4.5.17-18 (1543), and *Consilium de Luxu*, OC 10a.205. 36-38 [Eng. tr., *Interp.*, 19.2.194]: "Oh, if poverty were sometime hallowed in churches and in public, people would not be ashamed thereafter to admit it in private."

Christian. Cassiodorus, *Tripartite History*, 1.10 [CSEL 71.29-33]. See also LCC 20.19n17.

Lent. Cf. Clichtoveus, *Propugnaculum* (Cologne, 1526), 3.2 (p. 412f), 3 (pp. 418ff), 22 (pp. 530ff), 33 (pp. 599ff).

thug. Cassiodorus, *Tripartite History*, 8.1 [CSEL 71.455-458].

study. Augustine, *On the Works of Monks*, 14-17 [Eng. tr., NPNF¹ 3.511-513].

Christians. Epiphanius, Epistle to John Bishop of Jerusalem, tr. Jerome, *Letters*, 51.9 [Eng. tr., NPNF² 6.89]; cf. LCC 20.20n20.

rest. Ambrose, *De Abraham*, 1.9.80 [PL 14.472].

word. *Opus imperfectum in Matthaeum*, Hom 11 [PG 56.691.32-41, on Matt. 5:22]: "For if it is sinful and dangerous to transfer hallowed vessels to private uses, as we are taught by Belshazzar who, drinking from hallowed cups, was deposed from the kingdom and from life [Dan. 5:3,30], if therefore it is dangerous thus to transfer these hallowed vessels to private uses, in which is not the true body of Christ, but is contained the mystery of his body—how much more ought we not to yield up the vessels of our body (which God has prepared as a dwelling place for himself) to the devil to do those things which he desires?"

substantial. Cf. p. 104 below. A comparison with the *Institutes* of 1559 will show that this passage was substantially redrafted in 1543 after Calvin's Strasbourg sojourn. See LCC 20.20nn23-24.

other. Gratian, *Decr.*, 3.2.12 [Friedberg, 1.1318]: "The priest ought not to receive the body of Christ without the blood," quoting a supposed letter from Pope Gelasius to Bishops Maioricus and John: "We find that certain persons, taking only a portion of the sacred body, abstain from the cup of consecrated blood. These without doubt (since they are taught to abstain by some sort of superstition) are to receive the sacraments whole or be banned from the whole, for division of one part of the mystery from the other cannot occur without great sacrilege." Cf. *Augsburg Confession*, 2.1 [Eng. tr., Schaff, CC 3.29f]: "Both kinds of the sacrament in the Lord's Supper are given to the laity, because that this custom hath the commandment of the Lord: 'Drink ye all of this' [Matt. 26:27]; where Christ doth manifestly command concerning the cup that all should drink." Melanchthon subsequently cites the above-mentioned passage from Gratian. Calvin discusses withholding the cup from the laity at pp. 113f.

    blood. Cyprian, *Epist.*, 57.2 [Eng. tr., 53.2 ANF 5.337]: "For how do we teach or provoke them to shed their blood in confession of his name, if we deny to those who are about to enter on the warfare the blood of Christ? Or how do we make them fit for the cup of martyrdom, if we do not first admit them to drink, in the Church, the cup of the Lord by the right of communion." *On the Lapsed*, ch. 25 [Eng. tr., ANF 5.444]: "When, however, the solemnities were finished, and the deacon began to offer the cup to those present . . ." Cf. *Augsburg Confession*, 2.1 [Eng. tr., Schaff, CC 3.30]: "Cyprian in certain places doth witness that the blood was given to the people. . . ."

    reason. Council of Constance (1415), Session 13, Definition of communion in both kinds, confirmed by bull of Martin V, *In eminentis* (1418). Mansi, 27.727f, 1215, 1219. Cf. Clichtoveus, *Propugnaculum* (Paris, 1526), 1 [fol. 51].

Page 8.

    fasting. Eusebius, *Ecclesiastical History*, 5.18.

    law. Gratian, *Decr.*, 3.3.9 [Friedberg, 1.1354f]: "It is determined that all the churches should fast by priestly ordination and common decision, except on Sundays, and in Lent even on the Sabbath" [AD 506]. *Ibid.*, 3.3.3 [Friedberg, 1.1353f]: "It is determined that rogations, that is, litanies, are to be celebrated before the Ascension of our Lord, as follows: that the preparatory three-day fast is to be broken on the celebration of Ascension Sunday. By this three-day period man and maid-servants are to leave off work, in order that the whole people may assemble. During the three days all should abstain and use Lenten foods" [AD 511]. *Ibid.*, 3.3.7: "It is not permitted on the fifth day, brethren, of the last week to break the fast, and dishonor the whole of Lent, but rather to go through the whole of Lent abstaining sincerely" [AD 649].

    chastity. Cassiodorus, *Tripartite History*, 2.14 [CSEL 71.106f].

    opinion. Cf. Gratian, *Decr.*, 1.28.15 [AD 343] [Friedberg, 1.105]: "If anyone discerns a married priest and abstains from his oblation because by reason of wedlock he ought not to make offering, let him be anathema."

    limit. On clerical celibacy legislation see LCC 20.22n33.

    commanded. Cyprian, *Epist.*, 63.14 [Eng. tr., 62.14, ANF 5.362]: "There is then no reason, dearest brother, for any one to think that the custom of certain persons is to be followed, who have thought in time past that water alone should be offered in the cup of the Lord. For we must inquire whom they themselves have followed. For if in the sacrifice which Christ offered none is to be followed but Christ, assuredly it behooves us to obey and do that which Christ did, and what he commanded to be done, since he himself says in the gospel, 'If ye do whatsoever I command you, henceforth I call you not servants, but friends' [John 15:12f]. And that Christ alone ought to be heard, the

Father also testifies from heaven, saying: 'This is my well-beloved Son, in whom I am well pleased; hear him' [Matt. 17:5]."

keep it. Cf. for example, Clichtoveus, *Propugnaculum* (Cologne, 1526), 3.4 [pp. 422ff]; de Castro, *Adv. omnes haereses*, 1.5 [fol. 10D].

dialecticians. Tertullian, *On the Prescription of Heretics*, 7 [Eng. tr., LCC 5.35f; ANF 3.246]; Augustine, *Christian Doctrine*, 2.31 [Eng. tr., NPNF¹ 2.550]. Cf. Budé, *De Transitu* (1534/5) [Opera (1557/1966) 1.227], cited by Bohatec, *Budé und Calvin*, p. 70; and see Calvin, *Comm. Sen. De Clem.* [Eng. tr., Battles-Hugo, p.*54].

error. See Calvin, *Consilium de Luxu* [OC 10a.205.26f]: "The vices of individuals breed public error; in turn, public error breeds the vices of individuals." Cf. Seneca, *Epist. Mor.*, 94.54: "It is for this reason that the vices of the people exist in individuals, namely, that the people have imparted them."

evils. Cf. Erasmus, *Adagia*, 1.3.28 [LeClerc ed. 2.122f-23B].

Page 9.

men. Gratian, *Decr.*, 1.8.5 [Friedberg, 1.14]: "If you perchance oppose custom, you must be warned of what the Lord says: 'I am the truth.' He did not say, 'I am custom,' but 'truth.' And surely (as St. Cyprian expresses the idea) any custom, however ancient, however widespread is in every respect to be subordinated to truth, and usage contrary to truth is to be abolished." *Ibid.*, 1.8.9 [Friedberg, 1.15f]: "If Christ alone is to be heard, we ought not to pay attention to what anyone before us thought should be done, but what Christ, who is before all, previously has done. Nor ought we to follow the custom of man, but the truth of God, since God speaks through the prophet Isaiah in these words: 'Those who teach the commandments and doctrines of men are worshiping me without cause.' " Calvin's second marginal citation here seems to apply to *Extravagantes* (John XXII), "De Consuetudine" [Friedberg, 2.1237]. Cf. *Augsburg Confession*, 2.1 [Eng. tr., Schaff, CC 3.30]: "But it is manifest that a custom, brought in contrary to the commandments of God, is not to be approved, as the canons do witness. . . ."

Father. Cf. Bucer, *Enarrationes Perpetuae in Sacra Quatuor Evangelia* (Strasbourg, 1530) [Hereafter cited, following A. Ganoczy, as *EN*, I (Synoptic Gospels) and *EN*, II (Gospel of John)] [fol. 38ʳ.35-36, 40-41]: "For the commonwealth of Christians alone deserves to be called the kingdom of God and heavenly. . . . Truly [Christ] is utterly our sole king, who exercises in all the power of life and death. . . ."

world. On the imperishability of the church, see LCC 20.24n39. Further, *Augsburg Confession*, 1.7 [Eng. tr., Schaff, CC 3.11]: "Also they teach that one holy church is to continue forever."

confined. Cf. Bucer, *EN*, I [fol. 180ᵛ.30-46]: "Now certain ones cite this passage [Matt. 24:24] against the Romanists' and Mohammed's falsehoods, and do so rightly, insofar as Christ here testified that the kingdom of God consists in himself by faith, and is not to be attached in this world to a particular place, and does not know present happiness; yet the latter persons have taught men to seek the kingdom of God in outward things. But no one will be thus rightly saying what has, properly speaking, been set forth here concerning these matters. There are other passages as for example I Thess. 2, I Tim. 2, II Peter 2, dealing with these matters. Nor did the Pope say that he was Christ, that is, the restorer of freedom and all felicity, who would exhibit in the present time what the prophets foretold concerning Melchizedek. Yet Mohammed came closer to this madness. But because the Lord is here testifying that the kingdom here rests in faith, one cannot say of it, lo here, lo there [v. 26]; they infer nothing more definite from this passage than those who oppose to it the physical presence of Christ in the bread. For if the Lord here denies that the true Christ after his departure is to be proved to be in the world in a definite place, but is going to be present rather by the Spirit with the elect everywhere, that he will not return visibly, save with glory everywhere shining, they do not do rightly who wish so to shut up his body itself bodily and physically in bread and say lo here, lo there. Although one would derive some little support also from the argument of those who apply it against the monastic sects and other advocates of ceremonies. The kingdom of God is not connected to a place or to things visible: therefore, it is not in food, clothing, and other elements of the world."

hierarchy. Cf. Eck, *Enchiridion,* c. 3 [Eng. tr., Battles, p. 28ff]. Eck begins his chapter on the Primacy of the Apostolic See: "The supreme authority is within the church, which we observe in councils and in the Apostolic See. It is fitting that we affirm briefly the primacy of the Roman pontiff and of Peter." After quoting a string of scriptural and patristic prooftexts, Eck summarizes seven Protestant arguments against Petrine succession, refutes these; then turns to nineteen arguments against Peter (as founder of the Roman Church) and against the pope as its supreme ruler from postapostolic times, which he in turn refutes at length. He concludes: "Let us all submit to the authority of the church as reflected in the Apostolic See, the See of Rome."

admire. Cf. Bucer, *EN,* I [fol. 197^v.17-19]: "The kingdom of Christ is not of this world, that is, situated in outward dominion; hence its glory is destitute of riches and of outward might, as in the head of Christ, so also in the members. Therefore we must here be the off-scouring of the world, but at last are in regeneration going to reign with Christ."

sacraments. *Augsburg Confession,* 1.7 [Eng. tr., Schaff, CC 3.11f]: "But the church is the congregation of saints in which the gospel is rightly taught and the sacraments rightly administered."

remained. This discussion of Elijah and Micaiah (p. 10) should be compared to that of Zwingli, *Commentary,* 18.6 [Eng. tr., LWZ 3.218.10-17]: "Therefore let no man say, 'Who will put up with this? The whole world thinks differently.' Let him rather reflect that often an entire nation, except a few persons, has been in error, as happened in Noah's time [Gen. 6:17-18]. Elijah [I Kings 18:30] thought himself entirely alone, and Micaiah [I Kings 22:9-28] stood a true prophet against the entire crowd of reckless prophets. The truest is always known by the fewest." Note, however, that Calvin uses the minority argument in a general ecclesiological context while Zwingli applies it to the eucharist; also, Calvin includes Jeremiah and Jesus in his list of minority cases.

left. Cf. Dietrich of Niem's distinction between the universal Church (not capable of being reunified, since she cannot be divided by schism—her preservation in one faithful person being sure) and the Roman Church, which must be reformed and reunited to the Church Universal. See R. Petry, "Unitive Reform Principles of the Late Medieval Conciliarists," *Church History,* 31.2, p. 165.

Page 10.
Baal. Augustine, *De Unitate Ecclesiae,* c. 33 (PL 43.416) [Eng. tr., Giles, *Documents,* no. 167]: "For this reason that part of the people is by no means to be reckoned as having been an heretical sect. For God has ordered those same tribes to separate off, not in order that the faith, but that the Kingdom might be divided, and that in this way punishment might be meted out to the Kingdom of Judah. But God never orders a schism to be formed."

form. Cf. Bucer, *EN*, I [fol. 180ᵛ.30-46] (quoted at p. 9 note above).

courage. Here Calvin made an insertion in 1539 indicating that he had in the meantime read Hilary's *Against Auxentius*.

darkness. Guillaume Farel, *Sommaire et briefve declaration* (1525, republ. 1934) [fol. A.2ʳ], begins his introductory epistle in these words: "In this time when it pleases our Lord to reveal His holy brightness and light upon those who were in very deep darkness, a darkness greater than was felt and experienced in Egypt, there are several who cannot believe they have been in such darkness" (Pannier, 1.28a).

Eugenius. Eugenius IV had convoked the Council of Basel in 1439.

Amadeus. Dated 5 November 1439. Amadeus VIII was pope under the name Felix V.

Page 11.

two. Namely Martin V and Eugenius IV.

unscathed. Dated 7 February 1447.

hat. For a summary of these events, see LCC 20.27n45.

see. Cardinal Julius Cesarini.

imitated. Eck, *Enchiridion*, 6.2 [Eng. tr., Battles, p. 63]; cf. also John Fisher, *Confutatio* (1523), art. 36, p. 609f. Eck quotes the Emperor Basil's remarks at the end of the Eighth Council: "However much of religion and wisdom a lay person may manifest, or even if he may be inwardly endowed with all virtue, so long as he is a layman, he does not cease being called a sheep. This is the reason why, for those of you established in the order of sheep, pastors have the subtlety of discussing words, of seeking and striving after the things which are over us. Therefore we must with fear and sincere faith hear them and revere their faces, since they are ministers of Almighty God, and possess his form, and require nothing more than those things which are of our order. Hence by Christ the people are given leave to do not those things which princes, kings, tetrarchs or nobles might tell them; but 'whatever the scribes and Pharisees sitting on Moses' seat, have told you, this observe and practice' [Matt. 23:3]. But when the heretics seek popular applause, Jeremiah's prediction is fulfilled: 'the prophets prophesy falsely, as the priests applaud with their hands, and my people love such things, but what will happen to them when the end comes?' "

Sardanapalus. See LCC 20.28n47. Calvin in 1546 (*Epist.*, 771, OC 12.295) sarcastically gave Francis I the nickname Sardanapalus.

Page 12.

truth. Cf. Calvin, *Comm. Is.*, 6:10 [OC 36.136].

Catabaptists. It is at this point that Calvin introduces the second thrust of his double theological critique. While no specific section of the *Institutes* deals with the Anabaptists, the author picks up seriatim most of the articles of the *Schleitheim Confession* (1527), the earliest Anabaptist Confession, which is discussed and translated by John C. Wenger, "The Schleitheim Confession of Faith," *Mennonite Quarterly Review*, 19.4.244-253. Huldreich Zwingli, in his *Refutation of Baptist Tricks* (1527) [English translation by Henry Preble in SWHZ (1901)], gives a Latin version of the Confession, interspersing each article with his own refutation, as Calvin himself also later did in his *Brieve Instruction pour armer tous bons fideles contre les erreurs de la secte commune des Anabaptistes* (OC 7.49-142). This latter work is cited in its English translation, *A short instruction for to arme all good Christian people against the pestiferous errors of the common sect of the*

Anabaptistes, published in London by John Daye, 1549 [STC 4463]. For a brief discussion of Calvin's critique of Anabaptist beliefs, arranged according to the chief editorial strata of the *Institutes*, see W. E. Keeney, "An Analysis of Calvin's Treatment of the Anabaptists in the *Institutes*," in Battles, *An Analysis of the Institutes of the Christian Religion* (1972), pp. 74*ff. The following topics are discussed at the pages noted: oaths (pp. 29f), incarnation (pp. 68-72), ban or excommunication (pp. 82f), baptism (p. 135), the office of pastor (p. 227), perfection (pp. 152, 260). In the essay on Civil Government (Chapter 6, part 3, pp. 284ff) is to be found the greatest concentration of Anabaptist references, where separation from the world and the doctrine of the state (in its various ramifications) are discussed. It should be pointed out that Calvin is indebted to Bucer, *EN*, I-II (1530), for many insights concerning the Anabaptists. This dependence could well be the subject of a separate investigation. Bucer likewise alternates between the term "Catabaptists" (e.g., *EN*, I [fol. 75^v.39]) and "Anabaptists" (e.g., *EN*, I [fol. 149^r.37]).

Page 13.

scandals. This hint of the Nicodemite position should be compared with p. 199 below.

virtues. Herminjard [4.22n7] cites the testimonies of good character given by the magistrates of Strasbourg, Basel, and Bern to the French refugees, and calls attention to the letter of instruction dispatched from the Council of Bern to its ambassadors representing the Swiss Protestant cities in France (15 January 1537), no. 604 [Herminjard, 4.169-172].

gospel. As the Anabaptists at Münster had done by setting up their polygamous kingdom in 1534-35 under John of Leyden. See G. H. Williams, *The Radical Reformation* (1962), ch. 13 [pp. 362-386]. Calvin seems to allude to Münster again at pp. 204 and 207f below.

Page 14.

burnings. Cf. Calvin, *Comm. Sen. De Clem.* [Eng. tr., Battles-Hugo, p. 321].

September. On the date given in various editions of the *Institutes*, see LCC 20.31n51. Herminjard [4.23n9] cites three Swiss letters written shortly after the *Institutes* of 1536 came from the press. Marc Berthschi wrote from Basel to Vadian (28 March 1536): "Platter has printed: Julius Pollux, Galen's Works translated by Cornarius . . . Eusebius' *Chronicle*, a full and emended edition of Clement's *Letters*, Oecolampadius' *On Genesis*, Olympiodorus' *On Ecclesiastes*, Cyrus Theodorus' *Greek Poems on the Old Testament*, a certain Frenchman's *Catechism to the King of France*, Erasmus' *On the Purity of the Church* (Ps 15) with several selected letters, Erasmus' *Adagia*, etc." Conrad Pelican writing from Zurich to Vadian says: "You see what John Calvin writes to the King of the French, such open and solid truth that it cannot be despised. What is left but to hope for the best through Christ, and act boldly, recognizing the Lord's help and the hope that many will repent." Johan Jung at Basel in a letter to Ambrose Blaarer at Tübingen (5 August 1536) concludes: "On the 25th day of this month, our friend Mangold, reaching here, promises very soon to send you copies of Calvin."

CHAPTER I: THE LAW

Page 15.

Law. A. Ganoczy, *Le Jeune Calvin* (1966), p. 139, points out that the order and structure of *Institutes*, chs. 1-4, corresponds to that of Luther, *Small Catechism* (1522:

Latin eds., *Enchiridion piarum precationum cum calendrio et passionali;* 1525 [Strasbourg]; 1529 [Wittenberg]: Law, Faith, Prayer, Sacraments). On how Calvin came to know the *Small Catechism,* see W. G. Moore, *La Réforme allemande et la littérature française: Recherches sur la notoriété de Luther en France,* Strasbourg, 1930; P. Wernle, *Der evangelische Glaube nach den Hauptschriften der Reformatoren,* p. 86; cf. pp. 38, 52, 55, 94, 165. In our notes to Luther's *Small Catechism* and to his other catechetical materials for which parallels to Calvin have been adduced, we have generally cited *Enchiridion piarum precationum* in the 1543 Wittenberg edition from the copy in the Case Memorial Library, The Hartford Seminary Foundation, collating it where necessary with the German originals as printed in Weimarer Ausgabe, vols. 2, 10/2, 15, 30/1, and as cited in Barth-Niesel, *Opera Selecta Calvini* [OS], vols. 3-5. Additional parallels have been noted from Ganoczy, and some have been independently supplied.

God. For a strophic translation of pp. 15-18 ("the Kernel of Calvin's Faith"), see F. L. Battles, *The Piety of John Calvin* (1978), pp. 43-49.

doctrine. Cf. Guillaume Budé, *De Transitu,* Praef. [Opera, 1.131.33-37]: "And this is almost the sum of the philosophy which the zeal of the most Christian [king] ought to pursue: this diligent meditation upon the aforesaid dispensation of Christ our Savior, let down like a ladder from heaven for mankind, reaching from the depths to the heights, doubtless so that mortal followers of Him—whoever was not so firmly entangled in earthly bonds—could also mount up by this ladder to heaven."

ourselves. This key sentence of the *Institutes,* revised in the 1539 and subsequent editions to read, "Nearly all the wisdom we possess, that is.to say, true and sound wisdom, consists of two parts: the knowledge of God and of ourselves," has been compared with a number of earlier statements. For example, Clement of Alexandria, *Instructor,* 3.1 [Eng. tr., ANF 2.271] has the phrase: "If one knows himself, he will know God." Zwingli in his *Commentary on True and False Religion,* 2 [Eng. tr., LWZ 3.58.15-16] states: ". . . religion cannot be discussed rightly unless before all else you acknowledge [*agnoveris*] God and recognize [*cognoveris*] man." J. Bohatec, *Budé und Calvin* (1950), states that Calvin has undoubtedly taken this phrase from Guillaume Budé [p. 31, n.47] and discusses it at length [pp. 241ff]. See *De Transitu,* I [Opera, 1.239.5f]: "God willing that by every sort of teaching we be instructed in the knowledge of himself and of ourselves." One should, however, point out a very clear parallel to the phrase in Bucer, *EN,* I [fol. 66ᵛ.25-28], from a longer passage extensively used by Calvin in Chapter 3, "Prayer." Bucer says: ". . . if we know God and ourselves, we will ascribe to God glory in all things, but to ourselves confusion; all things in us insofar as they are of God are just and holy; but insofar as they are of us, we shall both acknowledge and confess them to be sin and iniquity."

Page 16.

conscience. To the long note on natural law in LCC 20.367n5 [*Inst.,* 2.8.1, 1559] (which includes, *inter alia,* John T. McNeill's important article, "Natural Law in the Teaching of the Reformers," *Journal of Religion* 26 (1946): 168-182) should be added Arthur C. Cochrane, "A New Approach to the Problem of Natural Law in Calvin," in *Church-State Relations in Ecumenical Perspective* (1966), pp. 176-217. In an unpublished Ph.D. dissertation by I. John Hesselink, entitled *Calvin's Concept of the Law,* chap. 2, "God's Witness in Creation and Nature," the voluminous literature on Calvin and natural law is skillfully and usefully reviewed. Especially to be noted is Hesselink's discussion of the continuity (McNeill) of the Reformers' (and Calvin's) natural law teaching with that of the scholastics, or its discontinuity (Karl Holl), for which see pp. 19ff. See also p. 216, below.

Page 19.

ourselves. Melanchthon, *Loci Communes* (1521), 4 [Eng. tr., LCC 19.55]: "You see, then, that the three commandments, that God must be trusted, that God must be praised, and that this work in us must be permitted, are comprehended in the one sentence: 'Love God with all your heart,' etc."

Egypt. Rom. 5:14; Rev. 11:8.

me. For most of the commandments Calvin uses an introductory formula similar to Luther's. Calvin says: "It is necessary that God be feared and loved by us"; Luther's expression is: "We ought to fear and love God." See Luther, *Enchiridion* (1543 ed.) [fol. 1.4^r-6^r]. Luther's familiar division of the exposition of each commandment into two parts—into what it forbids and what, by inference, it positively teaches, linked by an adversative conjunction—may be seen in Calvin's handling of the commandments. However, the two authors differ in their numbering and division of the commandments. Luther following medieval practice suppresses the commandment against making a graven image of God (Calvin, No. 2), then divides the last commandment into two. Luther includes three commandments in the first table, seven in the second; Calvin divides them four and six.

Page 20.

figure. Zwingli, *Commentary,* 29 [Eng. tr., LWZ 3.332.37f]: ". . . we worship God, who is invisible and forbids us to express him in any visible figure. . . . When therefore they say Christ can be expressed as God, they deceive themselves. . . ."

physical. Ganoczy, p. 158, n.140, glosses the words *carnale* and *carnaliter* as Zwinglian epithets but cites no reference.

religion. The short section here devoted to the Second Commandment, much enlarged in later editions of the *Institutes,* and distributed between 1.11 and 2.8 [1559] shows in the last edition Calvin's subsequent study. His fuller knowledge of the Iconoclastic Controversy (in 1536 reflected in his critique of conciliar infallibility—Constantinople AD 754 vs. Nicea II AD 787—at pp. 196f below) and of the "Caroline Books" is reflected in his final Latin edition. An English translation of the remains of the Iconoclastic Council of 754, set in contrast to the acts of Nicea II, has been prepared by F. L. Battles and Daniel Sahas. Calvin's later fuller treatment of the question indicates his subsequent reading in the Catholic controversialists on this.

gods. John Eck, *De non tollendis . . . imaginibus* [*Opp. Eckii,* II, fol. R 7^v]. See also Eck, *Enchiridion* (1532), c. 16 [fol. G.5^v]: ". . . they are to refer their veneration not to the image itself, but (as Basil teaches) to the prototype. . . ." Zwingli, *Commentary,* 29 [Eng. tr., LWZ 3.332.15-24]: "But contentiousness again objects that not the images are worshiped, but those whose images they are. I answer that neither were any of the heathen ever so stupid as to worship their images of stone, bronze, and wood for what they were in themselves; they reverenced in these their Joves and Apollos. Hence, although the Holy Scriptures frequently mock at the worship of images, as if the worshipers worshiped wood and stone, yet everybody knew that they did not in the least regard these things, but in them those rather whom they regarded as gods."

Page 21.
likenesses of God. Zwingli, *Commentary,* 29 [Eng. tr., LWZ 3.332.15-24].
evasion. Zwingli, *Commentary* [Eng. tr., LWZ 3.331.30-34; 331.39-332.3]: "And when some people say that man is taught by the images, and influenced to piety, this is an idea of their own. For Christ nowhere taught this method of teaching, and he certainly would not have omitted it if he had foreseen that it would be profitable. . . . We ought to be taught by the word of God externally, and by the Spirit internally, those things that have to do with piety, and not by sculpture wrought by the artist's hand." Cf. *Ibid.,* 3.336, and CR Zw 3.904n3, where Heinrich Lüty at the Second Zurich Disputation (26-28 October 1523) objects that "Pope Gregory called images 'the books of the laity.' " See also CR Zw 2.698.6f; 721.9ff; 3.169.16ff. Also: Kidd, Documents, no. 197; and Calvin, Sermon 115 on Deut. 19:16-21 (1555) [OC 27.579]: ". . . car il a semblé à ces bestes—la que c'estoyent livres des idiots (comme ils appellent) que les images. . . ."
uneducated. This allusion to Gregory the Great, *Epist.,* 9.105; 11.13, is made explicit by Calvin in eds. 1539ff.

Page 22.
evil one. The Anabaptists in the *Schleitheim Confession* (1527), art. 7, rejected all oaths on the grounds of Jesus' teaching in Matt. 5:33-37. Recognizing that such wholesale condemnation of oaths would subvert all government, Zwingli combatted this teaching point by point in his *Refutation of Baptist Tricks.* The key to Zwingli's position is in these words: ". . . you wish to destroy the magistracy and the power of which it consists. Take away the oath and you have dissolved all order" [SWHZ, p. 208]. Calvin, in his *Brieve Instruction* (1544), deals with the oath at fol. E.vii^r-F.viii [Eng. tr.].
prohibition. This view, reflecting the opinions of Zwingli expressed in his *Refutation of Baptist Tricks* [Eng. tr., SWHZ pp. 212f], asserts that Jesus in Matt. 5:33 is speaking against idle oath-taking in daily private conversation, not about the official oath or forum or court or magistracy, which is excepted from this prohibition. Calvin rejected this view in his 1539 edition of the *Institutes* and in all subsequent editions.

Page 23.
Holy Spirit. Melanchthon, *LC* (1521), 4 [Eng. tr., Hill, p. 120; cf. LCC 19.55]: "The third [=fourth] precept orders us to sanctify the Sabbath, to cease from our work, that is to suffer and to bear the work of God in us, which is our mortification. . . . The third [precept demands] the tolerance of the works of God in us. They who teach work-righteousness and the power of free will especially violate this precept. For it demands the mortification of free will. And when the people of the New Testament have a perpetual sabbath, it means that people whose flesh is zealously mortified and whose spirit is quickened."
conscience. Eph. 3:14-19; I Cor. 3:16; John 14:26; Rom. 8:14.
Scripture. Gregory the Great, *Moralia,* 35.8.15-17 [PL 76.757ff].

Page 24.
day. On the preceding, cf. Bucer, *EN* (1530), I [fol. 118^v.38-42]: "For because in the Sabbath commandment one is repeatedly reminded that God also rested on the seventh day, it seems to have been done to this end, that by the Sabbath day they might be mindful that the Lord has indeed done all things in order that they may be more and

more kindled to fear and love him and have faith in him, but at the same time may nevertheless learn to conquer all those things and rest from them, as the Epistle to the Hebrews [4:9-10] teaches that it is much more desirable, even as the Lord himself, to cease from tasks as yet to be accomplished."

sacraments. Cf. Bucer, *EN*, I [fol. 118ᵛ.24-26]: "Hence up to the time of the apostles, the custom persisted that on each Sabbath, the law and the prophets were to be read in the church, as is clear from Acts 13 and 15." *EN*, I [fol. 119ʳ.19-27]: "Now if to the end I have already mentioned, the Lord's day is to be celebrated and the notion of necessity removed from men's hearts (lest anyone believe either that that day is of itself holier than other days or in it sin is of itself active) and from our conduct is then to be banished that intemperance of life and luxury which in former times rendered Christian festivals more than disgraceful—I do not see what loss could come to godliness, rather I see a fruitful result, if on one day in seven, we especially take the time and effort thus publicly to hear the Word of God, to recall the Lord's benefits, to celebrate the Eucharist, to have prayers for the magistrate, and collections for the poor, to establish home and family in godliness, to admonish friends, to visit the infirm, and to do other deeds characteristic of Christians."

week. Cf. Albertus Magnus, *Compendium theologiae veritatis*, 5.62 [*Opera Omnia*, Paris (1895), 34.194f]: "In this precept there is something moral as the freeing [from labor] which is for praying, worshiping and meditating Godward; something ceremonial, as the appointing [*assignatio*] of the seventh day, which figured topically [*topice*] cessation from sin; allegorically, the repose of Christ's body in the tomb; anagogically, the everlasting rest in heaven. This precept therefore can be understood in three ways. First, generally, that we cease from vices. Secondly, specially, that we cease from physical labor, which hinders freeing us toward God. Thirdly, most especially, that is in contemplative men, who separate themselves from all earthly things, to free themselves totally for God." Also, Thomas Aquinas, *S. Th.*, PS 100.3.2; SS 122.4.1.

measure. Cassiodorus, *Tripartite History*, 9.38.

Page 25.

us. Peter Lombard, *Sent.*, 3.37.2 [p. 717.9f]: "The second precept is 'You will not take the name of your God in vain. . . .' " "The third is: 'Remember that you keep holy the day of Sabbath . . .' " [p. 717.14]. Cf. Thomas Aquinas, *S. Th.*, PT 100.4. Both Luther and Melanchthon omit the prohibition of image-making, thus reckoning, "You shall not take the name of your God in vain" (Third Commandment) as the Second Commandment. The number ten is restored by dividing the Tenth Commandment into "You shall not covet your neighbor's house" as the Ninth and "You shall not covet your neighbor's wife," etc., as the Tenth. See Luther, *Small Catechism*, Part I [Eng. tr., Schaff, CC 3.74, 76]; cf. also his *Enchiridion* (1543 ed.) [fol. A.4ʳ]. Also, Melanchthon, *LC* (1521), 4 [Eng. tr., LCC 19.54-57].

ours. Origen, *Hom. in Exod.*, Hom. 8.3 [GCS 29.221].

all. Augustine, *Against Two Letters of the Pelagians*, 3.4.10 [Eng. tr., NPNF¹ 5.406].

better. Augustine, *Questions on the Heptateuch*, 2.71 [PL 34.621.9-11]; cf. *Sermon*, 9.6.7 [PL 38.80.48-49]; *Sermon*, 33.3.3 [PL 38.208]; *Epist.*, 55.11.20 [Eng. tr., FC, 12.276f].

Page 26.

ordinance. Judocus Clichtoveus, *Propugnaculum* (Cologne, 1526), 2.25 [pp. 341ff]; Eck, *Enchiridion* (1532), c. 19 [Eng. tr., Battles, p. 147]: "If you look to nature, many other things are impossible for us; if you look to God's assisting grace, nothing is impossible, because those to whom it is given can receive. Therefore the wise man says: 'I know that I cannot otherwise be continent, unless God grant it; and this itself was wisdom: to know of whom the gift comes' [Wisd. 8:21]. The heretic brings us a fine sort of conquering the temptations of the flesh: so that we thus obey the desires of the flesh contrary to all scripture."

us. Cf. Luther, *Small Catechism*, I, 8th Comm. [Eng. tr., Schaff, CC 3.76, alt.]: "What does this mean? Answer: We ought so to fear and love God as not to entangle our neighbor in falsehoods, betray or slander him, nor do him any infamy, but we should excuse him, speak well of him, putting the best interpretation on everything [he does]." Cf. also Luther, *Enchiridion* (1543 ed.) [fol. 1ᵛ].

Page 27.

authority. Cf. p. 220 below on prayers for persons in authority.

Page 28.

love. Cf. Melanchthon, *LC* (1521), 4 [Eng. tr., LCC 19.56f]; see also A. Lang, "The Sources of Calvin's Institutes of 1536," *Ev.Q.*, Apr. 1936, p. 136. Melanchthon assigns the first portion of Jesus' summary of the law [Mark 12:30a] to the First Table (Commandments 1-3; Calvin's 1-4); the second (Mark 12:30b) he assigns to the Second Table (Commandments 4-10; Calvin's 5-10).

Page 29.

love. Augustine, *Christian Doctrine*, 1.23.22-26.27 [Eng. tr., NPNF¹ 2.528f].

can. Cf. Luther, *Enchiridion* (1543 ed.) [fol. B.4ᵛ]: "You will satisfy the last two commandments, if you everywhere promote your neighbor's welfare, nor ever for your own welfare's sake do injury to him or cause him trouble."

advantage. Cf. Luther, *Enchiridion* [fol. B.5ʳ⁻ᵛ]: "Therefore that man lives most uprightly who lives least for himself; conversely, no one lives a worse life than he who lives for himself. For the Decalogue requires something quite different."

obedience. Cf. Melanchthon, *LC* (1521), 5 [Eng. tr., LCC 19.77]: "They give over their hands, feet, and head to the law, but their heart they keep back."

spiritual. Cf. Melanchthon, *LC* (1521), 5 [Eng. tr., LCC 19.80]: "The law is spiritual, that is, it demands spiritual things. . . ."

law. Calvin's interpretation of the law, through the Sermon on the Mount, is one of inner intention, not external observance—a teaching that is fully elaborated in the edition of 1559 and that here bears a close resemblance to Melanchthon, *LC* (1521), 4 [Eng. tr., LCC 19.56]: "Secondly, the Sophists are under an illusion because they think that both these and other commandments can be fulfilled in our own strength. For they think that we are enjoined only in regard to outward acts that we not worship false gods, idols, etc., with external ceremonies and forms." Melanchthon then refers to Matt. ch. 5. He continues: "The apostle enumerates almost innumerable laws of love in Rom. ch. 12. But these also the Sophists have explained as dealing only with external acts, saying that the law is fulfilled if you do not commit murder, if you are not openly an adulterer, etc."

notion. Cf. *LC*, 5 [Eng. tr., LCC 19.74]: "We have called special attention to these matters in order that we might root out that common error which the godless Sophist professors of theology have spread abroad on the differences between law and gospel, and the Old Testament and the New. They say that Christ has become successor of Moses and has given a new law, and that this new law is called the gospel; it is found, they say, in Matt. chs. 5 to 6. For them the difference between the law of Moses and the law of Christ is that the former demands external works only, whereas Christ's law makes demands on the inner man also. As if Moses' law teaches some kind of hypocrisy and Pharisaical righteousness! For what else is this pretense of outward works than Pharisaism?"

Page 30.
obey. Cf. Thomas Aquinas, *S. Th.*, PS 108.4; Melanchthon, *LC* (1521), 4 [Eng. tr., LCC 19.57-59]: "In this realm too the Sophists have erred shamefully and godlessly, for they have made 'counsels' from divine law. That is, they have taught that certain things are not necessarily demanded by God, but only recommended, so that if anyone cares to, he may obey, and they absolve the one who does not obey. For the most part, they derive the counsels from Matt. ch. 5 . . . ," etc.

'counsels.' Cf. Thomas Aquinas, *S. Th.*, PS 108.4; *Determinatio Theologica facultatis Parisiensis, super doctrina Lutherana, hactenus per eam via* (1521) [CR Melanch., 1.382]. The Sorbonne thus summarized Luther's teaching on this point: "That word of Christ [Matt. 5:39], 'He who strikes you on the right cheek,' etc., and the passage in Romans [12:19], 'Not avenging yourselves, beloved,' etc., are not counsels, as many theologians seem erroneously to teach, but a command." Their refutation: "This proposition is false, excessively burdensome to Christian law and adverse to a sound understanding of scripture."

will. Augustine, *Conf.*, 10.29.40; 31.45 [Eng. tr., LCC 7.225, 228].

hearts. Cf. Melanchthon, *LC* (1521), 8 [Eng. tr., LCC 19.123]: "Those who have been renewed by the Spirit of Christ now conform voluntarily even without the law to what the law used to command. The law is the will of God; the Holy Spirit is nothing else than the living will of God and its being in action." Melanchthon then cites Augustine, *The Spirit and the Letter,* and quotes Jeremiah 31:31-34. Cf. p. 179, below.

Page 31.
dishonor. Cf. Melanchthon, *LC* (1521), 8 [Eng. tr., LCC 19.132]: "The Apostle Paul says in Phil. 3:8 that he considers as loss and dung all the righteousness which the efforts of his nature had produced in his law-dominated period."

Page 33.
law. Jacob Latomus, *De fide et operibus* [Opera, Louvain, 1550, fol. 135^r ff]; cf. II Clem. ch. 8.

Page 34.
gifts. Augustine, *Serm.*, 174.2.2 [PL 38.941.40-42].

Page 35.
sanctified. Cf. Melanchthon, *LC* (1521), 6 [Eng. tr., LCC 19.88]: "The gift is the Holy Spirit himself, whom he pours into the hearts of those on whom he has mercy. . . . The Holy Spirit is the gift that regenerates and sanctifies hearts. . . ."

alone. Cf. Bucer, *EN*, I [fol. 49ʳ.49-51]: "For he has added, 'but . . . in spirit and in truth,' that is, with a mind truly trusting in God and through love of neighbor and mortification of his own flesh, and declaring the proclamation of the Lord's glory, he truly and diligently magnifies God and truly worships Him as God."

are. Cf. Luther, *The Freedom of a Christian* [Eng. tr., LW 31.348]: "Although the commandments teach things that are good, the things taught are not done as soon as they are taught, for the commandments show us what we ought to do but do not give us the power to do it. They are intended to teach man to know himself, that through them he may recognize his inability to do good and may despair of his own ability. . . . For example, the commandment, 'You shall not covet' [Ex. 20.17], is a command which proves us all to be sinners, for no one can avoid coveting no matter how much he may struggle against it. Therefore, in order not to covet and to fulfil the commandment, a man is compelled to despair of himself, to seek the help which he does not find in himself elsewhere and from someone else. . . ." In his *Loci Communes* of 1521, Melanchthon posits two uses [*officia*] of the law; in the edition of 1535 there are three uses. However, he does hint in 1521 at the third or pedagogical Calvinian use. See *LC* (1521), 7 [Eng. tr., LCC 19.117f]: ". . . it is not the function of the law to justify. But the proper function of the law is to reveal sin and especially to confound the conscience." See also *Ibid.*, 5 [Eng. tr., LCC 19.77ff]. For Melanchthon's later tripartite scheme, see *LC* (1535) [Stupperich/Engelland, 2/1, p. 322 n.33]: "The first office of the law is civil, namely, to constrain all men by a certain discipline. . . . The second, the proper and chief office of divine law is to show sins, accuse, strike terror and condemn conscience. . . . The third office of the law in those who are just by faith, is to teach them concerning good works, which ones please God and to bid certain works in which they exercise obedience toward God." Zwingli, in his *Exposition of the Christian Faith*, 9 [Eng. tr., LCC 24.273], approaches Calvin's three uses in the following reason for preaching law and grace together: "For in the law the elect and believers learn the will of God, the ungodly are terror-struck, so that they either do something on behalf of neighbor out of fear, or show their own despair and treachery." Calvin's three uses of the law correspond more or less to the threefold use of punishment which he expounds from classical sources (Plato and Aulus Gellius) in his *Commentary on Seneca's De Clementia* (1532) [Eng. tr., Battles-Hugo, p. 125]. Also compare the three uses of church discipline at p. 61. I. John Hesselink, *Calvin's Concept and Use of the Law* (1961), chap. V, "The End and Use of the Law," reviews the vexed question of Luther, Melanchthon, and Calvin on the uses of the law, with a full sifting both of the sources and of contemporary interpreters. Especially valuable is his scrutiny of pertinent passages in Calvin's commentaries on this topic.

Then. Cf. Christian motives for using the law courts at pp. 218-219, below.

Page 36.

confusion. Cf. pp. 208f, below.

sight. Melanchthon does hint in his first edition of the *Loci Communes* (1521) at a third use of the law as the following two extracts show: 8 [Eng. tr., LCC 19.126]: "The reason why the saints keep the Decalogue is that it does not demand definite distinction of places and times, persons and things, beyond the righteousness of the heart, and also because the Spirit is actually the righteousness of the heart. Now that the law has been abrogated, the Decalogue cannot but be fulfilled." And further [p. 127]: "The Spirit of God cannot be in the human heart without fulfilling the Decalogue. The Decalogue is therefore observed by necessity. . . . The Decalogue contains mostly negative laws. This is in order that it may be clear that no definite work, circumscribed by persons, places or times is required, but rather the righteousness of the heart."

abrogated. That Calvin may have in mind here Melanchthon's remarks on the abrogation of the law is suggested by the following extracts from the *Loci Communes* (1521), 8 [Eng. tr., LCC 19.121]: "That part of the law called the Decalogue or the moral commandments has been abrogated by the New Testament." *Ibid.* [p. 122]: ". . . the Word of God, the law, preached before on Mount Zion . . . is abrogated by the new preaching, now that the message concerning his Son Christ is begun. If nothing is preached but that Christ is the Son of God, it follows that the righteousness of the law, or works, are not demanded, nor is anything else; and all that is commanded is that we embrace the Son." *Ibid.* [p. 124]: "You know now to what extent we are free from the Decalogue. We are free first because although we are sinners, it cannot condemn those who are in Christ. Secondly, those who are in Christ are led by the Spirit to do the law and they really act by the Spirit." *Ibid.* [p. 126]: ". . . there is one and the same reason why the entire law has been abrogated, not only ceremonial laws and judicial codes, but the Decalogue as well: it could not be fulfilled. . . . It has been abrogated, however, only in the case of those who have believed in the later covenant, namely the gospel. And so those in whom Christ's Spirit dwells are entirely free from all law." *Ibid.* [p. 127]: "I am content to point out that the Decalogue has been abrogated, not in order that it not be kept, but that it not condemn if we fail in anything; then too it has been abrogated that it may be kept. So this freedom is the freedom of a conscience which perceives by faith that sin is forgiven." *Ibid.* [p. 128]: "Scripture so discusses the abrogation of the law that everywhere in the discussion it commends the fullness of grace. It so abolishes ceremonies that it becomes evident that all law has been abrogated. It so rejects ceremonies that it is clear that because the Decalogue has been abrogated, ceremonies are done away with." Etc. With these references from Melanchthon should be placed also Zwingli's statement from his *Comm. on True and False Religion* (1525), 10 [Eng. tr., LWZ 3.141.18-21]: "A second kind of freedom from the law is that the law cannot condemn any more, which yet before wrought the wrath and indignation and just vengeance of God." Cf. p. 176, below.

Page 37.

follow him. This is the foundation of *Inst.*, 3.6-10, "The Short Treatise on The Christian Life," added in 1539.

Page 38.

fruits. Cf. Melanchthon, *LC* (1521), 7 [Eng. tr., LCC 19.109]: "Now, we must also consider that works as fruits of the Spirit are marks, testimonies, and signs of his presence. For Christ says in Matt. 7:20: 'You will know them by their fruits.' "

accord. Cochlaeus, *Philipp.*, 3.21.15 (17), 20, 62. Eck, *Enchiridion* (1532), c. 5 [Eng. tr., Battles, p. 55]: "Therefore sinners ought to be advised that without delay they carry out whatsoever their hand can do; they are not to turn aside or draw back from good works (something the Lutherans, haters of all good, do) and especially that they exercise works of piety not toward apostate monks and nuns fornicating and committing adultery under the honest title of marriage, but toward the true Catholic poor, according to the principle: 'Give to the merciful, and do not support the sinner; benefit the humble and give not to the impious' [Ecclus. 12]. . . . The whole error of the Lutherans concerning good works proceeds from ignorance of this distinction made in, and founded upon, the sacred scriptures."

do. Cf. Peter Lombard, *Sent.*, 2.27.8 [pp. 448f]: "Good will [*voluntas*] itself is both gift of God and merit of man, nay, of grace, because it is chiefly of grace, and is grace. Hence, Augustine [*Epist.*, 194.5.19, PL 33.880]: 'What is merit of man before grace, when all our good merit does not work in us save by grace?' For from grace as has been stated, which goes before and heals the will [*arbitrium*] of man, and from the will itself a good affection or good emotion of the mind is engendered in the soul; and this is the first good merit of man. Likewise on account of the word, from faith, virtue and man's will [*arbitrio*] is born in the mind a certain good and rewardable emotion, namely, that it believes, thus from love and free will [*arbitrio*] another very good emotion comes forth, namely to love; so should be understood concerning the remaining virtues. And these good emotions or affections are merits and gifts of God, by which we merit both the increase of them and others which consequently are added to us here and in the future."

Page 39.

sins. Cochlaeus, *Philipp.*, 3.21.

dung. Cf. Bonaventura, *In Sent.*, 4.15 [Quaracchi ed. min., 4.332ff]; Thomas Aquinas, *S. Th.*, PTS 12-15.

error. Cf. J. Faber *De fide et operibus*, c. 23, 25 [Opera, 3, fol. 103^v f].

Page 40.

well-doing. In the editions of 1539ff, a reference is here added to John Chrysostom, *Hom. in Gen.*, 26.5,6 [PG 53.235-9]. With the edition of 1539 of Calvin's *Institutes*, John Chrysostom was to assume a position next to that of Augustine in the patristic foundations of Calvin's thought. Luchesius Smits has shown the Augustinian ground in his study, *Saint Augustin dans l'oeuvre de Jean Calvin* (1957-58). John R. Walchenbach in an unpublished doctoral dissertation (U. of Pittsburgh, 1974), *John Calvin as Biblical Commentator: An Investigation into Calvin's Use of John Chrysostom as an Exegetical Tutor*, has demonstrated the growing importance of Chrysostom for Calvin in Scriptural exegesis. See also Calvin, *Preface to the Homilies of Chrysostom* [OC 9.831-838; Eng. tr., J. H. McIndoe, *Hartford Q.*, 5 (1965) 19-26].

Page 41.

slanders. See John Chrysostom, *Hom. in Matth.*, Hom. 24.3 (on Matt. 7:21) [Eng. tr., NPNF[1] 10.169].

recompense. Cf. Calvin-Cop, *Rectorial Address* (1533) [OS 1.6f; Eng. tr., App. III, below]: "Who would otherwise understand eternal life as a 'payment'? Who could be so senseless as to think and assert that eternal life is a repayment for other good deeds or that our good deeds are worthy of eternal life?" Etc.

CHAPTER II: FAITH

Page 42.

Faith. Max Dominicé In J. Pannier's edition of the *Institutes* of 1541, 2.369, summarizes previous literature contributory to Calvin's chapter, or at least reflecting the earliest Protestant materials in the French language. Luther's *Betbüchlein* (1522), first translated into Latin probably by Louis de Berquin (Strasbourg, 1525) as *Enchiridion precationum aliquot et piarum meditationum*. As A. Ganoczy shows, and as is set forth in our notes (employing the Wittenberg edition of 1543 since the 1525 and 1529 editions are unavailable), Calvin used several parts of this miscellany (including the section on the Creed in Luther's Catechism) in compiling the present chapter. Erasmus' *Symbolum Apostolorum* was translated into French by Berquin in 1533, a work censured by the Sorbonne in 1536. An English translation of the French title would read: *The Creed of the Apostles commonly called the "Credo," containing the articles of faith, in question and answer form*. Farel's *Sommaire* (1525, repr. 1934) discussed faith at ch. 11. François Lambert of Avignon's *Somme Chrestienne* (1529) dealt with faith at ch. 18: "Faith and its Fruits." Dominicé thinks Calvin read Farel but probably not Lambert. A comparison, however, with Farel's brief note on faith will disclose only a general concord. Farel states [fol. C.2.ᵛ-C.3ᵛ]: "Faith is a great and singular gift of God by which we are made children of God. It is a true feeling, experience and knowledge of God our Father, who is good, perfect, powerful and wise, and who for the love of his own has chosen us to be his children, saved and redeemed us by our Savior Jesus. Hence, doubt nothing of the holy promises of God, nor of what he has spoken by his own children, full of the Holy Spirit, but strengthened and confirmed by the word of him who cannot lie against all judgment, against all experience, against all human understanding. Judge and hold firmly what God has said and assured by unchangeable truth and illumined by true clarity, fear nothing. And without any doubt hold firm. And that which faith believes, it embraces through its sacred promises, being powerfully armed against all enemies, over whom it brings back victory. For nothing is impossible to it. Everything it requests, it obtains, and cannot fail—provided it is and goes by the word of God. And everything not in this faith, that is to say, according to the knowledge of the word, is sin. Faith cannot draw one to another than God; cannot maintain itself save in God; nothing pleases it save God and his voice. And insofar as it rests in him alone, it cannot be confounded, but perfectly obtains what it believes and hopes for." Actually, in addition to Luther, Melanchthon's *Loci Communes* (1521) and Bucer's *Enarrationes* (1530) were far more explicitly formative for Calvin here. Negatively, Calvin seems already at this early stage to be refuting Servetus' views as expressed in the latter's two earliest treatises.

faith. On explicit/implicit faith, cf. note to p. 4, "faith," above. Cf. also Biel, *Epitome et collectorium ex Occamo circa quatuor sententiarum Libros* [ed. Tübingen 1501/1965, fol. L.4ᵛ]. Biel's discussion, in part, is as follows: ". . . faith is twofold: explicit and implicit. According to this, one truth is explicitly believed, another implicitly. Explicit faith is actual assent to catholic truth whether universal or particular: thus whoever grasps some catholic truth and assents to it has explicit faith in that truth, as assent to this: all revelation from God is true; the canon of the Bible is true; Christ fed five thousand with five loaves and two fishes. Implicit faith is habitual faith or actual assent to any general proposition comprising in itself many particular truths. For a universal or general proposition is said to include all those particular ones which can be inferred in reasonable consequence immediately or mediately with respect to the truth assumed together with it. Here is an example of implicit faith: assent to this, that everything contained in the canonical Scriptures is true. Not only faith in everything contained in Scripture, etc., but faith in all particular truths contained in the canon, as for example: in the beginning God created heaven and earth; Adam was cast out of paradise; Christ supped with his disciples, etc." Melanchthon posits these two kinds of faith in *LC* (1521), 7. As Ganoczy points out [p. 153, nn.96, 98], Melanchthon in his *LC* (1521) excoriates at length the first sort of faith. [Eng. tr., LCC 19.89]: "It is well known that the common run of Sophists define faith as the assent to what is set forth in Scripture; therefore they say that even the godless have faith." *Ibid.* [p. 93]: "Scholastic faith is nothing but a dead opinion." *Ibid.* [p. 98]: "This faith [i.e., true faith] is no frigid opinion. . . ." *Ibid.* [p. 99]: "Therefore, when the author of Hebrews attributes faith to Abel and not to Cain, he does not mean some historical opinion, but faith which glorifies God, thinks well of God, trusts in the dvine mercy, etc." *Ibid.* [p. 100]: "For the ungodly do not believe, but hold to a frigid opinion but not from the bottom of the heart. . . . Likewise, the 'faith' of the Sophists is nothing but sheer pretense, a mere mockery of souls, and yet the impious and godless Sophists teach that this feigned faith of theirs can qualify as a good work." *Ibid.* [p. 112]: "Therefore the whole point that James is making is that dead faith, that frigid 'opinion' of the Parisian theologians, does not justify, but a living faith justifies." See also Luther, *Enchiridion* (1543 ed.) [fol. B.6^r]: ". . . there is a twofold reckoning of believing. The first is when I believe God exists and sense to be true what is reported about him, just as I sense to be true what is narrated concerning the Turks, the devil, or hell. This ought to be called a rather obscure knowledge or opinion rather than faith. The other sort of believing is when I believe in God, that is, when I not only believe the things said about him are true, but lodge in him all trust and hope, and so confirm my heart that I doubt not concerning his good will toward me."

Page 43.

conviction. Cf. Bucer, *Metaphr. Rom.* (1536) [fol. 14^v, 22^r], where he defines *fides* as a "*persuasio* of the mercy of God toward us." See Seeberg, *Lehrbuch der Dogmengeschichte*, 4th ed., 4.2, p. 552; Eng. tr., C. Hay, 2, p. 392. Seeberg, in the amplified first edition of his work represented by the English translation, notes on p. 402 (vol. 2): "The term *persuasio* (conviction) is characteristic of Calvin's exposition of faith—and was so from the beginning. . . . It appears to have been derived from Bucer." This note is omitted in the latest German edition.

certain. Bucer, *EN*, I (on Matthew ch. 8) [fol. 87^{r-v}], discusses faith, using among other passages Rom. 4:18, Hab. 2:4 and Heb. 11:1. His definition [fol. 87^v.7-11] is reminiscent of the famous Calvinian definition, here hinted at, but fully elaborated at *Inst.*, 3.2.7 (1559). Bucer's words are "This truly divine virtue in Hebrew called אמובה, in Greek πίστος, we call 'persuasion' [or 'conviction'], in common language, 'faith.' For it is a constant and firm conviction of the heart through the Holy Spirit of God's goodness and promises, whereby as it holds a sure faith of His words, so it undoubtingly promises itself all things from his goodness toward itself, then most zealously endeavors by deserving well of all persons both to gratify itself and make recompense." See also Luther, *Enchiridion* (1543 ed.) [fol. B.6^r]: "And that faith alone, when life is imperilled or death itself is imminent, establishes for certain that all those things are true which Scripture proclaims concerning God, produces the Christian and obtains whatever he desires of God. It is impossible for this faith to exist in an impure and hypocritical heart." M. Dominicé [Pannier, 2.369] cites here the definition of faith given in the *Catechism* of 1537/38 [para. 14: "Faith . . . is a firm and staunch confidence of the heart by which we securely repose in God's mercy promised us through the Gospel. For it is from the substance of the promises that the definition of faith is to be sought, which so rests on that foundation, that once it is removed, utterly falls or rather vanishes"] and asserts that Calvin's work on the *Commentary on Romans* (begun in 1538 in Strasbourg) is reflected in the fuller treatment of the definition in the second Latin edition of the *Institutes* (1539).

heart. Melanchthon teaches two kinds of faith. Ganoczy [p. 153, n. 97/100-3] gathers Melanchthon's description of the second kind of faith. [*LC* (1521), 7; Eng. tr., LCC 19.90]: Saul, says Melanchthon, ". . . did not believe (from the heart I mean). . . ." *Ibid.* [p. 92]: "Accordingly, faith is nothing else than trust in the divine mercy promised in Christ, and it makes no difference with what sign it has been promised." *Ibid.* [p. 90]: "I am speaking of an affliction of the heart." *Ibid.* [p. 97]: "Faith is the assurance of things hoped for, the conviction of things not seen. . . . But to have faith is to believe the promises, that is, to trust the mercy and goodness of God against the wickedness of the world, sin, death, and even the gates of hell. . . . You do not really believe, therefore, unless you believe that salvation has been promised to you also." *Ibid.* [p. 98]: "This faith concerning creation is . . . a very lively recognition of both the power and the goodness of God, pouring itself out on all creatures, ruling and governing them all."

Page 44.

thousand. Cf. Luther, *Enchiridion* (1543 ed.) [fol. B.6ᵛ]: "Since that faith or faithfulness of heart is to be lodged in no one except God, and yet that same faithfulness of heart is also lodged in Jesus Christ and in the Holy Spirit, here is proof that Christ Jesus with the Holy Spirit is participant in one and the same divinity with God the Father. For just as the same faith is attributed to all three persons, so also is the same divinity in all."

Page 45.

ineffable. This has reference to the name Jehovah as the 1539 revision of this passage makes clear (6.11).

man. Servetus, *On the Errors of the Trinity*, 1 [fol. 7ʳ; Eng. tr., Wilbur, p. 13]: "They have speculated ill, therefore in denying that the Son was a man, that they may make a Son of the Word; but the truth of the matter proves to be otherwise, and John thought it more fitting to say Word than Son."

Father. Cf. Servetus, *Errors*, 2 [fol. 66ᵛ; Eng. tr., Wilbur, p. 102]: "Moreover, as the whole Word is God, so is the whole Spirit. . . ." Etc. See also Calvin, *Contre la Secte des Libertins* (1545), esp. c. 10 [OC 7.176ff].

Page 46.

Scriptures. Cf. Servetus, *Errors*, 1 [fol. 32ʳ; Eng. tr., Wilbur, p. 50]: ". . . not one word is found in the whole Bible about the Trinity, nor about its Persons, nor about an Essence, nor about a unity of the Substance, nor about one Nature of the several beings, nor about their other babblings and disputes of words. . . ."

love. Bullinger, *Assertio orthodoxa* (1534) [fol. A.2ᵛ-3ʳ]. Cf. Servetus, *Errors*, 1 [fol. 36ʳff; Eng. tr., Wilbur, p. 56]: "Again, their defense may seem artificial, without the witness of the Scriptures; for the one God there is not in question, but of the three beings which they call Persons I find no mention, nor does Scripture speak of an Essence, nor of all their other doctrines, disputes of words, and profane babblings. 'O Timothy, turn away from the novelties of words, which some professing have erred concerning the faith' [I Tim. 4:20]. And elsewhere, 'Be not carried away by diverse and strange questions' [Heb. 13:9]. Again, Paul forbids us to be led astray by disputes about words [II Tim. 2:14]." In the passage following, Servetus sweepingly reviews the history of theological controversy from the early Church to the Scholastics, attributing the strife to the adoption of Greek philosophical terminology in place of straightforward Biblical language.

Scripture. Bullinger, *Assertio orthodoxa* (1534) [fol. 15ᵛ]. Cf. Servetus, as referred to in previous note.

occasion. Benoît [1.148n.1] notes that Calvin's defense of the traditional trinitarian terminology against criticism of its unbiblical character follows Luther's lead, as set forth, e.g., in *On Councils and the Church* (1539) [WA 50.572]. Bucer came more reluctantly to such a position; see, e.g., *Apology for the Confessio Tetrapolitana* (Strasbourg, 1531) [fol. K.4ᵛ]. It should be pointed out that Calvin found in an earlier work of Luther's, the *Enchiridion piarum precationum* (1522ff), a simple interpretation of the Apostles' Creed, the Athanasian Creed and the Te Deum [Wittenberg, 1543, fol. I.1ᵛff] wherein traditional theological terms and Biblical texts were woven together.

Page 47.

words. As cited previously, Servetus refers I Tim. 6:4, 20 ("novelties of words") to the orthodox and spends the balance of Book 1, *On the Errors of the Trinity* [Eng. tr., Wilbur, pp. 57ff], regaling his readers with the multifarious arguments over non-Scriptural theological terms throughout the history of the Church, at the last pleading that they "conform to the simplicity of the Scripture."

shifts. Cf. Augustine, *De Trin.*, 7.4.9 [PL 42.94.47-50].

Page 48.

quality. Cf. *Inst.* (1559), 1.13.22 [LCC 20.147.14-16].

Sabellius. Cf. Servetus, *Errors*, 1 [fol. 22ᵛ]. Servetus comments on John 10:30 ("I and the Father are one") by citing Augustine who brings it ". . . forward against Arius, because he said *one;* and against Sabellius, because he said *are*. And from this he argues the two beings as against Sabellius, and one Nature as against Arius." Servetus endeavors to resolve the question with Tertullian's aid, by remarking that *one* in the neuter (here used) refers to enemies of mind and harmony, while *one* in the masculine should have denoted the singleness of one and the same being." G. H. Williams, *The Radical Reformation*, p. 586: "We know that Calvin had a rendezvous with the author of *De-Trinitatis Erroribus* in Paris in 1534, shortly before the writing of the first draft of the *Psychopannychia*. Servetus, for some reason, failed to show up for the secret discussion." Williams cites R. H. Bainton, *Hunted Heretic,* p. 218. Yet the tenor of Calvin's guarded references to nameless opponents, especially in the initial section of chapter 2 (pp. 42-48) and in the second part of the Exposition of the Creed (pp. 49-57), suggests extensive conversations or at least contacts with persons holding such opinions in the early months of his new-found Evangelical faith. These pages of the *Institutes* seem a continuing and written chapter of previous oral discussions.

God. Cf. Servetus, *Errors,* 1 [fol. 9ᵛff]. The statements Calvin attributes to Arius refer both to the views of Arius and, probably, of Servetus. In the *Thalia* (see reconstruction of the text by F. L. Battles), Arius states "The Son is God's only-begotten" (line 36), "He was made by the will of God, and did not exist before" (line 24), "There was a time when the Son was not" (line 17), "Christ then is not true God; but the Father has adopted Him as His own Son, engodding Him by participation through grace" (lines 148-150). Servetus, in his summary of the history of the Trinitarian doctrine, characterizes Arius thus: "The Arians divide the second being from the Substance of the first, as being less than it" [*Errors,* 1 (fol. 38ᵛ); Eng. tr., p. 60]. However, in his own teaching

Servetus rejects the eternity of the Word in any sense but his own reading of the Hebrew word עולם, "which means nothing else than world, and the days of age; and, from the beginning, from everlasting, from the days of old, from everlasting days, are expressions taken in Scripture for the same thing, as is also shown by the adding of the word *days*, for that is eternal which is not limited to certain number of days; nor can it be understood how with its eternities of aeons a being is said to have begun to be, and how the Son is said to be begotten and brought forth from everlasting; for these are figments of the imagination which go beyond the limits of Scripture." [*Errors*, 3, fol. 81^v; Eng. tr., p. 126]. Thus John 1:1 would refer to the beginning of the world, not eternity philosophically understood. On this basis one cannot call Servetus Arian, although like Arius (though on different grounds) he subordinates Son to Father and assigned to him a beginning point in time.

beginning. Cf. Servetus, *Errors*, 2 [fol. 51^v ff; Eng. tr., p. 81]: "Nor does one ever read in Scripture of a begetting of the Word, or a begetting of the second being, which by a misuse of language they call the *logos*. But properly speaking it is called an utterance of the Word, upon which the begetting of the flesh follows." Servetus then describes Christ as "the creature of God" on the basis of Col. 1:15, 18 and other scriptures.

privilege. Cf. Servetus, *Errors*, 1 [fol. 23^v ff; Eng. tr., pp. 37f]. Servetus, in explaining John 17:21f (citing Origen) sees the oneness of Father and Son in sympathy and in harmony and in identity of will, but not in substance or nature [p. 37]. The Son's "singular privilege" he describes: ". . . he alone is in the bosom of the Father, he has one power together with the Father, has the duty and authority. Hence he is said to be one with the Father in a far higher way" [p. 38].

God. Servetus briefly characterizes the Sabellian position: they ". . . confuse the persons and the names of Christ and the Father; and are also called Patripassians, since they believe the Father suffered" [*Errors*, 1, fol. 39^r; Eng. tr., pp. 60f]. One might lay the charge of Sabellianism against Servetus, however, in his reading of the economy or dispositions of God (a modalistic concept): "And God, when he began to employ in himself those *dispositions* which he was afterwards to manifest to us in various ways, 'by his Word created the heavens, and all the powers of them by the breath of his mouth' [Ps. 33:6, Vg.]. Yet they all then existed only by a *disposition*, but now in very fact; and the appearance of the Persons which then in some secret way were *dispositions* with God, has now really taken place in diverse beings, and thus a real distinction of Persons has been made; one Person, that is, with the aspect of Deity, appearing in the Son, another in the Holy Spirit. And the absolute and distinct beings in which the Persons have appeared are, God the Father, a man the Son, and an angel the Holy Spirit" [*Errors*, 4, fol. 85^r; Eng. tr., p. 132].

Gods. Cf. Servetus, *Errors*, 1 [fol. 21^{r-v}]. Servetus, in rejecting the Scholastics' use of "three persons" in favor of "three *ousias* or beings," reasons that they have a plurality of Gods. The orthodox trinitarians, on this basis, ". . . contrive three Gods, or one threefold one. These three Gods of theirs form one composite *Ousia;* and although some will not use a word implying that the three have been put together, yet they do use a word implying that they are constituted together and that God is constituted out of three beings," etc.

Finger. Scriptural passages which Calvin probably has in mind here are Ex. 31:18 and Deut. 9:10, where the inspiration of the Law is expressed as "tables written with the finger of God"; Ps. 8:3 where creation, especially the heavens, are described as the work of God's fingers; and Luke 11:20 where Jesus speaks of casting out devils with the finger of God.

Page 49.

First Part. Ganoczy, pp. 140f, summarizes Calvin's structural indebtedness to Luther for his treatment of the Apostles' Creed. As Luther in his *Small Catechism* follows his discussion of the Law with one of the Apostles' Creed, so too Calvin. But Calvin's treatment is fuller, with more citations of Scripture. Luther divides the Creed into three articles (creation, redemption, sanctification) [*Enchiridion*, fol. 1.6^{r}ff]; Calvin adds to these three sections on Father, Son, and Spirit, a fourth section on the Church (for which last he draws material from Martin Bucer). Otherwise, Calvin structurally is close to Luther.

Sophists. The term "Sophist," popularized by Luther, and by Melanchthon *LC* (1521), as a term of opprobrium against the Scholastics and especially against the theologians of the Sorbonne, is used similarly by Calvin and other contemporary writers. Calvin (?) first used it in the Cop-Calvin Rectorial Address: see Appendix III.

idle. This picture of God which Calvin elsewhere describes as "Epicurean," is inferred by him as the picture of God of the Scholastics apparently because they seem to limit God's omnipotence by their emphasis on the contingency of events and the freedom of the human will. Already in the *Seneca Commentary*, Calvin had rejected this "Epicureanism": "The Epicureans, although they do not deny the existence of the gods, do the closest thing to it: they imagine the gods to be pleasure-loving, idle, not caring for mortals, lest anything detract from their pleasures . . ." [6:10f]. The picture of God idly sitting in his watch-tower is repeatedly set by Calvin in later editions of the *Institutes* over against his own Augustinian notion of a totally free, active and omnipotent God. Cf. Zwingli, *Commentary,* 3 [Eng. tr., LWZ 3.64.34-37]: "This good [=God], therefore, is not a thing idle or inert, so as to lie torpid and motionless, moving neither itself nor other things; for we saw above that it is the essence and constitution of all things."

service. and **faith.** Ganoczy [p. 141] remarks on the "astonishing correspondence" between Luther's and Calvin's descriptions of God's kindness to us and the gratitude we owe him. See Luther, *Small Catechism,* 2.1 [Eng. tr., Schaff, CC 3.78]: ". . . that he provides me richly and daily with all the necessaries of life, protects me from all danger, and preserves and guards me against all evil; and all this out of his pure paternal divine goodness and mercy, without any merit or worthiness of mine; for all which I am in duty bound to thank, praise, serve, and obey him. This is most certainly true." Cf. Luther, *Enchiridion* (1543 ed.) [fol. 1.8^v]: "I believe that God created me along with all creatures, that he gave me body and soul, eyes, ears and all members, reason and all senses and still sustains them. I believe that for these he provides me richly and daily with clothing and shoes, food and drink, house, wife and children, fields, beasts of burden and all goods with all things necessary for life. He defends me against all perils, and averts and keeps away all ills. Moreover, he does all these things not out of any merit of mine, but for his pure fatherly goodness and mercy. Accordingly, I ought to give thanks in return to him, praise him, obey his will and serve him. All these things are as sure as they are true."

Second Part. The discussion of the Christological Section of the Apostles' Creed which underwent extensive revision in subsequent editions of the *Institutes*, here strikes chiefly at what Calvin held to be a defective Anabaptist teaching on the incarnation. Actually, it is a refutation of the celestial flesh notion, by no means universally held by

Anabaptists. G. H. Williams, *The Radical Reformation*, has traced the history of this doctrine in detail. While the Anabaptists are not specifically mentioned in this passage, it is clear that Calvin has definite opponents in mind, whom he charges with Marcionite or Manichaean docetic views of Christ's humanity. The same reasoning, although differently ordered, is to be seen in his *Brieve Instruction* (1544), explicitly directed against the Anabaptists. See OC 7.103-110 [Eng. tr., fol. G.i^r-G.viii^r]. In addition to certain articles of the *Schleitheim Confession*, Calvin's tract deals with two additional articles: on the incarnation (here discussed) and on the sleep of souls (already treated in Calvin's first theological piece, the *Psychopannychia*). The *Brieve Instruction* first asserts that the Anabaptist Christology is reminiscent of the Marcionite, but especially of the Manichaean, view; then Calvin marshals his scriptural texts in support of Christ's real humanity. Finally, he disposes of the chief Anabaptist arguments that Jesus Christ is called David's Son, not because he took anything of the Virgin Mary, or that he was made of her substance, but only because she bore his heaven-sent body in her body as water passes through a pipe. These arguments include Phil. 2:7, I Cor. 15:47, the clause of the Apostles' Creed ("conceived of the Holy Spirit, born of the Virgin Mary"), and the assertion that attributing mere humanity like ours to him is to dishonor him. Calvin particularly refutes the Anabaptist view on soteriological grounds. For a critical note on Calvin's understanding of the Anabaptist position, see W. E. Keeney, "An Analysis of Calvin's Treatment of the Anabaptists in the *Institutes*," in Battles, *An Analysis* (1972, 1976), pp. 82*f. For the history of the doctrine of Christ's celestial flesh, see G. H. Williams, *The Radical Reformation*, index, "Celestial flesh of Christ." For an English translation of Calvin's Anabaptist writings see B. W. Farley, *John Calvin: Treatises Against the Anabaptists and Libertines* (Grand Rapids: Baker, 1982).

Page 50.

Power. The plural verb in the Hebrew of Gen. 1:26 [בעשה] after the Jewish exegesis of Rashi and David Kimchi (cf. Tertullian, *Against Praxeas*, c. 12) is by Servetus, *Dialogue on the Trinity* (1532), 1 [fol. A.6^r, Eng. tr., Wilbur, p. 195], interpreted as follows: "And the ministry of angels began in man, as God was at that time to be manifested to man through them. And the angels were not the creators of the world, but their office then began when God said, 'Let us make man' [Gen. 1:26]. For before this God had not spoken to the angels, but had created alone."

man. In the 1539 edition this is explicitly labelled as "Principio" (VG 1541, "le premier point") of our redemption; the "alterum caput" appears at p. 51, lines 8ff, below.

Page 51.

weakness. An instance of the exegetical principle of "accommodation."

humanity. "Those who despoil Christ of his humanity" are the advocates of Christ's celestial flesh. In his *Brieve Instruction* [Eng. tr., fol. E.viii^v] he describes their position, there identified as "Anabaptist": ". . . they do not beleue that Jesus Christe was a verye man: but rather do make hym touchynge hys bodye, a phantasy." Calvin's juxtaposition of these two opposing Christological tendencies is reminiscent of Luther, *Enchiridion* (1543 ed.) [fol. K.2^v3^r], "Exposition of Three Creeds of the Christian Faith": "Some have opposed his divinity. . . . Others have opposed his humanity."

Page 52.

two parts. Here the analogy, human soul : human body :: Christ's divinity : Christ's humanity, assumes Calvin's teaching on man created and fallen, and also the diversity of soul and body.

person. Cf. Augustine, *Sermon*, 186.1.1 [PL 38.999]; *Enchiridion*, 36.11 [Eng. tr., LCC 7.361f].

properties. On *communicatio idiomatum*, see LCC 20.483 n.4; also p. 105, below.

Page 53.

God. Cf. Augustine, *Unfinished Work against Julian*, 2.178; 3.186 [PL 45.1218-1219; 1325]. Calvin, *Brieve Instruction* [Eng. tr., fol. G.i^r]: "For the Maniches phantasied, that Jesus Christ, brought an heauenlye bodye, into the wombe of the Vyrgen his mother." Also [fol. G. vi^v]: "They [the Anabaptists] aledge further, that it was conceyued of the Holy Goste. But this vertue of the holy Goste is not to exclude the substaunce of hys mother." Etc. The identification of the Anabaptists, on this point, with the ancient Manichees, explicit in the tract, is not stated in the *Institutes*.

Most High. It is possible that Calvin infers a celestial flesh Christology from the use of these two texts by Servetus, *Errors*, 1 [fol. 6^r, Eng. tr., p. 12]: "Take note of what Luke says: 'This son whom thou shalt conceive and bring forth shall be called the Son of the Most High' [Luke 1:32]. . . . Has the second Person then, become great, and received from God the throne of his father David? Why did he not say, He shall be called the Son of the first Person, and the first Person shall give him the throne?" Cf. *Ibid*. [fol. 9^{r-v}; Eng. tr., pp. 16f]: "For with regard to Christ no such adoption is read of, but a real begetting by God, his Father. And he is called not merely a son, but his own Son [Rom. 8:32]: And God is called the Father of Jesus Christ with just as good right as earthly fathers are called the fathers of their own sons." Etc. Barth and Niesel [OS 3.468 n.1] also make reference to a letter from Berthold Haller of Berne to Henry Bullinger of Zurich (7 May 1534) which reports the difficulty with a former Neuchâtel colleague of Farel, Claude d'Aliad, a native of Savoy, who espoused the Christological views of Servetus. Haller's letter [Herminjard, 3.172-174, no. 469] reports that d'Aliad ". . . had asserted that Jesus Christ was a mere man; then when urged by us with the clearest Scripture passages, he admitted that Christ is God's son by nature, and is accordingly God but not eternal, nay, constituted and made in time. Secondly, he says that Christ although mere man, is the object of our faith." D'Aliad presented a confession of faith in August 1534 to the ministers of Constance, summing up his faith: ". . . I do not believe three persons to be one single God, but I know three men; three persons are three men, not one God." Haller expresses fear that ". . . Farel may be involved in this error."

two Christs. The traditional Christological position here expounded by Calvin is linked by Servetus [*Errors*, fol. 38^v; Eng. tr., p. 60] with Nestorius: "The Nestorians say that Jesus is one Son of God, and another son of man; and this in fact our brethren confess. For, as appears in the disputations of Maxentius of Constantinople, Nestorius never admitted that there were two sons, but defended himself by certain sophistical tricks, quite in the manner of men today. Read what is said there, and you shall clearly see that these are Nestorians." In the *Institutes* of 1559, Calvin explicitly refers to Nestorius at this point [2.14.7; LCC 20.491, lines 1f].

commingled. Cf. Chalcedonian Creed (AD 451): "without confusing the natures."

days. For Servetus' conflicting interpretation of this Hebraism, see note at p. 48, "God," above.

Page 54.

made. *Factus fuit*. Vg.: *factus est*; Gr.: γενομένον

deserve. Augustine, *Enchiridion*, 36.11.

divinity. Servetus, *Errors* [Eng. tr., p. 7]: "Of what Jesus do you suppose those things were said? Do you think they disputed these about a *hypostasis?*" Cf. p. 8: ". . . he, being distinguished above others by his anointing, is called Christ the King; because just as God made an angel chief over the angels, and a beast over the beasts, and a heavenly body over the heavenly bodies, so he made the man Christ chief over men."

humanity. From passages such as the following of Servetus, Calvin could have inferred this point, *Errors*, 2 [fol. 58ʳ; Eng. tr., pp. 90f]: "That you may therefore have knowledge of the true Christ apart from the imaginations of the philosophers, give heed how these more than Ebionites despoil the true Christ of all but his bare human nature, nor raise their eyes to regard his ineffable generation which took place from the beginning from the substance of God; nor regard him, all full of the divinity of the Father, all radiant with divine light." Cf. further [fol. 58, p. 91]: "For since God 'giveth not the Spirit by measure' [John 3:34], so great is the power of his spirit that all things that are said of him are more than human; and although they say that his being died and suffered even as a man, and that thus two died and were crucified, yet I maintain with the earlier writers that he was God and man . . . [and] admit that man was mingled with God, since God was born as a man Emmanuel." *Dialogues on the Trinity*, 1 [fol. A.6ᵛ; Eng. tr., p. 196]: ". . . he that went before the children of Israel was God himself, and was an angel, and was Christ, and all this is the face of Christ." And also [fol. A.7ᵛ; Eng. tr., p. 197]: "Note here in passing that this general statement about all the fulness of deity [Col. 1:19] cannot be verified in the humanity of Christ in accordance with the imagination of the philosophers, for the reason that the second being is united to it. But the whole fulness of God, the whole of God the Father together with all the fulness of his properties, whatever God has, this dwells fully in this man." Etc.

king. Here Calvin expresses a two-office view of Christ (king and priest) as he also does in *Catechism* (1538) [20.iii, p. 25]. In 1539 he added the office of prophet, possibly on the basis of Bucer, *EN* (1536), as noted by Benoît: "Christ is the King of kings, the high priest, and the chief of the prophets" [*EN* (1536), p. 607]. On the evolution of this doctrine in Calvin's thought, see J. F. Jansen, *Calvin's Doctrine of the Work of Christ* (1956).

Page 55.

hell. Cf. *Psychopannychia*, pp. 98, 36 (ed. Zimmerli) [Eng. tr., T&T 3.480f, 428f]: "And this is the confession which we make in the Creed, namely, that Christ 'descended into hell,' in other words, that He was subjected by the Father, on our account, to all the pains of death; that He endured all its agonies and terrors, and was truly effected, it having been previously said that 'he was buried.' " Cf. Smits 1.202: "In the *Institutes* of 1536, and more clearly still in that of 1539, he alludes to the *Explanatio Symboli* published in 1533 by Erasmus, which cast doubt upon the apostolic origin of the formation of the last article of the creed."

limbo. Cf. Thomas Aquinas, *S. Th.*, PTS, 69.4-7.

it. Thomas Aquinas, *S. Th.*, PT, 52.5: "When Christ descended into hell, by the power of his Passion he delivered the saints from the penalty whereby they were excluded from the life of glory. . . ."

authors. Cf. Irenaeus, *Against Heresies*, 4.2; 5.31 [Eng. tr., ANF 1.463f, 504f]; Tertullian, *On the Soul*, c. 7, 55 [Eng. tr., ANF 3.186f, 231].

story. Servetus, in his Letter 18 to Calvin (published in his *Christianismi Restitutio*, 1553), alludes to Calvin's non-literal interpretation of the descent into hell: "You slightingly allude to as a story the fact that hell now exists, that Christ descended into [it], and led out the saints with him: even though it chiefly displays Christ's redemption from his acknowledged victory over hell" [OC 8.682]. G. H. Williams, *The Radical Reformation*, p. 841, points out the surprising alliance of radicals generally with Catholics against ". . . the classical Protestant theologians Luther, Melanchthon, Bucer and Calvin [who] accepted the *descensus* in the tradition of the mystics as a spiritual *resignatio ad infernum*. . . . In contrast, representatives of all those of the main typological sectors of the Radical Reformation vigorously argued for the literal descent of Christ to the nether world in their manifest concern to safeguard the conviction that Christ in the fulness of time saved all who had lived by faith in anticipation of his advent. . . ."

time. Cf. *Psychopannychia* (ed. Zimmerli, p. 36) [Eng. tr., p. 429], where one finds the same figurative interpretation of 'prison' [carcer = exspectatio sanctorum patrum, qui redemptionem Christi exspectabant].

Page 56.

bosom. For Calvin's first exegesis of Abraham's bosom, see *Psychopannychia* [ed. Zimmerli, pp. 38ff]: "Scripture, by the bosom of Abraham . . ." means "the repose of the soul when, in sure trust in the divine promise, it is freed from the body" [p. 41]. Calvin's earliest exegesis of the fifth seal (the faithful souls under the altar of God [Rev. 6:9-11]) is at *Psychopannychia* [pp. 56f]. By "repose and quiet," Calvin does not mean soul-sleep, but a conscious, wakeful, yet tranquil state of waiting until the judgment.

Page 57.

himself. Cf. Luther, *Enchiridion* [1543 ed., fol. C.2^v]: "Not only do I believe the Holy Spirit to be true God with the Father and the Son, but this also: that no access is open to the Father through Christ's life, passion and death save with this Spirit leading and directing us; through him God the Father with the Son arouses me and his other followers, stirs up, calls and draws us through Christ and in Christ quickens and sanctifies, that we may be able to reach the Father. For this Spirit is he, all the works of whom the Father does through Christ and in Christ, and quickens all those."

Page 58.

elect. It is to be remarked that Calvin did not utilize Augustine's *On the Predestination of the Saints* until the 1539 edition of the *Institutes*. See A. Lang, *Der Evangelienkommentar Martin Butzers und die Grundzüge seiner Theologie* (1900/repr. 1972), p. 158: "We are quite aware of the importance of this investigation. For if it is true that directly Bucer's understanding of predestination became determinative for Calvin, then we would have to seek in the Strasbourg Reformer the primary and secondary meaning of this for the theology and practice of the Reformed Church's fundamental dogma. . . ." Lang quotes Max Scheibe, *Calvins Prädestinationslehre* (1897), pp. 20, 72, to the effect that Calvin was influenced by Bucer not only in the *Institutes* of 1536 but (presumably after studying the *Metaphrases* on Romans of 1536) also in the *Institutes* of 1539, where the doctrine takes on fuller development. It should be pointed out that the *Catechism* of 1537/38, 13, Election and Predestination (pp. 16f), seems for this doctrine to provide a bridge between the first and second Latin editions. Is this not evidence that Calvin's study of the *Metaphrases* began promptly after the publication of the 1536 *Institutes*, issuing not only in its sequel of 1539 but in the Romans Commentary of 1540 as well? The notes on the following pages adducing Bucerian parallels for Calvin's ecclesiology have been drawn from Ganoczy pp. 168-171. Cf. Bucer, *EN*, I [fol. 181ᵛ. 41-43]: "Also to be noted here is the phrase 'from the four winds' [Matt. 24:31], that is, the elect are to be gathered together everywhere in the world: therefore not only those are Christians who are under the Roman power."

Kingdom. Cf. Bucer, *EN*, I [fol. 197ᵛ.17-18]: "Christ's kingdom is not of this world, that is, set in outward rule, hence in Christ its head so also in its members is it destitute of glory, wealth and outward power." *EN*, II [fol. 20ʳ.38-41]: "Let it therefore be sufficient for anyone to be in the body of Christ, to live by his Spirit, whatsoever place he may at last obtain, whatsoever act he may perform." *EN*, II [fol. 89ᵛ.28-30]: "Hence it will be clear that I am in them, live, speak and fulfill all things. Thus at last they will be perfected into one, that all may be one body. . . ." *EN* [fol. 65ʳ.12-13]: "Thus it has become one flock, that is one church gathered from Gentiles and Jews, under one shepherd, the Head of this church, Christ.

Spirit. Cf. Bucer, *EN*, II [fol. 23ʳ.33-36]: "For those who have this faith, have the Spirit of God, are new men; as they truly know the Lord, so they can never be torn away from him. They have trust in the Lord and the Lord has trust in them, for they are one with him—the Lord in them and they in the Lord."

glorifies. Cf. Bucer, *EN*, II [fol. 44ᵛ.3-4]: "They are not glorified unless justified, not justified unless called, not called unless predestined" [Rom. 8:30; cf. fol. 44ʳ.25-26].

Holy Spirit. Cf. Bucer, *EN*, I [fol. 184ᵛ.30-32]: "Come and receive your inheritance of God's kingdom. For truly the Father has chosen you before the foundations of the world were laid, for this, which he made manifest by the blessing of his Spirit. . . ." Ganoczy [p. 170] also adduces two other Bucerian parallels: *EN*, I [fol. 37ʳ.44-46]: "Then are to be seen examples of innocence and piety in his disciples, even those acting on their own. As almost always in the elect, even before their conversion, and while they are dripping with misdeeds, yet they shine repeatedly as seedbeds of piety." And *EN*, II [fol. 71ᵛ.41-44]: "One might wonder why Christ entrusted money to Judas the thief. But this is the way God administers his matter of perdition to the reprobate, as he also does his matter of salvation to the elect; and it was fitting that Judas show himself unfaithful in a wicked deed and not in his own greed [*proprio Mammona*] that he might be openly seen to have been utterly unworthy of true and personal benefits."

election. In comparing Bucer's views on election as expressed in *EN* (1530) with those of Calvin in *Institutes* 1536, A. Ganoczy, pp. 170f, makes the following points: (1) for both, election is the constitutive factor of the Church Universal; (2) Bucer proceeds analytically on the biblical texts on which he is commenting while Calvin proceeds synthetically; (3) Bucer includes alongside the positive aspect of election the negative aspect of reprobation (cf. *EN*, I, 88B, 121D, 122AB, 146B; *EN*, II, 23A, 30A, 46A, 73D, 76D, 77A); (4) Bucer already treats expressly the outward society of the Church, "in which the proclamation of the 'outward word,' the administration of the sacraments and the discipline of 'warnings' constitute the visible and ministerial complement of the invisible aspect" while Calvin still prefers to consider the church under its invisible aspect. See *EN*, II, 73ʳ.16-45: "Obviously whatever of outward rites had been enjoined upon the ancient folk, it was enjoined to this end, that just as those more untutored than they might be shaped to some zeal for piety and honesty, then, separated from the

Gentiles, in observing God's word they might be preserved. When therefore the Spirit has been given, in order that the elect may the more perfectly be formed and inspired both to all godliness and to all honesty and decency of living at the same time, insofar as this could ever be accomplished by any outward institutions, then when the middle wall has been removed they become one people of God out of Jews and Gentiles, this is assuredly not reason why they should be joined together by those elements, namely little outward observances. Just as it would be absurd for the hand of him who especially possessed the art of writing to be instructed by another in the embellishment of letters, or to be delivered over to an elementary teacher after he had already attained perfect use of speaking and writing, or a man already adorned with morals worthy of man to be delivered over to those forms of morals which we prescribe for children. When what is perfect comes, what is in part is made void. Hence, in the coming age when the Spirit as teacher will show all things, when we shall know God as he really is, that is, when we attain to full manhood of the completely mature age of Christ, these external things will depart, of which there is also use in Christianity, namely the use of outward teaching and admonition, both of the sacraments by which the outward society of the church is initiated and restored in order to be more perfectly exercised in teaching, and of the order of ministers, whom the Lord willed us to have here to perform the office of teaching and warning. Thus surely since a much fuller spirit had touched the church than the ancients, and the saints had been led forth beyond childhood into an adolescence and youth of heavenly life, the pedagogy of the Law was rightly abolished, which had still been useful while the people of God was a child, that is, not yet endowed with the spirit of freedom but only with that of fear. Moreover, as some receive this spirit of freedom more richly than others even in Christianity, so also some rightly enjoy also a greater freedom from outward institutions than do others. It is useful sometimes to give more rudimentary injunctions to those clearly younger and more untutored in spirit, but which send forth righteous acts from the source of all holy injunction, namely these precepts— 'Love God with all your heart, etc., and your neighbor as yourself.' But the church as a whole is to be burdened with none of these injunctions save those which the Lord has given, who has given only those which I have spoken of. The use of the outward word, zeal of outward society for the sake of appropriately receiving the word, baptism and eucharist, by which we both enter upon and preserve this society appropriately, finally the order of ministers, who carry out the functions of teaching, warning and caring for other business of the church."

Page 59.

capacity. A prime exegetical principle, that of accommodation, is here suggested. Later editions of the *Institutes* saw a much more extensive use of the principle. Preeminently, it relates to the accommodation of language by God to make communication between God and man possible: God speaks "baby-talk" to man. He clothes ineffable truth in humanly experienced realities. But revelation in Scripture is not the only instance of divine accommodation to human capacity. The sacraments, the ministry of the church and other institutional forms translate divine ineffabilities into humanly grasped tangibles. There is a sense in which the incarnation itself—as the ultimate divine condescension— was the supreme act of accommodation. The notion (which Calvin never expresses in a noun, but only in verbs) is not original with him. In an unpublished paper entitled "The Doctrine of Scripture in Origen and Its Use in the Commentary on John" (1972), D. McKim cites R. P. C. Hanson, *Allegory and Event* (1959), p. 226, wherein Origen, *Frag. on*

Deut., 1:21 [PG 17.24] is quoted: ". . . father accommodating his language to the under-standing of his children." "He condescends and lowers himself to our weakness like a schoolmaster talking 'little language' συμφελλίζων to his children, like a father caring for his own children and adopting their ways." Origen's most carefully developed usage of "accommodation" is to explain how God can be said to repent or change his mind— *Hom. in Jeremiam*, 18.6 in Hanson, *Allegory*, pp. 226-228. The most extreme usage may be in *Hom. in Jeremiam*, 14.3 where "God can so accommodate himself to human ways as to deceive men for their own good" [PG 13.504f]. See Bruce Vawter, *Biblical Inspiration* (1972), passim. Cf. also Hilary, *Tractates on the Psalms*, Ps. 126:6: "For the divine Word tempers itself to the habit and nature of our understanding, by common words of things adapted to the signification of his doctrine and institution." The two verbs used by Calvin are *accommodare* and *attemperare*. On Calvin's earliest use of these, see *Comm. Sen. De Clem.*, pp. 46n., 175, 237, 337. In another unpublished paper, entitled "Accommodation: God's Revelation and Means adapted to our Level—Calvin's Understanding and Use of this Concept" (1974), Dennis R. Witt summarizes Calvin's teaching on accommodation and its application to such topics as specific Scriptural passages, the sacraments, the Lord's Prayer, Christian martyrs, etc. The name "Father" he sees as perhaps the supreme instance of accommodation, along with the incarnation itself, of divine ways to human capacity to understand. See also, F. L. Battles, "God was Accommodating Himself to Human Capacity," *Interp.* (Jan. 1977): 19-38.

God. Cf. Bucer, *EN*, I [fol. 138ᵛ.25-27]: "Thus therefore he also sent the disciples. First he gave the Spirit, for nothing can be done in the kingdom of God apart from the Spirit; then he ordered them to preach the Gospel, adding that as many as had faith would be saved, but as many as would not believe him would be condemned."

hand. Cf. Bucer, *EN*, II [fol. 65ᵛ.6-7]: "My sheep hear my voice" [John 10:16]. In these words he openly teaches that all things depend upon divine election, and those to whom he has once given the status of sheep can never perish. [*Ibid.*, 23-25]: "Therefore as from the Father's hand no one can seize the elect, so neither from Christ's hand while Christ's sheep forever stay in his saving hand, can they ever perish; and it is necessary for them to have eternal life. . . ." Also, *EN*, II [fol. 44ʳ.56-57]: "The remaining words commend once more to us Christ's incomparable dignity, the excellence of faith, and the unchangeable power of God's election."

lost. Cf. Bucer, *EN*, II [fol. 44ᵛ.4-6]: "Moreover, since they have been predestined to life eternal by God who cannot change, it is impious to think their life (once they had received it by faith) not to be eternal, and that they can perish against God's decree." Bucer then glosses "the elect" as those to whom "the Spirit of God has been given" [line 6].

Page 61.

church. Cf. Luther, *Enchiridion* (1543 ed.) [fol. c.3ʳ.8-11]: "I believe that no one can be saved, who is not in the number of these believers, who does not feel the same, who does not profess the same faith, gospel, sacrament, hope and love."

excommunications. This short section on excommunication was greatly elabo-rated on the basis of Calvin's later Geneva and Strasbourg pastoral experience. Here there is no mention of the Anabaptists, whose *Schleitheim Confession*, Article 2, deals with the ban. In his *Brieve Instruction*, [Eng. tr., fol. B.viʳ-D.iʳ], Calvin agrees with the Anabap-tists on the soundness of excommunication as a churchly practice (averring however that what "this ingrate people do knowe of thys matter they learned of us, and by their ignorance or presumption they have corrupted the doctrine" [fol. B.vi^v]), but disagrees with their strictness in rejecting table fellowship with all churches (even those in which doctrine is purely preached) where excommunication is not in full force [fol. B.vii^r]. Calvin considers this an imperfection, not a negation, of the true church. Perhaps this more moderate view of his has general reference to the Anabaptist strictness.

First. For the Anabaptist Dirk Philips' listing of almost the identical reason, see *BRN*, 10.358, 399-400, 660. The relationship of the three uses of church discipline, the three uses of the law, and the three classical uses of punishment is discussed in my note at Calvin, *Comm. Sen. De Clem.*, p. 125.14-26. For a comparative table, see Battles, *Analysis*, p. 119.

Page 63.

exists. Cf. *Augsburg Confession*, art. 7. While Calvin here speaks of two marks, in other places he mentions a third mark, discipline. E.g., *Reply to Sadolet* [OC 5.394]: "The holiness and strength of the church consists primarily in three things, namely: doctrine, discipline, and sacraments" [Benoît, 4.20n4]. Also see *Hom. Is.* [Suppl. Calv., 2.365.13-16, Is. 24:16, 2 June 1557]: "And in this also we see what is the true mark of the church: it is there where men so humble themselves that they condemn all their works and virtues, and confess that they hold their salvation only by God's freely-given bounty. If such a doctrine is preached and received, there is the church of God." Cf. *Ibid.* [lines 32-37]: "But there where there will be a confession of humility to recognize that in us there is only sin, and that all righteousness is in God and proceeds from him, and that so far as he is pleased to manifest his goodness toward us, we are righteous, but that however is necessary that we be shown that Jesus Christ has been given us for righteousness—there where this will be proclaimed, let us know that there is the church of God, and that we shall be avowed of him and of the angels of paradise, even though men despise and condemn us." *Ibid.* [Suppl. Calv., 2.381.3-10, Is. 24:33-25:1, 4 June 1557]: "Here then is a mark that God has put in his church: That it has elders to govern us, and that all may not take over mastery in his church, but that people may subject themselves willingly to those who have been appointed to conduct us on the right road, and who are in charge of preventing things from being confused and disordered or repressing scandals, of wiping out licentiousness. There then is how we shall be recognized by God and angels as the church. And when we reach that point—even though the world mistrust and reject us—that it is enough for us that God accepts us, and considers us agreeable, then it is that he has declared by his prophet's mouth that we are his flock" [cf. Ps. 79:13; 95:7].

others. Cf. Luther, *Enchiridion* (1543 ed.) [fol. C.3^v.2-17]: "I believe forgiveness of sins to exist in that assembly of saints and never anywhere else. I believe too that no works, however great and splendid, contribute anything to forgiveness of sins, if you are outside this assembly; no sins however great and frequent delay forgiveness. And this forgiveness of sins remains forever with and in the assembly of Christians. For Christ has given the keys to his church, when he says in Matt. 18:18: 'Verily I say to you, whatsoever you bind on earth will be bound in heaven,' etc. Likewise to Peter separately, who was bearing the type of the holy and sole church, he says in Matt. 16:19: 'Whoever you bind on earth will be bound in heaven.' "

salvation. Cyprian, *Epist.*, 73.21 = 72.2 [Eng. tr., ANF 5.380]: "But we who hold the head and root of the one church know, and trust for certain, that nothing is lawful there outside the church, and that the baptism which is one is among us. . . ."

Page 64.

death. For Calvin's earliest exegesis of Matt. 25:31ff and I Thess. 4:13 in response to Anabaptists who had used it as part of their Scriptural proof that before the Last Judgment no blessedness or misery was fixed, see *Psychopannychia* [ed. Zimmerli, pp. 76ff].

Page 65.

love. Peter Lombard, *Sent.*, 3.25.5 [p. 670]: "Do not understand that faith and hope causally or temporally precede love, the mother of all goods, but that love without them cannot be in anyone, but they can be without love, although there is no godly faith or hope without love. Therefore love is said to proceed from faith and hope, because it can come to no one without them." *Ibid.*, 3.23.3 [p. 656]: "Moreover, faith which is believed, if it be with love, is a virtue, because 'love' Ambrose says, 'is the mother of all virtues,' which shapes all virtues, without which no virtue is a true virtue. Faith therefore working through love [Gal. 5:6] is a virtue which, unseen, men believe." *Ibid.*, 3.23.9 [p. 661]: "Faith is not the foundation of love, because it is not love, but love is the cause of the very virtue faith: for love is the cause and mother of all virtues. . . . Love itself is therefore the cause of all the virtues, not of itself a cause of virtues, because it excels all gifts."

faith. Cf. Melanchthon, *LC* (1521), 7 [Eng. tr., LCC 19.111]: ". . . it is apparent how the love of God and love of the neighbor . . . have their source in faith," etc.

hope. With Calvin's remarks on hope, cf. Melanchthon, *LC* (1521), 7 [Eng. tr., LCC 19.111]: "Furthermore, hope also is a work of faith. For by faith man believes the Word, and in hope he expects what is promised through the Word. Faith in the Word of God causes us to expect what it promises," etc.

Page 66.

words. Peter Lombard, *Sent.*, 3.23.4 [p. 657]: "Through this faith 'is the ungodly man justified, so that faith itself then begins to work through love.' " [Augustine, *Enarr. in Ps.*, 67, n.41, PL 36.838.] Cf. Melanchthon, *LC* (1521), 7 [Eng. tr., LCC 19.111]: "I Cor. 13:2 is thrown in the teeth of those who contend for the righteousness of faith. . . ."

unformed faith. Cf. Melanchthon, *LC* (1521), 7 [Eng. tr., LCC 19.89]: "The other kind they call 'unformed'; it is found even in the godless, who lack love." See also LCC 19.91.

power. Peter Lombard, *Sent.*, 3.23.5 [p. 657.15-20]: "But if it is asked whether that unformed quality whereby an evil Christian believes everything that a good Christian believes with love accompanying, remains and becomes a virtue, or that quality is eliminated and another quality succeeds it, it can without peril be said which of the two is a virtue; yet it seems to some that that quality, which previously existed, remains and with the addition of love, becomes a virtue." Cf. Thomas Aquinas, *S. Th.*, PS 66.6; 113.4.1. Among contemporary 16th century Roman Catholic controversialists, see, e.g., John Fisher, *Confutatio*, art. 1 [p. 63]; Eck, *Enchiridion* (1532 ed.), c. 5 [Eng. tr., Battles, pp. 50-54]; de Castro, *Adv. haer.* (1534 ed.) [fol. 128B]; Cochlaeus, *Philipp.*, 3.10; Faber, *Cur noluerit . . .*, c. 14 [Opusc. t.2.a]; *De fide et operibus*, 1, c. 9 [fol. 73^r].

Page 67.

heart. Cf. Bucer, *EN*, I [fol. 63^r.22ff], Appendix II.

road. On the Calvinian doctrine of spiritual growth, here alluded to, see note to p. 112, "supply," below.

CHAPTER III: PRAYER

Page 68.

Prayer. For a strophic translation of this chapter, see F. L. Battles, *The Piety of John Calvin* (1973), pp. 101-143. On the amplified title of this chapter in the *Institutes* of 1559, see note to p. 102, "faith," below. Max Dominicé in J. Pannier's edition of the *Institutes* of 1541 [3.307f] provides a useful summary of previous works. Luther had published a treatise in German in 1519 translated into Latin as early as 1520 under the title *Explanation of the Lord's Prayer* then into French *The Lord's Prayer rendered in Translation and Dialogue by the Queen of Navarre* [BN MS Fr. 1723]. Luther published in 1522 his *Betbüchlein*, translated into Latin as *Handbook of some Prayers and Meditations* [*Enchiridion*, cited in this chapter as in previous chapters (see notes to pp. 15 and 42, above) in the Wittenberg edition of 1543] and published at Strasbourg in 1525. As previously noted, Louis de Berquin was the probable translator of the first Latin version, as also of the French version which appeared at Paris in 1528 as *The Book of True and Perfect Prayer,* censured by the Sorbonne in 1531. Berquin had also translated in 1525 an extract of Erasmus' Paraphrases on Matthew and Luke, as *Brief Admonition on the Manner of Prayer according to the Teaching of Jesus Christ, with a Brief Explanation of the Lord's Prayer,* also censured by the Sorbonne. Martin Bucer in his *Enarrationes perpetuae in sacra quatuor Evangelia* (1527, 1530) explicated Matthew 6:5-13; an English translation of this *locus* has been provided here as Appendix II. Alexandre Ganoczy, *Le Jeune Calvin,* pp. 171-175, makes a detailed comparison of Bucer and Calvin on prayer, here utilized in the documentation. See also P. Wernle, *Der evangelische Glaube nach den Hauptschriften der Reformatoren,* 3.81. A final French writer on prayer should be mentioned: Guillaume Farel, *Sommaire* (1525), 24 [fol. f.1^r-3^r], says of prayer: "Prayer is an ardent speaking with God in which man does not know what he ought to say or ask, but the Spirit which is in believers by great unspeakable groanings prays for us [Rom. 8:26]. In prayer the mouth is not required to speak, but only the heart. For as our Lord Jesus has taught us, when we pray we ought to say: 'Our Father who art in heaven.' It is not that one should say these words with the mouth only and that by them we have what we ask, for that would be like the superstition of magicians. But it is in order that in our heart we think of God just as this most beautiful prayer sets forth: that He is our Father; and that in true faith and good conscience we go to Him, lifting our hearts to heavenly things. Let us ask only what is contained in this most holy prayer: in order that we may see to it that all we ask which is not contained in it is not according to God. And from it comes [the fact] that all the prayers of the prophets and saints drawn from the Spirit of God, come down to what is asked for in this prayer. It is necessary therefore that our heart address it to God as to our good Father, and that it pray to him alone. For prayer is the true sacrifice of praise, by which one gives honor and glory to God. It is that it has pleased him alone to help us. And he wishes to be honored with this honor, and does not wish it to be given to another, as appears in his First Commandment. It is therefore gross idolatry and very displeasing to God that one have recourse to another than him. For that comes about by mistrusting his infinite goodness and mercy, as if there were something better and more merciful than he, or mistrust of his power and wisdom, as if he could not or knew not how to help us and to remove that faithlessness and mistrust by himself dwelling fully in his Son. He has redeemed us, he has saved us and cured us of all our ills [Gal. 3:13; Titus 2:14; Rev. 1:5]. Nevertheless we are warned that prayer not turn into sin, committing idolatry by praying to another than God. Not praying also in public to be seen, not mumbling or multiplying many words, but with great affection and few words, such that the tongue ceases much sooner than the heart, and that it begins to speak long after the heart and that the tongue never speaks or prays if the heart is not with God. For one must regard the dignity of him to whom one is speaking and what one says to him. For above all he hates hypocrisy. That one seek first the kingdom of God, that he may reign in us, destroying all sin, putting his righteousness in us, and nothing will be lacking to us."

philosophy. On the "Christian Philosophy," see LCC 20.6n8; also Cop/Calvin, *Academic Discourse*, at Appendix III, n.2.

to be in him. Cf. Bucer, *EN*, I [fol. 62^v.33ff]. For this, and all other notes to Bucer's *locus* on Matthew 6:1-13 [ed. 1530, fol. 62^r-67^v], see Appendix II, where Calvinian cross-references are provided in the margin.

Page 69.

ask. Luther, *Enchiridion* (1543 ed.) [fol. C.4^r]: "First of all, two things are required for true and God-pleasing prayer, which surely follows that which it asks. One is that we have God's promise. The other is that we have no doubt concerning that promise." Cf. *Treatise of Good Works*, 3rd Commandment, secs. IV, V [Eng. tr., PE 1.226-227].

you. Luther, *Enchiridion* (1543 ed.) [fol. C.4^v.23-C.5^r.19]: "Secondly, as we have said, this also is required for true prayer: that we have no doubt concerning the promise of our trustworthy and faithful God. For he has promised he will hear us, and has given the command to pray, that we might be sure and firmly believe, that he would hear us. As he says in Matt. 21:22 and Mark 11:24: 'I say to you, whatever you ask in prayer, believe that you will receive it, and it will be yours.' And in Luke 11:9ff: 'Ask, and it will be given you; seek, and you will find; knock, and it will be opened to you. For everyone who asks receives, and he who seeks finds, and to him who knocks it will be opened. What father among you, if one asks for bread, will give him a stone? Or if one asks for a fish, will instead of a fish give him a serpent; or if he asks for an egg, will give him a scorpion? If you, then, when you are evil, know how to give good gifts to your children, how much more will your heavenly Father give the Holy Spirit to those who ask him?' Our hearts ought by both these and like promises and precepts to be strengthened so that we may confidently pray, assured that all we ask we shall receive."

Page 70.

faith. Cf. Bucer, *EN*, I [fol. 63^v.57] (App. II).

them. Cf. Luther, *Enchiridion* (1543 ed.) [fol. C.4^v.9-22]: "And here you see, if we implore anything of God that it is to be rendered acceptable not by our prayers or our worthiness, but by God's inexhaustible goodness, which far and away anticipates our prayers and petitions, by his promise and command by which he arouses us to pray. As a consequence, by this means we learn that he is far more concerned for us and far readier to give than are we either to receive or ask. Moreover, because he offers us more of his benefits than we dare desire of him, this generosity of God ought to kindle and confirm us, that we should boldly and unhesitatingly pray to him."

tossed. Cf. Luther, *Enchiridion* (1543 ed.) [fol. C.5^r.20-C.5^v.10]: "Thirdly, if, when any persons pray and rashly pray, they doubt concerning God's will whether what they ask will come to pass or not, they commit two sins. First, that it comes to pass by their defect, whereby that prayer is somewhat lessened, and that they labor in vain. For thus also St. James says: 'If anyone asks anything of God, let him ask with faithfulness, with no doubting, for he who doubts is like a wave of the sea that is driven and tossed by the wind. For let that man not suppose he will receive anything from God' [James 1:6-8]. These words of James are to be so understood. Therefore, those who doubt, request nothing from God, because their hearts are not sure and calm. Faith moreover keeps the heart calm, that it may be able to receive the divine gifts."

Christ. Cf. Bucer, *EN,* I [fol. 63ᵛ.57] (App. II).

Page 71.

saints. Cf. *First Zurich Disputation* [SWHZ, pp. 62f]. See also, Zwingli, *Commentary,* 23, Invocation of the Saints [Eng. tr., LWZ 3.267-271]; *Exposition,* 1, Of God and the Worship of God [Eng. tr., LCC 24.247f]. Further, cf. Bucer, *EN,* I [fol. 64ʳ.1-4] (App. II).

Christ. Eck, *Enchiridion,* c. 15 (1532) [Eng. tr., Battles, p. 111], by a questionable exegesis of Scriptural and Apocryphal texts, defends the veneration of the saints and specifically saintly intercession for the living. Baruch 3:3 for him reads: "O Lord Almighty, God of Israel, hear now the prayer of the dead of Israel and their sons who have sinned before thee." II Macc. 15:12-14, the account of Judas Maccabeus' final dream, is also turned to account. Onias, the high priest, identifies the prophet Jeremiah as "the lover of the brethren and of the people of Israel, who prays much for the people and the whole holy city." Matt. 25:45 is glossed: "If honor is shown to the saints, honor will be shown to God." Ps. 36:6 ("For this every saint will pray to thee in a suitable time") is also glossed: "The Hebrews read 'every merciful one': the blessed moreover are saints and merciful." Absalom's two-year residence in Jerusalem without seeing his father is applied: "Thus, the sinner reconciled to God does not immediately present himself to God, but through mediators and intercessors" [II Sam. 14:28]. Solomon's placing a throne for his mother next to his own [I Kings 2:19] is related to Christ: "The true peacemaking Solomon, Christ, honoring his mother, did the same thing." The salutation of the Virgin as Queen of Heaven is to the Lutherans the supreme idolatry; their view is criticized by Eck as "the supreme injury imposed upon Christ who is our life, sweetness, hope and advocate with the Father." Cf. Thomas Aquinas, *S. Th.,* SS 86.11.

saints. Ambrose, *On Isaac or the Soul,* 8.75 [CSEL 52.1.694.6; PL 14.520].

Page 72.

heard. Eck, *Enchiridion* (1532), c. 15 [Eng. tr., Battles, p. 115]: "If therefore Christ the Head prays for us, why not also his members, the saints asking along with him, who conform themselves to Christ? . . . The living pray for one another, and often obtain their requests. . . . If therefore the living pray for one another, why would not also the blessed dead do this, who are more perfect in love, and more powerful before God, and purer of mind?" *Ibid.* [p. 120]: "We therefore honor, venerate, call upon and worship God and his saints, yet the former and the latter in different ways. God is the primal principle of being, conserving and governing for all, and alone gives grace and glory: therefore to him alone is owed *latria,* according to the text: 'You will worship the Lord your God, and serve him only'; again: 'To God alone be honor and glory.' . . . In the liturgy the church sets forth the distinction between the invocation or worship of God and the saints, where first the Holy Trinity is invoked under distinction of persons and unity of essence, to have pity on us. Then the intercession of the saints is implored, that they may pray for us. Finally, it returns to God that he deign to hear us, while the saints are praying along with us, to deliver us from evil, grant grace, and bestow eternal life."

thanksgiving. Cf. Bucer, *EN*, I [fol. 62^v.33-34] (App. II).

Page 73.
ceasing. *Ibid.* [fol. 63^v.11-12] (App. II).
all. *Ibid.* [fol. 63^r.45-46]. See Appendix II for this and the following references from Bucer's *locus*.

Page 74.
pray. *Ibid.* [fol. 62^v.24-25].
cares. *Ibid.* [fol. 62^v.39-40].
derision. *Ibid.* [fol. 62^v.36-38].
directions. *Ibid.* [fol. 62^v.39-40].
God. *Ibid.* [fol. 63^r.32].
example. *Ibid.* [fol. 62^v.50-51].
I Cor. 14:16-17. *Ibid.* [fol. 62^v.29].

Page 75.
headings. See Augustine, *Enchiridion,* 30.115 [Eng. tr., LCC 7.408]. In his *Enchiridion piarum precationum,* Luther has seven petitions, setting the sixth and seventh as follows [fol. 1.4^{r}ff]: "Sixth Petition: And lead us not &c. Indeed God tempts no one, yet we here ask that he be willing to defend us against the strategems of Satan, the world and our flesh, lest by them we be cast into unfaith, despair or other misdeeds. But if we be tempted by them, that we at last obtain victory. Seventh Petition: But free us from evil. Here we pray by way of summary, that our heavenly Father may defend and free us from all perils of body and soul, of possessions and reputation, and that at our last hour we may happily pass over from the calamitous life into life eternal" [tr. from the Latin text published at Wittenberg by Johann Lufft, 1529, as reproduced in WA 30/1, pp. 306/308]. It is to be noted that in the 1543 ed. of the *Enchiridion* [fol. m.2^{r-v}] the printer has placed the clue word [PETI-] at the bottom of fol. m.2^r, but has neglected to set above "Sed libera nos a Malo" the words "PETITIO VII" [fol. m.2^v]. Cf. Bucer, *EN,* I [fol. 67^r.45f] (App. II).

advantage. Bucer, *EN*, I [fol. 63^r.10-13] (App. II).

Page 76.
glory. Cf. Bucer, *EN*, I [fol. 83^r.10-12]: "Therefore in all prayers for external things, let the godly person add: 'Nevertheless let not my will, but thine, O Father, be done, if thou knowest I shall do it to thy glory, heal me, remove this or that evil, but not completely. . . .' "
First. Cf. Bucer, *EN,* I [fol. 64^r.20ff] (App. II).
himself. *Ibid.* [fol. 64^r.30-33].

Page 77.
demands. *Ibid.* [fol. 64^r.26-27, 33-35].

Page 78.
this. See note to p. 76, "himself."
Therefore. Cf. Luther, *Small Catechism,* 3.1 [Eng. tr., Schaff, CC 3.81]: "The name of God is indeed in itself holy; but we pray in the petition that it may be hallowed by us." See also *Enchiridion* (1543 ed.) [fol. 1.8^v].

Page 79.

works. Cf. Bucer, *EN*, I [fol. 184^v.31-32, 37^r.44-46]; *ibid.*, II [fol. 44^v.4-6]; *ibid.*, I [fol. 122^r].

power. See Bucer, *EN*, II [fol. 23^r.1-3]: "He blinds and hardens the reprobate, whatever the Spirit may do or say, as in Christ the Head of the saints, so also in all his members."

way. *Ibid.* [fol. 64^v.19-25] (App. II).

petition. Cf. Luther, *Small Catechism*, 3.3 [Eng. tr., Schaff, CC 3.82]: "God's good, gracious will is done indeed without our prayer; but we pray in this petition that it may be done also by us. . . . When God breaks and brings to nought every evil counsel and will which would hinder us from hallowing the name of God, and prevent his kingdom from coming to us (such as the will of the devil, of the world and of our own flesh); but makes us strong and steadfast in his Word and faith even unto our end; this is his gracious good will." Cf. *Enchiridion* (1543 ed.) [fol. m.1^{r-v}].

Page 80.

petition. With Calvin's treatment of the Fourth Petition, compare Bucer, *EN*, I [fol. 65^r.28-65^v.7] (App. II).

Page 81.

petition. Cf. Luther, *Small Catechism*, 3.5 [Eng. tr., Schaff, CC 3.83]: "We pray in this petition that our Father in heaven would not look upon our sins, nor on account of them deny our request; for we are not worthy of anything for which we pray, and have not merited it; but that he would grant us all things through grace; for we daily sin much, and deserve nothing but punishment. We will, therefore, also on our part, heartily forgive and willingly do good to those who sin against us." See also *Enchiridion* (1543 ed.) [fol. m.2^v]; Bucer, *EN*, I [fol. 65^v.8-42] (App. II).

Page 82.

varied. With Calvin's treatment of the Sixth Petition compare Bucer, *EN*, I [fol. 65^v.43-67^r.49]: "Lead us not into temptations"; and [fol. 67^r.45-67^v.19]: "but free us from the evil one" (App. II).

Page 84.

faith. With Calvin's brief comment on the concluding doxology, compare Bucer, *EN*, I [fol. 67^v.20-25] (App. II).

Amen. Cf. Luther, *Small Catechism*, 3.7 [Eng. tr., Schaff, CC 3.84]: "That I should be sure that such petitions are pleasing to our Father in heaven, and are heard by him; for he himself has commanded us thus to pray, and has promised that he will hear us. Amen, Amen: that is, Yea, yea, so shall it be." See also *Enchiridion* (1543 ed.) [fol. m.2^v].

Page 85.

him. Cf. Luther, *Enchiridion* (1543 ed.) [fol. C.7^r.3-12]: "Fifthly, that faith whereby we have trust in what is promised of God, is to be so tempered by us, that we not set any goal, time, place or measure for God, but we relinquish all things to his will, wisdom and omnipotence; then we shall be assured that what we ask may come to pass, even if neither place nor time nor even the reason by which they happen, may appear. For this is certain, that the divine wisdom knows and foresees these matters far better than we."

CHAPTER IV: THE SACRAMENTS

Page 87.

faith. Cf. pp. 120-121.

capacity. Yet another instance of the familiar Calvinian exegetical principle of *accommodation.*

it. From those matters which correspond to this cavil it seems to follow that Calvin here is referring to Bucer, *Apology* (1526) [fol. 12ᵛ, cf. Lang, p. 245]. Bucer says: "They teach that faith is strengthened by the use of those [sacraments], or just as herbs or other remedies contribute to bodily health, so they are like a divine instrument for the salvation of the soul, whomever else than the Holy Spirit they will prove to be the author of their doctrine. Just as faith is engendered by the help of the Spirit, so is it increased and confirmed by the same help; by the merit of Christ—not at all by the use of the sacraments—does the Father grant and promote the Spirit. Would these signs anywhere confirm faith in the word of God, signs of which you are ignorant unless you previously had faith in the word? It is just as if Caesar sent a document sealed with a new and unaccustomed sign, one never previously used on any other document. Ignorant of other proof as to the origin of that document, no one (never having seen that sign before) would be prompted to have faith in that document. In like manner, the symbols of Christians are certain protestations of faith, instituted the better to preserve the love of neighbors and the unity of the church—on scriptural authority we attribute nothing more to them."

adversaries. The words "our adversaries" have been supplied by the translator. The reference is to the Anabaptists as the *Brieve Instruction* makes clear [Eng. tr., fol. B.iiᵛ]: "And for the second parte, whyche is the promes of forgivenes of synnes, we canne haue no clearer probacion that thys sentence of S. Paule, where he sayeth, that circumcision was giuen to Abraham for a confirmacion, of the ryghtwysnes, which he frely obtayned of God, thorowe fayeth."

seal. Melanchthon, *LC* (1521), 9 [Eng. tr., LCC 19.133]: "The Scriptures add these signs to the promises as seals which remind us of the promises, and definitely testify of the divine will toward us. They testify that we shall surely receive what God has promised."

Page 88.

sows. Cf. VG: "Les Anciens pour confirmation de leurs appointemens avoyent accoustumé de tuer une truye." The reference is probably to the Latin *piaculum* or expiatory rite, described in Cato, *RR,* 139f. and Cicero, *Laws,* 2.22.57. Pagan Roman rituals had to be punctiliously performed, with the exact words before the act of sacrifice.

Augustine. Augustine, *John's Gospel,* 80.3 [Eng. tr., NPNF¹ 7.344]. *Against Faustus,* 19.16 [Eng. tr., NPNF¹ 4.244]. See also LCC 21.1281n8.

condemnation. Barth and Niesel [OS 5.263n3] cite A. Lang, *Der Evangelienkommentar Martin Butzers,* p. 418 [= *EN* (1530), I, fol. 18ʳ.43-50]: "Then how will it be a sure testimony of divine grace, to have been baptized and to have shared in the eucharist, when the pious have both in common with the impious? I ask, if anyone out of weak faith doubts concerning God's grace, but you, willing to confirm him, were to warn him of baptism and the eucharist, confidently saying, 'You cannot be unpleasing to God, after you have been baptized, after you have received the eucharist: those are sure testimonies of divine benevolence toward you.' his conscience in no wise fearful, would immediately respond—'How could these be sure indications of divine grace toward one, which I see to be shared with many impious persons, and even harmful to no small number of them?' "

believed. Augustine, *John's Gospel*, 80.3 [Eng. tr., NPNF[1] 7.344]

mercy. Zwingli, *Commentary*, 15 [Eng. tr., LWZ 3.184.9-11]: "For faith is that by which we rely on the mercy of God unwaveringly, firmly, and singlehandedly, as Paul shows us in many passages."

Page 89.

heart. Bucer, *EN* (1530), I [fol. 17[r].12-14] (= Lang, p. 413): "What else could we confer upon him through baptism, who with his whole heart believed in Jesus Christ than to add him to and receive him into the number of Christians?" *EN*, I [fol. 18[v].38-51] (= Lang p. 420): "Nothing of these things is present by the power or ministry of baptism; these are all works of the spirit of Christ. They are only represented by baptism, but those who are baptized are truly of those chosen to the kingdom of Christ. Surely Simon the Magician, and many others, who, without perfect faith, had still been baptized by the apostles, and absolved by it from sins, and even put on Christ, and were buried with Christ, so that they were going to walk in newness of life, commended to the church of Christ, yet never received anything of these, nor were even ever truly of Christ's flock. Just as it was not the intent of the apostles (who wished to baptize only those who believed and were divinely ordained to life) to join them to the flock. Hence Philip, before he baptized the eunuch who was seeking baptism, said: 'If you believe with your whole heart' [Acts 8:37]. Thus the pious wish to absolve no one of sins and declare no one a member of Christ, save those who have truly been chosen to it before the foundation of the world. Yet many spoiled fish are drawn up in the gospel net with the good, and many with Ananias and Sapphira lie to the Holy Spirit, who no one of sound mind will accordingly say that because they have been baptized with water, they truly have put on Christ and are of his flock." *EN*, II [fol. 50[r].39-43] (= Lang, p. 455): "No adult will not receive baptism to his destruction and the bread of the Supper as well, if he has not been renewed, and all the baptisms mentioned in the writings of the apostles were conferred on those who the apostles had not doubted were reborn. Thus Philip did not give baptism to the eunuch, without his professing that he believed in Christ with his whole heart."

learning. Cicero, *De Sen.*, 8.26.

consummate faith. Cf. Bucer, *EN* (1530), I [fol. 18[v].1-11] (= Lang, p. 419): "While our consciences begin to tremble with fear, not only are we not aroused by recalling the signs, but often even the eternal and undoubted word of God, the redemption of Christ and of our best Father, and his goodness shining everywhere cry out to us in vain—then there is need of the Spirit to confirm us, whom the God of all consolation [cf. Rom. 15:5] breathes upon us in time. To him alone let us yield this honor, that in all tribulation and temptation he will abundantly console us, even if we never recall the signs. Much more plausible and certain is what Paul has written in II Corinthians 1: [21-22]: 'Now it is God who confirms us, each one with you in Christ, and who has anointed us, who has also sealed us, and given the pledge of his spirit in our hearts.' He gives irrefragible testimony to our spirit that we are children and heirs of God [Rom. 8:17]. . . . What then of confirmation beyond this do we need?"

Page 90.

diminished. Cf. *Ibid.,* I [fol. 19ᵛ.3-14] (= Lang, pp. 422f): "Our ministry is concerned with the outward man, and does not always have the working of the Spirit conjoined. Truly therefore we diminish the glory of Christ and make too much of ourselves if we value our own ministry so highly that we say the Spirit of Christ is always conjoined to it. Nevertheless, we must strictly pray that he not be lacking to our ministry in order that we, together with Paul, may be found to be ministers of the New Covenant and the Spirit, not the letter [II Cor. 2]. Yet inasmuch as not only the Apostles but the Savior himself taught outwardly, yet the hearts of their hearers, when void of the Spirit, never felt anything of heavenly doctrine, we would be acting unworthily if we claimed for ourselves that, directly we pronounce the word of God, baptize with water, minister the bread and cup of the Lord—the Spirit of Christ perfects within what outwardly we either say or represent by symbols. 'The Spirit blows where it wills,' and they on whom it truly breathes are not unmindful of its power. Hence it is necessary for consciences to be confirmed, not by these [sacraments] which are done through men."

ensign. Cf. Zwingli, *Commentary,* 15 [Eng. tr., LWZ 3.180.25-29]: "Finally, there is also the so-called 'military sacrament,' by which soldiers are bound to obey their general according to the rights or laws of war. For wars also have laws, but laws of their own, for the regular laws are silent in the midst of arms." [Cf. Cicero, *Pro Milone,* 11; Calvin, *Comm. Sen. De Clem.,* 19.1.] Cf. Zwingli [LWZ 3.181.9-15]: "So I am brought to see that a sacrament is nothing else than an initiatory ceremony or a pledging. For just as those who were about to enter upon litigation deposited a certain amount of money, which could not be taken away except by the winner, so those who are initiated by sacraments bind and pledge themselves, and, as it were, seal a contract not to draw back." Etc. Cf. also [p. 184.12-25]: "So much for the meaning of the name. Christ left us two sacraments and no more, Baptism and The Lord's Supper. By these we are initiated, giving the name with the one, and showing by the other that we are mindful of Christ's victory and are members of His Church. In Baptism we receive a token that we are to fashion our lives according to the rule of Christ; by the Lord's Supper we give proof that we trust in the death of Christ, glad and thankful to be in that company which gives thanks to the Lord for the blessing of redemption which he freely gave us by dying for us. The other sacraments are rather ceremonials, for they have no initiatory function in the church of God. Hence it is not improper to exclude them; for they were not instituted by God to help us initiate anything in the church." Barth and Niesel [OS 5.270n1] remark that Calvin is here attacking Zwingli's opinion (as just quoted) and adduce as proof Calvin's letter [2187] of 20 April 1555 to Bullinger [CR 15.573]. Cf. also Zwingli, *Exposition of the 67 Articles,* Art. 18 [Eng. tr., Furcha, p. 112].

clearer. Cf. Zwingli, *Of Baptism* [Eng. tr., LCC 24.131].

ring. Cf. Calvin, *Comm. Sen. De Clem.,* 128.9f, note. Calvin's probable immediate source for this is Budé, *Annotationes in Pandectas,* 75A.

Page 91.

contrary. Cf. Luther, *Babylonian Captivity* [Eng. tr., PE 2.226; cf. LW 36.64]: "The great majority have supposed that there is some hidden spiritual power in the word or in the water, which works the grace of God in the soul of the recipient. Others deny this and hold that there is no power in the sacraments, but that grace is given by God alone, Who according to His covenant aids the sacraments He has instituted." This seems to refer to two scholastic views: that of the Thomists who held that the grace of the sacrament is contained in the sacramental sign and directly imparted by it and that of the Franciscans who held that the sign is merely a symbol, but that God, according to a *pactio*, or agreement, imparted the grace of the sacrament when the sign was being used. Luther, writing before the Zwinglian sacramental position came forward, is referring to the difference between the Thomist (normative Roman Catholic position of his day) and the Franciscan position. In using Luther's distinction, Calvin recasts the second tendency to describe the Zwinglian position which Luther had in the meantime combatted.

sorts. Cf. Luther, *Babylonian Captivity* [Eng. tr., PE 2.226f; cf. LW 36.64f]: "Hence they have been driven to attribute such great power to the sacraments of the New Law that in their opinion they benefit even such men as are in mortal sins, and that they do not require faith or grace; it is sufficient not to oppose a 'bar,' that is, an actual intention to sin again." Also, *Ibid.* [Eng. tr., PE 2.230; cf. LW 36.67]: "Hence, to seek the efficacy of the sacrament apart from the promise and apart from faith, is to labor in vain and to find damnation."

sin. Cf. Augustine, *Epist.* 98.10 (to Bonifacius) [Eng. tr., FC 18.138]; Duns Scotus, *In Sent.*, 4 dist. 1 q. 6, 10 [Opera 16.222]; Gabriel Biel, *Epitome*, 4 dist. 1 q. 3 art. 1.

judgment. Cf. Luther, *Babylonian Captivity* [Eng. tr., PE 2.227; cf. LW 36.65]: "For it is an error to hold that the sacraments of the New Law differ from those of the Old Law in the efficacy of their 'signifying.' The 'signifying' of both is equally efficacious. The same God who now saves me by baptism saved Abel by this sacrifice, Noah by the bow, Abraham by circumcision, and all the others by their respective signs."

give it. Augustine, *Enarrationes in Psalmos*, Ps. 73, praef. 2 [Eng. tr., LF 3.493 (margin)]. Augustine, *Epistle*, 138.18 (to Marcellinus) [Eng. tr., FC 20.41]. Augustine, *Questions on the Heptateuch*, 4.33 [PL 34.732.46-48].

power. Augustine, *John's Gospel*, 26.12 [Eng. tr., NPNF[1] 7.171f].

Others. In the edition of 1539, Calvin attributes this view not to a contemporary tendency (as it seems here) but to ancient writers overzealous for the dignity of the sacraments.

Page 92.

opposite. Pliny, *Natural History*, 2.60.150 [Eng. tr., LCL 1.286f]; Seneca, *Natural Questions*, 1.3 [Eng. tr., J. Clarke, *Physical Science in the Time of Nero*, pp. 16-22]. Calvin, with great irony, criticizes Aristotle for dealing with intermediate causes in his *De Meteor*, only to forget the ultimate cause of all, God; see *Comm. Gen.*, 19.22 [OC 23.277]; *Comm. Ps.*, 147.15 [OC 32.430]. Also in Calvin, *Comm. Sen. De Clem.*, p. 51.33f, note.

Hezekiah. Cf. Melanchthon, *LC*, (1521), 9 [Eng. tr., LCC 19.132]: "The Lord prolonged the life of Hezekiah through a revelation of Isaiah. God strengthened that promise by adding a sign that the king might know for certain that it would be kept: the shadow on the sundial went back ten steps [II Kings 20:8-11]. Gideon was strengthened by two signs lest he doubt that Israel would be liberated under his leadership [Judges 6:33-40]."

Page 93.

Lord's Supper. Cf. Melanchthon, *LC* (1521), 9 [Eng. tr., LCC 19.134]: " 'Neither circumcision counts for anything nor uncircumcision' [I Cor. 7:19]. So Baptism is nothing, and participation in the Lord's Supper is nothing, but they are testimonies and seals [καὶ σφαγίδες] of the divine will toward you which give assurance to your conscience if it doubts grace or God's good will toward itself."

Abraham. Cf. Melanchthon, *LC* (1521), 9 [Eng. tr., LCC 19.133f]: "You can most easily understand the nature of signs from Paul in Rom. 4.10ff, where he speaks of circumcision, as I shall here explain," etc.

Page 94.

Augustine. Augustine, *John's Gospel*, 15.8; 120.2 [Eng. tr., NPNF[1] 7.101, 434]: *Enarrationes in Psalmos*, Ps. 40:10; 126:7; 138:2 [Eng. tr., LF 2.174; 5.24, 192]; *Sermons*, 5.3 [PL 38.55.6-12].

profession. Zwingli, *De peccato originali declaratio* (1526) [CR Zw 5.392.24ff].

Word of life. The Greek New Testament text reads ῥήματι. Calvin is apparently using the Vulgate text here, which reads "in verbo vitae." In his *Comm. Eph.* he uses simply "in verbo."

Page 95.

remedies. Tertullian, *On Repentance*, 7.12 [Eng. tr., ANF 3.662]; Origen, *Hom. in Lev.*, Hom. 2.4 [PG 12.416f]; Cyprian, *Works and Alms*, 2 [Eng. tr., ANF 5.476]; *Lord's Prayer*, 32 [Eng. tr., ANF 5.456]. Cf. Gratian, *Decr.*, 2.33.3.1.72 [Friedberg, 1.1179], quoting Jerome, *Epist.*, 84.6: "The second plank after shipwreck is simply to confess. You have imitated one who errs; imitate now one corrected. We have erred in our youth; in our old age let us be changed; let us join together groanings and link tears."

baptism. Cf. Melanchthon, *LC* (1521), 9 [LCC 19.137]: "Sins terrify, death terrifies, other evils of the world terrify; but simply trust that because you have received the sign of God's mercy toward you, you will be saved no matter how the gates of hell storm against you."

Page 96.

apostles. The reformers were divided on the question of whether the baptism by John the Baptist and that by Christ were one and the same: Luther and Melanchthon held the two rites to be different, and in this they were followed by the Anabaptists. Melanchthon, *LC* (1521), 9 [Eng. tr., LCC 19.139] expresses the former view: "But John baptized with water because he was not the One in whom man should believe, the One who was to save. Since Christ is the Savior, he baptizes with the Holy Spirit and with fire. Those who have been washed by John were rebaptized even though they were justified, and there were justified Jews everywhere who had not been washed in the baptism of John. For the baptism of Christ gives assurance of grace already bestowed." Zwingli holds to the latter view as the following excerpts show: *Commentary*, 17 [Eng. tr., LWZ 3.189]: "How the baptism of John and that of Christ differ is a question much mooted both in the past and today, but plainly useless. For there is no difference at all as far as cause and end are concerned, although there is some difference with respect to use or form. Yet this is not a difference properly speaking, for we can variously use the same thing without loss of faith. John's baptism effected nothing; but we are speaking here of water baptism, not of inner cleansing, which is done through the Holy Spirit. Christ's baptism effects nothing; for Christ was content with John's baptism both for himself and for his disciples." Etc. For a discussion of Zwingli's interpretation of the baptism by John see G. W. Bromiley's remarks in LCC 24:123, and Zwingli's notes on Acts 19:1ff in *Of Baptism*, Eng. tr., LCC 24.160ff, where he refutes the argument of the

Anabaptists. Also see Zwingli's continuing discussion of the passage in *Commentary*, 17 [Eng. tr., LWZ 3.194.14-196.5].

Israel. Cf. Melanchthon, *LC* (1521), 9 [Eng. tr., LCC 19.136]: "Baptism was foreshadowed in the Israelites' crossing of the Arabian Gulf." Etc.

Page 97.

some. Alexander of Hales, *S. Th.*, 4 q. 20 membr. 1 art. 2; Bonaventura, *In Sent.*, 4 dist. 4 p. 1 art. 1 q.1 [ed. Quaracchi minor, 4.84-86]: "Whether Baptism in those worthy to receive it wipes out all guilt."

righteousness. Anselm, *On the Virgin Conception and Original Sin*, ch. 6; Eng. tr., D. Johnson and R. Phyles, in J. Hopkins and H. Richardson, *Anselm of Canterbury, Theological Treatises* (1967), 3.12: "Now although it is true that the absence of righteousness is nothing both where there ought to be righteousness and where it ought not to be, yet God rightly punishes sinners on account of something and not on account of nothing." Duns Scotus, *In Sent.* 2 Dist. 30 q. 2 *Opera* 13.293: "Whether original sin is the lack of original righteousness?" He answers that original sin is the lack of original righteousness in the will and is not concupiscence or ignorance. William of Ockham, *Quodlibeta*, 3 q. 10; *In Sent.*, 2 q. 26 U [vol. 4, fol. J.6^r]: "I say that original sin *de facto* according to Anselm in *On the Virgin Conception* [*and Original Sin*] is not anything positive in the soul, but only is the lack of owed righteousness. . . . But, to speak of original sin *de possibili*, I say it could happen through absolute power that one might speak of original sin as the lack of neither natural nor supernatural gift, but only that someone on account of preceding demerit in some respect may be unworthy of eternal life or of God's acceptance." Cf. Johannes Cochlaeus, *De libero arbitrio*, II [fol. M.3^v.3-26]: ". . . sin is not (as you [Melanchthon] foolishly think) any substance or positive being. Hear, I beg of you, what St. Dionysius (whom you impiously and blasphemously call more Platonic than Christian) both acutely and fully says on this: 'Substance is to be applied according to the accidents to evil, and on account of something else, not from its own beginning. As when something is done, it would seem indeed to be right, because it is done for the sake of good, but actually it is not right. For we think to be good what is not good. It is a wonder that what one aspires to is one thing; what one does, another. Now evil is beyond the way, beyond intention, beyond nature, beyond cause, beyond beginning beyond end, beyond limits, beyond will, beyond substance. Evil therefore is privation and defect, weakness, inconsistency, and frustration; deprived of goal, beauty, life, feeling, reason, perfection, foundation and cause, indefinite, unfruitful, idle, feeble, disordered, unlike, boundless, dark, lacking substance, and itself existing in no way, nowhere and nothing. How can anything evil exist at all? By mixture with good. That which is completely devoid of good is neither anything nor can be anything.' These are the words spoken by the holy man Dionysius, which you rashly found fault with before understanding them." Also see Cochlaeus, *Philipp.* 2.35 [fol. G.3^r]. Cf. Melanchthon, *LC* (1521), 3 [Eng. tr., LCC 19.31]: "Accordingly, when the Sophists say that original sin is the lack of original righteousness, as they express it, they are right. But why do they not add that where there is no original righteousness or the Spirit, there in reality is flesh, godlessness, a contempt for spiritual things?" The editors at this passage [LCC 19.31n.32] cite as "Sophists": Thomas Aquinas, *S. Th.*, PS 85.3; Gabriel Biel, *Epitome*, 2 dist. 30 q. 1 a. 3.

energy. Cf. Melanchthon, *LC* (1521), 3 [Eng. tr., LCC 19.30]: "Original sin is a native propensity and an innate force and energy by which we are drawn to sinning."

Ibid. [p. 33, alt.]: "Original sin is a living energy in every part of us, always bearing fruit—vices."

Page 98.

people. Cf. Luther, *Enchiridion* (1543 ed.) [fol. Q.6^v]: "Secondly, baptism is also an outward sign or mark which distinguishes us from all other men, who have not been baptized, so that we are recognized as being the people of our leader Jesus Christ, under whose sign (the cross) we assiduously struggle against sins."

Page 99.

sent. Cf. Luther, *Babylonian Captivity* [Eng. tr., PE 2.224; cf. LW 36.62]: "Hence, we ought to receive baptism at the hands of a man just as if Christ himself, nay, God himself, were baptizing us with his own hands."

minister. E.g., Augustine, *Enarr. in Ps.*, Ps. 10:5 [Eng. tr., LF 1.96]; *Epist.* 89.5 [Eng. tr., FC 18.38].

government. See *Schleitheim Confession*, Art. 1 [Wenger, p. 248]: "This excludes all infant baptism, the highest and chief abomination of the pope." Zwingli had in his *Commentary* (1525), 17, promised to refute this assertion [Eng. tr., LWZ 3.197], and done so in his *Of Baptism* (1525) [Eng. tr., LCC 24.149]; and in his *Refutation of Baptist Tricks* [Eng. tr., SWHZ, pp. 247-251]. See also LCC 21.1316n.26. Just as Calvin had identified Anabaptist teaching on the incarnation with the Manichees, so here he identifies their views on the sacraments with those of the Donatists. In his *Brieve Instruction* (1544) [Eng. tr., fol. A.vi^v-B.vi^r] Calvin refutes Article 1 at length. Cf. W. E. Keeney, in Battles, *Analysis*, pp. 80*f.

Page 100.

Paul. Bullinger, *In Act. Apostol.* [fol. H.1^v-3^r].

added. Wendel, *Evolution*, p. 135 n.77, cites this context as proof that Calvin had read Zwingli, *Commentary on True and False Religion.*

Page 101.

face. These lines represent a paraphrase of Calvin's rather compressed reasoning in a context suppressed in the edition of 1539.

preaching. On the Anabaptist rejection of infant baptism see p. 99, note to "government," above.

Page 102.

Lord's Supper. Zwingli, *Commentary*, 18.6 [Eng. tr., LWZ 3.228.13-16]: "The Lord's Supper [*caena dominica*], then, as Paul calls it [I Cor. 11:25-26], is a commemoration of Christ's death, not a remitting of sins, for that is the province of Christ's death alone." Cf. *Commentary*, 18; LWZ 3.199.38 [*caenae dominicae*].

Eucharist. Zwingli, *Commentary*, 18 [Eng. tr., LWZ 3.199.38-200.8]: "The Greeks gave the name Εὐχαριστία to the Dominical Supper, having always, if I may be permitted to say so, been more pious and more learned men than the Latins, as their written works bear witness clearer than day. And they undoubtedly gave it this name for the reason that they understood both from faith and from the meaning of the words of Christ and the apostles, that Christ wished to have a joyful commemoration of himself made by his supper and thanks given publicly for the blessing which he has bountifully bestowed upon us."

faith. The phrase, "exercises of faith" applied to the sacraments is reminiscent of Luther and also of Melanchthon. See, e.g., *LC* (1521), 9 [Eng. tr., LCC 19.137]: "From this it is evident that signs are nothing but reminders [μνημόσυνα] for exercizing faith." Pannier, *Institution*, 4.7, c (p. 302) claims Calvin is at this juncture referring to an Anabaptist view. Compare also Calvin's description of prayer as "the chief exercise of faith," as expressed in the amplified title of Chapter 3 [=3.20 in the edition of 1559]. On this see R. D. Loggie, "Chief Exercise of Faith: An Exposition of Calvin's Doctrine of Prayer," *Hartford Quarterly*, 5.65-81. Cf. also *Catechism* (1538) (ed., tr., F. L. Battles), 40.4f (on Prayer), and 43.7f (on the sacraments).

Page 103.

exchange. Cf. Luther, *The Freedom of a Christian*, 12 (German version) [Eng. tr., B. L. Woolf, *Reformation Writings of Martin Luther*, 1.363]: "If Christ has all good things, including blessedness, these will also belong to the soul. If the soul is full of trespasses and sins, these will belong to Christ. At this point a contest of happy exchanges takes place." Etc.

us. The doctrine of the mystical ascent of the believer, here sketched, was, in the course of controversy, more fully developed in later editions of the *Institutes*. In his *Second Defense of the Faith concerning the Sacraments in Answer to Joachim Westphal* of 1556 [Eng. tr., T&T 2.281], Calvin succinctly distinguishes his opinion from that of the Lutherans: ". . . a true and real communion . . . consists in our ascent to heaven, and requires no other descent in Christ than that of spiritual grace. It is not necessary for him to move his body from its place in order to infuse his vivifying virtue into us."

him. Cf. Calvin, *Catechism* (1538), 20, iii [Battles tr., p. 25]: "Indeed, he put on our flesh in order that having become Son of man he might make us sons of God with him; having received our poverty in himself, he might transfer his wealth to us; having submitted to our weakness, he might strengthen us by his power; having accepted our mortality, he might give us immortality; having descended to earth, he might raise us to heaven."

you. Luther, *Enchiridion* (1543 ed.) [fol. m.5^r]: "What benefit is there in so having eaten and drunk? I reply, These words ('It is given for you,' and 'it is shed for remission of sins') point it out to us. For in this sacrament remission of sins, life and eternal blessedness are given to us through these words. For remission of sins and blessedness of necessity go together."

salvation. Cf. Luther, *Enchiridion* (1543 ed.) [fol. T.8^v]: "And then indeed will it be opportune for you to confess and to lament to God concerning your misery, and to say, 'Lord Jesus, this sacrament was instituted by thee, and handed down to us, in order that through it we might obtain forgiveness of sins.' "

gladden. Luther, *Enchiridion* (1543 ed.) [fol. V.1^{r-v}]: "When therefore you are tried by death or conscience, you can arouse yourself by this sacrament and defy both Satan and sins as well; you can also confirm your faith and gladden your conscience, so that it no more fears God, but loves him."

Page 104.

interpret. Cf. de Castro, *Adv. haer.* (1534 ed.), 6 [fol. 108 F].

cross. This may be a reference to Wessel Gansforth's (c. 1420-1489) view of the

Supper, derived (as G. H. Williams points out in his *Radical Reformation*, p. 31) from Rupert of Deutz (d. 1129/1135): ". . . Christ descended into Hades for three days and three nights in order that the departed saints might receive his body, *in a wonderful manner in that kind [specie], wherein it hung on the cross.*" This notion of a Eucharistic *descensus* was picked up by Schwenckfeld and Servetus. The latter carried this teaching in his *On the Errors of the Trinity* (1531); it was refuted by Bucer in his lectures of December 1531. (Williams, *Radical Reformation*, p. 270).

body. This is apparently a brief reference to the doctrine of impanation, that the celestial flesh of the Son is, like manna from heaven, in the bread of the altar. See G. H. Williams, *The Radical Reformation*, pp. 328f.

under the bread. Cf. Luther, *The Blessed Sacrament of the Holy and True Body of Christ and the Brotherhoods* [Eng. tr., LW 35.60]: ". . . his flesh under the bread . . ."

forth. Zwingli, *Commentary*, 18, in his extended exposition of *est* as *significat* [Eng. tr., LWZ 3.240f] adduces from Tertullian, *Against Marcion*, 1.14, and especially from Augustine, the words "sign" and "figure" to apply to "body." Augustine, *Enarr. in Ps.*, 3.1 [Eng. tr., NPNF¹ 8.5]: ". . . the time at which he committed and delivered to his disciples the figure of his body and blood." Again, *John's Gospel*, 27.1-2 [Eng. tr., cf. NPNF¹ 7.174]: "The sign that one has eaten and drunk is, namely this: if one abides in him and is his abode, if one dwells and is dwelt in, if one clings and is not abandoned." Luther criticizes this position in *The Sacrament of the Body and Blood of Christ—Against the Fanatics* [Eng. tr., LW 36.346]: "There are only three words: 'This is my body.' So the one [Carlstadt] turns up his nose at the word 'this' and severs it from the bread, claiming that one should interpret it thus: 'Take, eat—this is my body': as if I were to say: 'Take and eat; here sits Hanns with the red jacket.' The second [Zwingli] seizes upon the little word 'is'; to him it is the equivalent of 'signifies.' The third [Oecolampadius] says, 'this is my body' means the same as, 'this is the figure of my body.' " See also *Ibid.* [p. 348]: ". . . these new preachers of ours . . . say that it is only a sign, by which one may recognize Christians and judge them, so that we have nothing more of it than the mere shell. So they come together, and eat and drink, in order that they may commemorate his death. All the power is said to be in this commemoration, the bread and the wine are no more than a sign and a color by which one may recognize that we are Christians."

Page 105.

heaven. See Ockham (?), *Centiloquium*, concl. 25, 28. *Opera plurima* [Lyon, 1494-96/1962], 4, fol. AA.7^{r-v}: "Christ's body can be everywhere just as God is everywhere" [concl. 25]. "The same body numerically extended can by extension be in many places at the same time" [concl. 28].

hell. Cf. Tertullian, *Against Marcion*, 3.8 [Eng. tr., ANF 3.327f]; *On the Flesh of Christ*, 5 [Eng. tr., ANF 3.525f].

heaven. Willibald Pirkheimer, *De vera Christi carne et vero eius sanguine, ad Joan. Oecolampadium responsio* (1526) [fol. F.5^v]; cf. Luther, *Dass diese Wort Christi "Das ist mein Leib" noch fest stehen* (1527) [WA 23.147.28ff].

properties. See p. 52, note on "properties," above, where LCC 20.483n.4 is cited. To the reference there given should be added Dedication of the *Praelectiones in Jeremiam* (Epist. 3986, 1563) [OC 20.72ff], as cited by Wallace, *Word and Sacrament*, p. 230.

way. On the *extra Calvinisticum*, See W. Niesel, *The Theology of Calvin* [Eng. tr.,

H. Knight (1956), pp. 118f]. Cf. *Inst.* (1559), 2.13.4; 2.14.1. A recent study of this is: E. Willis, *Calvin's Catholic Christology: The Function of the So-called Extra Calvinisticum.* Also see Leo I, *Tome*, c. 4 (p. 364): "The Son of God, descending from his seat in heaven, yet not departing from the glory of the Father, enters this lower world, born after a new order, by a new mode of birth."

evasion. See Caspar Schwenckfeld von Ossig, *Corpus Schwenckfeldianorum*, 14.117.34ff [Doc. 912 (1554)]; also *CS*, 7.780 [Doc. 354 (1541)]. Cf. Williams, *The Radical Reformation*, pp. 255-259. The doctrine here described by Calvin as a "subtle evasion" is a version of the celestial flesh eucharistic theory. Luther's view of it is unmistakable: in *The Sacrament of the Body and Blood of Christ—Against the Fanatics* (1526) [Eng. tr., LW 36.339f], he says: "How much easier it is with a glorified body than with a bodily voice!" Luther obviously prefers his doctrine of ubiquity over this adiaphoric assertion.

form. Biel, *Epitome*, 4 dist. 11 q. 1 D [1501/1965]; cf. also Pirkheimer, *De vera Christi carne* [fol. F.5^v].

Page 106.

glorious body. Cf. Luther, *The Sacrament of the Body and Blood of Christ* [Eng. tr., LW 36.342]: "Christ is around us and in us in all places. . . . He is present everywhere, but he does not wish that you grope for him everywhere."

truth. Augustine, *Epist.*, 187.3.10 (to Dardanus) [Eng. tr., FC 30.228f].

Page 107.

with us. No exact reference to this Roman Catholic argument has been found, but cf. Peter Lombard, *Sent.*, 4.10.1 [p. 798.20-24]: "Likewise, through the fact he is man, he is in heaven, that is, visibly; but he is invisibly in the altar, because he does not appear [there] in human form, but is covered by the form of bread and wine. Hence also his flesh which is on the altar is called 'invisible'; but because it does not appear in its own kind [or: form] it is called 'invisible.' "

there. cf. Luther, *The Blessed Sacrament* [Eng. tr., LW 35.59]: ". . . Christ . . . gave his true natural flesh in the bread. . . ."

flesh. Cf. *Deux Discours de Calvin au Colloque de Lausanne*, I (5 Oct. 1536) [OC 9.884]: "But that is a spiritual communication by which in power and effective working he makes us truly participants of all we can receive of grace in his body and his blood, but entirely spiritually, that is, by the bond of his spirit."

immortality. Irenaeus, *Against Heresies*, 4.18.5 [Eng. tr., ANF 1.486.33-40]: "For we offer to him his own, announcing consistently the fellowship and union of the flesh and Spirit. For as the bread, which is produced from the earth, when it receives the invocation of God, is no longer common bread, but the Eucharist, consisting of two realities, earthly and heavenly; so also our bodies, when they receive the Eucharist, are no longer corruptible, having the hope of the resurrection to eternity."

blood. Luther, *On the Sacrament of the Eucharist to the Waldensian Brethren* [WA 11.434ff].

faith. See p. 7, note to "word," above.

adoration. Zwingli, *Commentary*, 18 [Eng. tr., LWZ 3.249.30-33]: "For since God alone is to be worshiped [cf. Matt. 4:10], and absolutely no creature, so that even the theologians declare that Christ's pure humanity cannot be worshiped without risk of idolatry, is it not the height of impiety to worship the bread?"

Page 108.

there. Urban IV, *Transiturus de hoc* (1264) [Mansi 23.1077], quoted by *Clement. Decretal.*, 3.16, "On Relics and the Veneration of the Sacrament" [Friedberg, 2.1174-1177].

apostles. Zwingli, *Commentary*, 18 [Eng. tr., LWZ 3.238.22-24]: "Do we read that anyone of the apostles worshiped the supper when Christ was instituting this commemoration of himself?"

Page 109.

death. Zwingli, *Commentary*, 18 [Eng. tr., LWZ 3.237.32-35]: "The 'Eucharist,' then, or 'Synaxis,' or Lord's Supper, is nothing but the commemoration by which those who firmly believe that by Christ's death and blood they have become reconciled with the Father proclaim this life-giving death, that is, preach it with praise and thanksgiving."

intrude. This simile, used in *Didache*, 9.4, is elaborated by Cyprian, *Epist.*, 63.13 [ed. Bayard (1961) 2.208, Eng. tr., (*Epist.*, 62) ANF 5.362]: ". . . in which very sacrament our people are shown to be made one, so that in like manner as many grains, collected and ground, and mixed together into one mass, make one bread; so in Christ, who is the heavenly bread, we may know that there is one body, with which our member is joined and united." See also the following references: Augustine, *Sermon*, 272 [PL 38.1247f]; Peter Lombard, *Sent.*, 4.8.4 [p. 792]. Luther, *The Sacrament of the Body and Blood of Christ* [Eng. tr., LW 36.353]: "Just as each grain loses its form and takes on a common form from the others, so that you cannot see or distinguish one from the other, and all of them are identical, yet separately present; so too should Christendom be one, without sects. . . ." Luther, *The Blessed Sacrament of the Holy and True Body of Christ* [Eng. tr., LW 35.51]: "This fellowship consists in this, that all the spiritual possessions of Christ and his saints are shared with and become the common property of him who receives this sacrament. Again, all sufferings and sins also become common property; and thus love engenders love in return and [mutual love] unity." *Ibid.* [Eng. tr., LW 35.59]: "Thus in the sacrament we too become united with Christ, and are made one body with the saints, so that Christ comes for us and acts on our behalf." Zwingli, too, uses this theme. See *An Exposition of the Faith*, 5 [Eng. tr., LCC 24.263]: "For as bread is made up of many grains and wine of many grapes, so by a common trust in Christ which proceeds from the one Spirit the body of the Church is constituted and built up out of many members a single body, to be the true temple and body of the indwelling Spirit." Also see Oecolampadius, *Antisyngramma* [*Apologetica* (1526), fol. A.1ʳ]. As stated in the note to the title of Chapter 1, Calvin had access to Luther through a Latin translation of the *Betbüchlein (Enchiridion Piarum Precationum);* the relevant passage in the Latin edition of Wittenberg, 1543, is at fol. V.7ʳ.

Page 110.

love. Augustine, *John's Gospel*, 26.13 [Eng. tr., NPNF¹ 7.172].

another. Cf. Luther, *Enchiridion* (1543 ed.) [fol. V.2ᵛ.6-11]: "This moreover is the fruit [of the sacrament]: that as we eat the body of Christ and drink his blood, so we in turn may allow ourselves to be eaten and drunk by others, that is, that we may undertake all our actions, all our life to advance our neighbor's welfare."

body. Cf. Augustine, *On Baptism*, 5.8, 9 [PL 43.181]; *John's Gospel*, 6.15; 62.1 [PL 35.1432, 1801]. See Smits, 2.158, 189, 195.

Page 111.

cup. Ganoczy [p. 160, n.154-156] notes that both Zwingli and Calvin, in explaining the self-examination enjoined by Paul [I Cor. 11:28], link brotherly love and the conditions requisite to avoid unworthy partaking of the Supper. Zwingli, having quoted Paul, says [*Comm.*, 18, Eng. tr., LWZ 3.232.18-20; 238.1-4]: "For whosoever eats of this symbol shows himself to be a member of the church of Christ. . . . Those who come together for this practice or festival, to commemorate, that is, to proclaim the Lord's death, bear witness by this very fact that they are members of one body, are one bread. . . ." Ganoczy singles out especially the following words of Calvin for his comparison: "On this account, Paul enjoins that a man examine himself . . . whether, as he is considered a member by Christ, he in turn so holds all his brethren as members of his body. . . ." The correlation between "duties . . . of love" and "worthy eating" is also remarked.

himself. To our note at *Inst.* (1559), 1.5.3 [LCC 20.54n11] on this favorite phrase of Calvin for self-examination should be added: Erasmus, *Adagia*, 1.7.86: " 'To descend into oneself' is for one to inspect his own vices. It is derived either from pits or storage places into which men descend so they can know what is stored or hidden there. Alluded to are the caverns and recesses of the human heart, to which Momus wished the door to be closed." Erasmus then quotes Persius, *Sat.*, 4.23f, the same passage used by Calvin, *Comm. Sen. De Clem.*, 6.1. See also Calvin, *Sermons on Job*, 71 (Job 19:25) [OC 34.126.27f] and *Catechism* (1538), 23 (p. 34): ". . . we must diligently see to it, as often as we call upon the Lord, that we descend into the innermost recesses of our hearts." Bucer applies the phrase to the self-examination enjoined in prayer; see *EN*, I [fol. 63^v.6-8]: "Paul everywhere greatly urges his followers to be persistent in prayer, obviously desiring that they descend into themselves. . . ."

worthily. Cf. Luther, *Enchiridion* (1543 ed.) [fol. V.1^v.15-V.2^r.9]: "And this indeed is the true use of the sacrament and for this reason consciences are not tortured and receive consolation. For this sacrament was not instituted by God to be some sort of poison or cross, to strike terror in minds—an opinion spread abroad in the previous age by impious teachers, one that gripped all indiscriminately. For they so taught that we offer our righteousness as a sacrifice to God. Thus did it come to pass that those words which were full of consolation and life, by which consciences were aroused and strengthened, lay utterly despised and unknown. But so rather should it have come about that we felt there to be nothing in this sacrament but supreme grace, consolation and eternal life. A very present poison it is to those who take the sacrament rashly, who feel no infirmity, no vices, no urgent need, just as if they were previously already pure and righteous."

sin. Cf. Alexander of Hales, *S. Th.*, 4 q. 46 memb. 3 art. 3; Bonaventura, *In Sent.*, 4 dist. 12 p. 2, q. 1 [Quaracchi ed. minor 4.274f]: On the question whether this sacrament is efficacious in any righteous man, Bonaventura concludes: ". . . this sacrament is not efficacious in anyone except him who approaches it worthily. To approach it worthily consists in this, that a man prepares himself as he ought. Now it is not fitting or fruitful to receive this sacrament as one receives other food; and because in this sacrament divine Majesty and supreme love are expressed, it ought to be received with honor and devotion. And because such a noble guest is not received with honor and devotion in a dirty inn, it is necessary that a man prepare the inn for God through self-examination. And because he does not prepare the inn for the guest unless he know him, it is necessary that he distinguish this food from other foods. To the end then that this sacrament may be efficacious in anyone, first it is needful that one distinguish this food from others through faith; secondly, to prepare an inn through self-examination; thirdly, to receive [the guest] into the inn prepared with honor and devotion. . . . If a righteous man duly prepares himself, he receives; otherwise, if out of some sluggishness or distraction he does not duly prepare himself, it bears no or slight efficacy, although it does not incur a mortal offense." Etc. De Castro, *Adv. haer.,* 6 [fol. 116A ff].

satisfaction. Cf. Alexander of Hales, *Ibid.*; Biel, *Epitome,* 4 dist. 9 q. 2 B; de Castro, *Adv. haer.,* 6 [fol. 116F].

best. Alexander of Hales, *S. Th.,* 4 q. 46 memb. 3 art. 2; Biel, *Ibid.*

door. Cf. Luther, *Enchiridion* (1543 ed.) [fol. V.1^v.4-14]: "Thus it will come to pass that from day to day you will be rendered better, while otherwise you would act as an idle and lazy person. For the longer we abstain from this sacrament, the more unfitted to receive it we are rendered. But if you feel yourself unprepared, weak, even void of faith, how otherwise will you hope to be able to be strengthened? Will you wait until you are utterly pure and have absolute and perfect faith? Yet if you do that and never approach the sacrament, and come into its very presence, it will benefit you nothing."

Page 112.

him. Cf. Luther, *Enchiridion* (1543 ed.) [fol. V.2^r.9-15]: "For this sacrament requires a man who recognizes his own vices, and who sees how far away from true righteousness he is, and who yearns to be justified. The main thing therefore is to feel sin. For although as long as we live we have sins, yet not all of us recognize that fact."

God. Cf. Luther, *Enchiridion* (1543) [fol. V.2^r.16-24]: "Now these things should be enough: that you know how best to prepare yourself when you wish to receive this sacrament, that you exercise and confirm your faith by these words with which Christ instituted this sacrament, and that you feel Christ's body was truly given for you, Christ's blood truly poured out for you. These words clearly show what is the true use of the sacrament, and what it imparts to us if we partake of it."

love. *Ibid.* [fol. V.2^r.25-V.2^v.17]: "Now another thing follows, which flows as from a spring from the first, i.e., faith, that is, Christian love. Also it is fitting to cultivate it carefully, for God requires this of us, that the fruits which we appropriate from this sacrament shine like a light and that it be clear to all that we have used this sacrament with our other fruit."

supply. Cf. *Ibid.* (1543 ed.) [fol. V.6^r.6-V.6^v.20]: "Blessed Lord Jesus, I indeed come to this sacrament, but I feel no fruit from the thing itself, always I remain the same, as yet I feel concupiscence, anger, impatience, etc. And with me stays that huge idle treasure. Grant therefore that I may take some fruit from it, and that I may feel other emotions, likewise that other actions may by this sacrament be sown in my heart. But if once you begin to change, it will come to pass that you will be strengthened more and more, and from day to day put forth more good works. For this life is nothing else than an assiduous use of faith, love and the cross. Yet in no human being can these three perfectly exist. In Christ indeed these were perfect, who like the son was set forth as the example for us, that all may imitate even though we can never attain it. Therefore you should always find the stronger mixed with the weak; on the other hand some stronger with the latter also; and the weak are exercised by small calamities, the stronger by greater ones, so that thus all may be conformed to the image of Christ. For so ought our life to be that, from faith to faith, from love to love, from patience to patience, from cross to cross, we go forward. Nor ought this life to be called justice, but justification; not purity, but purification. Not yet have we attained that goal which has been set for us, but we are struggling toward it, and now are on the road. Some have been carried further, some follow the others at a distance. Our effort is approved by God, if he sees us striving toward the goal, even if we are as yet far from it. And when it seems fitting, he will meet and confirm us in faith and love. Then suddenly will come the passage from this world to heaven. But meanwhile while we are living here, let each of us bear one another, just as Christ also bore us, for no human being is perfect." We see here in Luther the same emphasis upon growth in the Christian life which was to be so central to Calvin's piety and preserved him from the pitfalls he found in both Roman Catholic and Anabaptist views of perfection. See p. 98, above.

attained. The charge laid by Calvin and others against the Anabaptists that they taught perfectionism is critically discussed by W. E. Keeney, *Dutch Anabaptist Thought and Practice 1539-1564* (1968), pp. 117-120. See also Keeney, "An Analysis of Calvin's Treatment of the Anabaptists in the *Institutes*," in Battles, *An Analysis of the Institutes of the Christian Religion of John Calvin* (1972), pp. 75*, 83*. Calvin's ground for such a charge (anticipated by Zwingli's *Refutation of Baptist Tricks,* 1527), is apparently in the *Schleitheim Confession,* Art. 2 [Wenger, p. 248]: "The ban shall be employed with all those who have given themselves to the Lord, to walk in his commandments, and with all those who are baptized into the one body of Christ and who are called brethren or sisters, and yet who slip sometimes and fall into error and sink, being inadvertently overtaken." Calvin discusses the impact of such a demand of perfection upon the administering of the Lord's Supper in his *Brieve Instruction* [Eng. tr., fol. C.iv^{r}ff]. Perfectionism is also hinted at in Art. 6 [Wenger, p. 250]: "The sword is ordained of God outside the perfection of Christ. . . . In the perfection of Christ, however, only the ban is used for a warning and for the excommunication of the one who has sinned. . . ." On this article, see note to p. 208, "man," below. Melanchthon had, in 1530, already explicitly charged the Anabaptists with perfectionism. The *Augsburg Confession,* 12 [Schaff, CC 3.14]: "They condemn the Anabaptists, who deny that men once justified can lose the Spirit of God, and do contend that some men may attain to such a perfection in their life that they cannot sin." Even earlier, in May 1525, Zwingli in his treatise *Of Baptism* explicitly lays the charge against them [Eng. tr., LCC 24.140.16-20]: "But the Anabaptists do hold that they live without sin. This is proved by what they and some others write and teach concerning the *perseverentia justorum,* or perseverance of saints. In this they are committed absolutely to the view that they can and do live without sin."

year. Fourth Lateran Council (1215) c. 21, quoted by *Decretal. Greg. IX.,* 5.38.12 [Friedberg, 2.887]: "All persons of both sexes, after they have reached the age of discretion, are, each by himself, to confess all their sins at least once a year faithfully to their own priest, and are to strive to fulfill with their own efforts the penance enjoined upon them, reverently partaking at least at Easter of the sacrament of the Eucharist, unless perchance at the advice of their own priest on account of some reasonable cause they should decide for the time being they must abstain from such partaking; otherwise the living are to be barred from entering the church and the dead are to be denied Christian burial." Note also a close paraphrase of this passage at p. 139, paragraph 24, below. See Zephyrinus (198-217). Cf. Platyna, *Lives of the Popes* [Eng. tr., W. Benham, 1.37].

Page 113.

shop. In the following lines Calvin undertakes a critique of the doctrine of "concomitance," whereby the sacramental cup is denied the laity. Cf. Luther, *Receiving Both Kinds in the Sacrament* [Eng. tr., LW 36.237-267] (LCC 21.1425n9). Pannier, *Institution,*

4.46, note a, refers here to Antoine Marcourt, *Le Livre des Marchands* (1534), a satire upon the Roman curia. See also p. 118, below.

men. Cf. Thomas Aquinas, *S. Th.*, PT 80.12.

Page 114.

also. Thomas Aquinas, *S. Th.*, PT 76.1,2.

Supper. Eck, *Enchiridion* (1532), c. 10 [Eng. tr., Battles, p. 87]: "We concede that Christ as consecrator instituted the sacrament under both kinds and gave it to the apostles under both kinds, who now were priests; thus today the celebrant priest partakes under both kinds, but why this to the layman? 'Drink, all of you' is said to the apostles and priests. This they do, that is, consecration in remembrance of Christ, for no others but the apostles were present, as is clear from the Gospel. Mark 14:23: 'and they all drank of it'—it is false to apply this to laymen." The following notes are from the margin of p. 264 of the original 1536 imprint. Eusebius, *Eccl. Hist.*, 6.34; Cassiodorus, *Tripartite Hist.*, 9.30 [CSEL 71.540-543]; Chrysostom, *Epist. to Innocent* [PG 52.533]; Augustine, *Epist.*, 217.5.16.8 (to Vitalis of Carthage) [Eng. tr., FC 32.87]; 54.2.2 (to Januarius) [Eng. tr., FC 12.253]; Jerome, *In Zephaniam*, c. 3.1-7 [PL 25.1375]; Tertullian, *On the Resurrection of the Flesh*, c. 8 [Eng. tr., ANF 3.551]; Cyprian, *On the Lapsed*, c. 25 [Eng. tr., ANF 5.444]; Tractatus "De Coena Domini" once ascribed to Cyprian; part is of the book of Ernaldus Bonaevallis, "De Cardinalibus operibus Christi" [PL 189.1644ff]; Cyprian, *Epist.*, 63 (to Caecilius), 1 [= *Epist.*, 62: Eng. tr., ANF 5.358f]; cf. *Epist.*, 57 (to Cornelius), 2 [= *Epist.*, 53: Eng. tr., ANF 5.337].

Page 115.

abomination. Cf. Luther, *Babylonian Captivity* [Eng. tr., PE 2.194; cf. LW 36.35]: "The third captivity of this sacrament is that abuse of all, in consequence of which there is today no more generally accepted and firmly believed opinion in the church than this— that the mass is a good work and a sacrifice."

sins. Peter Lombard, *Sent.*, 4.12.5 [p. 814.1-4]: "From this it is inferred that what is done on the altar is and is spoken of as a sacrifice, and that Christ was once offered and is daily offered, but in one way then, in another way now; and also, it shows what is the power of this sacrament, namely remission of venial sins and perfection of virtue." Thomas Aquinas, *S. Th.*, PT 83.1; Augustine, *Enchiridion*, 110.29 [Eng. tr., LCC 7.405].

Christ. Zwingli, *Commentary*, 18 [Eng. tr., LWZ 3.235.22-24]: "Why do we not bid all these mass-mongers to cease this atrocious insult to Christ?"

Christ. *Ibid.* [Eng. tr., LWZ 3.236.12-14, 20-31]: ". . . many men have argued a great deal about the priesthood of Christ, with the object of making themselves out his priesthood. . . . When, therefore, you come to the aforesaid passage, Heb. 5:1, you will find plainly that Paul is explaining the priesthood of Christ by comparison with the highpriest of old. It is not a series of sacrificing priests ordained in succession, with new men substituted for the dead. For how could Christ be 'a priest for ever' according to the utterance of the prophet [cf. Ps. 110:4], if any one were to succeed to his place? Is he dead or deprived of his office, that any one has to be substituted for him? Nay, since he sits forever at the right hand of the Father [Mark 16:19], and forever destroys our sins by the one offering made upon the cross, he does not need that any one should supply his place."

Page 116.

oracles. Plato, *Apology,* 30, quotes Socrates: "For I am now at the time when most men prophesy, the time just before death" [LCC 21.1432n5].

repeated. Cf. Eck, *Enchiridion* (1532), c. 17 [Eng. tr., Battles, p. 127]: "You cannot say that sacrifice was only on the cross, for he says it is sacrificed in every place and yet speaks of one offering; and there is no other sacrifice save the body of Christ so many times repeated in the mass." Cf. *Ibid.* [p. 130]: "But the other offering is sacramental, for Christ is daily offered in the church and taken by the priests in the sacrifice of the mass under the sacrament (that is, under the sacramental kinds, pure bread and wine) in remembrance of the passion, death, and prior offering once for all accomplished on the cross."

repeated. Zwingli, *Commentary,* 18 [Eng. tr., LWZ 3.235.24-26; 235.35-236.4]: "For if Christ has to be offered up daily, it must be because his being offered once on the cross is not sufficient for all time. . . . For as, before Christ was born, no one could effect that any offering should save us, now that he has reconciled us to God by having once for all suffered death on the cross, no congregation, no council, no fathers, can effect that he be offered up again."

Page 117.

again. Ganoczy asserts that, among the ideas Calvin picked up from Zwingli's critique of Emser was the equivalence between offering and sacrifice. He quotes Zwingli, *Comm.* [Eng. tr., LWZ 3.235.8f]: "For the offering is accomplished only when that which is offered has been slain. Christ can no more be offered up; for he cannot die." Beside this Ganoczy places these lines of Calvin: ". . . it is necessary that the victim offered be slain and sacrificed" [line 15f]. If ". . . we offer Christ to the Father in the Mass [lines 31f] . . . the Mass leads directly to the end that, if such can be, Christ is slain again" [lines 11f].

moment. Ganoczy [p. 168, n. 181] attributes to Emser's and scholasticism's inadequate statement of the Mass plus Zwingli's harsh exaggeration of 'immolationism' the fact that during his whole life Calvin 'tragically misread' the mass as a repeated immolation. The theology of the Placards of 1534 [see Appendix I] certainly expresses this view of the Mass very outspokenly.

death. Eck, *Enchiridion* (1532), c. 17 [Eng. tr., Battles, p. 132]: "Christ once for all accomplished this offering on the altar of the cross, and its effect is daily distributed to us, when the priest in the person of the church presents to God the Father the remembrance of this offering. Hence it comes to pass that while the first offering was of infinite merit, the second is limited and finite."

Passion. Eck, *Enchiridion* (1532), c. 17 [Battles, p. 131]: "There is therefore in this very celebration of the Mass the immolation of the body and blood of our Lord under the form of bread and wine, a true and proper sacrifice of the priesthood of Christ himself, according to the order of Melchizedek, whereby through the ministers of the church he is daily offered to God the Father as expiation of our sins."

Page 118.

sacrifice. Cf. Tertullian, *On Baptism,* c. 17 [Eng. tr., ANF 3.677]; *Exhortation to Chastity,* c. 7 [Eng. tr., ANF 4.54]; Cyprian, *Unity of the Church,* c. 17 [Eng. tr., ANF 5.427]; *Epist.,* 17.2 [= *Epist.,* 11: Eng. tr., ANF 5.292]; *Epist.,* 43.3 [= *Epist.,* 39: Eng.

tr., *Epist.*, 5.317]; *Epist.*, 55.10 [= *Epist.*, 51: Eng. tr., ANF 5.330]; *Epist.*, 61.1.4 [= *Epist.*, 58: Eng. tr., ANF 5.352f]; Chrysostom, *On the Priesthood*, 3.4, 5 [Eng. tr., NPNF[1] 9.46]; *Apostolic Constitutions*, 2.25 [Eng. tr., ANF 7.409]; *Apostolic Canons*, c. 3. See also Council of Ancyra (AD 314), c. 1-2 [Mansi 2.514]; Council of Laodicea (AD 364), c. 19 [Mansi 2.568].

private masses. See note on private masses in LCC 21.1436n12.

Helen. Paris, son of King Priam of Troy, in carrying away Helen, wife of Menelaus, precipitated the war between the Greeks and the Trojans, the theme of Homer's *Iliad*. Calvin here suggests this classical parallel for the captivity of the Lord's Supper under the Roman Mass.

traffickings. Pannier, *Institution*, 4.58, note *c* (p. 309), refers to Antoine Marcourt, *Livre des Marchands*.

Page 119.

God. Cf. Calvin, *Sermons on Deuteronomy*, 141 (ch. 24.19-22) [OC 28.209] (LCC 21.1441n22).

thanksgiving. εὐχαριστικὸν.

copper. The edition of 1545 adds the words: "according to the French reckoning." The French edition of 1541 renders the Latin *trigenta nummulis aereis* as "trente deniers de cuyvre."

Page 120.

thanksgiving. εὐχαριστικὸν.

Page 121.

Scriptures. Cf. p. 187, below.

Page 122.

thanksgiving. A comparison of this brief plan for the baptismal rite with *La Forme des Prieres et Chantz Ecclesiastiques* (1542): La Forme d'Administrer le Baptisme (OS 2.31-38) will show an exact correspondence: (1) Presentation of baptizand to assembly of believers (OS 2.31.13-16); (2) Explanation of Baptism (31.17-34.8); (3) Prayer over the baptizand (34.9-35.2); (4) Offering of the baptizand to God (35.3-7); (5) Recitation of the Confession of Faith (35.8-36.10); (6) Recounting of the promises taken in Baptism (36.11-37.16); (7) Baptizing in the name of the Trinity (37.20-38.3); (8) Dismissal with Prayers and Thanksgiving (38.4-9).

week. See *Articles concerning the Organization of the Church and of Worship at Geneva, proposed by the Ministers at the Council*, January 16, 1537 [Eng. tr., LCC 22.49f]: "It would be well to require that the Communion of the Holy Supper of Jesus Christ be held every Sunday at least as a rule. . . . But because the frailty of the people is still so great, there is danger that this sacred and so excellent mystery be misunderstood if it be celebrated so often. In view of this, it seemed good to us, while hoping that the people who are still so infirm will be the more strengthened, that use be made of the sacred Supper once a month in one of three places where preaching now takes place. . . ." "When the draft was put before the Council of Ministers, the proposal of a monthly observance was rejected in favor of continuing the customary quarterly observance" [OC 22.47].

Page 123.

peace. With some slight variations, this sketch of the order of Holy Communion was followed in the French liturgies prepared by Calvin (Strasbourg, 1539; Geneva, 1542; etc.). See *La Forme des Prieres* (1542), On the Sacrament of the Supper (OS 2.39-50). The items here mentioned correspond to the liturgy as follows: (1) Public Prayers (OS 2.45.6-46.5); (2) Sermon (44.35-39); (3) Placing of Bread and Wine on the Table (45.3); (4) Words of Institution (46.9-48.2); (5) Recital of Promises (48.3-35); (6) Excommunication (48.36); (7) Singing of Psalm (49.10); (8) Partaking of Supper (49.1-12); (9) Exhortation to and Confession of Faith (49.13-25); (10) Thanksgiving (49.36.); (11) Psalm of Praise (49.27f); (12) Benediction-Dismissal (49.28).

hands. Augustine, *Against the Writings of Petilian the Donatist*, 2.23.53 [Eng. tr., NPNF[1] 5.296].

Alexander. This is a reference to Pope Alexander I (AD 107-116). Cf. Platyna, *Lives of the Popes* [Eng. tr., W. Benham, 1.21f].

baptism. Tertullian, *On Baptism*, c. 7 [Eng. tr., ANF 3.672]; *Against Marcion*, 1.14 [Eng. tr., ANF 3.281]. Augustine, *Against Julian*, 2.120, 181; 4.77 [PL 45.1192.55-1193.1; 1220.35-40; 1383.31-33].

CHAPTER V: FALSE SACRAMENTS

Page 124.

Chapter V. Ganoczy, *Le Jeune Calvin*, p. 145, characterizes this chapter as a "personal and somewhat modified resumé of the famous treatise of Luther on the 'captivity' of the seven sacraments." On p. 185 [n. 304] Ganoczy gives details of correlation between Luther, *Babylonian Captivity of the Church* and (1) Gratian, (2) Peter Lombard. Wendel, *Evolution*, p. 133, cites Luther's *Babylonian Captivity* as a source on the false sacraments [See LCC 21.1448n1]. Max Dominicé [Pannier, 4.311] cites the following chapters of Farel's *Sommaire* as related to Calvin's treatment of the false sacraments: 20, Repentance; 29, Confession; 33, False Pastors; 38, Marriage. Zwingli, *Commentary on True and False Religion*, deals with the "false sacraments" in the following sections: Marriage [16 (LWZ 3.184f), 21 (3.257-260)], Confession [19 (3.253-256)], So-called Sacraments (Confirmation, Extreme Unction, Ordination) [20 (3.256-257)].

minds. Peter Lombard, *Sent.*, 4.2.1 [p. 751.21-26]: "Now let us take up the sacraments of the new law, which are: baptism, confirmation, the bread of blessing, that is, the eucharist, penance, extreme unction, order, marriage. Of these some furnish a remedy against sin and confer assisting grace, as baptism; others are only for a remedy, as marriage; still others support us with grace and power, as eucharist and order." Efforts to reunite the eastern and western Churches at the Council of Florence/Ferrara (AD 1438ff)—secession from the Council of Basel—led to conversations by the Latins with not only the Greek and Slavic churches, but with the Armenians and Jacobites as well. The bull of Eugenius IV, *Exultate Deo* (1439) attempted to bring Armenian belief and liturgical practice in line with the western tradition; here our concern is with the western scheme of seven sacraments which this bull (chapters 11-16) sets forth from Thomas Aquinas, *On the Articles of Faith and the Sacraments of the Church*. For the text, see Mansi, 31.1054ff; Denziger, *Enchiridion*, nos. 695-702 [Eng. tr., R. J. Deferrari, *The Sources of Catholic Dogma*, pp. 220-225]. The sacramental teaching of the bull [Denziger no. 695, Eng. tr., pp. 220-224] begins as follows: "In the fifth place we have reduced under this very brief formula the truth of the sacraments of the Church for the sake of an easier instruction of the Armenians, the present as well as the future. There are seven sacraments of the new law: namely, baptism, confirmation, Eucharist, penance, extreme unction, orders, and matrimony, which differ a great deal from the sacraments of the old law. For those of the old law did not effect grace, but only pronounced that it should be given through the passion of Christ; these sacraments of ours contain grace, and confer it upon those who receive them worthily." Etc.

Page 125.
Confirmation. Gratian, *Decr.*, 3.5.1-9 [Friedberg, 1.1413-1415]; Peter Lombard, *Sent.*, 4.7 [pp. 785-787]; Hugo of St. Victor, *On the Sacraments of the Christian Faith*, 2.7.4 [Eng. tr., R. J. Deferrari, p. 303]; Thomas Aquinas, *S. Th.*, PT 3.1; *Decretalia Greg. IX.*, 1.15.1 [Friedberg, 2.131.53-132.8, quoting Innocent III]: "We wish you to know that there are two kinds of anointing: outward, which is material and visible, and inward, which is spiritual and invisible. With outward anointing is the body visibly anointed; with inward, invisibly the heart. Of the first the Apostle James says [James 5:14]: 'Is any among you sick? Let him call for the presbyters of the church, and let them pray over him, anointing him with oil in the Lord's name; and the prayer of faith will save the sick man. . . .' Of the second the Apostle John says [I John 2:27]: 'But let the anointing which you have received from him remain in you, and you will have no need that anyone should teach you, as his anointing teaches you about anything.' Visible and outward anointing is a sign of inward and invisible anointing. But invisible and inward anointing is not only a sign, but also a sacrament, for, if it is worthily received, it either effects or increases, without doubt, what it designates." *Ibid.*, 1.15.7 [Friedberg, 2.133.46-66]: "Through the anointing of the forehead the laying on of hands is designated, which by another name is called 'confirmation,' because through it the Holy Spirit is given for increase and strength. Hence, although the simple priest or presbyter is capable of imparting certain anointings, only the supreme priest, that is, the bishop, ought to confer this, because of the apostles alone is it read (of whom the bishops are the vicars) that the Holy Spirit was given by the laying on of hands, as the passage in the Acts of the Apostles makes clear [Acts 8:14f]. . . ."

life. Gratian, *Decr.*, 3.5.2 [Friedberg, 1.1413.12-14, 16-18]: "The Holy Spirit who descends upon the waters of baptism by a salvation-bringing descent, and in the fount imparts his fulness for innocence, in confirmation supplies increase to grace. . . . In baptism we are regenerated to life, after baptism we are confirmed for battle."

Holy Spirit. Eugenius IV, *Exultate Deo* (AD 1439), Mansi, 31.1055E; Denziger, no. 697 [Eng. tr., p. 222].

sacrament. Augustine, *John's Gospel*, 80.3[Eng. tr., NPNF¹ 7.344].

rashly. See Chrysostom, *Homilies on Acts*, Hom. 18.3 [Eng. tr., NPNF¹ 11.114f].

Page 126.
confirm. Peter Lombard, *Sent.*, 4.7.3 [p. 785.19f]: "Now the power of this sacrament is the giving of the Holy Spirit for strengthening, who has been given in baptism for remission."

Page 127.
confirmation. Gratian, *Decr.*, 3.5.3 [Friedberg, 1.1413.36-38]: "But so conjoined are these two sacraments that, unless death intervenes, they can in no wise be separated from one another, and one without the other cannot be perfected."

combat. Gratian, *Decr.*, 3.5.2 [Friedberg, 1.1413.19-23]: "And although the benefits of regeneration are sufficient for those immediately about to pass over [from this life to the next], still the aids of confirmation are yet necessary for those about to live [in this life]. Regeneration by itself immediately saves those about to be received into the peace of the blessed world; confirmation arms and equips those about to be committed to the struggle and battles of this world."

Christians. Gratian, *Decr.*, 3.5.1 [Friedberg, 1.1413.5-8]: "All the faithful ought through the laying on of hands of the bishops to receive the Holy Spirit after baptism, that they may be found complete Christians, for, when the Holy Spirit is imparted, the faithful heart is opened to prudence and constancy."

Page 128.

confirmation. Gratian, *Decr.*, 3.5.6 [Friedberg, 1.1414.25-27]: ". . . he will never be a Christian, unless anointed with chrism by episcopal confirmation."

Christians. See Gratian, *Decr.*, 3.5.3 [Friedberg, 1.1413.27-28]. Here Gratian concludes that the sacrament of the laying on of the bishop's hands is more worthy than the sacrament of baptism because the former is both performed by those higher in the ecclesiastical hierarchy and perfects or completes what was begun in baptism.

Finally. Calvin's original marginal note, *c. spiritus eadem dist.*, is a false reference to Gratian, *Decr.*, dist. 5, c. 2.

sins. Peter Lombard, *Sent.*, 4.7.4 [p. 786.10-14]: "The sacrament of confirmation is called greater, possibly not because of the greater power or usefulness conferred by it, but because it is given by the more worthy, and on the worthier part of the body, that is, on the forehead; or possibly because it furnishes a greater increase of virtues, although baptism avails more for forgiveness."

minister. Augustine, *Sermon*, 266.1 [PL 38.1225-1229]; *Epist.*, 185.9.37 [Eng. tr., FC 30.176f]; *John's Gospel*, 4.11 [Eng. tr., LF 1.56]; *Enarr. in Ps.*, 10.5 [Eng. tr., LF 1.96].

Page 129.

Gregory. Gratian, *Decr.*, 1.95.1 [Friedberg, 1.331.28-35], quoting Gregory I, *Epist.*, 4.26 [MGH Ep. 1.261.28ff]: "It has also come to our attention that certain persons were offended that we forbade presbyters to touch with chrism those who were baptized. Now we have acted according to the ancient practice of our church. But if any are disturbed at all about this matter, where bishops are lacking, we concede that presbyters also ought to touch the baptized on the foreheads with chrism."

head. Gratian, *Decr.*, 3.5.5 [Friedberg, 1.1414.14-20]: "For the baptized person is marked with chrism by the priest on the top of the head; but by the bishop on the forehead, so that in the former anointing the descent of the Holy Spirit upon him to consecrate the dwelling to God is signified; in the second also, that the sevenfold grace of the Holy Spirit with all the fulness of holiness and knowledge and power is declared to come into man."

baptism. Peter Lombard, *Sent.*, 4.7.4.

confirmed. De Castro, *Adv. haer.* (1534), 4 [fol. 84B f]. See LCC 21.1460n26.

sacrament. Augustine, *Christian Doctrine*, 3.9.13 [Eng. tr., NPNF¹ 2.560]; *Epist.*, 54 (to Januarius), c. 1 [Eng. tr., FC 12.252].

citadel. Cf. Calvin, *Comm. Sen. De Clem.*, 118.5f, quoting Pliny, *Panegyric*, 49.3:

"This is an inaccessible citadel. . . ." The "citadel" referred to is the love of the king by his countrymen.

prayer. Augustine, *On Baptism against the Donatists*, 3.16.21; 5.23.33 [Eng. tr., NPNF¹ 4.443, 475].

Page 130.

birth. On Calvin's misreading of ancient ecclesiastical practice here, see Barth-Niesel, OS 5.439n; Benoît, *Institution* (1560), 4.472n1; LCC 21.1452n7.

exercise. Cf. *La Manière d'interroguer les enfans* (1553?) [OC 6.147-160]. See LCC 21.1461n27.

Penance. Gratian, *Decr.*, 2.33.3 (Treatise on Penance) [Friedberg, 1.1159-1247]; Peter Lombard, *Sent.*, 4.14-20 [pp. 819-880]. Eugenius IV, *Exultate Deo*, c. 13 [Mansi 31.1057; Denziger, *Enchiridion*, no. 699, Eng. tr., p. 223]: "The fourth sacrament is penance, the matter of which is, as it were, the acts of the penitent, which are divided into three parts."

vivification. Melanchthon, *LC* (1521), 9 [Eng. tr., LCC 19.140]: "For repentance truly is the mortification of our being, followed by life and renewal."

judgment. *Augsburg Confession*, 12 [Schaff, CC 3.14]: "Now repentance consists properly of these two parts: one is contrition, or terrors stricken into the conscience through the acknowledgment of sin. . . ."

contrition. See Melanchthon, *LC* (1521), 9 [Eng. tr., LCC 19.140]: "What we call 'mortification' the Scholastics preferred to call 'contrition'." Melanchthon himself uses the term in *Augsburg Confession*, 12 [Schaff, CC 3.14], calling the two parts of repentance, "contrition" and "faith."

Page 131

life. Among the passages in Melanchthon paralleling these lines of Calvin, see for example the following: *LC* (1521), 5 [Eng. tr. LCC 19.84]: "Those whom conscience has terrified in this manner would most surely be driven to despair, the usual condition of the condemned, if they were not lifted up and encouraged by the promise of the grace and mercy of God, commonly called the gospel. If the afflicted conscience believes the promise of grace in Christ, it is resuscitated and quickened by faith. . . ." *Ibid.*, 9 [19.137]: "The function of this sign [Baptism] is to testify that you are crossing through death to life, that the mortification of your flesh brings salvation." *Ibid.* [19.140]: "The Christian life is nothing else than this very repentance, that is, the regeneration of our being. Mortification is brought about through the law. . . . For the law terrifies and slays our conscience. Vivification takes place through the gospel or through absolution."

misery. Bucer has the terms "legal" and "evangelical" repentance; Melanchthon has the content, but not the terms themselves. See Bucer, *EN*, I [fol. 35ᵛ.39-44]: "This therefore is legal repentance or contrition of heart, hatred and detestation of sins together with sorrow and compunction of heart, which arises at the same time (when the law of God is recognized) as abomination of sins is also acknowledged. And it is common to the ungodly along with the godly. For Judas, Christ's betrayer, having acknowledged his own crime, felt compunction, so that he inflicted death upon himself. Evangelical repentance however is received on account of sins through faith in Christ; it is a perpetual but eager pursuit of, and an unremitting but willing meditation upon, the mortification of the life of the flesh and conformation to the Lord's will." Compare this with Melanchthon, *Apology of the Augsburg Confession*, 12.8.36 [Eng. tr., Tappert, *The Book of Concord*,

p. 186]: "This faith strengthens, sustains, and quickens the contrite according to the passage [Rom. 5:1], 'Since we are justified by faith, we have peace with God.' This faith obtains the forgiveness of sins. This faith justifies before God, as the same passage attests, 'We are justified by faith.' This faith shows the difference between the contrition of Judas and Saul on the one hand and that of Peter and David on the other."

majesty. For examples of legal repentance, see Melanchthon, *Apology*, 12.8.36: "The contrition of Judas and Saul did not avail because it lacked the faith that grasps the forgiveness of sins granted for Christ's sake." Luther, *Enarr. in I Lib. Mose* [42:6f, WA 44.469]: "Thus the Sophists once taught that one must long toil and sweat until contrition is sufficient. But what profit is there in being contrite over sins and not understanding even a tiny spark of divine mercy? For thus are Saul and Judas tried, vexed, purged, but only with a feeling of contrition; therefore they are broken, because there only the office of the law dominates. Even the devil has contrition and trembles with fear, as James [James 2:19] says, but this is not repentance unto salvation." Bucer gives instances of "legal repentance," in addition to Judas, the Ninevites and Manassas [*EN*, I, fol. 35ᵛ.16], the contrite Jews of Acts 2:37 when they first responded to Peter's preaching [*Ibid.*, fol. 35ᵛ.18-20].

hope. Melanchthon, *Apology*, 12.8.36: "The contrition of David and Peter did avail because it had the faith that grasps the forgiveness of sins granted for Christ's sake." Bucer sees an instance of evangelical repentance in Peter's call upon the Jews who had responded to his preaching [Acts 2:37] to change their lives: "It was therefore by the first kind of repentance that they felt compunction; . . . to the other kind Peter urged them."

Page 132.

penance. While Calvin does not offer the Hebrew and Greek words behind these lines on repentance, he seems to rest his statements on Bucer, *EN*, I [fol. 35ʳ.23ff]. Bucer there discusses שוב (converti), בתם (poenitere), and μετανοέω. Among the passages he cites are Jer. 3:14; Ezek. 18:50; Judges 21:6; Gen. 6:6; I Sam. 15:11.

sins. Bucer, commenting on Matt. 3:2 ("Repent for the kingdom is at hand"); 4:17 ("Repent, for the kingdom of heaven is at hand"); 10:7 ("And preach as you go, saying, 'The kingdom of heaven is at hand' "), speaks of the sum of the Gospel: "Very few words, but this is the sum of the whole Gospel preaching" [*EN*, I, fol. 15ᵛ.19-20]. "Surely this is the sum of the whole Gospel preaching, for it is proclaimed by these words: the kingdom of grace and reconciliation has come; at the same time it is explained to whom it has come, namely to those who are displeased with themselves, and recognize themselves as sinners" [*EN*, I, fol. 35ʳ.29-32]. "This at least was the sum and head of preaching of John, Christ and the Apostles to which diligent attention is to be paid lest any think they have preached only these words: 'The kingdom of heaven is at hand, repent' " [*EN*, I, fol. 102ᵛ.55-57].

sinners. Cf. Bucer, *EN*, I [fol. 35ʳ.29-32], quoted above.

Page 133.

death. Plato, *Phaedo*, 64AB, 67A-E, 81A; *Apology*, 29A, 41CD [Eng. tr., LCL Plato 1.222f, 232-235, 280ff; 1.106f, 142ff].

flesh. Cf. Bucer, *EN*, I [fol 35ᵛ.43], quoted above at p. 131, note on "misery." In this section on repentance lie at hand many of the materials later worked up in the edition of 1539 as the "Short Treatise on the Christian Life" [1559 ed., 3.6-10].

weep over. Gregory I, *Homilies on the Gospels*, 34.15 [PL 76.1256], quoted from Peter Lombard, *Sent.*, 4.14.2 [p. 820.5-6].

bewail. Pseudo-Ambrose, *Sermons*, 25.1 [PL 17.655], quoted from Peter Lombard, *Sent.*, 4.14.2 [p. 820.3-4]; Gratian, *Decr.*, 2.33.3.1.39 [Friedberg, 1.1168]. Cf. Luther, *Babylonian Captivity* [Eng. tr., LW 36.84].

committed. Pseudo-Augustine, *On True and False Repentance*, 8.22 [PL 40.1120], quoted from Peter Lombard, *Sent.*, 4.14.2 [p. 823.12-13, cf. also 18-19]; cf. Gratian, *Decr.*, 2.33.3.3.4 [Friedberg, 1.1211].

consented. Pseudo-Ambrose, *Sermons*, 25.1 [PL 17.655], quoted from Gratian, *Decr.*, 2.33.3.1.39 [Friedberg, 1.1168].

works. From supposed homily among John Chrysostom's works, ed. Erasmus, Basel 1530, 2.347A, "Provida mente"; ed. Paris, 1867, tome 5; quoted from Peter Lombard, *Sent.*, 4.16.1 [p. 839]; Gratian, *Decr.*, 2.33.3.1.40 [Friedberg, 1.1168]. Cf. Gregory I, *Hom I Kings*, 6.2,33 [PL 79.439]; Thomas Aquinas, *S. Th.*, PT 90.2; Eugenius IV, *Exultate Deo* (1439) [Mansi, 31.1057; Denziger, *Ench.*, no. 699, Eng. tr., pp. 223f]: "The first of these is contrition of heart, to which pertains grief for a sin committed together with a resolution not to sin in the future. The second is oral confession, to which pertains that the sinner confess integrally to his priest all sins of which he has recollection. The third is accomplished chiefly by prayer, fasting and alms." Etc.

Page 134.
full. Cf. Cyprian, *Epist.*, 51.18 [Eng. tr., ANF 5.331]: "Moreover, we do not prejudge when the Lord is to be the judge; save that if he shall find the repentance of the sinners full and sound, he will then ratify what shall have been determined by us."

us. Cf. Gabriel Biel, *Epitome*, 4.14.1.2. concl. 5U.

alone. Cf. Melanchthon, *LC* (1521), 9 [Eng. tr., LCC 19.141]: "From one point of view, confession involves acknowledging our sin before God and condemning ourselves. . . . On the other hand, when we make a confession in which we accuse and condemn ourselves and attribute to God true glory and righteousness, forgiveness must follow."

Page 135.
contrition. Cf. Thomas Aquinas, *S. Th.*, PTS 5.2.

theologians. Peter Lombard, *Sent.*, 4.17 [pp. 845-857]; Thomas Aquinas, *S. Th.*, PTS 6.

constitutions. Cf. Gratian, *Decr.*, 2.33.3.1.30-37 [Friedberg, 1.1165-67], esp. 2.33.3.1.37 [1.1167.37-39]: "Therefore it is not in confession that sin is forgiven, because it is proved to have been already forgiven. Therefore confession is made to show repentance, not to seek pardon. . . ." Peter Lombard, *Sent.*, 4.17.1-4 [pp. 845-854]. See especially: c. 1 [p. 848.25-27]: "Just as forgiveness of sins is a gift of God, so repentance and confession, through which sin is wiped away, cannot exist, save from God. . . ."

positive law. While no exact parallel for this has been found, Eck, *Enchiridion*, in answering the "heretics' " third argument ("He did not say to the adulteress, 'Go and confess to the priest,' but 'Go and sin no more': thus to Mary Magdalene") states: "Not yet did the power of loosing exist in the church, for the reason that confession had not yet been instituted. The adulteress, Mary Magdalene, was not held to confession. Now those things which were done with a special privilege are in consequence not to be treated according to the common theory" [Eng. tr., Battles, p. 76].

priests. Pseudo-Augustine, *On True and False Repentance*, 10.25 [PL 40.1122.9-27]: "He therefore who repents ought to repent completely, and show his sorrow by tears— let him set his life before God through the priest, let him anticipate God's judgment through confession. For the Lord has bidden those who are to be cleansed that 'they show themselves to the priests' [Luke 17:14], teaching that sins are to be confessed with one physically present, not revealed through a messenger or a written message. For he said: 'Show yourself' and all, not one for all. You are not to appoint another as messenger to offer for you the gift prescribed by Moses [Lev. 14:2]; but you who have sinned through yourself, are to blush with shame by yourself. For shame itself has a part in forgiveness; for out of his mercy the Lord commanded this: that no one repent secretly. For in that he speaks personally to the priest, and vanquishes shame by fear of offending God, pardon for sin is effected; for what was criminal in the committing becomes venial by confession; and if it is not immediately purged, yet what he had committed as a mortal sin becomes venial." Gratian, *Decr.*, 2.33.3.1.88 [Friedberg, 1.1187.56-1188.3]: "For the Lord bade those to be cleansed to show themselves to the priests, teaching that sins must be confessed by one physically present, not to be manifested through a messenger, or through a written message." Peter Lombard, *Sent.*, 4.18.6 [p. 862.24-26]: "In loosing or retaining sins therefore the Gospel priest acts just as the priest under the law once acted on those who were contaminated with leprosy, which is a figure of sin." Eck, *Enchiridion* (1532), c. 8 [Eng. tr., Battles, p. 75]: "In a figure of this thing Christ said to the cleansed leper: 'Go show yourself to the priest, and offer the gift prescribed by Moses'; he similarly enjoined the ten lepers."

Page 136.

go. The author of this allegory is Augustine; see *Enarr. in Ps.*, 101, Sermon 2.3 [PL 37.1306f]. Pseudo-Augustine, *On True and False Repentance*, 10.25 [PL 40.1122.42-55], quoted by Peter Lombard, *Sent.*, 4.18.5 [p. 861.12-21]: "Priests can spare those who confess; whom they forgive, God forgives. For he offered Lazarus raised from the tomb to be loosed by the disciples, showing through this the power of loosing granted to the priests. For he said: 'Whatever you loose on earth, will be loosed also in heaven,' that is, I God and all the orders of the heavenly host and all the saints in my glory praise with you and confirm whom you bind and loose. He did not say: 'whom you think you bind and loose,' but 'in whom you exercise the work of justice and mercy.' Otherwise even your other works toward sinners I do not recognize." Peter Lombard, *Sent.*, 4.18.6 [p. 862.21-23]: "Thus also the Lord offered the risen Lazarus to his disciples to be loosed—because even though someone may have been loosed in God's sight, he is not yet considered loosed in the eyes of the church save through the priest's judgment." Gratian, *Decr.*, 2.33.3.1.88 [Friedberg, 1.1188.26-29]: "Whom they forgive God forgives. For to his disciples he offered Lazarus risen from the tomb to be loosed, showing through this the power of loosing entrusted to the priests." Cf. Thomas Aquinas, *S. Th.*, PTS 8.1, etc. Also Eck, *Enchiridion* (1532), c. 8 [Eng. tr., Battles, p. 72f].

sins. Cf. Luther, *Babylonian Captivity*, Eng. tr., LW 36.85f: "There is no doubt that confession of sins is necessary and commanded of God in Matt. 3:6: 'They were baptized by John in the river Jordan, confessing their sins. . . .' "

another. Thomas Aquinas, *S. Th.*, PTS 6.6.2; 8.1.1; Eck, *Enchiridion* (1532), c. 8 [Eng. tr., Battles, p. 76]: "It is true that James did not determine with precision to whom confession is to be made, because Christ had already expressed the loosers of sinners; accordingly it was sufficient for James to express what was necessary for absolution, namely confession, not precisely indicating the judge."

Page 137.

ordained. Melanchthon, *LC* (1521), 9 [Eng. tr., LCC 19.144]: "The remaining confessions are traditions of men. For if you offer yourself voluntarily to the congregation and wish to be absolved, whether you have sinned privately or publicly, divine law does not demand a rehearsal of your acts. Christ forgave many in this way, and the apostles absolved several thousands in the same manner in Acts 2:38f. They did not demand that a catalog of sins be recited."

Innocent III. See p. 112, note to "year"; also LCC 20.630n14, on the Pseudo-Isidorian Decretals.

Sozomen. Cassiodorus, *Tripartite History,* 9.35 CSEL 71.552-554 (based on Sozomen, *HE,* 7.16).

office. Cf. Melanchthon, *LC* (1521), 9 [Eng. tr., LCC 19.142]: "The oldest custom was to make accusation of public crimes before the whole congregation and to receive absolution by the vote of the entire congregation. This custom has long since been abrogated. One of the presbyters was then designated before whom the charges were privately rehearsed even though they were for public crimes. . . . This is a custom which is diligently observed in the Western Churches and especially at Rome even to this day. In Roman practice, there is even a definite place for the guilty penitents to stand. . . ."

confession. Cf. Melanchthon, *LC* (1521), 9 [Eng. tr., LCC 19.143]: "But in Constantinople a presbyter presided over the penitents only until a certain woman of the highest nobility, after her confession, had lain several times with a deacon as she was doing penance in the church. When this was noised abroad, the common people rose against the presbyters because they had violated the church. Then it was that Bishop Nectarius ejected the deacon from his office and abrogated the ancient custom of penitents. . . ." Eck, *Enchiridion* (1532), c. 8 lists this as an argument of the "heretics" but does not there explicitly refute it.

Page 138.

pardon. Melanchthon, *LC* (1521), 9 [Eng. tr., LCC 19.141]: "From one point of view, confession involves acknowledging our sin before God and condemning ourselves."

heart. Melanchthon, *LC* (1521), 9 [Eng. tr., LCC 19.141]: "This confession is no different from mortification and contrition, of which I just spoke. Scripture often reminds us of this fact. I John 1:9: 'If we confess our sins, he is faithful and just and will forgive our sins.' David says in Ps. 51:3f: 'For I know my transgressions, and my sin is ever before me. Against thee, thee only, have I sinned, and done that which is evil in thy sight, so that thou art justified in thy sentences and blameless in thy judgment.' Ps. 32:5: 'I said, "I will confess my transgressions to the Lord"; then thou didst forgive the guilt of sins.' "

Page 139.

gift. While both Melanchthon and Calvin posit two kinds of private confession in a slightly different way, they share the same content. The latter's proof texts for his two scripturally approved forms of private confession—James 5:16 and Matt. 5:23-24—are lumped together by Melanchthon, *LC* (1521), 9 [Eng. tr., LCC 19.143f]: "In addition to public repentance there are private confessions. First are those by which we are privately reconciled with those whom we have offended [Matt. 5:23-24 and James 5:16 are now quoted]. . . . Then there are those ecclesiastical private confessions, the use of which is common today." With Melanchthon's view should be compared that of Luther, *Enchiridion piarum precationum*, 1543 ed. [fol S.5ᵛ ff]. Luther, like Melanchthon, posits three sorts of confession: (1) confession to God, (2) confession to neighbor, (3) auricular confession as commanded by the pope.

confess it. Peter Lombard, *Sent.*, 4.17.1 [p. 848.24-25]: "He who does not have the intent to confess is not truly penitent." Cf. Thomas Aquinas, *S. Th.*, PTS 10.1; Gabriel Biel, *Epitome*, 4.18.1.2 concl. 1 G.

open. Peter Lombard, *Sent.*, 4.17.3 [p. 853.5-7]: "From these and many other references it is shown beyond doubt that confession is to be offered to God first and then to the priest, nor can one enter into paradise in any other way unless a readiness to confess be present."

bind. Peter Lombard, *Sent.*, 4.18.2 [p. 858.3-6]: "These keys are not physical but spiritual, that is, 'the knowledge to discern and the power to judge,' that is, of binding and loosing, whereby the ecclesiastical judge, who has both the power of binding and loosing, 'ought to receive the worthy and exclude the unworthy from heaven.' " Adapted from Bede's gloss as found in Nicolas of Lyra at Matt. 16:19; cf. Hugo of Saint Victor (?), *Summa Sententiarum*, 6.14 [PL 176.152].

essence. Alexander of Hales, *S. Th.*, 4.79.3.1, cites and rejects this opinion without identifying its author.

power. Peter Lombard, *Sent.*, 4.18.2.

counselor. Hugo of Saint Victor (?), *Summa Sent.*, 6.14 (on the two keys) [PL 176.152A]; Thomas Aquinas, *S. Th.*, PTS 17.3; Duns Scotus, *In Sent.*, 4.18.1.3,8; Gabriel Biel, *Epitome*, 4.18.1 note 4 D.

but me. Peter Lombard, *Sent.*, 4.18.3 [p. 860.17-22]: "Therefore one is not freed from eternal wrath through the priest to whom one confesses; one is freed from it through the Lord, from whom he said, 'I shall confess.' Only God therefore cleanses man inwardly from the stain of sin and releases him from the debt of eternal punishment, as the prophet says: 'I alone blot out the iniquities and the sins of the people.' " Cf. Biel, *Epitome*, 4.18.1.1 note 2 B.

retained. Peter Lombard, *Sent.*, 4.18.6 [p. 863.13-14]: "The priests therefore remit or retain sins when they judge and point out those remitted or retained by God." Cf. Bonaventura, *In Sent.*, 4.18.1.1.1 [Quaracchi ed. minor, 4.452-454]; Duns Scotus, *In Sent.*, 4.19.1.4-6; William of Ockham, *In Sent.*, 4.8, 9 Q; Gabriel Biel, *Epitome*, 4.18.1.2.3,4 I K.

sacraments. Peter Lombard, *Sent.*, 4.18.7 [p. 863.17-19]: "Priests also bind when they impose the satisfaction of penance upon those who confess; they loose when they remit anything of it, or admit them purged through it to the partaking of the sacraments."

Page 140.

required. Peter Lombard, *Sent.*, 4.18.7 [p. 864.26-29]: "But this is to be understood as applying to those whose merits require binding or loosing. For the sentence of the priest then is approved and confirmed by the judgment of God and of the whole heavenly court, when it so proceeds from discretion that the merits of those accused do not contradict it."

promotion. Peter Lombard, *Sent.*, 4.19.1 [p. 866.24-26]: "These keys are given through the ministry of the bishops to each upon promotion to the priesthood; for at the same time as he receives the priestly order he also receives these keys."

bound. Cf. Alexander of Hales, *S. Th.*, 4.79.8.2; Thomas Aquinas, *S. Th.*, PTS 19.6.

locked. Alexander of Hales, *S. Th.*, 4.23.1; 4.23.3.1; 4.23.5; Albertus Magnus, *In Sent.*, 4.20.16 [*Opera omnia*, 29.848]: "Indulgence or relaxation is the remission of penalty enjoined from the power of the keys, and proceeding from the treasury of the supererogation of the perfect. In this treasury the church has the riches of the merits of Christ's passion, of the glorious Virgin Mary, of all the apostles, martyrs and God's saints, living and dead. And for the usefulness and necessity of the church, these riches can be expended for the support of those who serve the church when they are in need." Bonaventura, *In Sent.*, 4.20.2.1.3 [Quaracchi ed. minor, 4.522]: ". . . relaxations or indulgences are brought about from the merits of supererogation which are in the church, like a sort of spiritual treasury thereof. These merits are not for all to dispense, but only for the bishops; accordingly it belongs to the bishops alone to make relaxations." Thomas Aquinas, *S. Th.*, PTS 25.1.2. Cf. Clement VI, *Unigenitus* (1343), in *Extravag.*, 5.9.2 [Friedberg, 2.1304ff].

church. Alexander of Hales, *S. Th.*, 4.83.1.1.3,5; Thomas Aquinas, *ibid.*; Clement VI, *ibid.*

bishops. Innocent III, 4th Lateran Council (1215): *Decretal. Greg. IX*, 5.38.14 [Friedberg, 2.889]; Thomas Aquinas, *S. Th.*, PTS 26.3; cf. John Fisher, *Confut.*, art. 17, pp. 305ff.

sins. Eugenius IV, *Exultate Deo* (1439) [Mansi, 31.1057; Denziger, *Ench.*, no. 699; Eng. tr., pp. 223f]: ". . . that the sinner confess integrally to his priest all sins of which he has recollection. . . ."

Lord. Cf. *Augsburg Confession*, 2.4 [Schaff, CC 3.40f]: "But of Confession our churches teach that the enumeration of sins is not necessary, nor are consciences to be burdened with the care of enumerating all sins, inasmuch as it is impossible to recount all sins, as the Psalm [19:12] testifies: 'Who can understand his errors?' . . . But if no sins were remitted except what were recounted, consciences could never find peace, because very many sins they neither see nor can remember."

butchery. Cf. Melanchthon, *LC* (1521), 4 [Eng. tr., LCC 19.69]. In tracing the history of conciliar and papal laws burdensome to consciences, Melanchthon sees the power of the gospel obscured by satisfactions which had their birthplace at the Council of Nicaea, but in later centuries grew steadily more pernicious; he uses the same Latin word, *carnificina* (butchery, torture): "But a little later, what a torture of consciences did those satisfactions become!"

formulas. Cf., e.g., Jean Gerson, *De praeceptis decalogi, de confessione*, etc. [Works, E. du Pin, 1.442ff]; *Tractatus de differentia peccatorum venialium et mortalium* [Works, 2.486ff].

circumstances. Peter Lombard, *Sent.*, 4.16.1 [p. 840.10ff], quoting Pseudo-Augustine, *On True and False Repentance*, 14.29 [PL 40.1124]: "One should weigh the quality of the misdeed in place, in time, in perseverance, in variety of person, and by what sort of temptation he committed it, and in the execution of the manifold vice itself." Bonaventura, *In Sent.*, 4.16.1.7; 4.17.3.2.3 [Quaracchi ed. min., 4.382; 446-449]; Biel, *Epitome*, 4.17.1.2.4 note.

side. Virgil, *Aeneid*, 3.193.

Page 141.

knife. Cf. Plautus; *Captivi*, 617.

power. Cf. Alexander of Hales, *S. Th.*, 4.69.8.

consolation. Dominicé [Pannier, 2.395] notes: "One sees here the constant concern of the Reformation not to leave the sinner stuck in a consideration of his particular sins, but to make him aware of his sinful state."

slough. Latin: *lernam*. *Lerna* was the mythical abode of the Hydra. Cf. Luther, *Lectures on Romans*, Rom. 5:14 [LCC 15.168n29]. This sin [original sin] is Hydra, that extremely stubborn monster with many heads, with which we fight in the Lerna of this life until death. VG 1541 [Pannier 2.205] has "le secret abysme de vice." On the proverb *Lerna malorum*, see Erasmus, *Adagia*, 1.3.27 [Le Clerc, 2.122D-F], who concludes his comment with these words: "Therefore as often as we signify a man of violent wickedness, and befouled with every sort of turpitude or of pestilent human association, like the bilge water and dregs of criminals, we will rightly say, 'A Lerna of evils.' "

sinner. Cf. Farel, *Sommaire* (1525), ch. 29, Confession [fol. g.8ᵛ]: ". . . man, looking at himself and his misdeeds, condemns himself and judges himself to be totally other than God; he gives God the honor, who is good and just; while man is evil, unjust and wicked."

presence. Dominicé [Pannier, 2.396n] recalls Calvin's motto, that of a burning heart held forth in the palm of a hand with the device: *Prompte et Sincere*.

Page 142.

priestling. Latin: *in aurem sacrificuli cuiuspiam confessi.* Cf. VG 1541 ed. Pannier, t. 2, p. 207, lines 9f: ". . . ne sont pas ditz s'estre confusez en l'aureille de quelque messire JEAN." "To make one's confession in the ear of some Master John."

church. Dominicé [Pannier, 2.396n] cites Farel, *Sommaire* (1525), c. 29 [fol. h.3ᵛ]: "Say and palaver what he will, the Scot [Duns Scotus] however much he stammers, is not enough to weigh down the conscience. On the other hand, the Thomists (in disagreement with the Scot) will never by their teaching set man at peace."

indifferent. Cf. Luther, *Enchiridion piarum precationum* [ed. 1543, fol. S.7ʳ-8ʳ]: "The third sort of confession which the pope has commanded is auricular, which is done before the priest. God has not commanded this, but the pope has forced men to it. . . . But God does not approve of that confession, or any other work, if you do it against your will. . . . Truly therefore is that time called by the Germans 'passion week,' for their consciences are miserably tortured especially at that time with great peril to souls and salvation."

vengeance. Peter Lombard, *Sent.*, 4.17.4 [p. 852.20-25] quoting Pseudo-Aug., *TFR*, 10.25 (PL 40.1111): ". . . for the mind labors with suffering the blush of shame; and since shame is a great punishment, he who blushes for Christ is made worthy of mercy. Hence it is clear that, the more one will confess to many, in hope of pardon, the wickedness of a misdeed, the more easily he attains the grace of remission. For priests themselves can help more, the more they can spare those who confess."

Page 143.

swarms. Dominicé [Pannier, 2.396n] cites Farel, *Sommaire* (1525), c. 29 [fol. h.3ʳ]: "Who could reckon or count the great host of souls who, seduced by this confession have been drawn into hell? How many poor women sent into wickedness? How many virgins corrupted? Widows devoured? Orphans destroyed? Princes poisoned? Countries laid waste? Authorities and households set at nought?"

people. That is Nectarius, Bishop of Constantinople. See p. 137, above, with references to Melanchthon, *LC* (1521), 9.

power of the keys. Peter Lombard, *Sent.*, 4.18.19 [pp. 857-869]: Thomas Aquinas, *S. Th.*, PTS 17-24. John Fisher, *Confutatio* (1523), p. 244: "To Peter are committed the keys of heaven." Dominicé [Pannier, 2.396n] cites Farel, *Sommaire* (1525), c. 17, "On the Keys of the Kingdom of Heaven" [fol. d.3^{r-v}]: "It is in the knowledge of God, the word of God, the holy gospel, the feeding of souls, which man cannot give or commit to another, but God alone giving his Holy Spirit, opening the understanding of the Scriptures, sending the preaching of the holy Gospel. To him who truly believes, heaven is opened; he is loosed; his sins are pardoned. For by faith his heart is cleansed and he is saved. But he who does not believe, to him is heaven closed; he is bound; his sins are retained. For he does not believe in the name of the Son of God, and accordingly his sin remains."

goes. Cicero, *Familiar Letters*, 16.24.1.

two passages. Ganoczy [pp. 175-177] points out that in their criticism of the Roman penitential practice both Bucer and Calvin distinguish exegetically between Matthew 16 and John 20 on the one hand and Matthew 18. As the Bucerian parallels adduced in the following note will show, the first two passages are explained (to use Ganoczy's words [p. 175f]) by Bucer: "The power to bind and loose was promised and conferred in the first instance upon Peter only because he represented the whole community, and the same power was accorded to all the other apostles without distinction, to show that it belonged effectively to the whole church." The third passage is referred to the act of excommunication which is associated with the proclamation of the word and entrusted to the local congregation.

rest. Cf. Bucer, *EN*, I [fol. 23^{r}.22-29]: "For they say: how can we loose those whom we do not know to be bound? When therefore the sins by which they are bound are secret, it is necessary for them to confess them to us, and each one individually, for they cannot be freed of all of them at one time. We must answer them as follows: this loosing from sins and forgiveness of sins first promised to and conferred upon Peter in the name of the church, and thence to the rest likewise is the public admission into the church, into the number of those whom Christ saves from sins, that which is customarily done by the church of Christ first by baptism, thereafter as often as anyone who, cast out of the communion of the church on account of his misdeeds, by true repentance has deserved to be received." Also: *EN*, I [fol. 138^{v}.19-20]: Now in John 20[:21f] the Lord was speaking as follows to all the disciples: 'As my Father has sent me, even so I send you.' And when he had said this he breathed on them, and said to them, 'Receive the Holy Spirit.' "

Word. Cf. Bucer, *EN*, I [fol. 138^{v}.41-43]: "For these keys are nothing else than the Holy Spirit and the Word of God. The Holy Spirit is this power in the preacher, but it is put forth through the Word toward the hearers." Ganoczy in adducing this parallel [p. 176n248] also cites Lefèvre d'Étaples, *Comm. Matt.*, 16, n° 138, fol. 74^{v}: "Let no one say that Peter is the rock on which the church was founded. . . . Peter alone did not receive those [keys] from the Lord, but also all the rest who in faith built up the church upon Christ according to the will of Christ the Lord." Cf. also *EN*, I [fol. 138^{v}.51-54]: "Now out of the passage there was a huge struggle arising between the preachers of Christ and the flatterers of the Roman Pontiff, with the latter contending that all these things said by Christ pertain to Peter. For they mean to understand the promise to Peter, that the Church of Christ be built upon him and that he alone possess the keys of the kingdom of heaven, that is, the power of loosing and binding."

301

Page 144.

himself. Cf. LCC 21.1213n4: ". . . the divine authorship of Scripture is the authorship of its doctrine." Reference is there made to note on *Inst.*, 4.8.8 (1543): *"Verba quodammodo dictante Christi Spiritu"* [LCC 21.1155n7].

ministers. Cf. Bucer, *EN,* I [fol. 138ᵛ.30-35]: "They have not closed to believers the kingdom of heaven from the same Spirit and through the same word, that is, have denied the communion of the church. Thus have they bound and retained all sins by the power of the Spirit and through the word of God. It is proper, therefore, that not the bishops but Christ entrust the keys of the kingdom of heaven, that is, the power of receiving into the church and of excluding from it." Again, fol. 138ᵛ.43-45: "Thus Peter speaking from the Spirit announced salvation to the repentant Jews but condemnation to the impenitent, that is, he opened heaven to the former, but closed it to the latter."

passage. Ganoczy [p. 176] points out that, in exegeting Matthew 18, Bucer emphasizes the more disciplinary aspect of the power of the keys, that of excommunication. See above, p. 143, note to "rest," where Bucer mentions [*EN,* I, fol. 23ʳ.27-29] two kinds of public admission into the church—one at baptism, the other at the lifting of excommunication. It should be noted that Bucer in exegeting Matthew 18, and specifically in the matter of excommunication, has in mind not only the Roman Catholic alienation from Gospel teaching but also the erroneous Anabaptist view of excommunication which denied that Christ was present in the believers' fellowship where public excommunication was not the exclusive practice [EN, I, fol. 149ʳ.36ff].

Page 145.

church. Bucer, *EN,* I [fol. 75ʳ.55-56]: ". . . therefore he is not at all condemned, whatever of judgment charity exercises, when it investigates the diseases of the brethren, and judges, but in order to heal."

vote of the believers. Cf. Bucer, *EN,* I [fol. 149ʳ.22-31]: ". . . therefore in the public assemblies of the church, as today scarcely happens, excommunication cannot be publicly exercised save where the Lord has vouchsafed that the majority of the whole people, with the magistrates' office, has turned wholeheartedly to Christ. Where this is not the case, it is necessary that those who have more fully received Christ exercise this most holy and salutary institution of Christ among themselves, that they may diligently and freely admonish whatever acquaintances or neighbors they have, who have enrolled under Christ. When any members of the church—a society shared with one another by virtue of community of neighborhood or else of acquaintance, or finally by reason of kinship and family—undertake to despise its admonitions, then the rest are to abandon those despisers of the warning so the church will thereupon cast said despisers out of its communion, until this holy law is received by the majority."

sentence. Cf. Bucer, *EN,* I [fol. 23ʳ.30-32]: "Now to release [readmit] to the church, as has already been pointed out above concerning baptism, is nothing else but to pronounce them absolved by God."

midst of them. Cf. Bucer, *EN,* I [fol. 148ᵛ.27-33]: "You, striving on behalf of his Kingdom, will in such a way be regarded by the Father, that whatever you bind will be considered bound in heaven, that is, whomever thus warned you cast out of your fellowship, with the Father too they will be considered cast out; and, conversely, if you loose them (being repentant) and admit them back into your fellowship, with the Father also will this be ratified. For if even only two agree in my name upon the earth, whatever they pray the Father, they will get. Whenever at peace two or three gather in my name, with sure trust in me, I shall be in their midst and through me they can obtain all things."

confession. Cf. Peter Lombard, *Sent.*, 4.17.1.

excommunication. Thomas Aquinas, *S. Th.*, PTS 21; John Faber, *Malleus*, 5.14.1-2 [fol. 80ᵛ.22-24, 42-fol. 81ʳ.2]: "All your discourse tends to the conclusion that Peter could not be said to have the rights of earthly and heavenly authority together. Now tell me, Luther, whether the pontiff could not excommunicate? Certainly in my judgment he can do that . . . [scriptural and patristic proof texts follow]. But isn't the power from Peter which is in binding and loosing and is exercised on earth? As the gospel states, what Peter does on earth, Christ confirms in heaven. Then no great sin is committed, if Peter is said to have the rights of both authorities."

jurisdiction. Thomas Aquinas, *S. Th.*, PTS 17.2; John Faber, *Malleus* [fol. 80ᵛ-81ʳ]: see previous note.

indulgences. Thomas Aquinas, *S. Th.*, PTS 25.2.

what to do. Cf. Bucer, *EN*, II [fol. 13ʳ.11-14]: "And the church has no other power of remitting sins than the Holy Spirit: he moreover absolves those who believe in Christ of sins only and declares them freed, because the church could not otherwise remit sins than in recognizing and attesting them remitted for those who believe in Christ."

Holy Spirit. Peter Lombard, *Sent.*, 4.18.5 [p. 861.28-30]: "Note that he [Augustine] says that sins are remitted or retained by holy men, and yet he says that the Holy Spirit remits them." Peter Lombard has just quoted Pseudo-Augustine, *On True and False Repentance*, 10.25 [PL 40.1122.42-55].

Page 146.

indiscriminately. Peter Lombard, *Sent.*, 4.18.7 [p. 864.22-25]: "For sometimes they show loosed or bound those who are not with God; and meanwhile they bind or loose by the penalty of satisfaction or excommunication, the unworthy and admit the unworthy to the sacraments, and bar the worthy from being admitted."

knowledge. Peter Lombard, *Sent.*, 4.19.3 [p. 870.27-29]: The words of Malachi 2:2, "Woe to those who revive souls which are not alive, and make dead souls which are not dead," refer to priests ". . . who without the key of knowledge and the form of a good life presume to bind and loose."

power. Peter Lombard, *Sent.*, 4.19.1 [p. 867.17-20]: "Since it is now certain that not all priests have those two keys, because very many lack the knowledge of discerning, there is a question about the other key, that is the power of binding and loosing, whether all priests have it."

ministrants. Peter Lombard, *Sent.*, 4.19.3.

loosed. Peter Lombard, *Sent.*, 4.18.7 [pp. 864.29-865.2]: "Whomsoever therefore those priests possessing the key of discerning loose or bind according to the merits of the accused, are loosed or bound in heaven, that is, in God's sight; because by divine judgment the sentence of the priest so set forth is approved and confirmed."

rightly. Peter Lombard, *Sent.*, 4.19.1 [p. 867.4-16]: "Obviously it can be said that not all priests have the other one of these keys, that is, the knowledge of discerning— a fact to be regretted and to sorrow over. For many, although indiscreet and devoid of the knowledge in which priests should be eminent, presume to receive the rank of priest, yet unworthy of life and knowledge, who neither before priesthood nor after, have the knowledge of discerning which persons are to be bound or loosed. On this account they do not receive that key in consecration, because they always lack knowledge. But those who before becoming priests have been endowed with the knowledge of discerning, although they have discretion, still the key is not in them, because they do not have the power to shut or open; therefore, when one such is promoted to the office of priest, he is rightly said to receive the key of discretion, because his previously held discretion is increased and becomes a key in him, so that he now may use it to close and to open."

use. Peter Lombard, *Sent.*, 4.19.5 [p. 871.18-21], quoting Pseudo-Augustine, *TFR*, 20.36 [PL 40.1129f]: "Let the spiritual judge take care, just as he has not committed a wicked misdeed, so let him not lack the gift of knowledge; it is necessary that he know how to discern whatever he ought to judge: for judicial power demands this, that he discern what he ought to judge. . . . Let him take care not to corrupt, lest he rightly lose this judicial power."

Page 147.

indulgences. Cf. Thomas Aquinas, *S. Th.*, PTS 25.1.

taken away. Cf. e.g., *Gravimina nationis Germanicae adversus curiam Romanam* (1522-3), Kidd, *DCR*, no. 61, The Centum Gravimina, 3. De oneribus papalium indulgentiarum, pp. 113f: "On the burdens of papal indulgences. That unbearable burden of Roman indulgence long ago increased, when under the guise of piety although the Roman pontiffs promised either to construct Roman basilicas or to prepare an expedition against the Turks, they sucked out all from the simple-minded and too credulous Germans. And . . . through these impostures and the hired heralds of them . . . the genuine piety of Christians has been destroyed; while those who wished to sell these venal bulls, sang out praises for their wares; to condone wonderful and unheard of offenses sometimes something would be paid out, sometimes the right hand jingles coins. And by these traffickings of wares at the same time Germany has been despoiled of coins and devotion to Christ snuffed out, seeing that anyone for the price which he had paid out for these wares was promised for himself impunity from sinning. . . ."

benefit. Johan Wessels, *Adv. indulgentias*, disp. c. 50 [Walch, *Monimenta*, 1.1, p. 152].

Page 148.

sins. Thomas Aquinas, *S. Th.*, PTS 25.1; Eck, *Enchiridion* (1532), c. 24 [Eng. tr., Battles, p. 165]: "Know here that the treasury of indulgences is made from the superabundance of merits (insofar as they were capable of making satisfaction) of Christ and the saints. Concerning the superabundance of Christ's sufferings for us, it is said: 'He is the propitiation for our sins, not for ours only however, but for those of the whole world' [I John 2:2]. . . . Concerning the superabundance of sufferings and merits of the saints, for the office of satisfying for us, Job's statement is clear: 'O that my sins were weighed, for which I deserved wrath, and the calamity which I suffer in the balances appeared heavier than the sand of the sea' [Job 6:2-3]. From these words of Job it is clear that he suffered more than he ought to have suffered for his sins. In superabundance of sufferings consists superabundance of satisfactions. The same thing is very clear concerning many saints."

sense. Thomas Aquinas, *S. Th.*, PTS 25.1; Eck, *Enchiridion* (1532), c. 24 [Eng. tr., Battles, p. 166]: "Concerning the intention of the saints, namely that they willed to suffer and did freely suffer not only for themselves, but also for us, the apostle testifies: 'Now I rejoice in my sufferings for you, and in my flesh I complete those things which

are lacking in Christ's sufferings for the sake of his body, that is, the church' [Col. 1:24]."
See also John Fisher, *Confutatio*, p. 306.

Page 149.
    satisfaction. Peter Lombard, *Sent.*, 4.16.6 [p. 844.23-27], quoting Pseudo-Augustine, *Sermon*, 351.5.12 [PL 39.1549]: "As Augustine says, to do penance, 'it is not enough to change one's behavior for the better, and to forsake evil deeds, unless also from those which have been committed, satisfaction be made to the Lord through the sorrow of penance, through groaning of humiliation, through the sacrifice of a contrite heart, with accompanying alms.' "
    committed. Gratian, *Decr.*, 2.33.3.1.63 [Friedberg, 1.1177], also quoting Pseudo-Augustine, *Sermon* 351.12. His text differs slightly from that of Peter Lombard: "past evil deeds" and "alms and fasting."
    pardon. Gratian, *Decr.*, 2.33.3.1.76 [Friedberg, 1.1180], quoting Ambrose, *Sermon on Elijah and Fasting*, 20.75 [CSEL 32.II.458.4ff]: " 'The medicine of mercy removes great sins' [Eccl. 10:4]. We have very many aids, by which we redeem our sins; you have money, redeem your sin. The Lord is not for sale, but you are for sale. By your sins you have been put up for sale, redeem yourself by your works, redeem yourself by your money; money is cheap, but mercy is precious. 'Alms,' he says, 'frees from sin [Tobit 12:9].' " Gratian comments: "Therefore misdeeds are redeemed by alms." Calvin cites also in his marginal note, 1536 ed., p. 343, top left: "c. nullus. eadem dist." This refers to *Decr.*, 2.33.3.1.42, where Gratian quotes Augustine, *On Continence*, 6.15 [PL 40.358]: "No one receives pardon for a rather heavy penalty owed unless he has paid some penalty or other, even though it is far less than he owes. For thus does the Lord impart the gift of his mercy so that the justice of discipline is not relinquished." Ganoczy feels Calvin has here given a citation "renforcée ou deformée" [p. 181 n.287].

Page 151.
    remedies. Peter Lombard, *Sent.*, 4.16.6 [p. 844.18-22]: "For the Lord's Prayer with some fasting and alms, suffices, provided a bit of contrition precedes and confession is added, if readiness is present. . . . For graver sins however these means also are to be utilized, but much more forcibly and strictly. . . ."
    Lord's Prayer. Gratian, *Decr.*, 2.33.3.3.20 [Friedberg, 1.1214], quoting Augustine, *Enchiridion*, 7.19: "Concerning daily, short, and light sins, without which this life cannot be lived, the daily prayer of the faithful makes satisfaction. It is for them to say: 'Our Father which are in heaven.' Thus are they reborn to the Father by water and the Holy Spirit."
    Mass. Thomas Aquinas, *S. Th.*, PTS 86.4; 87.3.
    pardon. Cf. Melanchthon, *LC* (1521), 8 [Eng. tr., LCC 19.132]: "For every work of man is mortal sin if he is not in Christ. . . . On the contrary all the works of the saints are venial sins because, as we know, through the mercy of God they are forgiveness to those who believe."
    sins. Cicero, *Pro Murena*, 29.6: "All sins are equal." Diogenes Laërtius, 7.120; Lactantius, *Divine Institutes*, 3.23.8 [Eng. tr., ANF 7.93]: "But who approves of the equality of faults as laid down by Zeno?" Cyprian, *Epist.*, 51.16 [Eng. tr., ANF 5.331]: "The principle of the philosophers and Stoics is different, dearest brother, who say that all sins are equal, and that a grave man ought not easily to be moved. But there is a wide

difference between Christians and philosophers." Cf. Calvin, *Comm. Sen. De Clem.*, 49.1f. See also John Fisher, *Confutatio*, c. 5 [p. 160].

death. Calvin (here concerned with the Romanist critique of the Protestant rejection of classification of sins) has already in the *Psychopannychia* [ed. Zimmerli, pp. 65ff] dealt with these "death" texts, which had been used by the Anabaptists [Fragment II] in support of soul-death or soul-sleep. Their words: "The soul, although it had been given immortality, lapsed into sin, and by this ruin sunk and lost its immortality." Gen. 2:17, Rev. 6:23, and Ezek. 18:4 are then quoted by them in support of their view. Contending that the Scriptural imagery of physical death is divine accommodation of language to express in humanly understandable terms ineffable spiritual truth, Calvin asserts "that the immortality of the soul . . . consists in a perception of good and evil, exists even when it is dead, and that that death is something else than the annihilation" claimed by the Anabaptists [Zimmerli, p. 66]. Here Calvin, against the Romanists, takes the same exegetical position, but in answer to a different question.

to them. Cf. Cic., *De Off.*, 3.33.117.

Page 152.
paid. Thomas Aquinas, *S. Th.*, PT 86.4.

penalty. Thomas Aquinas, *S. Th.*, PTS 15.1; Bonaventura, *In Sent.*, 4.18.1.2.2 [Quaracchi ed. minor, 4. 458-461].

Page 153.
adultery. Thomas Aquinas, *S. Th.*, PT 86.4; Eck, *Enchiridion* (1532), c. 9 [Eng. tr., Battles, p. 77]: "David after having committed adultery and murder, repentant, said to Nathan: 'I have sinned against the Lord.' And Nathan said to him: 'The Lord also has put away your sin; you shall not die. But the son who is born to you shall die' [II Sam. 12:13-14]. 'And the sword will not depart from your house even for evermore' [II Sam. 12:10]. And these things came to pass which the Lord had threatened, that he was thus humbled by his son Absalom. From this example it is clear that after actual sins have been dismissed by repentance, the penitent remains bound to temporal satisfactions. This is more fully explained by Gregory and Augustine." (Cf. Gratian, *Decr.*, 2.33.3.1.83 [Friedberg, 1.11.82].)

guilt. Thomas Aquinas, *S. Th.*, PT 86.3.2; de Castro, *Adv. haer.* (1534) [fol. 181 C]; John Fisher, *Confutatio*, p. 160f.

alms. Hugo of St. Victor (?), *Summa Sententiarum*, 6.11 [PL 176.149A]; Eck, *Enchiridion* (1532), c. 9 [Eng. tr. Battles, p. 79]: "Daniel advised Nebuchadnezzar: 'Make recompense for your sins with alms, and your inequities with merciful acts toward the poor' [Dan. 4:27]." De Castro, *Adv. haer.* [fol. 181B].

much. Cf. Eck, *Enchiridion* (1532), c. 9 [Eng. tr., Battles, pp. 83-4]: And thus also he nevertheless spiritually converts the heart of man with such great agitation, that suddenly it perfectly achieves spiritual health, not only with guilt forgiven, but with all the rest of sin removed, as is clear concerning Mary Magdalene [Lk. 7:47]. He previously forgives sin through operating grace and afterwards he removes in succession the force of the penalty and other remaining sins." Cf. Thomas Aquinas, *S. Th.*, PT 49.1.

Page 154.
satisfaction. Ambrose, *Exposition of the Gospel of Luke*, 10.88 [CSEL 32 IV 489.8], as quoted from Gratian, *Decr.*, 2.33.3.1.1.1 [Friedberg, 1.1159]; cf. also Maximus of Turin, Hom. 53 (On Peter's Repentance) [PL 57.351].

Page 156.

Chrysostom. O. Balzer, *Die Sentenzen des Petrus Lombardus*, pp. 2f, summarizes Peter Lombard's use of Augustine (his chief source, with over 1000 citations) and also his use of later medieval compilations under Augustine's name: Fulgentius, *De Fide ad Petrum;* Vigilius Thaps., *Contra Felicianum;* Prosper, *Liber Sententiarum;* Gennadius, *De Dogmatibus Ecclesiae;* Cassian, *Collations;* and *On True and False Repentance* on which see following note below.

as his. Calvin's judgment on the inauthenticity of *On True and False Repentance* [PL 40.1113-1130], attributed to Augustine but actually an eleventh century compilation, is linked by Luchesius Smits, *Saint Augustin dans l'oeuvre de Jean Calvin* (1957), 1.190, to Erasmus' critical appraisal in his edition of Augustine [4.737]: "The book almost in its entirety was copied in the *Decretals and Sentences*, in such a way that the compiler had more zeal than judgment." Cf. Peter Lombard, *Sent.*, 4.14-22 [pp. 819-889].

purgatory. Peter Lombard, *Sent.*, 4.21.1-6 [pp. 880-883]. OS 4.138n.1; Bonaventura, *In Sent.*, 4.20.1.1.1-6 [Quaracchi ed. minor, 4.501-516].

obtained. This refers to Melanchthon's silence concerning purgatory in the *Augsburg Confession* and the *Apology*.

Page 157.

bulrush. Plautus, *Menaechmi*, 2.1.(247); Terence, *Andria*, 5.4.38 (921). Quoted in Erasmus, *Adagia*, 2.4.76.

heart. Peter Lombard, *Sent.*, 4.22.2 [p. 888.12-14]: "Some say that the Sacrament consists in what is done outwardly, that is, outward penance, which is a sign of inner repentance, that is, of contrition and humbling of heart." Cf. Luther, *Babylonian Captivity* [LW 36.62].

sacrament. Peter Lombard, *Sent.*, 4.22.2 [p. 888.24-26, 29-31; p. 889.3-7]: "If outward penance is the Sacrament, and inner repentance the sacramental matter, the sacramental matter more often precedes the sacrament than the sacrament precedes the matter. . . . Some moreover say that outward and inner penance are one sacrament, not two sacraments, as the species of bread and wine are not two sacraments but one. . . . For inner repentance is both the matter of the sacrament, that is of outward penance, and also the sacrament of the forgiveness of sin, which it both signifies and carries out. Also outward penance is both a sign of inner repentance and of forgiveness of sin."

understood. Augustine, *De Diversis quaestionibus LXXXIII, liber unus*, 43. [PL 40.28].

place. Augustine, *Sermon*, 272 [PL 38.1247.3-5].

arena. On *beluas conficere*, cf. Calvin, *Comm. Sen. De Clem.*, 103.16: "to slay the beast," obviously a proverbial saying.

Page 158.

represent. Augustine, *On the Merits and Remission of Sins*, 1.21.30 [Eng. tr., NPNF¹ 5.26].

sanctification. Augustine, *Questions on the Heptateuch*, 3.84 [PL 34.73.5-11].

alone. Augustine, *On Baptism*, 5.24.34 [Eng. tr., NPNF¹ 4.475].

penance. Cf. Luther, *Babylonian Captivity* [Eng. tr., LW 36.58]: "The source of these false opinions is that dangerous saying of St. Jerome either unhappily phrased or wrongly interpreted—in which he terms penance 'the second plank after shipwreck,' as if baptism were not penance." *Ibid.*, p. 61: "You will likewise see how perilous, indeed, how false it is to suppose that penance is 'the second plank after shipwreck,' and how pernicious an error it is to believe that the power of baptism is broken, and the ship dashed to pieces, because of sin. The ship remains one, solid, and invincible; it will never be broken up into separate 'planks.' " See also Peter Lombard, *Sent.*, 4.14.1 [p. 819.6ff]. Both writers are of course quoting Jerome, *Epist.* 84.6 [CSEL 55.128.5]; note also Calvin, *Comm. Sen. De Clem.*, 22.31n.

repentance. Cf. Luther, *Babylonian Captivity* [Eng. tr., LW 36.58]: ". . . as if baptism were not penance." Cf. Melanchthon, *LC* (1521), 9 [Eng. tr., LCC 19.140]: "The sacrament or sign of this [repentance] is simply baptism, which could most appropriately be called the 'sacrament of repentance.' "

call it. Peter Lombard, *Sent.*, 4.23 [pp. 889-892]. Thomas Aquinas, *S. Th.*, PTS 29-33; Eugenius IV, *Exultate Deo*, c. 14 [Mansi, 31.1058ff; Denziger, *Ench.*, no. 700 (Eng. tr., p. 224)]: "The fifth sacrament is extreme unction, whose matter is the olive oil blessed by the bishop. This sacrament should be given only to the sick of whose death there is fear; and he should be anointed in the following places: on the eyes because of sight, on the ears because of hearing, on the nostrils because of smell, on the mouth because of taste and speech, on the hands because of touch, on the feet because of gait, on the loins because of the delight that flourishes there."

tasting. Eugenius IV, *Ibid.* [Mansi, 31.1058A ff; Denziger, *Ench.*, no. 700, Eng. tr., p. 224]: "The form of this sacrament is the following, 'Through this holy anointing and his most kind mercy may the Lord forgive you whatever through seeing . . . etc.' And similarly on the other members."

soul. Peter Lombard, *Sent.*, 4.23.3 [p. 890.8-14]: "In this [James 5:1f] is shown that this sacrament was instituted for a double reason, namely for forgiveness of sins and for alleviation of bodily weakness. Hence it is clear that he who faithfully and devoutly receives this anointing is alleviated both in body and in soul, if it is expedient that he be alleviated in both. But if perchance it is not expedient for him to have health of body, in this sacrament he acquires that health which is of the soul." (Quoted from Hugo of St. Victor, *On the Sacraments of the Christian Faith*, 2.15.2 [cf. Eng. tr., R. J. Deferrari, p. 431; PL 176.577].)

forgiven. Peter Lombard, *Sent.*, 4.23.3 [p. 890.5-8], quoting James 5:14f. Cf. Innocent I, *Epist.*, 25 (to Decentius) c. 8 [PL 20.559B f]; Council of Ticino (Pavia) [AD 850] c. 8 [Mansi, 14.932E f]; Eugenius IV, *Exultate Deo* [Mansi, 31.1058A ff; Denziger, *Ench.*, no. 700, Eng. tr., p. 224]: "On this sacrament blessed James, the Apostle, says: 'Is any man sick among you? Let him bring in the priests of the church, and let them pray over him, anointing him with oil in the name of the Lord. And the prayer of faith shall save the sick man; and the Lord shall raise him up: and if he be in sins, they shall be forgiven him' [James 5:14f]."

Page 159.

healing. Cf. p. 5 above, where Calvin counters the Roman Catholic controversialists' demand that the "new" faith confirm itself by physical miracles. Augustine, *City of God*, 22.8, had accepted the view that miracles were performed to bring the world to believe in Christ, but considered that such miracles of healing had continued even to his own time. This was, of course, to become the teaching and practice of the medieval church, and of Romanism generally. Luther was the first of the Reformers to disallow physical miracles performed posteriorly to the Apostolic age, holding rather that God's proclaimed Word performs spiritual miracles to this day. See, *A Sermon on Keeping Children in School* (1530) [Eng. tr., PE 4.146ff]: "Though these [miracles] may not happen in a bodily way" (as they did with Jesus and the apostles) "yet they do happen spiritually in the soul, where the miracles are even greater." The minister is the instrument of the Word of God in this work, according to Luther.

anointing. Cf. Eugenius IV, *Exultate Deo* [Mansi, 31.1058A ff; Denziger, *Ench.*, no. 700, Eng. tr., p. 224]: "The minister of this sacrament is the priest. Now the effect is the healing of the mind and, moreover, in so far as it is expedient, of the body itself, also."

Page 160.

extremis. Peter Lombard, *Sent.*, 4.23.1 [p. 889.11-13]: "Besides the foregoing there is also another sacrament, namely, the anointing of the sick, which is done *in extremis*, with the oil consecrated by the bishop."

priests. Thomas Aquinas, *S. Th.*, PTS 31.3.

bishop. Cf. Innocent I, *Epist.*, 25 (to Decentius), c. 8 [PL 20.559B f]; Thomas Aquinas, *S. Th.*, PTS 29.6; Eugenius IV, *Exultate Deo* (1439), c. 14 [Mansi, 31.1058A ff].

balm. *Pontificale Romanum* [ed. Mechl., 1934], pp. 767, 769.

unction. Eugenius IV, *Exultate Deo*, c. 15 [Mansi, 31.1058D].

Page 161.

orders. Peter Lombard, *Sent.*, 4.24 [pp. 892-904]; Thomas Aquinas, *S. Th.*, PTS 34-40; Eugenius IV, *Exultate Deo*, c. 15; Denziger, *Ench.*, no. 701 [Eng. tr., p. 224]: "The sixth sacrament is that of order, the matter of which is that through whose transmission the order is conferred . . ." etc.

endowed. Peter Lombard, *Sent.*, 4.24.2 [p. 892.17-19]: "Moreover, there are seven orders on account of the sevenfold grace of the Holy Spirit; those who do not participate therein unworthily approach the grades of ecclesiastical orders."

promoted. Peter Lombard, *Sent.*, 4.24.2 [p. 892.19-22]: "But those in whose minds the sevenfold grace of the Holy Spirit is diffused, when they approach ecclesiastical orders are believed to receive a fuller grace in being promoted to a spiritual grade."

orders. Hugo of St. Victor counted seven orders in *On the Sacraments of the Christian Faith*, 2.3.5 [Eng. tr., R. J. Deferrari, p. 262]: "Among these seven grades of spiritual office. . . ."

nine. William of Paris, who numbers seven orders, mentions certain other writers who, he says, have numbered nine orders: *De Septem Sacramentis*, Operum Summa (Paris, 1516), 2.60.

in the orders. See P. Schanz, *Die Lehre von dem heil. Sakr. der Kath. Kirche* (1893), p. 676.

canons. Gratian, *Decr.*, 1.21.1 [Friedberg, 1.69] quoting Isidore of Seville, *Etymol.*, 7.12 [PL 82.290]: "Readers are so called from reading, psalmists from singing psalms. The former proclaim to the people what they are to follow; the latter sing to arouse the hearts of their hearers to compunction. . . ." Cf. 1.23.18 [Friedberg, 1.84]: "When the reader is ordained, the bishop is to make a statement concerning him to the people, commending his faith and life and character; after this, while the people look on, he is to deliver over to him the book in which he is going to read, saying: 'Receive this and be a bringer of God's Word, taking part (if you faithfully and usefully fulfil this office) with those who minister the word of God.' " This reference to *Decr.*, 1.23.18, is followed

in Calvin's marginal note [1536 ed., p. 369] by one to *Decr.*, 1.23.19 (c. *"ostiarius"*—
1.23.19). It would seem that Calvin really intends the next canon (1.23.20, *Psalmista*),
which reads as follows: "The psalmist or cantor can, without the knowledge of the bishop
and solely at the behest of the presbyter, undertake the office of singing. The presbyter
says to him: 'See to it that what you sing with the mouth, you believe in the heart, and
what you believe in the heart, you prove by your acts.' " Cf. *Statuta Ecclesiae antiquae*
= Council of Carthage IV (AD 398) [Mansi, 3.951f].

School. Peter Lombard, *Sent.*, 4.24.1 [p. 892.12]: "There are seven grades or
orders of spiritual offices. . . ."

portion. Gratian, *Decr.*, 1.21.1 [Friedberg, 1.67]: "We believe that the words
'clergy' and 'clerics' are derived from the fact that Matthias was chosen by lot [Acts
1:26], who we read was the first to be ordained by the apostles. Κλῆρος is used in Greek,
'lot' or 'inheritance' [*sors vel hereditas*] in Latin. On this account, then, they have been
called 'clerics,' because they are of the lot of the Lord, or because they have the Lord's
portion."

church. Gratian, *Decr.*, 2.12.1.7 [Friedberg, 1.678]: "There are two kinds of
Christians. There is one kind attached to the divine office, and dedicated to contemplation
and prayer, whom it befits to cease from all clangor of temporal affairs; such are the
clergy, devoted, that is converted, to God. For the Greek word κλῆρος in Latin means
'lot.' Hence men of this sort are called 'clergy,' that is, chosen by lot. . . . The other sort
of Christians is the laity. Λαός meant 'people.' These are permitted to possess temporal
goods, but only for use."

Page 162.

God. Cf. Luther, *The Freedom of a Christian* [Eng. tr., LW 31.356]: "Injustice is
done those words 'priest,' 'cleric,' 'spiritual,' 'ecclesiastic,' when they are transferred
from all Christians to those few who are now by a mischievous usage called 'ecclesiastics.' "

others. Gratian, *Decr.*, 2.12.1.7 [Friedberg, 1.678]: "For they [the clerics] are
kings, that is, they are ruling themselves and others in virtues, and thus have the kingdom
in God. This is what the crown on the head designates. They have this crown from the
foundation of the Roman church as a sign of the kingdom which they await in Christ.
The shaving of the head denotes the forsaking of all temporal goods. They, content with
food and clothing, hold no private property among themselves, but ought to hold all
things in common." Peter Lombard, *Sent.*, 4.24.4 [p. 893.9-13]: "The crown is a sign
whereby they are signified as a part of the allotted ministry of God. The crown signifies
royal dignity, and to serve God is to reign. Hence the ministers of the church ought to
be kings, that they may rule themselves and others; to them Peter says: 'You are a chosen
race, a royal priesthood.' "

cut off. Peter Lombard, *Sent.*, 4.24 [p. 893.17-19]; "The top of the head is made
bare to show their mind free to God so, 'with face unveiled,' to contemplate God's glory.
. . . Also the hair is cut even to the unveiling of the senses, namely the eyes and the
ears, in order that they may be taught that vices sprouting in heart and deed are to be
cut off. . . ."

things. Gratian, *Decr.*, 2.12.1.7 [Friedberg, 1.678].

Nazarites. Peter Lombard, *Sent.*, 4.24.4 [p. 893.22-23]: "The use of the ecclesiastical tonsure seems to have arisen from the Nazarites. . . ."

purified. Peter Lombard, *Sent.*, 4.24.4 [p. 893.27-29]: "In the Acts of the Apostles we read that Priscilla and Aquila did this: Paul also and certain other disciples of Christ did this."

Page 163.

ball. Gratian, *Decr.*, 1.23.21 [Friedberg, 1.85]: "Forbid, brethren, through all the regions of your churches, that clerics (according to the apostle) let their hair grow, but let them shave the head on top in the shape of a ball."

cords. Cf. Peter Lombard, *Sent.*, 4.24.5 [p. 894.21-22]: "The Lord fulfilled this office in his own person when he cast the buyers and sellers from the Temple with a whip made of cords."

door. *Ibid.*, 4.24.5 [p. 894.22-24]: "For he, signifying himself to be a doorkeeper, said: 'I am the door.' "

synagogue. *Ibid.*, 4.24.6 [p. 895.25-27]: "Christ fulfilled this office when, opening the book of Isaiah in the midst of the elders, he read clearly to be understood: 'The Spirit of the Lord is upon me,' " etc.

hearing. *Ibid.*, 4.24.7 [p. 896.17-19]: "The Lord performed this office when he touched with his spit the ears and tongue of the deaf mute . . ." etc.

darkness. Cf. *ibid.*, 4.24.8 [p. 897.16-17]: "The Lord testifies that he holds this office, saying: 'I am the light of the world; he who follows me does not walk in darkness.' "

feet. *Ibid.*, 4.24.9 [p. 898.14-15]: "The Lord performed this office when he girded himself with a linen cloth, and putting water in a basin, washed the disciples' feet and wiped their feet with the linen cloth."

apostles. *Ibid.*, 4.24.10 [p. 900.5-6]: "Christ performed this office when after the Supper he distributed the sacrament of flesh and blood to the disciples. . . ."

Father. *Ibid.*, 4.24.11 [p. 901.23-24]: "Christ performed this office when he offered himself on the altar of the cross." The editors of Lombard here cite Hebrews 10:11.

taperbearer. *Ibid.*, 4.24.8 [p. 897.4-6]: "They are called 'acolytes' in Greek, in Latin *ceroferarii* [taper bearers] from bearing tapers when the Gospel is to be read or the sacrifice to be offered."

cruet. *Ibid.*, 4.24.8 [p. 897.11-15]: "The acolyte's function includes the preparation of the lamps in the sanctuary; he carries the wax, prepares the cruet with the water and wine supplied for the eucharist for the subdeacons. They when ordained, after they have been instructed by the bishop as to how they ought to function in their office, receive the candlestick with the wax and the empty cruet from the archdeacon."

duties. De Castro, *Adv. haer.*, 1.13 [fol. 26ff].

Page 164.

demoniacs. Gratian, *Decr.*, 1.21.1 [Friedberg, 1.69]: "Exorcists are so called from the Greek; in Latin, adjurers or reprovers, for they invoke upon the catechumens or upon those who have an unclean spirit, the name of Lord Jesus, adjuring through him, that it come out of them."

after. Peter Lombard, *Sent.*, 4.24.12 [pp. 901.28-902.2,4f]: "Although they are all spiritual and sacred, yet they especially consider only two canons to be called 'sacred orders,' namely the diaconate and the presbyterate; for the ancient church is read to have held these alone, and they have a precept of the Apostle on these alone. But in the course of time the church established for itself subdeacons and acolytes."

sake. Peter Lombard cites I Tim. 3:2 and Acts 6:5 [p. 902.1-4].

gifts. Gratian, *Decr.*, 1.25.1.8 [Friedberg, 1.90.34-36]: "It is the duty of the presbyter to perform the sacrament of the Lord's body and blood on the altar, to say prayers, and to bless God's gifts."

consecrate. Peter Lombard, *Sent.*, 4.24.11 [p. 901.1-9]: "To the presbyter belongs the performing of the sacrament of the body and blood of the Lord on the altar of God, of saying prayers and of blessing God's gifts. When he is ordained his hands are anointed that he may know he has received the gift of consecrating, and ought to extend the works of charity to all. . . . Also he receives the chalice with the wine and the paten with the host, that through this he may know he has received the power of offering 'acceptable sacrifices to God' [Num. 5:8]."

priests. Cf. Luther, *The Freedom of a Christian* [Eng. tr., LW 31.354]: "Hence all of us who believe in Christ are priests and kings in Christ, as I Pt. 2:9 says: 'You are a chosen race, God's own people, a royal priesthood, a priestly kingdom, that you may declare the wonderful deeds of him who called you out of the darkness into his marvellous light.' "

successors. Cf. Irenaeus, *Against Heresies*, 3.3.2 [Eng. tr., ANF 1.415]: ". . . by indicating that tradition derived from the apostles, of the very great, the very ancient, and universally known church founded and organized at Rome by the two most glorious apostles, Peter and Paul; as also the faith preached to men, which comes down to our time by means of the successions of the bishops." Tertullian, *On Prescription against Heretics*, 32 [Eng. tr., ANF 3.258]: ". . . that bishop shall be able to show for his ordainer and predecessor some one of the apostles or of apostolic men,—a man, moreover, who continued steadfast with the apostles." Tertullian speaks of the bishops as "appointed to their episcopal places by apostles," and as "transmitters of the apostolic seed." Both of these statements are made in an effort to distinguish the authentic faith from the heretical which does not possess this continuity with the apostles. See also Augustine, *Against the Epistle Called Fundamental*, c. 4.5 [PL 42.175.34-37].

Page 165.

honor. Cf. Peter Lombard, *Sent.*, 4.24.11 [p. 901.14-20]: "Christ also 'chose twelve disciples' before, 'whom he also called apostles'; whose function in the church is carried out by the greater pontiffs. Then 'they designated seventy-two other disciples'; their function in the church is held by the priests. But one among the apostles, Peter, was the prince, whose vicar and successor is the supreme pontiff, hence called 'apostolic,' who also is called 'pope,' that is father of fathers." Also, Gratian, *Decr.*, 1.21.1 [Friedberg, 1.67f]: "The order of the bishops is fourfold: patriarchs, archbishops, metropolitans, and bishops. Patriarch in Greek means the chief one of the fathers, because he retains the first, that is, apostolic place, and therefore, because he discharges the highest honor, is accorded such a title, as the Roman, Antiochene, Alexandrine, patriarch. 'Archbishop' is the Greek word for the chief of the bishops, for he holds the apostolic place, and presides both over metropolitans and other bishops. Metropolitans are so called from the measure of cities; for they preside over individual provinces; to their authority and teaching other bishops are subject; apart from them it is not lawful for other bishops to take any action; for the oversight of the entire province is committed to them. All the above designated orders bear the single name of 'bishop'; but certain ones use their particular title on account of the distinction of powers which they have individually received."

bishops. Gratian, *Decr.*, 1.93.24 [Friedberg, 1.327]: ". . . since the Apostle clearly teaches that bishops are the same as presbyters . . ." Jerome, *On the Epistle of*

Titus, in Gratian, *Decr.*, 1.95.5 [Friedberg, 1.332]: "Once presbyter and bishop were one and the same, and before strife entered into religion through the devil's prompting, and it was said to the people: 'I am of Paul, I am of Apollos, I of Cephas,' the churches were governed by the common counsel of the presbyters."

rank. Peter Lombard, *Sent.*, 4.24.17 [p. 903.17-19]; also Gratian, *Decr.*, 1.21, intr., para. 3 [Friedberg, 1.67]: "The distinction of these [four orders of bishops] seems to have been introduced by the Gentiles who called some of their flamens simply flamens, others archiflamens, still others protoflamens." Note that Calvin has misapplied this quotation to the distinction between bishops and presbyters.

Lord. [Phil. 4:10-14; cf. Lk. 10:7].

busybodies. Theophylact, *Comm. in Epist. II Thess.* [PG. 124.1354].

Page 166.

task. Calvin here sets the apostles apart from all later ministers of the church. Revising this portion in 1543, he will make clearer the distinction (already used by Luther) between temporary and permanent church offices, resting upon the uniqueness of the Apostolic age. This handling of the apostolic office serves both to deny a factual "apostolic succession" to the Roman Catholics and the concentration on the inner call by certain early Anabaptists. For the latter, see W. E. Keeney, *Dutch Anabaptist Thought and Practice: 1539-1564* (1968), p. 46f. Note that Calvin does not explicitly criticize Article 5 of the *Schleitheim Confession* here.

Page 167.

alone. Third Lateran Council (AD 1179) [Mansi, 22.218]. Cf. Gratian, *Decr.*, 1.67.1, 2 [Friedberg, 1.253.32f]: "The bishop alone can confer honor upon priests and ministers; he alone cannot withdraw it."

title. Decree of the Third Lateran Council, c. 5, quoted in *Decretal Greg. IX*, 3.5.2, 4 [Friedberg, 2.454f], c. 2: "If any priest, that is, presbyter, deacon or subdeacon, suspected of the crime of fornication with any women, after the first, second or third admonition, be found to talk and in some way converse with her; he is to be laid under excommunication; the woman is to be judged canonically." *Ibid.*, c. 4: "Even as it is supremely fitting for us to see to the uprooting of vices which imperil souls, so also it befits us to spread the seeds of virtues, from which to effect an increase of salvation for the faithful, and the beauty of honesty for holy churches. Hence since there has for a long time and by a detestible custom prevailed in England the practice of clerics having prostitutes in their houses, we wishing to remove this very grave scandal from the people, and lead back the aforesaid clerics to ecclesiastical honesty, I bid Your Fraternity, through apostolic writings, to the best of your ability zealously to warn the clerics of your jurisdiction who in the subdiaconate and above have prostitutes in their houses, that they should remove these women from themselves, ceasing delays and appeals, not ever for the future admitting them. But if beyond forty days after your communication they perchance contemptuously acquiesce in these things, relying on apostolic authority, the remedy of appeal being removed, you are to suspend them from ecclesiastical benefices until appropriate satisfaction is made, and, if they undecided presume to retain such women, you are to take care to remove them permanently from those same benefices."

Page 168.

delegated. Cyprian, *Epist.*, 51.8 [ANF 5.329]: "Moreover Cornelius was made bishop by the judgment of God and of His Christ, by the testimony of almost all the clergy, by the vote of the people who were then present, and by the assembly of ancient priests and good men, when no one had been made so before him, when the place of Fabian, that is, when the places of Peter and the degree of the sacerdotal throne was vacant. . . ." Cf. also *Epist.*, 59(54).6 [ANF 5.341]; 67.3f [5.370f].

  interests. Virgil, *Aeneid*, 2.39.

  church. Decree of Third Lateran Council (AD 1179) can. 1, 3 [Mansi, 22.217ff].

Page 170.

  beginning. Peter Lombard, *Sent.*, 4.24.11 [p. 901.10-13]: "This order took its beginning from the sons of Aaron. For the high priests [supreme pontiffs] and lesser priests God established through Moses, who at God's command anointed Aaron as high priest, his sons as lesser priests." Gratian, *Decr.*, 1.21, Part I [Friedberg, 1.67.4-7]: "For the high priests and lesser priests were established by God through Moses, who from the Lord's precept anointed Aaron as high priest, his sons as lesser priests."

  character. Peter Lombard, *Sent.*, 4.24.13 [p. 902.8-11]: "If it is asked what it is that is here called 'order,' obviously it can be said that it is a certain sign, that is, something sacred, whereby spiritual power and office is transferred to the person ordained. Therefore the spiritual character where the promotion of power occurs, is called 'order' or 'grade.' " See also Thomas Aquinas, *S. Th.*, PT 63.6; PTS 35.2; Eugenius IV, *Exultate Deo* [Mansi, 31.1054; Denziger, *Ench.*, no. 695, Eng. tr., p. 221]: "Among these sacraments there are three, baptism, confirmation, and orders, which imprint an indelible sign on the soul, that is, a certain character distinctive from the others. Hence they should not be repeated in the same person." Cf. Luther, *Babylonian Captivity* [Eng. tr., LW 36.117]: "For that fiction of an 'indelible character' has long since become a laughingstock."

  sacrament. Gratian, *Decr.*, 2.1.54 [Friedberg, 1.379], quoting Augustine, *John's Gospel*, 80.3 [PL 35.1840]: "Withdraw the word, what is water but water? Add the word to the element, and it becomes a sacrament. Whence comes this great power of the water to teach the body and cleanse the heart, unless by the action of the word? Not because it is spoken, but because it is believed. For in the word itself, the transient sound is one thing, the abiding power another."

Page 171.

  deacons. Peter Lombard, *Sent.*, 4.24.10 [p. 899.20-21]: "This order was celebrated by the apostles when, as one reads in the Acts of the Apostles [6:3], they chose for this office 'seven men full of the Holy Spirit,' and having given a prayer, laid their hands upon them."

  poor. Cf. Luther, *Babylonian Captivity* [Eng. tr., LW 36.116]: "And the diaconate is the ministry, not of reading the Gospel or the Epistle, as is the present practice, but of distributing the church's aid to the poor. . . ."

Page 172.

  people. Peter Lombard, *Sent.*, 4.24.10 [p. 899.6-10]: "It is the office of the deacon to assist the priests and to minister in everything done in the sacraments of Christ, that is, in baptism, in chrism, in paten and chalice, to bring in the offerings and lay them on the altar, to set the Lord's table and cover it, to bear the cross and to pronounce the gospel and epistle."

  upon him. Gratian, *Decr.*, 1.23.11 [Friedberg, 1.83]: "When a deacon is ordained, the bishop alone who blesses him, is to place his hands upon the former's head because he is being consecrated not to the priesthood, but to the ministers." Cf. *Statuta ecclesiae antiquae*, c. 4 = Council of Carthage IV (AD 398) [Mansi, 3.951A].

of it. Peter Lombard, *Sent.*, 4.24.10 [pp. 899.27-900.2]: "When they are ordained, the bishop alone lays his hand upon him, because they apply to the ministry. He places a napkin, that is, a stole, upon the left shoulder, that through this they may understand that they have received 'the Lord's light yoke,' to subject the things pertaining to his left side to the fear of God. They receive also the text of the gospel, that they may understand themselves to be proclaimers of Christ's gospel." Cf. Eugenius IV, *Exultate Deo* [Mansi, 31.1058D; Denziger, *Ench.*, no. 701, Eng. tr., p. 225]: ". . . the diaconate [is transmitted] . . . by the giving of the book of the Gospels."

Levi. Peter Lombard, *Sent.*, 4.24.10 [p. 898.20f]: "This order derived its name in the Old Testament from the tribe of Levi, for they are also called 'Levites.' " Gratian, *Decr.*, 1.21.1 [Friedberg, 1.68f]: "The Levites are called from the name of their author. For from Levi the Levites took their origin; by them was fulfilled the ministry of the sacramental mystery in the temple of God. In Greek they are called 'deacons,' in Latin 'ministers,' for just as in the priest there is consecration, so in the deacon there is dispensation." *Ibid.*, 1.25.1 [Friedberg, 1.90.24-34]: "To the deacon belongs the assisting of the priests and the ministering in all things done in the sacrament of Christ: that is, in baptism, in chrism and paten and cup, also to bring in the offerings and lay them on the altar; to lay and cover the Lord's table, to bear the cross, and pronounce the gospel and epistle. For as the readers are bidden to read the Old Testament, so the deacons the New. To him also belongs the office of prayers and the recital of names; he forewarns the people to listen to God, exhorts them to pray, gives and announces peace." *Ibid.*, 1.25.3 [Friedberg, 1.92]: "A napkin is to be laid on the Levite's left shoulder because he prays, that is, speaks forth; but the right shoulder is to be left free that he may be free to move about in the priestly ministry."

order. Peter Lombard, *Sent.*, 4.24.13 [p. 902.12-14]: "And these orders are said to be sacraments, because in receiving them the sacramental matter, that is, grace, is conferred, which the things performed there figure."

Marriage. Peter Lombard, *Sent.*, 4.26.42 [pp. 912-994]; Thomas Aquinas, *S. Th.*, PTS 41-68; Eugenius IV, *Exultate Deo*, c. 16 [Mansi, 31.1058E f; Denziger, *Ench.*, no. 702, Eng. tr., p. 225]: "The seventh is the sacrament of matrimony, which is the sign of the joining of Christ and the church according to the Apostle who says: 'This is a great sacrament; but I speak in Christ and in the church' [Eph. 5:32]. The efficient cause of matrimony is regularly mutual consent expressed by words in person. Moreover, there is allotted a threefold good on the part of matrimony. First, the progeny is to be accepted and brought up for the worship of God. Second, there is faith which one of the spouses ought to keep for the other. Third, there is the indivisibility of marriage, because it signifies the indivisible union of Christ and the church. Although, moreover, there may be a separation of the marriage couch by reason of fornication, nevertheless, it is not permitted to contract another marriage, since the bond of marriage legitimately contracted is perpetual."

Gregory. Gregory VII (1073-1085); Peter Damian, *Sermo*, 69 [PL 161. 568]; Ives of Chartres, *Epist.*, 188 [PL 162.191]; *Decretum*, 8.9 [PL 161.568].

Page 173.

church. Peter Lombard, *Sent.*, 4.26.6 [p. 914.17-18]: "Since marriage is a sacrament, it is both a sacred sign and a sign of a sacred thing, namely, of the joining of Christ and the church. . . ."

hospital. Horace, *Satires*, 2.3.83. Anticyra was the name of two places in classical times famous for hellibore and frequented by hypochondriacs.

Page 174.

deceived them. Cf. Luther, *Babylonian Captivity* [Eng. tr., LW 36.93]: "For where we have [in the Vulgate] the word *sacramentum* the Greek original has *mysterium*, which the translator sometimes translated and sometimes retains in its Greek form. Thus our verse in the Greek reads: 'The two shall become one. This is a great mystery.' This explains how they came to understand a sacrament of the New Law here, a thing they would never have done if they had read *mysterium*, as it is in the Greek. Thus Christ himself is called a 'sacrament' in I Tim. 3[:16]: 'Great indeed, is the sacrament (that is the mystery). . . .' " Calvin's philological argument seems to echo also Zwingli's prior discussion. See *Commentary*, 15 [Eng. tr., LWZ 3.180.30-181.5]: "It does not appear that the word was used among the ancients to mean a sacred and secret thing. Hence I have given no space to this acception of the term, nor to the one which the Latin translation of the New Testament has, of 'sacramentum' for mystery [cf. Eph. 5:32]. For the word does not express that, nor do I know any Latin word which really gives the meaning of μυστήριον because 'arcanum' [secret] has a wider application than μυστήριον and 'sacrum' [sacred] is of somewhat narrower scope." Also, *Ibid.*, 16 [Eng. tr., LWZ 3.184.28]: "Of marriage I am going to say only enough here to prevent anyone's thinking its dignity impaired when I do not count it among the sacraments, while Paul nevertheless calls it a sacrament, Eph. 5:32. I will say this therefore, that two errors have been committed as to this passage: the first by the [Latin] translator, who as he should have rendered 'mystery' by 'secret' [*arcanum*], always translated it 'sacrament,' although the latter word does not correspond to the former. . . ." See also our note at *Inst.* (1559), 4.19.36 [LCC 21.1483n86]. A recent Roman Catholic translation of the Bible, *The Jerusalem Bible*, has "mystery" throughout.

memories. Quintilian, *Inst. of Oratory*, 4.2.91 [LCC 21.1483n86, for reference].

levity is this. Gratian, *Decr.*, 1.28.2 [Friedberg, 1.101], citing Innocent II, Council at Rome of 1139 [Mansi, 21.526]: "We decree that those who in the order of subdeacon and above take wives or have concubines lack the office and ecclesiastical benefice. For since they ought to be and be called the temple, the vessel of the Lord, the sanctuary of the Holy Spirit, it is unworthy of them to subject themselves to cohabitation and uncleanness." See also *Ibid.*, 1.82.3-4, quoting Pope Siricius' letter to Himericus, Bishop of Tarragona, AD 385 [Jaffe, no. 65].

sacrament. Cf. Luther, *Babylonian Captivity* [Eng. tr., LW 36.101]: "The 'impediment of ordination' is also the mere invention of man, especially since they prate that it annuls even a marriage already contracted." Cf. Zwingli, "Permission to Marry," Jackson, SWHZ pp. 30ff. Zwingli has a second selection on marriage in his *Commentary*, 21 [Eng. tr., LWZ 3.257-260], devoted to clerical celibacy and marriage.

copulation. Peter Lombard, *Sent.*, 4.26.6 [p. 915.1-4]: "The figure of copulation of two persons in marriage for the agreement of the spouses, signifies the spiritual copulation of Christ and the Church, which is done through love, but the commingling of the sexes signifies that copulation which is done through conformity of nature." Gratian, *Decr.*, 2.27.2.17 [Friedberg, 1.1066.32-36]: "Since the society of wedlock was established from the beginning in such a way that apart from the commingling of the sexes the marriage of Christ and the church does not in itself constitute a sacrament, there is no doubt that that woman is not married in whom it is shown that there was no

nuptial mystery [or: with whom it is shown that there was not sexual commingling]."
Cited from Leo I, Ep. 107 [Jaffe no. 320]. *Decr.,* 2.27.2.18 [Friedberg, 1.1067.16f]
(Comment on Gen. 2:24): ". . . man and woman can only become one flesh if they are
united to each other in carnal copulation."
   copulation. Peter Lombard, *Sent.,* 4.26.6 [p. 914.22-27]: "For as between spouses
the conjoining is according to the consent of minds or according to the mingling of
bodies, thus the Church is coupled to Christ by will and nature, because it wills the same
thing with him and he has taken form from the nature of man. Therefore bride is coupled
with bridegroom spiritually and corporeally, that is, in charity and in conformity of
nature." Gratian, *Decr.,* 2.32.2.4 [Friedberg, 1.1120f]: "Lawful marriages are indeed
free of sin, yet at that time when conjugal acts are performed, the presence of the Holy
Spirit will not be given, even though it is seen to be a prophet who is obeying the duty
of generation. But there are very many other offices in which human power alone is
sufficient, and nothing is lacking, and it is not fitting for the Holy Spirit to be present."

Page 175.
   men. Cf. Luther, *Babylonian Captivity* [Eng. tr., LW 36.96ff]. Luther rejects the
eighteen 'impediments' to marriage set forth in the *Summa de Casibus Conscientiae* of
Angelo Carletti di Chevasse (1411-1495). Note Luther's similar use of Lev. 18:6ff [p. 99]:
"Here, therefore, those inflexible impediments derived from affinity, by spiritual or legal
relationship, and from blood relationship must give way, so far as the Scriptures permit,
in which the second degree of consanguinity alone is prohibited. Thus it is written in
Lev. 18[:6-18], where there are twelve persons a man is prohibited from marrying: his
mother, step-mother, full sister, half-sister, daughter-in-law, brother's wife, wife's sister,
step-daughter, and his uncle's wife. Here only the first degree of affinity and the second
degree of consanguinity are forbidden; yet not without exception, as will appear on closer
examination, for the brother's or sister's daughter—the niece—is not included in the
prohibition, although she is in the second degree. Therefore, if a marriage has been
contracted outside of those degrees, which are the only ones which have been prohibited
by God's appointment, it should by no means be annulled on account of the laws of men."
   valid. Peter Lombard, *Sent.,* 4.36.4 [p. 964.17-23]: "This also is to be understood:
that boys before the age of fourteen and girls before the age of twelve according to the
laws cannot enter into matrimony. But if they enter into union before the aforesaid times,
they can be separated, although they have been joined by the will and assent of the
parents. But those who, having been joined together in childhood, after the years of
puberty do not want to leave one another, but rather to remain in union, are thereafter
on this basis made spouses, and cannot be separated." Gratian, *Decr.,* 2.30.2, intro.
[Friedberg, 1.1099.45-1100.4]: "Wedlock cannot be contracted before age seven. It can
be contracted only by consent; this can be interfered with only when it is understood by
either party what is going on between them. Wedlock is therefore proved not capable of
being contracted between children, the infirmity of whose age does not admit of consent."
   dissolved. Peter Lombard, *Sent.,* 4.40.1 [p. 979.1-2]: "Therefore kinsmen by
blood or by marriage in the seventh degree or closer ought not to be united in marriage."
Gratian, *Decr.,* 2.35.2/3.16 [Friedberg, 1.1267f]: "We decree that whatsoever progeny
of theirs are to preserve generation to the seventh degree, and so long as they recognize
themselves to be related by affinity, we deny them the right to be linked in marriage. But
if they contract marriage, let them be separated." *Ibid.,* 17: "On the basis of his kinship
no one is to marry a wife until after the seventh generation, or as far as the relationship

can be recognized. . . ." *Ibid.*, 19: "No persons are to take wives from their blood relation, up to the seventh degree, nor without the priest's blessing. . . ."

degrees. The relevant passage in Peter Lombard is *Sent.*, 4.41.1-2 [pp. 982-985]; in Gratian, *Decr.*, 2.35 [Friedberg, 1.1261-1288]. Peter Lombard deals with the various ancient laws of marriage in *Sent.*, 4.33.1/2 [pp. 948ff]; he discussed Lev. 18:6ff at 4.33.3 All this is in the context of a discussion of the polygamy of the patriarchs. Calvin may have this passage in mind in so commenting.

another. Peter Lombard, *Sent.*, 4.31.2 [p. 937.3-7]: "But the sacrament so inseparably adheres to the marriage of lawful persons that without it marriage does not seem to exist, for always while both live a conjugal bond remains, so that even when divorce supervenes on account of fornication, the firmness of the conjugal bond may not be dissolved." *Ibid.*, 4.34.5 [pp. 966f]: "On those men, also, who cohabit with two sisters or those women who do so with two brothers, let us see what the canons have to say: 'He who cohabits with two sisters and one was his wife before, has neither of them; nor are these adulterers joined in marriage.' " Etc.

matrimony. For this prohibition see Peter Lombard, *Sent.*, 4.42.3-4, "On the joining of god-children, or of adopted and natural children" [pp. 991f], and Gratian, *Decr.*, 2.30.3/4 [Friedberg, 1.1100f].

Epiphany. Peter Lombard, *Sent.*, 4.32.4 [p. 947.20-24]: "Not only in physical labor are these reasons to be observed, but also in celebrating marriage, according to the following: 'It is not fitting for marriage to be celebrated from Septuagesima to the octave of Easter, and in the three weeks before the feast of St. John, and from the Advent of our Lord until after Epiphany. If it be done, the couple is to be separated.' " Cf. Gratian, *Decr.*, 2.33.4.10 [Friedberg, 1.1249] where the identical words are cited.

asses. Cf. Erasmus, *Adagia*, 1.3.66: *"Induistis me leonis exuvium,"* where a similar saying is quoted from Lucian, *Pseudologista*.

CHAPTER VI: CHRISTIAN FREEDOM, ECCLESIASTICAL POWER, AND POLITICAL ADMINISTRATION

Page 176.

license. Cf. Luther, *The Freedom of a Christian* [Eng. tr., LW 31.372]: "There are very many who, when they hear of this freedom of faith, immediately turn it into an occasion for the flesh and think that now all things are allowed them." Max Dominicé, in Pannier, 4.129, note *c* (p. 325) refers this to the Anabaptists, Spiritual libertines, etc.

parts. Cf. Melanchthon, *LC* (1521), 8 [Eng. tr., LCC 19.124]: "You know now to what extent we are free from the Decalogue. We are free first because although we are sinners, it cannot condemn those who are in Christ. Secondly, those who are in Christ are led by the Spirit to do the law and they really act by the Spirit. They love and fear God, devote themselves to the needs of their neighbor, and desire to do those very things which the law demanded. They will do them even if no law had been given. Their will is nothing else than the Spirit, the living law." These two aspects of Christian freedom as set forth by Melanchthon correspond to the first two parts of Christian freedom. See also LCC 20.834n3.

law-righteousness. Cf. Melanchthon, *LC* (1521), 8 [Eng. tr., LCC 19.122]: "If nothing is preached but that Christ is the Son of God, it follows that the righteousness of the law, or works, are not demanded, nor is anything else: and all that is commanded is that we embrace the Son." Cf. Chap. I, sec. 27 above.

shown. Cf. Chap. I, sec. 33 above.

Page 177.

for believers. Cf., e.g., Servetus, *De Justicia Regni Christi* (1532), c. 3 [fol. D.7ʳ ff].

to good. Cf. Melanchthon, *LC* (1521), 8 [Eng. tr., LCC 19.125]: "Therefore the law has been abrogated, not that it not be kept, but in order that, even though not kept, it not condemn, and then too in order that it can be kept."

interpreters. De Castro, *Adv. haer.* (1534) [fol. 129 CD]; Cochlaeus, *Philipp.*, 3.32; cf. Jerome, *Comm. Gal.*, prol. [PL 26.309f]; Pelagius, *Comm. ad Gal.*, c. 2 [PL 30.810D]; Pseudo-Ambrose, *Comment. in Epist. ad Gal.* [PL 17.356C]. Melanchthon, *LC* (1521), 8 [Eng. tr., LCC 19.124f], rejects the Romanist notion that the abrogation of the law mentioned, e.g., in Acts 15:10, applies only to ceremonial law: "Would that those who have related freedom to judicial and ceremonial laws only had argued with more precision!"

Page 178.

in it. Cf. John Fisher, *Confutatio*, art. 31 (p. 492).

leading. Cf. Luther, *The Freedom of a Christian* [Eng. tr., LW 31.359]: "This [contrary will in his own flesh] the spirit of faith cannot tolerate, but with joyful zeal it attempts to put the body under control and hold it in check. . . ." "Nevertheless the works themselves do not justify him before God, but he does the works out of *spontaneous love* in obedience to God. . . ."

in vain. Cf. Melanchthon, *LC* (1521), 7 [Eng. tr., LCC 19.92]: "Therefore, no matter how many works of the law are done without faith, man sins." Etc.

Page 179.

"indifferent." Cf. Melanchthon, *Apology of the Augsburg Confession*, at 15.52 (*Bekenntnisschrift*, p. 307). Cf. also, Diogenes Laërtius, 7.102, 104; Seneca, *Epist. Mor.*, 82.10. For a discussion of adiaphora in Seneca, see Sevenster, *Paul and Seneca* (1961), pp. 201f, 221. See also LCC 20.838n9.

indifferently. Cf. Melanchthon, *LC* (1521), 8 [Eng. tr., LCC 19.123]: ". . . Christianity is freedom because . . . those who have been renewed by the Spirit of Christ now conform voluntarily even without the law to what the law used to command," etc.; cf. Chap. I, sec. 26 above.

frivolities. Jodocus Clichtoveus, *Antilutherus* (1524) 1.1.3 [fol. 4ᵛ.17-31]: "Luther seems very much like Jeroboam, King of Israel in this work, who, to turn his people aside from the true worship of God to be performed in the Jerusalem temple according to divine sanction, set up two golden calves on the borders of his kingdom, one in Bethel, and the other in Dan, to which, forsaking God [I Kings 12:26ff] the Israelite people flocked to worship. Surely the Christian and gospel freedom of Luther is thus described: there are two idols and golden calves, erected wherewith to deceive the Christian world: preferring the appearance of something honest in public, but hiding within the foulest plague of souls. His Christian freedom which he proclaims so much, is actually nothing else than the harshest bondage under the yoke of sin, arising out of disobedience toward God and the church. Also that one's gospel freedom ought to be called by the name of Babylonian captivity because through it men are led captive into the city of devilish confusion and the prison of sin."

NOTES TO PAGES 181 - 84

Page 181.

received. Calvin's reference to "the common distinction" between an offense given and one received closely parallels Melanchthon, *LC* (1521), 12 [Eng. tr., LCC 19.150]: "An offense is an injury by which either our neighbor's faith or his love is harmed." A number of parallels to Melanchthon's locus have been noted in the following pages.

Scripture. References to offense given include: Matt. 27:17; Mark 9:42f; Rom. 16:17; I Cor. 15:32f; Gal. 3:12f; 5:7-9; II Tim. 2:18; Rev. 2:14. References to offense received include: Mark 9:43; Luke 17:1; Matt. 11:16; 26:31; John 16:1. Examples of offense include Mark 6:13; Matt. 13:57; 15:12; John 6:60.

Page 182.

weakness. The principle of tempering freedom that the weak may not stumble had been succinctly stated by Melanchthon, *LC* (1521), 12 [Eng. tr., LCC 19.151]: "For the sake of freedom we must teach that human traditions may be violated so that the inexperienced understand that they do not sin even if they permit something contrary to the tradition of men. . . . As over against the weak and those who have not heard the gospel, the duty of love must be performed and human traditions must be kept, provided that we do nothing against divine law."

Pharisees. Calvin's remarks on "the offense of the Pharisees" closely parallel Melanchthon, *LC,* 12 [Eng. tr., LCC 19.151]: "In the presence of the Pharisees who demand the observance of their traditions as if they were necessary for salvation, these traditions should be violated without regard for offense. Paul did this with divine law when he refused to circumcise Titus [Gal. 2:3]. How much more should we do this with stupid papal traditions! Christ commands that those who are scandalized be let alone because they were blind leaders of the blind [Matt. 15:12-14]."

circumcised him. Luther, *The Freedom of a Christian,* [Eng. tr., LW 31.368f]: "St. Paul also circumcised his disciple Timothy, not because circumcision was necessary for his righteousness but that he might not offend or despise any man's weak faith and yielded to their will for a time, so he was also unwilling that the liberty of faith should be offended against or despised by stubborn, work-righteous men. He chose a middle way, sparing the weak for a time, but always withstanding the stubborn, that he might convert all to the liberty of faith. What we do should be done with the same zeal to sustain the weak in faith, as in Rom. 14[:1]; but we should firmly resist the stubborn teachers of works. Of this we shall say more later." See also Melanchthon, *LC* (1521), 8 [Eng. tr., LCC 19.125]: "Thus Paul circumcises one man and does not circumcise another; at one time he accommodated himself to those who were observing Jewish rites, and at another time he resisted them. Let our freedom be the same." Etc.

Page 183.

indifferent. Cf. Melanchthon, *LC* (1521), 12 [Eng. tr., LCC 19.150f]: "As for what is in the sphere of human law, so-called intermediate matters such as celibacy and abstaining from meats, human tradition does not obligate in case of necessity." Etc.

opinions. This refers to Gerard Roussel and the like. Cf. e.g., Calvin, *De Sacerdotio papali abiciendo* (1537) [OS 1.347f]. See LCC 20.846n18.

Page 184.

man. Calvin will return to the doctrine of the twofold government in man at p. 207 below. Cf. the doctrine of the two realms expressed in Luther, *Sermon on the Mount,* preface and exposition of Matthew 5:38-42 [LW 21.3-5, 105ff].

lawgivers. Here quite clearly Calvin picks up the thread of the apologetic argument from the conclusion of the Dedicatory Epistle (p. 14 above). As with Luther, so with Calvin the concept of two-fold government provides for Christian freedom without endangering the lawful political order.

eternal life. Cf. Clichtoveus, *Antilutherus* (1525), 1.10 [fol. 21ʳ.27-29]: "It is manifest, therefore, that general councils and chief officers of the church can obligate men to that which, the transgression of which is deadly for the soul." Also, *Compendium veritatum* (1529), c. 6.

Page 185.

Solons. Cf. Melanchthon, *LC* (1521), 4 [Eng. tr., LCC 19.67]: "Solons and legislators of the papacy."

burden. Clichtoveus, *Antilutherus,* 1.15 [fol. 28ᵛ.39-29ʳ.16]: "In the aforesaid council [Acts 15] the Apostles did not wish to impress upon the brethren, converted from heathenism to Christ, a yoke of legal ceremonies and observances of the Mosaic law. Paul also in his letters rejects the same: he proclaims freedom to them, and highly condemns the language of those old rites. Finally Christ our Lord adds the gentle and light yoke of his own law: for [that yoke], by no means burdened with the weight of Mosaic observances, frees us from the old law. Also the church pastors could not lay upon the shoulders of their subjects the yoke of the old law and its ceremonies already abolished once for all; nor do they even attempt to do so. Yet anyone could not at all deduce from this that the heads of the church could not establish new precepts—not ones to facilitate the observance of the old law, but the fuller observance of the new and evangelical law. Since these do not prejudice or detract from the true freedom of the new law, or drive man back into utter bondage, or render the Lord's yoke heavy among those who, aroused with a sincere and fervid love of God, eagerly walk in the law of the Lord. But if any bondage or difficulty in fulfilling the law arises in them, it originates only from our sluggishness or negligence, not from the character and conditions of the ecclesiastical precepts themselves. Therefore our wickedness ought not to be forced upon them or be ascribed to them."

contrary. Cf. Luther, *The Freedom of a Christian* [Eng. tr., LW 31.370]: "Anyone knowing this could easily and without danger find his way through those numberless mandates and precepts of pope, bishops, monasteries, churches, princes and magistrates upon which some ignorant pastors insist as if they were necessary to righteousness and salvation, calling them 'precepts of the church,' although they are nothing of the kind. For a Christian, as a free man, will say, 'I will fast, pray, do this and that as men command, not because it is necessary to my righteousness or salvation; but that I may show due respect to the pope, the bishop, the community, a magistrate, or my neighbor, and give them an example. I will do and suffer all things, just as Christ did and suffered far more for me, although he needed nothing of it all for himself, and was made under the law for my sake, although he was not under the law.' Although tyrants do violence or injustice in making their demands, yet it will do no harm as long as they demand nothing contrary to God."

constitutions. Eck, *Enchiridion,* c. 13 [Eng. tr., Battles, pp. 93-4]: "Ecclesiastical constitutions therefore are not only human laws, but also divine both because established by the fathers on divine authority, and because they are according to the divine scripture, and because they are for divine honor, the dignity and splendor of the church, the fulfillment of divine law and the salvation of souls. Hence they bind in the forum of conscience so that they make despisers and transgressors of them subject to eternal damnation, in accordance with the apostle's statement: 'Let every person be subject to the governing authorities. For there is no authority except from God, and those that exist have been instituted by God. Therefore he who resists the authorities, resists what God has appointed, and those who resist will incur judgment' [Rom. 13:1-2]."

ministry of God's Word. Cf. Calvin, *Catechism 1538*, 30 [tr. and ann. F. L. Battles (1972)]. The Pastors of the Church and their Power, p. 47. "But let us recall that that power which is allotted to pastors in Scripture is wholly bounded by the ministry of the Word. For Christ did not explicitly give this power to men, but to His Word, of which He made men ministers" [cf. Pannier, 4.151e, p. 328].

pastors. Latin: *ita et veris pastoribus praeclare sua constaret dignitas.* The French of 1541 [Pannier, 4.151] has "In this manner the dignity of the true pastors would be kept in its entirety." Dominicé in his note [p. 328] thinks that *en son entier,* a French legal term, is more expressive than *praeclare* ("preeminently").

Page 187.

mirror. The mirror is one of Calvin's most widely used figures of speech; for a list of occurrences and meanings in the *Institutes,* 1559, see Battles, *Analysis,* p. 36*. Dominicé [Pannier, 4.329n] comments that this comparison was used by Marguerite d'Angoulême, *Le Miroir de l'Âme Pecheresse* (1531).

passing. See p. 121 above. Cf. LCC 21.1155n6.

Page 188.

Word. This passage has been incorporated almost verbatim into *Catechism 1538,* p. 47, lines 22-31.

Page 189.

faith. Cf. Luther, *Babylonian Captivity* [Eng. tr., LW 36.28]: "Since the Roman bishop has ceased to be a bishop and has become a tyrant, I fear none of his decrees, for I know that it is not within his power, nor that of any general council, to make new articles of faith." Cf. Clichtoveus, *Antilutherus,* 1.15 [fol. 29^v.5-10]: "Therefore the reasonable and sound constitution of new precepts is not to be ascribed to the arrogance of church leaders, but rather to the good pleasure of God who has prompted him to make these, and to their sincere zeal for God's honor and the salvation of souls, to attend wisely and carefully to both through salutary regulations."

explicit faith. Cf. Cochlaeus, *De Auth. Eccl.* (1524), 1.6 [fol. D 1^r.12-16]: "I believe the Holy Catholic Church. That is I believe whatever Holy Mother Church adheres to most firmly in faith. For we priests in the Mass, after the Agnus Dei say: O Lord Jesus Christ, do not look upon our sins, but the faith of thy Holy Church."

ago. Cf. pp. 186 above.

Page 190.

from God. Eck, *Enchiridion* (1532), c. 13 [fol. E.7^r], quoted at p. 185, note to "constitutions," above. On the following critique of human traditions, cf. Farel, *Sommaire* (1525) [fol. c. 6^r-c.7^r], chap. 14, "On the Teaching and Tradition of Men": "Human teaching wishing to mix the things of God which belong to the salvation of the soul, of the adoration and service of God—this is nothing else than an abomination before God, vanity, a lie, and devilish doctrine, error and empty fraud, by which God is served in vain and his anger provoked on those who observe thusly whatever is given in a reprobate sense, serving the creature and not the Creator [Rom. 1:25]. For one is the servant of him whose commandments one keeps; and whose works one does, following and holding his doctrine and word. And the more human teaching has more appearance and color of sanctity, the more dangerous it is: as appears from that of the Pharisees: and above all that of the Antichrist, which having the appearance of being from Jesus is more efficacious and suitable to deceive and trick than any other: so that the elect, if possible, are led astray [Mark 13:22] on account of the covering that those have who make the statutes and ordinances; it is that they are assembled in the name of Jesus and that he is in the midst of them, and that the Holy Spirit directs them without letting them err, and such very dangerous fictions. One ought to look to the law of our Lord in proving all their ordinances, looking to such fruits as such constitutions and customs that they have introduced may bring: and thus one knows the tree by its fruits [Mark 13:22]." See also Calvin, *Catechism 1538*, 31 [Eng. tr., F. L. Battles, p. 48].

err. Eck, *Enchiridion* (1532), c. 1 [Eng. tr., Battles, pp. 9-10]: " 'And behold, I am with you all the days even to the end of the age.' Thus spoke Christ (who is the way, truth and life) to his disciples. It is clear that the church, the column of truth, with Christ as leader and the Holy Spirit as teacher, cannot err: how much less credible is it that for a thousand years the church erred, as the Lutherans rave." For a detailed note on this, see LCC 21.1158n10.

apostles. Dominicé [Pannier, 4.330n] cites the *Apostolic Constitutions* and notes that Book II of that work deals with forms of worship; Book VII, with various prayers.

writings. Cochlaeus, *De auth. eccl.*, 1.4 [fol. B.4^v.9-11]: "No, not all things were written down. And the primitive church was neither more imperfect nor more unworthy when as yet no gospels were written nor any epistles as was done afterwards." This is said by Cochlaeus in a context which itemizes articles and terms of the faith not expressly written down in Scripture.

blood. Clichtoveus, *Antilutherus*, 1.10 [fol. 21^v.11-36]: "That which is established and decreed by the Holy Spirit, pouring out his grace and introducing his will into the minds of those gathered together in Christ, is of no less or inferior level or condition than what has been openly established by Christ. For the Holy Spirit is also God, equal in authority and power to the Father and the Son. Things decreed in a general council of the church lawfully gathered, concerning the state and governance of the church universal are to be deemed established by the Holy Spirit, who presides over such a council and directs it, indeed by whose teaching office and government the whole church of Christ is directed and ruled, according to our Lord's statement to his disciples: 'I have many things to say to you which you cannot hear now. Yet when he, the Spirit of truth, comes, he shall teach you all the truth . . .' [John 16:12-13] of those things to be believed and done for the proper upbuilding of the church. Hence in the Acts of the Apostles, after a council was called by them on the question of whether to impose the ceremonies and observances of the Law of Moses upon the brethren, who had been converted from the Gentiles to Christ, the apostles wrote the sentence and decision of this synod to the absent brethren as follows: 'For it seemed good to the Holy Spirit and to us, to lay upon you no greater burden than these necessary things; that you abstain from things sacrificed to idols, and from blood, and from things strangled, and from fornication' [Acts 15:28-29]. In these words the apostles ascribe to the Holy Spirit as the first author the decision of that council, as it truly was. And concerning other conciliar sessions the same judgment ought to hold good. Therefore transgressors of constitutions ordained in councils of this sort, as rebellious and unjust toward the Holy Spirit, are adjudged guilty of mortal fault and liable to eternal death." Cochlaeus, *De auth. eccl.*, 1.3 [fol. B.3^v]. Eck, *Enchiridion* (1532), c. 1 [Eng. tr., Battles, p. 16]: " 'When Paul and Barnabas had no small dissension with them, Paul and Barnabas and some of the others were elected to go up to Jerusalem to the apostles and the presbyters about this question' [Acts 15:2]. See how that statement of Deuteronomy 17[:8ff] was fulfilled: what was the church—not the whole congregation. But they went up to the apostles and presbyters who represented the church."

Page 192.

church. Cf. Luther, *Babylonian Captivity* [Eng. tr., LW 36.71]: "For to be subjected to their statutes and tyrannical laws is indeed to become slaves of men."

declare. Eck, *Enchiridion* (1532), c. 13 [Eng. tr., Battles, p. 93]: " 'He who hears you, hears me; and he who despises you, despises me; and he who despises me, despises him who sent me' [Luke 10:16]. From this authority it is clearer than light that he who despises the prelates of the church and the ecclesiastical constitutions, despises Christ and the gospel." It is possible that Calvin here has in mind the various attacks of the Theological Faculty of the University of Paris upon the Protestants beginning in 1521 and especially that mounted against him personally after Nicolas Cop's Rectorial Address of All Saints Day, 1533. See Appendix III.

greater. Cf. *Reply to Sadolet* [Eng. tr., LCC 22.252].

truth. Eck, *Enchiridion* (1532), c. 1 [Eng. tr., Battles, p. 8]. Eck, having cited three parables of the kingdom [Matt. chs. 20, 22, 23], then says: "You will find many similar parables. If then the church is here called the kingdom of heaven, how could error and falsehood have reigned in it for a thousand years? The kingdom of heaven is the kingdom of truth. . . . The church does not err, not only because she has Christ as her bridegroom, but also because she is ruled by the teaching authority of the Holy Spirit who never forsakes her." De Castro, *Adv. haer.*, 4 [fol. 79B].

Page 193.

age. Cochlaeus, *De auth. eccl.* (1525), 1.3 [fol. B.3^r.19-28]: "For no less today is the pope, than Peter was then, the pastor of Christ's sheep, the head of the church, the prince of the priests. Not, not to Peter alone, but also, even unto the end of the age, to all his lawful successors in the Apostlic See, did Christ say: 'I give to you the keys of the kingdom of heaven, strengthen your brothers, feed my sheep, and other things of this sort, which pertain to the general governance of the whole church. Unless perchance you think either that Christ died not knowing how many times Peter was going to waver, or falsely said in Matthew, 'Behold I am with you alway, even unto the end of the age.' " Eck, *Enchiridion* (1532), c. 1.

truth. Clichtoveus, *Antilutherus*, 1.14 [fol. 28^v.19-23]: "Indeed to the apostles and to the rulers of his holy church in their name Christ promised he would give the Holy Spirit, to remain with them forever, not through certain periods of time, which having passed, the Holy Spirit would be withdrawn from the church, and no more be present in it."

Page 194.

spot. Eck, *Enchiridion* (1532), c. 1 [Eng. tr., Battles, p. 7], quotes Eph. 5:21-27 in support of the second part of his first proposition on the authority of the church: "The church is the body of Christ, the bride of Christ, the kingdom of heaven."

hear her. Clichtoveus, *Antilutherus*, 1.11 [fol. 22^r.26-33]: "In many decrees of church councils and supreme pontiffs this penalty is expressed: that the transgressors of these statutes incur a sentence of excommunication. In some the same is explained as the threat of eternal condemnation: which means it is to be inflicted upon those who transgressed against constitutions of this sort. And both of these are considered to be done rightly and in conformity to that saying of our Lord spoken to Peter on him who is deaf to the warnings of the church and refuses to obey her: 'If he does not hear the church, let him be to you as a Gentile and a publican' [Matt. 18:17]." Cochlaeus, *De auth. eccl.*, 1.3 [fol. B.4^r.18-21]: "From these things, then, which we have related concerning the council of the apostles and presbyters it is clear that no Christian is permitted to go against any decrees of sacred councils even in a single word. 'Let him who does not hear the church' (Christ himself says) 'be to you as a gentile and publican.' " *Ibid.*, 1.5 [fol. C.2^v.7-16]: "Concerning the church (which very many call 'the kingdom of heaven') he most gravely lays down this principle: 'If your brother sins against you, go and rebuke him privately. If he hears you, you have gained your brother. If he does not hear you, take with you one or two more. . . . But if he does not hear them, tell it to the church. If he does not hear the church, let him be to you as a gentile and publican.' How, then, is not Luther to us as a gentile and publican, Luther, who with the wickedest contempt reviles us now: church, church, church; council, council, council?" Cf. Eck, *Enchiridion*, c. 13, quoting Matt. 18:17.

say. Eck, *Enchiridion*, c. 2 [Eng. tr., Battles, p. 20], quotes Matt. 18:20, then comments: "No one can more clearly be proved not to have heard the church than if he did not hear a council. There is no greater agreement than in a council. In no place are more gathered in the Lord's name than in general councils."

Page 195.

councils. Eck, *Enchiridion*, c. 2 [Eng. tr., Battles, p. 20]: " 'Ask the bygone generation, and diligently seek out the memory of the fathers, for we are but of yesterday and know nothing, for our days on earth are a shadow; they will teach you, and tell you, and utter words out of their heart' [Job 8:8-10]. 'Wisdom is with the ancients, and prudence in length of days' [Job 12:12]. Therefore let us hear councils and fathers, not heretics recently born and apostates. If the authority of councils be taken away, then all things in the church will be ambiguous, doubtful, uncertain, unsure, for at once will all the heresies condemned by councils return. But if you fight against them with scripture, now, cut off from the authority of the church, they will reject whatever they please, as Luther rejected the Epistle of James, because it was in disagreement with him, and likewise Maccabees. And once the heretics did not accept the four gospels, just as the Manichees rejected the Old Testament." Etc.

times. Calvin draws a parallel between the prophetic critique of ancient Israel and his own critique of the Roman Catholic Church of his day. This parallel has already been suggested (with some of the same proof-texts) but not elaborated, by Melanchthon. See *LC* (1521), 4 [Eng. tr., LCC 19.63f]. Both Reformers are countering what they consider a wrong claim to continuity of tradition evidenced in the passage from Johannes Eck, quoted in the previous note.

knowledge of his Word. Cf. p. 185, paragraph 15, above.

sluggish. Cf. *Catechism 1538* [pp. 47f]: "But let them turn aside from this to their own dreams and figments of their own brains, then they are no longer to be considered to be pastors, but rather as pestilential wolves are to be driven out" [cited by Pannier, 4.174, note *a*; quoted from Battles tr.].

Page 196.
Ephesus. Cf. Calvin, *Comm. Act.*, 20:28: "Paul calls all the presbyters [= elders] by this name."

song. For this proverbial expression, widely used in 16th c. religious polemics, cf. Terence, *Phormio*, 3.2.10: *cantilenam eandem canis* = τὸ αὐτὸ ᾄδεις ᾆσμα, "ever the old song" [Lewis and Short, *Latin Dictionary*, 281].

Tatianists. This Romanist interpretation of I Tim. 4:1-3 is similarly rejected in Calvin's *Commentary on I Timothy* [OC 52.29f]. It is set forth by Eck, *Enchiridion*, c. 13 (14, ed. 1532), "On Feasts and Fasts," as the second objection of the heretics, which he refutes as follows (1529 edition) [Eng. tr., Battles, p. 108]: "Now here the Apostle Paul is not discussing fasting or softening of the flesh, but because the Tatianists and other heretics were saying that certain things were created by the evil principle. Paul tears this down, because every creature of God is good, and to be received with thanksgiving, which the Catholic does, although not for all the time, nor does Paul here enjoin this for all the time."

Page 197.
councils. Cf. Melanchthon, *LC* (1521), 4 [Eng. tr., LCC 19.64]: "When synods disagree, one must be in error." Calvin, pursuing the same theme, uses a different selection of disagreeing councils.

times. Eck, *Enchiridion* (1532), c. 2 [Eng. tr., Battles, p. 24]: "Plenary councils, which are concerned with morals and the governance of the church, make various decisions according to the quality and condition of times, persons, etc., without prejudice to the faith."

summoned. Synod of Constantinople (AD 754) under Constantine V Copronymus, son of Leo III; see acts of Nicea II [Mansi 13.215].

convened. 2nd Nicene Council (AD 787) [Mansi 13.378ff].

councils. Melanchthon, *LC* (1521), 4 [Eng. tr., LCC 19.63f], "quotes" the pope: "A council is ruled immediately by the Holy Spirit, and it cannot err."

weighed. Cf. Pliny, *Epist.*, 2.12: "Opinions are counted not weighed. . . ." For the principle that the weight of church councils is determined by the number of fathers in attendance, see Gratian, *Decr.*, 1.16.9-11 [Friedberg, 1.45f] (Note from Benoît, 4.178n1).

Page 198.
blame. Theodoret, *Ecclesiastical History*, 1.11.

salvation. Eck, *Enchiridion* (1532), c. 2 [Eng. tr., Battles, p. 25], cites *Decretal. Gregor. IX*, 4.14.8 [Friedberg, 2.703.53-57]: "It ought not to be judged reprehensible, if according to the variety of the times, human statutes may vary now and again, especially when urgent necessity or evident utility demands it, since God himself made some changes in the New Testament from those which he laid down in the Old."

from God. Cf. Melanchthon, *LC* (1521), 4 [Eng. tr., LCC 19.66]: "I hold that the other synods also must be evaluated in the light of Scripture."

apostles. Clichtoveus, *Antilutherus*, 1.4 [fol. 9ᵛ.5-8]: "And it is plainly to be understood, that, not only by the apostles but also by Christ, some things were instituted for all to observe, which have not been enjoined in written documents, but handed down by word of mouth, and conveyed even to us by the apostles and their successors."

letters. The ultimate source of this proverb is Plato, *Laws,* 3 [689D]: ". . . even although, in the words of the proverb, they know neither how to read nor how to swim." See Erasmus, *Adagia,* 1.4.13.

Page 199.

blood. In his *Commentary on Acts* Calvin notes the variation between the two forms of the decree (at Acts 15:20 and 15:29), but harmonizes the two. The word ἀλίσγημα, used at 15:20, means "pollutions," while εἰδυλόθυτα (15:29) means "what has been sacrificed to idols." However, the first expression can mean the same as the latter. He therefore takes the meaning for verse 20 from verse 29. See OC 48.358f.

decree. This exegesis of the "Apostolic Decree" of Acts 15 explicitly ties together the first and second essays of Chapter VI. In fact, both ecclesiastical government and civil are looked at in the light of Christian freedom, the theme that unites Chapter VI. This unifying theme was somewhat obscured in the editorial changes of subsequent editions of the *Institutes.*

without sin. The question of outward conformity to Romanist rites and regulations occupied Calvin throughout his career. In 1543 he wrote, "What a Faithful Man ought to do dwelling among the Papists" [OC 6.537-588; Eng. tr., 1548]. In 1544 he wrote his "Excuse à messieurs les Nicodemites" [OC 6.589-614], the various kinds of persons who adjust the Reformed doctrine and practice to avoid disrupting habitual piety and religious notions. These lines of the 1536 *Institutes* may well have afforded a nucleus for these later treatises.

scandals. The problem of scandals (obstacles to accepting the gospel) led Calvin in 1550 to write an extensive treatise, *De Scandalis.* See OS 2.162-340 for Latin text; for an English translation see *A little booke concernynge offences,* tr. A. Goldinge from the French ed. (London: W. Seres, 1557): STC 4434; also *Concerning Scandals,* tr. John Fraser (1978).

Page 200.

new laws. The Romanists had charged Reformed doctrine as "new" and "of recent birth"; here Calvin turns the charge of novelty against his opponents.

dominion. This refers to the *jus gladii* (see LCC 21.1220n15).

consciences. Cf. pp. 211ff below.

Page 201.

dominion. 1536 *falso:* "damnandi"; corr. 1539: "dominandi."

rulers. Cf. Clichtoveus, *Antilutherus,* 1.11 [fol. 22ᵛ.8-18]: "On the prelates of the church Christ, speaking under the name of the disciples, says . . ." [Luke 10:16 quoted]. "And again the Lord speaking to the crowd concerning those who have been put in charge of ecclesiastical affairs, says . . ." [Matt. 28:3-4 quoted]. "The Blessed Paul likewise writing to the Hebrews says . . ." [Heb. 13:17 quoted]. "And Peter [I Pet. 3:13]: 'Be subject to every ordinance of man for the Lord's sake.' And in very many other passages of the letters of the apostles the same thought is contained. From this it is very clear that those who despise the precepts of the church and of its prelates also despise God and are disobedient to him; consequently they incur the guilt of a deadly misdeed."

Page 202.

blood. Cf. Calvin, *Catechism 1538* [Battles tr., p. 48]: "But we are stoutly to resist those regulations which under the title of 'spiritual laws' are in force to bind consciences as if necessary for the worship of God. For they not only overturn the freedom which Christ won for us . . ." [cited by Pannier, 4.187, *b*, p. 335].

Page 203.

sword. Cf. p. 1, above.

Page 204.

human traditions. Note that the same order of discussion—pastors, then human traditions—is followed in Calvin's *Catechism* of 1537/38. See Battles tr., pp. 46-48; the correspondence is noted in Pannier, 4.191, note *f*, p. 336.

concord. Cf. pp. 207f below.

laws. Bohatec, *Budé und Calvin*, p. 446, here cites as possible classical backgrounds for this passage: Pindar (from Plutarch): "According to nature, the law is king of all mortals and immortals"; Aristotle, *Politics*, 4 (6) 1292a; Cicero, *Laws*, 2.5.12: "A state lacking laws . . . is to be held in no esteem." From medieval writers he cites Nicolas of Cusa, *De Concordantia:* "Where laws do not rule, no state exists." See Budé, *Annotationes in Pandectas*, 69A, where some of these authorities are quoted. Cf. also, Calvin, *Comm. Sen. De Clem.*, 25.4n.

sinews. Cf. *Reply to Sadolet* [OC 5.406]: "The body of the church, to be united, must be bound together by discipline, just as a body is by sinews." Benoît, 4.212n3. For Calvin's later use of sinew = discipline, see also *Inst.*, 4.12.1 (1543). Cf. also p. 215, paragraph 47 below, where sinew = law, a Platonic metaphor.

Page 205.

bare. Calvin in his *Discipline of the Reformed Churches* (1559) enjoined kneeling to correct the irreverence of many present at public and domestic prayers. In his *Prael. in Danielem*, 6.10 [OC 41.11]: ". . . not that kneeling is of itself necessary in prayers, but because we need stimuli." In his *Comm. Act.*, 9:40 [OC 48.220]: "Kneeling in prayers is the symbol of humility, with a two fold usefulness: to apply our whole self to the worship of God, and that outward bodily exercise may help the mind's weakness." *Ibid.*, 10:25 [OC 48.237]: "Certain stupid men are too much deceived in thinking that kneeling is condemned simply and of itself." *Ibid.*, 13:3 [OC 48.281], where it is stated that such ancient Jewish rites as kneeling and laying on of hands were retained by the apostles as useful for the exercise of piety. See also LCC 21.1208n50.

ditch. On the other hand, Calvin elsewhere enjoins against superfluous pomp in burial: "We must speak concerning funerals. Such pomp as we bring forth after death for our own pleasure yet cannot give to ourselves, we give rather to an insensible corpse, as if we were going to get back some delight from such a show." *Consilium de luxu* (1546/47?) [OC 10a.205.18ff, tr. F. L. Battles, *Interpretation*, 19.2.193, 198]. See also, *Projet d'Ordonnances Ecclesiastiques* (1541) [OC 10a.27], "On Burial."

Page 206.

decorum. Cf. Cicero, *Off.*, 1.27.93, where the Greek τὸ πρέπον and the Latin *decorum* are equated.

Page 207.

government. Cf. p. 184, paragraph 13, for note on the "twofold government in man." See LCC 21.1488n1 for a general introduction to Calvin's political thought.

freedom. This refers to the Münster Anabaptists. The early pages of the third essay of Chapter 6 dispose of this proposal to do away with civil government.

soul. In his earliest theological work, the *Psychopannychia*, Calvin clearly elucidated the difference, and different origin, of man's body and soul. Thus, the dichotomy between spiritual and temporal authority rests in Calvin's anthropology, in fact in his very doctrine of creation. After a lengthy discussion (Zimmerli, pp. 24-32) he concludes: "the spirit or soul of man is a substance distinct from the body" (p. 32).

Page 208.

man. *Schleitheim Confession*, Art. 6 (Wenger, p. 251), states: "The government magistracy is according to the flesh, but the Christians' is according to the Spirit; their houses and dwellings remain in the world, but the Christians' citizenship is in heaven. . . ." Etc. In addition to his refutation of this portion of Art. 6 in his *Brieve Instruction* [Eng. tr., fol. D.4^{r}ff], Calvin adverts to this question in his preaching, e.g., *Sermons sur le Livre de Michée*, 14 (1550), Suppl. Calv., 5.120.3-17: "However, it is true that we cannot exist in this world in the perfection looked for at the end. Why? Because the kingdom of our Lord Jesus Christ has only begun. In this, note the insanity of those fanatics who would abolish all power and authority among men. 'See here,' they say, 'the prophets Micah and Isaiah say that swords are to be turned into plowshares. And since our Lord Jesus Christ is manifested, there is no more any need of sword or magistrate.' See! But then it is that we have the greatest need, for as I have said, since the kingdom of our Lord Jesus Christ has only begun, it is necessary that it be ever increased more and more until it comes in its perfection. What then is to be done? We see that we are far from arriving at the peace of which he is speaking. But so it is that we can only arrive at it if we are ruled by our Lord Jesus Christ; and he wills not to lead us unless there are power and authority over us. Still, it is necessary that there be government, that we may see what part is our duty and why God has put us in the world, that is, in order that his kingdom may be increased more and more in us, since it has barely begun in this world; and since, on the other hand, that we may try to help and support our neighbors, and benefit them both in body and in soul."

trials. On the basis of Luke 12:14 and I Cor. 6:1-8, the Anabaptists rejected both serving as judges and also recourse to a court of law. In his answer to this objection, Zwingli offers another exegesis of the prior passage and concludes: "Therefore we see the office of judge rather confirmed than done away with, even among the devout." Zwingli [SWHZ, pp. 200f], as Calvin after him, interprets Paul's advice against Christian use of the law courts (I Cor. 6:1-8) as a warning against litigiousness. Melanchthon takes a somewhat different view toward the courts of law. See *LC* (1521), 4 [Eng. tr., LCC 19.128]: "The Christian is not allowed to take part in a lawsuit, but this is no reason for doing away with law. For although those who litigate sin in doing so, yet laws and courts are necessary in order to coerce evil men. Nor do they sin who pronounce judgment or give a legal decision."

tranquillity. Cf. "Confession de la Foy laquelle tous bourgeois et habitans de Genève et subietz du pays doibvent iurer de garder et tenir" (10 November 1536), 21. Magistrats [OC 9.700]: "We hold the dominion and rule of kings and princes as well as of other magistrates and superiors to be a holy and good ordinance of God. And while they in executing their office serve God and pursue a Christian calling, whether in defending the afflicted and innocent, or in correcting and punishing the wickedness of the evil, on our part we also ought to honor and reverence them, show them obedience and subjection, carry out their commands, carry the responsibilities imposed on us by them, insofar as it is possible for us without offending God. In short, we are to reckon them as God's vicars and lieutenants whom no one can resist without resisting God. And we are to regard their office as a holy commission of God which he has given them to govern and rule us. Accordingly, we understand that all Christians are bound to pray to God for the prosperity of the superiors and lords of the country where they live, to obey the statutes and ordinances which do not contravene God's commandments, promote public good, tranquillity and utility, applying themselves to support the honor of the superiors and the tranquillity of the people, without plotting anything to bring about what may stir up troubles or dissension. On the contrary, we declare that all those who conduct themselves unfaithfully toward their superiors and who lack a firm affection for the public good of the country where they dwell, in so doing show their faithlessness toward God." Cf. also the form of this confession in Calvin, *Catechismus sive Christianae Religionis Institutio* (1538) [1537], ed. and tr. F. L. Battles (Pittsburgh, 1972), pp. 61f.

    intact. Cicero, *Laws*, 1.6.19.

Page 209.

    magistrate. Cicero, *Laws*, 3.1.2.

    "gods." Cf. *Psychopannychia*, p. 91 (Zimmerli), where Calvin sets forth the same interpretation against the Anabaptists' view that gods = believers. The identification of magistrates with "gods" is found also in the thought of Luther and Zwingli. See Luther, *Eighty-Second Psalm Translated and Explained* (1530) [Eng. tr., Philadelphia ed. 4.289f]. Guillaume Farel also refers to the idea in his *Sommaire* (1525), c. 3.37 [fol. 1.1^r]: "For inasmuch as they are greater and are called gods, having such honor of being called sons of the Most High, inasmuch as the judgment will be more severe on them if they do not execute their duty, and keep holily the holy power that God has committed to them" [Ex. 23; Deut. 16; Ecclus. 20; Ps. 81 (82)]. While this lofty yet demanding view of the ruler rests chiefly upon such Biblical texts as Ps. 82:1, 6 and Rom. 13:1ff, its classical foundation had already been set forth by Calvin in *Comm. Sen. De Clem.* (1532): likeness to the gods at 55/7-9, 75/15, 81/6f; like an earthly Jupiter 7/36, 51/31, 119/22. See Battles-Hugo, *op. cit.*, pp. 110*. Cf. also Calvin, *Brieve Instruction contre les Anabaptistes* [OC Cal 7.83; Eng. tr., fol. D.i^v]: "Beholde the spirite of God, which doeth pronounce by S. Paule, that the magistrate is a minister of God, for our profitte and in sure favoure, to represse and to lette the violence of wicked people. And that for thys cause the swerde is putte into hys handes, to punysheth euil doers. Seying that God hat ordeyned hum to do thys: what are we that wyll let it? Lykewyse seynge that God doth offer vnto vs such a saugarge, why shall it not be lawful unto us to usë it?" The *Elizabethan Second Book of Homilies* (1563) [ed. Oxford, 1859, p. 554] clearly enunciates this teaching: ". . . so doth God himself in the same Scriptures sometime vouchsafe to communicate his name with earthly princes, terming them *gods*; doubtless after that similitude of government which they have, or should have, not unlike with God their king."

    vicegerents. Cf. Zwingli, *An Account of the Faith*, 11 [Eng. tr., LWZ 2.57]: "I know that magistracy when lawfully installed, holds God's place no less than prophecy."

Page 210.

God. Here Calvin applies Old Testament insights to the revolutionary tendencies of the 16th century.

governments. The *Schleitheim Confession*, 6.3 [Wenger, p. 251], asks the question, "Shall one be a magistrate if one should be chosen as such?" On the basis of John 6:15; 8:12; Matt. 16:24; 20:25; Rom. 8:29; I Pet. 2:21, the Confession concludes: "It is not appropriate for a Christian to serve as a magistrate." In his refutation of this teaching, Zwingli, *Refutation of Baptist Tricks* [Eng. tr., SWHZ, p. 200] asserts that in this interpretation of Scripture, the Anabaptists fail to "discriminate between Christ's omnipotence, providence and divinity, by which he governs all, and his mission which he performed here." Calvin, *Brieve Instruction*, [Eng. tr., fol. E.iii^r ff] takes up these Anabaptist proof-texts *seriatim* to confute their teaching. Earlier, Bucer, *EN* (1530), I [fol. 159^v.39-41] rejected this teaching: "Now here the Anabaptists think they can prove that to function as a magistrate is utterly alien to a Christian, nor can anyone at the same time serve as a magistrate and be a Christian, because the Lord said to his disciples 'but you are not so.' " Bucer then [lines 54-55] adduces the example of Moses as one of preeminent dignity and authority. In his advice to his disciples Christ is not dealing with governors or serving as a magistrate but is dissuading his followers from seeking preeminence and power for themselves.

Page 211.

reign. Cf. Calvin, *Praelectiones in Danielem*, 5:18 [OC 40.712]: "God wishes his providence to be seen in a special way in kingdoms. . . . His singular providence is reflected in the empires of this world." [Cf. Benoît, 4.512n1.]

private life. The classical distinction between public and private men, here alluded to, is examined in some detail in *Comm. Sen. De Clem.*, 55ff.

terms. Calvin here alludes to the tripartite classical typology of political forms (stemming from Plato, *Statesman*, 291D), widely discussed in his time. Zwingli discusses this in *Exposition of the Faith* [Eng. tr., LCC 24.266f] and in *First Fruits of a Commentary on the Prophet Isaiah*, Letter to the Reader, Eng. tr., H. Preble, published in Battles, *Huldreich Zwingli: A Comparative Essay on Forms of Government* (1970), pp. 1ff. In the latter work Zwingli boldly expresses his preference for the Swiss form of modified aristocracy over any ancient classical form.

sedition. Cf. Zwingli, *Exposition*, 7 [Eng. tr., LCC 24.267]: "When this form, i.e., democracy is corrupted the Greeks call it conspiracy or tumult, that is uproar, sedition and disturbance. . . ."

municipal officers. See Theodosian Code, 12.1, "De Decurionibus" [Eng. tr., C. Pharr, pp. 342-371]. The Latin phrase *liberis civitatibus senatus aut decuriones* is rather inexactly rendered in VG 1541: "et sur les peuple libres autres superieurs quelconques" [Benoît, 4.513].

Page 212.

oppressed. Cf. uses of the law, pp. 35f above. This corresponds to Seneca's and Gellius' third use of punishment, discussed in *Comm. Sen. De Clem.*, p. 124. Seneca says: "By removing bad men, to let the rest live in greater security." Gellius says: "To protect the dignity and authority of him against whom the sin has been committed" [p. 125.16]. For a comparative table, see Battles, *Analysis*, p. 71.

disturbed. Cf. Stobaeus, *Serm.*, 41.

dissolved. Pseudo-Cicero, *Letters to Brutus*, 1.15.3. This passage was quoted by Calvin in *Comm. Sen. De Clem.* at 23.33 and 125.12f.

arises. This "hard question" has been raised by the Anabaptists. In the *Schleitheim Confession* (1527), art. 6, they recognize the sword as ordained of God but outside the perfection of Christ to punish and put to death the wicked and guard and protect the good. However, Christians are not to serve as magistrates as such government is of the flesh, while Christian rule is of the Spirit. See John C. Wenger, pp. 250f. See also Calvin, *Comm. Sen. De Clem.*, 82.1; 96.15f: "Were kings also accustomed to kill? . . . The king also kills, but only when public welfare demands." These words of Seneca occur in a passage devoted to the contrast between king and tyrant. Cf. Augustine, *City of God*, 1.21.

Page 213.

men. Valerius Maximus, 3.7.9; Calvin earlier used this phrase at *Comm. Sen. De Clem.*, 47.5.

princes. Calvin, *Comm. Sen. De Clem.*, 29.31, earlier quotes this from Vospiscus, *Aurelian*, 44.1.

allowed. Dio Cassius, *Nerva*, Book 68.3. Since, however, the editio princeps of Dio Cassius' *History* is dated 1548 [R. Stephanus], the immediate source is unknown. At the time of the publication of the Seneca Commentary (1532) Calvin definitely did not know this author at first hand.

vengeance. Calvin in these lines sets forth a Christian doctrine of war against the pacifism of the Anabaptists. The same ground is covered by him in his *Brieve Instruction* [Eng. tr., fol. D.ii^{r-v}].

undertaken. Cf. Calvin, *Comm. Sen. De Clem.*, 124.7-9. Calvin's doctrine of humane war is in part influenced by this noble classical teaching. For a quite different (and pacifist) attitude, see Erasmus, *The Education of a Christian Prince* [Eng. tr., L. K. Born (1936)], c. 11.

Page 214.

magistrates. The caution here against anger on the ruler's part (intended for Francis I?) is a theme repeatedly expressed in *Comm. Sen. De Clem.*, e.g., at 9.23ff. See Battles-Hugo, p. 114*.

punishing. Cf. Augustine, *Epist.*, 153.3.8 (to Macedonius) [Eng. tr., FC 20.286]; also *Epist.*, 130.6.13 [Eng. tr., FC 18.386]; *Serm.* 13.7.3-8.4 [PL 48.110-111]. This use of Augustine is anticipated in *Comm. Sen. De Clem.*, 11.19f.

peace. Cicero, *Off.*, 1.23.79; 1.11.35. Calvin cites the latter of these two passages in *Comm. Sen. De Clem.*, 111.14ff.

defenses. That Calvin again, at this point, has the pacifism of the Anabaptists in mind is clear from his refutation of the fourth article of the *Schleitheim Confession*, e.g.: "Moreouer it is very euidente, that the intente of these poure phantasticals is to condempe all munitions, fortresses, engines of warre, and such lyke, whyche are done for the defence of the countrye . . ." [*Brieve Instruction*, Eng. tr., fol. D.ii^{r}].

people. Cf. Calvin, *Consilium de Luxu* [OC 10a.206.8; Eng. tr., F. L. Battles, "Against Luxury and License in Geneva," *Interpretation* 19.2 (April 1965)]: "All men bear the blood of the poor."

Page 215.

sinews. In *Comm. Sen. De Clem.*, 87.15, Calvin gives the source of this analogy: Cicero, *Pro Cluent.*, 53.146: "As our bodies without the mind, so also a state without law, cannot use its parts, which are analogous to sinews and blood and members."

Cicero. Cicero, *Laws*, 2.4ff. On Calvin's earlier use of the "organic analogy" see Battles-Hugo, p. 110*.

law. Cicero, *Laws*, 3.2. On Calvin's earlier use of the "living law" analogy, see Battles-Hugo, p. 112*; also *Comm. Sen. De Clem.*, 125.4.

nations. Cf. Melanchthon, *LC* (1521), 8 [Eng. tr., LCC 19.126]: "As for the rest, I should like Christians to use that kind of judicial code which Moses laid down and many of the ceremonial laws as well. For since in this life we have to have judicial laws, and, it seems to me, ceremonial ones, it would be better to use those given by Moses than either the Gentile laws or papal ceremonies." Bohatec, *Calvins Lehre von Staat und Kirche* (1937/58), pp. 14f, cites Melanchthon, *Commentary on the Third Book of Aristotle's Politics*, [CR Melanch 16.448]: "But some persons assign piety as a pretext to this case and deny that the laws of the Gentiles are to be used by the Christian. Therefore they try to pass new laws or call us back to the laws of Moses, as for example, Carlstadt, who very violently contended that, abandoning Roman laws, the laws of Moses were to be received." Bohatec includes in this group also Thomas Münzer and Eberlin von Günzberg. Barth and Niesel refer to RE 19.94.39 and to *Apol. Conf.*, 16.3 (Carlstadt).

judicial laws. Calvin's tripartite division of the "whole law of God" is like that of Melanchthon, *LC* (1521), 4 [Eng. tr., LCC 19.53]: "Divine laws are those which have been established by God through the canonical scriptures. They have been divided into three categories: moral, judicial, and ceremonial." [LCC 19.61]: "There remain judicial and ceremonial laws; a compendium is not the place to say very much on them. Judicial laws concerning legal decision, penalties, and especially public court cases were given to the Hebrew people in Scripture." "Ceremonial laws were given in regard to sacrificial rites, differences in days, vestments, victims and other like matters. In them there is undoubtedly a shadowing of the mysteries of the gospel as Hebrews and some passages in Corinthians teach." See also Thomas Aquinas, *S. Th.*, PS, q. 89, art. 4: the title of this section of the *Summa* is: "Whether there are in addition to moral and ceremonial precepts, judicial precepts as well."

writers. Some of the ancient writers who helped in the development of this distinction were the author of the Epistle of Barnabas, Tertullian, Origen, and Augustine. See C. Douais, "Saint Augustin et la Bible," *Révue Biblique*, 3 (1894): 420ff.

Page 216.

Equity. Cicero, *Topics*, 2.9.

equity. *Aequitas (epieikeia)*, already a central theme of Calvin's *Comm. Sem. De Clem.*, underlies as well his understanding of law in the Scriptures and his exegesis of it. See Battles-Hugo, p. 137* and *Comm. Sen. De Clem.*, 111.3ff, note.

men's hearts. On natural law, see LCC 21.1504n38.

God's Law. The passage that follows, while detached from Calvin's exposition of the Second Table of the Decalogue, has reference to Commandments 8, 9, 6, and 7, setting them in the larger context of comparative law in a manner reminiscent of Melanchthon's *Loci Theologici* (1535). Cf. Bohatec, *Calvins Lehre von Staat und Kirche*, p. 37. It bears the stamp of Calvin's recent legal studies already reflected in the *Seneca Commentary* where his interest in the question of the punishment for specific crimes is seen, e.g., at 48.26-29.

manifest. See Justinian, *Digest,* 47.2.2: "Of *furtum* there are two kinds, *manifestum* and *nec manifestum.*" In a "manifest theft" the thief is taken with the goods stolen [47.2.3]; in a "non-manifest theft" the thief is caught later [47.2.8]. Cf. Guillaume Budé, *Annotationes Reliquiae in Pandectas,* 292CD. The details here given by Calvin seem a rather inexact reference to Aulus Gellius, *Noctes Atticae,* 11.18, a chapter on the law of theft. Gellius was well known to the young classical humanist as evidenced by use of him in *Comm. Sen. De Clem.* Aulus Gellius states that under the earliest Greek lawgiver, Draco, all thefts brought capital punishment. Later, under Solon, this was scaled down to "double punishment." Among the Romans the Law of the XII Tables levied a variety of punishments for theft. A thief caught in the act might be scourged and then adjudged to the party wronged (if a slave, he was executed). A nocturnal thief or an armed thief could be killed. A non-manifest thief had to pay a "twofold" penalty (later increased to "fourfold"). See H. F. Jolowicz, *Digest XLVII.2 De Furtis* (1940), p. lxviii. It is possible that Calvin had in mind Gratian, *Decr.,* 2.33.3.1.6 [Friedberg, 1.1161].

punishment. See Girard, *Droit Romain,* 7th ed. (1924), p. 425.

cross. Cf. Mommsen, *Röm. Strafrecht* (1899), pp. 634f; 668f; 674ff.

death. Cf. *Ibid.,* p. 631f.

punishments. Cf. *Ibid.,* p. 698f.

Page 217.

God's law. Cf. Livy, *AUC,* 34.6 (cited by Calvin, *Consilium de Luxu,* OC 10a.206.47), distinguishing permanent vs. temporary laws.

all nations. Cf. Bohatec, *Calvins Lehre von Staat und Kirche,* p. 15: "This view, which would see in Moses an earthly lawgiver like Lycurgus and Solon, is considered by Calvin as dangerous, disordered and false. . . ."

law. Cf. Calvin, *Brieve Instruction* [Eng. tr., D.v^r]: ". . . we ought not to exclude from us the estate of civile iustice, neyther yet to chase it out of the Christen church. . . ." [Cf. Benoît, 4.524n2.]

Page 218.

society. Cf. the second use of the law, the restraining, p. 35 above.

Page 219.

vengeance. Another Anabaptist "misuse" of Rom. 12:19 is noted by Calvin in his *Brieve Instruction* [Eng. tr., fol. F.i^v]: "And S. Paule in the twelfthe of the Romayns doth lead us unto the same ende, that we might the better perceive what is our dutye. Therefore to saye that Moyses dyd but halfe teache the people of Israel to honour and serue God is a blasphemye, first forged by the Papistes, and now renued by these pore phantasticals, whyche take for a reuelation frome heauen, what so euer fabils they have heard of their grandmothers." In his *Contre la Secte des Libertins* (1545) [OC 7.243], Calvin refutes yet another application of the verse by Antoine Pocquet. Pocquet, after condemning government and also medicine, turns to war. "After he condemns in general all wars, without distinguishing whether waged for a just cause or not, even when a prince makes war only for his defense of his people, without incitement to ambition or greed, but solely for the duty of his office. To confirm this he alleges that He has commanded us to give place to anger [Rom. 12:19]. But St. Paul by the word 'anger' understands the vengeance of God, and his just punishment, which he has bidden princes to exercise."

coat. In the *Schleitheim Confession*, art. 4, we read: "To us then the command of the Lord is clear when He calls upon us to be separate from the evil and thus He will be our God and we shall be His sons and daughters. . . . Therefore there will also unquestionably fall from us the unchristian devilish weapons of force—such as sword, armor and the like, and all their use [either] for friends or against one's enemies—by virtue of the word of Christ, Resist not evil" [Wenger, p. 249f]. See also Zwingli, *Refutation of Baptist Tricks*, SWHZ, pp. 188-193, where the same article is quoted and refuted.

altogether. This refers to the second portion of the sixth article of the *Schleitheim Confession:* ". . . it will be asked concerning the sword, whether a Christian shall pass sentence in worldly dispute and strife such as unbelievers have with one another. This is our united answer: Christ did not wish to decide or pass judgment between brother and brother in the case of the inheritance, but refused to do so [Luke 12:14]. Therefore we should do likewise" [Wenger, p. 251]. For Calvin's refutation, see *Brieve Instruction contre les Anabaptistes* (1548) [Eng. tr., fol. E.i^v-E.ii^r]. Cf. Zwingli, *Refutation* [Eng. tr., SWHZ, pp. 200f].

Page 220.

office. Cicero, *Laws*, 3.2.5.

evil. Cf. *Schleitheim Confession*, 6.4 [Zw Opp. SS 3.399]. Zwingli, *Commentary*, 27 [Eng. tr., LWZ 3.303], cites this Anabaptist argument: "It is our own fault, then, that we are compelled to have magistrates, since we do not live according to Christ's directions; for if we did so live, we should have no need of magistrates." This he then refutes on Scriptural grounds.

defense. This brief mention of the duty of citizens to bear arms, if necessary, in the defense of their country, is more elaborately discussed in Calvin's *Brieve Instruction* [Eng. tr., fol. D.ii^v-D.iii^r]: "In thys case, if a christen man, after the order of the countrye, be called to serue hys prince, doeth not only not offende God in goynge to the warres, but is in a holye vocation, whiche cannot be reproued wythoute blasphemynge of God." He then cites Luke 3:14 and Acts 10:47ff in Scriptural support.

Page 221.

prince. Xenophon, *Cyropaedia*, 8.2.10; Apuleius, *De Mundo*, 26.

country. Cf. Calvin, *Comm. Sen. De Clem.*, 97.39-99.27, for detailed elucidation of this title; also introduction, where this and related titles of the king are discussed.

people. Homer, *Iliad*, 2.243, ποιμένα λαῶν, translated by Quintilian, *Inst. of Oratory*, 8.6.18, as *pastor populi*. See Calvin, *Comm. Sen. De Clem.*, Battles-Hugo, pp. 111*f; also 30.12n. Calvin eloquently uses the phrase in Sermon 12 on 2 Sam. 5:2 (1562) [Suppl. Calv. 1.102.30ff]: "Nevertheless those who have some superiority and dominion over the people must pay close attention to this fact: to know that they are pastors. Even among the pagans this was recognized for when they spoke of kings and princes, they called them 'pastors,' as their writings show. Who taught them such speech? God, who has inscribed it on their hearts, in order to render inexcusable those who employ tyranny."

innocence. While not an exact parallel, Cicero's *Pro Publio Sestio*, 65.137, may have been in Calvin's mind when he continued his list of titles of the magistrate: ". . . senatum republicae custodem, praesidem, propugnatorem collocaverunt." A parallel still less close is that of Cicero, *De Lege Agraria*, 2.16.15: ". . . per tribunum plebis, quem majores *praesidem libertatis, custodem esse voluerint, reges in civitate constituit."* Calvin had worked through these orations of Cicero already in his annotations of the *De Clementia* of Seneca.

favor. See Appendix IV.

office. Calvin asserts the power of the prince, whether good or bad, over his subjects, in *Comm. Sen. De Clem.*, 42.9f.

people. Cf. Plutarch, *On the Delay of Divine Vengeance, Moralia*, 552 [LCL 7.208].

Page 222.

to them. Cf. Calvin, *Comm. Acts,* 23:5 [OC 48.506]: "Although the administration of earthly or civil power may be confused and perverted, the Lord still wishes subjection to remain intact" [Benoît, 4.530n4].

pleases. These last pages of *Institutes* (1536), concerned with the contrast between king and tyrant (a commonplace in "mirrors of princes"), while bearing a dominantly Scriptural documentation, still reflect the classical philological treatment of the topic in *Comm. Sen. De Clem.*, 81.2ff. Cf. Zwingli, *Commentary,* 27 [Eng. tr., LWZ 3.298]: "I call it tyranny when dominion is assumed on one's own authority. If one man does this, he is a tyrant, and his sway is called a tyranny; if several, not all but some few, arrogate dominion to themselves, the Greeks called it an oligarchy. Tyranny, then, Christ altogether forbids; on the other hand, as even in a flock of sheep there must be some ram that leads the rest, so also there must be some headship in every state." Etc. Also see Zwingli, *Exposition of the Christian Faith,* 7 [Eng. tr., LCC 24.267].

Page 223.

servants. The same passage is quoted by Erasmus, *Education of a Christian Prince* [Eng. tr., Born, p. 166].

Jeremiah. Cf. *The Second Book of Homilies* (1563), "Against Wilful Rebellion," I, p. 557.29ff. For discussion of the right to resistance, see Bohatec, *Staat und Kirche,* pp. 247ff.

merits. This is a sort of reverse side to the doctrine of unmerited grace. God's arrangements for man transcend human effort. Just as man gets what he does not earn, so the ruler holds office not because of his goodness or skill but because he has been chosen so to function by God himself.

to us. Cf. Zwingli's "Sixty-Seven Articles" (1523), Art. 42 [Schaff, CC 3.204]: "But when the magistrates have acted falsely and outside the rule of Christ, they can be deposed with divine sanction [Latin: *cum Deo*]." Zwingli elaborates this in his *Auslegung und Begrundung der Schlussreden oder Artikel* (1523) [CR Zw 2.342.26ff].

David. David is similarly used as a model of obedience to an unjust king in *The First Book of Homilies* (1547), "Obedience," II (Oxford, 1859, pp. 110.17-112.11). Also, *The Second Book of Homilies* (1563), pp. 562.22-563.25. Cf. further Bohatec, *Staat und Kirche,* p. 250.

Page 224.

subjects. At this point, Calvin seems to direct his words expressly to the French evangelicals, thus asserting the continuity of these final pages with the message of the Epistle Dedicatory. The principle of *mutua obligatio* between rulers and subjects, reiterated here, is discussed at length by Bohatec, *Staat und Kirche,* pp. 64ff, and *Budé und Calvin,* pp. 450ff.

back. "Aesop's bag": Catullus, 22.21; Horace, *Sat.,* 2.3.298f; Seneca, *On Anger,*

2.28.2 (quoted by Calvin, *Comm. Sen. De Clem.*, 47.17). See also Erasmus, *Adagia*, 1.6.90.

sacrilegious. It is possible that in this brief characterization of various sorts of rulers Calvin has in mind his sketch of the Roman Emperors from Tiberius to Nero in *Comm. Sen. De Clem.*, 79.32-38, which he used again (1539) at *Inst.*, 3.14.2.

mind. That God intervenes to break the power of unjust rulers, a lesson eloquently driven home here, is presaged, if in pagan terms, by Calvin's words in *Comm. Sen. De Clem.*, 51.16f: ". . . let kings and emperors . . . recognize that there are gods who can weigh their misdeeds exactly by the same measure."

kingdoms. In his *Comm. Sen. De Clem.* (1532), Calvin omits any comment on Seneca's statement that to pity a cruel tyrant would be a crime. Further, he fails to note a more extreme view expressed by Seneca, *On Benefits*, 7.20.3, that a morally incurable tyrant may be lawfully assassinated. Prov. 21:1, here cited, is also used by Guillaume Budé, *L'Institution du Prince*, c. 21, p. 80. In later editions of the *Institutes*, Calvin used the same verse at 1.18.2 (1559) and 2.4.7 (1539). Budé explains the verse as follows: "Similarly, the king's heart is moved by the inspiration and impulsion of God, Who pushes and directs it according to His absolute good pleasure, to make the king's undertakings praiseworthy, honorable, useful and beneficial to his people, and salutary for himself; or conversely, according as he and his subjects deserve, he is inclined sinisterly and deviously, his passions being directed into dangerous paths, leading wayfarers and passersby to perdition and calamity."

Page 225.

governments. Cf. Calvin, *Comm. Sen. De Clem.*, 43.9f, 51.18, where the ultimate demise of wicked rulers is suggested.

wickedness. On this, see LCC 21.1518n54.

kings. Calvin, *Comm. Sen. De Clem.*, 80.40, after quoting Plutarch, *Moralia*, 779E, notes that it was during the reign of Theopompus, king of Sparta, "that the ephors had been instituted, to prevent royal whim from going to excess." He cites Cicero, *Off.*, 2.23.80, for this; cf. also *Laws*, 3.7.16; *Rep.*, 2.33.58. Cf. G. Budé, *Annotationes Reliquiae in Pandectas*, 366C. Also see Bohatec, *Staat und Kirche*, pp. 82f, citing Melanchthon, *Commentary on the Third Book of Aristotle's Politics* (before 1530) [CR Melanch 16.440]. Note how Zwingli, "Letter to the Reader," *Isaiah Commentary* [CR Zw 14.8; Eng. tr., H. Preble, in *Huldreich Zwingli: A Comparative Essay on Forms of Government*, ed. F. L. Battles, pp. 8f], uses the same material: "Was it not a republic rather than monarchy that Moses established when he established his chiliarchs and hecatontarchs and the rest of his associates in the government [cf. Ex. 18:21]? The very anger of God through which he so indignantly allowed the Jews a king [cf. I Sam. 8:4ff] shows that the government of Moses was not a kingdom or monarchy. Lacedaemon and Athens never gave kings such free rein that they could drive the chariot of state whithersoever they would. Hence the tenaciously obstructive power of the Ephors, as well as of the Tribunes of the Commons among the Romans."

submitted. Cf. Calvin, *Comm. Acts*, 17:7 [OC 48.398]: "If religion sometimes constrains us to resist certain tyrannical edicts which forbid . . . the service we owe God, at such a time we can with good reason affirm that we are in no way violating the king's power. For they haven't been raised to positions of high dignity so that like giants they may attempt to pull God down off his throne. . . . No one must accuse us in this matter of despising them because we value more the dominion and high majesty of God" [cited by Benoît, 4.536n2; tr. D. Deer]. Cf. also Zwingli, *Comm.*, 27 [Eng. tr., LWZ 3.301ff]: "Bear, then, and endorse any tyranny which does not interfere with faith; for it happens not in vain that you live under an impious ruler. God is either punishing your sins or testing your patience. But if the ruler attempt to wrest your faith from you, you will snap out even in this unpleasant situation: 'One must obey God rather than men' [Acts 5:29]." The same exception is made, and on the same Scriptural grounds (Acts 5:29), to obedience to the ruler when it contravenes God's will by *The First Book of Homilies* (1547), "Obedience," II (Oxford, 1859, pp. 112f): "Yet let us believe undoubtedly, good Christian people, that we may not obey kings, magistrates, or any other, though they be our own fathers, if they would command us to do anything contrary to God's commandments. In such a case we ought to say with the Apostles, 'We must rather obey God than men' (Acts 5:29)." Etc.

Page 226.

men. Cf. Calvin, *Praelectiones in Danielem*, 6:22 [OC 41.25-26]; also *Comm. Acts*, 4:19 [OC 48.88]: "We ought to obey princes and others who have been put in authority, but in such a way that they in no wise deprive God the supreme King, Father and Lord, of his right." [Cf. Benoît, 4.537n7.] Also note Melanchthon, *LC* (1521), 12 [Eng. tr., LCC 19.150]: "As for that which is demanded by divine law, what is so demanded must be obeyed, done, and taught without respect to offense. For faith must always be preferred to love. Acts 5:29 applies here: 'We must obey God rather than men.' Christ says: 'I have not come to bring peace, but a sword' [Matt. 10:34]. So Daniel did not obey the law demanding the worship of the golden statue. Neither should we obey godless rulers who condemn the gospel in our time."

APPENDIX I

THE PLACARDS OF 1534

Translated from the text established by Robert Hari, "Les Placards de 1534," in *Aspects de la Propaganda Religieuse* (Droz, 1957), pp. 114-119.

TRUSTWORTHY ARTICLES ON THE HORRIBLE, GREAT & UNBEARABLE ABUSES OF THE PAPAL MASS: devised directly against the Holy Supper of Jesus Christ.

I invoke heaven and earth in witness of the truth, against this pompous and proud papal Mass, by which the world (if God does not soon provide a remedy) is and will be totally desolated, ruined, lost, and laid low: for in the Mass our Lord is so outrageously blasphemed, and the people seduced and blinded— something which we ought no longer to suffer or endure. But, in order that the case may be more easily understood by each one, it is appropriate to proceed by articles.

First, it is and must be very certain to every faithful Christian that our Lord and Savior Jesus Christ as the Great Bishop and Pastor eternally ordained by God, has offered up his body, his soul, his life, and his blood for our sanctification in a most perfect sacrifice: which cannot and must never be repeated by any visible sacrifice. For this would be to renounce him as if he were ineffective, insufficient and imperfect. Not only to say such a thing, but even to think it is a horrible and frightful blasphemy. The earth has been and still at present is in several places loaded and filled with miserable sacrificers, who as if they were our redeemers put themselves in place of Jesus Christ, or make themselves of him, saying that they offer to God a sacrifice as agreeable and pleasing as that of Abraham, Isaac and Jacob, for the salvation both of the living and of sinners. This thing they do openly against the whole truth of Holy Scripture. For by the great and wonderful sacrifice of Jesus Christ all outward and visible sacrifice is abolished and voided, and never is another to remain. What I am saying is very simply shown in the Epistle to the Hebrews in chapters 7, 9, and 10, which I beg everyone diligently to ponder. Nevertheless, to touch on it a little and help the spirit of the smallest ones, in chapter 7 it is written as follows: "It was fitting that we should have a bishop, holy, blameless, unstained, who did not have need of offering sacrifices each day, first for his own sins, then

339

for those of the people; for he did this, in offering himself once for all." Note that he says: "In offering himself once for all." For never was this, never will this oblation be repeated, nor will there be any like it. Likewise in chapter 9: Christ bishop of benefits at his advent by his own blood entered once for all into the sanctuary. Here is where directly he says that by his being present once for all, eternal redemption is effected. For this reason it is clear that in our redemption we have no need of such sacrificers, unless we would renounce Jesus Christ's death. Likewise in chapter 10: "Lo, I have come to do thy will, Lord God," by which will we are sanctified by the offering of Christ's body made once for all. And also the Holy Spirit testifies to this, saying: "I will no longer remember their iniquities, and where their forgiveness is, there is no longer any offering for sin." This by St. Paul's inevitable argument I show thus, in chapters 5, 7, 8, and 10 of the Epistle to the Hebrews. The holy Apostle says: Because of the imperfection of the sacrifices of the old law, it was necessary daily to rebegin until something entirely perfect has been offered: this was done once for all by Jesus Christ. Therefore I ask of all sacrificers: whether their sacrifice is perfect or imperfect? If it is imperfect, why are they thus abusing the poor world? If it is perfect, is it necessary to repeat it? Come forward, sacrificers, and if you have the power to respond, respond.

Secondly, in this unhappy Mass one has provoked as it were the whole world to public idolatry, when one falsely gives to understand that under the species of bread and wine, Jesus Christ bodily, really, and actually, entirely and personally is flesh and bones, as great and perfect as at present he is living, is contained and hidden. This, Holy Scripture and our faith do not teach us, but completely to the contrary. For Jesus Christ after the resurrection ascended into heaven, seated at the right hand of God the Almighty Father, and will come to judge the living and the dead. Also St. Paul in Colossians 3 writes thus: "If you are raised up with Christ, seek the things that are above, where Christ is seated at the right hand of God." He does not say, "Seek Christ who is in the Mass, or at the altar," but in heaven. For this reason it may rightly be sensed: if his body is in heaven, during this same time he is not on earth; and if he were on the earth, he would not be in heaven, for certainly a true body is ever only in one place at one time. This St. Augustine well knew when in speaking of Jesus Christ, he wrote as follows: "Until the end of the world the Lord is above: yet the truth of the Lord is here with us. For the body in which he arose again must be in one place, but the truth is everywhere diffused."[1] Similarly, Fulgentius

1. Augustine, *John's Gospel*, 30.1 [PL 35.1632]. This passage, quoted in a collage of Augustinian passages by Gratian, *Decr.*, 3.2.44 [Friedberg, 1.1330.34-38], was used in sixteenth century debate on the eucharist. Zwingli, in his treatise *On the Lord's Supper* (1526), 2 [LCC 24.222], cited it as a medieval canonical refutation of scholastic interpretation of the dominical words of institution. Calvin cited the same passage from memory at the Lausanne Colloquy of 1536 and used it again in his *Second Defense* against the Lutheran Westphal in 1556. (See Introduction, p. li.) Thus it served both against Roman Catholic transubstantiation and against Lutheran ubiquity.

wrote as follows: "He was absent from heaven according to his human substance when he was on earth, and leaving the earth, when he ascended into heaven: but according to his divine and boundless substance, not leaving heaven when he descended from heaven, nor deserting the earth when he ascended to heaven."[2] Besides, we have infallible certification by Holy Scripture [Matt. 24:23ff.] that the advent of the Son of Man when it shall please him to leave heaven, will be visible and manifest: and if anyone tells you, Christ is here or there, do not believe it. Jesus Christ says: Do not believe it, and the sacrificers say: It is necessary to believe it. Dispose yourselves, poor idolators, to recognize your error, and to confess the truth; well now, in a short time it will befit you to respond to a little treatise, which (with God's help) will be composed particularly of this present matter, so clearly and openly that there will be neither woman nor child who does not recognize your damnable blindness.

Thirdly, these poor sacrificers, to heap error upon error, have in their madness said and taught that after having breathed or spoken over this bread that they take in their fingers and upon this wine that they put in the cup, that it does not remain either bread or wine, but as they speak in great and wonderful words, by Transubstantiation Jesus Christ is hidden and covered under the accidents of bread and wine, which is a doctrine of devils, against all truth, and manifestly against all Scripture. And I ask of these gross enclosers [*enchaperonez* — pun on "hood"?] where they discovered and found this gross word "transubstantiation". St. Paul, St. Matthew, St. Mark, St. Luke and the ancient fathers have not spoken this: but when they make mention of the Holy Supper of Jesus Christ, they openly and simply named bread and wine [I Cor. 11; Matt. 26; Mark 14; Luke 22]. See how St. Paul writes [I Cor. 11]: "Let a man examine himself." He does not say, Look to a tonsured one to examine you, but he says, let a man examine himself: then taste and eat of this bread; he does not say that the body of Jesus Christ is under the substance, under the species or appearance of bread, but only and purely he says, "Eat of this bread" [I Cor. 11]. Now it is certain that Scripture uses no deception: and that in this there is no fantasy, since he senses very well that it is bread. Similarly in another place it is written as follows: "On the Sabbath day when we are gathered together to break bread" [Acts 20]. In these very clear passages Holy Scripture expressly says and declares it to be bread, not species, appearance, or semblance of bread. Who will be able to sustain, bear and endure such mockers, such plagues, false antichrists? They, as presumptuous and arrogant men, according to their ordinary custom, have been so rash and stubborn as to conclude and decide to the contrary. For this reason, as enemies of God and of his Holy word, rightly one ought to reject and greatly detest them.

Fourthly, the fruit of the Mass is quite contrary to the fruit of the Holy Supper of Jesus Christ, which is not surprising, for between Christ and Belial there is nothing in common [II Cor. 6:15]. The fruit of the Holy Supper of Jesus

---

2. Fulgentius of Ruspe, *To Trasimund, King of the Vandals*, 2.17 [PL 65.265.10-14]. This passage was earlier cited by Zwingli against Luther in the Marburg Colloquy (1528).

Christ is publicly to make declaration of faith in him, and in certain assurance of salvation to have actual remembrance of the death and passion of Jesus Christ, by which we are redeemed from damnation and perdition. Also to have remembrance of the great love and charity with which he so loved us that he gave his life for us and by his blood cleansed us. Also in all of us taking the bread and the drink, we are admonished concerning the love and great union to which all of us of the same spirit ought to live and die in Jesus Christ. And this clearly restores the faithful soul, filling it with divine consolation, in complete humility increasing in faith from day to day, exercising itself in all goodness, most gentle and lovable charity. But the fruit of the Mass is quite different, just as experience shows us, for by it all knowledge of Jesus Christ is wiped out, and preaching of the Gospel rejected and hindered, time occupied in bell-ringing, cries, chantings, ceremonies, candlelightings, censings, disguises, and such sorts of buffooneries, by which the poor world is like a flock of sheep miserably deceived, and by these ravening wolves eaten, gnawed and devoured. And who could not ponder the thefts of these fornicators? By this Mass they have laid hold of all, destroyed all, engulfed all, they have disinherited princes and kings, merchants, lords, and all that one can say, whether dead or alive. By it they live in carefreeness, they need do nothing, strive still less, what more do you wish? One must not wonder that they maintain it so strongly: they kill, they burn, they destroy, they murder as brigands all those who have contradicted them, for anything else than force they do not have. Truth fails them; truth threatens them; truth pursues and catches them. Truth overcomes them. In short, by it they will be destroyed. So be it. So be it. Amen.

MARTIN BUCER ON THE LORD'S PRAYER

Translated from Bucer, *Enarrationes Perpetuae in Evangelia* (1530), I, fol. 62ʳ-67ᵛ, locus on Matthew 6:1-13, with cross-references in the margin to Calvin, *Institutes*, ch. 3, "Prayer."

[fol. 62ʳ.17] "Take heed that you do not do your alms before men," etc. [Matt. 6:1]. In the previous chapter Christ vindicated the law against the false inventions of the Pharisees; the present chapter he frees from the hypocrisy of those things which were commonly considered the special works of religion, namely alms, prayers and fasting. Then to render them more inclined to truly good works, namely the duties of love, he urges strongly that we entrust the whole care of our life to God our Father. The first place has been given to alms. According to the meaning of the word, it is the beneficence which is shown especially to the poor. For it is derived from the verb ἐλεεώ which means to show pity. Of this he requires nothing but the first fruits, of what is to be given by any petitioner, so that it may flow spontaneously from love of neighbor which he everywhere inculcates. Moreover, he very earnestly warns us to manifest with zeal that love solely to relieve the poor and to give thanks to God, drawing a contrast between the Pharisees and his own followers, seeing that he had proclaimed that their righteousness ought to be more abundant than that in which the Pharisees took pleasure.

[fol. 62ʳ.29] Now the sum of those things which he teaches is this: it is fitting for you to give alms most abundantly, seeing that it is your duty to recompense God the Father with the bounty and beneficence belonging even to your enemies. See to it that you not give alms before men, in order to be seen; that is, in benefiting the indigent, see to nothing else than that you live as brothers, show yourself approved of your heavenly Father, who most generously recompenses all things, rightly seeing even while you are concealed in mortal flesh, what benefits you have extended to your brothers, and recompenses with your great glory in the presence of all the saints, when you will truly hear from me: "Come, blessed of my Father, etc." [Matt. 25:34ff]. Otherwise, if you seek to be conspicuous to men, thus praised by them you will easily attain your reward, and receive nothing more empty than this, and then will be in no wise better than the Pharisees, than whom what could be more empty? For they do all their works in order to be visible to men, also cause trumpets to be sounded before them, in order to be seen by many, doing these acts out of their foolish ambition, so that in God's sight no vestige of grace remains to them.

[fol. 62ʳ.41] This discourse is full of common figures of speech. "To give alms in secret, that the left hand may not know what the right is doing" is hyperbole with metaphor, by which he intended to teach nothing other than that we be unwilling to seek men's admiration through our beneficence. By the word "reward" is to be understood what merit follows works, not what merit exists by works; on this we have stated something above, on the verse, "Rejoice and be glad for great will be your reward in heaven" [Matt. 5:12].

[fol. 62ʳ.46] The choice of the poor has been discussed elsewhere, on which there is a notable sermon of Johannes Oecolampadius. I consider it sufficient to have taught that alms are to be given to one's neighbor, that is, to him whom the Lord has offered to you, to be fostered by your kindness. On this there was more a little while ago where I explained who and to whom one is a neighbor. Surely, those whom the Lord has joined to us by physical kinship or fellowship of faith ought to be our first concern, as we are taught from Paul [Gal. 6:2; I Tim. 5:1ff] and we are to see to it that, as at other times, so also by giving alms, we should do as much good as possible to our brothers, and do it to the glory of God. And the Spirit will readily teach the concerned person to what ones it is most fitting to give alms.

[fol. 62ᵛ.1] "And when you pray, you will not pray as the hypocrites," etc. [Matt. 6:5]. Prayer is another thing with which those whom true religion holds are chiefly occupied. Now the Pharisees used vigorously to imitate this, as is clear enough from what Christ at ch. 23 below charges against them. Moreover, he instructs his followers that in praying they be free of two vices, one of the hypocritical Pharisees, the other of the Gentiles. He urges them against the first, captivation with human praise, with the same arguments which he used against ostentation in almsgiving. Undoubtedly these are his arguments: God is your Father; therefore you ought to render yourself acceptable to him alone, to pray to him, so that he, and not men, may see you. Secondly, he is your heavenly Father; therefore it is fitting that you also be his heavenly children, to whom all earthly commendation is a thing to be despised, much less to be striven for. Then, as you are God's children, so it is fitting that you far outstrip the hypocritical Pharisees, those striving for human approval; your care ought to be approved of God. Finally, if you chase after men's applause, the Father cannot recognize you to be serving him, and thus you are to expect no grace from him, having received men's applause, you have already received all the reward of your piety. What is viler or emptier than this? With two arguments he calls us away from another defect in praying, with which the Gentiles labor, namely futile heaping up of words. The first is: it is an error of the Gentiles so to lavish words on prayer, in the notion that they will be heard because of their vain repetitions, which is, at any rate, to think unworthily of God, as if he were obviously delighted at our vain repetitions, from which equally foolish and impious error, it is surely fitting for others to be children of God.

[fol. 62ᵛ.17] The second is: that toward God there is no need of words, as he already knows before we pray what our necessities are, and everyone who alone wishes to be considered religious, pitifully labors today under both defects, for such persons pray with an inexhaustible hodgepodge of words, and they, doubly blind and miserable, labor mightily to be seen in order that they may both commend and dearly sell to men their devotion as they call it. For unless they, shrieking with their many words, were confident they were going to ingratiate themselves with God, and with human praise, also to discern thence profit for their bellies, as they are work-haters and squeamish, they would obviously pray in very few words.

[fol. 62ᵛ.24] But the fact that [Jesus] commanded one to enter one's bedroom and with door closed pray to the Father meant nothing else than to flee ostentation in every way, if you utterly shunned this and by praying to the heavenly Father alone, strove to commend yourself to him, you rightly prayed in your closed chamber, even if you prayed in a vast throng of men. Nor is it a new custom to pray in the assembly of the church, as both the examples of the ancients—David, Solomon, and others—and the instruction of Paul [I Cor. 14:15f and I Tim. 2:1ff] prove. For just as God's benefits are best recalled in its assemblies, so is it fitting that the hearts of all be kindled to thanksgiving and to pray the Spirit for the will to live.

[fol. 62ᵛ.33] Yet inasmuch as prayer is a serious and burning conversation of the heart with God, whereby we both give him thanks for benefits received and pray for his beneficence to come, it especially delights in solitude. The Evangelists recall that Christ thus withdrew and Peter, about to pray at Joppa, climbed to the upper part of the building [Acts 10:9]. Surely as contempt of God is enormous, either you mindlessly pour out words to him, that is, pray not at all, but you imitate prayer with derision of God, or even beyond words, with vague musings you are caught up in the business of the flesh, when you have undertaken conversation with God, so pains must really be taken that the mind be rendered as empty as possible of human affairs, when prayer to God is entered upon. For we ought to reverence nothing as much as God our Creator; it is fitting that we yearn for nothing as much as our kindliest Father; it befits us to regard nothing as desirable as those things which exist for us to ask of him in prayer, obviously a truly good and right spirit [cf. Ps. 51:10]; finally, when our heart ought so to be rightly seized with the remembrance of his goodness toward us, if at that very point the heart can dissipate its energies in other things, this is obviously proof of a heart as yet too little knowing God and endowed with too weak a faith in him. Accordingly, since concern for earthly matters even more excessively obscures faith in and knowledge of God, and it cannot help but creep up on those who pay attention to carnal affairs, it is obviously preferable when one is disposed to pray, to withdraw from all concerns, not only of men, but also insofar as possible, of absolutely everything. Therefore, our Lord

345

74 and (after his example) the saints preferred nighttime for prayer. For in the assembly of the Church, the proclamation of the word of God and likewise the example of worshipers at prayer provide an alternate to solitude insofar as it pertains to calling the mind away from human business.

[fol. 62ᵛ.52] This is the first thing needed in order to pray in a worthy manner: call the mind away from all other thoughts, and with one's heart concentrating all its attention and yearning on God to talk with him, not showing derision toward God by evil acts or anger toward him, but in prayer giving thanks. Next, most diligently expend those benefits of his which he has bestowed and daily bestows both upon the whole of mankind and upon us individually, in order that, our heart being kindled, it may pour out itself completely in thanksgiving [fol. 63ʳ] and praise of our best Father, and then with full trust pray for itself and others, for whom by this it sees to it that there is need for the name of the Lord to be sanctified in us. "In this manner" surely we see very many psalms to have been composed, and also a form for praying to have been laid down by the Lord, when he sets forth for requests, "Our Father which art in heaven," indeed in few words, yet ones containing the fullest reminder of divine regard toward us, by which our eternal and heavenly Father has adopted us pitiable ones as his children and heirs of heavenly life; surely, as nothing more divine, nothing more blessed than this exists, so in it have all God's benefits been abundantly embraced.

[fol. 63ʳ.8] With the heart thus kindled, the memory of the Father's bounty, and thanksgiving, and requests freely follow, but that the heart itself having tasted God's bounty might rightly declare it over and over, thus nothing else 75 could conveniently supply these than duly recognized necessity. But the heart will not otherwise order these [prayers], and Christ's form of prayer prescribes that we chiefly pray for those things which make for God's glory, and likewise pray for things contrary thereto to be averted; and in the second place for those things which concern the present life. Although anything among those that daily happen to us, and for which the Father's kindliness ought to be urged, is especially also to be tempered, and only the heart itself, impelled by the Spirit of God, will teach when we are to rely more on thanksgiving, and when upon requests. Hence sometimes the heart will rather beg the Lord for health, sometimes for the striking down of poverty, sometimes against an enemy. Thus the greater is the sense of benefits, the more feeling here will be in thanksgiving, of the sort for which you see psalms to have been composed, as Psalm 9, 16, 18 and very many others. But if need pressed more closely, there will be much inclination to request and petition, as Psalm 3, 5, 6, 7 and many others indicate. But why waste words on these matters? True prayer is something more spiritual than our words can sketch, much less express.

74 [fol. 63ʳ.22] But lest I overlook this, there is no place in prayer for words, unless perchance the more ardent affection of the heart, ignorant of how to burst forth into prayer, while the heart is agitated with violent thoughts, succeeds (with no one present) in speaking with the mouth the same thoughts that occupy it

within. Thus, unless words well up from the heart, because of the excessive ardor of the affection, words will have no place in prayer. For prayer is conversation with God, who hears nothing more graciously than the discourse of the heart, but has no need of words. Yet there is use of words, where one prays publicly, or rather where an introductory formula precedes prayers, for it is equally fitting that through the words of prayer we signify and express to men the other thoughts and feelings of the heart. But then it is for the sake of others that words are employed, with whom we cannot otherwise act, not of our own or of God. Lastly, the Christian can read or even sing by himself alone with benefit, both psalms and other prayers of the saints, not so much that by reading 74 or singing these he prays, as that he reminds himself of the feelings with which the saints burned, and thence is both so displeased with his own lukewarmness and at the same time is kindled somewhat to pray.

[fol. 63^r.35] Surely to this end, psalms and other public prayers are used in churches, in order to warn the people that the saints should rely on God, that with confidence they may pray for and implore God's help, and that they may pour themselves out wholly in thanksgiving and the praise of God, and thus by their example be kindled to like things. Accordingly also these other public prayers are recited, and are framed by the presbyter for the church's need, for the same reason, namely they have been instituted to arouse the hearts of the people, to recognize their need, and to pray God to relieve it for their sake. Now in some way or other one can inquire from these what is the nature of true prayer, of what things it is prepared, and to what extent words can pertain to it. Lastly, that nothing less than prayers to God are those which under this name have been retailed wrongheadedly by the members of religious orders [*religiosulis*] without spirit and mind, mumbling and roaring a stream of words, long and loud.

[fol. 63^r.45] Hence it is perfectly clear that it is an unbearable madness 73, 85 to prescribe or even command, a certain time, manner and place of prayer— and that to have omitted anything would inflict deadly injury. I ask what mortal has the authority to determine time, place and necessary way for the expression either of feelings of rejoicing or sorrowing or of other yearning, when it is not even in man's power to be affected according to his own decision? Now without this most burning desire of heart and without enkindled hope and feeling of thanksgiving toward God, what else than unspeakable mockery of God is this presumptuous prayer? What else is it to pray without desire and to give thanks without a sense of benefit, than to rejoice without joy and to sorrow without sorrow? Who will incite such desires for spiritual things, who will establish a measure of desires, but the Spirit? His alone is the task of moving us to pray, and of establishing a manner of praying; any mortal who tried this would render himself a hypocrite hateful to God, and not render himself an intercessor pleasing to God. Accordingly we can call upon no one to pray except we have as diligently and well as possible placed in clear view both his need and misery and God's manifest goodness and kindness to all seeking it, [fol. 63^v] if then the will of

Christ is present and brings it to pass that he has faith in those things which we have preached to him, as he will now feel how poor he is and how pressed by the greatest need, thus he cannot but implore most ardently the aid of God whom he believes so kindly hears the poor; and as much as he recognizes his misery, so will he also be much in prayer.

[fol. 63ᵛ.5] Thus Paul and the other saints, because they always had before their eyes the needs of their own and of others, and the lack of the glory of God both in themselves and in others, were frequently at prayer. Consequently, Paul everywhere greatly urges his followers to be persistent in prayer, obviously desiring that they descend into themselves, recognize their own and others' diseases, rightly ponder God's unspeakable goodness, and thus more and more burn with desire for new life, a life established in conformity to God, that is continually and increasingly putting off man and putting on God. Surely that is what these passages mean: "Continue in prayer, and watch in the same with thanksgiving" [Rom. 12:12; Col. 4:2]. "Pray exceedingly" [I Thess. 3:10]. "In nothing be anxious but in everything by prayer and supplication with thanksgiving let your request be made known unto God" [Phil. 4:6].

[fol. 63ᵛ.14] Nor does he urge them to that sole perpetual desire of the glory of God which ought ever to be among Christians; this certain ill-advised persons have taught to be the prayer of the gospel scriptures and to be called Christian prayer. On the contrary, he warns that most frequently and as often as can be permitted, we should withdraw from crowds and business, devoting ourselves to fixed prayers, such as he continually used, in which he made mention of churches and brethren, whom he recalled in his letters and commended to their need. In order that these prayers might be kept much more intent, one will have to abstain from time to time from matrimonial intercourse and the pleasures of food, that is, to fast, of which Paul makes mention in I Cor 7. And in Matt. 17:21 Christ says that this kind of demon is cast out only by prayer and fasting, that is, by the intentest prayer, for which one prepares by fasting and by separating oneself from all concerns of the flesh, so that one's heart can be worthily occupied with God alone. Thus we read Paul and Barnabas prayed with fasting, and thus they commended the brethren to the Lord [Acts 14:23]. Why? Wherever Scripture mentions prayer, it speaks not otherwise of it than as a state of mental retirement to God, and never calls it by name, only that desire of God's glory, which ought continually to sit in the heart and hold first place in all our acts. That is rather called "the love of God," "the fear of God," "to seek the Lord," "to seek his kingdom" and such-like scriptural expressions. For prayer is more—as we have said—a serious conversation with God, which takes place only when other affairs are put aside.

[fol. 63ᵛ.31] So to converse with God and to lay down one's need before him is indeed rare today among those who wish to be seen of Christ; in fact many there are who are ignorant of what such acts mean. Here, indeed, is sure proof that such persons have as yet attained slender knowledge of their own sin and at the same time of God's goodness, especially since they see everywhere

348

such great contempt of the divine name, and such savage persecution of the gospel, and such great misdeeds reign everywhere, and circumscribe the most evangelical persons with the greatest infirmity. Nor is this stupor an obscure presentiment of the great vengeance of the threatening God, because we do not feel our own evil deeds, and, angered at the grace of the Judge, we cease (and indeed most strenuously) to pray.

[fol. 63ᵛ.39] Finally, lest these terms engender obscurity in anyone, Paul in Philippians 4:6, speaking of prayer, puts it this way: προσευχήν, δεήσειν, εὐχαριστίαν, αἰτήματα, that is, prayer, supplication, thanksgiving, requests; intercession he adds at I Tim. 2:1, among which I see no other distinction than that supplications are simple askings of those things which we especially pray from God, but intercessions, when we pray for others, we treat the need of others in the same way as our own, and pray for it to be lifted from them just as if we were ourselves pressed by it. Hence also Paul uses the word when he urges us to pray for other men and magistrates. Thanksgiving is that mark which, the more faithfully and ardently one prays, ought never to be absent from prayer.

[fol. 63ᵛ.48] In Hebrew prayer is usually called תפלה, that is, Thephilah, a word which according to its origin seems to signify a prayer that judgment or condemnation be averted [deprecation], just as תחנה, that is, Tehinnah, signifies prayer for grace; prayer always involves one or both of these; moreover we read here and there in scripture either term indiscriminately for what we call prayer, praying or deprecation.

[fol. 63ᵛ.53] From these matters it is also abundantly clear, to whom one must pray, namely God alone, our Father, for he alone can give the Spirit of salvation, to whom it is especially fitting for us and others to pray, and all the rest. For then no one could so befriend us as he, as he who gives up his own son to death for us, nor could anyone be as merciful, even to us sinners. It is quite clear that we must pray with faith, and to him through Christ; relying upon his satisfaction alone, we can trust that God is open to our prayers. Finally, it is also clear we must pray for our brothers, [fol. 64ʳ] inasmuch as we ought to love them as ourselves. On the dead saints' intercession for us, because Scripture promises nothing, we also will not be anxious, but will concern ourselves with praying to God rather than seeking out saints to pray for us, especially since we are not at all certain concerning their state as to whether they can hear us. To the present saints we can speak and write for them to pray for us, because it by no means ought to happen from lack of faith that God will hear our prayers as if we were too unworthy for him to listen to, if we alone prayed to the Father, but from the huge desire which we seek, in order obviously that we may desire all creatures to seek the same. For in all our prayers the chief one ought to be: "Hallowed be thy name, thy kingdom come,"—things clearly to be sought by all. So Paul similarly exhorted the brothers to pray for him, but only what made for God's glory, namely, that the door be opened both for him and for them to the preaching of the Gospel, that his message might hasten and bear fruit, and things of this sort. Neither Christ nor the Apostles bade us pray for the dead,

70

71

yet did not pass over in silence without greeting; therefore, I do not see, with what faith we can pray for them, especially since we do not know whether by our prayers they can be helped or not. Surely scripture has not even a word about the purgatory of the age to come.

[fol. 64^r.15] "In this manner you are to pray: Our Father which art in heaven." Note that he says, "pray in this manner," not "these words," as the crowd was to that point stupidly persuaded, thinking, after they had mumbled these words, they had prayed brilliantly. Some have at last fallen into the madness of supposing they would like to lay even the saints under obligation, offering this prayer repeated a definite number of times to some one of the saints in lieu of a votive offering. Prayer, as we have said, is a work of the mind not of the mouth: therefore it will not at all be lodged in words: here we are taught not with what words to pray but with what emotions of heart to request. First moreover let us request with that confidence with which sons could pray to a most kindly Father, sons reborn to a heavenly inheritance; likewise to a heavenly Father who not only is better than the best, but also has abundantly declared it in us, for whom he, to adopt us as his children into this heavenly dignity, gave his only-begotten Son over to death. This brief preface—nay, this appellation alone—most sweetly renews this very great kindness of his: "Our Father which art in heaven," and arouses and confesses in a wonderful manner this very faith that whatsoever it is fitting for heavenly children to request of their heavenly Father is to be obtained from him. Finally, the fact that he teaches us to say, "Our Father," commends the mutual love of the brotherhood, without which nothing could be made pleasing to God by us, as Christ testified in the previous chapter: "Therefore if you offer your gift," etc. And below at ch. 18:35: "So likewise shall my heavenly Father do also unto you, if you do not forgive everyone his brother from your hearts, their trespasses." Therefore these very few words warn, first, that God wishes to be our Father. What could be thought of that is either more desirable for us, or more fitting than God's goodness? Next: that he is that heavenly Father who is kindlier than everything earthly. Moreover, that we, as sons of the heavenly Father, ought at least to seek heavenly things. Finally, as we have him as the common Father of us all, who is our highest good, so much more should we have all things in common. Although he spoke in common with the disciples it was not his pleasure to teach them to say, "My Father," but "Our Father." It seems to me that he wished through this word "our" rather to commend the feeling of filial trust, that those who pray might be reminded and be certain that God wishes also to be their Father, and admonished that he would answer them no less than any other saints of the fellowship, in the fact that he taught them to pray thus in general and not each privately for himself.

[fol. 64^r.41] "Hallowed be thy name." They are commonly accustomed to divide this form of praying into seven petitions; as far as I am concerned, I think I have divided it quite enough and have shed enough light on it, if I apportion it into prayer and deprecation. For through it we are taught to pray for some things; on the other hand, to pray that some things be averted [*deprecor:* to deprecate, to pray that something be averted]. "To pray" includes both to pray for things spiritual and physical. The spiritual things Christ teaches us to pray for are that God may reign and be glorious in us, reshaped to his will. Physical things: that he may give us those things we need to carry on the present life from day to day. These include forgiveness of sins and guarding us from temptation lest we sin, or lest we put ourselves under the devil's thrall, to which prayer to avert physical ills (with which the devil exercises the elect) is joined a prayer to avert them, but only to the extent that they are truly evils and harmful to us. For quite often these outward evils wonderfully benefit us. Let me explain the individual words in order.

[fol. 64ʳ.52] "Hallowed be thy name" is just as if one said: "Grant that 78
thou mayest be honored and glorious on earth, that all the families of the nations may worship thee, that thy name may be glorious and blessed among all nations," of which Psalm 8 sings. For where through faith is recognized the goodness of God, set forth so kindly to us through Christ, then at last he is duly glorified by us, and God is truly worshiped, and we proclaim his glorious and great name, that is, hallow it. Hence Isaiah 52:5-7: "And now what does the Lord here say to me: Since my people is taken away for nought, [fol. 64ᵛ] they that rule over them make them howl, says the Lord, and my name continually every day is blasphemed. Therefore my people shall know my name; therefore they shall know in that day, since it is I myself who speak, behold it is I. How beautiful upon the mountains are the feet of him that preaches, that announces peace," etc. See: while the people of the Lord are held captive under wicked rulers, and God's kindness is not magnified among them, the ungodly arrogate all things to themselves and they blaspheme the name of God as it seems of one who has forsaken his own, and they say: "Where is their God?" Where moreover does he put forth his saving power, and redeem his people, something he has set forth preeminently through Christ, and has caused to be announced everywhere through the gospel: his holy and dread name is known and proclaimed, and he is known in his present glory. We are here taught to pray "in this manner," therefore, that through the gospel and the knowledge of his grace, the Father may render his name glorious in our Savior Jesus Christ. And "in this manner" is expressed the many oracles of the prophets, who foretold they would thus come to pass. This Ezekiel 39:7 holds, which he was pleased to write: "So will I make my holy name known in the midst of my people Israel, and I will not profane my holy name any more; and the heathen shall know that I am the Lord the Holy One in Israel." What else is this than that I render my name glorious and revered, when it will everywhere be known that I am the Lord, the Savior of my people.

[fol. 64ᵛ.17] But to be hallowed is the same thing as to be rendered illustrious and venerable, as is clear from what one reads in Exodus 20:11: "And God blessed the seventh day and hallowed it," that is, rendered it illustrious and sacred.

[fol. 64ᵛ.19] "Thy kingdom come." The same thing which is requested by 79

351

the previous petition is requested by this one: suppose the name of the Lord is rendered illustrious, in order that the Father may be known and worshiped everywhere, that is, that he may reign in us through his Spirit, unless the previous petition is explained in a measure through the latter, and at the same time it is declared in what manner the Lord's name is hallowed. For, with the Lord ruling over us, freed now from Satan's tyranny that we may enjoy God's bounty, we so confess his name to be holy and illustrious and glorify it, that he may reign over us, while he impels us by his Spirit to entrust ourselves wholly to him and to devote ourselves to being reconciled to our brothers with all our might. Isaiah in chs. 11-12 beautifully declares this consequence in another way: for after he has prophesied fully concerning the kingdom of God through Christ, he says in 12:4-6: "And in that day (that is, of the kingdom of Christ) you shall say: Confess to the Lord, call upon his name, declare his doings among the people, make mention that his name is exalted. Sing to the Lord, for he has made this excellent knowledge in all the earth. Cry out and shout, inhabitant of Zion, for great is the Holy One of Israel in the midst of you." For where this kingdom of God is blessed among us, it will be restored, and through faith, we enjoy God's presence, who would free us from all evils, and enrich us with a sheer abundance of good things; as we rightly know that all things are as nothing before him and in him there is nothing lacking to us that pertains to the most consummate happiness, so what else could we do than confess this to him, and everywhere testify and proclaim and commend to all his very great goodness toward us? The more widely the limits of this kingdom, by the esteem of the Lord, happen to extend among otherwise unhappy mortals, the more necessary it is that we break out into praise of him and rejoicing, howsoever much we cherish the glory of him who reigns in our midst.

[fol. 64ᵛ.39] We read many splendid things about the kingdom here and there in the Psalms and prophets. For it is a kingdom of righteousness and of both eternal freedom and happiness, which Christ (until the last enemy, death, is destroyed) administers in his elect through his Spirit. We are received into it indeed through faith, by love, so that we may prove by the authentic sign of this kingdom and by our own act, that we are citizens of it; it is the kingdom that was taken away from the Jews, and given to the elect from the Gentiles bringing forth fruit thereof [Matt. 21:43]. This is, I say, the kingdom of heaven, to which we are invited by the Gospel, which long ago came near to us in our misery. Would that it may truly come to individuals, in order that we, freed from the bondage of sin may dwell under Christ our King, free and blessed, with perfect faith and active love, until this kingdom of the eternal Father is utterly perfected in us, and he is all in all [I Cor. 15:28].

79

79

[fol. 64ᵛ.48] "Thy will be done, as in heaven so also on earth." That the Lord's name may be magnified, that is, that God's glorious goodness may be everywhere known and worshiped, was the first petition. The next is that "his kingdom come," which is obviously a consequence [of the first]. For who would not entrust himself to God's goodness once it is known, and through faith receive him as king, and prefer to act as a free and blessed man under his salvation-bringing sceptre, rather than serve as a miserable man Satan's pernicious authority? But while the flesh always causes trouble for us striving to accomplish this, and draws us back from this freedom of grace, back into the bondage of sin, this need consequently extorts from us likewise this third petition: "Thy will be done," etc. It is as if we said: We have prayed that thy kingdom, O God, the kingdom of heaven, may come, that, the strong armed man having been cast out through thy Christ, we may worship and follow thee as our sole king; from this our flesh calls us back and detains us. Grant then, after [fol. 65ʳ] thou hast deigned to receive us as citizens of thy kingdom, the kingdom of heaven, that we may devoutly so obey thy will on earth, as in heaven, in thy plainly spiritual minds, in which thou fully reignest, it is obeyed with the highest desire. Lest therefore there be in us also that very powerful law of our members, repugnant to thy law, away with the force of depraved desire which brings it about that the good we would do, we cannot, and we do the evil we hate [Rom. 7:15]! Grant that good will which the angels at Christ's birth announced would come to mankind through Christ, [Luke 2:14] that we may willingly and freely prepare ourselves for thy commandments through all things. This surely Ps. 110[:3] foretold concerning thine own: "Thy people (the prophet sings to thy Christ) should offer free-will offerings, or shall of their own free will be present; in the day of thy power thou shalt shine with holy beauty; they will be present from the womb of the morning, as the dew of thy youth." For when the day of power and of glory of thy Christ (he having been recalled from the dead) had arisen, and when he, your high priest (the Holy Spirit having been sent forth) had appeared in his holy beauty and magnificence, truly his people, the chosen apostles and others, betook both themselves and countless others as clean lambs, and a freewill offering, to follow the Father himself, and at once from the womb of the holy apostles came forth a huge throng of those regenerated through the Spirit of the youth of Christ, who when the day of salvation arose and the light of the Gospel shined, falling like dew at dawn, they fulfilled and made fruitful all things. Now, the added "As in heaven," admonishing heavenly minds to be intent upon doing at once the Father's will, seems to be borrowed from Psalm 103:21, where the Psalmist sings: "Praise the Lord, all his hosts, ministers of his, who do his pleasure." For as they know nothing can be better than what God wills, so do they strive with the greatest eagerness to accomplish it. Therefore it is fitting to pray that like zeal also come to us. In these matters consists prayer for spiritual things by which the glory of the Lord shines in us. For his name cannot be hallowed and glorified among us, unless he himself reigns among us by his good and salvation-bringing spirit, who, where it obtains among us, so forms us to the Father's will, that we give priority to nothing but obeying him and following him in all things, crucifying as we do our own will continually. Why the spiritual kingdom of God, and those holy minds obedient to God in all things, are called "heaven," we have said something above at Chapter 3 on verse 16: "The heavens were opened to him," etc. There follows the petition for physical things.

80-81
[fol. 65ʳ.28] "Give us this day our daily bread." I have called this the petition for physical things. For as we have need of these things also, and only by the Father's goodness do they come to us, so is it by no means unworthy, also to pray for those things by this petition. For there are those who by the words "epiousian bread" (as one commonly reads, "daily bread") understand the bread of the soul, because they deem it unworthy with such a heavenly prayer to request that bread which even the heathen receive from their parents. But when Christ added "today" as if limiting concern for food, lest we be concerned about tomorrow's [nourishment], I prefer with Chrysostom, to understand by this "daily bread," food and other necessities of the body. If we were praying for the spiritual food of the soul, we ought to add "forever" rather than "today." Nor is it unfitting by this heavenly prayer to request whatever food is needful for the body, since our heavenly Father does not consider himself unworthy to furnish us abundantly, nay asks that concern for this be entrusted to himself. In short, a great part of godliness is to pray with our faith, for food for the body from our heavenly Father, since we see that for so many concern for the body is an obstacle to their truly following Christ. Hence the saints of old were not at all ashamed urgently to seek the necessities of this life from God, as is clear even from the prayer of Jacob [Gen. 28:20], and Solomon [I Kings 8:15-61].

[fol. 65ʳ.43] Therefore by "epiousian bread" we shall understand food, and whatsoever the present life has need of. As these are gifts of God and necessary for those dwelling on earth, so will we rightly ask them of our heavenly Father, knowing indeed that all things are from his blessing, without which all our care and toil will be in vain. According to Prov. 10:22: "The blessing of the Lord will make rich, and that without sorrow." What Christ teaches must be attended to: to pray for our bread, and daily bread, and that today. By "ours" he curtails anything of superfluous desire, more than is required by necessary frugality. For our bread is that by which we are nourished usefully and needfully to live a godly life and serve our brothers, not that by which we may want beyond necessity in rioting and in destroying both ourselves and others. By the word "daily" he meant us to understand "easy to be had," depriving us of zeal for costly delicacies. By "today," finally, he removed concern for tomorrow, so that this is the sense of this petition: Our Father, thou didst so create us, that we need food while living in the flesh, just as thou didst make that necessary therefore for the body, so supply it generously, but according to the portion needed, so that we may eat only our bread which comes to us from thy institution; and furnish daily bread, easy to be had, [fol. 65ᵛ] which is at hand, and suitable to nourish our little body, we do not require costly delicacies. Finally, furnish it to us "today," for we shall pray again to thee for tomorrow. For day by day we must see, since nothing is lacking to thee whence thou feedest us and abundantly providest for our needs. But if anyone makes an analogy from this physical bread to spiritual, that is, spirit, in order that we may be aroused to hallow

354

God's name, and that his kingdom may prevail among us, and we may do his will—I will not quarrel with him, provided he does not think it unworthy of God's children to request in prayer from their father even these outward things which he deigns to promise.

[fol. 65ᵛ.8] "And forgive us our debts as we forgive our debtors." This is   81-82
the other part of this prayer by which we pray that spiritual evils be averted from us and those things by which God is offended. First, what we have already committed, then immediately what there is danger we may commit. Thus obviously it is fitting that our life be prepared ever to bear some good fruit in all our words and deeds to God's glory for our neighbors, for we are bidden to love God and them, and to fulfil his commandment to deserve well of our neighbor with all our heart, all our soul, and all our strength. From this anyone easily recognizes that no one lives so innocently as not to sin continually, for there is no one who does not sometimes either say or do and therefore think worthless things, much less things harmful to the brethren and obscuring the name of God. Therefore we render ourselves continually liable to new debts, which we are utterly unable to pay. For is there even a moment of time at which it is duly required of us that we should exert ourselves to God's glory? Far be it therefore from us to slough off ourselves of those debts we have previously contracted, because there is no time in which we do not contract still new ones. Consequently there is nothing left to us but to pray our debts be mercifully forgiven us by our Father, and that indeed at every moment. And because it is unworthy of us to seek mercy from our Father, if we ourselves are unkindly toward our brothers, nor is it fitting that God forgive us such great debts, if we have not previously forgiven our debtors all the debts they owe us, even the least important ones. Christ teaches us first to forgive our debtors their debts and so at last to pray the Father that, just as we ourselves forgive our debtors their debts, so he also wills to forgive us ours. For it is not the condition but the likeness that is noted here. And note, since the children of God are everywhere to pray in this manner, also that they are never free from debts and sins. When Christ (who came to free his own from sins) taught that there is no other satisfaction or remedy than to pray as suppliants for pardon from them, anyone sees they are teaching deceit that sins can be expiated through confession and certain works of satisfaction (as they call them) of ourselves and of other men or purchased remissions. It is God to whom alone we make ourselves debtors by sinning; he therefore alone it is also who by his goodness forgives these debts of ours, as is fitting, although not without satisfaction (but Christ's, not our own) inasmuch as it is impossible for us, never discharging our duty, even to make satisfaction for the least sin of all. Therefore we ought to pray to him alone also for forgiveness of sins, and await it solely from him. Whatever of this has been promised or requested elsewhere must be empty and of no account. Yet the extent to which we must confess both to individuals and to the church the sins we have committed, and must pray for their pardon, has been partly stated above in ch. 3, where we discussed confession. Yet all things will be in vain unless before

everything else we both recognize and are truly sorry for, the fact we have sinned before God, and both pray and entreat forgiveness from him, then confess our sins either to individuals whom we have offended or profitably to the church, and pray also to be received into favor by them.

[fol. 65ᵛ.42] "And lead us not into temptation." The temptation which Christ here teaches us to pray be averted, doubtless is of the same sort as that which was threatening his disciples on the Mount of Olives, when, while he was troubled even unto death, they were sleeping; hence he urged them to watch and pray, saying: "Watch and pray that you not come into temptation. The spirit indeed is ready but the flesh is weak" [Matt. 26:41]. This indeed is the temptation into which they soon fell, out of weak faith forsaking and denying him whom a little while before they had confessed as the author of salvation and had sworn that they would rather die with him than be left in peril. The meaning of this prayer to avert is as follows: Save us, O Father, from coming into that temptation by which we commit something unworthy of our faith in thee. For God tests, that is sounds out, men in various ways. He tried Abraham when he bade him sacrifice his son, and by that temptation brought to light what lay hidden in his heart: sure faith and ready obedience. He similarly tempted Job, and tempts any saints. He also tempted the Israelites with various afflictions in the wilderness, and thus brought it to pass that the majority deeply clung to their own unfaith hidden even to themselves, and contempt of God, when the same murmured against him, and vexed him with many blasphemies, betraying him. Thence it is that Moses in Deut. 8:2 said: "And you shall remember all the way which the Lord your God led you [fol. 66ʳ] these forty years through the wilderness, to humble you and to test you, to know what was in your heart, whether you would keep his commandments or not." For it was revealed when he afflicted them sometimes with hunger, sometimes with thirst, sometimes with other needs, that a sizable number of them had nothing of faith in their hearts, and by no means observed God's commandments, toward which they kept their minds utterly estranged. It is this sort of temptation that Christ teaches us to pray to be averted, not the previous kind, whereby all the saints are tempted and are tested as is gold by fire. On this, Peter [I Pet. 1:5-7] says: "You are kept by the power of God through faith unto salvation, ready to be revealed in the last time, wherein you greatly rejoice, though now afflicted for a short time in various temptations, if there is need, that the trial of your faith, much more precious than gold that perishes, though it be tested through fire," etc.

[fol. 66ʳ.10] In teaching us to pray the Father not to lead into that temptation, he hints that the Father leads into temptation those who [reading *qui* for *qua*] not so much show forth ungodliness as commit it; obviously he hints what the thing is, and scripture abundantly testifies to this. This plainly attests that God leads very many, not only into a fleeting temptation, tempted with which they sin indeed, but in no wise persevere in sin, but also they are perpetually inured to impiety. Of this sort was the temptation which stiffened and hardened Pharaoh's heart against hearing God's command and letting Israel go (Exodus chs. 4, 7; likewise Isaiah ch. 6). This is divinely enjoined upon the preacher of salvation: Make thick the heart of this people, and make heavy their ears, and cover over their eyes, so they may not see with their eyes, hear with their ears or understand with their heart and return and accept thy care. Look to Christ and to every preacher, God commands, how he clearly blinds the impious and those rejected by him, and renders them confounded in evil; this they do when the word of the Lord is announced to them. Thus surely Moses rendered Pharaoh, Christ the Pharisees, Paul very many Jews and Gentiles, only worse and utterly more obstinate in impiety, by preaching what would provide for their salvation, if they embraced it with a believing mind. The same comes by daily use, as many vessels of wrath as there are in the great house of God, when they are apprized of God's will, not only do they persevere in evil, but also as they attack the things that are of God, become savage. And thus they experience that what makes for the elect leads to resurrection, for them issues in ruin; in short, from this they derive death-dealing odor [cf. II Cor. 2:16], which for God's children is the breath of life.

[fol. 66ʳ.28] Those therefore whom God thus hardens and to whom he sends men to blind them to his word, he in this way leads into temptation. Paul testifies that certain ones "were given up by God unto a reprobate mind" (Rom. 1:28)—what else is this than to be led by him into temptation? And it was the same thing when the Spirit of the Lord departed from Saul, and an evil spirit from the Lord disturbed him (I Sam. 16:14). Thus also the Lord led David into temptation, when angered at Israel, he stirred up his heart, to hasten to make a census of the people, something it is written that Satan did (I Chron. 21:1). For as he sent the evil spirit into Saul to disturb him, and put a lying spirit into the mouth of the prophets of Ahab, to deceive him, so also he sent Satan against David, to stir up his heart to take a census of the people, that would turn out badly for the people toward whom he was doubtless angered, which was certainly a grievous temptation. Accordingly, open testimonies of Scripture show that the Lord leads into temptation both his own people and those rejected ones, and that he not only does this in order that they may be tested thereby in outward adversities—the particular temptation for the saints—but also that they thereby err, sin and involve themselves and others in evils. Hence in Isaiah 63:17 even the elect complain: "O Lord, why hast thou made us to err from thy ways, and hardened our heart not to fear thee? Return, for thy servants' sake, the tribes of thine inheritance," etc. Now, the temptation with which he deeply blinds and hardens certain ones is especially applied to the rejected who are vessels of wrath, prepared for destruction, "whom God shows and makes known to declare his wrath and power" [Rom. 9:22].

[fol. 66ʳ.44] These things seem hard to very many, because they cannot see how it is fitting for God to be angered by sins and to punish them, and yet testify concerning him that he hardens and stiffens some against obeying his word, and fleeing his vengeance. But these persons ought to ponder that God is so much greater than our reason, that it is no wonder, if its judgments are unable to see through how often the counsels of men, excellent in wisdom, seem absurd and unjust; when their consequence appears, we see how well framed they were. Undoubtedly, when we enter into the Lord's sanctuary and see God as he is, we will recognize nothing wicked, nothing absurd ever ordained by him. Meanwhile let us believe God to be, and we will not doubt him to be just, as he governs this whole system of the world (*mundi machinam*) in the most beautiful order and most fittingly, thus it will be easy for us to believe that he acts most equably with men. When therefore he testifies concerning himself in his scriptures, that he hardens and blinds, that is, leads certain ones into deadly temptations, we should believe and proclaim that this is both true and just.

[fol. 66ʳ.56] The fruit of this will be that the pious, to whom alone the Scriptures have been given for salvation, and ought to proclaim God's goodness [fol. 66ᵛ] toward them, will more greatly marvel at it, and more fervently will embrace it, because they ponder that they have been chosen by him from innumerable mortals, together with very few, and adopted into their number as long as he deigns to stir them up to good and to make clear how to know his will. This is the way they think: if God hardens, nobody can soften; on the other hand if he softens, nothing can harden; therefore there will be nothing set in me, nothing I may therefore do, if I sin; it will be the fault of God who hardens; when it pleases him he will soften me, etc. This will not be the thinking of men who fear God, to whom alone the scriptures speak. For faith in God, which knows him to be most righteous and best, does not allow such thoughts to steal in, but when one hears that others take Pharaoh's hardening in a false sense, one becomes more terrified, yet in such a way as at once to burn with wonderful rejoicing, pondering God's boundless goodness toward him who deigns to soften, not harden; to reveal, not blind. But the reprobate are offended not by this word of God alone, but to those who walk in darkness all things are an offense.

[fol. 66ᵛ.13] Then in like manner they ought to recognize and proclaim that it is a sin, punishable by God's righteous vengeance, for us either to ponder or desire anything contrary to his word, much less to devise by our own word or deed how by ourselves we can do nothing but sin, and the Lord himself leads us into temptation, and causes us to stray from his paths. This indeed not only the law comprised in the scriptures, but also which is engraved upon our hearts, proves. Created by the best Creator, we ought to be good, and ought duly to put ourselves under his will, but if it is lacking in us, surely this is sin, and not to be borne by the best Creator in his creation. If then we are unable to enter into the reason why God hardens, and delivers over to a reprobate sense, and yet punishes it as sin, let us nevertheless exclaim with Paul: "O depth of the riches both of the wisdom and knowledge of God! How unsearchable are his judgments and his ways past finding out!" etc. [Rom. 11:33]. Likewise, it is not known by us what happens when scripture testifies that God works all things in all, yet all our works at least have depravity attached to them, if they are not total depravity. These mysteries are by no means to be revealed to us in this age; if we know God and ourselves, we will ascribe to God glory in all things, but to ourselves confusion; all things in us insofar as they are of God are just and holy; but insofar as they are of us, we shall both acknowledge and confess them to be sin and iniquity.

[fol. 66ᵛ.29] Finally, these words: "I do not desire the death of the ungodly, or that one may die, but rather that he may repent and live" [Ezek. 18:23]. God desires that all men be saved and come to the knowledge of truth [cf. I Tim. 1:15, and similar passages]; they can by no means contend with these passages which we recall concerning hardening. Nonetheless it is an undoubted truth that God has rejected some, and hardened them and blinded them, as vessels of wrath prepared for destruction, something abundantly attested daily; therefore the fact that he says he does not will the death of an impious and dying man, but prefers that he repent and live, is to be understood concerning those whom he has chosen to the end that they repent and live, to whom the prophet chiefly spoke. "For he said to Pharaoh: I have raised you up, for the very purpose of showing my power in you, so that my name may be proclaimed in all the earth" [Ex. 9:16; Rom. 9:17]. He had hardened him just as he is wont to harden any rejected ones that they may not at all repent and live, but rather persist in their obstinacy, in their impiety, and perish, that in this he may magnify his power in the whole earth. To all he says: let it be just as if he had said, from all a few, or there is no race of men in which he does not also have his own. For frequently "all" in scripture is understood for "very many" or "anyone."

[fol. 66ᵛ.48] Concerning the temptations, therefore, into which God leads his own, the Christian should think as follows: the Lord leads his own into temptation when he puts their faith to the proof by adversity and examines it; we shall not at all fail to pray against being led into temptation, but rather when we are proved by this sort of temptation, tempted we stand together and pray together with perfect faith. For he sometimes also leads into temptation and turns us over to Satan for a time, to turn us toward sinning; in this sort of temptation he led David, Peter and many other elect and beloved of his. Concerning this sort of temptation one understands that statement of Paul: "Look to yourself, lest you be tempted" [Gal. 6:1]. And again, this passage: "I sent that I might know your faith, for fear that somehow the tempter had tempted you and that our labor would be in vain" [1 Thess. 3:5]. Likewise [I Cor. 7:5]: ". . . but then come together again, lest Satan tempt you [fol. 67ʳ] through lack of self-control." And those who wish to grow rich, fall into temptation and into the net. Although the Lord does not lead his own into this temptation to sin, unless the lapsed, to their own advantage, are afterwards to pray that they pay better attention to their weakness, and live a more modest and careful life. Indeed Christ urged his apostles on the Mount of Olives to pray that the temptation be averted although he knew the Father was going to lead them into it, and yet was only to accommodate it to their salvation. For it is our task, never to fail to pray that our offense toward God be averted, that indeed with a godly heart, and loving God beyond all things, nothing more serious can happen, so long as God himself, out of his boundless goodness will cause it to yield to his own glory and our good.

[fol. 67ʳ.10] Finally, the Lord leads into temptation (and an unending one) certain ones whom he straightway turns over as captives to Satan, stubborn in impiety, that they are goats not sheep, vessels of wrath not vessels of grace, enemies of God not children of God. We ought to have confidence we are never to be led into this by God, namely our Father, who lists us, apart from repentance, in the number of his children, unless we do not call upon that Father with sure faith. Nor do we truly believe him to be our Father, if we do not have confidence that he will so persist eternally in being our heavenly Father, who indeed knows those children whom he chose as his portion before the foundations of the world were laid [cf. Eph. 1:4], before they had done anything good or evil; when he gave it to his Son to save, from whose hand no one can seize them [John 10:29] and he does not at all cast away those who come to him [John 6:37]. Consequently, those who once were Christ's must never be estranged from him. When therefore there is in the faith of the one praying confidence that he is a true child of God and belief that God will be his Father forever, far away should that fear be of his deadly temptation, into which he leads only the rejected ones in whom he has determined to show forth his power, not his mercy.

[fol. 67ʳ.23] From that temptation, moreover, whereby daily even the saints are captivated with sinning and offending the most kindly Father, we have rightly deserved for ourselves, dwelling in this world, and are bidden, to pray with vigils and fasts to him to avert it, inasmuch as our flesh is not only weak toward good but also a persistent inciter to evil. The devil also goes about like a roaring lion, continually seeking someone to devour [I Pet. 5:8]. Against this temptation, therefore, is this sixth petition of this prayer. "And lead us not into temptation," that is, do not give us over to Satan to compel us to offend against thee; that is, its only purpose is to keep us from sin.

[fol. 67ʳ.30] Finally, let me not pass over that statement of James [1:13f], "Let not anyone when tempted say he is tempted by God. For, as God cannot be tempted, so neither does he tempt anyone; but every man is tempted, when he is drawn away by his own lust, and enticed." This passage, I think, is to be understood as follows: let no one so make God the author of temptation as to transfer to him his own guilt, as if the sin which the impious are wont to commit ought to be imputed to him and not to the sinner. Otherwise from these passages and that of II Sam. 24:1 (concerning David incited by God to take a census of the people), then Isaiah ch. 63 and countless other passages, it is clear enough that scripture is not afraid to make God the author of temptation, who repeatedly leads even the elect into temptation, a temptation by which they certainly fall and sin. Nevertheless sin ought to be ascribed to those committing it and not at all to God who leads into temptation. God acted justly and holily when he led David into that temptation rashly to take a census of the people; David moreover by committing it most gravely sinned nonetheless, and was most justly punished. God is true, and no less true and good is the work of God in sin called, but as a defect of right reason for us it is called evil. To these scripture adds also that the defect is so ordained by God that something good may come of it, that not even because of this can any sin be ascribed to God, however much he lets Satan incite men to it.

[fol. 67ʳ.45] "But deliver us from the evil one." This phrase is not so much a separate petition, as some persons have reckoned it the seventh, as part of the previous one. For Satan is called the tempter for the reason that he tempted us and, especially doing this, strives to deflect us from a right faith in God; if then he does not succeed in it, for whom it is an offense in us, he rejoices to overwhelm us and torture us with outward evils, as we read he did against Job and the other saints. Accordingly, rightly praying, "lead us not into temptation," that is, do not leave us to Satan to drag us to sin, we add, "but deliver us from the evil one," that is, the devil as tempter (as Chrysostom rightly seems to interpret). For he goes about like a lion seeking someone to devour, as Peter says [I Pet. 5:8], and if he cannot persuade any heart to evil he rages all the more impotently against bodies, to see if through bodily torture he can drag the heart from the right path. From him we are then at last fully delivered, when we shall fully receive citizenship in the heavenly Jerusalem, when all groaning and sorrow are banished, and no more will be heard the voice of weeping, and the voice of shouting, but all things will be full of joy and exultation—a future Isaiah has foretold in various passages, as have also the rest of the prophets. As long therefore as Satan is as it were our tormenter, by whose ministry [fol. 67ᵛ] also God outwardly exercises us, so long has this prayer to avert bodily evils been included as the last petition. Not expressly indeed has it been put forward as a prayer for physical goods, because bodily hardships are not evil of themselves, and so to be prayed to be averted, just as necessities are always, while we dwell here, good and to be prayed for. Nay, they often work together for us unto salvation, so that if we are tempted by them, we are yet proved at the same time, and moved to piety, so that it would be absolutely impious to pray that they be averted, as has been stated above. Therefore, he did not teach us to pray, "throw off from us the hardships of the body," just as he teaches us to request: "give us this day our daily bread, but deliver us from the evil one," that is the devil, who in this intends evils against the body, that he may estrange the mind from God. But if the Lord did not permit to him the evils he inflicts, to us they would by no means be evil but good. When at last the Father delivers us completely from him, and utterly releases us from sins, there will also be an end to all outward affliction, as we have been promised through Christ, and we piously hope, that it will so come to pass, and also piously pray that it will at last happen to us.

[fol. 67ᵛ.13] By the word "evil" here (with Chrysostom) I understand the devil as tempter: besides the article τοῦ, the reason is that through an adversative conjunction "Lead us not into temptation" is joined to this petition: "but deliver us from the evil one." From this it is obviously clear, that the same thing is sought through both, namely in this sense: "Mayest thou not leave us to the lust of the tempter, but utterly free us from him, that he may have no right at all over us, which will be when there is nothing of sin left in us." For this reason the devil is called ὅπονηϱός, that is, evil, depraved, at Matt. ch. 13; I John ch. 2; Eph. ch. 6, and in many other places.

84   [fol. 67ᵛ.20] "That thine is the kingdom and power and glory forever." This conclusion, whether added by the Lord himself, or afterwards added by somebody or other, is godly and according to scripture. The heart of one who truly prays is so accustomed to break out into pondering the greatness of God and praise of him, which also increases for him in a measure his confidence that his prayer will be answered. It seems therefore in this sense to support the foregoing petitions. We have prayed that thou mayest reign and be glorified in us, and that thou mayest impart to those who ask of thee what also pertains to the present life; we have prayed that punishment be averted from those sins we daily commit, and from temptation whereby the evil one continually urges us to offend against thy majesty, from whom we have prayed at last to be utterly freed; now thine is the kingdom; whatever power this evil one has over us is nothing but violent and most wicked tyranny. Therefore, claim us that thou (as is fitting) mayest truly be recognized by us as our King and worshiped. "Thine is the power": it will therefore be easy for thee to cast out whatever of opposing power hinders our striving to do thy will. It will be done to thy glory: I ask only that thou powerfully free us to show forth and spread, and as a father institute and promote, what ought at last to fill the whole earth and obtain eternity, in order that when we have been reformed to thine image and will and purged and freed of sins and evils, everything that is ours may praise thee, proclaim and extol thee.

THE ACADEMIC DISCOURSE
Delivered by Nicolas Cop
on Assuming the Rectorship of the University
of Paris on 1 November 1533.

The document here printed is a revision of the English translation by Dale Cooper and F. L. Battles published in *Hartford Quarterly* 6. 1 (1965): 76-85. The discourse has survived in two copies, a full text in the Archives of the St. Thomas Church, Strasbourg; and a fragment in Geneva. Our translation is made from the Strasbourg text as edited by P. Barth and W. Niesel, *Opera Selecta* (1926), vol. 1, pp. 4-10; the Geneva fragment variants are incorporated in brackets in the text in italic type. While a final determination of the authorship of this document cannot be made here, our notes point out a number of significant parallels with Calvin's later writings.

     The question of sources also cannot be disposed of with finality. A. Lang, *Die Bekehrung Johannes Calvins* (1897), suggested that especially the first half of the address shows some dependence upon a sermon of Luther preached on the festival of All Saints of 1522 as translated into Latin by Martin Bucer and printed in Strasbourg in 1526. [For bibliographic details, see WA 10.3.XX-XXI, CLXVIII.] The remarks on the "Christian philosophy," Lang attributes to Erasmus's Preface to the third edition of his New Testament. Neither of these "sources" accounts for very much of the content of the discourse, as our notes indicate. Two other sources have been marked: the rather guarded diatribe against the Sophists of the Sorbonne and the remarks about Law and Gospel suggest a familiarity with Melanchthon's *Loci Communes* of 1521; and the author's exposition of "reward" [Matt. 5:12] within a theology of grace seems to be in touch with Martin Bucer's *Enarrationes Perpetuae in Evangelia* (1530), although he does not seem to draw other exegetical details on the Beatitudes from Bucer.

Something great, something far excelling[1] expression or even comprehension by mind or thought is the Christian Philosophy,[2] a philosophy divinely given by Christ to a man, to show forth the true and surest felicity. Through it alone do we understand and believe ourselves to be God's children. This philosophy by its inherent brilliance and excellence has eclipsed the whole wisdom of the world. As I see it, those who excel in this wisdom excel over the rest of mankind almost as much as men surpass brute beasts.[3] This is undoubtedly so, for these men grasp with the heart [mind] things far greater and more excellent than do the rest. It is indeed fitting that this kind of philosophy be wonderful and holy, for, to bring it to men God willed to become man; being immortal he willed to become mortal. In my opinion, I shall surely speak the truth when I say that God's love toward us can be shown in no greater way than by his leaving his Word with us. What relationship could be closer or more certain? If we acclaim and admire for their usefulness the art of disputation, natural science, ethics and the rest of the arts, then what can possibly be compared with this kind of philosophy, a philosophy that reveals what all the philosophers have long sought but never found—the will of God?[4] Which pardons sins by the grace of God alone? Which promises the Holy Spirit to all Christians, a Spirit who sanctifies the hearts of all and brings eternal life? What a man who fails to praise the pursuit would judge praiseworthy is beyond my comprehension. For if delight of mind and relief from all cares be sought, (elements which look to [and avail for] the living of a good and blessed life), the Christian Philosophy more than fills the bill. [p. 5] It reins in, as it were, the troubled motions of the mind. So great [therefore] is the glory and worth of the Gospel, I am extremely delighted with the opportunity given me of explaining it, and I further rejoice that my present office demands this [of me].

But in the midst of such a full and immense mass of detail, where shall our discourse begin and where end? Since the subject for discussion is obviously wider than I could cover in one speech, I will deal chiefly with that Gospel

1. In the first few lines of the discourse, the author rings the changes on the verb *praestare* (to excel) and its derivatives, the comparative adjective *praestantior* (more excellent), and the noun *praestantia* (excellence). For comparable uses of the noun *praestantia* see F. L. Battles, *A Concordance of Calvin: Institutes of the Christian Religion* (1972, 1978), *ad verbum*.

2. On the "Christian Philosophy," see Calvin, *Inst.* (1559), "Subject Matter," LCC 20.6f, n.8; also 3.7.1, n.1 (1539); *Institutes* (1536), p. 68, keyword, "philosophy." There is some evidence that Calvin occasionally used distinctive Erasmian forms of Scriptural verses, but by no means consistently (signalled here by E). Calvin's later exegesis of Matt. 5:1-12 in his *Commentary on the Gospel Harmony*, and in his Sermons, tends to contrast not two "philosophies," but pagan philosophy and the "school of Christ."

3. Cf. Cicero, *On the Nature of the Gods*, 2.58.145.

4. See *Inst.* (1559), 3.6.1; cf. 2.2.15; 1.8.1.

passage which is usually read in church on this day.[5] But before I begin, I desire that you, with me, may with burning prayers beseech Christ, best and greatest, who is the one true intercessor with the Father,[6] to illumine our minds with his life-giving Spirit; as he himself is the glory of the Father [*and the Author of all good*] so may our discourse honor Him, savor of Him, breathe Him, and point Him out to us. We shall pray He may flow into our hearts [*minds*] and deign to shower us with the dew of His spiritual [*heavenly*] grace. I have hopes we shall attain this if we greet the most blessed Virgin with that solemn salutation [*and by far the most beautiful of all*]: "Hail, full of grace!" [Luke 1:28].[7]

"Blessed are the poor in spirit"—Matt. 5[:3]

To begin with, we must earnestly search out what is the aim of this Gospel passage, and all the matters that ought to be related to it; all this will readily be understood by describing the Law and describing the Gospel and then comparing them.[8] Therefore, the [*good*] Gospel is the message, the salvation-bringing proclamation concerning Christ that he was sent by God the Father to bring assistance to all, and to procure eternal life. The Law is contained in [*acts by*] precepts, it threatens, it burdens, it promises no goodwill. The Gospel acts without threats, it does not drive one on by precepts, but rather teaches us about the supreme goodwill of God toward us. Let whoever therefore is desirous of having a plain and honest understanding of the Gospel, test everything by the above descriptions [*the description of the Law and the Gospel*]. Those who do not follow this method of treatment will never be adequately versed in the Philosophy of Christ [*Christian philosophy*]. This is the difficulty those most wretched Sophists[9] have

5. In the Roman Lectionary the Gospel reading for the Feast of All Saints was Matt. 5:1-12.

6. Heb. 7:25. Cf. *Inst.* (1536), p. 70.

7. In *Sermons sur l'Harmonie Evangélique*, Sermon 6 (Luke 1:26-30) [OC 24.63], Calvin calls this verse (Luke 1:28) "the sum of the Gospel," inasmuch as it is intended not exclusively for the Virgin but "for the instruction of all God's children in order that they may recognize how God has taken pity on them, to draw them back from death's confusion where they were, and lead them to the hope of life, and of eternal salvation." Later he carefully distinguishes this from the superstitious development of the Romish "Ave Maria." In this later sermon is obviously the elaboration of what could only be hinted at in the Rectorial Address!

8. On Law/Gospel, cf. *Inst.*, 2.11.10.

9. The following strictures on the Sorbonne theologians (= *Sophistae*) seem to stem from Melanchthon, *LC* (1521), passim. By the mere use of this opprobrious epithet, Cop and his co-worker were thrust at once into the feud that had been raging since 1521 between the Paris Faculty of Theology and the Lutherans. The 1521 edition of the *Loci Communes* is loaded with such phrases as "Sophists," "stupid Scholastics," "hypocritical theologians," "so-called doctors of theology," "godless Sophist professors of theology," "Sophistic hypocrisy," etc. No wonder the Paris theologians identified the new rector and his young theological counsellor with the circle of religious dissent! Calvin was to use the epithet frequently in later writings.

run into; they argue interminably over goat's wool,[10] they quarrel, they dispute, they discuss (but nothing about faith, nothing about the love of God [*nothing about forgiveness of sins, nothing about grace* [p. 6] *nothing about justification*] nothing about true works). Or if they do discuss rightly they vilify and contaminate everything, and enclose it within their own sophistical laws. I beg of you all here present never to sit back and accept these heresies, these insults against God.

But let us go back to that point from which our discourse has digressed. We must see to it that we not regard Christ as having departed from the norm of the Gospel in this particular passage. For he seems to act through precepts [*and*] to bid us be poor [*in spirit*], gentle, pure in heart, and peacemakers. Why, he even sets before us [*promises us*] a reward, though one ought never be swayed by gifts, but should freely pay attention to Christ; seek after God's glory alone; do nothing out of fear of punishment or of hell. These are the thoughts of men who, so to speak, read the divine philosophy through a net,[11] who sample it with their upper lip,[12] but do nothing to advance the Gospel; to use Paul's words, "thinking themselves to be wise, they have become stupid" [Rom. 1:22]. Rather, the Gospel actually dispels the thickest of darkness and frees us from blindness so that he who could at one time see only with physical eyes may now also open the eyes of his mind. For, the precepts not clearly enough written for Moses, it now teaches more clearly[13] [*in this passage*]. Consequently, this Gospel does not impose any command, but rather [*solely*] reveals God's goodness, his mercy and benefits.

Do not be startled that[14] he equates "gifts" with the term "reward":[15] "Rejoice," he says, "because your *reward* is great in heaven" [Matt. 5:12, Vg]. Give me your full attention for a few moments. God's benefits are very frequently signified by the term "reward," even though they come to us for an altogether different reason—because of the grace of God alone, of course, and not because of our own virtues or worth. But while our obligations far outstrip our virtues, they also make satisfaction for them, and are denominated by the term "reward."

10. Horace, *Epist.*, 1.18.15; see Erasmus, *Adagia*, 1.3.53.

11. Cicero, *De oratore*, 1.35.162; see Erasmus, *Adagia*, 3.1.49.

12. Erasmus, *Adagia*, 1.9.92f; cf. Sen., *Epist.*, 10.3.

13. Cf. *Inst.* (1536), p. 29, keyword "notion," and note to Melanchthon, *LC* (1521) [Eng. tr., LCC 19.74].

14. End of Geneva fragment.

15. Cf. Luther, Sermon 58, on All Saints' Day [1 Nov. 1522], WA 10.3.400.19ff. On the interchangeability, for Calvin, of *praemium* (gift), *merces* (reward), and *retributio* (recompense) see *Inst.* (1536), p. 41, keyword "recompense." Also: *Harmonia Evangelica*, Matt. 5:12/Luke 6:23 [OC 23.165]; *Sermons sur l'Harmonie Evangélique*, Sermon 65 (Matt. 5:12) [OC 24.820], and other contexts in Calvin's writings. A theology of grace must thus radically view God's "reward" to man.

If I may employ a comparison[16] at this point it will make the whole matter much clearer: A son of the family[17] strives with all his might to please his father, and pays back all his obligations toward his father; but these actions are not great enough to merit the inheritance, which the son nonetheless receives. Consequently, one may call this a "reward," not because it is owed, but because it more than makes up for the obligation of the son toward the father. Thus is "reward" very commonly employed in the Scriptures.[18]

Who would otherwise understand eternal life as a "payment"? Who could be so senseless as to think and assert that eternal life is a repayment for our good deeds, or that our good deeds are worthy of eternal life? Let us all acknowledge then [p. 7] that in this particular passage of the Gospel (and in all the others as well) Christ is setting before our eyes his grace and his kindness; and is rightly interpreting Moses' teaching as to how the Law is to be understood.[19]

But let us listen to Matthew: "When he had seen the crowds, Jesus climbed the mountain, and after he had sat down, his disciples approached him; and he opened his mouth and taught them saying: 'Blessed are the poor in spirit' " [Matt. 5:1-3]. Listen, I beg of you, O Christian men, and meditate upon the extraordinary benefit of God toward us. He does not allow us to drowse any longer in darkness, but rouses us from our deep sleep; he smoothes out and perfects the rough and imperfect in us. A commandment was given to the ancients that they were to have no foreign gods [Ex. 20:3]. Since men dwelt in

16. A similar comparison is to be found in Bucer, *EN*, I [fol. 44ʳ.11-13], on Matt. 5:12: "Just as a father says to his little son: 'Pay close attention. You will receive a splendid reward from me, that is, new clothes, or something else.' Now this clothing is a reward and yet is not a reward. It is a reward because it follows work; it is not a reward because that work has not followed it but is contingent upon the free gift of the father unless that work is perfect."

17. Latin: *filius familias*. The archaic classical genitive in *-as*, used in the terms *paterfamilias*, *materfamilias*, etc., here connotes the absolute paternal control over the Roman family reflected in Roman law. It would seem, if Calvin be the author of this piece, that he is here mingling his legal knowledge with a reminiscence of the parable of the prodigal son.

18. *Merces* is the Vulgate rendering for μισθός, used in the New Testament in the sense of payment for work done, as reward (or punishment), recompense (usually by God) for "the moral quality of an action." Arndt-Gingrich, *Lexicon*, μισθός, q.v. Cf. Bucer, *EN*, I [fol. 44ʳ.19ff] (Matt. 5:12), with discussion of "reward" in such Old Testament passages as Gen. 15:1, Jer. 31:16, Ps. 127:3. Bucer concludes: "From these passages it is abundantly clear that 'reward' in the Scriptures denotes whatever benefits we receive from the Lord."

19. Here, in germ, is the whole exegetical basis of Calvin's handling of the decalogue: Jesus Christ in the Sermon on the Mount "interiorizes" and interprets according to the original lawgiver's intention the Ten Commandments. See *Inst.* (1559), 2.7-8. Cf. Luther, Sermon 58 [WA 10.3.401.33ff], correlating the Ten Commandments with the eight Beatitudes.

the deepest ignorance and were so deficient spiritually, they decided they must so understand idols as not to take up or worship anything as God [Ex. 20:4-5]. Now we ought not consider this as something altogether wicked. "For the idols of the nations are silver and gold, the work of men's hands; they have mouths . . . and will not speak," etc. [Ps. 135:15f, Vg 134:15f].[20] Even if they be the truest and most certain of idols, they still do not give satisfaction. The Lord desires a heart committed to no thing, to no created object; he declares that with a heart free and unattached to things man must give access to Him alone, that nothing is to be ascribed to human powers. He presses us to belittle all human good and have no concern for human honors. But I fear we prefer the world to God, and let flesh overcome the spirit. Who of us does not love to outrank his fellows? Who, in order to be esteemed among men, is not concentrating for the wrong reason on what I have called the "divine philosophy"? Who does not pant after human goods? Who does not prefer to please men with his silly trifles rather than to please God with the truth of the Gospel? O the monstrous stupidity of men, O the vainglory! Are we blind to the fact that "God searches hearts and reins" [Ps. 7:10; Rev. 2:23] or are we unaware that He "can destroy the soul utterly and send it to hell" [Matt. 10:28]? O brutish and foolish men, who, like the brute beasts, so stupidly occupy themselves only with the present. Or again, do we not know, brethren, that we shall all stand before the judgment-seat of Christ?[21] If we clearly understood it, we would give our energies to godliness[22] alone, to the Spirit alone. We would take joy in being disciplined by God with calamity, sickness, affliction and tribulation [cf. Rom. 8:35]. For Christ calls those blessed who mourn [Matt. 5:4], who despair of their own abilities, and yet who aspire to an upright life, attempt all things, press every nerve to be virtuous, and to draw others to embrace a better life and righteousness. But these are the very ones "who hunger and thirst after righteousness" [Matt. 5:6]. With it, if the Word of God cannot deceive us, they shall be filled.

And no wonder, seeing that the Gospel of God assures their consciences on forgiveness of sins, on the love of God, as to whether they have been accepted by God. Nothing more delightful, nothing better can happen to a Christian than this. Those who do not comprehend this must be living in the deepest error. Indeed what worship, what godliness, what religion can exist while the conscience doubts?[23] So Paul, in his Letter to the Romans, in order to dispel every

---

20. On idols, see *Inst.* (1536), pp. 19ff. Cf. Luther, Sermon 58 [WA 10.3.402.14ff], specifically linking the First Commandment with the First Beatitude.

21. See Rom. 14:10. Cf. the pleas of the minister and the layman before the divine judgment-seat in Calvin's *Reply to Sadolet* [Eng. tr., LCC 21.246ff, 250ff].

22. *Pietas* ("godliness") is a key word in Calvin's theology. In his "Letter to the Reader" (which introduces the *Institutes* of 1559) he announces his purpose: "I have no other purpose than to benefit the church by maintaining the true doctrine of godliness."

23. Cf. *Inst.* (1536), pp. 151f, and Melanchthon, *LC* (1521), 7 [Eng. tr., LCC 19.113].

doubt from their consciences, contends by a host of arguments that reconciliation and justification do not depend on our own worth or merits. Quoting from the Psalms [Ps. 32:1-2], he says, "Blessed are those whose iniquities have been forgiven, and whose sins covered; blessed is the man against whom the Lord has not reckoned his sin" [cf. Rom. 4:8]. Or again, after a long consideration of the righteousness of God, he asks, "Where, then, is your boasting? It has been shut out. On what principle? Of works? No, but rather through the principle of faith: for we hold that a man is justified by faith without works of the law" [Rom. 3:27f Vg]. But what could be more clearly stated than the words he wrote in the beginning of Chapter IV: "What then shall we say: Did Abraham discover our Father according to the flesh? For if he were justified by works, he has something to boast about, but not in the presence of God; for what does the Scripture say? 'Abraham believed God and it was reckoned to him as righteousness' " [Rom. 4:1-3 Vg]. And so on these grounds Paul argues that we are righteous because of Christ [cf. Rom. 4:23f]. And not without good reason. For otherwise if in any way the matter depended upon the worth of our works, moral or ceremonial, it would be completely unsure. The Law mentions the mercy of God, but only on a definite condition: provided the Law be fulfilled. The Gospel freely offers forgiveness of sins and justification. We have in fact not been accepted by God because we fulfill the Law's demands, but only because of the promise of Christ; if a man doubts this promise, he cannot live a godly life, and is preparing himself for the fire of hell. Indeed, if the Lord has concerned himself with the bodily vices of those who believe, he will forgive the sins of only those who have believed. Of all living creatures, therefore, we are the most miserable if we are uncertain whether God will forgive our sins [cf. I Cor. 15:19]. I am well aware that animal man does not understand whether he is worthy of either love or hate [Eccl. 9:1b].[24] "Animal man," in Paul's words, "does not receive the things of God, but the spiritual man discerns and perceives all things" [I Cor. 2:14ff]. All who deny this turn the whole of the Gospel upside down; they utterly bury Christ, and destroy all true worship of God, for God cannot be worshiped where doubt is present. The Gospel has led me to this belief: No greater evil could befall the Christian than doubt. And if at any time it does oppress and torment us, our cry ought to be: "Lord, help our unbelief!" [Matt. 5:3] and "those who hunger and thirst after righteousness" [v. 6] [p. 9] despair over their own abilities, these are nevertheless confident of the grace of God, of the forgiveness of sins, and of justification.[25]

But let us return to the Gospel. "Blessed are the peacemakers for they shall be called the children of God" [Matt. 5:9]. O what a worthy endeavor in

24. Cf. *Inst.* (1559), 3.2.38.

25. Certainty of salvation is a characteristic mark of the Pauline-Augustinian revival of the 16th century Reformation, from Luther onward. Calvin reflects on it in many places, e.g., in the Epistle Dedicatory to Francis I, *Inst.* (1559) [Eng. tr., LCC 20.13].

which all Christians are engaged! What is better than peace, than tranquility? If the Gentiles who knew not God made a peace so great that with the highest diligence they even provided for the building of a temple in its honor,[26] how much more ought the Christian man to work for the preservation of peace, and the renewal of concord among the discordant! The Gentiles seek after peace in order to live in tranquility; Christians, on the other hand, knowing they will be sons of God, look forward to things far greater and better. These work chiefly toward the attainment of spiritual peace, a peace without which the peace of the world is vain and of no consequence. The peace of the world consists in the removing of external evils [cf. John 14:27]; it lies in outwardly good things, with a friendly neighbor, but meanwhile the root of the discord which makes us enemies toward God still remains. Where there is enmity against God, how can the peace of the world long endure? Blessed therefore are they who set men's minds at peace,[27] who remove all dissensions from the church, temper all things with the word of truth, and never act by threats. For how can those who do not believe the word of God be moved to do so by torture? Should we not rather imitate Christ, our supreme leader who, though he could utterly have destroyed all the Gentiles and Jews, preferred to allure them by His word? O would that in this unhappy age of ours we might use the Word rather than the sword [cf. Matt. 10:34] in mending peace in the Church! For obviously either Satan is not overcome, or he is overcome by the Word of God. "When a strong man, fully armed, guards his house" [Luke 11:21] etc. But Christ is that "stronger one," not human reason, not the afflictions of men.[28] Men in perpetual disagreement are followers not so much of Christ as of those utterly depraved Pharisees. Who does not know that Christ demands a free, kind, and ready heart? "Blessed are the peacemakers" [Matt. 5:9] then who, by the word of truth reconcile those in disagreement.

More and more "blessed are they who suffer persecution for the sake of righteousness" [Matt. 5:10]. The Romans praise their Regulus,[29] a man who bore the ultimate and by far the most wretched of all torture to keep faith. The Athenians could not admire their staunch Socrates[30] enough for not hesitating

---

26. On the temple to Peace, see Suetonius, *Lives of the Caesars*, Vespasian, 9; also, Josephus, *Jewish War*, 7.5.7. After Titus's victory over the Jews, with the fall of Jerusalem in AD 70, and a defeat of the Germans at the same time, Vespasian had built at Rome with great speed, a temple dedicated to the Goddess Pax.

27. Cf. *Psychopannychia* (1534/5) [Eng. tr., T&T 3:435]; peace = tranquility of conscience.

28. Cf. Luke 11:22. The source of this rejected allegorization (if it ever was an interpretation and not merely a rhetorical heightening of his argument by Calvin) has not been determined.

29. On Atilius Regulus, see *Inst.* (1559), 2.4.8, n. 15. The author has obviously drawn this from Augustine, *City of God*, 1.15. The reference was previously used by Calvin in his *Commentary on Seneca's De Clementia* (1532), 1.25, p. 321.

30. Cf. *Inst.* (1559), 3.24.10.

to die after he had been charged in court with slighting the heathen gods. But who would adjudge such men blessed, men who knew nothing about the righteousness of God, and who were seeking their own glory, not God's glory.[31] There is no end to those who, because of the slander against good men or the insults against princes, suffer persecution; but there is no [Scriptural] passage in which God calls them blessed. "Blessed are they who" while seeking the righteousness of God "suffer persecution" [Matt. 5:10]. Indeed they seek God's righteousness who cling to his Word, despise all the silly trifles and dreams of men, and [p. 10] depart not a finger's breadth[32] from the Gospel in their speech. It is they who follow faithfully that passage from Paul: "Even if we or an angel from heaven should preach to you a Gospel other than the one we have preached to you, let him be accursed; as we have said before, I now say to you: If anyone preaches to you a Gospel other than what you received, let him be accursed" [Gal. 1:8f]. Happy and joyous must those be who suffer persecution on these charges. And may we not be so concerned about our prestige and our name that we become rather cold in our worship of God, in the setting forth of his will, and in the proclamation of truth.

"Blessed will you be," he says, "when men hurl insults at you, and reproach you, and say all evil against you falsely, for my sake" [Matt. 5:11]. When, then, do we conceal the truth rather than speak it out boldly? Is it right to please men rather than God [I Thess. 2:4; cf. Acts 4:19; Gal. 1:10]; to fear those who can destroy the body, but not the soul [Matt. 10:28; Luke 12:4f]? O the ingratitude of mankind which will not bear the slightest affliction in the name of him who died for the sins of all, him whose blood has freed us from eternal death and the shackles of Satan! The world and the wicked are wont to label as heretics, imposters, seducers and evil-speakers those who strive purely and sincerely to penetrate the minds of believers with the Gospel. "They think they are offering service to God" [John 16:2].[33] But happy and blessed are they who endure all this with composure, giving thanks to God in the midst of affliction and bravely bearing calamities. "Rejoice," he says, "for your reward is great in heaven" [Matt. 5:12].[34]

Onward then, O Christians. With our every muscle let us strive to attain this great bliss. May God, who begets faith, hope and love in all by his Word, breathe upon us with his favor and open our minds to believe the Gospel. And

---

31. On the blessedness of the righteous heathen, Calvin and Zwingli were in disagreement. Cf. Zwingli, *Exposition of the Faith*, 12. "Eternal Life" [Eng. tr., LCC 24.275f], and Calvin, *Inst.* (1559), 2.3.4; also 2.2.17, n. 64. Calvin's view reflects more closely that of Augustine, *City of God*, 2.17,23; 3.17.

32. Erasmus, *Adagia*, 1.5.6. Cf. Calvin, *Inst.* (1559), 3.15.8, n. 16a; 3.19.13, n. 18a; 4.18.12, n. 21a.

33. This verse is used in exactly the same way at *Inst.* (1559), 4.2.6.

34. The fate of the true "evangelicals" at the world's hands, here briefly sketched, is eloquently set forth in Calvin's Epistle Dedicatory to Francis I.

may we truly know that there is one God who alone must be served from the heart, and in whose name we must suffer and bear all. "May he fill us with all joy and peace in believing so that by the power of the Holy Spirit we may overcome in hope" [Rom. 15:13] and at last celebrate an everlasting victory in heaven. Amen.

John Calvin's Latin Preface
to Olivétan's French Bible (1535)

The Bible is that of Pierre Robert Olivétan (Olivetanus): *La Bible Qui est toute la Saincte escripture* . . . (Neuchâtel: Pierre de Wingle, 1535). The original text may be found in OC 9.787-790. For a complete description, and notice of locations, of this and all fifteenth and sixteenth century French Bibles, see: Bettye Thomas Chambers, *Bibliography of French Bibles* (Genève: Droz, 1983). Whereas Calvin's French preface to the New Testament was reprinted in all subsequent revisions of this Bible, this Latin preface appeared only in the 1535 edition. Efforts to obtain a license to print a "French Bible" in Geneva began in late 1532 and continued through the spring of 1533. Pierre de Wingle was to be the printer, but despite the assistance of Bern, he was exiled to Neuchâtel where (actually in Serriers, a small village outside Neuchâtel) the Bible emerged in May 1535. Calvin refers to this struggle in his preface. For documentation, see Herminjard, 2. no. 391 and 393; 3. no. 410.

John Calvin
To Emperors, Kings, Princes And
To All Peoples Subject to Christ's Rule,
Greeting

It was determined some time ago—not without reason or public benefit—that all new books must obtain a privilege [to be published]. If only today no book were to appear unless adorned with its privilege. [If only that privilege] were granted neither gratuitously nor by a monetary fee benefiting the prince by whom it was rashly recommended for the printer's profit, but that good and weighty testimony was proclaimed that [the book] truly was worthy to see the light and for human eyes. For this [is] proper to restrain that mad passion to write something[1] which continually produces for us so many swarms of books with no

1. Cf. Juvenal, *Sat.*, 8.50.

measure, no delight, no shame. Further, not a few so burn with the stupid desire for a name that they prefer to become notorious for some outrage or other rather than to remain unknown. Now with their immoderate self-serving they evilly counsel princes of republics who not only permit good [or] bad books to be published, but who have approved even the worst by their decision.

This present sacred work, which is neither newly born nor done by a man, hardly seems for that reason to require the testimony of men. And, obviously, it would have been a most wicked arrangement if the work were to have such paltry praises that nothing less than its very dignity were compromised. Therefore, the oracle and eternal truth of the Highest King, Lord of heaven, earth, and the sea, and King of Kings is the guarantor of the privileges [to publish it]. This magnificently and splendidly commends it to us. This commands that it be publicly and privately received with the highest reverence by all peoples, times, and classes. Here is an edict to which all men as one ought to be obedient.

But the ungodly voices of some are heard, shouting that it is a shameful thing to publish these divine mysteries among the simple common people. For among those who have spent their entire life [studying the mysteries], in general aided by the considerable support of innate ability and learning—yet in mid-life have often failed—few or perhaps none at all, are to be found who have attained their ultimate goal. How then, they ask, can these poor illiterates comprehend such things, untutored as they are in all liberal arts, and (if practice is involved) ignorant of all things?

But since the Lord has chosen prophets for Himself from the ranks of shepherds, apostles from the boats of fishermen, why should He not even now deign to choose like disciples? Indeed, if for these Rabbis (whose minds are so great and intrepid) learning with common and uneducated people is a shameful fate, how much more disgraceful it is to learn from such teachers who have in no respect surpassed the meanest persons except in what they have been taught by the Lord. Nor are these things said by me to the end that I would take away the calling[2] of teaching and learning from the church—provided that it is compelled to recognize the splendid goodness of God, [and] as long as it is properly instructed by prophets, doctors, and interpreters who have been sent by Him.

But I desire only this, that the faithful people be permitted to hear their God speaking and to learn from [Him] teaching. Seeing that He wills to be known by the least to the greatest; since all are promised to be God-taught [Is. 29:9]; since He confesses as yet always to be working among His own, whom He calls "weaned from milk, torn from the breasts" [Is. 28:9]; since He gives wisdom to children [Matt. 11:25], and directs that the gospel be preached to the poor [Matt. 11:5]. When, therefore, we see that there are people from all classes who are making progress in God's school, we acknowledge His truth which promised a pouring forth of His spirit on all flesh [Joel 2:28; Acts 2:17].

They [the above Rabbis] rage against this and are indignant. What is this

2. "ordinem"

but to reproach God for His bounty? Oh, if they had lived in that age when Philip had four prophesying daughters [Acts 21:9], how shamefully would they have carried them off? unless perhaps they had accepted them in a like shameful manner. But when indeed they strongly despise the word of God as often as they please, why do they not at least imitate the example of the Fathers to whom they pretend to be so deferential? Jerome did not disdain mere women as partners in his studies. Chrysostom and Augustine—when do they not urge the common people to this study—how frequently [don't] they insist that what they hear in church they should apply in [their] homes? Why is it that Chrysostom contends that the reading of holy scripture is more necessary for common people than for monks? That tossed about by various waves of care and business, they are immediately dashed into the shipwreck of this age unless they hold on to this anchor? Pamphilius the Martyr, who always had sacred codices ready at home to pass out to both men and women, was praised by Eusebius.

Nor was it only in that purer age, but for many years afterward this liberty prevailed—until at length the crowd, corrupted and immersed in its own lusts, out of its very own faithlessness and laziness, abandoned this kind of study. Now where it is beginning to be recovered, there emerges this tyranny which prohibits people access to the common good. It truly is just as if someone denied [men] fire and water and the common elements because it did not seem they were using them. Who would think there would be such cruelty in pastors (for pastors they wish to be considered and called) that do not tremble forcibly to snatch the fodder of life from the throats of sheep?

But there is a danger they say, that the crowd may fall into error out of the common man's simplemindedness, may corrupt things not understood, and thus swallow poison for food. How shamefully they reason at this point! The gospel is the smell of death unto death for those who die [II Cor. 2:16], for the Jews a stumbling-block, for the Greeks foolishness [I Cor. 1:23], therefore let it not be read, not be heard. Yet it is the power of God unto salvation for all believers, both Jew and Greek [I Cor. 1:18; 1:24, conflated]. Christ is the stone of stumbling on which many stumble, and by which many are shattered; therefore may Christ not be. But he is eternal life, the only way to the Father, and truth [John 14:6]. When they see these things not to be substantial enough, they add amidst the many heresies with which the world is now troubled, that it is better for people to be restrained by obedience than by learning. But then also all were burning with heresies when those to whom I referred, both Chrysostom and Augustine, were sharply urging their people to the study of heavenly doctrine. Certainly they were fortifying them against heresies with such medicine, equipping them with such arms.

Finally, they [the Rabbis] desperately complain that the crowd becomes haughty and furious as soon as it has grasped any taste of sacred letters. However, they say it is "to be haughty" not to hang from their lips, and not to adore as if from an accomplished oracle whatever they have thought up in their reveries.

375

Away, away with those tears.[3] Thus formerly the Roman Pontiff and his priestlings scarcely restrained their hands from him who wrote history for the people, the determination of which they wished to keep in their own power. In this way, since they are unable "to sell their smoke"[4] to the people except in darkness, it is no wonder that they cannot bear this light to be kindled. Indeed, this is worst to them to have their mysteries, in which there are more obscenities than either in the rites of the Goddess of Fertility, or even in the Bacchanals themselves, so openly revealed and exposed to ridicule.

Others, who wish to seem slightly more impartial, plead merely that the common people without distinction ought to be satisfied with that commonly used [i.e., Vulgate]. These versions which not only measure up to accuracy of translation but also to appropriate style, ought rather to be found in the libraries of the learned than to fall indiscriminately into the hands of the untutored, of whom, as they say, there are very few who can comprehend fully, but very many who may be offended by novelty. I do not see what they are driving at except that they alone wish to be wise. For when they deny there to be any use for a purer translation than what is now considered utterly corrupted in so many passages, they are plainly abusive toward the Holy Spirit, whose gift Paul declares to be the interpretation of tongues [I Cor. 12:10], and desires to be used for the edification of the church. If they despise the gift itself, they are sacrilegious; if they wish it to be suppressed so as not to serve many, they are envious and wicked. Novelty, indeed, I admit to be quite detestable, for many are the bellies who would not tolerate eating acorns even when fruit is found. Only that novelty deserves to be detested which of a certainty is not worth pursuing or adopting; but it is the most shameful ingratitude which digs up buried truth without embracing it with all favor. But if men's barbarity is such that they even badly use benefits themselves it is better to ignore disfavor and any sort of hatred, so that thanks to them truth may not be lost. Although I am unconcerned about people who, previously starving, regard such feasts longingly, far be it from me to shudder at novelty. But they need this excuse for their ill-will, [they] for whom it is not enough to luxuriate in such abundant treasures, but they even deny the people a coin struck with a better impression,[5] and even [begrudge them] their safe and unbroken treasures.

I speak more sparingly of the translator, lest I seem to be doing something for the sake of the kinship which exists between us, or for the sake of our old friendship. Nevertheless, I will say (something I would even dare promise on my word; nor could it be denied even by envy) that he is a man not slow in genius, not devoid of erudition. To the degree that he was able to exert himself with industry, zeal and earnestness he gained the highest trust in this office of translating. Nevertheless, I do not doubt there are certain things which, either

---

3. Terence, *Aud.*, 1.1.99
4. *Institutes* (1559), 4.16.11
5. Cf. *Calvin's Commentary on Seneca's De Clementia*, 145.1 (Battles-Hugo, p. 351).

because of the variety of critics, or because in a long work drowsiness steals in, will not please everybody. But I urge the readers, if anything of this sort happens, not to chew, rend and rail at a man well deserving of sacred letters, rather than moderately to admonish him for his slip. This generosity befits both Christian piety and liberal teaching; nor will they [the readers] be ungrateful to our Robert, who, distinguished by many other gifts, yet restrains himself with modesty. Yet such is that modesty, rather than immodest shame, that he was almost diverted from undertaking this very great holy labor, except that, overcome by the urging, and even the importunity of those holy men and witnesses of the unconquered word, Chusemeth and Chlorotes [Farel and Viret],[6] he was finally compelled to put his hand [to the task]. Those, indeed, who can in no way be restrained from depravity of tongue, will remember the art of slander to be very easy, if anyone wishes to contend with it, and which mere women practice on the street better than rhetoricians in the schools. Nor, indeed, is that [saying] of the comic poet less [apt]: "Ill reputed will they in turn be for their slander." They have [in Robert] a man whom they can exasperate with impunity, to the degree that retaliation relates to impudence. But I warn them not to expect great praise for their poisoned eloquence. As true as common is that expression: "Men are ready to criticize everything, but not to strive to excel the same." Farewell.

6. For the identification of these pseudonyms see: Herminjard, 3.290n, and OC 10.790.

INDEX OF BIBLICAL REFERENCES

380

COMPARATIVE TABLE OF 1536 AND 1559 INSTITUTES

The 1559 references are by book, chapter and section; the 1536 references are by page reference to the present translation. Cross-references include both substantial verbatim or near-verbatim parallel passages and also parallels obscured to varying degrees by Calvin's revision in the Latin editions of 1539–1559. For details see OS vols. 1, 3-5; also textual notes to the facsimile edition of the *Institution* of 1536 (Pittsburgh, 1972).

1559	1536	1559	1536	1559	1536	1559	1536
1.1.1	15	2.7.4	30	2.8.31	23	2.14.7	53
1.2.1	15	2.7.5	30	2.8.32	24	2.14.8	53
1.11.7	21	2.7.6	35	2.8.33	24	2.15.2	54
1.11.8	20	2.7.7	17	2.8.34	24	2.15.5	54
1.11.9	20	2.7.8	35	2.8.35	25	2.15.6	54
1.11.10	20	2.7.10	36	2.8.37	25	2.16.1	49
1.11.13	21	2.7.12	36	2.8.39	25		54
1.13.2	45	2.7.14	36	2.8.41	25	2.16.5	49
1.13.3	45	2.8.1	16	2.8.42	26		55
	47	2.8.2	16	2.8.44	26	2.16.6	55
1.13.4	47		17	2.8.45	26	2.16.7	49
1.13.5	48	2.8.3	17	2.8.46	26	2.16.9	55
1.13.9	45	2.8.4f	17		27	2.16.10	55
1.13.14	57	2.8.6	29	2.8.47	26	2.16.11	55
1.13.16	44	2.8.7	29	2.8.48	26	2.16.13	50
1.13.17	45	2.8.11	18	2.8.49	27		56
1.13.18	45	2.8.12	19	2.8.54	28	2.16.15	56
1.13.19	45		25	2.8.55	30	2.16.16	56
1.13.20	45	2.8.13	19	2.8.56	29	2.16.17	50
1.13.21	44	2.8.15	19		30		56
1.13.24	·50		22	2.8.57	30	2.16.18	42
1.15.3	15	2.8.17f	19	2.12.1	50	2.16.19	57
1.15.4	15	2.8.18	21	2.12.2	51	3.1	57
1.16.1	49	2.8.22	22	2.12.3	51	3.2.1	42
1.16.3	49	2.8.23	22	2.14.1	52		49
1.17.2	49	2.8.25	22	2.14.2	52	3.2.6	43
1.18.1	47	2.8.26	22		53	3.2.8	65
2.1.5	16	2.8.27	22	2.14.3	52	3.2.9	42
2.1.8	97	2.8.28	23	2.14.4	54		66
2.4.1-5	46	2.8.29	23	2.14.6	50	3.2.10	42
2.7.3	30	2.8.30	23			3.2.16	43

4.10.26	204	4.15.6	96	4.18.1	115	4.19.29	169
4.10.27	204		98	4.18.2	115	4.19.30	169
4.10.28	205	4.15.7	96	4.18.3	116	4.19.31	170
4.10.29	205	4.15.8	96	4.18.5	116	4.19.32	172
	206	4.15.9	96	4.18.6	117	4.19.33	172
4.10.31	205	4.15.10	97	4.18.7	117	4.19.34	172
4.10.32	206	4.15.11	97	4.18.9	118	4.19.35	173
4.11.1	143	4.15.13	98	4.18.13	119	4.19.36	174
4.11.2	144	4.15.14	98	4.18.14	119	4.19.37	174
	145	4.15.15	99	4.18.16	119	4.20.1	207
4.11.8	200	4.15.16	99		120	4.20.2	207
4.11.9	200	4.15.17	100	4.18.17	120	4.20.3	208
	201	4.15.18	100	4.18.18	118	4.20.4	208
4.11.10	201	4.15.19	122	4.18.19	120	4.20.6	210
4.11.14	201	4.17.1	102	4.18.20	121	4.20.7	210
4.12.5	61	4.17.2	102	4.19.1	124	4.20.8	211
	62	4.17.3	103	4.19.2	124	4.20.9	211
4.12.9	62	4.17.4	103		171	4.20.10	212
4.12.10	60	4.17.5	104	4.19.5	125	4.20.11	213
	62	4.17.17	105	4.19.6	125	4.20.12	214
4.12.23	196	4.17.18	107	4.19.7	126	4.20.13	214
4.13.3	26	4.17.22	107	4.19.8	127	4.20.14	215
4.14.1	87	4.17.24	106	4.19.9	127	4.20.15	215
4.14.3	87	4.17.26	107	4.19.10	128	4.20.16	216
4.14.5	87	4.17.29	105	4.19.11	129	4.20.17	217
4.14.6	88		106	4.19.12	129	4.20.18	217
4.14.7	88	4.17.30	105	4.19.13	130	4.20.19	218
4.14.8	89	4.17.32	107	4.19.14	130	4.20.20	219
4.14.12	89	4.17.33	104	4.19.15	157	4.20.21	219
4.14.13	90	4.17.35	107	4.19.16	157	4.20.22	220
4.14.14	91	4.17.36	108	4.19.17	158	4.20.23	220
4.14.17	91	4.17.37	109	4.19.18	158	4.20.24	221
4.14.18	92	4.17.38	109	4.19.19	159	4.20.25	221
4.14.19	93	4.17.40	110	4.19.20	159	4.20.26	222
4.14.20	93	4.17.41	111	4.19.21	160	4.20.27	223
4.14.21	93	4.17.42	111	4.19.22	161	4.20.28	223
4.14.22	94	4.17.43	122	4.19.23	163	4.20.29	224
4.14.26	91	4.17.44	112	4.19.24	163	4.20.30	224
4.15.1	94	4.17.46	112	4.19.25	162	4.20.31	225
4.15.2	94	4.17.47	113	4.19.26	162	4.20.32	225
4.15.3	95	4.17.48	114	4.19.27	164		
4.15.5	95	4.17.50	114	4.19.28	164		

REFERENCES TO CLASSICAL AUTHORS IN THE ENDNOTES

REFERENCES TO OTHER WORKS OF CALVIN IN THE ENDNOTES

AUTHOR, SOURCE, AND PERSON INDEX TO THE REFERENCES IN THE ENDNOTES